Classic Edition

Sources

Human Development

Contemporary Learning Series

2460 Kerper Blvd., Dubuque, IA 52001

Visit us on the Internet
www.mhcls.com

Classic Edition
Sources

Human Development

Edited by
RHETT DIESSNER
Lewis-Clarke State College

Contemporary Learning Series

2460 Kerper Blvd., Dubuque, IA 52001

Visit us on the Internet
www.mhcls.com

EDITORIAL STAFF

Larry Loeppke, Managing Editor
Jade Benedict, Developmental Editor
David Welsh, Developmental Editor
Joe Offredi, Developmental Editor
Nancy Meissner, Editorial Assistant
Rita Hingtgen, Production Service Assistant

PERMISSIONS STAFF

Lenny J. Behnke, Permissions Coordinator
Lori Church, Permissions Coordinator
Shirley Lanners, Permissions Coordinator

MARKETING STAFF

Julie Keck, Senior Marketing Manager
Mary Klein, Marketing Communications Specialist
Alice Link, Marketing Coordinator

PRODUCTION STAFF

Beth Kundert, Production Manager
DeAnna Dausener, Senior Administrative Assistant
Jane Mohr, Project Manager
Jean Smith, Project Manager
Sandy Wille, Project Manager
Tara McDermott, Design Specialist
Maggie Lytle, Cover Designer

Cataloging in Publication Data
Main entry under title: Sources Human Development, 3/e
1. Human Development. I. Diessner, Rhett, *comp.* II. Title: Sources Human Development.
ISBN-13: 978–0–07–337968–5   MHID-10: 0–07–337968–9   150   ISSN 1091-8795

Third Edition

Cover image © Siede Preis/Getty Images
Printed in the United States of America   234567890QDBQDB5432   Printed on Recycled Paper

RHETT DIESSNER
Lewis-Clark State College

Rhett Diessner is Professor of Psychology at Lewis-Clark State College in Lewiston, ID, where he has taught introductory, developmental, advanced developmental, adult, and educational psychology. He has also taught at Heritage College (Toppenish, WA; Yakama Indian Nation, 1983–85); Harvard Graduate School of Education (1985–1988); and Landegg International University (Switzerland, 1997–2002). He served as school psychologist for the Yakama Tribal Schools from 1982–1985. Professor Diessner's doctorate is in human development from Harvard University. His master's and bachelor's degrees are from the University of Oregon, in educational/school psychology and physiological psychology. His research interests include the aesthetics of moral development and the positive psychology of the human virtues, especially engagement with beauty. He was selected "2005 Carnegie Foundation for the Advancement of Teaching Idaho Professor of the Year" by The Carnegie Foundation for the Advancement of Teaching and the Council for Advancement and Support of Education; selected "Outstanding Professor" at LCSC by the students of the College Assistance Migrant Program (CAMP), in 2005 and 2006; and has been elected "Outstanding Academic Instructor" by the Associated Student Body of LCSC ten times. He has published in *The Journal of Moral Education, Journal of American Indian Education; Creative Child and Adult Quarterly; Peace and Conflict: Journal of Peace Psychology; Social Behavior and Personality; Converging Realities. A Journal of Art, Science and Religion; Peace Psychology Bulletin; The Journal of Social Psychology; Psychology and Aging; Counseling and Values; Psychology in the Schools; The Journal of Bahá'í Studies; The Journal of Genetic Psychology; The Journal of Early Adolescence, Educational and Psychological Measurement; Gifted/Creative/Talented;* and *The Teaching Professor.*

Dedication

I dedicate this book to my family, my crucible of human development: Ruth (mother), Wendy (wife), Lani (sister), Rory (brother), Jaleh and Maceo (daughter and grandson), David and Betty (son and his wife), Random and Mary (son and his wife). Love is the fundamental cause and goal of development.

Preface

*T*he study of human development is one of vigorous theoretical debate, as well as intense empirical research. It is a broad field that captures the attention and passion of psychologists, anthropologists, sociologists, educators, philosophers, theologians, policymakers, and social commentators. In addition to the interest in human development shown by academics and professionals, it is a domain of vital involvement of every human. Every one of us is currently in the midst of our own developmental trajectory. Human Development is of practical daily concern to parents in regard to their children, a common source of concern to adults with aging parents, and a topic of societal-wide responsibility. Human development is the aim and purpose of education and schooling. Therefore all political decisions that affect school systems need to be informed by an understanding of what human development is, what forms of development are desirable, and how that development can be fostered. *Classic Editions Sources: Human Development* sets the background to become an informed citizen on a wide range of human development issues.

This book, *Classic Editions Sources: Human Development*, is an introductory-level college text anthology that contains 46 carefully edited selections that have shaped the study of human development and our contemporary understanding of it. Most of the selections are well-known classics in the field of human development and developmental psychology, and are frequently and commonly cited in the leading textbooks. Included here are the works of a wide range of distinguished scientists, researchers, and theoreticians, both past and present. Each selection contains topics central to the field of human development. These selections offer findings from a variety of disciplines and are well suited to courses that attempt to examine, in some depth, topics related to human development. Each selection is preceded by a headnote that establishes the relevance of the selection and provides some background on the author(s) of that selection.

Organization of the Book

The selections are organized topically around the major areas of study in human development: the selections in Part 1 introduce the major theories in human development, including some non-western theories; Part 2 contains major selections in infancy and early childhood; Part 3, Middle Childhood; Part 4, Adolescence; Part 5, Early and Middle Adulthood; Part 6, Late Adulthood. Some of the articles are appropriate to several age groups, and were included in a particular section based on the general emphasis of the article.

This third edition has several changes from the second edition. Jane Loevinger's classic work on the stages of ego development has been added to Chapter 1, The Grand Theories. Likewise, Martin Seligman and Mihaly Csikszentmihalyi's manifesto on positive psychology has also been added to the chapter ("Positive Psychology: An Introduction," *American Psychologist*, 2000). Although the positive psychology movement is too recent to be considered classic, it has its roots in the classic approach to human strengths advocated by Humanistic Psychology, exemplified in the work of Abraham Maslow (see Chapter 11 of this volume). Positive psychology is beginning to have a huge influence on the field of human development and the fostering of character strengths and virtues. Positive psychology's "manual of the sanities," *Character Strengths and Virtues: A Handbook of Classification* (edited by C. Peterson & M. E. P. Seligman, Oxford University Press & American Psychological Association, 2004), includes chapters on twenty-four major human strengths (ranging from wisdom to love, from courage to appreciation of beauty and excellence), and each chapter has a section devoted to the development of that strength, a section on factors that enable and inhibit development of that strength, and a section on deliberate developmental interventions.

In Chapter 2, Non-Western Classics, Thich Nhat Hanh's (pronounced something like Tik Not Hahn) description of the Buddhist goals of human development are excerpted from his book *The Heart of the Buddha's Teaching* (Parallax Press, 1998). Buddhist explanations of human development are, of course, classic in the sense that they have influenced billions of human beings over the last two-and-a-half millennia. Also, Buddhism has had a strong influence in the practical aspects of human development in the last few decades in the West; in the great increase in the use of meditation by laypersons and psychotherapists; and in the practice of mindfulness, for which a strong empirical research base has been established in the psychology literature.

In Part Four, Adolescence, a section has been added from William G. Perry's classic study of the development of undergraduates, *Forms of Intellectual and Ethical Development in the College Years: A Scheme* (Holt, Rinehart & Winston, 1970). This is a fascinating new addition to *Classic Editions Sources: Human Development,* and is certain to make reflective, and hold the attention of, the majority of college students.

In Part Five, Early and Middle Adulthood, a new selection by the Bulgarian developmental psychologist Elena Mustakova-Possardt has been included. Mustakova's work on stages of "critical consciousness" integrate the critical and moral views of the great educator Paolo Freire with structural developmental stages of the Piagetian tradition. Her cross-cultural work, with Americans and Bulgarians, has reached modern classic status.

Also in Part Five, included in Chapter 11: Social and Personality Development, is a paper by William A. Barry, editor of the magazine *Human Development.* The title of the paper is "Christian Maturity Through Ignatian Spirituality." Religion, for better or worse, had and still has a huge impact on the psychological development of humans. Christianity is the most influential religion in the West, and the largest denomination of Christians is Catholic. Therefore we have included a paper by a psychologist on the development of Christians, in the context of the classic works on spiritual development by Ignatius of Loyola, founder of the Society of Jesus, of the Catholic Church.

A Word to the Instructor

An Instructor's Manual with Test Questions (multiple-choice and essay) is available through the publisher for the instructor using Sources in the classroom.

On the Internet

Each part of this book is preceded by an *On the Internet* page. This page provides a list of Internet site addresses that are relevant to that part of the book. Each URL that is mentioned also includes a description of the site.

Acknowledgments

I especially offer my gratitude to Joseph Offredi, Developmental Editor for this Classic Edition Sources line of books at McGraw-Hill Contemporary Learning Series, who effectively, eloquently, and warmly guided me through the twists and turns of producing the third edition of this text; Larry Loeppke, Managing Editor of the Contemporary Learning Series, as well as the efficient Nancy Meissner, Editorial Assistant. I also thank my students at Lewis-Clark State College, who provided the inspiration, and a variety of practical inputs, to complete this revision. My greatest gratitude is owed my beloved wife, Wendy, for her editorial assistance, and for her love, which has been the backdrop and home base of my psychological development for the last thirty years. I am forever appreciative of my mother Ruth, who launched my personal experience with human development, both genetically and environmentally. And I thank my colleague, Tim Richel, who has revised the *Instructor's Manual,* and let me bounce my human development ideas off his fertile and brilliant mind.

There are, due to space limitations, many excellent studies and approaches that have not been included in this text. We welcome your comments and observations about the selections in this volume and encourage you to write to us with suggestions for other selections to include or changes to consider. Please send your remarks to us in care of Classic Edition Sources, McGraw-Hill Contemporary Learning Series, 2460 Kerper Boulevard, Dubuque, IA, 52001.

Rhett Diessner
Lewis-Clark State College

Contents

> *"At a time when efforts are being made to eradicate discrimination between the sexes in the search for social equality and justice, the differences between the sexes are being rediscovered in the social sciences. This discovery occurs when theories formerly considered to be sexually neutral in their scientific objectivity are found instead to reflect a consistent observational and evaluative bias."*

> *"[W]e believe that human cognitive competence is better described in terms of a set of abilities, talents or mental skills, which we call 'intelligences.' All normal individuals possess each of these skills to some extent; individuals differ in the degree of skill and in the nature of their combination. We believe this theory of intelligence may be more humane and more veridical than alternative views of intelligence and this more adequately reflects the data of human 'intelligent' behavior."*

> *"Entering a new millennium, Americans face a historical choice. Left alone on the pinnacle of economic and political leadership, the United States can continue to increase its material wealth while ignoring the human needs of its people and those of the rest of the planet … At this juncture, the social and behavioral sciences can play an enormously important role."*

> *"There was a time when meadow, grove, and stream, /The earth, and every common sight, /To me did seem / Apparelled in celestial light, /The glory and the freshness of a dream, /It is not now as it hath been of yore."*

Non-Western Classics   *58*

> *"The basic structures of consciousness are, in effect, what is known as the Great Chain of Being. Some versions of the Great Chain give only two levels (matter and spirit) … Some are very sophisticated, giving literally dozens of the basic structures of the overall spectrum…. For this presentation, I have selected what seem to be the nine most central and functionally dominant structures."*

> *"The stages that mark the wayfarer's journey from the abode of dust to the heavenly homeland are said to be seven. Some have called these Seven Valleys, and others, Seven Cities. And they say that until the wayfarer taketh leave of self, and traverseth these stages, he shall never reach to the ocean of nearness and union, nor drink of the peerless wine."*

"The Way of learning to be great (or adult education) consists in manifesting the clear character, loving the people, and abiding (chih) in the highest good."

"There has been a rapid evolution in the thinking about the psychology of African Americans since 1970. That evolution has progressed from a self-negating perspective which viewed the model human being as necessarily non-Black to a self-affirmative perspective which sees the African as a model of universal man."

"The heredity-environment problem is still very much alive. Its viability is assured by the gradual replacement of the questions, 'Which one?' and 'How much?' by the more basic and appropriate question, 'How?' "

"It is our hypothesis that the personality is shaped by the constant interplay of temperament and environment."

"Intelligence does not by any means appear at once derived from mental development, like a higher mechanism, and radically distinct from those which have preceded it. Intelligence presents, on the contrary, a remarkable continuity with the acquired of even inborn processes on which it depends and at the same time makes sense of."

"Whether the context is feeding, close bodily contact, face-to-face interaction, or indeed the situation defined by the infant's crying, mother-infant interaction provides the baby with opportunity to build up expectations of the mother and, eventually, a working model of her as more or less accessible and responsive."

"A pasteboard model ... was made to represent three mountains. From his [sic] initial position in front of the model the child sees a green mountain occupying the foreground a little to his right."

Cognitive Development in Middle Childhood 133

Social and Personality Development in Middle Childhood

146

Physical and Cognitive Development in Adolescence

164

Social and Personality Development in Adolescence

Cognitive Development in Early and Middle Adulthood

Social and Personality Development in Early and Middle Adulthood

221

Development During the Elder Years

242

Internet References

General Internet Sites for Human Development

http://classweb.gmu.edu/awinsler/div7/homepage.shtml
Division 7 of the American Psychological Association is Developmental Psychology. Division 7 "promotes research in the field of developmental psychology and high standards in the application of scientific knowledge to educational, child care, policy, and related settings." "Division 7 was organized to (a) promote research in the field of Developmental Psychology; (b) foster the development of researchers through providing information about educational opportunities and recognizing outstanding contributions to the discipline; (c) facilitate exchange of scientific information about developmental psychology through publications such as the division's newsletter and through national and international meetings; and (d) promote high standards for the application of scientific knowledge on human development to public policy issues."

http://www.srcd.org/index.html
The Society for Research in Child Development "is a multidisciplinary, not-for-profit, professional association with a membership of approximately 5,500 researchers, practitioners, and human development professionals from over 50 countries. The purposes of the Society are to promote multidisciplinary research in the field of human development, to foster the exchange of information among scientists and other professionals of various disciplines, and to encourage applications of research findings. Our goals are pursued through a variety of programs with the cooperation and service of our governing council, standing committees, and members."

http://www.adultdevelopment.org/
"The international membership of the Society for Research in Adult Development includes people from all disciplines who are interested in positive adult development. Positive adult development refers to development starting in late adolescence and continuing through life. The focus is on expanded capabilities and changes that improve the quality of life."

http://www.apa.org/divisions/div37/
"The Division of Child, Youth, and Family Services (Division 37 of the American Psychological Association) is committed to the application of psychological knowledge to advocacy, service delivery, and public policies affecting children, youth, and families. The Division advances research, education, training, and practice through a multidisciplinary perspective. Division activities, which include published works, have focused on such topics as: divorce and custody, child abuse prevention, pediatric AIDS, drug-exposed infants, latchkey children, homelessness, and systems of care."

http://www.apa.org/about/division/div53.html
"Division 53—Society of Clinical Child and Adolescent Psychology represents psychologists who are active in teaching, research, clinical services, administration, and advocacy in clinical child psychology to the APA and the public. Division 53 publishes the *Journal of Clinical Child and Adolescent Psychology* and the *Clinical Child & Adolescent Psychology Newsletter* and sponsors a full program at the annual APA convention. The Division has established research and professional service awards, including an annual student research award, and also sponsors publications describing graduate programs and clinical internships that provide specialized training in clinical child psychology. The Division also supports task forces on the development and evaluation of evidence-based treatments for childhood disorders and coordinates efforts for dissemination of information about evidence-based services."

http://www.sshdonline.org/
"The newly organized Society for the Study of Human Development (SSHD) is a professional society formed by a group of scholars from multiple disciples (e.g., medicine, biology, psychology, sociology, economics, and history). The central focus of SSHD is to provide an organization that moves beyond age-segmented scholarly organizations to take an integrative, interdisciplinary approach to ages/stages across the life span, generational and ecological contexts of human development, and research and applications to human development policies and programs. SSHD currently includes 150 members."

Chapter 1

http://www.apsa.org/
"The American Psychoanalytic Association (APsaA), the oldest national psychoanalytic organization in the nation, was founded in 1911. APsaA, as a professional organization for psychoanalysts, focuses on education, research and membership development." APsaA keeps Freud's development work alive and progressive.

http://www.piaget.org/
"The Jean Piaget Society, established in 1970, has an international, interdisciplinary membership of scholars, teachers and researchers interested in exploring the nature of the developmental construction of human knowledge. The Society was named in honor of the Swiss developmentalist, Jean Piaget, who made major theoretical and empirical contributions to our understanding of the origins and evolution of knowledge."

http://tigger.uic.edu/~lnucci/MoralEd/overview.html#kohlberg
These pages, posted by Prof. Larry Nucci, of the University of Illinois at Chicago, contain a good summary of Kohlberg's work on moral development.

http://www.webster.edu/~woolflm/gilligan.html
These pages, posted by Prof. Linda Wolff of Webster University, offer a good summary of Carol Gilligan's life and work.

http://www.ship.edu/~cgboeree/erikson.html
These pages, posted by Prof. George Boeree (pronounced boo-RAY) of Shippensburg University, are an excellent and broad summary of Erik Erikson's work on human development.

http://www.webster.edu/~woolflm/loevinger.html
These pages, posted by Prof. Linda Wolff of Webster University, offer biographical information about Jane Loevinger as well as an outline of her work.

http://www.howardgardner.com/
Explore Howard Gardner's (creator of the Theory of Multiple Intelligences) own web pages.

http://www.authentichappiness.sas.upenn.edu/
Check out the web pages of Prof. Martin E. P. Seligman's Authentic Happiness Web site. Dr. Seligman was one of the founders of the Positive Psychology movement.

Chapter 2

http://wilber.shambhala.com/index.cfm/
Ken Wilber is "out there," but his work is very influential among "new agers." Check out these pages from his publisher that have a host of information about his current thinking.

http://www.ship.edu/~cgboeree/buddhapers.html
These pages contain a fine introduction to the life of the Buddha, Buddhism, and Buddhist psychology, posted by Prof. C. George Boeree (pronounced boo-RAY) of Shippensburg University.

http://info.bahai.org/bahaullah-teachings.html
This site contains further information on a Bahá'í viewpoint of human development, from the Bahá'í International Community's Web pages.

http://www.comparative-religion.com/confucianism/
These pages offer a brief biography of Confucius, as well as online access to all the books he is credited with writing. A background in Confucian texts will help you better understand Confucius' outlook on human development.

http://www.naimakbar.com/
Explore Prof. Na'im Akbar's own Web pages to learn more about his cogent explanations of human development from an African Psychology perspective.

Chapter 3

http://www.genome.gov/
"The Human Genome Project (HGP) was one of the great feats of exploration in history—an inward voyage of discovery rather than an outward exploration of the planet or the cosmos; an international research effort to sequence and map all of the genes—together known as the genome—of members of our species, *Homo sapiens*. Completed in April 2003, the HGP gave us the ability to, for the first time, read nature's complete genetic blueprint for building a human being."

http://www.personalityresearch.org/bg.html
The pages are posted by Prof. G. Scott Acton of the Rochester Institute of Technology, and provide a good introduction to behavioral genetics.

Chapter 4

http://www.waimh.org/
"The World Association for Infant Mental Health (WAIMH) is a not-for-profit organization for scientific and educational professionals. WAIMH's central aim is to promote the mental well-being and healthy development of infants throughout the world, taking into account cultural, regional, and environmental variations, and to generate and disseminate scientific knowledge." Specifically the WAIMH "seeks to facilitate increased knowledge about mental development and disorder in children from conception to three years of age; the dissemination of scientific knowledge about services for care, intervention and prevention of mental disorder, and impairment in infancy; and the dissemination of evidence-based knowledge about ways to support the developmental transition to parenthood, as well as the healthy aspects of parenting and caregiving environments."

http://classweb.gmu.edu/awinsler/div7/homepage.shtml
Division 7 of the American Psychological Association is Developmental Psychology. Division 7 "promotes research in the field of developmental psychology and high standards in the application of scientific knowledge to educational, child care, policy, and related settings. Division 7 was organized to (a) promote research in the field of Developmental Psychology; (b) foster the development of researchers through providing information about educational opportunities and recognizing outstanding contributions to the discipline; (c) facilitate exchange of scientific information about developmental psychology through publications such as the division's newsletter and through national and international meetings; and (d) promote high standards for the application of scientific knowledge on human development to public policy issues."

Chapter 5

http://www.apa.org/about/division/div54.html
Division 54 of the American Psychological Association is the Society of Pediatric Psychology (SPP). SPP "is dedicated to research and practice addressing the relationship between children's physical, cognitive, social, and emotional functioning and their physical well-being, including maintenance of health, promotion of positive health behaviors, and treatment of chronic or serious medical conditions. In recognition of the close interplay between children's psychological and physical health, SPP has developed liaisons with several pediatric societies and many pediatric psychologists have become experts in the behavioral and developmental aspects of acute and chronic diseases."

http://www.naeyc.org/
"The National Association for the Education of Young Children (NAEYC) is dedicated to improving the well-being of all young children, with particular focus on the quality of educational and developmental services for all children from birth through age 8. NAEYC is committed to becoming an increasingly high performing and inclusive organization. Founded in 1926, NAEYC is the world's largest organization working on behalf of young children with nearly 100,000 members, a national network of over 300 local, state, and regional Affiliates, and a growing global alliance of like-minded organizations. Membership is open to all individuals who share a desire to serve and act on behalf of the needs and rights of all young children."

http://www.srcd.org/index.html
The Society for Research in Child Development "is a multidisciplinary, not-for-profit, professional association with a membership of approximately 5,500 researchers, practitioners, and human development professionals from over 50 countries. The purposes of the Society are to promote multidisciplinary research in the field of human development, to foster the exchange of information among scientists and other professionals of various disciplines, and to encourage applications of research findings. Our goals are pursued

through a variety of programs with the cooperation and service of our governing council, standing committees, and members."

Chapter 6

http://www.piaget.org/
"The Jean Piaget Society, established in 1970, has an international, interdisciplinary membership of scholars, teachers and researchers interested in exploring the nature of the developmental construction of human knowledge. The Society was named in honor of the Swiss developmentalist, Jean Piaget, who made major theoretical and empirical contributions to our understanding of the origins and evolution of knowledge."

http://www.cdc.gov/ncbddd/child/middlechildhood.htm
The Center for Disease Control (CDC) posts useful summary pages of expected cognitive development milestones for children in middle childhood. Check them out at this URL.

Chapter 7

http://www.cyfernet.org/
"If you're a professional serving children, youth and families or a parent with your own children, you know that finding reliable, high quality, research-based information on the Web can be a major challenge. That's where CYFERnet can help you. CYFERnet's Web site brings together the best, children, youth and family resources of all the public land-grant universities in the country. Materials are carefully reviewed by college and university faculty."

http://www.iaccp.org/
"The International Association for Cross-Cultural Psychology (IACCP) was founded in 1972 and has a membership of over 800 persons in more than 65 countries. The aims of the Association are to facilitate communication among persons interested in a diverse range of issues involving the intersection of culture and psychology. IACCP is affiliated with the International Union of Psychological Science (IUPsyS)." The influence of culture is huge on children's cognitive, social, and personality development. Developmental psychologist's at the IACCP are particularly focused on those issues.

http://www.mpib-berlin.mpg.de/en/institut/dok/full/
keller/acrosscu/ISSBD.pdf
Check out this short paper by Monika Keller, from the Max Planck Institute for Human Development, Berlin, Germany, on cross-cultural issues of friendship.

http://www.apa.org/divisions/div37/
"The Division of Child, Youth, and Family Services (Division 37 of the American Psychological Association) is committed to the application of psychological knowledge to advocacy, service delivery, and public policies affecting children, youth, and families. The Division advances research, education, training, and practice through a multidisciplinary perspective. Division activities, which include published works, have focused on such topics as: divorce and custody, child abuse prevention, pediatric AIDS, drug-exposed infants, latchkey children, homelessness, and systems of care."

Chapter 8

http://www.iub.edu/~cafs/adol/adol.html
"Adolescence Directory On-Line (ADOL) is an electronic guide to information on adolescent issues. It is a service of the Center for Adolescent Studies at Indiana University. Educators, counselors, parents, researchers, health practitioners, and teens can use ADOL to find Web resources for" a very wide variety of topics, including health issues, counseling resources, mental health, conflict and violence.

http://www.ericdigests.org/pre-925/perry.htm
These pages contain a brief paper, written by D. Battaglini & R. Schenkat, summarizing William Perry's and Stephen Toulmin's approaches to cognitive and moral development among college students.

http://chiron.valdosta.edu/whuitt/col/cogsys/piaget.html
These pages, posted by W. Huitt of Valdosta University, contain an excellent summary of Piaget's work on cognitive development, especially the formal operational stage that is typical of adolescence and adulthood.

Chapter 9

http://www.apa.org/about/division/div53.html
"Division 53—Society of Clinical Child and Adolescent Psychology represents psychologists who are active in teaching, research, clinical services, administration, and advocacy in clinical child psychology to the APA and the public. Division 53 publishes the *Journal of Clinical Child and Adolescent Psychology* and the *Clinical Child & Adolescent Psychology Newsletter* and sponsors a full program at the annual APA convention. The Division has established research and professional service awards, including an annual student research award, and also sponsors publications describing graduate programs and clinical internships that provide specialized training in clinical child psychology. The Division also supports task forces on the development and evaluation of evidence-based treatments for childhood disorders and coordinates efforts for dissemination of information about evidence-based services."

http://www.s-r-a.org/index.html
"The Society for Research on Adolescence (SRA) is a rapidly growing, dynamic society focused on the theoretical, empirical, and policy research issues of adolescence. Established in the winter 1984 as an international, multidisciplinary, nonprofit professional association, the goal of the Society is to promote the understanding of adolescence through research and dissemination. SRA currently serves over 1,100 members representing 25 countries throughout the world."

Chapter 10

http://www.adultdevelopment.org/
"The international membership of the Society for Research in Adult Development includes people from all disciplines who are interested in positive adult development. Positive adult development refers to development starting in late adolescence and continuing through life. The focus is on expanded capabilities and changes that improve the quality of life."

http://www.webster.edu/~woolflm/wwok.html
These pages, posted by Prof. Linda Wolff of Webster University, offer background information about the Women's Ways of Knowing Project, completed by the researchers Mary Field Belenky, Blythe McVicker Clinchy, Nancy Rule Goldberger, and Jill Mattuck Tarulet.

http://www.esrea.org/
The European Society for Research on the Education of Adults (ESREA) "promotes and disseminates theoretical and empirical research on the education of adults and adult learning in Europe through research networks, conferences

and publications." Learning and cognitive development are almost synonyms; check out these pages concerning these topics in a European venue.

Chapter 11

http://www.authentichappiness.sas.upenn.edu/
Check out the Web pages of Prof. Martin E. P. Seligman's Authentic Happiness Web site. Dr. Seligman was one of the founders of the Positive Psychology movement. These pages have many reliable and valid personality tests that adults can complete, free of charge, and thus evaluate their own levels of social and personality development.

http://www.mpib-berlin.mpg.de/
"Founded in 1963, the Max Planck Institute for Human Development is a multidisciplinary research institute dedicated to the study of human development and education, and their evolutionary, social, historical, and institutional contexts. Considering human development and education from a life-span and life-course perspective is another facet of the Institute's research agenda." The institute is one of the world's leading research institutions on the topic of life-span human development and is located near Berlin, Germany.

http://www.dushkin.com/connectext/psy/ch03/levinson.mhtml
Check out a summary of Levinson's theory of adult development at the McGraw-Hill Higher Education site.

Chapter 12

http://apadiv20.phhp.ufl.edu/
These are the official pages of the American Psychological Association's Division 20. This Division is dedicated to studying the Psychology of Adult Development and Aging.

http://geron.psu.edu/index.html
"The Penn State Gerontology Center strives to carry out research, instruction, and community-service programs of the highest quality and to make those resources available to the Commonwealth and the nation. Building on its 35-year history of accomplishments, the Gerontology Center seeks to advance the study of aging in the biological, behavioral, and social sciences; stimulate communication among scholars of different disciplines and among teachers, researchers, practitioners, government officials, and the elderly; promote development of undergraduate and graduate courses in adult development and aging; and foster applied research that improves the quality of life and promotes the welfare of adults and the elderly." Included at this Web site are information about and links to the Seattle Longitudinal Study, and K. Warner Schaie's current work on that study.

http://www.lifespirals.com/TheMindSpiral/Fowler/fowler.html
These pages contain an interesting interview with Prof. James Fowler, the author of *Stages of Faith: The Psychology of Human Development and the Quest for Meaning* (1981, Harper & Row).

The Grand Theories

The Development of the Sexual Function

Sigmund Freud

Sigmund Freud's psychoanalytic ideology is one of the most influential theories in the history of psychology, and his impact on art, literature, and all of social science is astounding. Born in 1856, he lived most of his life in Vienna, Austria. He earned his medical degree from Vienna University in 1881, and he died in London in 1939. Freud is often considered the first great psychologist to put forth a systematic theory of human development. He considered the sexual urge the most fundamental motive and thus identified five stages of psychosexual development: oral, anal, phallic, latent, and genital. These psychosexual stages were first identified in the second essay of his book *Three Essays on the Theory of Sexuality* (1915).

By the 1890s Freud was beginning to put forth in writing his hypotheses concerning the sexual nature of child development. Freud's belief that sexuality was at the core of human development shocked the Victorian world. Initially, most psychiatrists considered Freud's work untenable, but within a couple of decades he was taken very seriously throughout the professional psychiatric world, as well as by other forms of the intelligentsia of Western society. His *Three Essays on the Theory of Sexuality* was in its fourth edition by 1920. Freud was very serious about "testing" his theory with his clinical research approach, and he constantly improved his theory. He made significant revisions in each of the four editions of *Three Essays*.

The following excerpt was written in 1938, one year before Freud's death, and first published in 1940 as chapter 3 of *An Outline of Psychoanalysis*. It is essentially a final revision and synopsis of his theory of psychosexual development, as found in the second essay of *Three Essays on the Theory of Sexuality*.

Key Concept: psychosexual stages

According to the popular view, human sexual life consists essentially in the impulse to bring one's own genitals into contact with those of someone of the opposite sex. With this are associated, as accessory phenomena and introductory acts, kissing this extraneous body, looking at and touching it. This impulse is supposed to make its appearance at puberty, that is, at the age of sexual maturity, and to serve the purposes of reproduction. Nevertheless, certain facts have always been known that fail to fit into the narrow framework of this view. (1) It is a remarkable fact that there are people who are only attracted by the persons and genitals of members of their own sex. (2) It is equally remarkable that there are people whose desires behave in every way like sexual ones, but who at the same time entirely disregard the sexual organs or their normal use; people of this kind are known as "perverts." (3) And finally it is striking that many children (who are on that account regarded as degenerates) take a very early interest in their genitals and show signs of excitation in them.

It may well be believed that psychoanalysis provoked astonishment and denials when, partly upon the basis of these three neglected facts, it contradicted all the popular opinions upon sexuality. Its principal findings are as follows:

(a) Sexual life does not begin only at puberty, but starts with clear manifestations soon after birth.

(b) It is necessary to distinguish sharply between the concepts of "sexual" and "genital." The former is the wider concept and includes many activities that have nothing to do with the genitals.

(c) Sexual life comprises the function of obtaining pleasure from zones of the body—a function which is subsequently brought into the service of that of reproduction. The two functions often fail to coincide completely.

The chief interest is naturally focused upon the first of these assertions, the most unexpected of all. It has been found that in early childhood there are signs of bodily activity to which only ancient prejudice could deny the name of sexual, and which are connected with mental phenomena that we come across later in adult love, such as fixation to a particular object, jealousy, and so on. It is further found that these phenomena which emerge in early childhood form part of a regular process of development, that they undergo a steady increase and reach a climax toward the end of the fifth year, after which there follows a lull. During this lull, progress is at a standstill and much is unlearned and undone. After the end of this period of latency, as it is called, sexual life is resumed with puberty, or, as we might say, it has a second efflorescence. Here we come upon the fact that the onset of sexual life is *diphasic*, that it occurs in two waves; this is unknown except in man and evidently has an important bearing upon his genesis.[1] It is not a matter of indifference that, with few exceptions, the events of the early period of sexuality fall a victim to *infantile amnesia*. Our understanding of the etiology of the neuroses and the technique of analytic therapy are derived from these views; and the tracing of the process of development in this early period has also provided evidence for yet other conclusions.

The first organ to make its appearance as an erotogenic zone and to make libidinal demands upon the mind is, from the time of birth onward, the mouth. To begin with, all mental activity is centered upon the task of providing satisfaction for the needs of that zone. In the first instance, of course, the latter serves the purposes of self-preservation by means of nourishment; but physiology should not be confused with psychology. The baby's obstinate persistence in sucking gives evidence at an early stage of a need for satisfaction which, although it originates from and is stimulated by the taking of nourishment, nevertheless seeks to obtain pleasure independently of nourishment and for that reason may and should be described as "sexual."

Sadistic impulses already begin to occur sporadically during the oral phase along with the appearance of the teeth. Their extent increases greatly during the second phase, which we describe as the sadistic-anal phase, because satisfaction is then sought in aggression and in the excretory function. We justify our inclusion of aggressive impulses in the libido by supposing that sadism is an instinctual fusion of purely libidinal and purely destructive impulses, a fusion which thenceforward persists without interruption.[2]

The third phase is the so-called phallic one, which is, as it were, a forerunner of the final shape of sexual life, and already greatly resembles it. It is to be noted that what comes in question at this stage is not the genitals of both sexes but only those of the male (the phallus). The female genitals long remain unknown: in the child's attempt at understanding sexual processes, he pays homage to the venerable cloacal theory*—a theory which has a genetic justification.[3]

With the phallic phase and in the course of it the sexuality of early childhood reaches its height and approaches its decline. Thenceforward boys and girls have different histories. To begin with, both place their intellectual activity at the service of sexual research; both start off from the presumption of the universal presence of the penis. But now the paths of the sexes divide. The boy enters the Oedipus phase**; he begins to manipulate his penis, and simultaneously has phantasies of carrying out some sort of activity with it in relation to his mother; but at last, owing to the combined effect of a threat of castration and the spectacle of women's lack of a penis, he experiences the greatest trauma of his life, and this introduces the period of latency with all its attendant consequences. The girl, after vainly attempting to do the same as the boy, comes to recognize her lack of a penis or rather the inferiority of her clitoris, with permanent effects upon the development of her character; and, as a result of this first disappointment in rivalry, she often turns away altogether from sexual life.

It would be a mistake to suppose that these three phases succeed one another in a clear-cut fashion: one of them may appear in addition to another, they may overlap one another, they may be present simultaneously.

In the earlier phases the separate component instincts set about their pursuit of pleasure independently of one another; in the phallic phase there are the first signs of an organization which subordinates the other trends to the primacy of the genitals and signifies the beginning of a co-ordination of the general pursuit of pleasure into the sexual function. The complete organization is not attained until puberty, in a fourth, or genital, phase†. A state of affairs is then established in which (1) many earlier libidinal cathexes are retained, (2) others are included in the sexual function as preparatory or auxiliary acts, their satisfaction producing what is known as fore-pleasure, and (3) other tendencies are excluded from the organization, and are either entirely suppressed (repressed) or are employed in the ego in some other way, forming character-traits or undergoing sublimation with a displacement of their aims.

This process is not always carried out perfectly. Inhibitions in the course of its development manifest themselves

---

* ["Cloacal theory" is based on the notion that our excretory and reproductive organs have a common and connected evolutionary origin.—Eds.]

** [The "Oedipal phase" is a metaphor that Freud borrowed from a Greek myth in which a young man unknowingly marries his mother. Freud believed that all young boys (aged approximately 3–6) fall "in love" with their mothers. Freud's writings are inconsistent about whether or not young girls fall "in love" with their fathers.—Eds.]

† [In most human development textbooks, the fourth stage is referred to as the "latent stage" and the genital stage is termed the fifth and final stage. Herein Freud is not considering the latent stage as a sexual stage because sexuality is latent and not manifest during the middle childhood years.—Eds.]

as the various disturbances of sexual life. Fixations of the libido to conditions at earlier phases are then found, the trend of which, moving independently of the normal sexual aim, is described as *perversion*. One example of an inhibition in development of this kind is homosexuality, if it is manifest. Analysis shows that in every case a homosexual attachment to an object has at one time been present and in most cases has persisted in a latent condition. The situation is complicated by the fact that the processes necessary for bringing about a normal outcome are not for the most part either completely present or completely absent; they are as a rule *partially* present, so that the final result remains dependent upon *quantitative* relations. Thus genital organization will be attained, but will be weakened in respect of those portions of the libido which have not proceeded so far but have remained fixated to pregenital objects and aims. Such weakening shows itself in a tendency, if there is an absence of genital satisfaction or if there are difficulties in the real world, for the libido to return to its earlier pregenital cathexes (*i.e.* to *regress*).

During the study of the sexual functions it has been possible to gain a first, preliminary conviction, or rather suspicion, of two pieces of knowledge which will later be found to be important over the whole of our field. Firstly, the normal and abnormal phenomena that we observe (that is, the phenomenology of the subject) require to be described from the point of view of dynamics and of economies (*i.e.,* in this connection, from the point of view of the quantitative distribution of the libido). And secondly, the etiology of [such] disturbances . . . is to be found in the developmental history of the individual, that is to say, in the early part of his life.

Notes

1. Cf. the hypothesis that man is descended from a mammal which reached sexual maturity at the age of five, but that some great external influence was brought to bear upon the species and interrupted the straight line of development of sexuality. This may also have been related to some other transformations in the sexual life of man as compared with that of animals, such as the suppression of the periodicity of the libido and the exploitation of the part played by menstruation in the relation between the sexes.

2. The question arises whether satisfaction of purely destructive instinctual impulses can be felt as pleasure, whether pure destructiveness without any libidinal component occurs. Satisfaction of what remains in the ego of the death instinct seems not to produce feelings of pleasure, although masochism represents a fusion which is precisely analogous to sadism.

3. The occurrence of early vaginal excitations is often asserted. But it is most probably a question of excitations in the clitoris, that is, in an organ analogous to the penis, so that this fact would not preclude us from describing the phase as phallic.

The Genetic Approach to the Psychology of Thought

Jean Piaget

Swiss psychologist Jean Piaget (1896–1980) is considered the most influential developmental psychologist in Western history. He earned his Ph.D. in zoology from the University of Neuchatel in 1918, and this background in the scientific observation of organisms helped him to become an astute researcher of the human child. Piaget's deep study of philosophy led him to examine the most fundamental categories of the developing human mind, as evidenced by the titles of but a few of his many published texts: *The Language and Thought of the Child* (1923), *Judgment and Reasoning in the Child* (1924), *The Child's Conception of the World* (1926), *The Child's Conception of Physical Reality* (1927), *The Moral Judgment of the Child* (1932), *The Origins of Intelligence in the Child* (1936), *The Construction of Reality in the Child* (1937), *The Child's Conception of Time* (1946), *The Child's Conception of Movement and Speed* (1946), and *Psychology and Epistemology: Towards a Theory of Knowledge* (1970).

Piaget's lifework focused upon mapping the stages of cognitive development. Piaget referred to his theory as "genetic epistemology," meaning the study of the emergence of the capacity "to know." His use of the term *genetic* does not simply mean the endowment of our genes. Piaget was both an interactionist and a constructivist. He believed that children intentionally construct their own minds and are simultaneously influenced by their genes and the environment while so doing.

The following selection comes from a presentation given at the New York Academy of Sciences' Conference on the Psychology of Thinking on April 28–29, 1960. It was later translated by Ruth Golbin and then published as "The Genetic Approach to the Psychology of Thought" in the *Journal of Educational Psychology* (December 1961).

Key Concept: cognitive-developmental stages

From a developmental point of view, the essential in the act of thinking is not contemplation—that is to say, that which the Greeks called "theorema"—but the action of the dynamics.

Taking into consideration all that is known, one can distinguish two principal aspects:

1. The formal viewpoint which deals with the configuration of the state of things to know—for instance, most perceptions, mental images, imageries.
2. The *dynamic* aspect, which deals with transformations—for instance, to disconnect a motor in order to understand its functioning, to disassociate and vary the components of a physical phenomenon, to understand its causalities, to isolate the elements of a geometrical figure in order to investigate its properties, etc.

The study of the development of thought shows that the dynamic aspect is at the same time more difficult to attain and more important, because only transformations make us understand the state of things. For instance: when a child of 4 to 6 years transfers a liquid from a large and low glass into a narrow and higher glass, he believes in general that the quantity of the liquid has increased, because he is limited to comparing the initial state (low level) to the final state (high level) without concerning himself with the transformation. Toward 7 or 8 years of age, on the other hand, a child discovers the preservation of the liquid, because he will think in terms of transformation. He will say that nothing has been taken away and nothing added, and, if the level of the liquid rises, this is due to a loss of width, etc.

The formal aspect of thought makes way, therefore, more and more in the course of the development to its dynamic aspect, until such time when only transformation gives an understanding of things. To think means, above all, to understand; and to understand means to arrive at the transformations, which furnish the reason for the state of things. All development of thought is resumed in the following manner: a construction of operations which stem from actions and a gradual subordination of formal aspects into dynamic aspects.

The operation, properly speaking, which constitutes the terminal point of this evolution is, therefore, to be conceived as an internalized action reversible (example: addition and subtraction, etc.) bound to other operations, which form with it a structured whole and which is characterized by well defined laws of totality (example: the groups, the lattice, etc.). Dynamic totalities are clearly different from the "gestalt" because those are characterized by their nonadditive composition, consequently irreversible.

So defined, the dynamics intervene in the construction of all thought processes; in the structure of forms and classifications, of relations and serialization of correspondences, of numbers, of space and time, of the causality, etc. One could think at first glance that space and geometry add to the formal aspect of thought. In this way one conceived of the geometric science in the past, considering it impure mathematics, but applicable to perception and intuition. Modern geometry, since *Le Programme d'Erlangen* by F. Klein, has tended, like all other precise disciplines, to subordinate the formal to the dynamic. The geometries are, indeed, understood today as relying all on groups of transformation, so that one can go from one to the other by characterizing one less general "subgroup" as part of a more inclusive group. Thus geometry too rests on a system of dynamics.

Any action of thought consists of combining thought operations and integrating the objects to be understood into systems of dynamic transformation. The psychological criteria of this is the appearance of the notion of conservation or "invariants of groups." Before speech, at the purely sensory-motor stage of a child from 0 to 18 months, it is possible to observe actions which show evidence of such tendencies. For instances: From 4–5 to 18 months, the baby constructs his first invariant, which is the schema of the permanent object (to recover an object which escaped from the field of perception). He succeeds in this by coordinating the positions and the displacements according to a structure, which can be compared to what the geometricians call "group displacements."

When, with the beginning of the symbolic function (language, symbolic play, imagerie, etc.), the representation through thought becomes possible, it is at first a question of reconstructing in thought what the action is already able to realize. The actions actually do not become transformed immediately into operations, and one has to wait until about 7 to 8 years for the child to reach a functioning level. During this preoperative period the child, therefore, only arrives at incomplete structures characterized by a lack in the notion of combinations and, consequently, by a lack of logic (in transitivity, etc.).

In the realm of causality one can especially observe these diverse forms of precausality, which we have previously described in detail. It is true that a certain number of authors—Anglo-Saxon above all—have severely criticized these conclusions, while others have recognized the same facts as we have (animism, etc.). Yet, in an important recent book (which will appear soon) two Canadian authors, M. Laurendeau and A. Pinard, have taken the whole problem up once again by means of thorough statistics. In the main points they have come to a remarkable verification of our views, explaining, moreover, the methodological reasons for the divergencies among the preceding authors.

At about 7 to 8 years the child arrives at his first complete dynamic structures (classes, relations, and numbers), which, however, still remain concrete—in other words, only at the time of a handling of objects (material manipulation or, when possible, directly imagined). It is not before the age of 11 to 12 years or more that operations can be applied to pure hypotheses. At this latter level, a logic of propositions helps complete the concrete structures. This enlarges the structures considerably until their disposition.

The fundamental genetic problem of the psychology of thought is hence to explain the formation of these dynamic structures.

Practically, one would have to rely on three principal factors in order to explain the facts of development: maturation, physical experience, and social interaction. But in this particular case none of these three suffice to furnish us with the desired explanations—not even the three together.

Maturation. First of all, none of these dynamic structures are innate, but they form very gradually. (For example: The transitivity of equalities is acquired at approximately 6½ to 7 years, and the ability of linear measure comes about only at 9 years, as does the full understanding of weights, etc.) But progressive construction does not seem to depend on maturation, because the achievements hardly correspond to a particular age. Only the order of succession is constant. However, one witnesses innumerable accelerations or retardations for reasons of education (cultural) or acquired experience. Certainly one cannot deny the inevitable role which maturation plays, but it is determined above all by existing possibility (or limitation). They still remain to be actualized, which brings about other factors. In addition, in the domain of thought, the factors of innateness seem above all limitative. We do not have, for example, an intuition of space in the fourth dimension; nevertheless we can deduce it.

Physical experience. Experiencing of objects plays, naturally, a very important role in the establishment of dynamic structures, because the operations originate from actions and the actions bear upon the object. This role manifests itself right from the beginning of sensory-motor explorations, preceding language, and it affirms itself continually in the course of manipulations and activities which are appropriate to the antecedent stages. Necessary as the role of experience may be, it does not sufficiently describe the construction of the dynamic structures—and this for the following three reasons.

First, there exist ideas which cannot possibly be derived from the child's experience—for instance, when one changes the shape of a small ball of clay. The child will declare, at 7 to 8 years, that the quantity of the matter is conserved. It does so before discovering the conservation of weight (9 to 10 years) and that of volume (10 to 11 years). What is the quantity of a matter independently of its weight and its volume? This is an abstract notion corresponding to the "substance" of the pre-Socratic physicists. This notion is neither possible to be perceived nor measurable. It is, therefore, the product of a dynamic deduction and not part of an experience. (The problem would not be solved either by presenting the quantity in the form of a bar of chocolate to be eaten.)

Secondly, the various investigations into the learning of logical structure, which we were able to make at our International Center of Genetic Epistemology, lead a very unanimous result:[1] one does not "learn" a logical structure as one learns to discover any physical law. For instance, it is easy to bring about the learning of the conservation of weight because of its physical character, but it is difficult to obtain the one of the transitivity of the relationship of the weight:

$$A = C \quad \text{if } A = B \text{ and } B = C$$

or the one of the relationship of inclusion, etc. The reason for this is that in order to arrive at the learning of a logical structure, one has to build on another more elementary logical (or prelogical) structure. And such structures consequently never stem from experience alone, but suppose always a coordinating activity of the subject.

Thirdly, there exist two types of experiences:

1. The physical experiences show the objects as they are, and the knowledge of them leads to the abstraction directly from the object (example: to discover that a more voluminous matter is more or less heavy than a less voluminous matter).

2. The logicomathematical experience supposes to interrelate by action individual facts into the world of objects, but this refers to the result of these actions rather than to the objects themselves. These interrelations are arrived at by process of abstractions from the actions and their coordinates. For instance, to discover that 10 stones in a line always add up to 10, whether they are counted from left to right or from right to left. Because then the order and the total sum have been presented. The new knowledge consists

simply in the discovery that the action of adding a sum is independent of the action of putting them in order. Thus the logicomathematical experience does not stem from the same type of learning as that of the physical experience, but rather from an equilibration of the scheme of actions, as we will see.

Social interaction. The educative and social transmission (linguistic, etc.) plays, naturally, an evident role in the formation of dynamic structures, but this factor does not suffice either to entirely explain its development, and this for two reasons:

First, a certain number of structures do not lend themselves to teaching and are prior to all teaching. One can cite, as an example, most concepts of conservation, of which, in general, the pedagogs agree that they are not problematic to the child.

The second, more fundamental, reason is that in order to understand the adult and his language, the child needs means of assimilation which are formed through structures preliminary to the social transmission itself—for instance, an ancient experience has shown us that French-speaking children understand very early the expression *"quelques unes de mes fleurs"* [some of my flowers] in contrast to *"toutes mes fleurs"* [all my flowers], and this occurs when they have not yet constructed the relation of inclusion:

Some A are part of all B;   therefore A < B

In conclusion, it is not exaggerated to maintain that the basic factors invoked before in order to explain mental development do not suffice to explain the formation of the dynamic structures. Though all three of them certainly play a necessary role, they do not constitute in themselves sufficient reason and one has to add to them a fourth factor, which we shall try to describe now.

This fourth factor seems to us to consist of a general progression of equilibration. This factor intervenes, as is to be expected, in the interaction of the preceding factors. Indeed, if the development depends, on one hand, on internal factors (maturation), and on the other hand on external factors (physical or social), it is self-evident that these internal and external factors equilibrate each other. The question is then to know if we are dealing here only with momentary compromises (unstable equilibrium) or if, on the contrary, this equilibrium becomes more and more stable. This shows that all exchange (mental as well as biological) between the organisms and the milieu (physical and social) as composed of two poles: (*a*) of the *assimilation* of the given external to the previous internal structures, and (*b*) of the *accommodation* of these structures to the given ones. The equilibrium between the assimilation and the accommodation is proportionately more stable than the assimilative structures which are better differentiated and coordinated.

It is this equilibrium between the assimilation and accommodation that seems to explain to us the functioning of the reversible operations. This occurs, for instance, in the realm of notions of conservation where the invariants of groups do not account for the maturation and the physical experience, nor for the sociolingual transmission. In fact, dynamic reversibility is a compensatory system of which the idea of conservation constitutes precisely the result. The equilibrium (between the assimilation and the accommodation) is to be defined as a compensation of exterior disturbances through activities of the subject orientated in the contrary direction of these disturbances. This leads us directly to the reversibility.

Notice that we do not conceive of the idea of equilibrium in the same manner as the "gestalt theory" does, which makes great use of this idea too, but in the sense of an automatical physical equilibrium. We believe, on the contrary, that the mental equilibrium and even the biological one presumes an activity of the subject, or of the organism. It consists in a sort of matching, orientated towards compensation—with even some overcompensation—resulting from strategies of precaution. One knows, for instance, that the homeostasis does not always lead to an exact balance. But it often leads to overcompensation, in response to exterior disturbances. Such is the case in nearly all occurrences except precisely in the case of occurrences of a superior order, which are the operations of reversible intelligence, the reversible logic of which is characterized by a complete and exact compensation (inverted operation).

The idea of equilibrium is so close to the one of reversibility that G. Brunner, in a friendly criticism of one of our latest books appearing in the *British Journal of Psychology*, proposes to renounce the idea of equilibrium because the notion of the reversibility seems sufficient to him. We hesitate to accept this suggestion for the following three reasons:

First, reversibility is a logical idea, while the equilibrium is a causal idea which permits the explanation of reforms by means of a probabilistic schema. For instance, in order to explain the formation of the idea of conservation, one can distinguish a certain number of successive stages, of which each is characterized by the "strategy" of a progress of compensation. Now it is possible to show[2] that the first of these strategies (only bearing upon one dimension, to the neglect of others) is the most probable at the point of departure, and further, that the second of these strategies (with the emphasis on a second dimension) *becomes* the most likely—as a function of the result of the first. And, finally, that the third of these strategies (oscillation between the observed modifications upon the different dimensions and the discovery of their solidarity) *becomes* the most likely in the functioning of the results of the preceding, etc. From such a point of view the process of equilibration is, therefore, characterized by a sequential control with increasing probabilities. It furnishes a beginning for causal explanations of the reversibility and does not duplicate the former idea.

Secondly, the tendency of equilibrium is much broader for the operation than the reversibility as such, which leads us to explain the reversibility through the equilibrium and not the reverse. In effect, it is at this level of the obvious regulations and sensory-motor feedbacks that the process of equilibration starts. This in its higher form becomes intelligence. Logical reversibility is therefore conceivable as an end result and not as a beginning and the entire reversibility follows the laws of a semi-reversibility of various levels.

Thirdly, the tendency to equilibrate does not only explain this final reversibility, but also certain new synthesis between originally distinct operations. One can cite in this regard an example of great importance: the serial of whole numbers. [Bertrand] Russell and [Alfred North] Whitehead have tried to explain the basic set of numbers through the idea of equivalent classes, without recourse to the serial order. This means that two classes are believed to be equivalent, if one can put their respective elements into a reciprocal arrangement. Only when this relationship relies on the quality of the objects (an A put into relation with an A, a B with a B, etc.) one does not get the quantity. If this relationship is made exclusive of the qualities (an Individual A or B put into relationship with an Individual B or A) then there exists only one way to distinguish the elements from each other. In order not to forget one, or not to count the same twice, one must deal with them in succession and introduce the serial factor as well as the structure of classes. We may then say, psychologically speaking, that the sequence of whole numbers is synthesis between two groupings qualitatively distinct, the fitting of the classes and serialization, and that this synthesis takes place as soon as one excludes the qualities of the elements in question. But how does this synthesis occur? Precisely by a gradual process of equilibration.

On the one hand the child who develops his ideas from numbers is in possession of structures enabling him to fit them into classes (classifications). But if he wants to be exclusive of qualities in order to answer to the question "how many," he becomes unable to distinguish the elements. The disequilibrium which appears, therefore, obliges the child to resort to the idea of order and take recourse to arranging these elements into a lineal row. On the other hand, if the child arranges the elements as 1, 1, 1, etc., how would he know, for instance, how to distinguish the second from the third? This new disequilibrium brings him back to the idea of classification: The "second" is the element which has but one predecessor, and the "third" is one that has two of them. In short, every new problem provokes a disequilibrium (recognizable through types of dominant errors) the solution of which consists in a re-equilibration, which brings about a new original synthesis of two systems, up to the point of independence.

During the discussion of my theories, Brunner has said that I have called disequilibrium what others describe as motivation. This is perfectly true, but the advantage of this language is to clarify that a cognitive or dynamic structure is never independent of motivational factors. The motivation in return is always solidary to structural (therefore cognitive) determined level. The language of the equilibrium presents that activity, that permits us to reunite into one and the same totality those two aspects of behavior which always have a functional solidarity because there exists no structure (cognition) without an energizer (motivation) and vice versa.

Notes

1. See *Etudes d'Epistomologie Genetique*, Vols. 7 and 10.
2. *Logique et Equilibre,* Vol. 2 of *Etudes d'Epistemologie Genetique.*

Eight Stages of Man

Erik Erikson

Erik Erikson (1902–1994) was born in Germany, studied psychoanalysis under Sigmund Freud and his daughter Anna Freud in Vienna, and moved to America in 1933, taking a position at Harvard Medical School. Based on his observations of human development in Europe and America, including his studies among the Sioux in South Dakota and the Yurok in northern California, he posited that social relationships are more influential on human development than the inner sexual tensions posited by Freud. He was also the first influential researcher in human development to emphasize stages of adult development beyond adolescence. Both Freud's psychosexual stages and Jean Piaget's cognitive-developmental stages end at puberty. Erikson, however, asserted that there are distinct stages of human functioning and interaction in young, middle, and late adulthood.

Erikson's theory of the eight stages of human development, spanning infancy to old age, was first published in his classic text *Childhood and Society* in 1950. These stages are outlined in the following excerpt from the second edition of *Childhood and Society* (W. W. Norton, 1963). In this text Erikson establishes that humans experience psychological "crises" during each of these stages. This revision of Freudian theory has inspired countless researchers, child psychologists, and educators in the last five decades.

Key Concept: psychosocial stages

Basic Trust vs. Basic Mistrust

The first demonstration of social trust in the baby is the ease of his feeding, the depth of his sleep, the relaxation of his bowels. The experience of a mutual regulation of his increasingly receptive capacities with the maternal techniques of provision gradually helps him to balance the discomfort caused by the immaturity of homeostasis with which he was born. In his gradually increasing waking hours he finds that more and more adventures of the senses arouse a feeling of familiarity, of having coincided with a feeling of inner goodness. Forms of comfort, and people associated with them, become as familiar as the gnawing discomfort of the bowels. The infant's first social achievement, then, is his willingness to let the mother out of sight without undue anxiety or rage, because she has become an inner certainty as well as an outer predictability. Such consistency, continuity, and sameness of experience provide a rudimentary sense of ego identity which depends, I think, on the recognition that there is an inner population of remembered and anticipated sensations and images which are firmly correlated with the outer population of familiar and predictable things and people. . . .

The firm establishment of enduring patterns for the solution of the nuclear conflict of basic trust versus basic mistrust in mere existence is the first task of the ego, and thus first of all a task for maternal care. But let it be said here that the amount of trust derived from earliest infantile experience does not seem to depend on absolute quantities of food or demonstrations of love, but rather on the quality of the maternal relationship. Mothers create a sense of trust in their children by that kind of administration which in its quality combines sensitive care of the baby's individual needs and a firm sense of personal trustworthiness within the trusted framework of their culture's life style. This forms the basis in the child for a sense of identity which will later combine a sense of being "all right," of being oneself, and of becoming what other people trust one will become. There are, therefore (within certain limits previously defined as the "musts" of child care), few frustrations in either this or the following stages which the growing child cannot endure if the frustration leads to the ever-renewed experience of greater sameness and stronger continuity of development, toward a final integration of the individual life cycle with some meaningful wider belongingness. Parents must not only have certain ways of guiding by prohibition and permission; they must also be able to represent to the child a deep, an almost somatic conviction that there is a meaning to what they are doing. Ultimately, children become neurotic not from frustrations, but from the lack or loss of societal meaning in these frustrations.

But even under the most favorable circumstances, this stage seems to introduce into psychic life (and become prototypical for) a sense of inner division and universal nostalgia for a paradise forfeited. It is against this powerful combination of a sense of having been deprived, of having been divided, and of having been abandoned—that basic trust must maintain itself throughout life.

Each successive stage and crisis has a special relation to one of the basic elements of society, and this for the simple reason that the human life cycle and man's institutions have evolved together. In this [essay] we can do little more than mention, after the description of each stage, what basic element of social organization is related to it. This relation is twofold: man brings to these institutions the remnants of his infantile mentality and his youthful fervor, and he receives from them—as long as they manage to maintain their actuality—reinforcement of his infantile gains.

The parental faith which supports the trust emerging in the newborn, has throughout history sought its institutional safeguard (and, on occasion, found its greatest enemy) in organized religion. Trust born of care is, in fact, the touchstone of the *actuality* of a given religion. All religions have in common the periodical childlike surrender to a Provider or providers who dispense earthly fortune as well as spiritual health; some demonstration of man's smallness by way of reduced posture and humble gesture; the admission in prayer and song of misdeeds, of misthoughts, and of evil intentions; fervent appeal for inner unification by divine guidance; and finally, the insight that individual trust must become a common faith, individual mistrust a commonly formulated evil, while the individual's restoration must become part of the ritual practice of many, and must become a sign of trustworthiness in the community.[1] . . . [T]ribes dealing with one segment of nature develop a collective magic which seems to treat the Supernatural Providers of food and fortune as if they were angry and must be appeased by prayer and self-torture. Primitive religions, the most primitive layer in all religions, and the religious layer in each individual, abound with efforts at atonement which try to make up for vague deeds against a maternal matrix and try to restore faith in the goodness of one's strivings and in the kindness of the powers of the universe.

Each society and each age must find the institutionalized form of reverence which derives vitality from its world-image—from predestination to indeterminacy. The clinician can only observe that many are proud to be without religion whose children cannot afford their being without it. On the other hand, there are many who seem to derive a vital faith from social action or scientific pursuit. And again, there are many who profess faith, yet in practice breathe mistrust both of life and man.

Autonomy vs. Shame and Doubt

In describing the growth and the crises of the human person as a series of alternative basic attitudes such as trust vs. mistrust, we take recourse to the term a "sense of," although, like a "sense of health," or a "sense of being unwell," such "senses" pervade surface and depth, consciousness and the unconscious. They are, then, at the same time, ways of *experiencing* accessible to introspection; ways of *behaving,* observable by others; and unconscious *inner states* determinable by test and analysis. It is important to keep these three dimensions in mind, as we proceed.

Muscular maturation sets the stage for experimentation with two simultaneous sets of social modalities: holding on and letting go. As is the case with all of these modalities, their basic conflicts can lead in the end to either hostile or benign expectations and attitudes. Thus, to hold can become a destructive and cruel retaining or restraining, and it can become a pattern of care: to have and to hold. To let go, too, can turn into an inimical letting loose of destructive forces, or it can become a relaxed "to let pass" and "to let be."

Outer control at this stage, therefore, must be firmly reassuring. The infant must come to feel that the basic faith in existence, which is the lasting treasure saved from the rages of the oral stage, will not be jeopardized by this about-face of his, this sudden violent wish to have a choice, to appropriate demandingly, and to eliminate stubbornly. Firmness must protect him against the potential anarchy of his as yet untrained sense of discrimination, his inability to hold on and to let go with discretion. As his environment encourages him to "stand on his own feet," it must protect him against meaningless and arbitrary experiences of shame and of early doubt. . . .

Shame is an emotion insufficiently studied, because in our civilization it is so early and easily absorbed by guilt. Shame supposes that one is completely exposed and conscious of being looked at: in one word, self-conscious. One is visible and not ready to be visible; which is why we dream of shame as a situation in which we are stared at in a condition of incomplete dress, in night attire, "with one's pants down." Shame is early expressed in an impulse to bury one's face, or to sink, right then and there, into the ground. But this, I think, is essentially rage turned against the self. He who is ashamed would like to force the world not to look at him, not to notice his exposure. He would like to destroy the eyes of the world. Instead he must wish for his own invisibility. This potentiality is abundantly used in the educational method of "shaming" used so exclusively by some primitive peoples. Visual shame precedes auditory guilt, which is a sense of badness to be had all by oneself when nobody watches and when everything is quiet—except the voice of the superego. Such shaming exploits an increasing sense of being small, which can develop only as the child stands up and as his awareness permits him to note the relative measures of size and power. . . .

Doubt is the brother of shame. Where shame is dependent on the consciousness of being upright and exposed, doubt, so clinical observation leads me to believe, has much to do with a consciousness of having a front and a back—and especially a "behind." For this reverse area of the body, with its aggressive and libidinal focus in the sphincters and in the buttocks, cannot be seen by the child, and yet it can be dominated by the will of others. The "behind" is the small being's dark continent, an area of the body which can be magically dominated and effectively invaded by those who would attack one's power of autonomy and who would designate as evil those products of the bowels which were felt to be all right when they were being passed. This basic sense of doubt in whatever one has left behind forms a substratum for later and more verbal forms of compulsive doubting; this finds its adult expression in paranoiac fears concerning hidden persecutors and secret persecutions threatening from behind (and from within the behind).

This stage, therefore, becomes decisive for the ratio of love and hate, cooperation and willfulness, freedom of self-expression and its suppression. From a sense of self-control without loss of self-esteem comes a lasting sense of good will and pride; from a sense of loss of self-control and of foreign overcontrol comes a lasting propensity for doubt and shame. . . .

We have related basic trust to the institution of religion. The lasting need of the individual to have his will reaffirmed and delineated within an adult order of things which at the same time reaffirms and delineates the will of others has an institutional safeguard in the *principle of law and order*. In daily life as well as in the high courts of law—domestic and international—this principle apportions to each his privileges and his limitations, his obligations and his rights. A sense of rightful dignity and lawful independence on the part of adults around him gives to the child of good will the confident expectation that the kind of autonomy fostered in childhood will not lead to undue doubt or shame in later life. Thus the sense of autonomy fostered in the child and modified as life progresses, serves (and is served by) the preservation in economic and political life of a sense of justice.

Initiative vs. Guilt

There is in every child at every stage a new miracle of vigorous unfolding, which constitutes a new hope and a new responsibility for all. Such is the sense and the pervading quality of initiative. The criteria for all these senses and qualities are the same: a crisis, more or less beset with fumbling and fear, is resolved, in that the child suddenly seems to "grow together" both in his person and in his body. He appears "more himself," more loving, relaxed

and brighter in his judgment, more activated and activating. He is in free possession of a surplus of energy which permits him to forget failures quickly and to approach what seems desirable (even if it also seems uncertain and even dangerous) with undiminished and more accurate direction. Initiative adds to autonomy the quality of undertaking, planning and "attacking" a task for the sake of being active and on the move, where before self-will, more often than not, inspired acts of defiance or, at any rate, protested independence. . . .

The danger of this stage is a sense of guilt over the goals contemplated and the acts initiated in one's exuberant enjoyment of new locomotor and mental power: acts of aggressive manipulation and coercion which soon go far beyond the executive capacity of organism and mind and therefore call for an energetic halt on one's contemplated initiative. While autonomy concentrates on keeping potential rivals out, and therefore can lead to jealous rage most often directed against encroachments by younger siblings, initiative brings with it anticipatory rivalry with those who have been there first and may, therefore, occupy with their superior equipment the field toward which one's initiative is directed. Infantile jealousy and rivalry, those often embittered and yet essentially futile attempts at demarcating a sphere of unquestioned privilege, now come to a climax in a final contest for a favored position with the mother; the usual failure leads to resignation, guilt, and anxiety. The child indulges in fantasies of being a giant and a tiger, but in his dreams he runs in terror for dear life. This, then, is the stage of the "castration complex," the intensified fear of finding the (now energetically erotized) genitals harmed as a punishment for the fantasies attached to their excitement.

. . . [I]t is well to look back at the blueprint of the life-stages and to the possibilities of guiding the young of the race while they are young. And here we note that according to the wisdom of the ground plan the child is at no time more ready to learn quickly and avidly, to become bigger in the sense of sharing obligation and performance than during this period of his development. He is eager and able to make things cooperatively, to combine with other children for the purpose of constructing and planning, and he is willing to profit from teachers and to emulate ideal prototypes. He remains, of course, identified with the parent of the same sex, but for the present he looks for opportunities where work-identification seems to promise a field of initiative without too much infantile conflict or oedipal guilt and a more realistic identification based on a spirit of equality experienced in doing things together. At any rate, the "oedipal" stage results not only in the oppressive establishment of a moral sense restricting the horizon of the permissible; it also sets the direction toward the possible and the tangible which permits the dreams of early childhood to be attached to the goals of an active adult life. Social institutions, therefore, offer children of this age an *economic ethos*, in the form of ideal adults recognizable by their uniforms and their functions, and fascinating enough to replace, the heroes of picture book and fairy tale.

Industry vs. Inferiority

Thus the inner stage seems all set for "entrance into life," except that life must first be school life, whether school is field or jungle or classroom. The child must forget past hopes and wishes, while his exuberant imagination is tamed and harnessed to the laws of impersonal things—even the three R's. For before the child, psychologically already a rudimentary parent, can become a biological parent, he must begin to be a worker and potential provider. With the oncoming latency period, the normally advanced child forgets, or rather sublimates, the necessity to "make" people by direct attack or to become papa and mama in a hurry: he now learns to win recognition by producing things. He has mastered the ambulatory field and the organ modes. He has experienced a sense of finality regarding the fact that there is no workable future within the womb of his family, and thus becomes ready to apply himself to given skills and tasks, which go far beyond the mere playful expression of his organ modes or the pleasure in the function of his limbs. He develops a sense of industry—i.e., he adjusts himself to the inorganic laws of the tool world. He can become an eager and absorbed unit of a productive situation. To bring a productive situation to completion is an aim which gradually supersedes the whims and wishes of play. . . .

In all cultures, at this stage, children receive some *systematic instruction*, although . . . it is by no means always in the kind of school which literate people must organize around special teachers who have learned how to teach literacy. In preliterate people and in non-literate pursuits much is learned from adults who become teachers by dint of gift and inclination rather than by appointment, and perhaps the greatest amount is learned from older children. Thus the *fundamentals of technology* are developed, as the child becomes ready to handle the utensils, the tools, and the weapons used by the big people. Literate people, with more specialized careers, must prepare the child by teaching him things which first of all make him literate, the widest possible basic education for the greatest number of possible careers. The more confusing specialization becomes, however, the more indistinct are the eventual goals of initiative; and the more complicated social reality, the vaguer are the father's and mother's role in it. School seems to be a culture all by itself, with its own goals and limits, its achievements and disappointment.

The child's danger, at this stage, lies in a sense of inadequacy and inferiority. If he despairs of his tools and skills or of his status among his tool partners, he may be discouraged from identification with them and with a section of the tool world. To lose the hope of such "industrial" association may pull him back to the more isolated, less tool-conscious familial rivalry of the oedipal time. The child despairs of his equipment in the tool world and

in anatomy, and considers himself doomed to mediocrity or inadequacy. It is at this point that wider society becomes significant in its ways of admitting the child to an understanding of meaningful roles in its technology and economy. Many a child's development is disrupted when family life has failed to prepare him for school life, or when school life fails to sustain the promises of earlier stages. . . .

On the other hand, this is socially a most decisive stage: since industry involves doing things beside and with others, a first sense of division of labor and of differential opportunity, that is, a sense of the *technological ethos* of a culture, develops at this time. . . .

Identity vs. Role Confusion

With the establishment of a good initial relationship to the world of skills and tools, and with the advent of puberty, childhood proper comes to an end. Youth begins. But in puberty and adolescence all samenesses and continuities relied on earlier are more or less questioned again, because of a rapidity of body growth which equals that of early childhood and because of the new addition of genital maturity. The growing and developing youths, faced with this physiological revolution within them, and with tangible adult tasks ahead of them are now primarily concerned with what they appear to be in the eyes of others as compared with what they feel they are, and with the question of how to connect the roles and skills cultivated earlier with the occupational prototypes of the day. In their search for a new sense of continuity and sameness, adolescents have to refight many of the battles of earlier years, even though to do so they must artificially appoint perfectly well-meaning people to play the roles of adversaries; and they are ever ready to install lasting idols and ideals as guardians of a final identity.

The integration now taking place in the form of ego identity is, as pointed out, more than the sum of the childhood identifications. It is the accrued experience of the ego's ability to integrate all identifications with the vicissitudes of the libido, with the aptitudes developed out of endowment, and with the opportunities offered in social roles. The sense of ego identity, then, is the accrued confidence that the inner sameness and continuity prepared in the past are matched by the sameness and continuity of one's meaning for others, as evidenced in the tangible promise of a "career."

The danger of this stage is role confusion.[2] Where this is based on a strong previous doubt as to one's sexual identity, delinquent and outright psychotic episodes are not uncommon. If diagnosed and treated correctly, these incidents do not have the same fatal significance which they have at other ages. In most instances, however, it is the inability to settle on an occupational identity which disturbs individual young people. To keep themselves together they temporarily overidentify, to the point of apparent complete loss of identity, with the heroes of cliques and crowds. This initiates the stage of "falling in love," which is by no means entirely, or even primarily, a sexual matter—except where the mores demand it. To a considerable extent adolescent love is an attempt to arrive at a definition of one's identity by projecting one's diffused ego image on another and by seeing it thus reflected and gradually clarified. This is why so much of young love is conversation. . . .

Intimacy vs. Isolation

The strength acquired at any stage is tested by the necessity to transcend it in such a way that the individual can take chances in the next stage with what was most vulnerably precious in the previous one. Thus, the young adult, emerging from the search for and the insistence on identity, is eager and willing to fuse his identity with that of others. He is ready for intimacy, that is, the capacity to commit himself to concrete affiliations and partnerships and to develop the ethical strength to abide by such commitments, even though they may call for significant sacrifices and compromises. Body and ego must now be masters of the organ modes and of the nuclear conflicts, in order to be able to face the fear of ego loss in situations which call for self-abandon: in the solidarity of close affiliations, in orgasms and sexual unions, in close friendships and in physical combat, in experiences of inspiration by teachers and of intuition from the recesses of the self. The avoidance of such experiences because of a fear of ego loss may lead to a deep sense of isolation and consequent self-absorption.

The counterpart of intimacy is distantiation: the readiness to isolate and, if necessary, to destroy those forces and people whose essence seems dangerous to one's own, and whose "territory" seems to encroach on the extent of one's intimate relations. Prejudices thus developed (and utilized and exploited in politics and in war) are a more mature outgrowth of the blinder repudiations which during the struggle for identity differentiate sharply and cruelly between the familiar and the foreign. The danger of this stage is that intimate, competitive, and combative relations are experienced with and against the selfsame people. But as the areas of adult duty are delineated, and as the competitive encounter, and the sexual embrace, are differentiated, they eventually become subject to that *ethical sense* which is the mark of the adult. . . .

Generativity vs. Stagnation

In this [essay] the emphasis is on the childhood stages, otherwise the section on generativity would of necessity be the central one, for this term encompasses the evolutionary development which has made man the teaching and instituting as well as the learning animal. The fashionable insistence on dramatizing the dependence of children on adults often blinds us to the dependence of the older generation on the younger one. Mature man needs

to be needed, and maturity needs guidance as well as encouragement from what has been produced and must be taken care of.

Generativity, then, is primarily the concern in establishing and guiding the next generation, although there are individuals who, through misfortune or because of special and genuine gifts in other directions, do not apply this drive to their own offspring. And indeed, the concept generativity is meant to include such more popular synonyms as *productivity* and *creativity*, which, however, cannot replace it.

It has taken psychoanalysis some time to realize that the ability to lose oneself in the meeting of bodies and minds leads to a gradual expansion of ego-interests and to a libidinal investment in that which is being generated. Generativity thus is an essential stage on the psychosexual as well as on the psychosocial schedule. Where such enrichment fails altogether, regression to an obsessive need for pseudo-intimacy takes place, often with a pervading sense of stagnation and personal impoverishment. Individuals, then, often begin to indulge themselves as if they were their own—or one another's—one and only child; and where conditions favor it, early invalidism, physical or psychological, becomes the vehicle of self-concern. The mere fact of having or even wanting children, however, does not "achieve" generativity. In fact, some young parents suffer, it seems, from the retardation of the ability to develop this stage. The reasons are often to be found in early childhood impressions; in excessive self-love based on a too strenuously self-made personality; and finally (and here we return to the beginnings) in the lack of some faith, some "belief in the species," which would make a child appear to be a welcome trust of the community.

As to the institutions which safeguard and reinforce generativity, one can only say that all institutions codify the ethics of generative succession. Even where philosophical and spiritual tradition suggests the renunciation of the right to procreate or to produce, such early turn to "ultimate concerns," wherever instituted in monastic movements, strives to settle at the same time the matter of its relationship to the Care for the creatures of this world and to the Charity which is felt to transcend it.

If this were [an essay] on adulthood, it would be indispensable and profitable at this point to compare economic and psychological theories (beginning with the strange convergencies and divergencies of Marx and Freud) and to proceed to a discussion of man's relationship to his production as well as to his progeny.

Ego Integrity vs. Despair

Only in him who in some way has taken care of things and people and has adapted himself to the triumphs and disappointments adherent to being, the originator of others or the generator of products and ideas—only in him may gradually ripen the fruit of these seven stages. I know no better word for it than ego integrity. Lacking a clear definition, I shall point to a few constituents of this state of mind. It is the ego's accrued assurance of its proclivity for order and meaning. It is a post-narcissistic love of the human ego—not of the self—as an experience which conveys some world order and spiritual sense, no matter how dearly paid for. It is the acceptance of one's one and only life cycle as something that had to be and that, by necessity, permitted of no substitutions: it thus means a new, a different love of one's parents. It is a comradeship with the ordering ways of distant times and different pursuits, as expressed in the simple products and sayings of such times and pursuits. . . .

The lack or loss of this accrued ego integration is signified by fear of death: the one and only life cycle is not accepted as the ultimate of life. Despair expresses the feeling that the time is now short, too short for the attempt to start another life and to try out alternate roads to integrity. . . .

Each individual, to become a mature adult, must to a sufficient degree develop all the ego qualities mentioned, so that a wise Indian, a true gentleman, and a mature peasant share and recognize in one another the final stage of integrity. But each cultural entity, to develop the particular style of integrity suggested by its historical place, utilizes a particular combination of these conflicts, along with specific provocations and prohibitions of infantile sexuality. Infantile conflicts become creative only if sustained by the firm support of cultural institutions and of the special leader classes representing them. In order to approach or experience integrity, the individual must know how to be a follower of image bearers in religion and in politics, in the economic order and in technology, in aristocratic living and in the arts and sciences. Ego integrity, therefore, implies an emotional integration which permits participation by followership as well as acceptance of the responsibility of leadership.

Webster's Dictionary is kind enough to help us complete this outline in a circular fashion. Trust (the first of our ego values) is here defined as "the assured reliance on another's integrity," the last of our values. I suspect that Webster had business in mind rather than babies, credit rather than faith. But the formulation stands. And it seems possible to further paraphrase the relation of adult integrity and infantile trust by saying that healthy children will not fear life if their elders have integrity enough not to fear death.

Notes

1. This is the communal and psychosocial side of religion. Its often paradoxical relation to the spirituality of the individual is a matter not to be treated briefly and in passing (see *Young Man Luther*). (E. H. E.)
2. See "The Problem of Ego-Identity," *J. Amer. Psa. Assoc.*, 4:56–121.

The Concept of Ego Development

Lê Xuân Hy and Jane Loevinger

Jane Loevinger completed her baccalaureate (in psychology, magna cum laude at age nineteen) and masters at the University of Minnesota. Later, at Berkeley, she was Erik Erikson's research assistant, and wrote her doctoral dissertation (1944) there on the construction and evaluation of tests of ability. Her subsequent work in psychometrics earned her national and international recognition, including the presidency of the American Psychological Association's Division of Evaluation, Measurement and Statistics.

Loevinger was one of the first psychologists to focus on studies of women by developing an objective test of mothers' attitudes, funded by the National Institute for Mental Health. She has written, "My interest had turned to the problems of mothers and of women in general. My personal experiences, those of my friends, particularly, two who had had severe postpartum depressions, added to the impression that most research in psychology had used male subjects, and that it was time to focus on women." Her eventually famous Sentence Completion Test was originally designed to investigate the development of women, and has now been used in hundreds of studies with both sexes and has been translated into Spanish, Dutch, Hebrew, Vietnamese, and Japanese.

Washington University has recognized her outstanding research and teaching with the William R. Stuckenberg Professor Emeritus of Human Values in Arts and Sciences. She has won a variety of prizes and awards in recognition of her work, including the Bruno Kolpfer Award for Outstanding Lifetime Contribution from the Society of Personality Assessment and the Murray Award from APA Division 8, Society for Personality and Social Psychology.

Loevinger is best known for her work on ego development. She has published more than 50 scientific articles, and several books, including *Measuring Ego Development* (1970, Jossey-Bass), *Ego Development* (1976, Jossey-Bass) and *Paradigms of Personality* (1987, Freeman). The chapter we include below comes from *Measuring Ego Development* (2nd ed.; Lawrence Erlbaum Associates), a book coauthored with Lê Xuân Hy. Professor Hy earned his doctorate at Washington University in 1986; Loevinger, who particularly enjoys working with culturally diverse students, was his mentor. In 1989 he was the recipient of the Samuel J. and Anne G. Beck Award for Outstanding Early Research from the Society of Personality Assessment. Professor Hy was born and raised in Vietnam, and is currently associate professor of psychology, Director of the Institute for Human Development, and holder of the Pigott-McCone endowed chair at Seattle University.

The concept of *ego development* has roots in ancient Greek, Hebrew, and Hindu cultures. Contrary to common belief, it did not originate with Freud or with later psychoanalysts. Psychoanalysis, in fact, originated in part as a rebellion against 19th-century ego psychology. Freud (1926/1959) consciously avoided using the term *ego*; he preferred words chosen from common speech to those of Latin origin, a preference that was ignored by his translators.

Once granted that the original sources were not written in English, it follows that one must look under other terms, the I (*das Ich*), the me (*le moi*), the self, and so on, to trace the relevant literature. There have been many similar or related conceptions, variously termed *moral development* (Kohlberg, 1964), *character development* (Peck & Havighurst, 1960), *interpersonal relatability* (Isaacs, 1956), *cognitive complexity* (Harvey, Hunt, & Schroder, 1961), and *interpersonal integration* (C. Sullivan et al., 1957). Many of the foregoing authors acknowledged as sources H. S. Sullivan (1953) *Interpersonal Theory of Psychiatry* and Piaget (1932) *Moral Judgment of the Child*. Although the definitions of the various stages and their sequence are not identical from author to author, there are many similarities, too many to be considered independent phenomena (Loevinger, 1976).

Interest in all aspects of development was stimulated at the end of the 19th century by the impact of Darwin's theory of evolution. For this and other reasons, in the early 20th century a child study movement in the United States led to the founding of child welfare institutes and incorporation of the topic of child development in texts and college curricula. The standard approaches to child development, at least in the past, tended to blur the topic of ego development. Children's growth was studied in terms of chronology, taking in order the behaviors characteristic of average and not-so-average children of each successive age.

Such atheoretical approaches have the weakness that all kinds of development are occurring together. Observation by itself will never yield a concept such as ego development nor distinguish signs of ego development from signs of intellectual development, of psychosexual development, or even of adjustment. Ego development is an abstraction, and the essence of science is that abstract ideas guide observations, and observations in turn alter abstract ideas.

A long-standing issue in the study of ego development is whether the ego is derived from and more or less explained in terms of instinctual drives, as Freud and many of his followers believed in the early years of psychoanalysis. That issue separated Freud and Adler in 1911. Adler maintained that the drives were largely subordinate to the ego and the ego strove spontaneously to develop. Freud countered that to adopt Adler's view would be to give up the hard-won gains of psychoanalytic insights, but many of his followers believed that the two views could be reconciled. Some years later, Freud returned to the topic of ego development and made major theoretical contributions whose importance is not always recognized either by psychoanalysts or by their opponents (Loevinger, 1966, 1987). At the same time, some psychoanalysts and some behaviorists found common ground in the instinct-derivative view of ego development. Although that remains a major theoretical issue, it does not bear directly on the enterprise of this book.

Ego as Frame of Reference

A second theoretical issue, one more closely related to the present enterprise, is whether ego development is best characterized as a gradual evolutionary process or as a set of discrete stages, with distinct jumps from one stage to the next. There are problems either way.

One of Adler's best-known concepts is "style of life," which at various times he equated with self or ego, the unity of personality, individuality, the method of facing problems, opinion about oneself and the problems of life, and the whole attitude toward life (H. Ansbacher & R. Ansbacher, 1956, p. 174). Seemingly, according to Adler, those terms were meant to be different ways of describing a single thing or function. That is what is here called the *ego*. That view contrasts with that found in some psychoanalytic writings, where the ego is spoken of as a collection of different functions, with its "synthetic function" just one among many. Adler's view was elaborated in somewhat different style by H. S. Sullivan (1953), who preferred the term *self-system*.

The ego is remarkable for its relative stability; it changes slowly. Accounting for this stability is not always recognized as a major theoretical problem. Simply calling the ego a structure, as some psychoanalytic theorists do, and then adding that structures are, by definition, relatively stable is not a solution.

H. S. Sullivan (1953) formulated a theory of ego stability in terms of *anxiety gating*: A major purpose of the self-system is to avoid or minimize anxiety. A person tends to recognize only what is in accord with his or her already existing self-system, that is, his or her frame of reference. Discordant observations are anxiety producing, and they are consequently avoided by selective inattention. (Fingarette, 1963, preferred to say that the failure to integrate an observation into one's current frame of reference is what anxiety is, rather than the cause of an emotion called anxiety. Anxiety, to Fingarette, was meaninglessness.)

Thus, the search for coherent meanings in experience is the essence of the ego or of ego functioning, rather than just one among many ego functions. The ego maintains its stability, its identity, and its coherence by selectively gating out observations inconsistent with its current state—granting that one person's coherence is another person's gibberish. This assumption is the theoretical foundation for the use of sentence completions and other projective techniques to measure ego development. Projective techniques call on subjects to project their own frame of reference on the test material. In contrast, objective tests constrain subjects' responses within the test constructor's frame of reference.

Thus, the issue of ego stability is illuminated by Sullivan's theory of ego (self-system, he would say) coherence; the issue of how the ego develops remains, and is perhaps made even more difficult. Sullivan called on other aspects of development, including the drives, as impetus for renewed development. In psychoanalytic theory, *mastery* becomes a key term in accounting for development, although not exactly in Adler's terms (Loevinger, 1976).

If coherence is the hallmark of ego stability, then how does one identify the stable configurations? A working list of ego stages is presented in Table 4.1. This list is almost the same as the version used in the 1970 edition of this manual. However, it differs from other authors' lists of stages, but there are large overlaps. So far it has proved impossible to show by research that some configurations called *stages* are in any demonstrable way different from patterns that have been called *transitions* between stages. In some cases, what were originally seen as transitions are now labeled as stages. For methodological reasons that are detailed shortly, no quick solution to this problem seems likely.

Stages

One of the newborn's earliest tasks is to construct for him or herself a stable world of objects. Constructing the world of objects and constructing the self are correlative.

Table 4.1 Some Characteristics of Levels of Ego Development

Level	Code	Characteristics		
		Impulse Control	**Interpersonal Mode**	**Conscious Preoccupations**
Impulsive	E2 (I-2)	Impulsive	Egocentric, dependent	Bodily feelings
Self-Protective	E3 (Delta)	Opportunistic	Manipulative, wary	"Trouble," control
Conformist	E4 (I-3)	Respect for rules	Cooperative, loyal	Appearances, behavior
Self-Aware	E5 (I-3/4)	Exceptions allowable	Helpful, self-aware	Feelings, problems, adjustment
Conscientious	E6 (I-4)	Self-evaluated standards, self-critical	Intense, responsible	Motives, traits, achievements
Individualistic	E7 (I-4/5)	Tolerant	Mutual	Individuality, development, roles
Autonomous	E8 (I-5)	Coping with conflict	Interdependent	Self-fulfillment, psychological causation
Integrated	E9 (I-6)		Cherishing individuality	Identity

Note. The code for the previous version used I-levels and Delta; the current code uses E-levels. Adapted from Loevinger (1976, 1987).

Many authors, especially many psychoanalytic theorists, refer to this period alone as ego development, but that leaves no distinctive term for the remaining stages that are the topic of our inquiry. This stage of ego formation is called the *first stage* and is acknowledged for theoretical completeness. It is beyond the scope of our work.

E2: *Impulsive Stage*

The lowest stage that is accessible by our methods of study is the Impulsive stage. The child at this stage is a creature of physical needs and impulses, dependent on others for control. Deep and dependent attachment to caretakers is colored by physical needs. Other people are understood in terms of the simplest dichotomies, good and bad, clean and dirty. Good guys give to me, mean ones do not. The growing sense of self is affirmed by the word "No." There is little sense of causation. Punishment is arbitrary or retaliatory. Rules are poorly understood. Lacking the ability to conceptualize inner life, the child cannot distinguish physical from emotional malaise. This is normal behavior for the very young child; by school age, children optimally have advanced beyond it, but those who do not may be diagnosed as "impulsive personalities."

E3: *Self-Protective Stage*

The Self-protective stage, the first step toward control of impulses and hence of character development, occurs when the child becomes capable of delay for immediate advantage. Children at this stage appreciate rules and know it is to their advantage to play by them. They are creatures of more or less opportunistic hedonism; they lack long-term goals and ideals. They want immediate gratification and, if they can, will exploit others for their ends. Seeing interpersonal relationships as exploitative, they are themselves wary and self-protective. If they "get in trouble," it is because they were with the "wrong people." Thus, blame is understood but assigned to others, to

circumstances, or sometimes to a part of themselves for which they do not feel responsible ("my eyes"). In small children passing through this stage in normal time, rituals and traditions tend to be prominent, a kind of embodiment of rules and controls. Older children and adults who remain at this stage see life as a zero-sum game; they may become hostile, opportunistic, or even psychopathic. However, most adults go beyond this stage, and probably most self-protective persons find a place in normal society and may even be successful, given good luck, good looks, intellectual brilliance, or inherited wealth.

E4: *Conformist Stage*

In normal development, at school age or somewhere in the school years, the child negotiates the transition from the egocentric Self-protective stage to the group-centered Conformist stage. More psychologists and philosophers have described Conformity than any other stage. At this stage, the child identifies self with the group or its authority—be it parents, teachers, or peers. Rules are accepted just because they are the rules. This is the period of greatest cognitive simplicity: There is a right way and a wrong way, and it is the same for everyone all the time, or at least for broad classes of people described in demographic terms. What is conventional and socially approved is right. That is usually true with respect to conventional gender roles. However, a person who rigidly conforms to some unconventional gender norms is still a Conformist. Friendliness and social niceness are highly valued; disapproval is a potent sanction. The person is preoccupied with appearance, material things, reputation, and social acceptance and belonging. Inner states are perceived in the simplest language (sad, happy, glad, angry, love, and understanding), contrasting with an almost physical version of inner life at lower levels (sick, upset, mad, excited) and a richly differentiated inner life at higher levels. People, including the self, are perceived in terms of stereotypes based on social groups rather than in terms of individual differences. The way people are and the way they ought to be are not sharply differentiated. People at this stage usually describe themselves and others of their ingroup in socially acceptable terms. Interpersonal interaction is seen primarily in terms of actions, not feelings, and the prototypic action is talking.

Group pressure can presumably encourage transition from the Self-protective to the Conformist stage. But what impels the transition out of pure conformity? Possibly, the young person during the primary school and secondary school years finds him or herself a member of different groups that demand conformity to somewhat disparate standards. One woman, for example, said that her mother punished her for some infraction by forbidding her to go to mass. She feared punishment in the Hereafter, but her mother was the clear and present danger. An individual can hardly endure such a dilemma without abandoning his or her absolute faith in at least one of the competing authorities.

E5: Self-Aware Stage

By whatever means, the person at the Self-aware stage has become aware that not everyone, including his or her own self, conforms perfectly all the time to the characteristics that stereotypes seem to demand. Once "what I am" is untied from "what I ought to be," the way is open to begin examination of self. The ability to conceptualize inner life expands; interpersonal relationships are described not merely as actions but also in terms of feelings. In many people at this stage, there is an acute sense of the distinction between self and group; emotions such as self-consciousness and loneliness are described. At the same time, the person perceives that there may be alternative possibilities in many situations that for the Conformist are covered by absolute rules or statements. Qualifications and contingencies are allowed, although they still tend to be stated in broadly demographic terms rather than in terms of individual differences: For example, some activity is okay if you are an adult, or if you are a boy, rather than if you are personally qualified or have a deep desire for it. Such modification of absolute rules may apply to anything from sexual mores to a woman having a career. The Self-aware stage is still basically a version of Conformity.

E6: Conscientious Stage

Growth to the Conscientious stage is another major and mysterious shift, for, as Freud (1930/1961) pointed out, so long as sanctions for misdeeds come from outside oneself, they can be escaped, but a bad conscience is ineluctable punishment. How are people induced to make that shift? The psychoanalytic answer is by identification with others admired, loved, or even feared; the social learning answer is that in the long run a person without conscience is punished or socially disapproved. The social learning answer seems more adequate to account for growth to Conformity than to growth past that stage, and intuitively conscience seems to be less calculating than is implied by social learning theory. However, research has no clear answers.

The distinctive mark of the Conscientious stage is self-evaluated standards: I approve or disapprove of a given conduct not just because my family or my schoolmates or the authorities do, but because that is what I personally feel. Of course, most people at this level do choose to adopt conformity as an everyday rule, so the difference between this stage and the Conformist and Self-aware stages is not the behavior itself. At this stage, one is guilty not primarily, or not only, when one has broken a rule, but rather when one has hurt another person. Motives and consequences are more important than rules per se; *ought* is differentiated from *is*. Inner states and individual differences are described in vivid and differentiated terms. Long-term goals and ideals are characteristic.

The Conscientious person is reflective; self and others are described in terms of reflexive traits. The only reflexive traits that regularly appear at a lower level are self-consciousness and self-confidence. The Conscientious person is self-critical but not totally rejecting of self, as are some persons at the lowest levels (as well as depressed people of any level). The recognition of multiple possibilities in situations leads to a sense of choice; decisions are made for reasons. The person strives for goals, tries to live up to ideals, and to improve the self.

The moral imperative remains, but it is not just a matter of doing right and avoiding wrong; priorities and appropriateness are considered. Moral issues are separated from conventional rules and from esthetic standards or preferences. To make such distinctions entails greater conceptual complexity than at the Conformist level or lower. Achievement is highly valued, not only in terms of competition or social approval (which always retain some importance), but in terms of one's own standards. Work, rather than being purely onerous, is an opportunity for achievement, so long as it is not dull or boring. People at this level are more likely than those at lower levels to think beyond their own personal concerns to those of society. The conscientious character has the negative aspect that the person may feel excessive responsibility for others.

E7: Individualistic Stage

Where the Conscientious person has a vivid sense of individual differences, the person at the next stage (Individualistic) has a sense of individuality, of the personality as a whole or the style of life. There is a greater tolerance for individual differences than at earlier stages. The inner self and the outer self are often differentiated, a distinction anticipated at the Conscientious level in concern about deceptive behavior. Although a concern for the problems of dependence and independence is a recurrent one, at this stage the person distinguishes physical, financial, and emotional dependence; there is particular concern for emotional dependence. Relationships with other people, which have been becoming deeper and more intensive as the person grew from the Conformist to the Conscientious stage, are recognized as being partly antagonistic to the striving for achievement and the sometimes excessive moralism and responsibility for others at the Conscientious level.

There are other new elements at the Individualistic level, more fully developed at the Autonomous stage. These ideas include psychological causation and psychological development. Below the Conscientious stage, almost no one ever mentions spontaneously the development of personality or of traits. Another new element is a concept of people as having and being different in different roles. The prime example of role differentiation—that a modern woman is expected to serve as wife, mother, housekeeper, lover, working woman, and so on—has become such a staple topic of women's magazines that it turns up at lower levels too. It illustrates the fact that not all clichés are Conformist.

E8: Autonomous Stage

Autonomy is a need that recurs throughout life in different forms. Erikson (1950) used the term *autonomous* for the stage here designated as Self-protective. The young child, even in the Impulsive stage, asserts him or herself by demanding to "do it by self." Here the term *autonomy* is reserved for a stage at the other end of the scale. Its chief characteristic is the recognition of other people's need for autonomy. There is also some freeing of the person from the excessive striving and sense of responsibility characteristic of the Conscientious stage. Moral dichotomies are no longer typical. They are replaced by a feeling for the complexity and multifaceted character of real people and real situations. There is a deepened respect for other people and their need to find their own way and even make their own mistakes. Crucial instances are members of one's own family, particularly one's children.

Conflicts between needs and desires are recognized and often acknowledged as part of the human condition, and thus they are not totally solvable. There is a high toleration for ambiguity and recognition of paradoxes. Humor is not hostile but tends instead to be existential, touching on the droll aspects of the nature of things. The Conscientious person's striving for achievement is transmuted into a search for self-fulfillment.

E9: Integrated Stage

Only a few individuals, probably less than 1% of an urban population in the United States, for example, reach the theoretical highest point, the Integrated stage. Data at present do not suffice to describe fully this theoretical high point. Maslow (1954) probably provides what is the best description of the self-actualizing person. Because this stage is rare in most samples and there are major differences among qualified raters both as to the description of

this level and application of the description in particular cases, under most circumstances it is best combined with the Autonomous stage.

There is a temptation to see the stages of ego development as a kind of ladder to be climbed and to suppose that the people at the highest stages are the best adjusted. There are probably well-adjusted people of all stages; surely, many children are well-adjusted, and they cannot be at the highest stages. In principle, ego maturity and adjustment must be described independently in order to ascertain empirically the relation between them. Those who remain below the Conformist level at maturity may be described as maladjusted from the point of view of some pillars of society; nonetheless, they may become quite successful in life. Because acknowledgment of inner conflict is one of the clearest signs of high ego level, some of those at the highest level may appear to be or may in fact be among those who are not well adjusted. On the other hand, some persons in the Conformist to Conscientious range may also have conflicts, acknowledged or not.

The relation between adjustment and ego level depends on one's definition of terms. From one point of view, each ego level has its own appropriate mode of adjustment, but in that case, not much is added by asserting a relation of ego development to adjustment. From another point of view, there are meanings to adjustment that do permit comparison of different ego levels. Then they must be defined independently, and one could argue that the result does not do justice to the characteristic adjustment of the highest levels.

Understandably, there is special interest in the lowest and highest stages, because both have some aura of mystery. The origins of the ego are fascinating for some of the same reasons as the origins of any psychological function. The highest stages are fascinating in part because they embody so much of what each of us aspires to or believes that he or she has achieved. But to describe ego development as simply the progression from the Impulsive stage to the Autonomous or Integrated stage, implying that the developmental course is a steady progression from low to high, would be a grievous mistake. The vast majority of people would not be described that way, and the process itself would be distorted, because neither the individual differences in ego development nor the dialectics of the most populous stages would be represented. What is most observable, either in slow progression or in individual differences within a cohort, is the range from the Self-Protective to the Conformist and from the Conformist to the Conscientious stages.

Methodological Difficulties

Table 4.1 summarizes our current views on the substance of the successive stages. In one way or another it differs from what any of the other investigators in the field has drawn up or would do when making a similar table. All of us deal with data, with hundreds or even thousands of cases, so why should there be such unresolved differences?

First, there is no one-to-one correspondence between any bit of behavior and its underlying disposition—in this case, ego level. No bit of behavior is or can be assumed to be more than probabilistically related to ego level.

Second, all kinds of development are occurring at the same times. There is no completely error-free method of separating one strand of development from another. A particular bit of behavior may, and in general must be assumed to, reflect more than one strand of development. Ego development is conceptually distinct from intellectual development and psychosexual development, but it is bound to be correlated with them during childhood and adolescence. There is not even a guarantee of "local independence"; that is, even for a group of constant chronological age, there may be a correlation between ego development and other strands of development. Thus, there is a confounding of variance that no amount of data will resolve into its component sources. If one depends entirely on empirical methods, one is at the mercy of confounded variance; so theory must always temper reliance on data, even more so because our data inevitably contain gaps.

Third, there is no error-free method of distinguishing probable signs of one ego level from signs of a probable correlate. To the extent that the correlates are other developmental variables, this principle is the same as the second one. Other correlates, such as socioeconomic status (SES), are not developmental. How can one be sure whether a particular kind of behavior results from low ego level or associated low economic and social level? In principle, with infinite amounts of data, one could decide; in practice, with the kinds of data available, one cannot be sure.

Fourth, no task can be guaranteed to display just what one wants to know about ego level. In a structured test, the investigator is projecting his or her own frame of reference rather than tapping the frame of reference of the subjects, which is what reveals their ego level. In unstructured tests, one cannot control what the subject will choose to reveal. Testers become very adept at interpreting minimal signs, but there is always the chance a person will conceal all or respond in a way that conceals usual ego level, in whatever sense others reveal theirs.

Fifth, every person in principle displays behavior at more than one level. Every behavior sample must be assumed to be diverse with respect to level. The basic tasks of psychometrics are to translate qualitative aspects of behavior to quantitative and to reduce diverse observations to single scores. There is no unique way to do either. Different psychometric procedures may lead to at least slightly different pictures of successive stages.

Sixth, there are intrinsic difficulties in assigning behavioral signs to any developmental level. A sign that appears at one level in tentative or embryonic version appears at higher levels in increasingly clear and elaborated versions. In sentence completions, a thought that appears at one level as a cliché appears in deeper, more convincing, and more complex versions at higher levels. A paradoxical result is that when similar responses are grouped together as a category and the most representative response is used as category title, the title response will often be the one that comes from a protocol rated a level lower.

Seventh, a behavioral sign may be discriminating in one direction only; thus, there is an intrinsic ambiguity in assigning it to any level within those to which it applies.

Eighth is the issue of base rates (Meehl & Rosen, 1955). Given a particular replicated response, what is the probability that the subject comes from a given level? If one is concerned only with the particular sample, the answer is the obvious one, the central tendency of those who give the response. But test constructors are not concerned just with the sample before them. Most samples contain few extreme cases; so this rule will ordinarily yield no signs that would receive extreme scores. The proper question is more like: Given a particular ego level, what is the probability of showing this sign? Because extreme cases are rare, most decisions about extreme ratings will be based on small numbers of cases, leaving the test constructor at the mercy of the idiosyncrasies of a few people. The same consideration holds for all uncommon responses at median levels. Thus, particularly for ratings at extreme levels, theory is indispensable as a supplement to data.

Finally, consider the question about clinical insight as arbiter of the appropriate level for a given sign or response type. Clinicians rarely think of data in terms of the complex probabilities detailed earlier. They tend to think of every bit of behavior as determined by the patient's particular constellation of traits and circumstances. Responses that the ground rules of this manual (see chapter 3) call for rating, clinicians would say do not reveal ego level. Indeed, that is correct, for they are equivocal. Thus, the psychometric frame of reference is different from the clinical frame of reference. There is also a deeper reason why the clinician's intuitive perceptions may be misleading. Every developmental level builds on and transmutes the previous one. The unconscious or preconscious components of the attitudes of one level are the corresponding attitudes of earlier levels. Precisely because clinicians see the patient more deeply than any test can, they may misjudge the level of a particular sign or of a patient. Hence, clinical judgment fails as a court of last appeal, though with proper precautions it is a valuable line of evidence additional to theory and test and experimental data.

The Child as a Moral Philosopher

Lawrence Kohlberg

Lawrence Kohlberg (1927–1987) is considered the most influential of all psychologists who have studied and written about the psychology of moral development and moral education. He began his doctoral dissertation on stages of moral development at the University of Chicago in 1955 and completed the majority of his research as a professor at the Harvard Graduate School of Education. Kohlberg's theory coordinates both an ancient and a modern tradition; it is based upon the Socratic notion that justice is the end of all moral reasoning and on the Piagetian notion that development occurs in discrete qualitative stages. Whereas Jean Piaget posited developmental stages of scientific reasoning, Kohlberg applied Piaget's stages to the domain of moral reasoning.

Kohlberg's work also illustrates one of the most important research designs in developmental psychology and educational outcomes research: the *longitudinal design*. Kohlberg's initial sample was a group of 75 boys, aged 10 to 16. In the mid-1950s he asked these boys how to solve a series of moral dilemmas. The boys' responses were then stage-coded, based on the "structure" of their explanations. These boys were then reinterviewed with the same dilemmas every 3 to 5 years. They are still being contacted and interviewed now, over 40 years later!

Kohlberg's work has been highly controversial, with much support and criticism from many quarters, including philosophers, feminists, anthropologists, educators, sociologists, and other psychologists. Nonetheless, most agree that his longitudinal data collection is one of the best storehouses of empirical data that the world has with regard to the ontogeny (individual development) of reasoning about justice. As an educational psychologist, Kohlberg extended educator John Dewey's work in democratizing schooling by creating "just community" schools in several places in Massachusetts and New York. Kohlberg worked from Dewey's lament that schools "told" students about democracy but did not let them live in democratic classrooms or schools.

Kohlberg published many articles in education, psychology, religion, and philosophy journals. He also authored or coauthored *Child Psychology and Childhood Education: A Cognitive-Developmental View* (Longman, 1987), *Lawrence Kohlberg's Approach to Moral Education* (Columbia University Press, 1989), *The Measurement of Moral Judgment*, 2 vols. (Cambridge University Press, 1987), *The Philosophy of Moral Development: Moral Stages and the Idea of Justice* (Harper & Row, 1981), and *Psychology of Moral Development: Essays on Moral Development* (Harper & Row, 1984). The following selection comes from "The Child as a Moral Philosopher," *Psychology Today* (1968). Kohlberg's explanation of the moral reasoning of children and youth is the most influential theory studied by schoolteachers with regard to the structure and development of moral thought in the twentieth century.

Key Concept: stages of moral reasoning

How can one study morality? Current trends in the fields of ethics, linguistics, anthropology and cognitive psychology have suggested a new approach which seems to avoid the morass of semantical confusions, value-bias and cultural relativity in which the psychoanalytic and semantic approaches to morality have foundered. New scholarship in all these fields is now focusing upon structures, forms and relationships that seem to be common to all societies and all languages rather than upon the features that make particular languages or cultures different.

For 12 years, my colleagues and I studied the same group of 75 boys, following their development at three-year intervals from early adolescence through young manhood. At the start of the study, the boys were aged 10 to 16. We have now followed them through to ages 22 to 28. In addition, I have explored moral development in other cultures—Great Britain, Canada, Taiwan, Mexico and Turkey.

Inspired by Jean Piaget's pioneering effort to apply a structural approach to moral development, I have gradually elaborated over the years of my study a typological scheme describing general structures and forms of moral thought which can be defined independently of the specific content of particular moral decisions or actions.

The typology contains three distinct levels of moral thinking, and within each of these levels distinguishes two related stages. These levels and stages may be considered separate moral philosophies, distinct views of the sociomoral world.

We can speak of the child as having his own morality or series of moralities. Adults seldom listen to children's moralizing. If a child throws back a few adult cliches and behaves himself, most parents—and many anthropologists and psychologists as well—think that the child has adopted or internalized the appropriate parental standards.

Actually, as soon as we talk with children about morality, we find that they have many ways of making judgments which are not "internalized" from the outside, and which do not come in any direct and obvious way from parents, teachers or even peers.

Moral Levels

The *preconventional* level is the first of three levels of moral thinking; the second level is *conventional*, and the third *postconventional* or autonomous. While the preconventional child is often "well-behaved" and is responsive to cultural labels of good and bad, he interprets these labels in terms of their physical consequences (punishment, reward, exchange of favors) or in terms of the physical power of those who enunciate the rules and labels of good and bad.

This level is usually occupied by children aged four to 10, a fact long known to sensitive observers of children. The capacity of "properly behaved" children of this age to engage in cruel behavior when there are holes in the power structure is sometimes noted as tragic (*Lord of the Flies, High Wind in Jamaica*), sometimes as comic (Lucy in *Peanuts*).

The second or *conventional* level also can be described as conformist, but that is perhaps too smug a term. Maintaining the expectations and rules of the individual's family, group or nation is perceived as valuable in its own right. There is a concern not only with *conforming* to the individual's social order but in *maintaining*, supporting and justifying this order.

The *postconventional* level is characterized by a major thrust toward autonomous moral principles which have validity and application apart from authority of the groups or persons who hold them and apart from the individual's identification with those persons or groups.

Moral Stages

Within each of these three levels there are two discernable stages. At the preconventional level we have:

Stage 1: Orientation toward punishment and unquestioning deference to superior power. The physical consequences of action regardless of their human meaning or value determine its goodness or badness.

Stage 2: Right action consists of that which instrumentally satisfies one's own needs and occasionally the needs of others. Human relations are viewed in terms like those of the marketplace. Elements of fairness, of reciprocity and equal sharing are present, but they are always interpreted in a physical, pragmatic way. Reciprocity is a matter of "you scratch my back and I'll scratch yours" not of loyalty, gratitude or justice.

And at the conventional level we have:

Stage 3: Good-boy–good-girl orientation. Good behavior is that which pleases or helps others and is approved by them. There is much conformity to stereotypical images of what is majority or "natural" behavior. Behavior is often judged by intention—"he means well" becomes important for the first time, and is overused, as by Charlie Brown in *Peanuts*. One seeks approval by being "nice."

Stage 4: Orientation toward authority, fixed rules and the maintenance of the social order. Right behavior consists of doing one's duty, showing respect for authority and maintaining the given social order for its own sake. One earns respect by performing dutifully.

At the postconventional level, we have:

Stage 5: A social-contract orientation, generally with legalistic and utilitarian overtones. Right action tends to be defined in terms of general rights and in terms of standards which have been critically examined and agreed upon by the whole society. There is a clear awareness of the relativism of personal values and opinions and a corresponding emphasis upon procedural rules for reaching consensus. Aside from what is constitutionally and democratically agreed upon, right or wrong is a matter of personal "values" and "opinion." The result is an emphasis upon the "legal point of view," but with an emphasis upon the possibility of *changing* law in terms of rational considerations of social utility, rather than freezing it in the terms of Stage 4 "law and order." Outside the legal realm, free agreement and contract are the binding elements of obligation. This is the "official" morality of American government, and finds its ground in the thought of the writers of the Constitution.

Stage 6: Orientation toward the decisions of conscience and toward self-chosen *ethical principles* appealing to logical comprehensiveness, universality and consistency. These principles are abstract and ethical (the Golden Rule, the categorical imperative); they are not concrete moral rules like the Ten Commandments. Instead, they are universal principles of *justice*, of the *reciprocity* and *equality* of human rights, and of respect for the dignity of human beings as *individual persons*.

Up to Now

In the past, when psychologists tried to answer the question asked of Socrates by Meno, "Is virtue something that can be taught (by rational discussion), or does it come by practice, or is it a natural inborn attitude?", their answers usually have been dictated, not by research findings on children's moral character, but by their general theoretical convictions.

Behavior theorists have said that virtue is behavior acquired according to their favorite general principles of learning. Freudians have claimed that virtue is superego-identification with parents generated by a proper balance of love and authority in family relations.

The American psychologists who have actually studied children's morality have tried to start with a set of labels—the "virtues" and "vices," the "traits" of good and bad character found in ordinary language. The earliest major psychological study of moral character, that of Hugh Hartshorne and Mark May in 1928–1930 focused on a bag of virtues including honesty, service (altruism or generosity), and self-control. To their dismay, they found that there were *no* character traits, psychological dispositions or entities which corresponded to words like honesty, service or self-control.

Regarding honesty, for instance, they found that almost everyone cheats some of the time, and that if a person cheats in one situation, it doesn't mean that he *will* or *won't* in another. In other words, it is not an identifiable character trait, *dis*honesty, that makes a child cheat in a given situation. These early researchers also found that people who cheat express as much or even more moral disapproval of cheating as those who do not cheat.

What Hartshorne and May found out about their bag of virtues is equally upsetting to the somewhat more psychological-sounding names introduced by psycho-analytic psychology: "superego-strength," "resistance to temptation," "strength of conscience," and the like. When recent researchers attempt to measure such traits in individuals, they have been forced to use Hartshorne and May's old tests of honesty and self-control and they get exactly the same results —"superego strength" in one situation predicts little to "superego strength" in another. That is, virtue-words like honesty (or superego-strength) point to certain behaviors with approval, but give us no guide to understanding them.

So far as one can extract some generalized personality factor from children's performance on tests of honesty or resistance to temptation, it is a factor of ego-strength or ego-control, which always involves non-moral capacities like the capacity to maintain attention, intelligent-task performance, and the ability to delay response. "Ego-strength" (called "will" in earlier days) has something to do with moral action, but it does not take us to the core of morality or to the definition of virtue. Obviously enough, many of the greatest evildoers in history have been men of strong wills, men strongly pursuing immoral goals.

Moral Reasons

In our research, we have found definite and universal levels of development in moral thought. In our study

of 75 American boys from early adolescence on, these youths were presented with hypothetical moral dilemmas, all deliberately philosophical, some of them found in medieval works of casuistry.

On the basis of their reasoning about these dilemmas at a given age, each boy's stage of thought could be determined for each of 25 basic moral concepts or aspects. One such aspect, for instance, is "Motive Given for Rule Obedience or Moral Action." In this instance, the six stages look like this:

1. Obey rules to avoid punishment.
2. Conform to obtain rewards, have favors returned, and so on.
3. Conform to avoid disapproval, dislike by others.
4. Conform to avoid censure by legitimate authorities and resultant guilt.
5. Conform to maintain the respect of the impartial spectator judging in terms of community welfare.
6. Conform to avoid self-condemnation.

In another of these 25 moral aspects, the value of human life, the six stages can be defined thus:

1. The value of a human life is confused with the value of physical objects and is based on the social status or physical attributes of its possessor.
2. The value of a human life is seen as instrumental to the satisfaction of the needs of its possessor or of other persons.
3. The value of a human life is based on the empathy and affection of family members and others toward its possessor.
4. Life is conceived as sacred in terms of its place in a categorical moral or religious order of rights and duties.
5. Life is valued both in terms of its relation to community welfare and in terms of life being a universal human right.
6. Belief in the sacredness of human life as representing a universal human value of respect for the individual.

I have called this scheme a typology. This is because about 50 per cent of most people's thinking will be at a single stage, regardless of the moral dilemma involved. We call our types *stages* because they seem to represent an *invariant developmental sequence*. "True" stages come one at a time and always in the same order.

All movement is forward in sequence, and does not skip steps. Children may move through these stages at varying speeds, of course, and may be found half in and half out of a particular stage. An individual may stop at any given stage and at any age, but if he continues to move, he must move in accord with these steps. Moral reasoning of the conventional or Stage 3–4 kind never occurs before the preconventional Stage-1 and Stage-2 thought has taken place. No adult in Stage 4 has gone through Stage 6, but all Stage-6 adults have gone at least through 4.

While the evidence is not complete, my study strongly suggests that moral change fits the stage pattern just described. (The major uncertainty is whether all Stage 6s go through Stage 5 or whether these are two alternate mature orientations.)

How Values Change

As a single example of our findings of stage-sequence, take the progress of two boys on the aspect "The Value of Human Life." The first boy Tommy, is asked "Is it better to save the life of one important person or a lot of unimportant people?" At age 10, he answers "all the people that aren't important because one man just has one house, maybe a lot of furniture, but a whole bunch of people have an awful lot of furniture and some of these poor people might have a lot of money and it doesn't look it."

Clearly Tommy is Stage 1: he confuses the value of a human being with the value of the property he possesses. Three years later (age 13) Tommy's conceptions of life's value are most clearly elicited by the question, "Should the doctor 'mercy kill' a fatally ill woman requesting death because of her pain?" He answers, "Maybe it would be good to put her out of her pain, she'd be better off that way. But the husband wouldn't want it, it's not like an animal. If a pet dies you can get along without it—it isn't something you really need. Well, you can get a new wife, but it's not really the same."

Here his answer is Stage 2: the value of the woman's life is partly contingent on its hedonistic value to the wife herself but even more contingent on its instrumental value to her husband, who can't replace her as easily as he can a pet.

Three years later still (age 16) Tommy's conception of life's value is elicited by the same question, to which he replies: "It might be best for her, but her husband—it's a human life—not like an animal; it just doesn't have the same relationship that a human being does to a family. You can become attached to a dog, but nothing like a human you know."

Now Tommy has moved from a Stage 2 instrumental view of the woman's value to a Stage-3 view based on the husband's distinctively human empathy and love for someone in his family. Equally clearly, it lacks any basis for a universal human value of the woman's life, which would hold if she had no husband or if her husband didn't love her. Tommy, then, has moved step by step through three stages during the age 10–16. Tommy, though bright (I.Q. 120), is a slow developer in moral judgment. Let us take another boy, Richard, to show us sequential movement through the remaining three steps.

At age 13, Richard said about the mercy-killing, "If she requests it, it's really up to her. She is in such terrible pain, just the same as people are always putting animals out of their pain," and in general showed a mixture of

Stage-2 and Stage-3 responses concerning the value of life. At 16, he said, "I don't know. In one way, it's murder, it's not a right or privilege of man to decide who shall live and who should die. God put life into everybody on earth and you're taking away something from that person that came directly from God, and you're destroying something that is very sacred, it's in a way part of God and it's almost destroying a part of God when you kill a person. There's something of God in everyone."

Here Richard clearly displays a Stage-4 concept of life as sacred in terms of its place in a categorical moral or religious order. The value of human life is universal, it is true for all humans. It is still, however, dependent on something else, upon respect for God and God's authority; it is not an autonomous human value. Presumably if God told Richard to murder, as God commanded Abraham to murder Isaac, he would do so.

At age 20, Richard said to the same question: "There are more and more people in the medical profession who think it is a hardship on everyone, the person, the family, when you know they are going to die. When a person is kept alive by an artificial lung or kidney it's more like being a vegetable than being a human. If it's her own choice, I think there are certain rights and privileges that go along with being a human being. I am a human being and have certain desires for life and I think everybody else does too. You have a world of which you are the center, and everybody else does too and in that sense we're all equal."

Richard's response is clearly Stage 5, in that the value of life is defined in terms of equal and universal human rights in a context of relativity ("You have a world of which you are the center and in that sense we're all equal"), and of concern for utility or welfare consequences.

The Final Step

At 24, Richard says: "A human life takes precedence over any other moral or legal value, whoever it is. A human life has inherent value whether or not it is valued by a particular individual. The worth of the individual human being is central where the principles of justice and love are normative for all human relationships."

This young man is at Stage 6 in seeing the value of human life as absolute in representing a universal and equal respect for the human as an individual. He has moved step by step through a sequence, culminating in a definition of human life as centrally valuable rather than derived from or dependent on social or divine authority.

In a genuine and culturally universal sense, these steps lead toward an increased *morality* of value judgment, where morality is considered as a form of judging, as it has been in a philosophic tradition running from the analyses of Kant to those of the modern analytic or "ordinary language" philosophers. The person at Stage 6 has disentangled his judgments of—or language about—human life from status and property values

(Stage 1), from its uses to others (Stage 2), from interpersonal affection (Stage 3), and so on; he has a means of moral judgment that is universal and impersonal. The Stage-6 person's answers use moral words like "duty" or "morally right," and he uses them in a way implying universality, ideals, impersonality: He thinks and speaks in phrases like "regardless of who it was," or "... I would do it in spite of punishment."

Across Cultures

When I first decided to explore moral development in other cultures, I was told by anthropologist friends that I would have to throw away my culture-bound moral concepts and stories and start from scratch learning a whole new set of values for each new culture. My first try consisted of a brace of villages, one Atayal (Malaysian aboriginal) and the other Taiwanese.

My guide was a young Chinese ethnographer who had written an account of the moral and religious patterns of the Atayal and Taiwanese villages. Taiwanese boys in the 10–13 age group were asked about a story involving theft of food. A man's wife is starving to death but the store owner won't give the man any food unless he can pay, which he can't. Should he break in and steal some food? Why? Many of the boys said, "He should steal the food for his wife because if she dies he'll have to pay for her funeral and that costs a lot."

My guide was amused by these responses, but I was relieved: they were of course "classic" Stage-2 responses.

In the Atayal village, funerals weren't such a big thing, so the Stage-2 boys would say, "He should steal the food because he needs his wife to cook for him."

This means that we need to consult our anthropologists to know what content a Stage-2 child will include in his instrumental exchange calculations, or what a Stage-4 adult will identify as the proper social order. But one certainly doesn't have to start from scratch. What made my guide laugh was the difference in form between the children's Stage-2 thought and his own, a difference definable independently of particular cultures.

[Figures] 5.1 and 5.2 indicate the cultural universality of the sequence of stages which we have found. [Figure] 5.1 presents the age trends for middle-class urban boys in the U.S., Taiwan and Mexico. At age 10 in each country, the order of use of each stage is the same as the order of its difficulty or maturity.

In the United States, by age 16 the order is the reverse, from the highest to the lowest, except that Stage 6 is still little-used. At age 13, the good-boy, middle stage (Stage 3), is not used.

The results in Mexico and Taiwan are the same, except that development is a little slower. The most conspicuous feature is that at the age of 16, Stage-5 thinking is much more salient in the United States than in Mexico or Taiwan. Nevertheless, it *is* present in the other countries, so we know that this is not purely an American democratic construct.

[Figure] 5.2 shows strikingly similar results from two isolated villages, one in Yucatan, one in Turkey. While

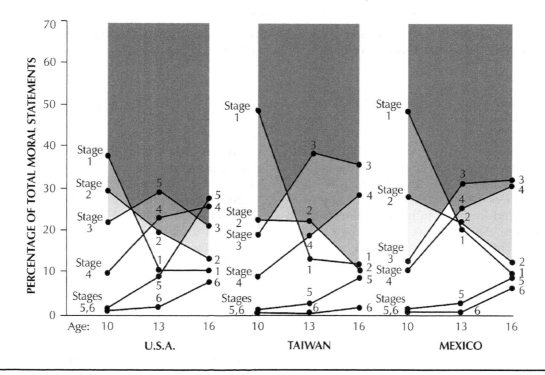

Figure 5.1 Note: Middle-class urban boys in the U.S., Taiwan and Mexico. At age 10 the stages are used according to difficulty. At age 13, Stage 3 is most used by all three groups. At age 16 U.S. boys have reversed the order of age 10 stages (with the exception of 6). In Taiwan and Mexico, conventional (3–4) stages prevail at age 16, with Stage 5 also little used.

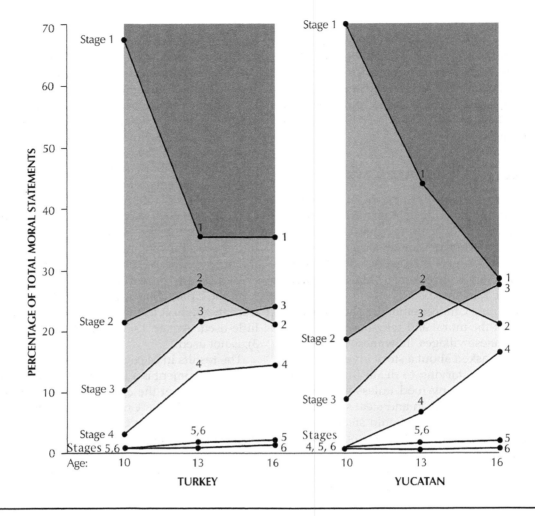

Figure 5.2   Note: Two isolated villages, one in Turkey, the other in Yucatan, show similar patterns in moral thinking. There is no reversal of order, and preconventional (1–2) thought does not gain a clear ascendancy over conventional stages at age 16.

conventional moral thought increases steadily from ages 10 to 16 it still has not achieved a clear ascendancy over preconventional thought.

Trends for lower-class urban groups are intermediate in the rate of development between those for the middle-class and for the village boys. In the three divergent cultures that I studied, middle-class children were found to be more advanced in moral judgment than matched lower-class children. This was not due to the fact that the middle-class children heavily favored some one type of thought which could be seen as corresponding to the prevailing middle-class pattern. Instead, middle-class and working-class children move through the same sequences, but the middle-class children move faster and farther.

This sequence is not dependent upon a particular religion, or any religion at all in the usual sense. I found no important differences in the development of moral thinking among Catholics, Protestants, Jews, Buddhists, Moslems and atheists. Religious values seem to go through the same stages as all other values.

Trading Up

In summary, the nature of our sequence is not significantly affected by widely varying social, cultural or religious conditions. The only thing that is affected is the *rate* at which individuals progress through this sequence.

Why should there be such a universal invariant sequence of development? In answering this question, we need first to analyze these developing social concepts in terms of their internal logical structure. At each stage, the same basic moral concept or aspect is defined, but at each higher stage this definition is more differentiated, more integrated and more general or universal. When one's concept of human life moves from Stage 1 to Stage 2 the value of life becomes more differentiated from the value of property, more integrated (the value of life enters an organizational hierarchy where it is "higher" than property so that one steals property in order to save life) and more universalized (the life of any sentient being is valuable regardless of status or property). The same advance is true at each stage in the hierarchy. Each step of development then is a better cognitive organization than the one before it, one which takes account of everything present in the previous stage, but making new distinctions and organizing them into a more comprehensive or more equilibrated structure. The fact that this is the case has been demonstrated by a series of studies indicating that children and adolescents comprehend all stages up to their own, but not more than one stage beyond their own. And importantly, *they prefer this next stage.*

We have conducted experimental moral discussion classes which show that the child at an earlier stage of development tends to move forward when confronted by the views of a child one stage further along. In an argument between a Stage-3 and Stage-4 child, the child in the third stage tends to move toward or into Stage 4, while the Stage-4 child understands but does not accept the arguments of the Stage-3 child.

Moral thought, then, seems to behave like all other kinds of thought. Progress through the moral levels and stages is characterized by increasing differentiation and increasing integration, and hence is the same kind of progress that scientific theory represents. Like acceptable scientific theory—or like *any* theory or structure of knowledge—moral thought may be considered partially to generate its own data as it goes along, or at least to expand so as to contain in a balanced, self-consistent way a wider and wider experiential field. The raw data in the case of our ethical philosophies may be considered as conflicts between roles, or values, or as the social order in which men live.

The Role of Society

The social worlds of all men seem to contain the same basic structures. All the societies we have studied have the same basic institutions—family, economy, law, government. In addition, however, all societies are alike because they *are* societies—systems of defined complementary roles. In order to *play* a social role in the family, school or society, the child must implicitly take the role of others toward himself and toward others in the group. These role-taking tendencies form the basis of all social institutions. They represent various patternings of shared or complementary expectations.

In the preconventional and conventional levels (Stages 1–4), moral content or value is largely accidental or culture-bound. Anything from "honesty" to "courage in battle" can be the central value. But in the higher postconventional levels, Socrates, Lincoln, Thoreau and Martin Luther King tend to speak without confusion of tongues, as it were. This is because the ideal principles of any social structure are basically alike, if only because there simply aren't that many principles which are articulate, comprehensive and integrated enough to be satisfying to the human intellect. And most of these principles have gone by the name of justice.

Behavioristic psychology and psychoanalysis have always upheld the Philistine view that fine moral words are one thing and moral deeds another. Morally mature reasoning is quite a different matter, and does not really depend on "fine words." The man who understands justice is more likely to practice it.

In our studies, we have found that youths who understand justice act more justly, and the man who understands justice helps create a moral climate which goes far beyond his immediate and personal acts. The universal society is the beneficiary.

Woman's Place in Man's Life Cycle

Carol Gilligan

Carol Gilligan (b. 1936) is currently a professor of human development at the Harvard Graduate School of Education. Originally an English major at Swarthmore College, she added to her interest of reading books the reading and interpreting of humans and their development. As a student at Harvard she followed Erik Erikson's work closely, and she became a research associate to Lawrence Kohlberg, with whom she published on the topic of adolescent development. During her collaboration with Kohlberg, she noticed that females tended to respond in a qualitatively different way than males to the hypothetical moral dilemmas that Kohlberg used in his research. This led her to realize not only that the most influential developmental psychologists were male but that their theories contained a masculine bias. She found that either data that were collected about women were forced to fit into what was considered "normal" for a man's development or the data from women's lives were considered aberrant.

Gilligan wrote several papers revealing this problem, which were later collected, revised, and included in her text *In a Different Voice: Psychological Theory and Women's Development* (Harvard University Press, 1982). It immediately caught the attention of academics and psychologists, and it became a nonfiction best-seller. It has inspired a whole new generation of gender-related research, and it has influenced a variety of academic fields, from English literature to philosophy and education. The following selection is an excerpt from the first chapter of this text, entitled "Woman's Place in Man's Life Cycle." An earlier version of that chapter was originally published in the *Harvard Educational Review*.

Key Concept: women's distinct developmental path

In the second act of *The Cherry Orchard*, Lopahin, a young merchant, describes his life of hard work and success. Failing to convince Madam Ranevskaya to cut down the cherry orchard to save her estate, he will go on in the next act to buy it himself. He is the self-made man who, in purchasing the estate where his father and grandfather were slaves, seeks to eradicate the "awkward, unhappy life" of the past, replacing the cherry orchard with summer cottages where coming generations "will see a new life." In elaborating this developmental vision, he reveals the image of man that underlies and supports his activity: "At times when I can't go to sleep, I think: Lord, thou gavest us immense forests, unbounded fields and the widest horizons, and living in the midst of them we should indeed be giants"—at which point, Madame Ranevskaya interrupts him, saying, "You feel the need for giants—They are good only in fairy tales, anywhere else they only frighten us."

Conceptions of the human life cycle represent attempts to order and make coherent the unfolding experiences and perceptions, the changing wishes and realities of everyday life. But the nature of such conceptions depends in part on the position of the observer. The brief excerpt from Chekhov's play suggests that when the observer is a woman, the perspective may be of a different sort. Different judgments of the image of man as giant imply different ideas about human development, different ways of imagining the human condition, different notions of what is of value in life.

At a time when efforts are being made to eradicate discrimination between the sexes in the search for social equality and justice, the differences between the sexes are being rediscovered in the social sciences. This discovery occurs when theories formerly considered to be sexually neutral in their scientific objectivity are found instead to reflect a consistent observational and evaluative bias. Then the presumed neutrality of science, like that of language itself, gives way to the recognition that the categories of knowledge are human constructions. The fascination with point of view that has informed the fiction of the twentieth century and the corresponding recognition of the relativity of judgment infuse our scientific understanding as well when we begin to notice how accustomed we have become to seeing life through men's eyes.

A recent discovery of this sort pertains to the apparently innocent classic *The Elements of Style* by William Strunk and E. B. White. A Supreme Court ruling on the subject of sex discrimination led one teacher of English to notice that the elementary rules of English usage were being taught through examples which counterposed the birth of Napoleon, the writings of Coleridge, and statements such as "He was an interesting talker. A man who had traveled all over the world and lived in half a dozen countries," with "Well, Susan, this is a fine mess you are in" or, less drastically, "He saw a woman, accompanied by two children, walking slowly down the road."

Psychological theorists have fallen as innocently as Strunk and White into the same observational bias. Implicitly adopting the male life as the norm, they have tried to fashion women out of a masculine cloth. It all goes back, of course, to Adam and Eve—a story which shows, among other things, that if you make a woman out of a man, you are bound to get into trouble. In the life cycle, as in the Garden of Eden, the woman has been the deviant.

The penchant of developmental theorists to project a masculine image, and one that appears frightening to women, goes back at least to Freud (1905), who built his theory of psychosexual development around the experiences of the male child that culminate in the Oedipus complex. In the 1920s, Freud struggled to resolve the contradictions posed for his theory by the differences in female anatomy and the different configuration of the young girl's early family relationships. After trying to fit women into his masculine conception, seeing them as envying that which they missed, he came instead to acknowledge, in the strength and persistence of women's pre-Oedipal attachments to their mothers, a developmental difference. He considered this difference in women's development to be responsible for what he saw as women's developmental failure.

Having tied the formation of the superego or conscience to castration anxiety, Freud considered women to be deprived by nature of the impetus for a clear-cut Oedipal resolution. Consequently, women's superego—the heir to the Oedipus complex—was compromised: it was never "so inexorable, so impersonal, so independent of its emotional origins as we require it to be in men." From this observation of difference, that "for women the level of what is ethically normal is different from what it is in men," Freud concluded that women "show less sense of justice than men, that they are less ready to submit to the great exigencies of life, that they are more often influenced in their judgments by feelings of affection or hostility" (1925, pp. 257–258).

Thus a problem in theory became cast as a problem in women's development, and the problem in women's development was located in their experience of relationships. Nancy Chodorow (1974), attempting to account for "the reproduction within each generation of certain general and nearly universal differences that characterize masculine and feminine personality and roles," attributes these differences between the sexes not to anatomy but rather to "the fact that women, universally, are largely responsible for early child care." Because this early social environment differs for and is experienced differently by male and female children, basic sex differences recur in personality development. As a result, "in any given society, feminine personality comes to define itself in relation and connection to other people more than masculine personality does" (pp. 43–44).

In her analysis, Chodorow relies primarily on Robert Stoller's studies which indicate that gender identity, the unchanging core of personality formation, is "with rare exception firmly and irreversibly established for both sexes by the time a child is around three." Given that for both sexes the primary caretaker in the first three years of life is typically female, the interpersonal dynamics of gender identity formation are different for boys and girls. Female identity formation takes place in a context of ongoing relationship since "mothers tend to experience their daughters as more like, and continuous with, themselves." Correspondingly, girls, in identifying themselves as female, experience themselves as like their mothers, thus fusing the experience of attachment with the process of identity formation. In contrast, "mothers experience their sons as a male opposite," and boys, in defining themselves as masculine, separate their mothers from themselves, thus curtailing "their primary love and sense of empathic tie." Consequently, male development entails a "more emphatic individuation and a more defensive firming of experienced ego boundaries." For boys, but not girls, "issues of differentiation have become intertwined with sexual issues" (1978, pp. 150, 166–167).

Writing against the masculine bias of psychoanalytic theory, Chodorow argues that the existence of sex differences in the early experiences of individuation and relationship "does not mean that women have 'weaker' ego boundries than men or are more prone to psychosis." It means instead that "girls emerge from this period with a basis for 'empathy' built into their primary definition of self in a way that boys do not." Chodorow thus replaces Freud's negative and derivative description of female psychology with a positive and direct account of her own: "Girls emerge with a stronger basis for experiencing another's needs or feelings as one's own (or of thinking that one is so experiencing another's needs and feelings). Furthermore, girls do not define themselves in terms of the denial of preoedipal relational modes to the same extent as do boys. Therefore, regression to these modes tends not to feel as much as a basic threat to their ego. From very early, then, because they are parented by a person of the same gender . . . girls come to experience themselves as less differentiated than boys, as more continuous with and related to the external object-world, and as differently oriented to their inner object-world as well" (p. 167).

Consequently, relationships, and particularly issues of dependency, are experienced differently by women and men. For boys and men, separation and individuation are critically tied to gender identity since separation from the mother is essential for the development of masculinity. For girls and women, issues of femininity or feminine identity do not depend on the achievement of separation from the mother or on the progress of individuation. Since masculinity is defined through separation while femininity is defined through attachment, male gender identity is threatened by intimacy while female gender identity is threatened by separation. Thus males tend to have difficulty with relationships, while females tend to have problems with individuation. The quality of embeddedness in social interaction and personal relationships that characterizes women's lives in contrast to men's, however, becomes not only a descriptive difference but also a developmental liability when the milestones of childhood and adolescent development in the psychological literature are markers of increasing separation. Women's failure to separate then becomes by definition a failure to develop.

The sex differences in personality formation that Chodorow describes in early childhood appear during the middle childhood years in studies of children's games. Children's games are considered by George Herbert Mead (1934) and Jean Piaget (1932) as the crucible of social development during the school years. In games, children learn to take the role of the other and come to see themselves through another's eyes. In games, they learn respect for rules and come to understand the ways rules can be made and changed.

Janet Lever (1976), considering the peer group to be the agent of socialization during the elementary school years and play to be a major activity of socialization at that time, set out to discover whether there are sex differences in the games that children play. Studying 181 fifth-grade, white, middle-class children, ages ten and eleven, she observed the organization and structure of their playtime activities. She watched the children as they played at school during recess and in physical education class, and in addition kept diaries of their accounts as to how they spent their out-of-school time. From this study, Lever reports sex differences: boys play out of doors more often than girls do; boys play more often in large and age-heterogeneous groups; they play competitive games more often, and their games last longer than girls' games. The last is in some ways the most interesting finding. Boys' games appeared to last longer not only because they required a higher level of skill and were thus less likely to become boring, but also because, when disputes arose in the course of a game, boys were able to resolve the disputes more effectively than girls: "During the course of this study, boys were seen quarrelling all the time, but not once was a game terminated because of a quarrel and no game was interrupted for more than seven minutes. In the gravest debates, the final word was

always, to 'repeat the play,' generally followed by a chorus of 'cheater's proof'" (p. 482). In fact, it seemed that the boys enjoyed the legal debates as much as they did the game itself, and even marginal players of lesser size or skill participated equally in these recurrent squabbles. In contrast, the eruption of disputes among girls tended to end the game.

Thus Lever extends and corroborates the observations of Piaget in his study of the rules of the game, where he finds boys becoming through childhood increasingly fascinated with the legal elaboration of rules and the development of fair procedures for adjudicating conflicts, a fascination that, he notes, does not hold for girls. Girls, Piaget observes, have a more "pragmatic" attitude toward rules, "regarding a rule as good as long as the game repaid it" (p. 83). Girls are more tolerant in their attitudes toward rules, more willing to make exceptions, and more easily reconciled to innovations. As a result, the legal sense, which Piaget considers essential to moral development, "is far less developed in little girls than in boys" (p. 77).

The bias that leads Piaget to equate male development with child development also colors Lever's work. The assumption that shapes her discussion of results is that the male model is the better one since it fits the requirements for modern corporate success. In contrast, the sensitivity and care for the feelings of others that girls develop through their play have little market value and can even impede professional success. Lever implies that, given the realities of adult life, if a girl does not want to be left dependent on men, she will have to learn to play like a boy.

To Piaget's argument that children learn the respect for rules necessary for moral development by playing rule-bound games, Lawrence Kohlbert (1969) adds that these lessons are most effectively learned through the opportunities for role-taking that arise in the course of resolving disputes. Consequently, the moral lessons inherent in girls' play appear to be fewer than in boys'. Traditional girls' games like jump rope and hopscotch are turn-taking games, where competition is indirect since one person's success does not necessarily signify another's failure. Consequently, disputes requiring adjudication are less likely to occur. In fact, most of the girls whom Lever interviewed claimed that when a quarrel broke out, they ended the game. Rather than elaborating a system of rules for resolving disputes, girls subordinated the continuation of the game to the continuation of relationships.

Lever concludes that from the games they play, boys learn both the independence and the organizational skills necessary for coordinating the activities of large and diverse groups of people. By participating in controlled and socially approved competitive situations, they learn to deal with competition in a relatively forthright manner—to play with their enemies and to compete with their friends—all in accordance with the rules of the game. In contrast, girls' play tends to occur in smaller, more intimate groups, often the best-friend dyad, and in private places. This play replicates the social pattern of primary human relationships in that its organization is more cooperative. Thus, it points less, in Mead's terms, toward learning to take the role of "the generalized other," less toward the abstraction of human relationships. But it fosters the development of the empathy and sensitivity necessary for taking the role of "the particular other" and points more toward knowing the other as different from the self.

The sex differences in personality formation in early childhood that Chodorow derives from her analysis of the mother-child relationship are thus extended by Lever's observations of sex differences in the play activities of middle childhood. Together these accounts suggest that boys and girls arrive at puberty with a different interpersonal orientation and a different range of social experiences. Yet, since adolescence is considered a crucial time for separation, the period of "the second individuation process" (Blos, 1967), female development has appeared most divergent and thus most problematic at this time.

"Puberty," Freud says, "which brings about so great an accession of libido in boys, is marked in girls by a fresh wave of *repression*," necessary for the transformation of the young girls' "masculine sexuality" into the specifically feminine sexuality of her adulthood (1905, pp. 220–221). Freud posits this transformation on the girl's acknowledgment and acceptance of "the fact of her castration" (1931, p. 229). To the girl, Freud explains, puberty brings a new awareness of "the wound to her narcissism" and leads her to develop, "like a scar, a sense of inferiority" (1925, p. 253). Since in Erik Erikson's expansion of Freud's psychoanalytic account, adolescence is the time when development hinges on identity, the girl arrives at this juncture either psychologically at risk or with a different agenda.

The problem that female adolescence presents for theorists of human development is apparent in Erikson's scheme. Erikson (1950) charts eight stages of psychosocial development, of which adolescence is the fifth. The task at this stage is to forge a coherent sense of self, to verify an identity that can span the discontinuity of puberty and make possible the adult capacity to love and work. The preparation for the successful resolution of the adolescent identity crisis is delineated in Erikson's description of the cries that characterize the preceding four stages. Although the initial crisis in infancy of "trust versus mistrust" anchors development in the experience of relationship, the task then clearly becomes one of individuation. Erikson's second stage centers on the crisis of "autonomy versus shame and doubt," which marks the walking child's emerging sense of separateness and agency. From there, development goes on through the crisis of "initiative versus guilt," successful resolution of which represents a further move in the direction of autonomy. Next, following the inevitable disappointment of the magical wishes of the Oedipal period, children realize that to compete with their parents, they must first join them and learn to do what they do so well. Thus

in the middle childhood years, development turns on the crisis of "industry versus inferiority," as the demonstration of competence becomes critical to the child's developing self-esteem. This is the time when children strive to learn and master the technology of their culture, in order to recognize themselves and to be recognized by others as capable of becoming adults. Next comes adolescence, the celebration of the autonomous, initiating, industrious self through the forging of an identity based on an ideology that can support and justify adult commitments. But about whom is Erikson talking?

Once again it turns out to be the male child. For the female, Erikson (1968) says, the sequence is a bit different. She holds her identity in abeyance as she prepares to attract the man by whose name she will be known, by whose status she will be defined, the man who will rescue her from emptiness and loneliness by filling "the inner space." While for men, identity precedes intimacy and generativity in the optimal cycle of human separation and attachment, for women these tasks seem instead to be fused. Intimacy goes along with identity, as the female comes to know herself as she is known, through her relationships with others.

Yet despite Erikson's observation of sex differences, his chart of life-cycle stages remains unchanged: identity continues to precede intimacy as male experience continues to define his life-cycle conception. But in this male life cycle there is little preparation for the intimacy of the first adult stage. Only the initial stage of trust versus mistrust suggests the type of mutuality that Erikson means by intimacy and generativity and Freud means by genitality. The rest is separateness, with the result that development itself comes to be identified with separation, and attachments appear to be developmental impediments, as is repeatedly the case in the assessment of women.

Erikson's description of male identity as forged in relation to the world and of female identity as awakened in a relationship of intimacy with another person is hardly new. In the fairy tales that Bruno Bettelheim (1976) describes an identical portrayal appears. The dynamics of male adolescence are illustrated archetypically by the conflict between father and son in "The Three Languages." Here a son, considered hopelessly stupid by his father, is given one last chance at education and sent for a year to study with a master. But when he returns, all he has learned is "what the dogs bark." After two further attempts of this sort, the father gives up in disgust and orders his servants to take the child into the forest and kill him. But the servants, those perpetual rescuers of disowned and abandoned children, take pity on the child and decide simply to leave him in the forest. From there, his wanderings take him to a land beset by furious dogs whose barking permits nobody to rest and who periodically devour one of the inhabitants. Now it turns out that our hero has learned just the right thing: he can talk with the dogs and is able to quiet them, thus restoring peace to the land. Since the other knowledge he acquires serves him equally well, he emerges triumphant from his adolescent confrontation with his father, a giant of the life-cycle conception.

In contrast, the dynamics of female adolescence are depicted through the telling of a very different story. In the world of the fairy tale, the girl's first bleeding is followed by a period of intense passivity in which nothing seems to be happening. Yet in the deep sleeps of Snow White and Sleeping Beauty, Bettelheim sees that inner concentration which he considers to be the necessary counterpart to the activity of adventure. Since the adolescent heroines awake from their sleep, not to conquer the world, but to marry the prince, their identity is inwardly and interpersonally defined. For women, in Bettelheim's as in Erikson's account, identity and intimacy are intricately conjoined. The sex differences depicted in the world of fairy tales, like the fantasy of the woman warrior in Maxine Hong Kingston's (1977) recent autobiographical novel which echoes the old stories of Troilus and Cressida and Tancred and Chlorinda, indicate repeatedly that active adventure is a male activity, and that if a woman is to embark on such endeavors, she must at least dress like a man.

These observations about sex difference support the conclusion reached by David McClelland (1975) that "sex role turns out to be one of the most important determinants of human behavior; psychologists have found sex differences in their studies from the moment they started doing empirical research." But since it is difficult to say "different" without saying "better" or "worse," since there is a tendency to construct a single scale of measurement, and since that scale has generally been derived from and standardized on the basis of men's interpretations of research data drawn predominantly or exclusively from studies of males, psychologists "have tended to regard male behavior as the 'norm' and female behavior as some kind of deviation from that norm" (p. 81). Thus, when women do not conform to the standards of psychological expectation, the conclusion has generally been that something is wrong with the women.

What Matina Horner (1972) found to be wrong with women was the anxiety they showed about competitive achievement. From the beginning, research on human motivation using the Thematic Apperception Test (TAT) was plagued by evidence of sex differences which appeared to confuse and complicate data analysis. The TAT presents for interpretation an ambiguous cue—a picture about which a story is to be written or a segment of a story that is to be completed. Such stories, in reflecting projective imagination, are considered by psychologists to reveal the ways in which people construe what they perceive, that is, the concepts and interpretations they bring to their experience and thus presumably the kind of sense that they make of their lives. Prior to Horner's work it was clear that women made a different kind of sense than men of situations of competitive achievement, that in some way they saw the situations differently or the situations aroused in them some different response.

On the basis of his studies of men, McClelland divided the concept of achievement motivation into what appeared to be its two logical components, a motive to approach success ("hope success") and a motive to avoid failure ("fear failure"). From her studies of women, Horner identified as a third category the unlikely motivation to avoid success ("fear success"). Women appeared to have a problem with competitive achievement, and that problem seemed to emanate from a perceived conflict between femininity and success, the dilemma of the female adolescent who struggles to integrate her feminine aspirations and the identifications of her early childhood with the more masculine competence she has acquired at school. From her analysis of women's completions of a story that began, "after first term finals, Anne finds herself at the top of her medical school class," and from her observation of women's performance in competitive achievement situations, Horner reports that, "when success is likely or possible, threatened by the negative consequences they expect to follow success, young women become anxious and their positive achievement strivings become thwarted" (p. 171). She concludes that this fear "exists because for most women, the anticipation of success in competitive achievement activity, especially against men, produces anticipation of certain negative consequences, for example, threat of social rejection and loss of femininity" (1968, p. 125).

Such conflicts about success, however, may be viewed in a different light. Georgia Sassen (1980) suggests that the conflicts expressed by the women might instead indicate "a heightened perception of the 'other side' of competitive success, that is, the great emotional costs at which success achieved through competition is often gained—an understanding which, though confused, indicates some underlying sense that something is rotten in the state in which success is defined as having better grades than everyone else" (p. 15). Sassen points out that Horner found success anxiety to be present in women only when achievement was directly competitive, that is, when one person's success was at the expense of another's failure.

In his elaboration of the identity crisis, Erikson (1968) cites the life of George Bernard Shaw to illustrate the young person's sense of being co-opted prematurely by success in a career he cannot wholeheartedly endorse. Shaw at seventy, reflecting upon his life, described his crisis at the age of twenty as having been caused not by the lack of success or the absence of recognition, but by too much of both: "I made good in spite of myself, and found, to my dismay, that Business, instead of expelling me as the worthless impostor I was, was fastening upon me with no intention of letting me go. Behold me, therefore, in my twentieth year, with a business training, in an occupation which I detested as cordially as any sane person lets himself detest anything he cannot escape from. In March 1876 I broke loose" (p. 143). At this point Shaw settled down to study and write as he pleased. Hardly interpreted as evidence of neurotic anxiety about achievement and competition, Shaw's refusal suggests to Erikson "the extraordinary workings of an extraordinary personality [coming] to the fore" (p. 144).

We might on these grounds begin to ask, not why women have conflicts about competitive success, but why men show such readiness to adopt and celebrate a rather narrow vision of success. Remembering Piaget's observation, corroborated by Lever, that boys in their games are more concerned with rules while girls are more concerned with relationships, often at the expense of the game itself—and given Chodorow's conclusion that men's social orientation is positional while women's is personal—we begin to understand why, when "Anne" becomes "John" in Horner's tale of competitive success and the story is completed by men, fear of success tends to disappear. John is considered to have played by the rules and won. He has the *right* to feel good about his success. Confirmed in the sense of his own identity as separate from those who, compared to him, are less competent, his positional sense of self is affirmed. For Anne, it is possible that the position she could obtain by being at the top of her medical school class may not, in fact, be what she wants.

"It is obvious," Virginia Woolf says, "that the values of women differ very often from the values which have been made by the other sex" (1929, p. 76). Yet, she adds, "it is the masculine values that prevail." As a result, women come to question the normality of their feelings and to alter their judgments in deference to the opinion of others. In the nineteenth century novels written by women, Woolf sees at work "a mind which was slightly pulled from the straight and made to alter its clear vision in deference to external authority." The same deference to the values and opinions of others can be seen in the judgments of twentieth century women. The difficulty women experience in finding or speaking publicly in their own voices emerges repeatedly in the form of qualification and self-doubt, but also in intimations of a divided judgment, a public assessment and private assessment which are fundamentally at odds.

Yet the deference and confusion that Woolf criticizes in women derive from the values she sees as their strength. Women's deference is rooted not only in their social subordination but also in the substance of their moral concern. Sensitivity to the needs of others and the assumption of responsibility for taking care lead women to attend to voices other than their own and to include in their judgment other points of view. Women's moral weakness, manifest in an apparent diffusion and confusion of judgment, is thus inseparable from women's moral strength, an overriding concern with relationships and responsibilities. The reluctance to judge may itself be indicative of the care and concern for others that infuse the psychology of women's development and are responsible for what is generally seen as problematic in its nature.

Thus women not only define themselves in a context of human relationship but also judge themselves in terms of their ability to care. Women's place in man's life cycle has been that of nurturer, caretaker, and helpmate, the weaver of those networks of relationships on which she in turn relies. But while women have thus taken care of men, men have, in their theories of psychological development, as in their economic arrangements, tended to assume or devalue that care. When the focus on individuation and individual achievement extends into adulthood and maturity is equated with personal autonomy, concern with relationships appears as a weakness of women rather than as a human strength (Miller, 1976).

The discrepancy between womanhood and adulthood is nowhere more evident than in the studies on sex-role stereotypes reported by Broverman, Vogel, Broverman, Clarkson, and Rosenkrantz (1972). The repeated finding of these studies is that the qualities deemed necessary for adulthood—the capacity for autonomous thinking, clear decision-making, and responsible action—are those associated with masculinity and considered undesirable as attributes of the feminine self. The stereotypes suggest a splitting of love and work that relegates expressive capacities to women while placing instrumental abilities in the masculine domain. Yet looked at from a different perspective, these stereotypes reflect a conception of adulthood that is itself out of balance, favoring the separateness of the individual self over connection to others, and leaning more toward an autonomous life of work than toward the interdependence of love and care.

The discovery now being celebrated by men in midlife of the importance of intimacy, relationships, and care is something that women have known from the beginning. However, because that knowledge in women has been considered "intuitive" or "instinctive," a function of anatomy coupled with destiny, psychologists have neglected to describe its development. In my research, I have found that women's moral development centers on the elaboration of that knowledge and thus delineates a critical line of psychological development in the lives of both of the sexes. The subject of moral development not only provides the final illustration of the reiterative pattern in the observation and assessment of sex differences in the literature on human development, but also indicates more particularly why the nature and significance of women's development has been for so long obscured and shrouded in mystery.

The criticism that Freud makes of women's sense of justice, seeing it as compromised in its refusal of blind impartiality, reappears not only in the work of Piaget but also in that of Kohlberg. While in Piaget's account (1932) of the moral judgment of the child, girls are an aside, a curiosity to whom he devotes four brief entries in an index that omits "boys" altogether because "the child" is assumed to be male, in the research from which Kohlberg derives his theory, females simply do not exit. Kohlberg's (1958, 1981) six stages that describe the development of moral judgment from childhood to adulthood are based empirically on a study of eighty-four boys whose development Kohlberg has followed for a period of over twenty years. Although Kohlberg claims universality for his stage sequence, those groups not included in his original sample rarely reach his higher stages (Edwards, 1975; Holstein, 1976; Simpson, 1974). Prominent among those who thus appear to be deficient in moral development when measured by Kohlberg's scale are women, whose judgments seem to exemplify the third stage of his six-stage sequence. At this stage morality is conceived in interpersonal terms and goodness is equated with helping and pleasing others. This conception of goodness is considered by Kohlberg and Kramer (1969) to be functional in the lives of mature women insofar as their lives take place in the home. Kohlberg and Kramer imply that only if women enter the traditional arena of male activity will they recognize the inadequacy of this moral perspective and progress like men toward higher stages where relationships are subordinated to rules (stage four) and rules to universal principles of justice (stages five and six).

Yet herein lies a paradox, for the very traits that traditionally have defined the "goodness" of women, their care for and sensitivity to the needs of others, are those that mark them as deficient in moral development. In this version of moral development, however, the conception of maturity is derived from the study of men's lives and reflects the importance of individuation in their development. Piaget (1970), challenging the common impression that a developmental theory is built like a pyramid from its base in infancy, points out that a conception of development instead hangs from its vertex of maturity, the point toward which progress is traced. Thus, a change in the definition of maturity does not simply alter the description of the highest stage but recasts the understanding of development, changing the entire account.

When one begins with the study of women and derives developmental constructs from their lives, the outline of a moral conception different from that described by Freud, Piaget, or Kohlberg begins to emerge and informs a different description of development. In this conception, the moral problem arises from conflicting responsibilities rather than from competing rights and requires for its resolution a mode of thinking that is contextual and narrative rather than formal and abstract. This conception of morality as concerned with the activity of care centers moral development around the understanding of responsibility and relationships, just as the conception of morality as fairness ties moral development to the understanding of rights and rules.

This different construction of the moral problem by women may be seen as the critical reason for their failure to develop within the constraints of Kohlberg's system. Regarding all constructions of responsibility as evidence of a conventional moral understanding, Kohlberg defines the highest stages of moral development as deriving from a reflective understanding of human rights. That the morality of rights differs from the morality of responsibility in its emphasis on separation rather than connection, in its consideration of the individual rather than the relationship as primary, is illustrated by two responses to interview questions about the nature of morality. The first comes from a twenty-five-year-old man, one of the participants in Kohlberg's study:

> [*What does the word morality mean to you?*] Nobody in the world knows the answer. I think it is recognizing the right of the individual, the rights of other individuals, not interfering with those rights. Act as fairly as you would have them treat you. I think it is basically to preserve the human being's right to existence. I think that is the most important. Secondly, the human being's right to do as he pleases, again without interfering with somebody else's rights.
>
> [*How have your views on morality changed since the last interview?*] I think I am more aware of an individual's rights now. I used to be looking at it strictly from my point of view, just for me. Now I think I am more aware of what the individual has a right to.

Kohlberg (1973) cites this man's response as illustrative of the principled conception of human rights that exemplifies his fifth and sixth stages. Commenting on the response, Kohlberg says: "Moving to a perspective outside of that of his society, he identifies morality with justice (fairness, rights, the Golden Rule), with recognition of the rights of others as these are defined naturally or intrinsically. The human's being right to do as he pleases without interfering with somebody else's rights is a formula defining rights prior to social legislation" (pp. 29–30).

The second response comes from a woman who participated in the rights and responsibilities study. She also was twenty-five and, at the time, a third-year law student:

> [*Is there really some correct solution to moral problems, or is everybody's opinion equally right?*] No, I don't think everybody's opinion is equally right. I think that in some situations there may be opinions that are equally valid, and one could conscientiously adopt one of several courses of action. But there are other situations in which I think there are right and wrong answers, that sort of inhere in the nature of existence, of all individuals here who need to live with each other to live. We need to depend on each other, and hopefully it is not only a physical need but a need of fulfillment in ourselves, that a person's life is enriched by cooperating with other people and striving to live in harmony with everybody else, and to that end, there are right and wrong, there are things which promote that end and that move away from it, and in that way it is possible to choose in certain cases among different courses of action that obviously promote or harm that goal.
>
> [*Is there a time in the past when you would have thought about these things differently?*] Oh, yeah, I think that I went through a time when I thought that things were pretty relative, that I can't tell you what to do and you can't tell me what to do, because you've got your conscience and I've got mine.
>
> [*When was that?*] When I was in high school. I guess that it just sort of dawned on me that my own ideas changed, and because my own judgment changed, I felt I couldn't judge another person's judgment. But now

I think even when it is only the person himself who is going to be affected. I say it is wrong to the extent it doesn't cohere with what I know about human nature and what I know about you, and just from what I think is true about the operation of the universe, I could say I think you are making a mistake.

[*What led you to change, do you think?*] Just seeing more of life, just recognizing that there are an awful lot of things that are common among people. There are certain things that you come to learn promote a better life and better relationships and more personal fulfillment than other things that in general tend to do the opposite, and the things that promote these things, you would call morally right.

This response also represents a personal reconstruction of morality following a period of questioning and doubt, but the reconstruction of moral understanding is based not on the primacy and universality of individual rights, but rather on what she describes as a "very strong sense of being responsible to the world." Within this construction, the moral dilemma changes from how to exercise one's rights without interfering with the rights of others to how "to lead a moral life which includes obligations to myself and my family and people in general." The problem then becomes one of limiting responsibilities without abandoning moral concern. When asked to describe herself, this woman says that she values "having other people that I am tied to, and also having people that I am responsible to. I have a very strong sense of being responsible to the world, that I can't just live for my enjoyment, but just the fact of being in the world gives me an obligation to do what I can to make the world a better place to live in, no matter how small a scale that may be on." Thus while Kohlberg's subject worries about people interfering with each other's rights, this woman worries about "the possibility of omission, of your not helping others when you could help them."

The issue that this woman raises is addressed by Jane Loevinger's fifth "autonomous" stage of ego development, where autonomy, placed in a context of relationships, is defined as modulating an excessive sense of responsibility through the recognition that other people have responsibility for their own destiny. The autonomous stage in Loevinger's account (1970) witnesses a relinquishing of moral dichotomies and their replacement with "a feeling for the complexity and multifaceted character of real people and real situations" (p. 6). Whereas the rights conception of morality that informs Kohlberg's principled level (stages five and six) is geared to arriving at an objectively fair or just resolution to moral dilemmas upon which all rational persons could agree, the responsibility conception focuses instead on the limitations of any particular resolution and describes the conflicts that remain.

Thus it becomes clear why a morality of rights and noninterference may appear frightening to women in its potential justification of indifference and unconcern. At the same time, it becomes clear why, from a male perspective, a morality of responsibility appears inconclusive and diffuse, given its insistent contextual relativism. Women's moral judgments thus elucidate the pattern observed in the description of the developmental differences between the sexes, but they also provide an alternative conception of maturity by which these differences can be assessed and their implications traced. The psychology of women that has consistently been described as distinctive in its greater orientation toward relationships and interdependence implies a more contextual mode of judgment and a different moral understanding. Given the differences in women's conceptions of self and morality, women bring to the life cycle a different point of view and order human experience in terms of different priorities.

The myth of Demeter and Persephone, which McClelland (1975) cites as exemplifying the feminine attitude toward power, was associated with the Eleusinian Mysteries celebrated in ancient Greece for over two thousand years. As told in the Homeric *Hymn to Demeter*, the story of Persephone indicates the strengths of interdependence, building up resources and giving, that McClelland found in his research on power motivation to characterize the mature feminine style. Although, McClelland says, "it is fashionable to conclude that no one knows what went on in the Mysteries, it is known that they were probably the most important religious ceremonies, even partly on the historical record, which were organized by and for women, especially at the onset before men by means of the cult of Dionysos began to take them over." Thus McClelland regards the myth as "a special presentation of feminine psychology" (p. 96). It is, as well, a life-cycle story par excellence.

Persephone, the daughter of Demeter, while playing in a meadow with her girlfriends, sees a beautiful narcissus which she runs to pick. As she does so, the earth opens and she is snatched away by Hades, who takes her to his underworld kingdom. Demeter, goddess of the earth, so mourns the loss of her daughter that she refuses to allow anything to grow. The crops that sustain life on earth shrivel up, killing men and animals alike, until Zeus takes pity on man's suffering and persuades his brother to return Persephone to her mother. But before she leaves, Persephone eats some pomegranate seeds, which ensures that she will spend part of every year with Hades in the underworld.

The elusive mystery of women's development lies in its recognition of the continuing importance of attachment in the human live cycle. Woman's place in man's life cycle is to protect this recognition while the developmental litany intones the celebration of separation, autonomy, individuation, and natural rights. The myth of Persephone speaks directly to the distortion in this view by reminding us that narcissism leads to death, that the fertility of the earth is in some mysterious way tied to the continuation of the mother-daughter relationship, and that the life cycle itself arises from an alternation between the world of women and that of men. Only when life-cycle theorists divide their attention and begin to live with women as they have lived with men will their vision encompass the experience of both sexes and their theories become correspondingly more fertile.

References

Bettelheim, Bruno. *The Uses of Enchantment.* New York: Alfred A. Knopf, 1976.

Blos, Peter. "The Second Individuation Process of Adolescence." In A. Freud, ed., *The Psychoanalytic Study of the Child*, vol. 22. New York: International Universities Press, 1967.

Broverman, I., Vogel, S., Broverman, D., Clarkson, F., and Rosenkrantz, P. "Sex-role Stereotypes: A Current Appraisal." *Journal of Social Issues* 28 (1972): 59–78.

Chekhov, Anton. *The Cherry Orchard* (1904). In *Best Plays by Chekhov*, trans. Stark Young. New York: The Modern Library, 1956.

Chodorow, Nancy. "Family Structure and Feminine Personality." In M. Z. Rosaldo and L. Lamphere, eds., *Woman, Culture and Society.* Stanford: Stanford University Press, 1974.

———. *The Reproduction of Mothering.* Berkeley: University of California Press, 1978.

Edwards, Carolyn P. "Societal Complexity and Moral Development: A Kenyan Study," *Ethos* 3 (1975): 505–527.

Erikson, Erik H. *Childhood and Society.* New York: W. W. Norton, 1950.

———. *Identity: Youth and Crisis.* New York: W. W. Norton, 1968.

Freud, Sigmund. *Three Essays on the Theory of Sexuality* (1905). Vol. VII.

———. "Some Psychical Consequences of the Anatomical Distinction Between the Sexes" (1925). Vol. XIX.

———. "Female Sexuality" (1931). Vol. XXI.

Holstein, Constance, "Development of Moral Judgment: A Longitudinal Study of Males and Females." *Child Development* 47 (1976): 51–61.

Horner, Matina S. "Sex Differences in Achievement Motivation and Performance in Competitive and Noncompetitive Situations." Ph.D. Diss., University of Michigan, 1968. University Microfilms #6912135.

———. "Toward an Understanding of Achievement-related Conflicts in Women." *Journal of Social Issues* 28 (1972): 157–175.

Kingston, Maxine Hong. *The Woman Warrior.* New York: Alfred A. Knopf, 1977.

Kohlberg, Lawrence. "The Development of Modes of Thinking and Choices in Years 10 to 16." Ph.D. Diss., University of Chicago, 1958.

———. "Stage and Sequence: The Cognitive-Development Approach to Socialization." In D. A. Goslin, ed., *Handbook of Socialization Theory and Research.* Chicago: Rand McNally, 1969.

———. "Continuities and Discontinuities in Childhood and Adult Moral Development Revisited." In *Collected Papers on Moral Development and Moral Education.* Moral Education Research Foundation, Harvard University, 1973.

———. *The Philosophy of Moral Development.* San Francisco: Harper and Row, 1981.

Kohlberg, L., and Kramer, R. "Continuities and Discontinuities in Child and Adult Moral Development." *Human Development* 12 (1969): 93–120.

Lever, Janet. "Sex Differences in the Games Children Play." *Social Problems* 23 (1976): 478–487.

Loevinger, Jane, and Wessler, Ruth. *Measuring Ego Development.* San Francisco: Jossey-Bass, 1970.

McClelland, David C. *Power: The Inner Experience.* New York: Irvington, 1975.

Mead, George Herbert. *Mind, Self, and Society.* Chicago: University of Chicago Press, 1934.

Miller, Jean Baker. *Toward a New Psychology of Women.* Boston: Beacon Press, 1976.

Piaget, Jean. *The Moral Judgment of the Child* (1932). New York: The Free Press, 1965.

———. *Structuralism.* New York: Basic Books, 1970.

Sassen, Georgia, "Success Anxiety in Women: A Constructivist Interpretation of Its Sources and Its Significance." *Harvard Educational Review* 50 (1980): 13–25.

Simpson, Elizabeth L. "Moral Development Research: A Case Study of Scientific Cultural Bias." *Human Development* 17 (1974): 81–106.

Stoller, Robert, J. "A Contribution to the Study of Gender Identity." *International Journal of Psycho-Analysis* 45 (1964): 220–226.

Strunk, William Jr., and White, E. B. *The Elements of Style* (1918). New York: Macmillan, 1958.

Woolf, Virginia. *A Room of One's Own.* New York: Harcourt, Brace and World, 1929.

A Rounded Version

Howard Gardner and Joseph Walters

Howard Gardner was born in Pennsylvania and earned both his bachelor's and doctorate degrees from Harvard University. He is currently a professor of human development at the Harvard Graduate School of Education. Gardner's book *Frames of Mind: The Theory of Multiple Intelligences* (Basic Books, 1983) has been deeply influential in the lively, ongoing debate concerning the nature of intelligence in both the field of psychology and the popular press. It earned the Best Book Award from the American Psychological Association in 1984.

Since the beginning of scientific psychology about 100 years ago, there has been an ongoing argument over whether intelligence is best considered a single, broad, general ability (referred to as "g-factor") or whether it is more accurately depicted as a set of specific abilities that are largely discrete and independent. In *Frames of Mind* Gardner presented a variety of strong evidence—ranging from physiological-psychological brain research to studies of precocity and genius—to demonstrate that there are at least seven basic different intelligences. In the last decade and a half, Gardner's Theory of Multiple Intelligences (TMI) has had a big impact on the practice of human development, particularly in schools. It has transformed curriculum and teaching methods in every part of the United States, from preschool to college, in that school districts across the nation have been inspired with a vision of teaching to all seven intelligences.

The following excerpt is taken from the second chapter of *Multiple Intelligences: The Theory in Practice* (Basic Books, 1993). Coauthored by Joseph Walters, it is essentially a revised and updated summary of Gardner's TMI, one decade after it was first made public.

Key Concept: multiple intelligences

Two eleven-year-old children are taking a test of "intelligence." They sit at their desks laboring over the meanings of different words, the interpretation of graphs, and the solutions to arithmetic problems. They record their answers by filling in small circles on a single piece of paper. Later these completed answer sheets are scored objectively: the number of right answers is converted into a standardized score that compares the individual child with a population of children of similar age.

The teachers of these children review the different scores. They notice that one of the children has performed at a superior level; on all sections of the test, she answered more questions correctly than did her peers. In fact, her score is similar to that of children three to four years older. The other child's performance is average—his scores reflect those of other children his age.

A subtle change in expectations surrounds the review of these test scores. Teachers begin to expect the first child to do quite well during her formal schooling, whereas the second should have only moderate success. Indeed these

predictions come true. In other words, the test taken by the eleven-year-olds serves as a reliable predictor of their later performance in school.

How does this happen? One explanation involves our free use of the word "intelligence": the child with the greater "intelligence" has the ability to solve problems, to find the answers to specific questions, and to learn new material quickly and efficiently. These skills in turn play a central role in school success. In this view, "intelligence" is a singular faculty that is brought to bear in any problem-solving situation. Since schooling deals largely with solving problems of various sorts, predicting this capacity in young children predicts their future success in school.

"Intelligence," from this point of view, is a general ability that is found in varying degrees in all individuals. It is the key to success in solving problems. This ability can be measured reliably with standardized pencil-and-paper tests that, in turn, predict future success in school.

What happens after school is completed? Consider the two individuals in the example. Looking further down the road, we find that the "average" student has become a highly successful mechanical engineer who has risen to a position of prominence in both the professional community of engineers as well as in civic groups in his community. His success is no fluke—he is considered by all to be a talented individual. The "superior" student, on the other hand, has had little success in her chosen career as a writer; after repeated rejections by publishers, she has taken up a middle management position in a bank. While certainly not a "failure," she is considered by her peers to be quite "ordinary" in her adult accomplishments. So what happened?

This fabricated example is based on the facts of intelligence testing. IQ tests predict school performance with considerable accuracy, but they are only an indifferent predictor of performance in a profession after formal schooling (Jencks, 1972). Furthermore, even as IQ tests measure only logical or logical linguistic capacities, in this society we are nearly "brain-washed" to restrict the notion of intelligence to the capacities used in solving logical and linguistic problems.

To introduce an alternative point of view, undertake the following "thought experiment." Suspend the usual judgment of what constitutes intelligence and let your thoughts run freely over the capabilities of humans—perhaps those that would be picked out by the proverbial Martian visitor. In this exercise, you are drawn to the brilliant chess player, the world-class violinist, and the champion athlete; such outstanding performers deserve special consideration. Under this experiment, a quite different view of *intelligence* emerges. Are the chess player, violinist, and athlete "intelligent" in these pursuits? If they are, then why do our tests of "intelligence" fail to identify them? If they are not "intelligent," what allows them to achieve such astounding feats? In general, why does the contemporary construct "intelligence" fail to explain large areas of human endeavor?

[Here] we approach these problems through the theory of multiple intelligences (MI). As the name indicates, we believe that human cognitive competence is better described in terms of a set of abilities, talents, or mental skills, which we call "intelligences." All normal individuals possess each of these skills to some extent; individuals differ in the degree of skill and in the nature of their combination. We believe this theory of intelligence may be more humane and more veridical than alternative views of intelligence and that it more adequately reflects the data of human "intelligent" behavior. Such a theory has important educational implications, including ones for curriculum development.

What Constitutes an Intelligence?

The question of the optimal definition of intelligence looms large in our inquiry. Indeed, it is at the level of this definition that the theory of multiple intelligences diverges from traditional points of view. In a traditional view, intelligence is defined operationally as the ability to answer items on tests of intelligence. The inference from the test scores to some underlying ability is supported by statistical techniques that compare responses of subjects at different ages; the apparent correlation of these test scores across ages and across different tests corroborates the notion that the general faculty of intelligence, g, does not change much with age or with training or experience. It is an inborn attribute or faculty of the individual.

Multiple intelligences theory, on the other hand, pluralizes the traditional concept. An intelligence entails the ability to solve problems or fashion products that are of consequence in a particular cultural setting or community. The problem-solving skill allows one to approach a situation in which a goal is to be obtained and to locate the appropriate route to that goal. The creation of a *cultural* product is crucial to such functions as capturing and transmitting knowledge or expressing one's views or feelings. The problems to be solved range from creating an end for a story to anticipating a mating move in chess to repairing a quilt. Products range from scientific theories to musical compositions to successful political campaigns.

MI theory is framed in light of the biological origins of each problem solving skill. Only those skills that are universal to the human species are treated. Even so, the biological proclivity to participate in a particular form of problem solving must also be coupled with the cultural nurturing of that domain. For example, language, a universal skill, may manifest itself particularly as writing in one culture, as oratory in another culture, and as the secret language of anagrams in a third.

Given the desire of selecting intelligences that are rooted in biology, and that are valued in one or more cultural settings, how does one actually identify an "intelligence"? In coming up with our list, we consulted evidence from several different sources: knowledge about normal development and development in gifted individuals; information about the breakdown of cognitive skills under conditions of brain damage; studies of exceptional populations, including prodigies, idiots savants, and autistic children; data about the evolution of cognition over the millenia; cross-cultural accounts of cognition; psychometric studies, including examinations of correlations among tests; and psychological training studies, particularly measures of transfer and generalization across tasks. Only those candidate intelligences that satisfied all or a majority of the criteria were selected as bona fide intelligences. A more complete discussion of each of these criteria for an "intelligence" and the seven intelligences that have been proposed so far, is found in *Frames of mind* (1983). This book also considers how the theory might be disproven and compares it to competing theories of intelligence.

In addition to satisfying the aforementioned criteria, each intelligence must have an identifiable core operation or set of operations. As a neurally based computational system, each intelligence is activated or "triggered" by certain kinds of internally or externally presented information.

For example, one core of musical intelligence is the sensitivity to pitch relations, whereas one core of linguistic intelligence is the sensitivity to phonological features.

An intelligence must also be susceptible to encoding in a symbol system—a culturally contrived system of meaning, which captures and conveys important forms of information. Language, picturing, and mathematics are but three nearly worldwide symbol systems that are necessary for human survival and productivity. The relationship of a candidate intelligence to a human symbol system is no accident. In fact, the existence of a core computational capacity anticipates the existence of a symbol system that exploits that capacity. While it may be possible for an intelligence to proceed without an accompanying symbol system, a primary characteristic of human intelligence may well be its gravitation toward such an embodiment.

The Seven Intelligences

Having sketched the characteristics and criteria of an intelligence, we turn now to a brief consideration of each of the seven intelligences. We begin each sketch with a thumbnail biography of a person who demonstrates an unusual facility with that intelligence. These biographies illustrate some of the abilities that are central to the fluent operation of a given intelligence. Although each biography illustrates a particular intelligence, we do not wish to imply that in adulthood intelligences operate in isolation. Indeed, except for abnormal individuals, intelligences always work in concert, and any sophisticated adult role will involve a melding of several of them. Following each biography we survey the various sources of data that support each candidate as an "intelligence."

Musical Intelligence
When he was three years old, Yehudi Menuhin was smuggled into the San Francisco Orchestra concerts by his parents. The sound of Louis Persinger's violin so entranced the youngster that he insisted on a violin for his birthday and Louis Persinger as his teacher. He got both. By the time he was ten years old, Menuhin was an international performer (Menuhin, 1977).

Violinist Yehudi Menuhin's musical intelligence manifested itself even before he had touched a violin or received any musical training. His powerful reaction to that particular sound and his rapid progress on the instrument suggest that he was biologically prepared in some way for that endeavor. In this way evidence from child prodigies supports our claim that there is a biological link to a particular intelligence. Other special populations, such as autistic children who can play a musical instrument beautifully but who cannot speak, underscore the independence of musical intelligence.

A brief consideration of the evidence suggests that musical skill passes the other tests for an intelligence. For example, certain parts of the brain play important roles in perception and production of music. These areas are characteristically located in the right hemisphere, although musical skill is not as clearly "localized," or located in a specifiable area, as language. Although the particular susceptibility of musical ability to brain damage depends on the degree of training and other individual differences, there is clear evidence for "amusia" or loss of musical ability.

Music apparently played an important unifying role in Stone Age (paleolithic) societies. Birdsong provides a link to other species. Evidence from various cultures supports the notion that music is a universal faculty. Studies of infant development suggest that there is a "raw" computational ability in early childhood. Finally, musical notation provides an accessible and lucid symbol system.

In short, evidence to support the interpretation of musical ability as an "intelligence" comes from many different sources. Even though musical skill is not typically considered an intellectual skill like mathematics, it qualifies under our criteria. By definition it deserves consideration; and in view of the data, its inclusion is empirically justified.

Bodily-Kinesthetic Intelligence
Fifteen-year-old Babe Ruth played third base. During one game his team's pitcher was doing very poorly and Babe loudly criticized him from third base. Brother Mathias, the coach, called out, "Ruth, if you know so much about it, YOU pitch!" Babe was surprised and embarrassed because he had never pitched before, but Brother Mathias insisted. Ruth said later that at the very moment he took the pitcher's mound, he KNEW he was supposed to be a pitcher and that it was "natural" for him to strike people out. Indeed, he went on to become a great major league pitcher (and, of course, attained legendary status as a hitter) (Connor, 1982).

Like Menuhin, Babe Ruth was a child prodigy who recognized his "instrument" immediately upon his first exposure to it. This recognition occurred in advance of formal training.

Control of bodily movement is, of course, localized in the motor cortex, with each hemisphere dominant or controlling bodily movements on the contra-lateral side. In right-handers, the dominance for such movement is ordinarily found in the left hemisphere. The ability to perform movements when directed to do so can be impaired even in individuals who can perform the same movements reflexively or on a nonvoluntary basis. The existence of specific *apraxia* constitutes one line of evidence for a bodily-kinesthetic intelligence.

The evolution of specialized body movements is of obvious advantage to the species, and in humans this adaptation is extended through the use of tools. Body movement undergoes a clearly defined developmental schedule in children. And there is little question of its universality across cultures. Thus it appears that bodily-kinesthetic "knowledge" satisfies many of the criteria for an intelligence.

The consideration of bodily-kinesthetic knowledge as "problem solving" may be less intuitive. Certainly carrying out a mime sequence or hitting a tennis ball is not solving a mathematical equation. And yet, the ability to use one's body to express an emotion (as in a dance), to play a game (as in a sport), or to create a new product (as in devising an invention) is evidence of the cognitive features of body usage. The specific computations required to solve a particular bodily-kinesthetic *problem*, hitting a tennis ball, are summarized by Tim Gallwey:

At the moment the ball leaves the server's racket, the brain calculates approximately where it will land and where the racket will intercept it. This calculation includes the initial velocity of the ball, combined with an input for the progressive decrease in velocity and the effect of wind and after the bounce of the ball. Simultaneously, muscle orders are given: not just once, but constantly with refined and updated information. The muscles must cooperate. A movement of the feet occurs, the racket is taken back, the face of the racket kept at a constant angle. Contact is made at a precise point that depends on whether the order was given to hit down the line or cross-court, an order not given until after a split-second analysis of the movement and balance of the opponent.

To return an average serve, you have about one second to do this. To hit the ball at all is remarkable and yet not uncommon. The truth is that everyone who inhabits a human body possesses a remarkable creation (Gallwey, 1976).

Logical-Mathematical Intelligence

In 1983 Barbara McClintock won the Nobel prize in medicine or physiology for her work in microbiology. Her intellectual powers of deduction and observation illustrate one form of logical-mathematical intelligence that is often labeled "scientific thinking." One incident is particularly illuminating. While a researcher at Cornell in the 1920s McClintock was faced one day with a problem: while *theory* predicted 50 percent pollen sterility in corn, her research assistant (in the "field") was finding plants that were only 25 to 30 percent sterile. Disturbed by this discrepancy, McClintock left the cornfield and returned to her office where she sat for half an hour, thinking:

Suddenly I jumped up and ran back to the (corn) field. At the top of the field (the others were still at the bottom) I shouted "Eureka, I have it! I know what the 30% sterility is!" . . . They asked me to prove it. I sat down with a paper bag and a pencil and I started from scratch, which I had not done at all in my laboratory. It had all been done so fast; the answer came and I ran. Now I worked it out step by step—it was an intricate series of steps—and I came out with [the same result]. [They] looked at the material and it was exactly as I'd said it was; it worked out exactly as I had diagrammed it. Now, why did I know, without having done it on paper? Why was I so sure? (Keller, 1983, p. 104).

This anecdote illustrates two essential facts of the logical-mathematical intelligence. First, in the gifted individual, the process of problem solving is often remarkably rapid—the successful scientist copes with many variables at once and creates numerous hypotheses that are each evaluated and then accepted or rejected in turn.

The anecdote also underscores the *nonverbal* nature of the intelligence. A solution to a problem can be constructed *before* it is articulated. In fact, the solution process may be totally invisible, even to the problem solver. This need not imply, however, that discoveries of this sort—the familiar "Aha!" phenomenon—are mysterious, intuitive, or unpredictable. The fact that it happens more frequently to some people (perhaps Nobel prize winners) suggests the opposite. We interpret this as the work of the logical-mathematical intelligence.

Along with the companion skill of language, logical-mathematical reasoning provides the principal basis for IQ tests. This form of intelligence has been heavily investigated by traditional psychologists, and it is the archetype of "raw intelligence" or the problem-solving faculty that purportedly cuts across domains. It is perhaps ironic, then, that the actual mechanism by which one arrives at a solution to a logical-mathematical problem is not as yet properly understood.

This intelligence is supported by our empirical criteria as well. Certain areas of the brain are more prominent in mathematical calculation than others. There are idiots savants who perform great feats of calculation even though they remain tragically deficient in most other areas. Child prodigies in mathematics abound. The development of this intelligence in children has been carefully documented by Jean Piaget and other psychologists.

Linguistic Intelligence
At the age of ten, T. S. Eliot created a magazine called "Fireside" to which he was the sole contributor. In a three-day period during his winter vacation, he created eight complete issues. Each one included poems, adventure stories, a gossip column, and humor. Some of this material survives and it displays the talent of the poet (see Soldo, 1982).

As with the logical intelligence, calling linguistic skill an "intelligence" is consistent with the stance of traditional psychology. Linguistic intelligence also passes our empirical tests. For instance, a specific area of the brain, called "Broca's Area," is responsible for the production of grammatical sentences. A person with damage to this area can understand words and sentences quite well but has difficulty putting words together in anything other than the simplest of sentences. At the same time, other thought processes may be entirely unaffected.

The gift of language is universal, and its development in children is strikingly constant across cultures. Even in deaf populations where a manual sign language is not explicitly taught, children will often "invent" their own manual language and use it surreptitiously! We thus see how an intelligence may operate independently of a specific input modality or output channel.

Spatial Intelligence

Navigation around the Caroline Islands in the South Seas is accomplished without instruments. The position of the stars, as viewed from various islands, the weather patterns, and water color are the only sign posts. Each journey is broken into a series of segments; and the navigator learns the position of the stars within each of these segments. During the actual trip the navigator must envision mentally a reference island as it passes under a particular star and from that he computes the number of segments completed, the proportion of the trip remaining, and any corrections in heading that are required. The navigator cannot *see* the islands as he sails along; instead he maps their locations in his mental "picture" of the journey (Gardner, 1983).

Spatial problem solving is required for navigation and in the use of the notational system of maps. Other kinds of spatial problem solving are brought to bear in visualizing an object seen from a different angle and in playing chess. The visual arts also employ this intelligence in the use of space.

Evidence from brain research is clear and persuasive. Just as the left hemisphere has, over the course of evolution, been selected as the site of linguistic processing in right-handed persons, the right hemisphere proves to be the site most crucial for spatial processing. Damage to the right posterior regions causes impairment of the ability to find one's way around a site, to recognize faces or scenes, or to notice fine details.

Patients with damage specific to regions of the right hemisphere will attempt to compensate for their spatial deficits with linguistic strategies. They will try to reason aloud, to challenge the task, or even make up answers. But such nonspatial strategies are rarely successful.

Blind populations provide an illustration of the distinction between the spatial intelligence and visual perception. A blind person can recognize shapes by an indirect method: running a hand along the object translates into length of time of movement, which in turn is translated into the size of the object. For the blind person, the perceptual system of the tactile modality parallels the visual modality in the seeing person. The analogy between the spatial reasoning of the blind and the linguistic reasoning of the deaf is notable.

There are few child prodigies among visual artists, but there are idiots savants such as Nadia (Selfe, 1977). Despite a condition of severe autism, this preschool child made drawings of the most remarkable representational accuracy and finesse.

Interpersonal Intelligence

With little formal training in special education and nearly blind herself, Anne Sullivan began the intimidating task of instructing a blind and deaf seven-year-old Helen Keller. Sullivan's efforts at communication were complicated by the child's emotional struggle with the world around her. At their first meal together, this scene occurred:

> Annie did not allow Helen to put her hand into Annie's plate and take what she wanted, as she had been accustomed to do with her family. It became a test of wills—hand thrust into plate, hand firmly put aside. The family, much upset, left the dining room. Annie locked the door and proceeded to eat her breakfast while Helen lay on the floor kicking and screaming, pushing and pulling at Annie's chair. After half an hour Helen went around the table looking for her family. She discovered no one else was there and that bewildered her. Finally, she sat down and began to eat her breakfast, but with her hands. Annie gave her a spoon. Down on the floor it clattered, and the contest of wills began anew (Lash, 1980, p. 52).

Anne Sullivan sensitively responded to the child's behavior. She wrote home: "The greatest problem I shall have to solve is how to discipline and control her without breaking her spirit. I shall go rather slowly at first and try to win her love."

In fact, the first "miracle" occurred two weeks later, well before the famous incident at the pumphouse. Annie had taken Helen to a small cottage near the family's house, where they could live alone. After seven days together, Helen's personality suddenly underwent a profound change—the therapy had worked:

> My heart is singing with joy this morning. A miracle has happened! The wild little creature of two weeks ago has been transformed into a gentle child (p. 54).

It was just two weeks after this that the first breakthrough in Helen's grasp of language occurred; and from that point on, she progressed with incredible speed. The key to the miracle of language was Anne Sullivan's insight into the *person* of Helen Keller.

Interpersonal intelligence builds on a core capacity to notice distinctions among others; in particular, contrasts in their moods, temperaments, motivations, and intentions. In more advanced forms, this intelligence permits a skilled adult to read the intentions and desires of others, even when these have been hidden. This skill appears in a highly sophisticated form in religious or political leaders, teachers, therapists, and parents. The Helen Keller–Anne Sullivan story suggests that this interpersonal intelligence does not depend on language.

All indices in brain research suggest that the frontal lobes play a prominent role in interpersonal knowledge. Damage in this area can cause profound personality changes while leaving other forms of problem solving unharmed—a person is often "not the same person" after such an injury.

Alzheimer's disease, a form of presenile dementia, appears to attack posterior brain zones with a special ferocity, leaving spatial, logical, and linguistic computations severely impaired. Yet, Alzheimer's patients will often remain well groomed, socially proper, and continually apologetic for their errors. In contrast, Pick's disease, another variety of presenile dementia that is more frontally oriented, entails a rapid loss of social graces.

Biological evidence for interpersonal intelligence encompasses two additional factors often cited as unique to humans. One factor is the prolonged childhood of primates, including the close attachment to the mother. In those cases where the mother is removed from early development, normal interpersonal development is in serious jeopardy. The second factor is the relative importance in humans of social interaction. Skills such as hunting, tracking, and killing in prehistoric societies required participation and cooperation of large numbers of people. The need for group cohesion, leadership, organization, and solidarity follows naturally from this.

Intrapersonal Intelligence

In an essay called "A Sketch of the Past," written almost as a diary entry, Virginia Woolf discusses the "cotton wool of existence"—the various mundane events of life. She contrasts this "cotton wool" with three specific and poignant memories from her childhood: a fight with her brother, seeing a particular flower in the garden, and hearing of the suicide of a past visitor:

> These are three instances of exceptional moments. I often tell them over, or rather they come to the surface unexpectedly. But now for the first time I have written them down, and I realize something that I have never realized before. Two of these moments ended in a state of despair. The other ended, on the contrary, in a state of satisfaction.
>
> The sense of horror (in hearing of the suicide) held me powerless. But in the case of the flower, I found a reason; and was thus able to deal with the sensation. I was not powerless.
>
> Though I still have the peculiarity that I receive these sudden shocks, they are now always welcome; after the first surprise, I always feel instantly that they are particularly valuable. And so I go on to suppose that the shock-receiving capacity is what makes me a writer. I hazard the explanation that a shock is at once in my case followed by the desire to explain it. I feel that I have had a blow; but it is not, as I thought as a child, simply a blow from an enemy hidden behind the cottonwood of daily life; it is or will become a revelation of some order; it is a token of some real thing behind appearances; and I make it real by putting it into words (Woolf, 1976, pp. 69–70).

This quotation vividly illustrates the intrapersonal intelligence—knowledge of the internal aspects of a person: access to one's own feeling life, one's range of emotions, the capacity to effect discriminations among these emotions and eventually to label them and to draw upon them as a means of understanding and guiding one's own behavior. A person with good intrapersonal intelligence has a viable and effective model of himself or herself. Since this intelligence is the most private, it requires evidence from language, music, or some other more expressive form of intelligence if the observer is to detect it at work. In the above quotation, for example,

linguistic intelligence is drawn upon to convey intrapersonal knowledge; it embodies the interaction of intelligences, a common phenomenon to which we will return later.

We see the familiar criteria at work in the intrapersonal intelligence. As with the interpersonal intelligence, the frontal lobes play a central role in personality change. Injury to the lower area of the frontal lobes is likely to produce irritability or euphoria; while injury to the higher regions is more likely to produce indifference, listlessness, slowness, and apathy—a kind of depressive personality. In such "frontal-lobe" individuals, the other cognitive functions often remain preserved. In contrast, among aphasics who have recovered sufficiently to describe their experiences, we find consistent testimony: while there may have been a diminution of general alertness and considerable depression about the condition, the individual in no way felt himself to be a different person. He recognized his own needs, wants, and desires and tried as best he could to achieve them.

The autistic child is a prototypical example of an individual with impaired intrapersonal intelligence; indeed, the child may not even be able to refer to himself. At the same time, such children often exhibit remarkable abilities in the musical, computational, spatial, or mechanical realms.

Evolutionary evidence for an intrapersonal faculty is more difficult to come by, but we might speculate that the capacity to transcend the satisfaction of instinctual drives is relevant. This becomes increasingly important in a species not perennially involved in the struggle for survival.

In sum, then, both interpersonal and intrapersonal faculties pass the tests of an intelligence. They both feature problem-solving endeavors with significance for the individual and the species. Interpersonal intelligence allows one to understand and work with others; intrapersonal intelligence allows one to understand and work with oneself. In the individual's sense of self, one encounters a melding of inter- and intra-personal components. Indeed, the sense of self emerges as one of the most marvelous of human inventions—a symbol that represents all kinds of information about a person and that is at the same time an invention that all individuals construct for themselves.

Summary: The Unique Contributions of the Theory

As human beings, we all have a repertoire of skills for solving different kinds of problems. Our investigation has begun, therefore, with a consideration of these problems, the contexts they are found in, and the culturally significant products that are the outcome. We have not approached "intelligence" as a reified human faculty that is brought to bear in literally any problem setting; rather, we have begun with the problems that humans *solve* and worked back to the "intelligences" that must be responsible.

Evidence from brain research, human development, evolution, and cross-cultural comparisons was brought to bear in our search for the relevant human intelligences: a candidate was included only if reasonable evidence to support its membership was found across these diverse fields. Again, this tack differs from the traditional one: since no candidate faculty is *necessarily* an intelligence, we could choose on a motivated basis. In the traditional approach to "intelligence," there is no opportunity for this type of empirical decision.

We have also determined that these multiple human faculties, the intelligences, are to a significant extent *independent*. For example, research with brain damaged adults repeatedly demonstrates that particular faculties can be lost while others are spared. This independence of intelligences implies that a particularly high level of ability in one intelligence, say mathematics, does not require a similarly high level in another intelligence, like language or music. This independence of intelligences contrasts sharply with traditional measures of IQ that find high correlations among test scores. We speculate that the usual correlations among subtests of IQ tests come about because all of these tasks in fact measure the ability to respond rapidly to items of a logical-mathematical or linguistic sort; we believe that these correlations would be substantially reduced if one were to survey in a contextually appropriate way the full range of human problem-solving skills.

Until now, we have supported the fiction that adult roles depend largely on the flowering of a single intelligence. In fact, however, nearly every cultural role of any degree of sophistication requires a combination of intelligences. Thus, even an apparently straightforward role, like playing the violin, transcends a reliance on simple musical intelligence. To become a successful violinist requires bodily-kinesthetic dexterity and the interpersonal skills of relating to an audience and, in a different way, choosing a manager; quite possibly it involves an intrapersonal intelligence as well. Dance requires skills in bodily kinesthetic, musical, interpersonal, and spatial intelligences in varying degrees. Politics requires an interpersonal skill, a linguistic facility, and perhaps some logical aptitude. Inasmuch as nearly every cultural role requires several intelligences, it becomes important to consider individuals as a collection of aptitudes rather than as having a singular problem-solving faculty that can be measured directly through pencil-and-paper tests. Even given a relatively small number of such intelligences, the diversity of human ability is created through the differences in these profiles. In fact, it may well be that the "total is greater than the sum of the parts." An individual may not be particularly gifted in any intelligence; and yet, because of a particular combination or blend of skills, he or she may be able to fill some niche uniquely well. Thus it is of paramount importance to assess the particular combination of skills that may earmark an individual for a certain vocational or avocational niche.

Positive Psychology: An Introduction

Martin E. P. Seligman and Mihaly Csikszentmihalyi

Martin E. P. Seligman is currently the Robert A. Fox Leadership Professor of Psychology at the University of Pennsylvania, Department of Psychology, and he is a past president of the American Psychological Association. By the 1980s he was well known for his work on the development of learned helplessness; in the 1990s he became acclaimed for his work on learned optimism. This century has found him as a leader, if not the leader, of the positive psychology movement. Among his twenty-some published books are *The Optimistic Child: Proven Program to Safeguard Children from Depression & Build Lifelong Resilience* (1996, Houghton Mifflin) and *Authentic Happiness* (2002, Free Press).

Mihaly Csikszentmihalyi is currently the director of the Quality of Life Research Center at the Drucker School of the Claremont Graduate School, California. He is the former head of the Department of Psychology at the University of Chicago. He is best known for his work on *flow*, a psychological state in which the person is fully engaged in what she or he is doing; flow is like meditative action, in which a person loses track of time, is energized but calm, and totally absorbed in their current activity. Csikszentmihalyi has documented his work in such texts as, *Flow: The Psychology of Optimal Experience* (1990, Harper and Row), *Creativity: Flow and the Psychology of Discovery and Invention* (1996, Harper Perennial), and Finding *Flow: The Psychology of Engagement with Everyday Life* (1998, Basic Books).

Seligman and Csikszentmihalyi coauthored the seminal paper, almost a manifesto, on the positive psychology movement, "Positive Psychology: An Introduction," in the *American Psychologist* (2000), which is included below. This paper includes reference to human development in the context of character strengths and virtues. Recent research shows that the development of character strengths, such as courage, optimism, appreciation of beauty, hope, love, fairness, and so on, brings both happiness and meaningfulness to the life of children, adolescents, and adults. This paper, and the positive psychology movement, is having and will have a huge impact on the scientific study and the practice of human development far into the 21st century.

Key concept: positive psychology and character strengths

A science of positive subjective experience, positive individual traits, and positive institutions promises to improve quality of life and prevent the pathologies that arise when life is barren and meaningless. The exclusive focus on pathology that has dominated so much of our discipline results in a model of the human being lacking the positive features that make life worth living. Hope, wisdom, creativity, future mindedness, courage, spirituality, responsibility, and perseverance are ignored or explained as transformations of more authentic negative impulses. The 15 articles in this millennial issue of the *American Psychologist* discuss such issues as what enables happiness, the effects of autonomy and self-regulation, how optimism and hope affect health, what constitutes wisdom, and how talent and creativity come to fruition. The authors outline a framework for a science of positive psychology, point to gaps in our knowledge, and predict that the next century will see a science and profession that will come to understand and build the factors that allow individuals, communities, and societies to flourish.

Entering a new millennium, Americans face a historical choice. Left alone on the pinnacle of economic and political leadership, the United States can continue to increase its material wealth while ignoring the human needs of its people and those of the rest of the planet. Such a course is likely to lead to increasing selfishness, to alienation between the more and the less fortunate, and eventually to chaos and despair.

At this juncture, the social and behavioral sciences can play an enormously important role. They can articulate a vision of the good life that is empirically sound while being understandable and attractive. They can show what actions lead to well-being, to positive individuals, and to thriving communities. Psychology should be able to help document what kinds of families result in children who flourish, what work settings support the greatest satisfaction among workers, what policies result in the strongest civic engagement, and how people's lives can be most worth living.

Yet psychologists have scant knowledge of what makes life worth living. They have come to understand quite a bit about how people survive and endure under conditions of adversity. (For recent surveys of the history of psychology, see, e.g., Benjamin, 1992; Koch & Leary, 1985; and Smith, 1997.) However, psychologists know very little about how normal people flourish under more benign conditions. Psychology has, since World War II, become a science largely about healing. It concentrates on repairing damage within a disease model of human functioning. This almost exclusive attention to pathology neglects the fulfilled individual and the thriving community. The aim of positive psychology is to begin to catalyze a change in the focus of psychology from preoccupation only with repairing the worst things in life to also building positive qualities.

The field of positive psychology at the subjective level is about valued subjective experiences: well-being, contentment, and satisfaction (in the past); hope and optimism (for the future); and flow and happiness (in the present). At the individual level, it is about positive individual traits: the capacity for love and vocation, courage, interpersonal skill, aesthetic sensibility, perseverance, forgiveness, originality, future mindedness, spirituality, high talent, and wisdom. At the group level, it is about the civic virtues and the institutions that move individuals toward better citizenship: responsibility, nurturance, altruism, civility, moderation, tolerance, and work ethic.

Two personal stories, one told by each author, explain how we arrived at the conviction that a movement toward positive psychology was needed and how this special issue of the *American Psychologist* came about. For Martin E. P. Seligman, it began at a moment a few months after being elected president of the American Psychological Association:

The moment took place in my garden while I was weeding with my five-year-old daughter, Nikki. I have to confess that even though I write books about children, I'm really not all that good with children. I am goal oriented and time urgent, and when I'm weeding in the garden, I'm actually trying to get the weeding done. Nikki, however, was throwing weeds into the air, singing, and dancing around. I yelled at her. She walked away, then came back and said,

"Daddy, I want to talk to you."

"Yes, Nikki?"

"Daddy, do you remember before my fifth birthday? From the time I was three to the time I was five, I was a whiner. I whined every day. When I turned five, I decided not to whine anymore. That was the hardest thing I've

ever done. And if I can stop whining, you can stop being such a grouch."

This was for me an epiphany, nothing less. I learned something about Nikki, about raising kids, about myself, and a great deal about my profession. First, I realized that raising Nikki was not about correcting whining. Nikki did that herself. Rather, I realized that raising Nikki is about taking this marvelous strength she has—I call it "seeing into the soul"—amplifying it, nurturing it, helping her to lead her life around it to buffer against her weaknesses and the storms of life. Raising children, I realized, is vastly more than fixing what is wrong with them. It is about identifying and nurturing their strongest qualities, what they own and are best at, and helping them find niches in which they can best live out these strengths.

As for my own life, Nikki hit the nail right on the head. I was a grouch. I had spent 50 years mostly enduring wet weather in my soul, and the past 10 years being a nimbus cloud in a household full of sunshine. Any good fortune I had was probably not due to my grumpiness, but in spite of it. In that moment, I resolved to change.

However, the broadest implication of Nikki's teaching was about the science and profession of psychology: Before World War II, psychology had three distinct missions: curing mental illness, making the lives of all people more productive and fulfilling, and identifying and nurturing high talent. The early focus on positive psychology is exemplified by work such as Terman's studies of giftedness (Terman, 1939) and marital happiness (Terman, Buttenwieser, Ferguson, Johnson, & Wilson, 1938), Watson's writings on effective parenting (Watson, 1928), and Jung's work concerning the search for and discovery of meaning in life (Jung, 1933). Right after the war, two events—both economic—changed the face of psychology: In 1946, the Veterans Administration (now Veterans Affairs) was founded, and thousands of psychologists found out that they could make a living treating mental illness. In 1947, the National Institute of Mental Health (which, in spite of its charter, has always been based on the disease model and should now more appropriately be renamed the National Institute of Mental Illness) was founded, and academics found out that they could get grants if their research was about pathology.

This arrangement has brought many benefits. There have been huge strides in the understanding of and therapy for mental illness: At least 14 disorders, previously intractable, have yielded their secrets to science and can now be either cured or considerably relieved (Seligman, 1994). The downside, however, was that the other two fundamental missions of psychology—making the lives of all people better and nurturing genius—were all but forgotten. It wasn't only the subject matter that was altered by funding, but the currency of the theories underpinning how psychologists viewed themselves. They came to see themselves as part of a mere subfield of the health professions, and psychology became a victimology. Psychologists saw human beings as passive foci: Stimuli came on and elicited responses (what an extraordinarily passive word!). External reinforcements weakened or strengthened responses. Drives, tissue needs, instincts, and conflicts from childhood pushed each of us around.

Psychology's empirical focus shifted to assessing and curing individual suffering. There has been an explosion in research on psychological disorders and the negative effects of environmental stressors, such as parental divorce, the deaths of loved ones, and physical and sexual abuse. Practitioners went about treating the mental illnesses of patients within a disease framework by repairing damage: damaged habits, damaged drives, damaged childhoods, and damaged brains.

Mihaly Csikszentmihalyi realized the need for a positive psychology in Europe during World War II: As a child, I witnessed the dissolution of the smug world in which I had been comfortably ensconced. I noticed with surprise how many of the adults I had known as successful and self-confident became helpless and dispirited once the war removed their social supports. Without jobs, money, or status, they were reduced to empty shells. Yet there were a few who kept their integrity and purpose despite the surrounding chaos. Their serenity was a beacon that kept others from losing hope. And these were not the men and women one would have expected to emerge unscathed: They were not necessarily the most respected, better educated, or more skilled individuals. This experience set me thinking: What sources of strength were these people drawing on?

Reading philosophy and dabbling in history and religion did not provide satisfying answers to that question. I found the ideas in these texts to be too subjective, to be dependent on faith or to be dubious assumptions; they lacked the clear-eyed skepticism and the slow cumulative growth that I associated with science. Then, for the first time, I came across psychology: first the writings of Jung, then Freud, then a few of the psychologists who were writing in Europe in the 1950s. Here, I thought, was a possible solution to my quest—a discipline that dealt with the fundamental issues of life and attempted to do so with the patient simplicity of the natural sciences.

However, at that time psychology was not yet a recognized discipline. In Italy, where I lived, one could take courses in it only as a minor while pursuing a degree in medicine or in philosophy, so I decided to come to the United States, where psychology had gained wider acceptance. The first courses I took were somewhat of a shock. It turned out that in the United States, psychology had indeed became a science, if by science one means only a skeptical attitude and a concern for measurement. What seemed to be lacking, however, was a vision that justified the attitude and the methodology. I was looking for a scientific approach to human behavior, but I never dreamed that this could yield a value-free understanding. In human behavior, what is most intriguing is not the average, but the improbable. Very few people kept their decency during the onslaught of World War II; yet it was those few

who held the key to what humans could be like at their best. However, at the height of its behaviorist phase, psychology was being taught as if it were a branch of statistical mechanics. Ever since, I have struggled to reconcile the twin imperatives that a science of human beings should include: to understand what *is* and what *could be*.

A decade later, the "third way" heralded by Abraham Maslow, Carl Rogers, and other humanistic psychologists promised to add a new perspective to the entrenched clinical and behaviorist approaches. The generous humanistic vision had a strong effect on the culture at large and held enormous promise. Unfortunately, humanistic psychology did not attract much of a cumulative empirical base, and it spawned myriad therapeutic self-help movements. In some of its incarnations, it emphasized the self and encouraged a self-centeredness that played down concerns for collective well-being. Future debate will determine whether this came about because Maslow and Rogers were ahead of their times, because these flaws were inherent in their original vision, or because of overly enthusiastic followers. However, one legacy of the humanism of the 1960s is prominently displayed in any large bookstore: The "psychology" section contains at least 10 shelves on crystal healing, aromatherapy, and reaching the inner child for every shelf of books that tries to uphold some scholarly standard.

Whatever the personal origins of our conviction that the time has arrived for a positive psychology, our message is to remind our field that psychology is not just the study of pathology, weakness, and damage; it is also the study of strength and virtue. Treatment is not just fixing what is broken; it is nurturing what is best. Psychology is not just a branch of medicine concerned with illness or health; it is much larger. It is about work, education, insight, love, growth, and play. And in this quest for what is best, positive psychology does not rely on wishful thinking, faith, self-deception, fads, or hand waving; it tries to adapt what is best in the scientific method to the unique problems that human behavior presents to those who wish to understand it in all its complexity.

What foregrounds this approach is the issue of prevention. In the past decade, psychologists have become concerned with prevention, and this was the presidential theme, of the 1998 American Psychological Association convention in San Francisco. How can psychologists prevent problems like depression or substance abuse or schizophrenia in young people who are genetically vulnerable or who live in worlds that nurture these problems? How can psychologists prevent murderous schoolyard violence in children who have access to weapons, poor parental supervision, and a mean streak? What psychologists have learned over 50 years is that the disease model does not move psychology closer to the prevention of these serious problems. Indeed, the major strides in prevention have come largely from a perspective focused on systematically building competency, not on correcting weakness.

Prevention researchers have discovered that there are human strengths that act as buffers against mental illness: courage, future mindedness, optimism, interpersonal skill, faith, work ethic, hope, honesty, perseverance, and the capacity for flow and insight, to name several. Much of the task of prevention in this new century will be to create a science of human strength whose mission will be to understand and learn how to foster these virtues in young people.

Working exclusively on personal weakness and on damaged brains, however, has rendered science poorly equipped to effectively prevent illness. Psychologists need now to call for massive research on human strengths and virtues. Practitioners need to recognize that much of the best work they already do in the consulting room is to amplify strengths rather than repair the weaknesses of their clients. Psychologists working with families, schools, religious communities, and corporations, need to develop climates that foster these strengths. The major psychological theories have changed to undergird a new science of strength and resilience. No longer do the dominant theories view the individual as a passive vessel responding to stimuli; rather, individuals are now seen as decision makers, with choices, preferences, and the possibility of becoming masterful, efficacious, or in malignant circumstances, helpless and hopeless (Bandura, 1986; Seligman, 1992). Science and practice that rely on this worldview may have the direct effect of preventing many of the major emotional disorders. They may also have two side effects: They may make the lives of clients physically healthier, given all that psychologists are learning about the effects of mental well-being on the body. This science and practice will also reorient psychology back to its two neglected missions—making normal people stronger and more productive and making high human potential actual.

About This Issue

The 15 articles that follow this introduction present a remarkably varied and complex picture of the orientation in psychology—and the social sciences more generally —that might be included under the rubric of positive psychology. Of course, like all selections, this one is to some extent arbitrary and incomplete. For many of the topics included in this issue, the space allotted to an entire issue of the *American Psychologist* would be needed to print all the contributions worthy of inclusion. We hope only that these enticing hors d'oeuvres stimulate the reader's appetite to sample more widely from the offerings of the field.

As editors of this special issue, we have tried to be comprehensive without being redundant. The authors were asked to write at a level of generality appealing to the greatly varied and diverse specialties of the journal's readership, without sacrificing the intellectual rigor of their arguments. The articles were not intended to be specialized reviews of the literature, but broad overviews with an eye turned to cross-disciplinary links and practical applications. Finally, we invited mostly seasoned scholars to contribute, thereby excluding some of the most promising young researchers—but they are already preparing to edit a section of this journal devoted to the latest work on positive psychology.

There are three main topics that run through these contributions. The first concerns the positive experience. What makes one moment "better" than the next? If Daniel Kahneman is right, the hedonic quality of current experience is the basic building block of a positive psychology (Kahneman, 1999, p. 6). Diener (2000, this issue) focuses on subjective well-being, Massimini and Delle Fave (2000, this issue) on optimal experience, Peterson (2000, this issue) on optimism, Myers (2000, this issue) on happiness, and Ryan and Deci (2000, this issue) on self-determination. Taylor, Kemeny, Reed, Bower, and Gruenwald (2000, this issue), and Salovey, Rothman, Detweiler, and Steward (2000, this issue) report on the relationship between positive emotions and physical health.

These topics can, of course, be seen as statelike or traitlike: One can investigate either what accounts for moments of happiness or what distinguishes happy from unhappy individuals. Thus, the second thread in these articles is the theme of the positive personality. The common denominator underlying all the approaches represented here is a perspective on human beings as self-organizing, self-directed, adaptive entities. Ryan and Deci (2000) focus on self-determination, Baltes and Staudinger (2000, this issue) on wisdom, and Vaillant (2000, this issue) on mature defenses. Lubinski and Benbow (2000, this issue), Simonton (2000, this issue), Winner (2000, this issue), and Larson (2000, this issue) focus on exceptional performance (i.e., creativity and talent). Some of these approaches adopt an explicit developmental perspective, taking into account that individual strengths unfold over an entire life span.

The third thread that runs through these contributions is the recognition that people and experiences are embedded in a social context. Thus, a positive psychology needs to take positive communities and positive institutions into account. At the broadest level, Buss (2000, this issue) and Massimini and Delle Fave (2000) describe the evolutionary milieu that shapes positive human experience. Myers (2000) describes the contributions of social relationships to happiness, and Schwartz (2000, this issue) reflects on the necessity for cultural norms to relieve individuals of the burden of choice. Larson (2000) emphasizes the importance of voluntary activities for the development of resourceful young people, and Winner (2000) describes the effects of families on the development of talent. In fact, to a degree that is exceedingly rare in psychological literature, every one of these contributions looks at behavior in its ecologically valid social setting. A more detailed introduction to the articles in this issue follows.

Evolutionary Perspectives

The first section comprises two articles that place positive psychology in the broadest context within which it can be understood, namely that of evolution. To some people, evolutionary approaches are distasteful because they deny the importance of learning and self-determination, but this need not be necessarily so. These two articles are exceptional in that they not only provide ambitious theoretical perspectives, but—mirabile dictu—they also provide uplifting practical examples of how a psychology based on evolutionary principles can be applied to the improvement of the human condition.

In the first article, David Buss (2000) reminds readers that the dead hand of the past weighs heavily on the present. He focuses primarily on three reasons why positive states of mind are so elusive. First, because the environments people currently live in are so different from the ancestral environments to which their bodies and minds have been adapted, they are often misfit in modern surroundings. Second, evolved distress mechanisms are often functional—for instance, jealousy alerts people to make sure of the fidelity of their spouses. Finally, selection tends to be competitive and to involve zero-sum outcomes. What makes Buss's article unusually interesting is that after identifying these major obstacles to well-being, he then outlines some concrete strategies for overcoming them. For instance, one of the major differences between ancestral and current environments is the paradoxical change in people's relationships to others: On the one hand, people live surrounded by many more people than their ancestors did, yet they are intimate with fewer individuals and thus experience greater loneliness and alienation. The solutions to this and other impasses are not only conceptually justified within the theoretical framework but are also eminently practical. So what are they? At the risk of creating unbearable suspense, we think it is better for readers to find out for themselves.

Whereas Buss (2000) bases his arguments on the solid foundations of biological evolution, Fausto Massimini and Antonella Delle Fave (2000) venture into the less explored realm of psychological and cultural evolution. In a sense, they start where Buss leaves off: by looking analytically at the effects of changes in the ancestral environment and by looking specifically at how the production of *memes* (e.g., artifacts and values) affect and are affected by human consciousness. They start with the assumption that living systems are self-organizing and oriented toward increasing complexity. Thus, individuals are the authors of their own evolution. They are continuously involved in the selection of the memes that will define their own individuality, and when added to the memes selected by others, they shape the future of the culture. Massimini and Delle Fave make the point—so essential to the argument for positive psychology—that psychological selection is motivated not solely by the pressures of adaptation and survival, but also by the need to reproduce optimal experiences. Whenever possible, people choose behaviors that make them feel fully alive, competent, and creative. These authors conclude their visionary call for individual development in harmony with global evolution by providing instances drawn from their own experience of cross-cultural interventions, where psychology has been applied to remedy traumatic social conditions created by runaway modernization.

Positive Personal Traits

The second section includes five articles dealing with four different personal traits that contribute to positive psychology: subjective well-being, optimism, happiness, and self-determination. These are topics that in the past three decades have been extensively studied and have produced an impressive array of findings—many of them unexpected and counterintuitive.

The first article in this set is a review of what is known about subjective well-being written by Edward Diener (2000), whose research in this field now spans three decades. Subjective well-being refers to what people think and how they feel about their lives—to the cognitive and affective conclusions they reach when they evaluate their existence. In practice, subjective well-being is a more scientific-sounding term for what people usually mean by happiness. Even though subjective well-being research relies primarily on rather global self-ratings that could be criticized on various grounds, its findings are plausible and coherent. Diener's account begins with a review of the temperament and personality correlates of subjective well-being and the demographic characteristics of groups high in subjective well-being. The extensive cross-cultural research on the topic is then reviewed, suggesting interesting links between macrosocial conditions and happiness. A central issue is how a person's values and goals mediate between external events and the quality of experience. These investigations promise to bring psychologists closer to understanding the insights of such philosophers of antiquity as Democritus or Epictetus, who argued that it is not what happens to people that determines how happy they are, but how they interpret what happens.

One dispositional trait that appears to mediate between external events and a person's interpretation of them is optimism. This trait includes both *little optimism* (e.g., "I will find a convenient parking space this evening") and *big optimism* (e.g., "Our nation is on the verge of something great"). Christopher Peterson (2000) describes the research on this beneficial psychological characteristic in the second article of this set. He considers optimism to involve cognitive, emotional, and motivational components. People high in optimism tend to have better moods, to be more persevering and successful, and to experience better physical health. How does optimism work? How can it be increased? When does it begin to distort reality? These are some of the questions Peterson addresses. As is true of the other authors in this issue, this author is aware that complex psychological issues cannot be understood in isolation from the social and cultural contexts in which they are embedded. Hence, he asks questions such as the following: How does an overly pessimistic culture affect the well-being of its members? And conversely, does an overly optimistic culture lead to shallow materialism?

David Myers (2000) presents his synthesis of research on happiness in the third article of this section. His perspective, although strictly based on empirical evidence, is informed by a belief that traditional values must contain important elements of truth if they are to survive across generations. Hence, he is more attuned than most to issues that are not very fashionable in the field, such as the often-found association between religious faith and happiness. The other two candidates for promoting happiness that Myers considers are economic growth and income (not much there, after a minimum threshold of affluence is passed) and close personal relationships (a strong association). Although based on correlational survey studies of self-reported happiness, the robustness of the findings, replicated across time and different cultures, suggests that these findings ought to be taken seriously by anyone interested in understanding the elements that contribute to a positive quality of life.

In the first of two articles that focus on self-determination, Richard Ryan and Edward Deci (2000) discuss another trait that is central to positive psychology and has been extensively researched. Self-determination theory investigates three related human needs: the need for competence, the need for belongingness, and the need for autonomy. When these needs are satisfied, Ryan and Deci claim personal well-being and social development are optimized. Persons in this condition are intrinsically motivated, able to fulfill their potentialities, and able to seek out progressively greater challenges. These authors consider the kinds of social contexts that support autonomy, competence, and relatedness, and those that stand in the way of personal growth. Especially important is their discussion of how a person can maintain autonomy even under external pressures that seem to deny it. Ryan and Deci's contribution shows that the promises of the *humanistic psychology* of the 1960s can generate a vital program of empirical research.

Is an emphasis on autonomy an unmitigated good? Barry Schwartz (2000) takes on the subject of self-determination from a more philosophical and historical angle. He is concerned that the emphasis on autonomy in our culture results in a kind of psychological tyranny— an excess of freedom that may lead to dissatisfaction and depression. He finds particularly problematic the influence of rational-choice theory on our conception of human motivation. The burden of responsibility for autonomous choices often becomes too heavy, leading to insecurity and regrets. For most people in the world, he argues, individual choice is neither expected nor desired. Cultural constraints are necessary for leading a meaningful and satisfying life. Although Ryan and Deci's (2000)

self-determination theory takes relatedness into account as one of the three components of personal fulfillment, Schwartz's argument highlights even further the benefits of relying on cultural norms and values.

Implications for Mental and Physical Health

One of the arguments for positive psychology is that during the past half century, psychology has become increasingly focused on mental illness and, as a result, has developed a distorted view of what normal—and exceptional—human experience is like. How does mental health look when seen from the perspective of positive psychology? The next three articles deal with this topic.

Beethoven was suicidal and despairing at age 31, yet two dozen years later he composed the "Ode to Joy," translating into sublime music Schiller's lines, "Be embraced, all ye millions . . ." What made it possible for him to overcome despair despite poverty and deafness? In the first article of this section, the psychiatrist George Vaillant (2000) reminds readers that it is impossible to describe positive psychological processes without taking a life span, or at least a longitudinal, approach. "Call no man happy till he dies," for a truly positive psychological adaptation should unfold over a lifetime. Relying on the results obtained from three large samples of adults studied over several decades, Vaillant summarizes the contributions of mature defenses—altruism, sublimation, suppression, humor, anticipation—to a successful and joyful life. Even though Vaillant still uses the pathocentric terminology of *defenses*, his view of mature functioning, which takes into full account the importance of creative, proactive solutions, breaks the mold of the victimology that has been one legacy of psychoanalytic approaches.

It is generally assumed that it is healthy to be rigorously objective about one's situation. To paint a rosier picture than the facts warrant is often seen as a sign of pathology (cf. Peterson, 2000; Schwartz, 2000; and Vaillant, 2000, in this issue). However, in the second article of this section, Shelley Taylor and her collaborators argue that unrealistically optimistic beliefs about the future can protect people from illness (Taylor et al., 2000). The results of numerous studies of patients with life-threatening diseases, such as AIDS, suggest that those who remain optimistic show symptoms later and survive longer than patients who confront reality more objectively. According to these authors, the positive effects of optimism are mediated mainly at a cognitive level. An optimistic patient is more likely to practice habits that enhance health and to enlist social support. It is also possible, but not proven, that positive affective states may have a direct physiological effect that retards the course of illness. As Taylor et al. note, this line of research has enormously important implications for ameliorating health through prevention and care.

At the beginning of their extensive review of the impacts of a broad range of emotions on physical health,

Peter Salovey and his coauthors (Salovey et al., 2000) ruefully admit that because of the pathological bias of most research in the field, a great deal more is known about how negative emotions promote illness than is known about how positive emotions promote health. However, as positive and negative emotions are generally inversely correlated, they argue that substituting the former for the latter can have preventive and therapeutic effects. The research considered includes the direct effects of affect on physiology and the immune system, as well as the indirect effects of affect, such as the marshalling of psychological and social resources and the motivation of health-promoting behaviors. One of the most interesting sets of studies they discuss is the one that shows that persons high in optimism and hope are actually more likely to provide themselves with unfavorable information about their disease, thereby being better prepared to face up to realities even though their positive outcome estimates may be inflated.

Fostering Excellence

If psychologists wish to improve the human condition, it is not enough to help those who suffer. The majority of "normal" people also need examples and advice to reach a richer and more fulfilling existence. This is why early investigators, such as William James (1902/1958), Carl Jung (1936/1969), Gordon Allport (1961), and Abraham Maslow (1971), were interested in exploring spiritual ecstasy, play, creativity, and peak experiences. When these interests were eclipsed by medicalization and "physics envy," psychology neglected an essential segment of its agenda. As a gesture toward redressing such neglect, the last section of this issue presents six articles dealing with phenomena at the opposite end of the pathological tail of the normal curve—the end that includes the most positive human experiences.

Wisdom is one of the most prized traits in all cultures; according to the Old Testament, its price is above rubies (Job 28:18). It is a widespread belief that wisdom comes with age, but as the gerontologist Bernice Neugarten used to say, "You can't expect a dumb youngster to grow up to be a wise senior." Although the first president of the American Psychological Association, G. Stanley Hall, tried to develop a model of wisdom in aging as far back as 1922 (Hall, 1922), the topic has not been a popular one in the intervening years. Recently, however, interest in wisdom has revived, and nowhere more vigorously than at the Max Planck Institute of Berlin, where the "Berlin wisdom paradigm" has been developed. Paul Baltes and Ursula Staudinger (2000) report on a series of studies that has resulted in a complex model that views wisdom as a cognitive and motivational heuristic for organizing knowledge in pursuit of individual and collective excellence. Seen as the embodiment of the best subjective beliefs and laws of life that have been sifted and selected through the experience of succeeding generations, wisdom is defined as an expert knowledge system concerning the fundamental pragmatic issues of existence.

The second article in this section, by David Lubinski and Camilla Benbow (2000), deals with excellence of a different sort. In this article, the authors review the large literature concerning children with exceptional intellectual abilities. If one asked a layperson at what point in the distribution of intelligence the largest gap in ability is found, the modal answer would probably be that it is the gifted people in the top 1% or 2% who differ most in ability from the rest of the population. As the authors point out, however, one third of the total ability range is found within the top 1%—a child with an IQ of 200 is quite different and needs a different educational environment from a gifted student with "only" an IQ of 140. Lubinski and Benbow consider issues of how to identify, nurture, counsel, and teach children in these high ability ranges, arguing that neglecting the potentialities of such exceptional children would be a grievous loss to society as a whole.

One of the most poignant paradoxes in psychology concerns the complex relationships between pathology and creativity. Ever since Cesare Lombroso raised the issue over a century ago, the uneasy relationship between these two seemingly opposite traits has been explored again and again (on this topic, cf. also Vaillant, 2000, in this issue). A related paradox is that some of the most creative adults were reared in unusually adverse childhood situations. This and many other puzzles concerning the nature and nurture of creativity are reviewed in Dean K. Simonton's (2000) article, which examines the cognitive, personality, and developmental dimensions of the process, as well as the environmental conditions that foster or hinder creativity. For instance, on the basis of his exhaustive historiometric analyses that measure rates of creative contributions decade by decade, Simonton concludes that nationalistic revolts against oppressive rules are followed a generation later by greater frequencies of creative output.

The topics of giftedness and exceptional performance dealt with in the previous two articles are also taken up by Ellen Winner (2000). Her definition of giftedness is more inclusive than the previous ones: It relates to children who are precocious and self-motivated and approach problems in their domain of talent in an original way. Contrary to some of the findings concerning creative individuals just mentioned, such children tend to be well-adjusted and to have supportive families. Winner describes the current state of knowledge about this topic by focusing on the origins of giftedness; the motivation of gifted children; and the social, emotional, and cognitive correlates of exceptional performance. As is true of most other contributors to this issue, this author is sensitive throughout to the practical implications of research findings, such as what can be done to nurture and to keep giftedness alive.

Developing excellence in young people is also the theme of Reed Larson's (2000) article, which begins with the ominous and often replicated finding that the average student reports being bored about one third of the time he or she is in school. Considering that people go to school for at least one fifth of their lives, this is not good news. Larson argues that youths in our society rarely have the opportunity to take initiative, and that their education encourages passive adaptation to external rules instead. He explores the contribution of voluntary activities, such as participation in sport, art, and civic organizations, to providing opportunities for concentrated, self-directed effort applied over time. Although this article deals with issues central also to previous articles (e.g., Massimini & Delle Fave, 2000; Ryan & Deck, 2000; Winner, 2000), it does so from the perspective of naturalistic studies of youth programs, thereby adding a welcome confirmatory triangulation to previous approaches.

Challenges for the Future

The 15 articles contained in this issue make a powerful contribution to positive psychology. At the same time, the issues raised in these articles point to huge gaps in knowledge that may be the challenges at the forefront of positive psychology. What, can we guess, are the great problems that will occupy this science for the next decade or two?

The Calculus of Well-Being

One fundamental gap concerns the relationship between momentary experiences of happiness and long-lasting well-being. A simple hedonic calculus suggests that by adding up a person's positive events in consciousness, subtracting the negatives, and aggregating over time, one will get a sum that represents that person's overall well-being. This makes sense, up to a point (Kahneman, 1999), but as several articles in this issue suggest, what makes people happy in small doses does not necessarily add satisfaction in larger amounts; a point of diminishing returns is quickly reached in many instances, ranging from the amount of income one earns to the pleasures of eating good food. What, exactly, is the mechanism that governs the rewarding quality of stimuli?

The Development of Positivity

It is also necessary to realize that a person at time N is a different entity from the same person at time $N + 1$; thus, psychologists can't assume that what makes a teenager happy will also contribute to his or her happiness as an adult. For example, watching television and hanging out with friends tend to be positive experiences for most teenagers. However, to the extent that TV and friends become the main source of happiness, and thus attract increasing amounts of attention, the teenager is likely to grow into an adult who is limited in the ability to obtain positive experiences from a wide range of opportunities. How much delayed gratification is necessary to increase the

chances of long-term well-being? Is the future mindedness necessary for serious delay of gratification antagonistic to momentary happiness, to living in the moment? What are the childhood building blocks of later happiness or of long-lasting well-being?

Neuroscience and Heritability

A flourishing neuroscience of pathology has begun in the past 20 years. Psychologists have more than rudimentary ideas about what the neurochemistry and pharmacology of depression are. They have reasonable ideas about brain loci and pathways for schizophrenia, substance abuse, anxiety, and obsessive-compulsive disorder. Somehow, it has gone unobserved (and unfunded) that all of these pathological states have their opposites (LeDoux & Armony, 1999). What are the neurochemistry and anatomy of flow, good cheer, realism, future mindedness, resistance to temptation, courage, and rational or flexible thinking?

Similarly, psychologists are learning about the heritability of negative states, like aggression, depression, and schizophrenia, but they know very little of the genetic contribution of gene-environment interaction and covariance. Can psychologists develop a biology of positive experience and positive traits?

Enjoyment versus Pleasure

In a similar vein, it is useful to distinguish positive experiences that are *pleasurable* from those that are *enjoyable*. Pleasure is the good feeling that comes from satisfying homeostatic needs such as hunger, sex, and bodily comfort. Enjoyment, on the other hand, refers to the good feelings people experience when they break through the limits of homeostasis—when they do something that stretches them beyond what they were—in an athletic event, an artistic performance, a good deed, a stimulating conversation. Enjoyment, rather than pleasure, is what leads to personal growth and long-term happiness, but why is that when given a chance, most people opt for pleasure over enjoyment? Why do people choose to watch television over reading a challenging book, even when they know that their usual hedonic state during television is mild dysphoria, whereas the book can produce flow?

Collective Well-Being

This question leads directly to the issue of the balance between individual and collective well-being. Some hedonic rewards tend to be zero-sum when viewed from a systemic perspective. If running a speedboat for an hour provides the same amount of well-being to Person A as reading from a book of poems provides to Person B, but the speedboat consumes 10 gallons of gasoline and irritates 200 bathers, should the two experiences be weighed equally? Will a social science of positive community and positive institutions arise?

Authenticity

It has been a common but unspoken assumption in the social sciences that negative traits are authentic and positive traits are derivative, compensatory, or even inauthentic, but there are two other possibilities: that negative traits are derivative from positive traits and that the positive and negative systems are separate systems. However, if the two systems are separate, how do they interact? Is it necessary to be resilient, to overcome hardship and suffering to experience positive emotion and to develop positive traits? Does too much positive experience create a fragile and brittle personality?

Buffering

As positive psychology finds its way into prevention and therapy, techniques that build positive traits will become commonplace. Psychologists have good reason to believe that techniques that build positive traits and positive subjective experiences work, both in therapy and perhaps more importantly in prevention. Building optimism, for example, prevents depression (Seligman, Schulman, DeRubeis, & Hollon, 1999). The question is, how? By what mechanisms does courage or interpersonal skill or hope or future mindedness buffer against depression or schizophrenia or substance abuse?

Descriptive or Prescriptive

Is a science of positive psychology descriptive or prescriptive? The study of the relations among enabling conditions, individual strengths, institutions, and outcomes such as well-being or income might merely result in an empirical matrix. Such a matrix would describe, for example, what talents under what enabling conditions lead to what kinds of outcomes. This matrix would inform individuals' choices along the course of their lives, but would take no stand on the desirability of different life courses. Alternatively, positive psychology might become a prescriptive discipline like clinical psychology, in which the paths out of depression, for example, are not only described, but also held to be desirable.

Realism

What is the relationship between positive traits like optimism and positive experiences like happiness on the one hand, and being realistic on the other? Many doubt the possibility of being both. This suspicion is well illustrated in the reaction attributed to Charles de Gaulle, then President of the French Republic, to a journalist's inquiry:

"Mr. President, are you a happy man?"

"What sort of a fool do you take me for?"

Is the world simply too full of tragedy to allow a wise person to be happy? As the articles in this issue suggest, a person can be happy while confronting life realistically and while working productively to improve the conditions of existence. Whether this view is accurate only time will tell; in the meantime, we hope that you will find what follows enjoyable and enlightening to read.

Conclusions

We end this introduction by hazarding a prediction about psychology in the new century. We believe that a psychology of positive human functioning will arise that achieves a scientific understanding and effective interventions to build thriving in individuals, families, and communities.

You may think that this is pure fantasy. You may think that psychology will never look beyond the victim, the underdog, and the remedial, but we want to suggest that the time is finally right for positive psychology. We well recognize that positive psychology is not a new idea. It has many distinguished ancestors, and we make no claim of originality. However, these ancestors somehow failed to attract a cumulative, empirical body of research to ground their ideas.

Why didn't they attract this research, and why has psychology been so focused on the negative? Why has psychology adopted the premise—without a shred of evidence—that negative motivations are authentic and positive emotions are derivative? There are several possible explanations. Negative emotions and experiences may be more urgent and therefore may override positive ones. This would make evolutionary sense. Because negative emotions often reflect immediate problems or objective dangers, they should be powerful enough to force people to stop, increase their vigilance, reflect on their behavior, and change their actions if necessary. (Of course, in some dangerous situations, it is most adaptive to respond without taking a great deal of time to reflect.) In contrast, when people are adapting well to the world, no such alarm is needed. Experiences that promote happiness often seem to pass effortlessly. Therefore, on one level, psychology's focus on the negative may reflect differences in the survival value of negative versus positive emotions.

Perhaps, however, people are blinded to the survival value of positive emotions precisely because they are so important. Like the fish who is unaware of the water in which it swims, people take for granted a certain amount of hope, love, enjoyment, and trust because these are the very conditions that allow them to go on living. These conditions are fundamental to existence, and if they are present, any number of objective obstacles can be faced with equanimity and even joy. Camus wrote that the foremost question of philosophy is why one should not commit suicide. One cannot answer that question just by curing depression; there must be positive reasons for living as well.

There are also historical reasons for psychology's negative focus. When cultures face military threat, shortages of goods, poverty, or instability, they may most naturally be concerned with defense and damage control. Cultures may turn their attention to creativity, virtue, and the highest qualities in life only when they are stable, prosperous, and at peace. Athens in the 5th century B.C., Florence in the 15th century, and Victorian England are examples of cultures that focused on positive qualities. Athenian philosophy focused on the human virtues: What is good action and good character? What makes life most worthwhile? Democracy was born during this era. Florence chose not to become the most important military power in Europe, but to invest its surplus in beauty. Victorian England affirmed honor, discipline, valor, and duty as central human virtues.

We are not suggesting that American culture should now erect an aesthetic monument. Rather, we believe that the nation—wealthy, at peace, and stable—provides the world with a historical opportunity. Psychologists can choose to create a scientific monument—a science that takes as its primary task the understanding of what makes life worth living. Such an endeavor will move all of the social sciences away from their negative bias. The prevailing social sciences tend to view the authentic forces governing human behavior to be self-interest, aggressiveness, territoriality, class conflict, and the like. Such a science, even at its best, is by necessity incomplete. Even if utopianly successful, it would then have to proceed to ask how humanity can achieve what is best in life.

We predict that positive psychology in this new century will allow psychologists to understand and build those factors that allow individuals, communities, and societies to flourish. Such a science will not need to start afresh. It requires for the most part just a redirecting of scientific energy. In the 50 years since psychology and psychiatry became healing disciplines, they have developed a highly transferable science of mental illness. They developed a usable taxonomy, as well as reliable and valid ways of measuring such fuzzy concepts as schizophrenia, anger, and depression. They developed sophisticated methods—both experimental and longitudinal—for understanding the causal pathways that lead to such undesirable outcomes. Most important, they developed pharmacological and psychological interventions that have allowed many untreatable mental disorders to become highly treatable and, in a couple of cases, even curable. These same methods and in many cases the same laboratories and the next generation of scientists, with a slight shift of emphasis and funding, will be used to measure, understand, and build those characteristics that make life most worth living. As a side effect of studying positive human traits, science will learn how to buffer against and better prevent mental, as well as some physical, illnesses. As a main effect, psychologists will learn how to build the qualities that help individuals and communities, not just to endure and survive, but also to flourish.

References

Allport, G. W. (1961). *Pattern and growth in personality.* New York: Holt, Rinehart & Wilson.

Baltes, P. B., & Staudinger, U. M. (2000). Wisdom: A metaheuristic (pragmatic) to orchestrate mind and virtue toward excellence. *American Psychologist, 55,* 122–136.

Bandura, A. (1986). *Social foundations of thoughts and action.* Englewood Cliffs, NJ: Prentice-Hall.

Benjamin, L. T., Jr. (Ed.). (1992). The history of American psychology [Special issue]. *American Psychologist, 47*(2).

Buss, D. M. (2000). The evolution of happiness. *American Psychologist, 55,* 15–23.

Diener, E. (2000). Subjective well-being: The science of happiness and a proposal for a national index. *American Psychologist, 55,* 34–43.

Hall, G. S. (1922). *Senescence: The last half of life.* New York: Appleton.

James, W. (1958). *Varieties of religious experience.* New York: Mentor. (Original work published 1902)

Jung, C. (1933). *Modern man in search of a soul.* New York: Harcourt.

Jung, C. G. (1969). *The archetypes of the collective unconscious: Vol. 9. The collective works of C. G. Jung.* Princeton, NJ: Princeton University Press. (Original work published 1936)

Kahneman, D. (1999). Objective happiness. In D. Kahneman, E. Diener, & N. Schwartz (Eds.), *Well-being: The foundations of hedonic psychology* (pp. 3–25). New York: Russell Sage Foundation.

Koch, S., & Leary, D. E. (Eds.). (1985). *A century of psychology as science.* New York: McGraw-Hill.

Larson, R. W. (2000). Toward a psychology of positive youth development. *American Psychologist, 55,* 170–183.

LeDoux, J., & Armony, J. (1999). Can neurobiology tell us anything about human feelings? In D. Kahneman, E. Diener, & N. Schwartz (Eds.), *Well-being: The foundations of hedonic psychology* (pp. 489–499). New York: Russell Sage Foundation.

Lubinski, D., & Benbow, C. P. (2000). States of excellence. *American Psychologist, 55,* 137–150.

Maslow, A. (1971). *The farthest reaches of human nature.* New York: Viking.

Massimini, F., & Delle Fave, A. (2000). Individual development in a bio-cultural perspective. *American Psychologist, 55,* 24–33.

Myers, D. G. (2000). The funds, friends, and faith of happy people. *American Psychologist, 55,* 56–67.

Peterson, C. (2000). The future of optimism. *American Psychologist, 55,* 44–55.

Ryan, R. M., & Deci, E. L. (2000). Self-determination theory and the facilitation of intrinsic motivation, social development, and well-being. *American Psychologist, 55,* 68–78.

Salovey, P., Rothman, A. J., Detweiler, J. B., & Steward, W. T. (2000). Emotional states and physical health. *American Psychologist, 55,* 110–121.

Schwartz, B. (2000). Self-determination: The tyranny of freedom. *American Psychologist, 55,* 79–88.

Seligman, M. (1992). *Helplessness: On depression, development, and death.* New York: Freeman.

Seligman, M. (1994). *What you can change & what you can't.* New York: Knopf.

Seligman, M., Schulman, P., DeRubeis, R., & Hollon, S. (1999). The prevention of depression and anxiety. *Prevention and*

Treatment, 2, Article 8. Available on the World Wide Web: http://journals.apa.org/prevention/volume2/pre0020008a.html

Simonton, D. K. (2000). Creativity: Cognitive, personal, developmental, and social aspects. *American Psychologist, 55,* 151–158.

Smith, R. (1997). *The human sciences.* New York: Norton.

Taylor, S. E., Kemeny, M. E., Reed, G. M., Bower, J. E., & Gruenewald, T. L. (2000). Psychological resources, positive illusions, and health. *American Psychologist, 55,* 99–109.

Terman, L. M. (1939). The gifted student and his academic environment. *School and Society, 49,* 65–73.

Terman, L. M., Buttenwieser, P., Ferguson, L. W., Johnson, W. B., & Wilson, D. P. (1938). *Psychological factors in marital happiness.* New York: McGraw-Hill.

Vaillant, G. E. (2000). Adaptive mental mechanisms: Their role in a positive psychology. *American Psychologist, 55,* 89–98.

Watson, J. (1928). *Psychological care of infant and child.* New York: Norton.

Winner, E. (2000). The origins and ends of giftedness. *American Psychologist, 55,* 159–169.

Ode: Intimations of Immortality from Recollections of Early Childhood

William Wordsworth

William Wordsworth (1770–1850) was one of the greatest of the romantic period poets. He was born in Cumberland, England, and earned his degree in 1791 from Cambridge University. Wordsworth became friends with another great romantic poet, Samuel Taylor Coleridge, and their coauthored book of poems, *Lyrical Ballads* (1798), is credited with launching the English romantic movement.

Like other Romantics, one of Wordsworth's contributions was integrating the beauty and grandeur of nature with the human heart and mind. Of particular interest to students of human development is his masterpiece, *The Prelude,* which is credited with being the first grand autobiographical poem. In words that the developmental psychologist Howard Gardner might use, it was an extravaganza of "intrapersonal" intelligence. Wordsworth was appointed Poet Laureate of England in 1843, a station that he occupied until his death.

The following poem is Wordsworth's "Ode: Intimations of Immortality from Recollections of Early Childhood," which was written in 1802–1804 and first published in *Poems in Two Volumes* (1807). It is considered one of Wordsworth's greatest poems, and it echoes the classic lament that adults lose the childhood power to see the radiance, the glory, and the freshness of the world.

Key Concept: the beauty of child development

The Child is father of the Man;
And I could wish my days to be
Bound each to each by natural piety.

I.

There was a time when meadow, grove, and stream,
The earth, and every common sight,
To me did seem
Apparelled in celestial light,
The glory and the freshness of a dream.
It is not now as it hath been of yore;—
Turn wheresoe'er I may,
By night or day,
The things which I have seen I now can see no more.

II.

The Rainbow comes and goes,
And lovely is the Rose,

The Moon doth with delight
Look round her when the heavens are bare,
Waters on a starry night
Are beautiful and fair;
The sunshine is a glorious birth;
But yet I know, where'er I go,
That there hath past away a glory from the earth.

III.

Now, while the birds thus sing a joyous song,
And while the young lambs bound
As to the tabor's sound,
To me alone there came a thought of grief;
A timely utterance gave that thought relief,
And I again am strong:
The cataracts blow their trumpets from the steep;
No more shall grief of mine the season wrong;
I hear the Echoes through the mountains throng,
The Winds come to me from the fields of sleep,

And all the earth is gay;
Land and sea
Give themselves up to jollity,
And with the heart of May
Doth every Beast keep holiday;—
Thou Child of Joy,
Shout round me, let me hear thy shouts, thou happy
Shepherd-boy!

IV.

Ye blessèd Creatures, I have heard the call
Ye to each other make; I see
The heavens laugh with you in your jubilee;
My heart is at your festival,
My head hath its coronal,
The fulness of your bliss, I feel—I feel it all.
Oh evil day! if I were sullen
While Earth herself is adorning,
This sweet May-morning,
And the Children are culling
On every side,
In a thousand valleys far and wide,
Fresh flowers; while the sun shines warm,
And the Babe leaps up on his Mother's arm:—
I hear, I hear, with joy I hear!
—But there's a Tree, of many, one,
A single Field which I have looked upon,
Both of them speak of something that is gone:
The Pansy at my feet
Doth the same tale repeat:
Whither is fled the visionary gleam!
Where is it now, the glory and the dream!

V.

Our birth is but a sleep and a forgetting:
The Soul that rises with us, our life's Star,
Hath had elsewhere its setting,
And cometh from afar:
Not in entire forgetfulness,
And not in utter nakedness,
But trailing clouds of glory do we come
From God, who is our home:
Heaven lies about us in our infancy!
Shades of the prison-house begin to close
Upon the growing Boy,
But He beholds the light, and whence it flows,
He sees it in his joy;
The Youth, who daily farther from the east
Must travel, still is Nature's Priest,
And by the vision splendid
Is on his way attended;
At length the Man perceives it die away,
And fade into the light of common day.

VI.

Earth fills her lap with pleasures of her own;
Yearnings she hath in her own natural kind,
And, even with something of a Mother's mind,
And no unworthy aim,
The homely Nurse doth all she can
To make her Foster-child, her Inmate Man,
Forget the glories he hath known,
And that imperial palace whence he came.

VII.

Behold the Child among his new-born blisses,
A six years' Darling of a pigmy size!
See, where 'mid work of his own hand he lies,
Fretted by sallies of his mother's kisses,
With light upon him from his father's eyes!
See, at his feet, some little plan or chart,
Some fragment from his dream of human life,
Shaped by himself with newly-learned art;
A wedding or a festival,
A mourning or a funeral;
And this hath now his heart,
And unto this he frames his song:
Then will he fit his tongue
To dialogues of business, love, or strife:
But it will not be long
Ere this be thrown aside,
And with new joy and pride
The little Actor cons another part;
Filling from time to time his "humorous stage"
With all the Persons, down to palsied Age,
That Life brings with her in her equipage;
As if his whole vocation
Were endless imitation.

VIII.

Thou, whose exterior semblance doth belie
Thy Soul's immensity;
Thou best Philosopher, who yet dost keep
Thy heritage, thou Eye among the blind,
That, deaf and silent, read'st the eternal deep,
Haunted for ever by the eternal mind,—
Mighty Prophet! Seer blest!
On whom those truths do rest,
Which we are toiling all our lives to find,
In darkness lost, the darkness of the grave;
Thou, over whom thy Immortality
Broods like the Day, a Master o'er a Slave,
A Presence which is not to be put by;
[To whom the grave
Is but a lonely bed without the sense or sight
Of day or the warm light,
A place of thought where we in waiting lie;[1]]

Thou little Child, yet glorious in the might
Of heaven-born freedom on thy being's height,
Why with such earnest pains dost thou provoke
The years to bring the inevitable yoke,
Thus blindly with thy blessedness at strife?
Full soon thy Soul shall have her earthly freight,
And custom lie upon thee with a weight,
Heavy as frost, and deep almost as life!

IX.

O joy! that in our embers
Is something that doth live,
That nature yet remembers
What was so fugitive!
The thought of our past years in me doth breed
Perpetual benediction: not indeed
For that which is most worthy to be blest;
Delight and liberty, the simple creed
Of Childhood, whether busy or at rest,
With new-fledged hope still fluttering in his breast:—
Not for these I raise
The song of thanks and praise;
But for those obstinate questionings
Of sense and outward things,
Fallings from us, vanishings;
Blank misgivings of a Creature
Moving about in worlds not realised,
High instincts before which our mortal Nature
Did tremble like a guilty Thing surprised:
But for those first affections,
Those shadowy recollections,
Which, be they what they may,
Are yet the fountain-light of all our day,
Are yet a master-light of all our seeing;
Uphold us, cherish, and have power to make
Our noisy years seem moments in the being
Of the eternal Silence: truths that wake,
To perish never:
Which neither listlessness, nor mad endeavour,
Nor Man nor Boy,
Nor all that is at enmity with joy,
Can utterly abolish or destroy!
Hence in a season of calm weather
Though inland far we be,
Our Souls have sight of that immortal sea
Which brought us hither,
Can in a moment travel thither,

And see the Children sport upon the shore,
And hear the mighty waters rolling evermore.

X.

Then sing, ye Birds, sing, sing a joyous song!
And let the young Lambs bound
As to the tabor's sound!
We in thought will join your throng,
Ye that pipe and ye that play,
Ye that through your hearts today
Feel the gladness of the May!
What though the radiance which was once so bright
Be now for ever taken from my sight,
Though nothing can bring back the hour
Of splendour in the grass, of glory in the flower;
We will grieve not, rather find
Strength in what remains behind;
In the primal sympathy
Which having been must ever be;
In the soothing thoughts that spring
Out of human suffering;
In the faith that looks through death,
In years that bring the philosophic mind.

XI.

And O, ye Fountains, Meadows, Hills, and Groves,
Forebode not any severing of our loves!
Yet in my heart of hearts I feel your might;
I only have relinquished one delight
To live beneath your more habitual sway.
I love the Brooks which down their channels fret,
Even more than when I tripped lightly as they;
The innocent brightness of a new-born Day
Is lovely yet;
The Clouds that gather round the setting sun
Do take a sober colouring from an eye
That hath kept watch o'er man's mortality;
Another race hath been, and other palms are won.
Thanks to the human heart by which we live,
Thanks to its tenderness, its joys, and fears,
To me the meanest flower that blows can give
Thoughts that do often lie too deep for tears.

Note

1.   Found in edd. 1807 and 1815; omitted from ed. 1820 and all subsequent issues in consequence of Coleridge's adverse criticism. See *Biographia Literaria*, chap. xxii.—ED.

Non-Western Classics

The Spectrum of Development

Ken Wilber

Ken Wilber is a prolific author in the field of human development, with more than a dozen texts and hundreds of articles to his credit. He works within the humanistic and transpersonal approach to psychology. Humanistic psychology (the school of which Abraham Maslow was a founder) is often referred to as the "third force" in the general discipline of psychology, Freudian and neo-Freudian psychology being the first force and behaviorism the second. Humanistic and transpersonal approaches to human development are often criticized as being weak "scientifically," as they seldom use experimental designs (which humanists, in turn, criticize as "artificial"). The strength of these approaches lies in addressing the enduring and meaningful questions of human development: What is the purpose of development? What is most important in the human experience? and, How can life be made more meaningful?

The following selection is from "The Spectrum of Development," in Ken Wilber, Jack Engler, and Daniel P. Brown, eds., *Transformations of Consciousness: Conventional and Contemplative Perspectives on Development* (New Science Library, 1986). In it, Wilber compares stages of human development based on Hindu and Buddhist thought to Jean Piaget's stages of cognitive development. To maintain a worldwide view of human development, one must realize that approximately 1 billion Hindus are influenced by the Hindu view of development. Likewise, 500 million Buddhists are influenced by the Buddhist approach to human development (and if one counts the strong Buddhist influence that still exists in China, the number swells to more than 1.5 billion people affected by that approach).

The contemplative approach to human knowledge, outlined by Wilber, is based on the belief that most of the important knowledge that a human can gain may come from inner meditation rather than from external experimental manipulation of the environment.

Key Concept: structures of consciousness, or stages of contemplation

The Spectrum of Consciousness . . .

The Basic Structures

The most notable feature about a basic structure or level of consciousness is that, once it emerges in human development, it tends to *remain in existence* in the life of the individual during subsequent development. Even though it is eventually transcended, subsumed, and subordinated by the self's movement to higher basic structures, it nevertheless retains a relative autonomy and functional independence.

The basic structures of consciousness are, in effect, what is known as the Great Chain of Being. Some versions of the Great Chain give only two levels (matter and spirit); others give three (matter, mind, and spirit); still others give four or five (matter, body, mind, soul, and spirit). Some are very sophisticated, giving literally dozens of the basic structures of the overall spectrum.

. . . For this presentation, I have selected what seem to be the nine most central and functionally dominant structures. . . .

The basic structures of consciousness development shown in Fig. 10.1 may be very briefly (and somewhat simplistically) outlined as follows (proceeding up the hierarchy):

1. *Sensoriphysical*—the realms of matter, sensation, and perception (the first three Buddhist *skandhas*); Piaget's sensorimotor level, etc.
2. *Phantasmic-emotional*—the emotional-sexual level (the sheath of bioenergy, *élan vital*, libido, or *prana*; the fourth Buddhist *skandha*, the *pranamayokosa* in Vendata, [a form of Hinduism] etc.) and the phantasmic level (Arietís term for the lower or *image* mind, the simplest form of mental "picturing" using only images).
3. *Rep-mind*—an abbreviation for "representational mind," or Piaget's preoperational thinking

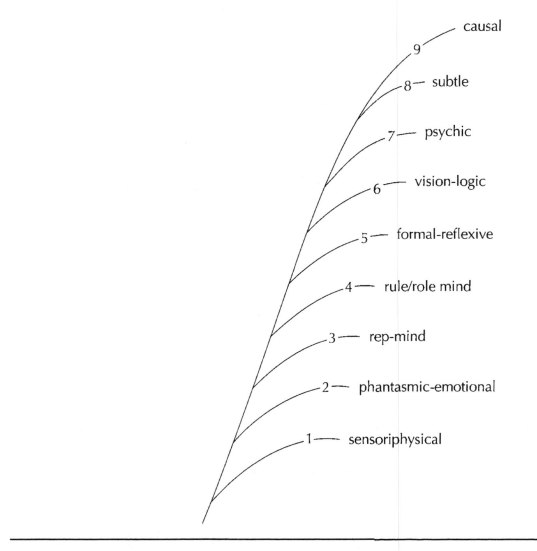

Figure 10.1   The Basic Structures of Consciousness.

("preop"). The rep-mind develops in two stages—that of *symbols* (2–4 yrs), and that of *concepts* (4–7 yrs). A symbol goes beyond a simple image (the phantasmic mind) in this essential respect; an image represents an object pictorially, while a symbol can represent it nonpictorially or verbally. Thus, for example, the mental image of a tree looks more or less like a real tree, whereas the word-symbol "t-r-e-e" does not look like a tree at all; symbolic representation is a higher, more difficult, and more sophisticated cognitive operation. A *concept* is a symbol that represents, not just one object or act, but a *class* of objects or acts—an even more difficult cognitive task. A symbol denotes; a concept connotes. But no matter how advanced the rep-mind is over its phantasmic predecessor, one of its most striking features is that it *cannot easily take the role of other*. It is, as Piaget would say, still very egocentric. This is very similar to Aurobindo's "will-mind," the third chakra in Yoga psychology, etc.

4. *Rule/role mind*—This is, for example, Piaget's concrete operational thinking ("conop"). Conop, unlike its rep-mind predecessor, can begin to take the *role* of others. It is also the first structure that can clearly perform *rule* operations, such as multiplication, division, class inclusion, hierarchization, etc. Aurobindo describes this structure as the mind that operates on sensory or concrete objects—very similar to Piaget.

5. *Formal-reflexive mind*—This is essentially Piaget's formal operational thinking ("formop"). It is the first structure that can not only think about the world but think about thinking; hence, it is the first structure that is clearly self-reflexive and introspective (although this begins in rudimentary form with the rule/role mind). It is also the first structure capable of hypothetico-deductive or propositional reasoning ("if a, then b"), which, among other things, allows it to take genuinely pluralistic and more universal views. Aurobindo calls this level the "reasoning mind," a mind that

is not bound to sensory or concrete objects, but instead apprehends and operates on *relationships* (which are not "things").

6. *Vision-logic*—Numerous psychologists have pointed out that there is much evidence for a cognitive structure beyond or higher than Piaget's "formal operational." It has been called "dialectical," "integrative," "creative synthetic," and so forth. I prefer the term "vision-logic." In any case, it appears that whereas the formal mind establishes relationships, vision-logic establishes *networks* of those relationships (i.e., just as formop "operates on" conop, so vision-logic "operates on" formop). Such vision or panoramic logic apprehends a mass network of ideas, how they influence each other and interrelate. It is thus the beginning of truly higher-order synthesizing capacity, or making connections, relating truths, coordinating ideas, integrating concepts. Interestingly, this is almost exactly what Aurobindo called "the higher mind," which "can freely express itself in single ideas, but its most characteristic movement is a mass ideation, a system or totality of truth-seeing at a single view; the relations of idea with idea, of truth with truth, self-seen in the integral whole." This, obviously is a highly *integrative* structure; indeed in my opinion it is the highest integrative structure in the *personal* realm; beyond it lie transpersonal developments.

7. *Psychic*—The psychic level may be thought of as the culmination of vision-logic and visionary insight; it is perhaps best epitomized by the sixth chakra, the "third eye," which is said to mark the beginning or opening of transcendental, transpersonal, or contemplative developments: the individual's cognitive and perceptual capacities apparently become so pluralistic and universal that they begin to "reach beyond" any narrowly personal or individual perspectives and concerns. According to most contemplative traditions, at this level an individual *begins* to learn to very subtly inspect the mind's cognitive and perceptual capacities, and thus to that extent begins to *transcend* them. This is Aurobindo's "illumined mind," the "preliminary stages" of meditation in Hinduism and Buddhism, etc, According to Aurobindo,

> The perceptual power of the inner [psychic] sight is greater and more direct than the perceptual power of thought. As the higher mind [i.e., vision-logic] brings a greater consciousness into the being than the idea and its power of truth [formop], so the illumined mind [psychic level] brings a still greater consciousness through a Truth sight and Truth Light and its seeing and seizing power; it illumines the thought-mind with a direct inner vision and inspiration; it can embody a finer and bolder revealing outline and

a larger comprehension and power of totality than thought-conception can manage.

8. *Subtle*—The subtle level is said to be the seat of actual archetypes, of Platonic Forms, of subtle sounds and audible illuminations (*nada, shabd*), of transcendent insight and absorption. Some traditions, such as Hinduism and Gnosticism, claim that, according to direct phenomenological apprehension, this level is the home of personal deity-form (*ishtadeva* in Hinduism, *yidam* in Mahayana, *demiurge* in Gnosticism, etc.), cognized in a state known as *savikalpa samadhi* in Hinduism. In Theravadin Buddhism, this is the realm of the four "*jhanas* with form," or the four stages of concentrative meditation into archetypal "planes of illumination" or "Brahma realms." In *vipassana* meditation, this is the stage-realm of pseudonirvana, the realm of illumination and rapture and initial transcendental insight.

9. *Causal*—The causal level is said to be the unmanifest source or transcendental ground of all the lesser structures; the Abyss (Gnosticism), the Void (Mahayana), the Formless (Vedanta). It is realized in a state of consciousness known variously as *nirvikalpa samadhi* (Hinduism), *jnana samadhi* (Vendanta), the eighth of the ten ox-herding pictures (Zen [Buddhism]); the seventh and eighth *jhanas*; the state of effortless insight culminating in *nirvana* (*vipassana*). Alternatively, this state is described as a universal and formless Self (Atman), common in and to all beings. Aurobindo: "When the Overmind [causal] descends, the predominance of the centralizing ego-sense is entirely subordinated, lost in largeness of being and finally abolished; a wide cosmic perception and feeling of boundless universal self replaces it . . . an unlimited consciousness of unity which pervades everywhere . . . a being who is in essence one with the Supreme Self."

10. *Ultimate*—Passing fully through the state of cessation or unmanifest causal absorption, consciousness is said finally to re-awaken to its prior and eternal abode as absolute Spirit, radiant and all-pervading, one and many, only and all—the complete integration and identity to manifest Form with the unmanifest Formless. This is classical *sahaj* and *bhava samadhi* [terminology for Hindu psychology]; the state of *turiya* (and *turiyatita*), absolute and unqualifiable Consciousness as Such, Aurobindo's "Supermind," Zen's "One Mind," Brahman-Atman, the *Svabhavikakaya*. Strictly speaking, the ultimate is not one level among others, but the reality, condition, or suchness of all levels. By analogy, the paper on which Fig. 10.1 is drawn represents this fundamental ground of empty-suchness.

The Seven Valleys and the Four Valleys

Bahá'u'lláh

Bahá'u'lláh was born in Tehran in 1817. In 1863 he initiated the Bahá'í movement, which had among its several objectives the reform of Islam. In Islamic countries, human development is conceived as closely linked to religious development. The separation of church and state does not exist in many Muslim countries and is a recent phenomenon in others. Differentiating religion and science is also foreign to Muslim culture; the two tend to be more integrated than they are in the West.

The following excerpt from Bahá'u'lláh's *The Seven Valleys and the Four Valleys*, translated by Marzieh Gail (Bahá'í Publishing Trust, 1976), is in some sense a modernized adaptation of 'Attár's famous epic poem *The Conference of the Birds*. 'Attár, one of the main protagonists of the mystic Sufi movement within Islam, lived in Persia in the twelfth century A.D. Bahá'u'lláh wrote *Seven Valleys* in this style in response to a query he received from a noted Sufi sheikh concerning the mystical stages of human development.

In terms of a worldview of human development, it is helpful to keep in mind that about 300 million Muslim people live in Africa, close to 50 million are in the former Soviet Union, and around 750 million Muslims live in other parts of Asia.

Key Concept: stages of mystic development

The stages that mark the wayfarer's journey from the abode of dust to the heavenly homeland are said to be seven. Some have called these Seven Valleys, and others, Seven Cities. And they say that until the wayfarer taketh leave of self, and traverseth these stages, he shall never reach to the ocean of nearness and union, nor drink of the peerless wine. The first is

THE VALLEY OF SEARCH

The steed of this Valley is patience; without patience the wayfarer on this journey will reach nowhere and attain no goal. Nor should he ever be downhearted; if he strive for a hundred thousand years and yet fail to behold the beauty of the Friend, he should not falter. For those who seek the Ka'bih[1] of "for Us" rejoice in the tidings: "In Our ways will We guide them."[2] In their search, they have stoutly girded up the loins of service, and seek at every moment to journey from the plane of heedlessness into the realm of being. No bond shall hold them back, and no counsel shall deter them.

It is incumbent on these servants that they cleanse the heart—which is the wellspring of divine treasures—from every marking, and that they turn away from imitation, which is following the traces of their forefathers and sires, and shut the door of friendliness and enmity upon all the people of the earth.

In this journey the seeker reacheth a stage wherein he seeth all created things wandering distracted in search of the Friend. How many a Jacob will he see, hunting after his Joseph; he will behold many a lover, hasting to seek the Beloved, he will witness a world of desiring ones searching after the One Desired. At every moment he findeth a weighty matter, in every hour he becometh aware of a mystery; for he hath taken his heart away from both worlds, and set out for the Ka'bih of the Beloved. At every step, aid from the Invisible Realm will attend him and the heat of his search will grow. . . .

And if, by the help of God, he findeth on this journey a trace of the traceless Friend, and inhaleth the fragrance of the long-lost Joseph from the heavenly messenger,[3] he shall straightway step into

THE VALLEY OF LOVE

and be dissolved in the fire of love. In this city the heaven of ecstasy is upraised and the world-illuming sun of yearning shineth, and the fire of love is ablaze; and when the fire of love is ablaze, it burneth to ashes the harvest of reason.

Now is the traveler unaware of himself, and of aught besides himself. He seeth neither ignorance nor knowledge, neither doubt nor certitude; he knoweth not the morn of guidance from the night of error. He fleeth both from unbelief and faith, and deadly poison is a balm to him. Wherefore 'Attár[4] saith:

For the infidel, error—for the faithful, faith;
For 'Attár's heart, an atom of Thy pain.

The steed of this Valley is pain; and if there be no pain this journey will never end. In this station the lover hath no thought save the Beloved, and seeketh no refuge save the Friend. At every moment he offereth a hundred lives in the path of the Loved One, at every step he throweth a thousand heads at the feet of the Beloved. . . .

And if, confirmed by the Creator, the lover escapes from the claws of the eagle of love, he will enter

THE VALLEY OF KNOWLEDGE

and come out of doubt into certitude, and turn from the darkness of illusion to the guiding light of the fear of God. His inner eyes will open and he will privily converse with his Beloved; he will set ajar the gate of truth and piety, and shut the doors of vain imaginings. He in this station is content with the decree of God, and seeth war as peace, and findeth in death the secrets of everlasting life. With inward and outward eyes he witnesseth the mysteries of resurrection in the realms of creation and the souls of men, and with a pure heart apprehendeth the divine wisdom in the endless Manifestations of God. In the ocean he findeth a drop, in a drop he beholdeth the secrets of the sea. . . .

The wayfarer in this Valley seeth in the fashionings of the True One nothing save clear providence, and at every moment saith: "No defect canst thou see in the creation of the God of Mercy: Repeat the gaze: Seest thou a single flaw?"[5] He beholdeth justice in injustice, and in justice, grace. In ignorance he findeth many a knowledge hidden, and in knowledge a myriad wisdoms manifest. He breaketh the cage of the body and the passions, and consorteth with the people of the immortal realm. He mounteth on the ladders of inner truth and hasteneth to the heaven of inner significance. He rideth in the ark of "we shall show them our signs in the regions and in themselves,"[6] and journeyeth over the sea of "until it become plain to them that (this Book) is the truth."[6] And if he meeteth with injustice he shall have patience, and if he cometh upon wrath he shall manifest love. . . .

After passing through the Valley of knowledge, which is the last plane of limitation, the wayfarer cometh to

THE VALLEY OF UNITY

and drinketh from the cup of the Absolute, and gazeth on the manifestations of Oneness. In this station he pierceth the veils of plurality, fleeth from the worlds of the flesh, and ascendeth into the heaven of singleness. With the ear of God he heareth, with the eye of God he beholdeth the mysteries of divine creation. He steppeth into the sanctuary of the Friend, and shareth as an intimate the pavilion of the Loved One. He stretcheth out the hand of truth from the sleeve of the Absolute; he revealeth the secrets of power. He seeth in himself neither name nor fame nor rank, but findeth his own praise in praising God. He beholdeth in his own name the name of God; to him, "all songs are from the King,"[7] and every melody from Him. He sitteth on the throne of "Say, all is from God,"[8] and taketh his rest on the carpet of "There is no power or might but in God."[9] He looketh on all things with the eye of oneness, and seeth the brilliant rays of the divine sun shining from the dawning-point of Essence alike on all created things, and the lights of singleness reflected over all creation. . . .

Peace be upon him who concludeth this exalted journey and followeth the True One by the lights of guidance.

And the wayfarer, after traversing the high planes of this supernal journey, entereth

THE VALLEY OF CONTENTMENT

In this Valley he feeleth the winds of divine contentment blowing from the plane of the spirit. He burneth away the veils of want, and with inward and outward eye, perceiveth within and without all things the day of: "God will compensate each one out of His abundance."[10] From sorrow he turneth to bliss, from anguish to joy. His grief and mourning yield to delight and rapture.

Although to outward view, the wayfarers in this Valley may dwell upon the dust, yet inwardly they are throned in the heights of mystic meaning; they eat of the endless bounties of inner significances, and drink of the delicate wines of the spirit.

The tongue faileth in describing these three Valleys, and speech falleth short. The pen steppeth not into this region, the ink leaveth only a blot. In these planes, the nightingale of the heart hath other songs and secrets, which make the heart to stir and the soul to clamor, but this mystery of inner meaning may be whispered only from heart to heart, confided only from breast to breast. . . .

After journeying through the planes of pure contentment, the traveler cometh to

THE VALLEY OF WONDERMENT

and is tossed in the oceans of grandeur, and at every moment his wonder groweth. Now he seeth the shape of wealth as poverty itself, and the essence of freedom as sheer impotence. Now is he struck dumb with the beauty of the All-Glorious; again is he wearied out with his own life. How many a mystic tree hath this whirlwind of wonderment snatched by the roots, how many a soul hath it exhausted. For in this Valley the traveler is flung into confusion, albeit, in the eye of him who hath attained, such marvels are esteemed and well beloved. At every moment he beholdeth a wondrous world, a new creation, and goeth from astonishment to astonishment, and is lost in awe at the works of the Lord of Oneness. . . .

After scaling the high summits of wonderment the wayfarer cometh to

THE VALLEY OF THE TRUE POVERTY
AND ABSOLUTE NOTHINGNESS

This station is the dying from self and the living in God, the being poor in self and rich in the Desired One. Poverty as here referred to signifieth being poor in the things of the created world, rich in the things of God's world. For when the true lover and devoted friend reacheth to the presence of the Beloved, the sparkling beauty of the Loved One and the fire of the lover's heart will kindle a blaze and burn away all veils and wrappings. Yea, all he hath, from heart to skin, will be set aflame, so that nothing will remain save the Friend.

> When the qualities of the Ancient of Days stood revealed,
> Then the qualities of earthly things did Moses burn away.[7]

He who hath attained this station is sanctified from all that pertaineth to the world. Wherefore, if those who have come to the sea of His presence are found to possess none of the limited things of this perishable world, whether it be outer wealth or personal opinions, it mattereth not. For whatever the creatures have is limited by their own limits, and whatever the True One hath is sanctified therefrom; this utterance must be deeply pondered that its purport may be clear. . . .

This is the plane whereon the vestiges of all things are destroyed in the traveler, and on the horizon of eternity the Divine Face riseth out of the darkness, and the meaning of "All on the earth shall pass away, but the face of thy Lord. . . . "[11] is made manifest.

O My friend, listen with heart and soul to the songs of the spirit, and treasure them as thine own eyes. . . .

Now hast thou abandoned the drop of life and come to the sea of the Life-Bestower. This is the goal thou didst ask for; if it be God's will, thou wilt gain it.

Notes

1. The holy Sanctuary at Mecca. Here the word means "goal."
2. Qur'án 29:69: "And whoso maketh efforts for Us, in Our ways will We guide them."
3. Refer to the story of Joseph in the Qur'án and the Old Testament.
4. Farídu'd-Dín 'Attár (ca. 1150–1230 A.D.), the great Persian Súfí poet.
5. Qur'án 67:3.
6. Qur'án 41:53.
7. Jalálu'd-Dín Rúmí (1207–1273 A.D.), The *Mathnaví*. Jalálu'd-Dín, called Mawláná ("our Master"), is the greatest of all Persian Súfí poets, and founder of the Mawlaví "whirling" dervish order.
8. Qur'án 4:80.
9. Qur'án 18:37.
10. Qur'án 4:129.
11. Qur'án 55:26, 27.

The Great Learning

K'ung Fu-tzu (Confucius)

Confucius is one of the most influential people in human history. Born in 551 B.C., his family name was K'ung, and his personal name was Ch'iu. "Fu-tzu" is Chinese for "Master," and "Confucius" is a Latinized form of "K'ung Futzu," or "Master K'ung." Confucius's teachings were often directed toward the practical side of human development, both development of the individual and development of the state. Historians of China say that if we were to characterize the Chinese way of life for the last two-and-a-half millennia, we would say "Confucian." Although the Maoist revolution attempted to replace Confucius's teachings with Marxist beliefs, it has only been partially successful; Confucius's explanations concerning human development are still highly influential, both theoretically and in everyday family socialization.

The following selection comes from the classic essay *The Great Learning*, which is one of four Confucian works included in a single-bound text called *The Four Books*. *The Four Books* is considered the greatest classic in Chinese history; it served as the basis for the civil service examinations in China for six centuries (1313–1905). The Chinese title for *The Great Learning* is "Ta hsüeh," which may be translated as "adult development" or "higher education." At first glance a Westerner might say, "This selection seems to be a study of political science, not a study of human development or developmental psychology." As cross-cultural psychologists point out, however, the Chinese culture is a collectivist culture. The Chinese tend to look at the individual in a different context than Westerners do. The Chinese would not want to distinctly separate individual development from development of the society, as is more common in the West.

It is unclear who actually wrote The *Great Learning*, although there is consensus among scholars that it is clearly a "Confucian" work. Some attribute its writing to Tseng Tzu, one of Confucius's pupils, or to his grandson Tzu Ssu.

Key Concept: the way of the great learning

The Great Learning *is originally ch. 42 of the* Li chi *(Book of Rites). Not much attention was paid to it until the time of Ssu-ma Kuang (1019–1086), who wrote a commentary on it, treating it as a separate work for the first time. This commentary is now lost. Ch'eng Hao (Ch'eng Ming-tao, 1032–1085) and his younger brother Ch'eng I (Ch'eng I-ch'uan, 1033–1107) each rearranged the text. Chu Hsi did the same and, moreover, added a "supplement." He further divided the work into one "text" and ten "chapters of commentary," and contended that the former was Confucius' own words handed down by his pupil Tseng Tzu (505–c. 436 B.C.) and that the latter were the views of Tseng Tzu recorded by his pupils. There is no evidence for this contention. Recent scholars, equally without evidence, have dated the work as late as around 200 B.C. Regardless of its date and authorship, which has also been attributed to Confucius' grandson Tzu-ssu (492–431 B.C.), it was Chu Hsi who made it important in the last 800 years. He grouped it with the* Analects, *the* Book of Mencius, *and the* Doctrine of the Mean *as the "Four Books"*

and wrote commentaries on them. Since then they were honored as Classics, and from 1313 till 1905 they were the basis of civil service examinations. Thus they replaced the other Classics in importance and influence.

The Way of learning to be great (or adult education) consists in manifesting the clear character, loving the people, and abiding *(chih)* in the highest good.

Only after knowing what to abide in can one be calm. Only after having been calm can one be tranquil. Only after having achieved tranquility can one have peaceful repose. Only after having peaceful repose can one begin to deliberate. Only after deliberation can the end be attained. Things have their roots and branches. Affairs have their beginnings and their ends. To know what is first and what is last will lead one near the Way.

The ancients who wished to manifest their clear character to the world would first bring order to their states. Those who wished to bring order to their states would first regulate their families. Those who wished to regulate their families would first cultivate their personal lives. Those who wished to cultivate their personal lives would first rectify their minds. Those who wished to make their wills sincere would first extend their knowledge. The extension of knowledge consists in the investigation of things. When things are investigated, knowledge is extended; when knowledge is extended, the will becomes sincere; when the will is sincere, the mind is rectified; when the mind is rectified, the personal life is cultivated; when the personal life is cultivated, the family will be regulated; when the family is regulated, the state will be in order; and when the state is in order, there will be peace throughout the world. From the Son of Heaven down to the common people, all must regard cultivation of the personal life as the root or foundation. There is never a case when the root is in disorder and yet the branches are in order. There has never been a case when what is treated with great importance becomes a matter of slight importance or what is treated with slight importance becomes a matter of great importance.

Chu Hsi's Remark. The above is the text in one chapter. It is the words of Confucius, handed down by Tseng Tzu. The ten chapters of commentary which follow are the views of Tseng Tzu and were recorded by his pupils. In the traditional version there have been some mistakes in its arrangement. Now follows the new version fixed by Master Ch'eng I, and in addition, having examined the contents of the text, I (Chu Hsi) have rearranged it as follows:

Chapters of Commentary

1. In the "Announcement of K'ang" it is said, "He was able to manifest his clear character." In the "T'ai-chia" it is said, "He contemplated the clear Mandates of Heaven." In the "Canon of Yao" it is said, "He was able to manifest his lofty character." These all show that the ancient kings manifested their own character.

Chu Hsi's Remark. The above first chapter of commentary explains manifesting the clear character.

2. The inscription on the bath-tub of King T'ang read, "If you can renovate yourself one day, then you can do so every day, and keep doing so day after day." In the "Announcement of K'ang," it is said, "Arouse people to become new." The Book of Odes says, "Although Chou is an ancient state, the mandate it has received from Heaven is new." Therefore, the superior man tries at all times to do his utmost [in renovating himself and others].

Chu Hsi's Remark. The above second chapter of commentary explains the renovating of the people.

3. The Book of Odes says, "The imperial domain of a thousand li is where the people stay (chih)." The Book of Odes also says, "The twittering yellow bird rests (chih) on a thickly wooded mount." Confucius said, "When the bird rests, it knows where to rest. Should a human being be unequal to a bird?" The Book of Odes says, "How profound was King Wen! How he maintained his brilliant virtue without interruption and regarded with reverence that which he abided (chih)." As a ruler, he abided in humanity. As a minister, he abided in reverence. As a son, he abided in filial piety. As a father, he abided in deep love. And in dealing with the people of the country, he abided in faithfulness.

The Book of Odes says, "Look at that curve in the Ch'i River. How luxuriant and green are the bamboo trees there! Here is our elegant and accomplished prince. [His personal life is cultivated] as a thing is cut and filed and as a thing is carved and polished. How grave and dignified! How majestic and distinguished! Here is our elegant and accomplished prince. We can never forget him!" "As a thing is cut and filed" refers to the pursuit of learning. "As a thing is carved and polished" refers to self-cultivation. "How grave and how dignified" indicates precaution. "How majestic and distinguished" expresses awe-inspiring appearance. "Here is our elegant and accomplished prince. We can never forget him" means that the people cannot forget his eminent character and perfect virtue. The Book of Odes says, "Ah! the ancient kings are not forgotten." [Future] rulers deemed worthy what they deemed worthy and loved what they loved, while the common people enjoyed what they enjoyed and benefited from their beneficial arrangements. That was why they are not forgotten even after they passed away.

Chu Hsi's Remark. The above third chapter of commentary explains abiding in the highest good.

4. Confucius said, "In hearing litigations, I am as good as anyone. What is necessary is to enable people not to have litigations at all." Those who would not tell the truth will not dare to finish their words, and a great awe would be struck into people's minds. This is called knowing the root.

Chu Hsi's Remark. The above fourth chapter of commentary explains the root and the branches.

5. This is called knowing the root. This is called the perfecting of knowledge.

Chu Hsi's Remark. The above fifth chapter of commentary explains the meaning of the investigation of things and the extension of knowledge, which is now lost. I have ventured to take the view of Master Ch'eng I and supplement it as follows: The meaning of the expression "The perfection of knowledge depends on the investigation of things (ko-wu)" is this: If we wish to extend our knowledge to the utmost, we must investigate the principles of all things we come into contact with, for the intelligent mind of man is certainly formed to know, and there is not a single thing in which its principles do not inhere. It is only because all principles are not investigated that man's knowledge is incomplete. For this reason, the first step in the education of the adult is to instruct the learner, in regard to all things in the world, to proceed from what knowledge he has of their principles, and investigate further until he reaches the limit. After exerting himself in this way for a long time, he will one day achieve a wide and far-reaching penetration. Then the qualities of all things, whether internal or external, the refined or the coarse, will all be apprehended, and the mind, in its total substance and great functioning, will be perfectly intelligent. This is called the investigation of things. This is called the perfection of knowledge.

6. What is meant by "Making the will sincere" is allowing no self-deception, as when we hate a bad smell or love a beautiful color. This is called satisfying oneself. Therefore the superior man will always be watchful over himself when alone. When the inferior man is alone and leisurely, there is no limit to which he does not go in his evil deeds. Only when he sees a superior man does he then try to disguise himself, concealing the evil and showing off the good in him. But what is the use? For other people see him as if they see his very heart. This is what is meant by saying that what is true in a man's heart will be shown in his outward appearance. Therefore the superior man will always be watchful over himself when alone. Tseng Tzu said, "What ten eyes are beholding and what ten hands are pointing to—isn't it frightening?" Wealth makes a house shining and virtue makes a person shining. When one's mind is broad and his heart generous, his body becomes big and is at ease. Therefore the superior man always makes his will sincere.

Chu Hsi's Remark. The above sixth chapter of commentary explains the sincerity of the will.

7. What is meant by saying that cultivation of the personal life depends on the rectification of the mind is that when one is affected by wrath to any extent, his mind will not be correct. When one is affected by fear to any extent, his mind will not be correct. When he is affected by fondness to any extent, his mind will not be correct. When he is affected by worries and anxieties, his mind will not be correct. When the mind is not present, we look but do not see, listen but do not hear, and eat but do not know the taste of the food. This is what is meant by saying that the cultivation of the personal life depends on the rectification of the mind.

Chu Hsi's Remark. The above seventh chapter of commentary explains the rectification of the mind in order to cultivate the personal life.

8. What is meant by saying that the regulation of the family depends on the cultivation of the personal life is this: Men are partial toward those for whom they have affection and whom they love, partial toward those whom they despise and dislike, partial toward those whom they fear and revere, partial toward those whom they pity and for whom they have compassion, and partial toward those whom they do not respect. Therefore there are few people in the world who know what is bad in those whom they love and what is good in those whom they dislike. Hence it is said, "People do not know the faults of their sons and do not know (are not satisfied with) the bigness of their seedlings." This is what is meant by saying that if the personal life is not cultivated, one cannot regulate his family.

Chu Hsi's Remark. The above eighth chapter of commentary explains the cultivation of the personal life in order to regulate the family.

9. What is meant by saying that in order to govern the state it is necessary first to regulate the family is this: There is no one who cannot teach his own family and yet can teach others. Therefore the superior man (ruler) without going beyond his family, can bring education into completion in the whole state. Filial piety is that with which one serves his ruler. Brotherly respect is that with which one serves his elders, and deep love is that with which one treats the multitude. The "Announcement of K'ang" says, "Act as if you were watching over an infant." If a mother sincerely and earnestly looks for what the infant wants, she may not hit the mark but she will not be far from it. A young woman has never had to learn about nursing a baby before she marries. When the individual families have become humane, then the whole country will be aroused toward humanity. When the individual families have been compliant, then the whole country will be aroused toward compliance. When one man is greedy or avaricious, the whole country will be plunged into disorder. Such is the subtle, incipient activating force of things. This is what is meant by saying that a single word may spoil an affair and a single man may put the country in order. (Sage-emperors) Yao and Shun led the world with humanity and the people followed them. (Wicked kings) Chieh and Chou led the world with violence and the people followed them. The people did not follow their orders which were contrary to what they themselves liked. Therefore the superior man must have the good qualities in himself before he may require them in other people. He must not have the bad qualities in himself before he may require others not to have them. There has never been a man who does not cherish altruism (shu) in himself and yet can teach other people. Therefore the order of the state depends on the regulation of the family.

The *Book of Odes* says, "How young and pretty is that peach tree! How luxuriant is its foliage! This girl is going to her husband's house. She will rightly order her household." Only when one has rightly ordered his household can he teach the people of the country. The *Book of Odes* says, "They were correct and good in their elder brothers. They were correct and good to their younger brothers." Only when one is good and correct to one's elder and younger brothers can one teach the people of the country. The *Book of Odes* says, "His deportment is all correct, and he rectifies all the people of the country." Because he served as a worthy example as a father, son, elder brother, and younger brother, therefore the people imitated him. This is what is meant by saying that the order of the state depends on the regulation of the family.

Chu Hsi's Remark. The above ninth chapter of commentary explains regulating the family to bring order to the state.

10. What is meant by saying that peace of the world depends on the order of the state is this: When the ruler treats the elders with respect, then the people will be aroused toward filial piety. When the ruler treats the aged with respect, then the people will be aroused toward brotherly respect. When the ruler treats compassionately the young and the helpless, then the common people will not follow the opposite course. Therefore the ruler has a principle with which, as with a measuring square, he may regulate his conduct.

What a man dislikes in his superiors, let him not show it in dealing with his inferiors; what he dislikes in those in front of him, let him not show it in preceding those who are behind; what he dislikes in those behind him, let him not show it in following those in front of him; what he dislikes in those on the right, let him not apply it to those on the left; and what he dislikes in those on the left, let him not apply it to those on the right. This is the principle of the measuring square.

The *Book of Odes* says, "How much the people rejoice in their prince, a parent of the people!" He likes what the people like and dislikes what the people dislike. This is what is meant by being a parent of the people. The *Book of Odes* says, "Lofty is the Southern Mountain! How massive are the rocks! How majestic is the Grand Tutor Yin (of Chou)! The people all look up to you!" Thus rulers of states should never be careless. If they deviate from the correct path, they will be cast away by the world. The *Book of Odes* says, "Before the rulers of the Yin (Shang) dynasty lost the support of the people, they could have been counterparts of Heaven. Take warning from the Yin dynasty. It is not easy to keep the Mandate of Heaven." This shows that by having the support of the people, they have their countries, and by losing the support of the people, lose their countries. Therefore the ruler will first be watchful over his own virtue. If he has virtue, he will have the people with him. If he has the people with him, he will have the territory. If he has the territory, he will have wealth. And if he has wealth, he will have its use. Virtue is the root, while wealth is the branch. If he regards the root as external (or secondary) and the branch as internal (or essential), he will compete with the people in robbing each other. Therefore when wealth is gathered in the ruler's hand, the people will scatter away from him; and when wealth is scattered [among the people], they will gather round him. Therefore if the ruler's words are uttered in an evil way, the same words will be uttered back to him in an evil way; and if he acquires wealth in an evil way, it will be taken away from him in an evil way. In the "Announcement of K'ang" it is said, "The Mandate of Heaven is not fixed or unchangeable." The good ruler gets it and the bad ruler loses it. In the *Book of Ch'u* it is said, "The State of Ch'u does not consider anything as treasure; it considers only good [men] as treasure. Uncle Fan (maternal uncle to a prince of Chin in exile) said, 'Our exiled prince has no treasure; to be humane toward his parents is his only treasure.' " In the "Oath of Ch'in" it is said, "Let me have but one minister, sincere and single-minded, not pretending to other abilities, but broad and upright of mind, generous and tolerant toward others. When he sees that another person has a certain kind of ability, he is as happy as though he himself had it, and when he sees another man who is elegant and wise, he loves him in his heart as much as if he said so in so many words, thus showing that he can really tolerate others. Such a person can preserve my sons, and grandsons and the black-haired people (the common people). He may well be a great benefit to the country. But when a minister sees another person with a certain kind of ability, he is jealous and hates him, and when he sees another person who is elegant and wise, he blocks him so he cannot advance, thus showing that he really cannot tolerate others. Such a person cannot preserve my sons, grandsons, and the black-haired people. He is a danger to the country." It is only a man of humanity who can send away such a minister and banish him, driving him to live among the barbarian tribes and not allowing him to exist together with the rest of the people in the Middle Kingdom (China). This is what is meant by saying that it is only the man of humanity who can love or who can hate others. To see a worthy and not be able to raise him to office, or be able to raise him but not to be the first one to do so—that is negligence. To see bad men and not be able to remove them from office, or to be able to remove them but not to remove them as far away as possible—that is a mistake. To love what the people hate and to hate what the people love—that is to act contrary to human nature, and disaster will come to such a person. Thus we see that the ruler has a great principle to follow. He must attain it through loyalty and faithfulness and will surely lose it through pride and indulgence.

There is a great principle for the production of wealth. If there are many producers and few consumers, and if people who produce wealth do so quickly and those who spend it do so slowly, then wealth will always be sufficient. A man of humanity develops his personality by means of his wealth, while the inhumane person develops wealth at the sacrifice of his personality. There has never been a case of a ruler who loved humanity and whose people did not love righteousness. There has never been a case where the people loved righteousness and yet the affairs of the state have not been carried to completion. And there has never been a case where in such a state the wealth collected in the national treasury did not continue in the possession of the ruler.

The officer Meng-hsien said, "He who keeps a horse [one who has just become an official] and a carriage does not look after poultry and pigs. [The higher officials] who use ice [in their sacrifices] do not keep cattle and sheep. And the nobles who can keep a hundred carriages do not keep rapacious tax-gathering ministers under them. It is better to have a minister who robs the state treasury than to have such a tax-gathering minister. This is what is meant by saying that in a state financial profit is not considered real profit whereas righteousness is considered to be the real profit. He who heads a state or a family and is devoted to wealth and its use must have been under the influence of an inferior man. He may consider this man to be good, but when an inferior man is allowed to handle the country or family, disasters and injuries will come together. Though a good man may take his place, nothing can be done. This is what is meant by saying that in a state financial profit is not considered real profit whereas righteousness is considered the real profit.

Chu Hsi's Remark. The above tenth chapter of commentary explains ordering the state to bring peace to the world. There are altogether ten commentary chapters. The first four generally discuss the principal topics and the basic import. The last six chapters discuss in detail the items and the required effort involved. Chapter five deals with the essence of the understanding of goodness and chapter six deals with the foundation of making the personal life sincere. These two chapters, especially, represent the immediate task, particularly for the beginning student. The reader should not neglect them because of their simplicity.

The Evolution of Human Psychology for African Americans

Na'im Akbar

Na'im Akbar took his undergraduate and doctoral degrees at the University of Michigan, completing his Ph.D. in Clinical Psychology in 1970. He is currently on the faculty of the Department of Psychology at Florida State University. Previously he had served as Chair of the Morehouse College Psychology Department, and was an Associate Professor at Norfolk State University. In 1987 he was elected president of the National Association of Black Psychologists, after serving several terms on its Board of Directors. He has also been Associate Editor, for over 10 years, of the *Journal of Black Psychology*, and has served on the Editorial Board of the *Journal of Black Studies*.

He has received the "Distinguished Black Psychologist" award from the National Association of Black Psychologists for his outstanding scholarship and research in African Psychology. In fact, his activist scholarship has led the mayors of four American cities—in Jackson, MI, Cincinnati, OH, Atlantic City, NJ, and Cleveland, OH—to declare "Na'im Akbar Days" in their communities. Florida State University has awarded him the Dr. Martin Luther King, Jr. Distinguished Scholar Award, and Lincoln University and Edinboro University (both in Pennsylvania) have awarded him honorary Doctorates of Humane Letters. He has given hundreds of lectures and presentations on African psychology at universities, colleges, and conferences throughout the United States, Africa, Asia, South America, and Europe. Akbar has written several books, including *Breaking the Chains of Psychological Slavery* (rev. ed., 1996, Mind Productions & Associates); *The Community of Self* (rev. ed., 1985, Mind Productions & Associates); *Visions for Black Men* (1992, Mind Productions & Associates); *Know Thy Self* (1998, Mind Productions & Associates); and most recently, *Akbar Papers in African Psychology* (2004, Mind Productions).

The first edition of the anthology, *Black Psychology*, edited by Reginald Jones, was published in 1972 (by Harper & Row), and is mentioned as an important historical event on the Web pages of the American Psychological Association. Akbar has written a chapter, "The Evolution of Human Psychology for African Americans," which has been included in the now-classic text *Black Psychology* (4th ed., 2004, Cobb & Henry Publishers). This chapter, excerpted below, details the development of the field of African-American psychology from its early stages when it was initially dominated by a European-American perspective. Next, Akbar describes what he calls the Black Psychology perspective, which was partially a reaction against the earlier Euro-American perspective. The development of African American psychology culminates in a more radical perspective, that of African Psychology. This selection takes a macro view of human development, explaining both the evolution of the field of African-American psychology, and describing psychological factors that have influenced the development of both African Americans and Euro Americans at conceptual, cultural, axiological, and epistemological levels.

Key Concept: Black psychology, African psychology

There has been a rapid evolution in the thinking about the psychology of African Americans since 1970. That evolution has progressed from a self-negating perspective which viewed the model human being as necessarily non-Black to a self-affirmative perspective which sees the African as a model of universal man. In a relatively brief time, scholars have dissected the youthful psychology which has grown-up in Europe and America over the last 100 years and have sought to salvage human psychology from the precipice of mechanized, human destruction. This discussion is a brief review of the evolution of that thinking about the psychology of African Americans.

Several scholars have presented extensive comparisons regarding the philosophical basis of conceptualizing the world from European vs. African perspectives

(Akbar, 1976; Ani, 1994; Clark, 1972; Clark (X), et al. 1975, Dixon, 1976, Kambon, 1996, 1998 & Nobles, 1986). The differences in these philosophical perspectives have been cited as the basis of the differences in European and African behavior as well as differences in the methods of observation of those behaviors (Baldwin, 1976; Jackson, 1976, 1979 & Nobles, 1974, 1976). Jackson (1979), in a provocative study, reviewed the origin and development of "Black Psychology" and some of the key issues regarding the development of that field of inquiry. This discussion draws upon the valuable discussion of Jackson and perhaps extends his observations a step further into analyzing the conceptual development that has occurred in the thinking of, particularly, African American psychologists over the last 25 years of the twentieth century.

We shall characterize the three major developments in the conceptualization of African-American psychology as "European American," "Black," and "African" perspectives. This classification is probably very similar to the categories identified as the "Schools of Black Psychology" identified by Karenga (1993) as "Traditional," "Reformed," and "Radical." These three orientations have certain characteristics that define their methodology and, by implication, structure the definitions and ontology that emerge from these perspectives.

Conceptual Orientations

These three stages of conceptual growth have first evolved in terms of their orientation. An orientation determines one's reference point for assessing normality. Throughout most of the history of observations of African American behavior in the West, that reference point has clearly been European American or Eurocentric. Baldwin (1976) observes that the standards of observation which have led to persistent conclusions of the "social pathology" of Black behavior has resulted from the Eurocentric assumptions in the use of measures of Black behavior. Baldwin (1976) continues:

> The traditional social pathology view of Black behavior is therefore based on a European conception or definition of reality, or more precisely, a European distortion of the reality of Black people. Its rise to prominence in the psychological literature, naturally then, merely reflects the vested social power of Euro-American psychology (and White people generally in European American culture) to legitimate European definitions of reality rather than the necessary objective credibility appeal of its presumed validity (p. 8).

From this Eurocentric reference point, normality is established on a model of the middle class, Caucasian, male of European descent. The more one approximates this model in appearance, values and behavior, the more "normal" a person is considered to be. The major problem with such normative assumptions for non-European people is the inevitable conclusion of deviance on the part of anyone, unlike this model. In fact, the more distinct or

distant you are from this model the more pathological one is considered to be. The obvious advantage for Europeans is that such norms confirm their reality as the reality and flaunts statements of their supremacy as scientifically based "fact."

Even a casual observation of the history of psychology will well-demonstrate that the volumes of psychological literature from the last 100 years have been based on observations primarily on Europeans, exclusively Caucasian, predominantly male and overwhelmingly middle class. Robert Guthrie (1998)—in his book *Even the Rat was White*, and Thomas and Sillen (1972) in their extensive review of *Racism and Psychiatry*—have well-demonstrated this fact. The formulations of such notable thinkers who have shaped the thought of Euro-American psychology such as Sigmund Freud (1953), G. Stanley Hall (1904), Carl Jung (1953), William McDougall (1908) and B. F. Skinner (1971) have all directly or indirectly asserted the superiority of European races over non-European races. Despite the diversity of the so-called "Schools" of Western psychology, they seem to merge unequivocally in their assumption of the Eurocentric point of view and the superiority of people of European descent. It is not surprising that the conclusion reached from the application of their concepts and methods the inevitable inferiority of non-Caucasian peoples. The use of this Eurocentric reference point by non-European (Caucasian) observers has resulted in many non-Caucasian observers having become advocates of their own inferiority. It is for this reason that many so-called "Black psychologists" have been identified with the same racist tradition that has characterized the majority of Western psychology and its research findings. Such findings have obsessively dealt with the alleged self-rejection, inferior intellect, defective families and contorted motivations of African Americans. These conclusions are not unlike the typical conclusions of the European American psychologist. As I have observed elsewhere (Weems, 1973):

> The logical fallacy in this inappropriate attribution of normative statements about non-White people is the assumption that to be intelligent (or for that matter, psychologically healthy in general) is to act like a European rather than as an agent of your own culture.

The orientation of "Black psychology" is "ghetto-centric." Jackson (1979) has accurately portrayed the early development of Black Psychology as "reactive." He further observes:

> Black psychology can be readily traced to the 1920's when Afro-American psychologists first published research studies to dispel the notion of Afro-American inferiority and sought to increase the psychological services rendered to the Afro-American community. These heuristic works and pioneering efforts were, for the most part, a reaction to the existence of institutional racism and individual acts of discrimination, and, therefore, merely constituted a racist perspective (p. 271).

This reactive aspect of Black psychology was necessary and served a vital purpose in the evolution of thought about the psychology of African Americans. It was probably one of the initial insights of the African American scholars that one of the primary shortcomings of traditional psychology was its fallacious normative definitions. It was clearly perceived by writers such as Clark (1965)—who has condemned the Black Psychology movement since its inception—that the insistence upon viewing African American behavior in the light of European American norms was clearly conceptually faulty. The response was to decry the Caucasian, middle class norm and to assert the necessity of analyzing African American behavior in the context of its own norms. These norms were assumed to be the behaviors of southern-born, working class, African American ghettos-dwellers. Such a norm, though introducing bias against large numbers of African Americans was certainly more valid than the traditional norms which had been applied.

Joseph White (1972) in his landmark piece asserted the need for this new norm. He states:

> . . . it is vitally important that we develop, out of the authentic experience of Black people in this country, an accurate workable theory of Black Psychology, It is very difficult, if not impossible to understand the life styles of Black people using traditional theories developed by White psychologists to explain White people. Moreover, when these traditional theories are applied to the lives of Black folks many incorrect, weakness-dominated, and inferiority-oriented conclusions come about (p. 43).

White (1972) asserts quite correctly that the effort to use the norm of middle class, European American behavior results in serious distortions in the analysis of African American behavior. An example that he offers is of the designation of "culturally deprived" to a group of Black youngsters who he describes as having developed the kind of "mental toughness and survival skills, in terms of coping with life, which make them in many ways superior to their White age-mates." He continues:

> These Black youngsters know how to deal effectively with bill collectors, building superintendents, corner grocery stores, hypes, pimps, whores and sickness and death. They know how to jive school counselors, principals, teachers, welfare workers, juvenile authorities, and in doing so, display a lot of psychological cleverness and originality. They recognize very early that they exist in an environment which is sometimes both complicated and hostile (p. 44).

The irony of this Black norm assertion is that it invariably validates itself in comparison with Whites. White's assertion that such a perspective actually makes "them superior to their White age-mates" is the consistent conclusion from the Black norm. Ultimately, the Eurocentric norm continues to influence your analysis since African American behavior is still being compared with the rejected norm. The statement of what it meant to be "Black" was never considered an adequate statement

unless that condition was in some way compared with Whites. The consequence is an inevitable entrapment in the same circle. The other limitation of the "Black norm" as adopted in the Black Psychology movement is the assumption that the adaptation to the conditions of America by African Americans constitutes a reasonable normative statement about African American behavior. The problem with such a conclusion is the acceptance of many adaptive but ultimately self-destructive behaviors as legitimate. For example, the pimp becomes glorified as a cultural hero because of his culturally distinct flair, style and his materialistic flamboyance. For very much the same reason, the drug pusher can become a hero because he, in White's words, "is the Black culture hero who messes with the system and gets away with it." As a consequence, such destructive adaptations emerge as new cultural norms for the African American community.

Utilization of the "ghetto-centric" norms rendered "Black Psychology" irrelevant to a large middle class of African Americans who were, ironically, the authors of Black Psychology. A classic example of this irony was the robust condemnation of the Moynihan conclusions about the African American family. Based on the Eurocentric norm and models of Freudian psychology, Moynihan concluded that the "Black family" was essentially pathogenic or responsible for the origin of many psychological and social problems of African Americans. The outcry was intense and extreme from Black and "liberal" White psychologists, sociologists, and other social scientists. Typical of this outcry was the statement by psychologist Joseph White (1972):

> When the Black family is viewed from a middle-class frame of reference, which assumes that the psychologically healthy family contains two parents, one male and one female, who remain with the child until he or she becomes a young adult, the fact that the same Black male is not consistently visible to the White observer of the Black family leads to a conclusion that the Black family unit has a matriarchal structure . . . A closer look at the Black family might show that the matriarchal or one parent view fails to take into consideration the extended nature of the Black family (pp. 44–45).

Though the description of an extended family is true from a point of view, it inadvertently establishes a new and equally biased norm based upon the ghetto-centric perspective. The large number of intact African American families are then suspect in regard to the "Black norm." Though the extended family concept is valid as a structure of African American families, it is important to realize that the nuclear family can also have validity for African Americans. The assumption that one must choose one or the other due to majority participation raised serious questions about the validity of the norm being applied. As we shall see below, the application of a more universal norm could legitimize either pattern.

The weakness of the Eurocentric and ghetto-centric perspectives is their reliance on a statistical norm as the model of human order. Implicit in both perspectives is an assumption that a majority in a particular context can effectively determine what is natural for human beings. In fact, throughout European American psychology, there is a serious fallacy that confuses normative (or normal) with natural. We have seriously criticized this tendency, which we call "democratic sanity," elsewhere (Akbar, 1979). The orientation of African Psychology is nature-centric. It takes as its norm, the nature of the human being and the functioning of nature in general. It is important to note at this juncture that we use the term "African" advisedly. In fact, we might more appropriately describe this approach as "natural psychology" (Akbar, 1995). This reservation is crucial because of the numerous distorted images that can be observed in post-colonial, modern Africa. A misapplication of the concepts of African Psychology has come from the effort to document or disprove the African Psychology model by conducting field surveys or studies of contemporary urban African behavior. The assumption of the African Psychology theoreticians has been since its inception that the philosophical foundations of African Psychology (Nobles, 1972) represent a pure model of the African person in particular and universal man in general. "African Psychology" (and Afrocentricity) has gained growing popular usage over the last several years, so we use it here, but with the aforementioned reservations.

The writer is aware that the use of vague language like "human nature" is a harping back to the "pre-scientific" assertions of 19th century European philosophy. Precisely because of the false security in such pseudo-objective notions as "behavior" and "statistical norms," we reassert the validity of concepts such as "human nature." The use of a "nature-centric" perspective maintains that there are absolute standards and principles guiding human behaviors.

For example, one of the principles of African Psychology is "survival of the tribe" or the principle of collective survival. Under the influence of this principle, one can observe a wide variety of behaviors geared towards that end. Many behaviors can fit this standard of human nature. The critical point is that the norm is not a statistical majority, but a life concept of collective survival. From this point of view, we can more fully appreciate Nobles' (1978) description of the African American family structure as "elastic." Such a family can be as effectively nuclear as extended, depending upon what kinds of circumstances were necessary for survival of the family (tribe). The same point is true of functions within the family. According to Nobles (1978): "Functionality, or the performance of its (family) functions, would be fluid or elastic. That is, the performance of a particular function does or can "expand" into many other functions. The whole notion of fixed and inflexible role definitions does not become a criterion of effective family functioning." As a consequence, arguments for the presence or absence of a physical father is a moot question regarding family effectiveness. Instead, the issue becomes adequacy

of function rather than the presence of a particular role occupant. The concept of a matriarchy or a patriarchy is a meaningless analysis. Equally useless, is the argument of a nuclear as opposed to an extended family, for the same reasons.

There are other absolute norms about the nature of humans that are drawn from both historical, philosophical, religious and esoteric descriptions of the human being. Assumptions about the perfectibility of man, our capacities for self-mastery, consciousness and conscience an well as our inseparability form each other, are viewed as pre-eminent influences in human nature from the African psychological perspective.

Axiology (Values)

Issues of values are seldom discussed in scientific enterprises. This is in part due to a pervasive denial of the role of values in guiding so-called "scientific" activity. In fact, it is the erroneous claim that values are absent in the "objectivity" of science that rather systematically excludes values as an issue in the discussion of science. Dr. Jacob Carruthers (1972) observes rather astutely:

. . . the science or (experimental) methodology is neutral or objective, it is the science of control through intervention and/or the unnatural alteration (if possible) of all objects (p. 3). So, what is assumed to be value-free is itself a value. The choice of values or the values guiding ones pursuit constitutes one of the critical distinctions between approaches to the study of man.

The essential value position taken by the European American psychological perspective is the value of objectivity. It starts as Carruthers (1972) continues by assuming:

. . . a theory about harnessing certain forces and subduing certain oppositions to the deserved change. Western science assumes that any desirable modification of nature is dictated . . . Thus not only is it right to modify nature to supply needs, but it is also right to conform nature to all other tastes, in keeping with the doctrine of enlightened self-interest. (pp. 3–4). In other words, the value of objectivity adopts a point of view the essential relationship in nature to be man-over-object. Man is viewed as the instrument of control and all other things (and occasionally people of lesser power) are objects subject to that control. The individual self is viewed as the center of reality and all else is object. So if self is male then all that is female is object; if self is Caucasian, then all that is non-Caucasian is object and is therefore subject to male, Caucasian, control or unnatural alteration.

Social science is replete with examples of this tendency to objectify by ordinal or nominal classification. Again, Dr. Carruthers (1972) observes:

. . . modern methodology is based upon ordinal classifications. The various phenomena are ranked according to imagined or imposed objective values such as magnitude or complexity or natural arrangements derived from so-called systematic comparisons (p. 4). Classifications

which are frequently encountered in social science literature of the European American variety frequently reduce
people to categories like "the aged," "the schizophrenic
subjects," "the culturally deprived," etc. Such categories which are initially nominal are invariably treated in
some qualitative fashion resulting in an ordinal classification based on superordiate-subordinate arrangement.
The necessity to refer to people involved in psychological
studies as "subjects" is clearly instructive about the goal
of such studies to subject. This is the value of the "value-
less" European American experimental methodology.

A final value implication of the European American
methodology is the assumption that the observer is not
a participant in what he observes. This arbitrary suspen-
sion of universal interconnection is an astounding feat
of logical fallacy. By altering the classification or deper-
sonalizing the personalities into an (E)xperimenter and a
S(ubject), there is an assumption that the E is free to peek
without detection or intrusion. Such an assumption per-
petuates the platonic notion that man and nature are two
different realms of being. This assumption frees man to
run amok in his role as master over nature. In fact, Carruthers (1972) goes on to point out:

> The assumptions are based on the so-called self-evident
> notion that nature is uneven in supplying the needs of
> man; thus, the maximization of individual survival can
> be achieved by modification of natural supply (p. 3).

The axiological position of Black Psychology is racialism. This value assumes race to be the critical human
issue in the study of African American behavior. As the
European American operates effectively from his position
of man-to-object, the Black Psychologist views the critical
relationship of Black-to-White as the paradigmatic relationship. The condition of White oppression of Blacks is
accepted as a given and the essential value of Black Psychology is mastery over oppression and the oppressor. In
fact, psychiatrist Frances Welsing (1974) defines "Black
Psychiatry" as "counter-racism."

The works of eminent Black scholars such as Clark
(1965), Fanon (1967), Grier and Cobbs (1968) and non-
Black scholars such as Kardiner and Ovesey (1951),
and many others have well-illustrated this position.
The assumption that Black personality is a cumulative
by-product of sustained oppression is one of the major
positions of these writers. Furthermore, it is assumed
that the only meaningful approach to the study of Black
persons is from the perspective of oppression and in
terms of the Black experience with White's in America.
In fact, the idea is that African Americans would be just
like European Americans or perhaps, more appropriately,
would be European Americans if it were not for oppression. There is also an assumption of commonality among
those who have experienced oppression. It is not unusual for some African American social scientists to adopt
a Marxist position which uncritically equates the racial
oppression of people of African descent with other economically and/or socially oppressed peoples.

The extension of this value perspective asserts that
essentially whatever is Black is of positive value and what
is White is of negative value. This is in direct contrast to the
Caucasian domination and exploitative use of "objective"
methodology which has objectively concluded everything
"White" to be positive and everything "Black" negative. The
reactive quality of Black psychology is reflected in
this mirror image of European American psychology. The
"Black Psychologist" involves himself with the process of
delineating those Black positive characteristics and those
White negative ones. In other words, it follows the tradition of Dr. Welsing's "counter-racist psychiatry."

The essential value of the African Psychological system is the centrality of the human being. According to
Nobles (1980) in the African Cosmology, the Supreme
Being and spiritual beings are above and humans are in
the center. "The animals, plants, and natural phenomena
constitute the environment in which man lives." Nobles
(1980) continues: "everything was functionally connected; to destroy one category completely would cause
the destruction of the whole of existence, including the
Creator." Man and his world are clearly interdependent
and the objective approach which completely excludes
subjectivity is logically fallacious. The African approach
identifies the relevance of psycho-historical trauma such
as slavery and the barbaric behavior of certain cultures
but these considerations are not reactive. Though the
experiences of oppression are critical in terms of assessing the contemporary African experience, this cosmology evolved long before the coming of the European
and it would be self-effacing to reduce its perspective to
"racialism" or experiences with the European. The Axiology of African Psychology identifies a Divine Creator
as the originator and sustainer of man. Nature is in harmony with herself and the desirable state is a harmonious relationship with nature. Consequently, mastery over
the environment is not the essential value of African Psychology. Neither is mastery over oppression viewed as
a preeminent concern because without oppression man
would find himself in a teleological vacuum. However,
the preeminent value is self-mastery which presupposes
the active elimination of oppressive yokes in order to
realize this value. Man is conceived as a microcosm of the
universe, therefore, in mastering self one has mastered
the essential processes of nature.

Those things that facilitate effective human development are valued. Human values are paramount and
objects are evaluated as they impact upon the human
situation. Objects are never evaluated as having greater
prominence than people.

Conceptions of Self

The three orientations also differ in terms of how they
define self. The definition of self or "person" in psychology is critical because such a definition determines both
the approach to description, assessment and ultimately

reconstruction, if such should become necessary. In other words, ones conception of consciousness is at the foundation of the approach or method in the study of the human mind.

European American psychology takes as its arena of study the individual ego, behavior and consciousness. The commonality in the European American approach to personality is its emphasis on individuality. From Adler's "creative self" through Maslow's "actualized self" and Mead's "looking glass self," the conception is consistent that self is an individual phenomenon. All of these approaches agree on the validity of the individual as the authentic subject matter of psychology. So from Skinnerian to Freudian psychology, we can observe that there is a common emphasis on individual differences as being the best description of human experience.

Black Psychology describes the arena of study as being the collective experience of oppression. What must be studied to understand the human experience is the shared experience of oppression or the shared phenomenon of being an oppressor. The degree to which one is conscious of shared oppression is assumed to be a measure of "Black awareness" or "Black personality." Therefore, we get models of Black personality such as the Cross (1971) model which describes development of Black personality as growing from Negro (or unawareness of oppressive realities) to Black (hyper-awareness of oppression and the oppressor) to transcendence (where Blackness is integrated). Semaj (1980) introduces an excellent critique of the limitations of this analysis, which would take this discussion somewhat a field to fully review. However, the essential issue is that personality for African Americans is conceptualized as the emergence of consciousness of oppression. This approach that begins to see personality as a collective phenomenon is a critical contribution of Black psychology. It makes a radical departure from the European American preoccupation with the individual and his isolated experience. There is a "quantum leap" in this conceptualization though the intention was to merely address the shared reality of oppression.

African Psychology conceptualizes self as an unqualified collective phenomenon while respecting the uniqueness of the individual self as a component of the collectivity. Nobles' (1980) description of the African ethos as a "collective consciousness" typifies this notion. Akbar (1999) offers even a broader conception of this notion in his description of the dimensions of the African Self in a recent publication entitled *Know Thy Self*. The African conception of personality is captured in the formula given by Mbiti (1970): "I am because we are; and because we are therefore I am." Whatever happened to the individual impacted on the corporate body, the tribe and whatever happened to the tribe reverberated into the individual. This conception identified the appropriate arena of study as being the collective consciousness or again, what Nobles (1980) refers to as the "experiential communality" or the sharing of particular experience by a group of people. Nobles (1980) argues that the experiential communality is important in determining society's fundamental principles—its beliefs about the nature of man and what kind of society humans should create for themselves. In other words, description, assessment and even reconstruction is assumed to be a collective rather than an individual phenomenon. This is critical not only in terms of how people define their psychology, but also in terms of the kind of society that people give their energies to. To the extent that this self-conception of African people is alien to that of the European American society, one would expect many Africans well-adjusted to their "experiential communality" to be quite deviant in an alien society (see, Akbar, 1979).

Time Orientations

Another distinction in the approaches is in terms of how time is conceptualized. Time orientations are critical in that they determine people's relationship to each other and to their world. The values that are most important get expressed in people's concept of time. Most importantly time becomes that which maintains the cadence of people's lives. It determines their rate and intensity of activity as well as their priorities about life. Their motivations and orientations are determined through the cadence established by their time orientation. Time is such a powerfully subjective factor that people seldom consider that their time orientation is actually idiosyncratic. They rather automatically assume that everyone else is out of order if they are not moving consistent with their rhythm. This is particularly true when there is a strong investment in objective measures of time.

Certainly, the most extreme of these objective time-measuring cultures is the European American culture. Their approach or orientation to time is predominantly futuristic. Their rhythm as a consequence is exceedingly urgent and pressured since it is essentially impossible to ever catch-up with the future.

This futuristic orientation is played-out in their study of human psychology. The objectives of their study are focused on the goal of prediction and control. The concepts, instruments and methods of European American psychology are ones that are geared towards future outcomes as opposed to enhancement of the present or elaboration of the past. For example, there is often greater credibility given to predictive assessment devices than is given to the actual here-and-now performance of people or the prior history of their performance.

Child-rearing practices, learning methods and even psychotherapy are future-oriented. Non-Europeans have often been described as deficient because of an inadequate future-orientation. This is another example of the attribution that emanates from the ethnocentrism. As we commented above, ethnocentric time is probably the most notorious of the projections that comes from ethnocentrism. Time is as idiosyncratic as is the heartbeat responding directly to ones own life (cultural) experience and reality.

Time in the European American system is a concrete commodity: it is bought and sold as is any other product. In many systems of psychotherapy, for instance, the time is viewed as a critical dimension of the psychotherapy. The "clock time" is strictly adhered to regardless of the emotional state of the client. Scheduled meeting times are viewed as sacred and clients are routinely charged for their appointment times whether they keep them or not. Though elaborate theoretical justifications are given for such actions, this is still a graphic illustration of the concrete conception of time in the European American's orientation. The mathematical reality of the clock has the same tyrannical hold on European American's conception of reality as does quantification throughout their science. The symbolic numbers that are associated with the rhythm of time are assumed to literally be the reality of time. With the projection towards the future working with this concretizing of time, human conduct actually becomes a servant to time and behavior is judged by its adequacy in responding to time.

The Black Psychology time focus is on the recent past of the African American experience and the present conditions of oppression and its multifarious manifestations. The future is not considered as relevant. There is actually no consideration of prediction since racism is considered a constant and the experiences and behaviors of African Americans are determined by racism. The African American rhythm is assumed to be actually determined by its reaction to racist oppression.

The time orientation is primarily past and present in this system of thought. The assumption is that to understand current behaviors, one need only understand the history of racism and to be conscious of contemporary expressions of oppression. Time is actually reckoned by the pain of oppression. This condition and when it has been manifest is the focus of the rhythm of time. So one is a victim of time because time itself actually becomes a part of the oppressive process in an oppressive environment.

In the African system, time is viewed as cyclical rather than linear. Consequently, "now" is the past and the future since those dimensions are immersed in the present. The past was focused upon as the source of instruction because "the direction of one's life system was from the present dimension backward to the past dimension" (Nobles, 1980). Nobles goes on to describe the African conception of time thus:

> For the people, time itself was simply a composition of past events. Very little concern was given to time in and of itself. It existed, but the African time concept was (is) very elastic . . . Time was reckoned by phenomena . . . In order to make sense, or be real, to the West African, time had to be experienced. The way in which one experienced time was partly through one's own individual life and partly through the life of the tribe which went back many generations before one's birth. We see in this description a very

distinct orientation to time from the European American perspective that we described above. There is first of all, a basic acceptance of the notion that time is a subjective phenomenon, so the likelihood that one feels compelled to impose their time perspective on others is reduced in the African system. This might in part account for the absence of colonizing and proselytizing activities historically on the part of Africans. Many of the differences in motivations and behaviors among people of African descent and people of European descent can be seen to be attributable to their differences in conceptualizing the rhythm of life, which we call time. Jackson (1979) makes a compelling argument for the African American's treatment of time as growing out of this African conception of time. It is important to observe however that though the future orientation does not predominate in the African system, there is a consideration of the future. History informs us that the first clocks and calendars were established by Ancient African people. The ability to plan and develop for crops, migrations, etc., was well entrenched in the African lifestyle. Certainly, much of the metaphysical life of African people was relegated by a future orientation, but the future was understood to be contained in the present. The future is conceptualized as a repetition of the infinite cycles of being that all meet in the powerful experience of the present. The future is actually viewed as a reenactment of the past and progress is the application of the best lessons of the past and the avoidance of repeating disastrous errors from the past (p. 71).

Human Goals

The next area of difference in the orientations to human psychology is in terms of the projected goal of the human being. The conceptualization of goals determines the basis for effectiveness of the human being. Therefore, mental health and mental disorder are determined by effectiveness in achieving the goals of the self or personality. So, the theoretical import of hypothesized goals is critical in terms of evaluating the adequacy, effectiveness, i.e., sanity of the person. Variation in perception of goals can lead to serious discrepancies in the assessment of mental health as well as the prioritizing of energies for groups of people.

The European American approach sees the person as essentially directed towards pleasurable gratification. The Behaviorists suggest that all behavior hinges on rewards and punishments. Freud assumes the primal need of immediate gratification of either sexual or aggressive drives and Maslow assumes a hierarchy of needs for gratification at various levels. Again, the diversity of the schools converge in the shared assumption that the critical goal of human personality is the desire for individual gratification.

The emphasis of Black Psychology is that the essential goal of human behavior is survival. The emphasis on survival skills characterizes the majority of the literature in this area: Grier and Cobbs (1968), White (1978) and other similar writers have emphasized the survival skills of African Americans as being the primary goal and objective of personality. The constant confrontation with racism and oppression is viewed as the consistent reality and strategies to out-maneuver threats to survival by African Americans is the goal of personality. Staples (1974) for example, builds his theory of the Black family on a survival-adaptation basis. His assumption is that confrontation with slavery and subsequent oppression shaped the African American family through its struggles to survive. The essential goal of the Black Psychology orientation was formulated as in this example as: "how do we overcome the oppression of European Americans?"

Though survival, no doubt represents a basic goal of human existence as it is a goal of all life forms, the limitation of the Black Psychology orientation is that it views the goal of survival only vis-a-vis the oppressive European American. It does not address the goal of personality in the absence of oppression. The goal of African American existence again takes its form in reaction to the conditions of oppression.

African Psychology offers the goal of self-affirmation and self-perpetuation as the objective of human personality. It advocates that the affirmation of ones unique history and the perpetuation of ones collective self and cultural reality is the goal of human personality. The human being is focused on the full manifestation and perpetuation of who he is as a collective phenomenon. This clearly is not opposed to the Black Psychology perspective of "survival against oppression." African Psychology sees oppression as an incidental but disturbing obstacle to human self-affirmation which is not unlike many similar issues.

Epistemology

Epistemology defines "how we know, what we know." What is the legitimate form of acquiring knowledge and how do we identify that knowledge has been acquired? The latter part of this question has, of course, become a major objective of the psychologist and educator. The way that the psychologist defines what's actually knowledge and how it is acquired becomes paramount in his determination of who has adequate knowledge facility. The degree to which measurement of intelligence has permeated the concern of psychology throughout its history is an indication of how critical this question is. The fact that alleged discrepancies in intellectual faculties has served as the justification for the discriminatory treatment of African Americans also indicates why this issue of epistemology is so important for conceptualizing human functioning.

In European American psychology, knowledge of the outer environment particularly as it is experienced by the European American person is considered as the basis of legitimate knowledge. The concept of IQ is rooted in the idea that the greater is ones store of information about the typical middle class, Caucasian American environment, its attitudes, values and techniques, the greater is ones IQ=Intelligence=Knowledge. The issue of self-mastery, the applicability or even the validity (Truth) of the acquired knowledge is not an issue. The European American epistemology identifies knowledge as essentially recall or recognition of essential objects, processes, or experiences within the typical European American experience. The key assumption of this epistemology is that what is to be known is external to the person and ones knowledge is assessed by what is known of the European-American external world.

The reactive quality of Black Psychology is again reflected in its epistemology. The assumption of Black Psychology is also that intelligence is a mastery of the outer environment. From this perspective intelligence is determined by the knowledge that the African American has of the southern working class traditional African American environment. This is well-demonstrated in Robert Williams' (Wright & Isenstein, 1975) approach of culture-specific testing that he bases on a principle of cultural match or mismatch:

> Learning one activity either facilitates or hampers the learning of another, contingent upon the similarity or dissimilarity between the learner's cultural background and the material to be learned (p. 9).

On this basis, Williams established the Black Intelligence Test of Cultural Homogeneity (BITCH). He devised the test by drawing from a glossary compiled of African American slang, "his personal experiences and that of his friends who had lived in the African American community" Dr. Williams' approach is not unlike that of Drs. Wechsler, Binet and others (in this regard) who have developed European American instruments for measuring "intelligence." The difference, of course, is the cultural experience being identified as the context or source of knowledge. The limitation in both the European-American and Black Psychology orientations is the epistemological conclusion that what is knowable is external and the inevitable bias that comes from variations in experience of the external environment. Williams concludes that European Americans are "victims of innate intellectual inferiority as demonstrated by their consistently lower performance on the BITCH test." This is the parallel conclusion of his Caucasian counterparts in their assessment of African American performance on their tests.

African Psychology assumes a universal knowledge rooted in knowledge of the makeup of the human being. The most direct experience of the self is through emotion or affect. Vernon Dixon (1976) observes:

> Homeland and overseas African persons know reality predominantly through the interaction of affect and symbolic imagery, i.e., the synthesis of these two factors produce knowledge. In the "pure" Africanized worldview of the unity of man and the phenomenal world, there is no empty perceptual space between the self and phenomena.

Affect refers to the feeling self, the emotive self engaged in experiencing phenomena holistically (p. 70).

Dixon (1976) makes another important distinction in this regard, relating to African epistemology. He says:

Affect, however, is not intuition, for the latter term means direct or immediate knowledge (instinctive knowledge) without recourse to inference from or reasoning about evidence. Affect does interact with evidence, in the form of symbolic imagery (p. 70).

This knowledge via "self" or holistic knowledge is critical in terms of understanding African Psychology. The relationship to reality inferred by African Psychology is one that views as doubtful any of the measures that exclusively assess knowledge of external reality. The measure of intelligence in African psychology would be assessed by "effective living and development." Effective living would not be demonstrated on a typical European American IQ measure. Instead, one would need a more dynamic evaluation of a person's experience of him or herself as well as an evaluation of the socio-cultural environment surrounding the person. In other words, knowledge would be reflected in the degree to which a person is capable of maneuvering an environment offering obstacles to their development. So, intelligence would entail (1) knowledge of the collective and historical reality of self, (2) knowledge of environmental obstacles to effective (collective) self-development, (3) actions initiated to remove or master such obstacles, and ultimately (4) knowledge of the Divine and universal laws that guide human development into ultimate knowledge of the Creator. These components of knowledge are most directly "known" through the "affect-symbolic imagery" as described by Dixon above. Dixon (1976) notes that "symbolic imagery is the use of phenomena (words, gestures, tones, rhythms, objects, etc.) to convey meaning." Consequently, an adequate inference of intelligence would require effectively tapping the full-range of a people's symbolic imagery as well as ascertaining the most effective ways that such imagery is used for self and environmental mastery. One could not evaluate a person's "knowledge" without knowing how effectively that person has mastered themselves and their relationship with the world and others. Therefore, the possibility of a man being adjudged a genius on the basis of his external knowledge yet proving to be morally inept would be impossible in African Psychology. Genius, by definition, would identify not only what you knew, but the kinds of judgments and prudent uses made of what you know. The four dimensions of the African Psychological conception of intelligence identified above must be understood as interdependent. There should be a level of harmony and balance among these competencies in order to assess intelligence.

Another example would be that knowledge can only be adjudged or assessed as adequate if it is used in the service of the collective self, which is ones community.

Cognition is not presumed to exist independent of self-liberating action. Unlike the European American and Black Psychology approaches which assess both knowledge (cognition) and achievement independent of self-affirming activity, the holistic approach of African Psychology could not hypothesize such an inconsistency. The most "intelligent" among those assessed through African Psychology would demonstrate the greatest self-knowledge, knowledge of the Creator and the mission for humanity as understood through universal wisdom. In the light of such an approach, it is not surprising that the leaders perceived as most intelligent by the majority of African Americans (looking at their experience from this perspective) would be people such as Nat Turner, Harriet Tubman, Martin Luther King, Malcolm (X) Shabazz, Elijah Muhammad, Marcus Garvey, and others. All of these models invariably came equipped with Universal wisdom as well as secular knowledge of the external world. The kind of response to such leadership (knowledge) as well as the expression of such knowledge is done by way of the affective-symbolic imagery defined above. The ideas are communicated and received, not by words alone, but from the full range of affective and symbolic imagery.

The intelligent being from the perspective of African Psychology is a moral being. Morality represents the imperative of ordered life functioning for the purpose of effective human development. Knowledge of such principles and, of course, the implementation of them is as much a measure of intelligence as is the shrewd and facile manipulation of principles of material creation. The holistic conception of human life requires attention to and progressive understanding of laws that regulate the outer life "and" the inner life. The degree to which the person understands and utilizes these laws for the purpose of collective self-liberation is the supreme measure of intelligence and well-adjusted functioning. In the light of such an approach to intelligence, the assessment of intelligence is not a quantitative phenomenon. It is seen in the quality of life that a person gives to himself. Such an approach makes moot the issue of racial superiority/inferiority and nature/nurture controversies as they relate to intelligence. The assessment of superiority and inferiority is done on the basis of the quality of life chosen and the utilization of human growth potential. Again, the assertion is that material accoutrements constitute only a limited portion of life quality, and such achievements must be evaluated in the light of humane and just usage of such resources. Ultimately, the intelligent person finds peace for themselves and helps to bring it to others. Such is viewed as the nature of the harmonious universe and is therefore within the natural potential of all human beings.

Another aspect of epistemology that directly proceeds from the above discussion is the assumption made about the essence of things. Particularly, in attempting to understand the human being, ones definition of the human essence is crucial. The definition of essence identifies the conception of the lowest possible form to which the human being can be reduced. European American psychology views this essence as material. It is this materialism which has devolved psychology. From the study of the psyche (or soul) to its current status as the study of behavior, the European American preoccupation with mind-brain formulations, hypothesizing that the totality of human life can be understood from brain functioning, represents the epitome of the European American concept of essence as material. The pervasive conviction that what can be observed by the senses identities the essence of human life defines this epistemology. The direct inference, epistemologically, is: what can be observed and is material is real and therefore knowable. What is unobservable and not material represents the unknowable or nonreality. Therefore, the equation of external or outer technology with human superiority and even reality becomes understandable in the light of their epistemology. It is not surprising how people with less opulent outer appearance are adjudged inferior, uncivilized, undeveloped, unintelligent or savage, even when such people may far surpass European Americans injustice, charitableness, compassion, contentment and peacefulness. Black psychology followed a similar course because of its emphasis on the physical exploitation of oppression. The tendency to view the essence of human life as the outcome of struggle and oppression results in a material conception of the human being. The view that Blackness is sacrosanct is the obverse of the view that Whiteness is supreme. Frances Welsing's "counter-racist psychiatry" epitomizes such an approach. As the European American has justified his exploitation of non-Caucasians on the basis of his superior material (i.e., White skin color), Welsing (1979) argues that the basis of such exploitation is due to their inferior material (i.e., color inadequacy) and their fear of the superior material (i.e., significant skin pigment) of Black, brown, red and yellow peoples. The goal of "counter-racism" according to Dr. Welsing (1974) is to "efficiently and effectively checkmate the behavioral system of racism (White supremacy)." The essence of this counter strategic conceptualization of the human being is material.

As we have suggested throughout this discussion, there is considerable justification for the spokespersons of "Black Psychology" to focus on the exploitation of African people by Europeans as a central issue in conceptualizing the psychology of African Americans. As Baldwin (1986) concludes in his analysis: "(Black) Psychology is therefore proactive as well as reactive, and it is most certainly political. Notwithstanding its reactive aspects, however, its thrust is clearly toward proactivity, that is self-definition and self-determination" (p. 246). The urgency of the historical oppression of African people by Europeans demands urgent and unprecedented attention. However, it is ultimately debilitating to ones conceptual development if a battle strategy becomes ones "Weltanschauung." Fanon (1968) insightfully notes:

But, if nationalism is not made explicit, if it is not enriched and deepened by a very rapid transformation into a consciousness of social and political needs, in other words into humanism, it leads up a blind alley (p. 204).

There are some who would argue that such a position is accomodationist and advocates a transcendence beyond the persisting realities of racism and oppression. Such is clearly, not the position of this discussion. What is described as an evolution is that which has become increasingly more expansive in addressing the total needs of human beings, particularly the historically exploited and excluded from conceptualizations of humanity. It also recognizes the real limitations of field weaponry when the struggle has moved into the halls of scholarship addressing the control of minds rather than bodies. African Psychology affirms itself and in so doing counteracts whatever is destructively alien.

African Psychology maintains that the essence of the human being is spiritual. This means that humans reduced to their lowest terms are invisible and of a universal substance. This writer (Akbar, 1976, 1999) has discussed elsewhere that the African conception of personality is fundamentally built on the notion of a force that defines the man's continuity with all things within the world. This implies that man is ultimately reducible to the universe itself which gives man universal potential. This assumption of the ultimate spiritual nature of the human being hypothesizes the potential harmony of people with each other and the remainder of the universe. There is no assumption of essential conflict in an interdependent cosmos. Material by its very nature is fragmented and in conflict. The material world operates on principles of polarity and conflict and if ones system of thought remains at this level, conflict becomes inevitable. The Freudian conclusion of the essence of man being a conflict between life force (libido) and death force (thanatos) is not surprising. The Skinnerian notion of the essence of man's development centering around the conflict of avoidance of punishment and the acquisition of rewards is also consistent with this view. We can even understand the vital relationship of Black/White conflict being the essential element in the materially based Black Psychology epistemology.

African Psychology sees the person reducible ultimately to a universal substance that affirms their oneness with the essence of the universe. Humans are considered as harmonious and integrated with all components of nature itself. The human being is considered as related to and vast as the universe itself. With such a definition of the essence of the human being, we can better understand the conceptions of intelligence that were discussed above.

As a final aspect of "epistemology," the issue of "how" we know becomes a point of significant departure among the various approaches to human psychology that we have identified in this discussion. The conceptualizations of intelligence and essence identify what is knowable within an epistemological framework. How what is knowable becomes known is highly significant in conceptualizing the workings of human psychology.

European American psychology identifies this process as rational thought or cognition. Cognition or thinking is considered to be a rather mechanical process that follows certain systematic rules of logic. Logic, objectivity and rationality automatically preclude affect in terms of Western thought. Thinking is considered to be effective only when it is free of subjectivity (i.e., emotion or affect). The only things that are validly known are known by this process. As we discussed above, objectivity is a prime value in the European American axiology because it is presumed to be the only appropriate and reliable way to obtain knowledge. Feeling is identified as a contaminant to "good and pure" thought.

> Syed Khatib (a.k.a Cedric Clark, 1972) observes that:
> Our philosophical heritage—that is, what is taught in our public schools—is firmly grounded in European conceptions of reality. The dualistic conception of Descartes, as defined by the British Empiricist thinkers, particularly Hume, Locke, and Mill, still stands as the scientific foundation of contemporary psychology. The only "truth" that matters according to these thinkers, is that which is given to us by our sensory experience with things. The mind may exist, but it is totally independent of matter, and what "matters" (i.e., is important) is the reality of the matter. Matter is sense; the mind is nonsense, or would result in nonsense if one philosophized on it too long (p. 12).

This observation well-characterizes the modality of the European American epistemology. From such an orientation we can see how psychology has reduced human intelligence to a score on an IQ test or human misery to a score over 70 on the MMPI. We can also see why a psychotherapist who "feels" with a suffering client is described as experiencing "counter-transference" rather than sharing with another human being. Khatib (Clark, 1972) quotes the historian of psychology, Boring, as claiming that the science of psychology "first lost its soul, then its consciousness." He goes on to observe that, "at least one contemporary writer has since added that psychology threatens to go out of its mind completely" (Clark, 1972). Even human identity is characterized through rational experience: cogito ergo sum ("I think therefore I am"), which comes from Descartes, captures this cognitive orientation of European American psychology. It is a brief step to conclude that one who is not adequately cognitive (i.e., with a low IQ score) is an inferior human being.

Black Psychology takes a completely opposite point of view. The assumption in Black Psychology is that the best way to know what we know is through affect or feeling. Joseph White describes the culture of African Americans as a feeling oriented culture. White (1972) says: "In a feeling-oriented culture, apparent and when examined closely, superficial logical contradictions do not have the same meaning as they might have in the Anglo culture." White (1972) continues:

> Closely related to the easy style of handling contradictions, it can also be stated that Black people have a greater tolerance for conflict, stress, ambiguity, and ambivalence. White psychologists fail to take this into consideration when they assume that because we have a lower class background, Black people are therefore more impulsive, emotionally mature and have less tolerance for stress. (pp. 46–47).

Such an approach to characterizing "Black culture" is appropriate in the light of the negative characterizations of African American affectivity that have grown out of the Anglo approach to psychology. The Black psychologist reacted in self-defense in declaring Black culture as a feeling culture and therefore appropriate in many ways of its responses viewed as pathological by European American Psychology.

Again, because of the focus of Black Psychology on oppression as the critical human experience, there is a focusing on the hatred or negative feeling of the racist and the suffering and pain (feelings) experienced by the victims of oppression. One is tempted to conclude from the analysis of Black Psychology that the predominant human feeling modality is pain or suffering. African Psychology assumes a rhythmic balance between affect and cognition. As we quoted Dixon (1976) above: Affect does interact with material evidence, but with evidence in the form of symbolic imagery. This process of synthesis is essential to the African Psychological perspective because it gives a balanced perspective on feeling and cognition. There is recognition that knowledge is acquired from sensory experience as well as the subjective experience of affect. African Psychology assumes that the perimeters of knowledge are rational, affectional and moral boundaries. Rationality represents the order of exoteric or outer principles of reality and morality represents the order of principles of esoteric or inner reality. Feeling is the mediating process between these dimensions. Such an approach provides a guide and a context for the often ungrounded nature of rational knowledge. The classic example is the kind of human suffering that has emerged from the exclusively rational commitment to nuclear weapons in contrast to the potentially great human contribution which could come from a morally guided use of the knowledge of nuclear energy.

As we observed previously in this discussion, balance is considered critical in African Psychology. Moral or affective dimensions unchecked by rational or cognitive dimensions results in a human imbalance that ultimately lays the conceptual foundation for human destruction.

Summary

Black Psychology emerged from the kinds of negative evaluations of African Americans that have characterized the vast majority of the European American psychological literature. Black Psychology was a reaction. It remains the political or militant arm of the study of African Americans within the European American context. Black Psychology is self-affirmative, particularly in its denial of the denigrating conceptualizations of European American psychology.

African Psychology attempts to look at human behavior from the perspective of the basic philosophical assumptions about the nature of man and the universe as it is understood from classical African Philosophy and worldview. It attempts to identify the characteristics of the human being in the light of Divine revelation as well as modern science.

This discussion has looked at the basic philosophical assumptions of the three approaches to the study of human (primarily African American) behavior as stages III the evolution of our thought about the psychology of African Americans. The conclusion that we draw shows a growth in our concepts that give us an ever-expanding horizon for study. European American concepts are appropriate for a time and a context, i.e., the time and context that views the African American as a deviant from the Anglo world for those observers who maintain the insignificance of race and cultural plurality may still find such an approach appropriate and valuable. Black Psychology represents an effort to come to grips with the overwhelming ethnocentrism of European American psychology with a counter-ethnocentrism. The approach is emphatically reactive and predicates its existence on the postulates of European American Psychology. African Psychology may more properly be characterized as natural psychology in that it attempts to identify the natural laws of the universal human experience. It does not deny the necessity of the often militant stance of Black Psychology nor does it deny the considerable distance of Europeans from this model of natural human form. It asserts, however, that the principles of African Psychology represent the Creator's model whereby a people most in accord with the original and natural laws of human nature are likely to find compatibility with these principles. In order to do so, the human being must be liberated from the contaminants of materialism, individualism, dualism and hedonism that obscure universal vision and proper human evolution.

References

Akbar, N. (1976). Rhythmic patterns in African personality. In L. King (Ed.), *African philosophy: Assumptions and paradigms for research on Black persons.*

Akbar, N. (1991). Mental disorder among African Americans. In R. Jones (Ed.), *Black psychology.* (3rd. ed.). Hampton, VA: Cobb & Henry Publishers.

Akbar, N. (1995). *Natural psychology and human transformation.* Tallahassee, FL: Mind Productions & Associates.

Akbar, N. (1999). *Know thy self.* Tallahassee, FL: Mind Productions & Associates.

Ani, M. (1994). *Yurugu: An African-centered critique of European cultural thought and behavior.* Trenton, NJ: African World Press.

Azibo, D. (1996). *African psychology in historical perspective and related commentary.* Trenton, NJ: Africa World Press.

Baldwin, J. (1976). Black psychology and Black personality. *Black Books Bulletin, 4, 3, 6–11, 65.*

Baldwin, J. (1986). African (Black) psychology: Issues and synthesis. *Journal of Black Studies, 16, 3, 235–249.*

Carruthers, J. (1972). *Science and oppression.* Chicago: Center for Inner City Studies. Northeastern Illinois University.

Clark, C. (1972). Black studies or the study of Black people? In R. Jones (Ed.), *Black psychology.* New York: Harper & Row.

Clark, K. (1965). *Dark ghetto.* New York: Harper & Row.

Cross, W. E. (1971). Negro to Black conversion experience: Toward a psychology of Black liberation. *Black World, 20, 9, 13–27.*

Dixon, V. (1976). Worldviews and research methodology. In L. King (Ed.), *African philosophy: Assumptions and paradigms for research on Black persons.* Los Angeles, CA: Fanon R & D Center.

Fanon, F. (1968). *The wretched of the earth.* New York: Grove Press.

Freud, S. (1953–74). *The standard edition of the complete psychological works.* J. Strachey (Ed.). London: Hogarth Press.

Grier, W. & Cobbs, P. (1968). *Black rage.* New York: Basic Books.

Guthrie, R. V. (1998). *Even the rat was White: An historical view of psychology.* (2nd. ed. revised). Boston: Allyn & Bacon.

Hall, G. (1904). *Adolescence.* New York: Appleton.

Jackson, G. C. (1976) Cultural seedbeds of the Black backlash in mental health. *Journal of Afro-American Issues, 4, 1, 70–91.*

Jackson, G. G. (1979). The origin and development of Black psychology: Implications for Black studies and human behavior. *Studia Africana, 1, 3, 270–293.*

Jung, C. C. (1953–78). *Collected works.* H. Read, M. Fordham, & G. Adler (Eds.). Princeton: Princeton University Press.

Kambon, K. (1992). *The African personality in America: An African centered framework.* Tallahassee, FL: Nubian Nation Publications.

Kambon, K. (1998). *African/Black psychology in the American context: An African-centered approach.* Tallahassee, FL: Nubian Nation Publications.

Kardiner, A., & Ovesey L. (1962). *The mark of oppression.* Cleveland: World Publishing Company.

Karenga, M. (1993). *Introduction to Black studies.* (2nd. ed.). Inglewood, CA: Kawaida Publications.

Khatib, S. (Cedric X), McGee, D. P., Nobles, W. and Akbar, N. (Luther X). (1975). Voodoo or IQ: An introduction to African psychology. *Journal of Black Psychology, 1(2), 9–29.*

Mbiti, J. (1970). *African religions and philosophy.* Garden City, NY: Anchor Books.

McDougall, W. (1908). *Social psychology.* New York: Luce.

Mosby, D. (1972). Toward a new specialty of Black psychology. In R. Jones (Ed.), *Black psychology.* New York: Harper & Row.

Nobles, W. (1974). Africanity: Its role in Black families. *The Black Scholar, 5, 9, 10–17.*

Nobles, W. (1976). African science: The consciousness of self. In L. King, V. Dixon, W. Nobles (Eds.), *African philosophy: Assumptions and paradigms for research on Black persons.* Los Angeles, CA: Fanon Research for Development Center.

Nobles, W. (1978). The Black family and its children: The survival of humanness. *Black Books Bulletin, 6, 2, 6–14.*

Nobles, W. (1980). African philosophy: Foundations for Black psychology. In R. Jones (Ed.), *Black psychology.* New York: Harper & Row.

Nobles, W. (1986). *African psychology: Towards its reclamation, reascension and revitalization.* Oakland, CA: Black Family Institute Publications.

Semaj, L. (1980). *Models for an Africentric psychology*. Presented at the Community Clinical Psychology Conference. Southern Regional Education Board, Atlanta.

Skinner, B. F. (1971). *Beyond freedom and dignity*. New York: Knopf.

Staples, R. (1974). The Black family in evolutionary perspective. *Black Scholar*, 5, 9, 2–9.

Thomas, A., & Sillen, S. (1972). *Racism and psychiatry*. New York: Bruner/Mazel Publishers.

(Weems) X, L. (1972). *Guidelines for African humanism*. Presented at the meeting of the international Association for Cross-Cultural Psychology. Ibadan, Nigeria.

Welsing, F. (1974). *Definitions in counter-racist psychiatry*. Unpublished manuscript. Washington, D.C.

Welsing, F. (1974). *The cress color confrontation theory*. (Private printing). Washington, D.C.

White, J. (1972). Toward a Black psychology. In R. Jones (Ed.), *Black psychology*. New York: Harper and Row.

Wright, B. J. & Isenstein, V. (1975). *Psychological tests and minorities*. Mental Health Studies and Reports Branch, NIMH.

Genes and Environmental Influence

Heredity, Environment, and the Question "How?"

Anne Anastasi

Ann Anastasi was born in New York City in 1908, earned her Ph.D. at Columbia University, and spent the majority of her career teaching at Fordham University. She had the honor of serving as president of the American Psychological Association from 1965 to 1967, and she is best known for her outstanding work in the theory and application of psychological testing. Revised editions of her famous text *Psychological Testing*, first published in 1954, are still widely used today.

Throughout the twentieth century psychologists have debated the "nature versus nurture" controversy. This debate asks, Which has a bigger effect on personality or intelligence, or personal happiness: nature (heredity) or nurture (environmental influences)? Anastasi joined this fray, arguing that nearly all human attributes are influenced by both. Her article "Heredity, Environment, and the Question 'How?' " *Psychological Review* (1958), from which the following selection has been taken, has become the definitive statement on this topic.

Key Concept: environmental versus hereditary influences

Two or three decades ago, the so-called heredity-environment question was the center of lively controversy. Today, on the other hand, many psychologists look upon it as a dead issue. It is now generally conceded that both hereditary and environmental factors enter into all behavior. The reacting organism is a product of its genes and its past environment, while present environment profiles the immediate stimulus for current behavior. To be sure, it can be argued that, although a given trait may result from the combined influence of hereditary and environmental factors, a specific difference in this trait between individuals or between groups may be traceable to either hereditary or environmental factors alone. The design of most traditional investigations undertaken to identify such factors, however, has been such as to yield inconclusive answers. The same set of data has frequently led to opposite conclusions in the hands of psychologists with different orientations.

Nor have efforts to determine the proportional contribution of hereditary and environmental factors to observed individual differences in given traits met with any greater success. Apart from difficulties in controlling conditions, such investigations have usually been based upon the implicit assumption that hereditary and environmental factors combine in an additive fashion. Both geneticists and psychologists have repeatedly demonstrated, however, that a more tenable hypothesis is that of interaction (15, 22, 28, 40). In other words, the nature and extent of the influence of each type of factor depend upon the contribution of the other. Thus the proportional contribution of heredity to the variance of a given trait, rather than being a constant, will vary under different environmental conditions. Similarly, under different hereditary conditions, the relative contribution of environment will differ. Studies designed to estimate the proportional contribution of heredity and environment, however, have rarely included measures of such interaction. The only possible conclusion from such research would thus seem to be that both heredity and environment contribute to all behavior traits and that the extent of their respective contributions cannot be specified for any trait. Small wonder that some psychologists regard the heredity-environment question as unworthy of further consideration!

But is this really all we can find out about the operation of heredity and environment in the etiology of behavior?

Perhaps we have simply been asking the wrong questions. The traditional questions about heredity and environment may not be intrinsically unanswerable. Psychologists began by asking *which* type of factor, hereditary or environmental, is responsible for individual differences in a given trait. Later, they tried to discover *how much* of the variance was attributable to heredity and how much to environment. It is the primary contention of this paper that a more fruitful approach is to be found in the question *"How?"* There is still much to be learned about the specific *modus operandi* of hereditary and environmental factors in the development of behavioral differences. And there are several current lines of research which offer promising techniques for answering the question "How?"

Variety of Interaction Mechanisms

Hereditary Factors. If we examine some of the specific ways in which hereditary factors may influence behavior, we cannot fail but be impressed by their wide diversity. At one extreme, we find such conditions as phenylpyruvic amentia and amaurotic idiocy.* In these cases, certain essential physical prerequisites for normal intellectual development are lacking as a result of hereditary metabolic disorders. In our present state of knowledge, there is no environmental factor which can completely counteract this hereditary deficit. The individual will be mentally defective, regardless of the type of environmental conditions under which he is reared.

A somewhat different situation is illustrated by hereditary deafness, which may lead to intellectual retardation through interference with normal social interaction, language development, and schooling. In such a case, however, the hereditary handicap can be offset by appropriate adaptations of training procedures. It has been said, in fact, that the degree of intellectual backwardness of the deaf is an index of the state of development of special instructional facilities. As the latter improve, the intellectual retardation associated with deafness is correspondingly reduced.

A third example is provided by inherited susceptibility to certain physical diseases, with consequent protracted ill health. If environmental conditions are such that illness does in fact develop, a number of different behavioral effects may follow. Intellectually, the individual may be handicapped by his inability to attend school regularly. On the other hand, depending upon age of onset, home conditions, parental status, and similar factors, poor health may have the effect of concentrating the individual's energies upon intellectual pursuits. The curtailment of participation in athletics and social functions may serve to strengthen interest in reading and other sedentary activities. Concomitant circumstances would also determine the influence of such illness upon personality development. And it is well known that the latter effects could run the gamut from a deepening of human sympathy to psychiatric breakdown.

Finally, heredity may influence behavior through the mechanism of social stereotypes. A wide variety of inherited physical characteristics have served as the visible cues for identifying such stereotypes. These cues thus lead to behavioral restrictions or opportunities and—at a more subtle level—to social attitudes and expectancies. The individual's own self concept tends gradually to reflect such expectancies. All of these influences eventually leave their mark upon his abilities and inabilities, his emotional reactions, goals, ambitions, and outlook on life.

The geneticist Dobzhansky illustrates this type of mechanism by means of a dramatic hypothetical situation. He points out that, if there were a culture in which the carriers of blood group AB were considered aristocrats and those of blood group O laborers, then the blood-group genes would become important hereditary determiners of behavior (12, p. 147). Obviously the association between blood group and behavior would be specific to that culture. But such specificity is an essential property of the causal mechanism under consideration.

More realistic examples are not hard to find. The most familiar instances occur in connection with constitutional types, sex, and race. Sex and skin pigmentation obviously depend upon heredity. General body build is strongly influenced by hereditary components, although also susceptible to environmental modification. That all these physical characteristics may exert a pronounced effect upon behavior within a given culture is well known. It is equally apparent, of course, that in different cultures the behavioral correlates of such hereditary physical traits may be quite unlike. A specific physical cue may be completely unrelated to individual differences in psychological traits in one culture, while closely correlated with them in another. Or it may be associated with totally dissimilar behavior characteristics in two different cultures.

It might be objected that some of the illustrations which have been cited do not properly exemplify the operation of hereditary mechanisms in behavior development, since hereditary factors enter only indirectly into the behavior in question. Closer examination, however, shows this distinction to be untenable. First it may be noted that

---

* ["Phenylpyruvic amentia" is better known as phenylketonuria. It is a rare genetic disorder in which the body lacks the means to break down one of the necessary amino acids: phenylalanine. When the excessive phenylalanine accumulates in the spinal fluid it damages the nervous system, causing severe or profound mental retardation. If some of these words sound vaguely familiar to you, it's likely you have read about them on the warning labels of foods and drinks sweetened with aspartame (NutriSweet). "Amaurotic idiocy" is better known as Tay-Sach's disease, a rare genetic disorder of the body's metabolism that causes paralysis, blindness, mental retardation and death. The disorder is most common among Jews of Eastern Europe ancestry (the Ashkenazi).—Eds.]

the influence of heredity upon behavior is always indirect. No psychological trait is ever inherited as such. All we can ever say directly from behavioral observations is that a given trait shows evidence of being influenced by certain "inheritable unknowns." This merely defines a problem for genetic research; it does not provide a casual explanation. Unlike the blood groups, which are close to the level of primary gene products, psychological traits are related to genes by highly indirect and devious routes. Even the mental deficiency associated with phenylketonuria is several steps removed from the chemically defective genes that represent its hereditary basis. Moreover, hereditary influences cannot be dichotomized into the more direct and less direct. Rather do they represent a whole "continuum of indirectness," along which are found all degrees of remoteness of casual links. The examples already cited illustrate a few of the points on this continuum.

It should be noted that as we proceed along the continuum of indirectness, the range of variation of possible outcomes of hereditary factors expands rapidly. At each step in the causal chain, there is fresh opportunity for interaction with other hereditary factors as well as with environmental factors. And since each interaction in turn determines the direction of subsequent interactions, there is an ever-widening network of possible outcomes. If we visualize a simple sequential grid with only two alternatives at each point, it is obvious that there are two possible outcomes in the one-stage situation, four outcomes at the second stage, eight at the third, and so on in geometric progression. The actual situation is undoubtedly much more complex, since there will usually be more than two alternatives at any one point.

In the case of the blood groups, the relation to specific genes is so close that no other concomitant hereditary or environmental conditions can alter the outcome. If the organism survives at all, it will have the blood group determined by its genes. Among psychological traits, on the other hand, some variation in outcome is always possible as a result of concurrent circumstances. Even in cases of phenylketonuria, intellectual development will exhibit some relationship with the type of care and training available to the individual. That behavioral outcomes show progressive diversification as we proceed along the continuum of indirectness is brought out by the other examples which were cited. Chronic illness *can* lead to scholarly renown or to intellectual immaturity; a mesomorphic physique [strong, muscular build] *can* be a contributing factor in juvenile delinquency or in the attainment of a college presidency! Published data on Sheldon somatotypes provide some support for both of the latter outcomes.

Parenthetically, it may be noted that geneticists have sometimes used the term "norm of reaction" to designate the range of variation of possible outcomes of gene properties (cf. 13, p. 161). Thus heredity sets the "norm" or limits within which environmental differences determine the eventual outcome. In the case of some traits, such as blood groups or eye color, this norm is much narrower than in the case of other traits. Owing to the rather different psychological connotations of both the words "norm" and "reaction," however, it seems less confusing to speak of the "range of variation" in this context.

A large portion of the continuum of hereditary influences which we have described coincides with the domain of somatopsychological relations, as defined by Barker et al. (6). Under this heading, Barker includes "variations in physique that affect the psychological situation of a person by influencing the effectiveness of his body as a tool for actions or by serving as a stimulus to himself or others" (6, p. 1). Relatively direct neurological influences on behavior, which have been the traditional concern of physiological psychology, are excluded from this definition, Barker being primarily concerned with what he calls the "social psychology of physique." Of the examples cited in the present paper, deafness, severe illness, and the physical characteristics associated with social stereotypes would meet the specifications of somatopsychological factors.

The somatic factors to which Barker refers, however, are not limited to those of hereditary origin. Bodily conditions attributable to environmental causes operate in the same sorts of somatopsychological relations as those traceable to heredity. In fact, heredity-environment distinctions play a minor part in Barker's approach.

Environmental Factors: Organic. Turning now to an analysis of the role of environmental factors in behavior, we find the same etiological mechanisms which were observed in the case of hereditary factors. First, however, we must differentiate between two classes of environmental influences: (a) those producing organic effects which may in turn influence behavior and (b) those serving as direct stimuli for psychological reactions. The former may be illustrated by food intake or by exposure to bacterial infection; the latter, by tribal initiation ceremonies or by a course in algebra. There are no completely satisfactory names by which to designate these two classes of influences. In an earlier paper by Anastasi and Foley (4), the terms "structural" and "functional" were employed. However, "organic" and "behavioral" have the advantage of greater familiarity in this context and may be less open to misinterpretation. Accordingly, these terms will be used in the present paper.

Like hereditary factors, environmental influences of an organic nature can also be ordered along a continuum of indirectness with regard to their relation to behavior. This continuum closely parallels that of hereditary factors. One end is typified by such conditions as mental deficiency resulting from cerebral birth injury or from prenatal nutritional inadequacies. A more indirect etiological mechanism is illustrated by severe motor disorder—as in certain cases of cerebral palsy—*without* accompanying injury to higher neurological centers. In such instances, intellectual retardation may occur as an indirect result of the motor handicap, through the curtailment of educational and social activities. Obviously this casual mechanism corresponds closely to that of hereditary deafness cited earlier in the paper.

Finally, we may consider an environmental parallel to the previously discussed social stereotypes which were mediated by hereditary physical cues. Let us suppose that a young woman with mousy brown hair becomes transformed into a dazzling golden blonde through environmental techniques currently available in our culture. It is highly probable that this metamorphosis will alter, not only the reactions of her associates toward her, but also her own self concept and subsequent behavior. The effects could range all the way from a rise in social poise to a drop in clerical accuracy!

Among the examples of environmentally determined organic influences which have been described, all but the first two fit Barker's definition of somatopsychological factors. With the exception of birth injuries and nutritional deficiencies, all fall within the social psychology of physique. Nevertheless, the individual factors exhibit wide diversity in their specific *modus operandi*—a diversity which has important practical as well as theoretical implications.

Environmental Factors: Behavioral. The second major class of environmental factors—the behavioral as contrasted to the organic—are by definition direct influences. The immediate effect of such environmental factors is always a behavioral change. To be sure, some of the initial behavioral effects may themselves indirectly affect the individual's later behavior. But this relationship can perhaps be best conceptualized in terms of breadth and permanence of effects. Thus it could be said that we are now dealing, not with a continuum of indirectness, as in the case of hereditary and organic-environmental factors, but rather with a continuum of breadth.

Social class membership may serve as an illustration of a relatively broad, pervasive, and enduring environmental factor. Its influence upon behavior development may operate through many channels. Thus social level may determine the range and nature of intellectual stimulation provided by home and community through books, music, art, play activities, and the like. Even more far-reaching may be the effects upon interests and motivation, as illustrated by the desire to perform abstract intellectual tasks, to surpass others in competitive situations, to succeed in school, or to gain social approval. Emotional and social traits may likewise be influenced by the nature of interpersonal relations characterizing homes at different socio-economic levels. Somewhat more restricted in scope than social class, although still exerting a relatively broad influence, is amount of formal schooling which the individual is able to obtain.

A factor which may be wide or narrow in its effects, depending upon concomitant circumstances, is language handicap. Thus the bilingualism of an adult who moves to a foreign country with inadequate mastery of the new language represents a relatively limited handicap which can be readily overcome in most cases. At most, the difficulty is one of communication. On the other hand, some kinds of bilingualism in childhood may exert a retarding influence upon intellectual development and may under certain conditions affect personality development adversely (2, 5, 10). A common pattern in the homes of immigrants is that the child speaks one language at home and another in school, so that his knowledge of each language is limited to certain types of situations. Inadequate facility with the language of the school interferes with the acquisition of basic concepts, intellectual skills, and information. The frustration engendered by scholastic difficulties may in turn lead to discouragement and general dislike of school. Such reactions can be found, for example, among a number of Puerto Rican children in New York City schools (3). In the case of certain groups, moreover, the child's foreign language background may be perceived by himself and his associates as a symbol of minority group status and may thereby augment any emotional maladjustment arising from such status (34).

A highly restricted environmental influence is to be found in the opportunity to acquire specific items of information occurring in a particular intelligence test. The fact that such opportunities may vary with culture, social class, or individual experiential background is at the basis of the test user's concern with the problem of coaching and with "culture-free" or "culture-fair" tests (cf. 1, 2). If the advantage or disadvantage which such experiential differences confer upon certain individuals is strictly confined to performance on the given test, it will obviously reduce the validity of the test and should be eliminated.

In this connection, however, it is essential to know the breadth of the environmental influence in question. A fallacy inherent in many attempts to develop culture-fair tests is that the breadth of cultural differentials is not taken into account. Failure to consider breadth of effect likewise characterizes certain discussions of coaching. If, in coaching a student for a college admission test, we can improve his knowledge of verbal concepts and his reading comprehension, he will be better equipped to succeed in college courses. His performance level will thus be raised, not only on the test, but also on the criterion which the test is intended to predict. To try to devise a test which is not susceptible to such coaching would merely reduce the effectiveness of the test. Similarly, efforts to rule out cultural differentials from test items so as to make them equally "fair" to subjects in different social classes or in different cultures may merely limit the usefulness of the test, since the same cultural differentials may operate within the broader area of behavior which the test is designed to sample.

Methodological Approaches

The examples considered so far should suffice to highlight the wide variety of ways in which hereditary and environmental factors may interact in the course of behavior development. There is clearly a need for identifying explicitly the etiological mechanism whereby any given hereditary or environmental condition ultimately leads to a behavioral characteristic—in other words, the "how" of heredity and environment. Accordingly, we may now take a quick look at some promising methodological approaches to the question "how."

Within the past decade, an increasing number of studies have been designed to trace the connection between specific factors in the hereditary backgrounds or in the reactional biographies of individuals and their observed behavioral characteristics. There has been a definite shift away from the predominantly descriptive and correlational approach of the earlier decades toward more deliberate attempts to verify explanatory hypotheses. Similarly, the cataloguing of group differences in psychological traits has been giving way gradually to research on *changes* in group characteristics following altered conditions.

Among recent methodological developments, we have chosen seven as being particularly relevant to the analysis of etiological mechanisms. The first represents an extension of selective breeding investigations to permit the identification of specific hereditary conditions underlying the observed behavioral differences. When early selective breeding investigations such as those of Tryon (36) on rats indicated that "maze learning ability" was inherited, we were still a long way from knowing what was actually being transmitted by the genes. It was obviously not "maze learning ability" as such. Twenty—or even ten—years ago, some psychologists would have suggested that it was probably general intelligence. And a few might even have drawn a parallel with the inheritance of human intelligence.

But today investigators have been asking: Just what makes one group of rats learn mazes more quickly than the other? Is it differences in motivation, emotionality, speed of running, general activity level? If so, are these behavioral characteristics in turn dependent upon group differences in glandular development, body weight, brain size, biochemical factors, or some other organic conditions? A number of recent and ongoing investigations indicate that attempts are being made to trace, at least part of the way, the steps whereby certain chemical properties of the genes may ultimately lead to specified behavior characteristics.

An example of such a study is provided by Searle's (31) follow-up of Tryon's research. Working with the strains of maze-bright and maze-dull rats developed by Tryon, Searle demonstrated that the two strains differed in a number of emotional and motivational factors, rather than in ability. Thus the strain differences were traced one step further, although many links still remain to be found between maze learning and genes. A promising methodological development within the same general ares is to be found in the recent research of Hirsch and Tryon (18). Utilizing a specially devised technique for measuring individual differences in behavior among lower organisms, these investigators launched a series of studies on selective breeding for behavioral characteristics in the fruit fly, *Drosophila*. Such research can capitalize on the mass of available genetic knowledge regarding the morphology of *Drosophila*, as well as on other advantages of using such an organism in genetic studies.

Further evidence of current interest in the specific hereditary factors which influence behavior is to be found in an extensive research program in progress at the Jackson Memorial Laboratory, under the direction of Scott and Fuller (30). In general, the project is concerned with the behavioral characteristics of various breeds and crossbreeds of dogs. Analyses of some of the data gathered to date again suggest that "differences in performance are produced by differences in emotional, motivational, and peripheral processes, and that genetically caused differences in central processes may be either slight or nonexistent" (29, p. 225). In other parts of the same project, breed differences in physiological characteristics, which may in turn be related to behavioral differences, have been established.

A second line of attack is the exploration of possible relationships between behavioral characteristics and physiological variables which may in turn be traceable to hereditary factors. Research on EEG, autonomic balance, metabolic processes, and biochemical factors illustrates this approach. A lucid demonstration of the process of tracing a psychological condition to genetic factors is provided by identification and subsequent investigation of phenylpyruvic amentia. In this case, the causal chain from defective gene, through metabolic disorder and consequent cerebral malfunctioning, to feeble-mindedness and other overt symptoms can be described step by step (cf. 32; 33, pp. 389–391). Also relevant are the recent researches on neurological and biochemical correlates of schizophrenia (9). Owing to inadequate methodological controls, however, most of the findings of the latter studies must be regarded as tentative (19).

Prenatal environmental factors provide a third avenue of fruitful investigation. Especially noteworthy is the recent work of Pasamanick and his associates (27), which demonstrated a tie-up between socioeconomic level, complications of pregnancy and parturition, [the process of giving birth] and psychological disorders of the offspring. In a series of studies on large samples of whites and Negroes in Baltimore, these investigators showed that various prenatal and paranatal disorders are significantly related to the occurrence of mental defect and psychiatric disorders in the child. An important source of such irregularities in the process of childbearing and birth is to be found in deficiencies of maternal diet and in other conditions associated with low socioeconomic status. An analysis of the data did in fact reveal a much higher frequency of all such medical complications in lower than in higher socioeconomic levels, and a higher frequency among Negroes than among whites.

Direct evidence of the influence of prenatal nutritional factors upon subsequent intellectual development is to be found in a recent, well controlled experiment by Harrell et al. (16). The subjects were pregnant women in low-income groups, whose normal diets were generally quite deficient. A dietary supplement was administered to some of these women during pregnancy and lactation, while an equated control group received placebos. When tested at the ages of three and four years, the offspring of the experimental group obtained a significantly higher mean IQ than did the offspring of the controls.

Mention should also be made of animal experiments on the effects of such factors as prenatal radiation and neonatal asphyxia upon cerebral anomalies as well as upon subsequent behavior development. These experimental studies merge imperceptibly into the fourth approach to be considered, namely, the investigation of the influence of early experience upon the eventual behavioral characteristics of animals. Research in this area has been accumulating at a rapid rate. In 1954, Beach and Jaynes (8) surveyed this literature for the *Psychological Bulletin*, listing over 130 references. Several new studies have appeared since that date (e.g., 14, 21, 24, 25, 35). The variety of factors covered ranges from the type and quantity of available food to the extent of contact with human culture. A large number of experiments have been concerned with various forms of sensory deprivation and with diminished opportunities for motor exercise. Effects have been observed in many kinds of animals and in almost all aspects of behavior, including perceptual responses, motor activity, learning, emotionally, and social reactions.

In their review, Beach and Jaynes pointed out that research in this area has been stimulated by at least four distinct theoretical interests. Some studies were motivated by the traditional concern with the relative contribution of maturation and learning to behavior development. Others were designed in an effort to test certain psychoanalytic theories regarding infantile experiences, as illustrated by studies which limited the feeding responses of young animals. A third relevant influence is to be found in the work of the European biologist Lorenz (23) on early social stimulation of birds, and in particular on the special type of learning for which the term "imprinting" has been coined. A relatively large number of recent studies have centered around Hebb's (17) theory regarding the importance of early perceptual experiences upon subsequent performance in learning situations. All this research represents a rapidly growing and promising attack on the *modus operandi* of specific environmental factors.

The human counterpart of these animal studies may be found in the comparative investigation of child-rearing practices in different cultures and subcultures. This represents the fifth approach in our list. An outstanding example of such a study is that by Whiting and Child (38), published in 1953. Utilizing data on 75 primitive societies from the Cross-Cultural Files of the Yale Institute of Human Relations, these investigators set out to

test a number of hypotheses regarding the relationships between child-rearing practices and personality development. This analysis was followed up by field observations in five cultures, the results of which have not yet been reported (cf. 37).

Within our own culture, similar surveys have been concerned with the diverse psychological environments provided by different social classes (11). Of particular interest are the study by Williams and Scott (39) on the association between socioeconomic level, permissiveness, and motor development among Negro children, and the exploratory research by Milner (26) on the relationship between reading readiness in first-grade children and patterns of parent-child interaction. Milner found that upon school entrance the lower-class child seems to lack chiefly two advantages enjoyed by the middle-class child. The first is described as "a warm positive family atmosphere or adult-relationship pattern which is more and more being recognized as a motivational prerequisite of any kind of adult-controlled learning." The lower-class children in Milner's study perceived adults as predominantly hostile. The second advantage is an extensive opportunity to interact verbally with adults in the family. The latter point is illustrated by parental attitudes toward mealtime conversation, lower-class parents tending to inhibit and discourage such conversation, while middle-class parents encourage it.

Most traditional studies on child-rearing practices have been designed in terms of a psychoanalytic orientation. There is need for more data pertaining to other types of hypotheses. Findings such as those of Milner on opportunities for verbalization and the resulting effects upon reading readiness represent a step in this direction. Another possible source of future data is the application of the intensive observational techniques of psychological ecology developed by Barker and Wright (7) to widely diverse socioeconomic groups.

A sixth major approach involves research on the previously cited somatopsychological relationships (6). To date, little direct information is available on the precise operation of this class of factors in psychological development. The multiplicity of ways in which physical traits—whether hereditary or environmental in origin—may influence behavior thus offers a relatively unexplored field for future study.

The seventh and final approach to be considered represents an adaptation of traditional twin studies. From the standpoint of the question "How?" there is need for closer coordination between the usual data on twin resemblance and observations of the family interactions of twins. Available data already suggest, for example, that closeness of contact and extent of environmental similarity are greater in the case of monozygotic tan in the case of dizygotic twins (cf. 2). Information on the social reactions of twins toward each other and the specialization of roles is likewise of interest (2). Especially useful would be longitudinal studies of twins, beginning in early infancy and following the subjects through school age. The operation of differential environmental pressures, the development of specialized roles, and other environmental influences could thus be more clearly identified and correlated with intellectual and personality changes in the growing twins.

Parenthetically, I should like to add a remark about the traditional applications of the twin method, in which persons in different degrees of hereditary and environmental relationships to each other are simply compared for behavioral similarity. In these studies, attention has been focus principally upon the amount of resemblance of monozygotic as contrasted to dizygotic twins. Yet such a comparison is particularly difficult to interpret because of the many subtle differences in the environmental situations of the two types of twins. A more fruitful comparison would seem to be that between dizygotic twins and siblings, for whom the hereditary similarity is known to be the same. In Kallmann's monumental research on psychiatric disorders among twins (20), for example, one of the most convincing bits of evidence for the operation of hereditary factors in schizophrenia is the fact that the degrees of concordance for dizygotic twins and for siblings were practically identical. In contrast, it will be recalled that in intelligence test scores dizygotic twins resemble each other much more closely than do siblings—a finding which reveals the influence of environmental factors in intellectual development.

Summary

The heredity-environment problem is still very much alive. Its viability is assured by the gradual replacement of the questions, "Which one?" and "How much?" by the more basic and appropriate question, "How?" Hereditary influences—as well as environmental factors of an organic nature—vary along a "continuum of indirectness." The more indirect their connection with behavior, the wider will be the range of variation of possible outcomes. One extreme of the continuum of indirectness may be illustrated by brain damage leading to mental deficiency; the other extreme, by physical characteristics associated with social stereotypes. Examples of factors falling at intermediate points include deafness, physical diseases, and motor disorders. Those environmental factors which act directly upon behavior can be ordered along a continuum of breadth or permanence of effect, as exemplified by social class membership, amount of formal schooling, language handicap, and familiarity with specific test items.

Several current lines of research offer promising techniques for exploring the *modus operandi* of hereditary and environmental factors. Outstanding among them are investigations of: (a) hereditary conditions which underlie behavioral differences between selectively bred groups of animals; (b) relations between physiological variables and individual differences in behavior, especially in the case of pathological deviations; (c) role of prenatal physiological factors in behavior development; (d) influence of early experience upon eventual behavioral characteristics; (e) cultural differences in child-rearing practices in relation to intellectual and emotional development; (f) mechanisms of somatopsychological relationships; and (g) psychological development of twins from infancy to maturity, together with observations of their social environment. Such approaches are extremely varied with regard to subjects employed, nature of psychological functions studies, and specific experimental procedures followed. But it is just such heterogeneity of methodology that is demanded by the wide diversity of ways in which hereditary and environmental factors interact in behavior development.

References

1. Anastasi, Anne. *Psychological testing.* New York: Macmillan, 1954.
2. Anastasi, Anne. *Differential psychology,* (3rd ed.) New York: Macmillan, 1958.
3. Anastasi, Anne, & Cordova, F. A. Some effects of bilingualism upon the intelligence test performance of Puerto Rican children in New York City. *J. educ. Psychol.,* 1953, **44**, 1–19.
4. Anastasi, Anne, & Foley, J. P., Jr. A proposed reorientation in the heredity-environment controversy. *Psychol. Rev.,* 2948, **55**, 239–249.
5. Arsenian, S. Bilingualism in the post-war world. *Psychol. Bull.,* 1945, **42**, 65–86.
6. Barker, R. G., Wright, Beatrice A., Myerson, L., & Gonick, Mollie R. Adjustment to physical handicap and illness: A survey of the social psychology of physique and disability. *Soc. Sci. Res. Coun. Bull.,* 1953, No. 55 (Rev.).
7. Barker, R. G., & Wright, H. F. *Midwest and its children: The psychological ecology of an American town.* Evanston, Ill.: Row, Peterson, 1955.
8. Beach, F. A., & Jaynes, J. Effects of early experience upon the behavior of animals. *Psychol. Bull.,* 1954, **51**, 239–263.
9. Brackbill, G. A. Studies of brain dysfunction in schizophrenia. *Psychol. Bull.,* 1956, **53**, 210–226.
10. Darcy, Natalie T. A review of the literature on the effects of bilingualism upon the measurement of intelligence. *J. genet. Psychol.,* 1953, **82**, 21–57.
11. Davis. A., & Havighurst, R. J. Social class can color differences in child rearing. *Amer. sociol. Rev.,* 1946, **11**, 698–710.
12. Dobzhansky, T. The genetic nature of differences among men. In S. Persons (ed.), *Evolutionary thought in America.* New Haven: Yale Univer. Press, 1950, pp. 86–155.
13. Dobzhansky, T. Heredity, environment, and evolution. *Science,* 1950, **111**, 161–166.
14. Forgus, R. H. The effect of early perceptual learning on the behavioral organization of adult rats. *J. comp. physiol. Psychol.,* 1954, **47**, 331–336.
15. Haldane, J. B. S. *Heredity and politics.* New York: Norton, 1938.
16. Harrell, Ruth F., Woodyard, Ella, & Gates, A. I. *The effect of mothers' diets on the intelligence of the offspring.* New York: Bur. Publ., Teach. Coll., Columbia Univ., 1955.
17. Hebb, D. O. *The organization of behavior.* New York: Wiley, 1949.

18. Hirsch, J., & Tryon, R. C. Mass screening and reliable individual measurement in the experimental behavior genetics of lower organisms. *Psychol. Bull.*, 1956, **53**, 402–410.

19. Horwitt, M. K. Fact and artifact in the biology of schizophrenia. *Science*, 1956, **124**, 429–430.

20. Kallmann, F. J. *Heredity in health and mental disorder; Principles of psychiatric genetics in the light of comparative twin studies.* New York: Norton, 1953.

21. King, J. A., & Gurney, Nancy L. Effect of early social experience on adult aggressive behavior in C57BL10 mice. *J. comp. physiol. Psychol.*, 1954, **47**, 326–330.

22. Loevinger, Jane. On the proportional contributions of differences in nature and in nurture to differences in intelligence. *Psychol. Bull.*, 1943, **40**, 725–756.

23. Lorenz, K. Der Kumpan in der Umwelt des Vogels. Der Artgenosse als auslösendes Momemt sozialer Verhaltungsweisen. *J. Orn., Lpz.*, 1935, **83**, 137–213; 289–413.

24. Luchins. A. S., & Forgus, R. H. The effect of differential postweaning environment on the rigidity of an animal's behavior. *J. genet. Psychol.*, 1955, **86**, 51–58.

25. Melzack, R. The genesis of emotional behavior: An experimental study of the dog. *J. comp. physiol. Psychol.*, 1954, **47**, 166–168.

26. Milner, Esther A. A study of the relationships between reading readiness in grade one school children and patterns of parent-child interaction. *Child Develpm.*, 1951, **22**, 95–112.

27. Pasamanick, B., Knobloch, Hilda, & Lilienfeld, A. M. Socioeconomic status and some precursors of neuropsychiatric disorder. *Amer. J. Orthopsychiat.*, 1956, **26**, 594–601.

28. Schwesinger, Gladys C. *Heredity and environment.* New York: Macmillan, 1933.

29. Scott, J. P., & Charles, Margaret, S. Some problems of heredity and social behavior. *J. gen. Psychol.*, 1953, **48**, 209–230.

30. Scott, J. P., & Fuller, J. L. Research on genetics and social behavior at the Roscoe B. Jackson Memorial Laboratory, 1946–1951—A progress report. *J. Hered.*, 1951, **42**, 191–197.

31. Searle, L. V. The organization of hereditary maze-brightness and maze-dullness. *Genet. Psychol. Monogr.*, 1949, **39**, 279–325.

32. Snyder, L. H. The genetic approach to human individuality. *Sci. Mon., N. Y.*, 1949, **68**, 165–171.

33. Snyder, L. H., & David, P. R. *The principles of heredity.* (5th ed.) Boston: Heath, 1957.

34. Spoerl, Dorothy T. Bilinguality and emotional adjustment. *J. abnorm. soc. Psychol.*, 1943, **38**, 37–57.

35. Thompson, W. R., & Melzack, R. Early environment. *Sci. Amer.*, 1956, **194** (1), 38–42.

36. Tyron, R. C. Genetic differences in maze-learning ability in rats. *Yearb. nat. Soc. Stud. Educ.*, 1940, **39**, Part I, 111–119.

37. Whiting, J. W. M., et al. *Field guide for a study of socialization in five societies.* Cambridge, Mass.: Harvard Univer., 1954 (mimeo.).

38. Whiting, J. W. M., & Child, I. L. *Child training and personality: A cross-cultural study.* New Haven: Yale Univer. Press, 1953.

39. Williams, Judith R., & Scott, R. B. Growth and development of Negro infants: IV. Motor development and its relationship to child rearing practices in two groups of Negro infants. *Child Develpm.*, 1953, **24**, 103–121.

40. Woodworth, R. S. Heredity and environment: A critical survey of recently published material on twins and foster children. *Soc. Sci. Res. Coun. Bull.*, 1941, No. 47.

The Origin of Personality

Alexander Thomas, Stella Chess, and Herbert G. Birch

Alexander Thomas and Stella Chess, both pediatric physicians, launched one of the most famous longitudinal studies of infants in the field of human development in the late 1950s. Their study of 140 children from birth to adolescence became renowned as the New York Longitudinal Study. Longitudinal studies are critical to the field of human development, but they are particularly expensive and difficult to perform. Most developmental research is "cross-sectional." For example, researchers may test a group of 4-year-olds, a group of 8-year-olds, and a group of 12-year-olds, and then compare the differences. However, this is not as good for revealing developmental changes as testing a group of 4-year-olds, then four years later retesting them, and four years later retesting them again. The reason such longitudinal research is better is because cross-sectional research is influenced by "cohort" environmental impacts. For instance, in the cross-sectional example above, if the 12-year-olds had grown up without television until age 8 but the 4- and 8-year-olds had television for all or even half of their lives, it might skew the results.

One of the long-standing questions in human development research is, Do children have specific temperaments? That is, do children have personalities that are based on genes and not on their environmental influences? The following selection, which is from "The Origin of Personality," *Scientific American* (1970), helps to answer that question. Herbert G. Birch collaborated with Thomas and Chess on this article, in which over a decade of their longitudinal research into the biological roots of personality is summarized.

Key Concept: temperament

others, nurses and pediatricians are well aware that infants begin to express themselves as individuals from the time of birth. The fact that each child appears to have a characteristic temperament from his earliest days has also been suggested by Sigmund Freud and Arnold Gesell. In recent years, however, many psychiatrists and psychologists appear to have lost sight of this fact. Instead they have tended to emphasize the influence of the child's early environment when discussing the origin of the human personality.

As physicians who have had frequent occasion to examine the family background of disturbed children, we began many years ago to encounter reasons to question the prevailing one-sided emphasis on environment. We found that some children with severe psychological problems had a family upbringing that did not differ essentially from the environment of other children who developed no severe problems. On the other hand, some children were found to be free of serious personality disturbances although they had experienced severe family disorganization and poor parental care. Even in cases where parental mishandling was obviously responsible

for a child's personality difficulties there was no consistent or predictable relation between the parents' treatment and the child's specific symptoms. Domineering, authoritarian handling by the parents might make one youngster anxious and submissive and another defiant and antagonistic. Such unpredictability seemed to be the direct consequence of omitting an important factor from the evaluation: the child's own temperament, that is, his own individual style of responding to the environment.

It might be inferred from these opinions that we reject the environmentalist tendency to emphasize the role of the child's surroundings and the influence of his parents (particularly the mother) as major factors in the formation of personality, and that instead we favor the constitutionalist concept of personality's being largely inborn. Actually we reject both the "nurture" and the "nature" concepts. Either by itself is too simplistic to account for the intricate play of forces that form the human character. It is our hypothesis that the personality is shaped by the constant interplay of temperament and environment.

We decided to test this concept by conducting a systematic long-term investigation of the differences in the behavioral reactions of infants. The study would be designed to determine whether or not these differences persist through childhood, and it would focus on how a child's behavioral traits interact with specific elements of his environment. Apart from satisfying scientific curiosity, answers to these questions would help parents and teachers—and psychiatrists—to promote healthy personality development.

After much preliminary exploration we developed techniques for gathering and analyzing information about individual differences in behavioral characteristics in the first few months of life, for categorizing such differences and for identifying individuality at each stage of a child's life. This technique consisted in obtaining detailed descriptions of children's behavior through structured interviews with their parents at regular intervals beginning when the child had reached an age of two to three months. Independent checks by trained observers established that the descriptions of the children's behavior supplied by the parents in these interviews could be accepted as reliable and significant.

Analyzing the data, we identified nine characteristics that could be reliably scored on a three-point scale (medium, high and low): (1) the level and extent of motor activity; (2) the rhythmicity, or degree of regularity, of functions such as eating, elimination and the cycle of sleeping and wakefulness; (3) the response to a new object or person, in terms of whether the child accepts the new experience or withdraws from it; (4) the adaptability of behavior to changes in the environment; (5) the threshold, or sensitivity, to stimuli; (6) the intensity, or energy level, of responses; (7) the child's general mood or "disposition," whether cheerful or given to crying, pleasant or cranky, friendly or unfriendly; (8) the degree of the child's distractibility from what he is doing; (9) the span of the child's attention and his persistence in an activity.

The set of ratings in these nine characteristics defines the temperament, or behavioral profile, of a child, and the profile is discernible even as early as the age of two or three months. We found that the nine qualities could be identified and rated in a wide diversity of population samples we studied: middle-class children, children of working-class Puerto Ricans, mentally retarded children, children born prematurely and children with congenital rubella ("German measles"). Other investigators in the U.S. and abroad have identified the same set of characteristics in children.

Equipped with this means of collecting and analyzing the required data on individual children through standard interviews with their parents, we proceeded to our long-term study of the development of a large group of children. We obtained the willing collaboration of 85 families, with a total of 141 children, who agreed to allow us to follow their children's development from birth over a period of years that by now extends to more than a decade. Our parents have cooperated magnificently in all the

interviews and tests, and in the 14 years since the study was started only four families (with five children) have dropped out. In order to avoid complicating the study by having to consider a diversity of socioeconomic influences we confined the study to a homogeneous group, consisting mainly of highly educated families in the professions and business occupations.

We have observed the children's development throughout their preschool period and their years in nursery and elementary school. Their parents have been interviewed at frequent intervals, so that descriptions of the children's behavior have been obtained while the parents' memory of it was still fresh. The interviews have focused on factual details of how the children behaved in specific situations, avoiding subjective interpretations as much as possible. We have supplemented the parental interviews with direct observation and with information obtained from the children's teachers. The children have also been examined with various psychological tests. Youngsters who have shown evidence of behavioral disturbances have received a complete psychiatric examination. The detailed behavioral data collected on all the children have been analyzed both in statistical and in descriptive terms.

Our preliminary exploration had already answered our first question: Children do show distinct individuality in temperament in the first weeks of life, independently of their parents' handling or personality style. Our long term study has now established that the original characteristics of temperament tend to persist in most children over the years. This is clearly illustrated by two striking examples. Donald exhibited an extremely high activity level almost from birth. At three months, his parents reported, he wriggled and moved about a great deal while asleep in his crib. At six months he "swam like a fish" while being bathed. At 12 months he still squirmed constantly while he was being dressed or washed. At 15 months he was "very fast and busy"; his parents found themselves "always chasing after him." At two years he was "constantly in motion, jumping and climbing." At three he would "climb like a monkey and run like an unleashed puppy." In kindergarten his teacher reported humorously that he would "hang from the walls and climb on the ceiling." By the time he was seven Donald was encountering difficulty in school because he was unable to sit still long enough to learn anything and disturbed the other children by moving rapidly about the classroom.

Clem exemplifies a child who scored high in intensity of reaction. At four and a half months he screamed every time he was bathed, according to his parents' report. His reactions were "not discriminating—all or none." At six months during feeding he screamed "at the sight of the spoon approaching his mouth." At nine and a half months he was generally "either in a very good mood, laughing or chuckling," or else screaming. "He laughed so hard playing peekaboo he got hiccups." At two years his parents reported: "He screams bloody murder when he's being dressed." At seven they related: "When he's frustrated, as for example when he doesn't hit a ball very far, he stomps around, his voice goes up to its highest level, his eyes get red and occasionally fill with tears. Once he went up to his room when this occurred and screamed for half an hour."

Of course a child's temperament is not immutable. In the course of his development the environmental circumstances may heighten, diminish or otherwise modify his reactions and behavior. For example, behavior may become routinized in various areas so that the basic temperamental characteristics are no longer evident in these situations. Most children come to accept and even take pleasure in the bath, whatever their initial reactions may have been. The characteristics usually remain present, however, and may assert themselves in new situations even in the form of an unexpected and mystifying reaction. An illustration is the case of a 10-year-old girl who had been well adjusted to school. Entering the fifth grade, Grace was transferred from a small school to a large new one that was strongly departmentalized and much more formal. The change threw her into a state of acute fear and worry. Her parents were puzzled, because Grace had many friends and had been doing very well in her studies. On reviewing her history, however, we found that she had shown withdrawal reactions to new situations during infancy and also on entrance into kindergarten and the first and second grades. Her parents and Grace had forgotten about these early reactions, because from the third grade on she was entirely happy in school. In the light of the early history it now became apparent that Grace's fear at the transfer to the new school, confronting her with a new scholastic setup, new fellow-students and a new level of academic demand, arose from her fundamental tendency to withdraw from new situations and to be slow to adapt to them.

Not all the children in our study have shown a basic constancy of temperament. In some there have apparently been changes in certain characteristics as time has passed. We are analyzing the data in these cases to try to determine if changes in the children's life situations or in specific stresses are responsible for the apparent fluctuations in temperament. We may find that inconsistency in temperament is itself a basic characteristic in some children. When we analyzed the behavioral profiles of the children in an endeavor to find correlations among the nine individual attributes, we found that certain characteristics did cluster together. The clusters defined three general types of temperament (although some of the children did not fit into any of the three).

One type is characterized by positiveness in mood, regularity in bodily functions, a low or moderate intensity of reaction, adaptability and a positive approach to, rather than withdrawal from, new situations. In infancy these children quickly establish regular sleeping and feeding schedules, are generally cheerful and adapt quickly to new routines, new foods and new people. As they grow older they learn the rules of new games quickly, participate readily in new activities and adapt easily to school. We named this group the "easy children," because they present so few problems in care and training. Approximately 40 percent of the children in our total sample could be placed in this category.

In contrast, we found another constellation of characteristics that described "difficult children." These children are irregular in bodily functions, are usually intense in their reactions, tend to withdraw in the face of new stimuli, are slow to adapt to changes in the environment and are generally negative in mood. As infants they are often irregular in feeding and sleeping, are slow to accept new foods, take a long time to adjust to new routines or activities and tend to cry a great deal. Their crying and their laughter are characteristically loud. Frustration usually sends them into a violent tantrum. These children are, of course, a trial to their parents and require a high degree of consistency and tolerance in their up-bringing. They comprised about 10 percent of the children in our sample.

The third type of temperament is displayed by those children we call "slow to warm up." They typically have a low activity level, tend to withdraw on their first exposure to new stimuli, are slow to adapt, are somewhat negative in mood and respond to situations with a low intensity of reaction. They made up 15 percent of the population sample we studied. Hence 65 percent of the children could be described as belonging to one or another of the three categories we were able to define; the rest had mixtures of traits that did not add up to a general characterization.

Among the 141 children comprising our total sample, 42 presented behavioral problems that called for psychiatric attention. Not surprisingly, the group of "difficult children" accounted for the largest proportion of these cases, the "slow to warm up children" for the next-largest proportion and the "easy children" for the smallest proportion. About 70 percent of the "difficult children" developed behavioral problems, whereas only 18 percent of the "easy children" did so.

In general easy children respond favorably to various child-reading styles. Under certain conditions, however, their ready adaptability to parental handling may itself lead to the development of a behavioral problem. Having adapted readily to the parents' standards and expectations early in life, the child on moving into the world of his peers and school may find that the demands of these environments conflict sharply with the behavior patterns he has learned at home. If the conflict between the two sets of demands is severe, the child may be unable to make an adaptation that reconciles the double standard.

The possible results of such a dissonance are illustrated in the case of an "easy child" we call Isobel. Reared by parents who placed great value on individuality, imagination and self-expression, she developed these qualities to a high degree. When she entered school, however, her work fell far below her intellectual capabilities. She had difficulties not only in learning but also in making friends. It was found that the problems arose from her resistance to taking instruction from her teacher and to accepting her schoolmates' preferences in play. Once the nature of the conflict was recognized it was easily remedied in this case. We advised the parents to combine their encouragement of Isobel's assertions of individuality with efforts to teach her how to join constructively in activities with her teacher and schoolmates. The parents adopted this strategy, and within six months Isobel began to function well in school life.

*I*n the case of difficult children the handling problem is present from the outset. The parents must cope with the child's irregularity and the slowness with which he adapts in order to establish conformity to the family's rules of living. If the parents are inconsistent, impatient or punitive in their handling of the child, he is much more likely to react negatively than other children are. Only by exceptionally objective, consistent treatment, taking full account of the child's temperament, can he be brought to get along easily with others and to learn appropriate behavior. This may take a long time, but with skillful handling such children do learn the rules and function well. The essential requirement is that the parents recognize the need for unusually painstaking handling; tactics that work well with other children may fail for the difficult child.

For children in the "slow to warm up" category the key to successful development is allowing the child to adapt to the environment at his own pace. If the teacher or parents of such a child pressure him to move quickly into new situations, the insistence is likely to intensify his natural tendency to withdraw. On the other hand, he does need encouragement and opportunity to try new experiences. Bobby was a case in point. His parents never encouraged him to participate in anything new; they simply withdrew things he did not like. When, as an infant, he rejected a new food by letting it dribble out of this mouth, they eliminated it from his diet. When he backed away from other children in the playground, they kept him at home. By the age of 10 Bobby was living on a diet consisting mainly of hamburgers, applesauce and medium-boiled eggs, and in play he was a "loner." Any activity that required exposure to new people or new demands was distasteful or even impossible for him. Yet he was adept and took pleasure in activities he could pursue by himself and at his own speed.

*I*n general our studies indicate that a demand that conflicts excessively with any temperamental characteristics and capacities is likely to place a child under heavy and even unbearable stress. This means that parents and teachers need to recognize what a specific child can and cannot do. A child with a high activity level, for example, should not be required to sit still through an eight-hour automobile trip; frequent stops should be made to allow him to run around and give vent to his energy. A persistent child who does not like to be distracted from a project should not be expected to come running when he is called unless he has been told in advance how much time he will have before he is called.

Obviously a detailed knowledge of a child's temperamental characteristics can be of great help to parents in handling the child and avoiding the development of behavioral problems. A highly adaptable child can be expected to accept new foods without resistance and even welcome them. On the other hand, a nonadaptable, intense child may need to have the same food offered at each meal for several days until he comes to accept it; if the mother takes away a rejected food, tries it again some weeks later and again retreats in the face of protests, the child simply learns that by fussing enough he will have his way. An adaptable child who is caught sticking things into electric sockets may need only one lecture on the danger to give up this practice; an easily distractible child may merely need to have his attention diverted to some other activity; a persistent child may have to be removed bodily from the hazard.

Understanding a child's temperament is equally crucial in the school situation. His temperamental traits affect both his approach to a learning task and the way he interacts with his teacher and classmates. [Table 15.1] If the school's demands on him go against the grain of these traits, learning may be difficult indeed. Hence the teacher has a need to know not only the child's capacities for learning but also his temperamental style.

A pupil who wriggles about a great deal, plays continually with his pencils and other objects and involves himself in activities with the student next to him—in short, a child with a high activity level—obviously requires special handling. If the teacher decides the child does not want to learn and treats him accordingly, the youngster is apt to conclude that he is stupid or unlikable and react with even worse behavior. The teacher is best advised to avoid expressions of annoyance and to provide the child with constructive channels for his energy, such as running necessary errands, cleaning the blackboard and so on. Similarly, a "slow to warm up" child requires patience, encouragement and repeated exposure to a learning task until he becomes familiar with it and comfortable in attacking it. Children with the "difficult" constellation of traits of course present the most taxing problem. They respond poorly to a permissive, *laissez faire* attitude in the teacher and angrily to learning tasks they cannot master immediately. The teacher needs to be firm and patient; once the child has been tided over the period (which may be long) of learning rules or becoming familiar with a new task, he will function well and confidently. *Laissez faire* treatment is also detrimental for youngsters who are low in persistence and easily distracted from their work. Such a child will do poorly if few demands are made and little achievement is expected of him. He must be required to function up to his abilities.

Table 15.1

	"Easy"	Type of Child "Slow to Warm Up"	"Difficult"
ACTIVITY LEVEL The proportion of active periods to inactive ones.	VARIES	LOW TO MODERATE	VARIES
RHYTHMICITY Regularity of hunger, excretion, sleep and wakefulness.	VERY REGULAR	VARIES	IRREGULAR
DISTRACTIBILITY The degree to which extraneous stimuli alter behavior.	VARIES	VARIES	VARIES
APPROACH WITHDRAWAL The response to a new object or person.	POSITIVE APPROACH	INITIAL WITHDRAWAL	WITHDRAWAL
ADAPTABILITY The ease with which a child adapts to changes in his environment.	VERY ADAPTABLE	SLOWLY ADAPTABLE	SLOWLY ADAPTABLE
ATTENTION SPAN AND PERSISTENCE The amount of time devoted to an activity, and the effect of distraction on the activity.	HIGH OR LOW	HIGH OR LOW	HIGH OR LOW
INTENSITY OF REACTION The energy of response, regardless of its quality or direction.	LOW OR MILD	MILD	INTENSE
THRESHOLD OF RESPONSIVENESS The intensity of stimulation required to evoke a discernible response.	HIGH OR LOW	HIGH OR LOW	HIGH OR LOW
QUALITY OF MOOD The amount of friendly, pleasant, joyful behavior as contrasted with unpleasant, unfriendly behavior.	POSITIVE	SLIGHTLY NEGATIVE	NEGATIVE

TEMPERAMENT of a child allows him to be classified as "easy," "slow to warm up" or "difficult" according to how he rates in certain key categories in the authors' nine-point personality index. The categories are only a general guide to temperament. Of the 141 subjects 65 percent could be categorized, but 35 percent displayed a mixture of traits. Such a child might, for example, be rated "easy" in some ways and "difficult" in others.

*T*he paramount conclusion from our studies is that the debate over the relative importance of nature and nurture only confuses the issue. What is important is the interaction between the two—between the child's own characteristics and his environment. If the two influences are harmonized, one can expect healthy development of the child; if they are dissonant, behavioral problems are almost sure to ensue.

It follows that the pediatrician who undertakes to supervise the care of a newborn child should familiarize himself with his young patient's temperamental as well as physical characteristics. He will then be able to provide the parents with appropriate advice on weaning, toilet training and the handling of other needs as the child develops. Similarly, if a behavioral disorder arises, the psychiatrist will need to understand both the child's temperament and the environmental demands in conflict with it in order to find a helpful course of action. His function then will often be to guide rather than "treat" the parents. Most parents, once they are informed of the facts, can change their handling to achieve a healthier interaction with the child.

Theory and practice in psychiatry must take into full account the individual and his uniqueness: how children differ and how these differences act to influence their psychological growth. A given environment will not have the identical functional meaning for all children. Much will depend on the temperamental makeup of the child. As we learn more about how specific parental attitudes and practices and other specific factors in the environment of the child interact with specific temperamental, mental and physical attributes of individual children, it should become considerably easier to foster the child's healthy development.

Development in Infancy

The Origins of Intelligence in Children

Jean Piaget

Jean Piaget (1896–1980), perhaps the most influential of all developmental psychologists, studied children from birth through adolescence. He is, however, particularly well known for his studies of infants. Indeed, the concept whose name he coined "object permanence" is studied by every student of human development.

Piaget's text *The Origins of Intelligence in Children* was first published in French in 1936 and later in English in 1952. It inaugurated a new generation of studies in both Europe and North America on the development of infants. Although more recent researchers find fault with his methods (he primarily studied his own children) and disagree with the age-related milestones he suggested, few can find fault with the accuracy of the developmental sequence he established.

In the following excerpt from *The Origins of Intelligence in Children*, Piaget refers to six stages of development. These should not be confused with his four broad stages of development that span infancy to adolescence: sensorimotor, preoperational, concrete operational, and formal operational. The six stages he discusses may all be considered substages of the sensorimotor stage.

Key Concept: cognitive substages of the sensorimotor stage

Intelligence does not by any means appear at once derived from mental development, like a higher mechanism, and radically distinct from those which have preceded it. Intelligence presents, on the contrary, a remarkable continuity with the acquired or even inborn processes on which it depends and at the same times makes use of. Thus, it is appropriate, before analyzing intelligence as such, to find out how the formation of habits and even the exercise of the reflex prepare its appearance. . . .

The First Stage: The Use of Reflexes

If, in order to analyze the first mental acts, we refer to hereditary organic reactions, we must study them not for their own sake but merely so that we may describe *in toto* the way in which they affect the individual's behavior. We should begin, therefore, by trying to differentiate between the psychological problem of the reflexes and the strictly biological problem.

Behavior observable during the first weeks of life is very complicated, biologically speaking. At first there are very different types of reflexes involving the medulla, the bulb, the optic commissures, the ectoderm itself; moreover, from reflex to instinct is only a difference of degree. Next to the reflexes of the central nervous system

are those of the autonomic nervous system and all the reactions due to "protopathic" sensibility. There is, above all, the whole group of postural reflexes [that are important] for the beginnings of the evolution of the mind. . . . It is hard to envisage the organization of the foregoing mechanisms without giving the endocrine processes their just due as indicated by so many learned or spontaneous reactions. Physiological psychology is confronted at the present time by a host of problems which consist of determining the effects on the individual's behavior of each of these separate mechanisms. . . .

[I]t seems to us difficult at the present time to go beyond a general description when it comes to grasping the continuity between the earliest behavior of the nursling and the future intellectual behavior. That is why, although in complete sympathy with [the] attempt to identify psychic mechanisms with those of life itself, we believe we should limit ourselves to emphasizing functional identity, from the point of view of simple external behavior.

In this respect the problem which arises in connection with reactions in the first weeks is only this: How do the sensorimotor, postural, and other reactions, inherent in the hereditary equipment of the newborn child, prepare him to adapt himself to his external environment and to acquire subsequent behavior distinguished by the progressive use of experience?

The psychological problem begins to pose itself as soon as the reflexes, postures, etc., are considered no longer in connection with the internal mechanism of the living organism, but rather in their relationships to the external environment as it is subjected to the individual's activity. Let us examine, from this point of view, the various fundamental reactions in the first weeks: sucking and grasping reflexes, crying and vocalization, movements and positions of the arms, the head or the trunk, etc.

What is striking about this is that such activities from the start of their most primitive functioning, each in itself and some in relation to others, give rise to a systematization which exceeds their automatization. Almost since birth, therefore, there is "behavior" in the sense of the individual's total reaction and not only a setting in motion of particular or local automatizations only interrelated from within. In other words, the sequential manifestations of a reflex such as sucking are not comparable to the periodic starting up of a motor used intermittently, but constitute an historical development so that each episode depends on preceding episodes and conditions those that follow in a truly organic evolution. In fact, whatever the intensive mechanism of this historical process may be, one can follow the changes from the outside and describe things as though each particular reaction determined the others without intermediates. This comprises total reaction, that is to say, the beginning of psychology.

Sucking Reflexes

Let us take as an example the sucking reflexes or the instinctive act of sucking; these reflexes are complicated, involving a large number of afferent fibers of the trigeminal and the glossopharyngeal nerves as well as the efferent fibers of the facial, the hypoglossal and the masseteric nerves, all of which have as a center the bulb of the spinal cord. First here are some facts:

Observation 1. From birth sucking-like movements may be observed: impulsive movement and protrusion of the lips accompanied by displacements of the tongue, while the arms engage in unruly and more or less rhythmical gestures and the head moves laterally, etc.

As soon as the hands rub the lips the sucking reflex is released. The child sucks his fingers for a moment but of course does not know either how to keep them in his mouth or pursue them with his lips. Lucienne and Laurent, a quarter of an hour and a half hour after birth, respectively, had already sucked their hand like this: Lucienne, whose hand had been immobilized due to its position, sucked her fingers for more than ten minutes.

A few hours after birth, first nippleful of collostrum. It is known how greatly children differ from each other with respect to adaptation to this first meal. For some children like Lucienne and Laurent, contact of the lips and probably the tongue with the nipple suffices to produce sucking and swallowing. Other children, such as Jacqueline, have slower coördination: the child lets go of the breast every moment without taking it back again by himself or applying himself to it as vigorously when the nipple is replaced in his mouth. There are some children, finally, who need real forcing: holding their head, forcibly putting the nipple between the lips and in contact with the tongue, etc.

Observation 2. The day after birth Laurent seized the nipple with his lips without having to have it held in his mouth. He immediately seeks the breast when it escapes him as the result of some movement.

During the second day also Laurent again begins to make sucking-like movements between meals while thus repeating the impulsive movements of the first day: His lips open and close as if to receive a real nippleful, but without having an object. This behavior subsequently became more frequent and we shall not take it up again.

The same day the beginning of a sort of reflex searching may be observed in Laurent, which will develop on the following days and which probably constitutes the functional equivalent of the gropings characteristic of the later stages (acquisition of habits and empirical intelligence). Laurent is lying on his back with his mouth open, his lips and tongue moving slightly in imitation of the mechanism of sucking, and his head moving from left to right and back again, as though seeking an object. These gestures are either silent or interrupted by grunts with an expression of impatience and of hunger.

Observation 3. The third day Laurent makes new progress in his adjustment to the breast. All he needs in order to grope with open mouth toward final success is to have touched the breast or the surrounding teguments with his lips. But he hunts on the wrong side as well as on the right side, that is to say, the side where contact has been made.

Observation 4. Laurent at 0;0 (9) is lying in bed and seeks to suck, moving his head to the left and to the right. Several times he rubs his lips with his hand which he immediately sucks. He knocks against a quilt and a wool coverlet; each time he sucks the object only to relinquish it after a moment and begins to cry again. When he sucks his hand he does not turn away from it as he seems to do with the woolens, but the hand itself escapes him through lack of coördination; he then immediately begins to hunt again.

Observation 5. As soon as his cheek comes in contact with the breast, Laurent at 0;0 (12) applies himself to seeking until he finds drink. His search takes its bearings: immediately from the correct side, that is to say, the side where he experienced contact.

At 0;0 (20) he bites the breast which is given him, 5 cm. from the nipple. For a moment he sucks the skin which he then lets go in order to move his mouth about 2 cm. As soon as he begins sucking again he stops. In one of his attempts he touches the nipple with the outside of his lips and he does not recognize it. But, when his search subsequently leads him accidentally to touch the nipple with the mucosa of the upper lip (his mouth being wide open), he at once adjusts his lips and begins to suck.

The same day, same experiment: after having sucked the skin for several seconds, he withdraws and begins to cry. Then he begins again, withdraws again, but without crying, and takes it again 1 cm. away; he keeps this up until he discovers the nipple.

Observation 6. The same day I hold out my crooked index finger to Laurent, who is crying from hunger (but intermittently and without violence). He immediately sucks it but rejects it after a few seconds and begins to cry. Second attempt: same reaction. Third attempt: he sucks it, this time for a long time and thoroughly, and it is I who retract it after a few minutes. . . .

The Use of Reflexes

Concerning its *adaptation,* it is interesting to note that the reflex, no matter how well endowed with hereditary physiological mechanism, and no matter how stable its automatization, nevertheless needs to be used in order truly to adapt itself, and that it is capable of gradual accommodation to external reality.

Let us first stress this element of *accommodation.* The sucking reflex is hereditary and functions from birth, influenced either by diffuse impulsive movements or by an external excitant (Obs. 1); this is the point of departure. In order that a useful function may result, that is to say, swallowing, it often suffices to put the nipple in the mouth of the newborn child, but, as we know (Obs. 1), it sometimes happens that the child does not adapt at the first attempt. Only practice will lead to normal functioning. That is the first aspect of accommodation: contact with the object modifies, in a way, the activity of the reflex, and, even if this activity were oriented hereditarily to such contact, the latter is no less necessary to the consolidation of the former. This is how certain instincts are lost or certain reflexes cease to function normally, due to the lack of a suitable environment. Moreover, contact with the environment not only results in developing the reflexes, but also in coördinating them in some way. Observations 2, 3, [and] 5 . . . show how the child, who first does not know how to suck the nipple when it is put in his mouth, grows increasingly able to grasp and even to find it, first after direct touch, then after contact with any neighboring region.

How can such accommodations be explained? It seems to us difficult to invoke from birth the mechanism of acquired associations, in the limited sense of the term, or of "conditioned reflexes," both of which imply systematic training. On the contrary, the examining of these behavior patterns reveals at once the respects in which they differ from acquired associations: Whereas with regard to the latter, including conditioned reflexes, association is established between a certain perception, foreign to the realm of the reflex, and the reflex itself (for example, between a sound, a visual perception, etc., and the salivary reflex),

according to our observations, it is simply the reflex's own sensibility (contact of the lips with a foreign body) which is generalized, that is to say, brings with it the action of the reflex in increasingly numerous situations. In the case of Observations 2, 3, [and] 5 . . . , for example, accommodation consists essentially of progress in the continuity of the searching. In the beginning (Obs. 2 and 3) contact with any part of the breast whatever sets in motion momentary sucking of this region, immediately followed by crying or a desultory search, where as after several days (Obs. 5), the same contact sets in motion a groping during which the child is headed toward success. It is very interesting, in the second case, to see how the reflex, excited by each contact with the breast, stops functioning as soon as the child perceives that sucking is not followed by any satisfaction, as is the taking of nourishment (see Obs. 5 . . .), and to see how the search goes on until swallowing begins. In this regard, Observations 2 to 6 confirm that there is a great variety of kinds of accommodation. Sucking of the eider-down quilt, of the coverlet, etc., leads to rejection, that of the breast to acceptance; sucking of the skin (the child's hand, etc.) leads to acceptance if it is only a matter of sucking for the sake of sucking, but it leads to rejection (for example when it involves an area of the breast other than the nipple) if there is great hunger; the paternal index finger (Obs. 6) is rejected when the child is held against the breast, but is accepted as a pacifier, etc. In all behavior patterns it seems evident to us that learning is a function of the environment.

Surely all these facts admit of a physiological explanation which does not at all take us out of the realm of the reflex. The "irradiations," the "prolonged shocks," the "summations" of excitations and the intercoördination of reflexes probably explains why the child's searching becomes increasingly systematic, why contact which does not suffice to set the next operation in motion, does suffice in doing so a few days later, etc. Those are not necessarily mechanisms which are superposed on the reflex such as habit or intelligent understanding will be, later. But it remains no less true that the environment is indispensable to this operation, in other words, that reflex adaptation is partly accommodation. Without previous contact with the nipple and the experience of imbibing milk, it is very likely that the eider-down quilt, the wool coverlet, or the paternal index finger, after setting in motion the sucking reflex, would not have been so briskly rejected by Laurent.

But if, in reflex adaptation, allowances must be made for accommodation, accommodation cannot be dissociated from progressive *assimilation,* inherent in the very use of the reflex. In a general way, one can say that the reflex is consolidated and strengthened by virtue of its own functioning. Such a fact is the most direct expression of the mechanism of assimilation. Assimilation is revealed, in the first place, by a growing need for repetition which characterizes the use of the reflex (functional assimilation) and, in the second place, by this sort of entirely practical or sensorimotor recognition which enables the child to adapt himself to the different objects with which his lips come in contact (recognitory and generalizing assimilations). . . .

The Second Stage: The First Acquired Adaptations and the Primary Circular Reaction

The hereditary adaptations are doubled, at a given moment, by adaptations which are not innate to which they are subordinated little by little. In other words, the reflex processes are progressively integrated into cortical activity. These new adaptations constitute what are ordinarily called "acquired associations," habits or even conditioned reflexes, to say nothing of intentional movements characteristic of a third stage. Intent, which is doubtless imminent to the more primitive levels of psychological assimilation, could not, in effect, be aware of itself, and thus differentiate behavior, before assimilation through "secondary" schemata, that is to say, before the behavior patterns born of the exercise of prehension and contemporaneous with the first actions brought to bear on things. We can therefore ascribe to the present stage intentional movements as the higher limit and the first nonhereditary adaptations as the lower limit. . . .

Acquired Sucking Habits

Superimposed on the reflex behavior patterns . . . are, from the second or third month, certain forms of sucking which are unquestionably new. We shall begin by describing the two principal circular reactions—the systematic protrusion of the tongue (later with the action of saliva, of the lips, etc.), and the sucking of the thumb. These two activities will provide us with the type of that which is spontaneous acquired habit, with active assimilation and accommodation. Thereupon we shall discuss some facts concerning accommodation, commonly called "association transfers" or "sensorimotor associations" (setting in motion of sucking by various signals: position, noises, optical signals, etc.) and we shall see that these partial accommodations, however mechanical and passive they may appear to be, in reality constitute simple, isolated and abstract links of the cycles inherent in circular reaction. Finally we shall speak of certain coördinations between sucking and vision.

Here are examples of the first group of facts (circular reactions):

Observation 11. Laurent at 0;0 (30) stays awake without crying, gazing ahead with wide open eyes. He makes sucking-like movements almost continually, opening and closing his mouth in slow rhythm, his tongue constantly moving. At certain moments his tongue, instead of remaining inside his lips, licks the lower lip; the sucking recommences with renewed ardor.

Two interpretations are possible. Either at such times there is searching for food and then the protrusion of the tongue is merely a reflex inherent in the mechanism of sucking and swallowing, or else this marks the beginning of circular reaction. It seems, for the time being, that both are present. Sometimes protrusion of the tongue is accompanied by disordered movements of the arms and leads to impatience and anger. In such a case there is obviously a seeking to suck, and disappointment. Sometimes, on the other hand, protrusion of the tongue is accompanied by slow, rhythmical movements of the arms and an expression of contentment. In this case the tongue comes into play through circular reaction. . . .

The Intentional Sensorimotor Adaptations [Stages Three to Six]

The coördination of vision and prehension . . . inaugurates a new series of behavior patterns: the intentional adaptations. Unfortunately, nothing is more difficult to define than intention. Shall it be said, as is frequently done, that an act is intentional when it is determined by representation, contrary to the elementary associations in which the act is controlled by an external stimulus? But if representation is taken in the strict sense of the word, there would not then be intentional acts prior to language—that is to say, before the faculty of thinking of reality by means of signs making up the deficiency of action. Now intelligence presupposes intention. If, on the other hand, one extends the term representation so that it comprises all consciousness of meanings, intention would exist ever since the simplest associations and almost since the beginning of reflex use. Shall it be said that intention is connected with the power of evoking images and the searching for the fruit in a closed box, for instance, is an intentional act to the extent that it is determined by the representation of the fruit in the box? But, as we shall see, it appears according to all probabilities that even this kind of representations, by images and individual symbols, makes a tardy appearance. The mental image is a product of the internalization of the acts of intelligence and not a datum preliminary to these acts. Since then we see only one method of distinguishing intentional adaptation from the simple circular reactions peculiar to sensorimotor habit: this is to invoke the number of intermediaries coming between the stimulus of the act and its result. When a 2-month-old baby sucks his thumb this cannot be called an intentional act because the coördination of the hand and of sucking is simple and direct. It therefore suffices for the child to maintain, by circular reaction, the favorable movements which satisfy his need, in order that this behavior become habitual. On the other hand, when an 8-month-old child sets aside an obstacle in order to attain an objective, it is possible to call this intention, because the need set in motion by the stimulus of the act (by the object to be grasped) is only satisfied after a more or less lengthy series of intermediary acts (the obstacles to be set aside). Intention is thus determined by consciousness of desire, or of the direction of the act, this awareness being itself a function of the number of intermediary actions necessitated by the principal act. In a sense, there is therefore only a difference of degree between the elementary adaptations and the intentional adaptations. The intentional act is only a more complex totality subsuming the secondary values under the essential values and subordinating the intermediary movements or *means* to the principal steps which assign an end to the action. But, in another sense, intention involves a reversing in the data of consciousness. There is henceforth the influence of recurrent consciousness of direction impressed on the action or no longer only on its result. Consciousness arises from disadaptation and thus proceeds from the periphery to the center.

In practice, we can acknowledge—provided we bear in mind that this division is artificial and that all the transitions connect the acts of the second stage to those of the third—that intentional adaptation begins as soon as the child transcends the level of simple corporal activities (sucking, listening and making sounds, looking and grasping) and acts upon things and uses the interrelationships of objects. In effect, to the extent that the subject is limited to sucking, looking, listening, grasping, etc., he satisfies in a more or less direct way his immediate needs, and, if he acts upon things, it is simply in order to perform his own functions. In such a case it is hardly possible to speak of ends and means. The schemata serving as means become mingled with those which assign an end to the action and there is no occasion for this influence of consciousness *sui generis* [constituting a class in itself; unique] which determines intention. On the contrary, as soon as the subject, possessing the coördinated schemata of prehension, vision, etc., utilizes them in order to assimilate to himself the totality of his universe, the multiple combinations which then present themselves (by generalizing assimilation and accommodation, combined) bring with them the momentary hierarchies of ends and means; that is to say, there is the influence of consciousness of the direction of the act or of its intention.

From the theoretical point of view, intention therefore denotes the extension of the totalities and relationships acquired during the preceding stage and, by the fact of their extension, their greater dissociation into real totalities and ideal totalities in relationships of fact and relationships of value. As soon as there is intention, in effect, there is a goal to reach and means to use, consequently the influence of consciousness of values (the value or the interest of the intermediary acts serving as *means* is subordinated to that of the goal) and of the ideal (the act to be accomplished is part of an ideal totality or *goal*, in relation to the real totality of the acts already organized). Thus it may be seen that the functional categories related to the function of organization will henceforth become more precise, from the time of the global schemata of the preceding stage.

Concerning the functions of assimilation and accommodation, intentional adaptation also brings with it a more pronounced differentiation of their respective categories, ever since the relatively undifferentiated state of the first stages. Assimilation, after having proceeded as hitherto, by nearly rigid schemata (the sensorimotor schemata of sucking, prehension, etc.) will henceforth engender more mobile schemata, capable of various involvements and in which we shall find the functional equivalent of the qualitative concepts and of the quantitative relationships peculiar to reflective intelligence. With regard to accommodation, by clasping more tightly the external universe, it will clarify the space-time relationships as well as those of substance and causality, hitherto enveloped in the subject's psycho-organic activity.

In other words, we now arrive at the problem of intelligence . . . with regard to stages III to VI. Hitherto we have stayed on this side of actual intelligence. During the first stage this was self-evident, since pure reflexes were involved. Concerning the second stage it was not known how, despite the functional resemblances, to identify habit and intelligent adaptation, since it is precisely intention that separates them. This is not the place to define this structural difference which analyzing the facts alone will permit us to fathom. . . . Let us say only that the sequence of our stages corresponds in the main to the system outlined by Claparède in a remarkable article on intelligence published in 1917. To Claparède intelligence is an adaptation to new situations as opposed to reflexes and habitual associations which also constitute adaptations, either hereditary or due to personal experience, but adaptations to situations which repeat themselves. Now these new situations to which the child will have to adapt himself appear precisely when the habitual schemata, elaborated during the second stage, will be applied for the first time to the external environment in its complexity.

Furthermore, there may be distinguished, among the intentional acts which constitute intelligence, two relatively opposite types, corresponding in the main to what Claparède calls empirical intelligence and systematic intelligence. The first consists in operations controlled by the things themselves and not by deduction alone. The second consists in operations controlled from within by the consciousness of relationships and thus marks the beginning of deduction. We shall consider the first of these behavior patterns as characteristic of the stages III to V and shall make the appearance of the second behavior patterns the criterion of a sixth stage.

On the other hand, the concept of "empirical intelligence" remains a little vague as long as one does not put into effect, in the sequence of facts, some divisions intended, not to make discontinuous an actual continuity, but to permit analysis of the increasing complication of the behavior patterns. This is why we shall distinguish three stages between the beginnings of the action upon things and those of systematic intelligence: stages III to IV.

The third stage appearing with the prehension of visual objectives is characterized by the appearance of a behavior pattern which is already almost intentional, in the sense indicated before, which also foretells empirical intelligence but which nevertheless remains intermediary between the acquired association belonging to the second stage and the true act of intelligence. This is the "secondary circular reaction," that is to say, the behavior which consists in rediscovering the gestures which by chance exercised an advantageous action upon things. Such a behavior pattern, in effect, goes beyond acquired association to the extent that almost intentional searching is necessary to reproduce the movements until then performed fortuitously. But it does not yet constitute a typical act of intelligence since this searching simply consists in rediscovering that which has just been done and not in inventing again or applying the known to new circumstances: the "means" are hardly yet differentiated from the "ends" or at least they are only differentiated after the event, at the time the act is repeated.

A fourth stage begins at around 8 to 9 months and lasts until the end of the first year. It is characterized by the appearance of certain behavior patterns which are superimposed on the preceding ones and their essence is "the application of known means to new situations." Such behavior patterns differ from the preceding ones both in their functional meaning and in their structural mechanism. From the functional point of view for the first time they fully correspond to the current definition of intelligence: adaptation to new circumstances. Given a habitual goal temporarily thwarted by unforeseen obstacles, the problem is to surmount these difficulties. The simplest procedure consists in trying out different known schemata and in adjusting them to the goal pursued: in this consist the present behavior patterns. From the structural point of view they therefore constitute a combination of schemata among themselves, so that some are subordinated to others in the capacity of "means"; hence two results: a greater mobility of the schemata and a more accurate accommodation to external conditions. If this stage is to be distinguished from the preceding one with respect to the functioning of intelligence, it is to be distinguished still more with regard to the structure of objects, space and causality: it marks the beginnings of the permanence of things, of "objective" spatial "groups" and of spatial and objectified causality.

At the beginning of the second year a fifth stage makes itself manifest, characterized by the first real experimentations; hence the possibility of a "discovery of new means through active experimentation." This is the impetus of the instrumental behavior patterns and the acme of empirical intelligence.

Finally, this totality of the behavior patterns, the application of which determines the beginning of the sixth stage, will be crowned by the "invention of new means through mental combination."

Infant–Mother Attachment

Mary D. Salter Ainsworth

Mary D. Salter Ainsworth (b. 1913) received her Ph.D. from the University of Toronto in 1939. She worked as a consultant to the director of personnel selection in the Canadian Women's Army Corps and later worked with child and family researcher John Bowlby at the Tavistock Institute in London, England. She also taught at Johns Hopkins University and the University of Virginia in the United States. Like Bowlby, Ainsworth took an ethological approach to studying human development, focusing on the influences of evolution on human behavior in her subjects' natural environments.

Ainsworth is most recognized for her work in human attachment. Besides studying infants in Europe and America, she conducted research in Africa, which led to the publication of *Infancy in Uganda: Infant Care and the Growth of Love* in 1967. Her creative research methodology, particularly the "strange situation," has greatly influenced a generation of researchers in the field of human development. The "strange situation" assesses toddlers' attachment patterns by introducing the child, a parent, and a stranger into a laboratory setting. Based on a sequence of experimentally manipulated events, the child's behavior can then be reliably coded as "securely attached," "insecure avoidantly attached," or "insecure ambivalently attached." The following selection, excerpted from "Infant–Mother Attachment," *American Psychologist* (October 1979), summarizes 10 years of Ainsworth's studies on attachment.

Key Concept: patterns of attachment

Bowlby's (1969) ethological–evolutionary attachment theory implies that it is an essential part of the ground plan of the human species—as well as that of many other species—for an infant to become attached to a mother figure. This figure need not be the natural mother but can be anyone who plays the role of principal caregiver. This ground plan is fulfilled, except under extraordinary circumstances when the baby experiences too little interaction with any one caregiver to support the formation of an attachment. The literature on maternal deprivation describes some of these circumstances, but it cannot be reviewed here, except to note that research has not yet specified an acceptable minimum amount of interaction required for attachment formation.

However, there have been substantial recent advances in the areas of individual differences in the way attachment behavior becomes organized, differential experiences associated with the various attachment patterns, and the value of such patterns in forecasting subsequent development. These advances have been much aided by a standardized laboratory situation that was devised to supplement a naturalistic, longitudinal investigation of the development of infant–mother attachment in the first

year of life. This *strange situation*, as we entitled it, has proved to be an excellent basis for the assessment of such attachment in 1-year-olds (Ainsworth, Blehar, Waters, & Wall, 1978).

The assessment procedure consists of classification according to the pattern of behavior shown in the strange situation, particularly in the episodes of reunion after separation. Eight patterns were identified, but I shall deal here only with the three main groups into which they fell—Groups A, B, and C. To summarize, Group B babies use their mothers as a secure base from which to explore in the preseparation episodes; their attachment behavior is greatly intensified by the separation episodes so that exploration diminishes and distress is likely; and in the reunion episodes they seek contact with, proximity to, or at least interaction with their mothers. Group C babies tend to show some signs of anxiety even in the preseparation episodes; they are intensely distressed by separation; and in the reunion episodes they are ambivalent with the mother, seeking close contact with her and yet resisting contact or interaction. Group A babies, in sharp contrast, rarely cry in the separation episodes and, in the reunion episodes, avoid the mother, either mingling proximity-seeking and avoidant behaviors or ignoring her altogether.

Comparison of Strange-Situation Behavior and Behavior Elsewhere

Groups A, B, and C in our longitudinal sample were compared in regard to their behavior at home during the first year. Stayton and Ainsworth (1973) had identified a security–anxiety dimension in a factor analysis of fourth-quarter infant behavior. Group B infants were identified as securely attached because they significantly more often displayed behaviors characteristic of the secure pole of this dimension, whereas both of the other groups were identified as anxious because their behaviors were characteristic of the anxious pole. A second dimension was clearly related to close bodily contact, and this was important in distinguishing Group A babies from those in the other two groups, in that Group A babies behaved less positively to being held and yet more negatively to being put down. The groups were also distinguished by two behaviors not included in the factor analysis—cooperativeness and anger. Group B babies were more cooperative and less angry than either A or C babies; Group A babies were even more angry than those in Group C. Clearly, something went awry in the physical-contact interaction Group A babies had with their mothers, and as I explain below, I believe it is this that makes them especially prone to anger.

Ainsworth et al. (1978) reviewed findings of other investigators who had compared A–B–C groups of 1-year-olds in terms of their behavior elsewhere. Their findings regarding socioemotional behavior support the summary just cited, and in addition three investigations using cognitive measures found an advantage in favor of the securely attached.

Comparison of Infant Strange-Situation Behavior with Maternal Home Behavior

Mothers of the securely attached (Group B) babies were, throughout the first year, more sensitively responsive to infant signals than were the mothers of the two anxiously attached groups, in terms of a variety of measures spanning all of the most common contexts for mother–infant interaction (Ainsworth et al., 1978). Such responsiveness, I suggest, enables an infant to form expectations, primitive at first, that moderate his or her responses to events, both internal and environmental. Gradually, such an infant constructs an inner representation—or "working model" (Bowlby, 1969)—of his or her mother as generally accessible and responsive to him or her. Therein lies his or her security. In contrast, babies whose mothers have disregarded their signals, or have responded to them

belatedly or in a grossly inappropriate fashion, have no basis for believing the mother to be accessible and responsive; consequently they are anxious, not knowing what to expect of her.

In regard to interaction in close bodily contact, the most striking finding is that the mothers of avoidant (Group A) babies all evinced a deep-seated aversion to it, whereas none of the other mothers did. In addition they were more rejecting, more often angry, and yet more restricted in the expression of affect than were Group B or C mothers. Main (e.g., in press) and Ainsworth et al. (1978) have presented a theoretical account of the dynamics of interaction of avoidant babies and their rejecting mothers. This emphasizes the acute approach–avoidance conflict experienced by these infants when their attachment behavior is activated at high intensity—a conflict stemming from painful rebuff consequent upon seeking close bodily contact. Avoidance is viewed as a defensive maneuver, lessening the anxiety and anger experienced in the conflict situation and enabling the baby nevertheless to remain within a tolerable range of proximity to the mother.

Findings and interpretations such as these raise the issue of direction of effects. To what extent is the pattern of attachment of a baby attributable to the mother's behavior throughout the first year, and to what extent is it attributable to built-in differences in potential and temperament? I have considered this problem elsewhere (Ainsworth, 1979) and have concluded that in our sample of normal babies there is a strong case to be made for differences in attachment quality being attributable to maternal behavior. Two studies, however (Connell, 1976; Waters, Vaughn, & Egeland, in press), have suggested that Group C babies may as newborns be constitutionally "difficult." Particularly if the mother's personality or life situation makes it hard for her to be sensitively responsive to infant cues, such a baby seems indeed likely to form an attachment relationship of anxious quality.

Contexts of Mother–Infant Interaction

Of the various contexts in which mother–infant interaction commonly takes place, the face-to-face situation has been the focus of most recent research. By many (e.g., Walters & Parke, 1965), interaction mediated by distance receptors and behaviors has been judged especially important in the establishment of human relationships. Microanalytic studies, based on frame-by-frame analysis of film records, show clearly that maternal sensitivity to infant behavioral cues is essential for successful pacing of face-to-face interaction (e.g., Brazelton, Koslowski, & Main, 1974; Stern, 1974). Telling evidence of the role of vision, both in the infant's development of attachment to the mother and in the mother's responsiveness to the infant, comes from Fraiberg's (1977) longitudinal study of blind infants.

So persuasive have been the studies of interaction involving distance receptors that interaction involving close bodily contact has been largely ignored. The evolutionary perspective of attachment theory attributes focal importance to bodily contact. Other primate species rely on the maintenance of close mother–infant contact as crucial for infant survival. Societies of hunter–gatherers, living much as the earliest humans did, are conspicuous for very much more mother–infant contact than are western societies (e.g., Konner, 1976). Blurton Jones (1972) presented evidence suggesting that humans evolved as a species in which infants are carried by the mother and are fed at frequent intervals, rather than as a species in which infants are left for long periods, are cached in a safe place, and are fed but infrequently. Bowlby (1969) pointed out that when attachment behavior is intensely activated it is close bodily contact that is specifically required. Indeed, Bell and Ainsworth (1972) found that even with the white, middle-class mothers of their sample, the most frequent and the most effective response to an infant's crying throughout the first year was to pick up the baby. A recent analysis of our longitudinal findings (Blehar, Ainsworth, & Main, Note 1) suggests that bodily contact is at least as important a context of interaction as face-to-face is, perhaps especially in the first few months of life. Within the limits represented by our sample, however, we found that it was *how* the mother holds her baby rather than *how much* she holds him or her that affects the way in which attachment develops.

In recent years the feeding situation has been neglected as a context for mother–infant interaction, except insofar as it is viewed as a setting for purely social, face-to-face interaction. Earlier, mother's gratification or frustration of infant interest to both psychoanalytically oriented and social-learning research, on the assumption that a mother's gratification or frustration of infant instinctual drives, or her role as a secondary reinforcer, determined the nature of the baby's tie to her. Such research yielded no evidence that methods of feeding significantly affected the course of infant development, although these negative findings seem almost certainly to reflect methodological deficiencies (Caldwell, 1964). In contrast, we have found that sensitive maternal responsiveness to infant signals relevant to feeding is closely related to the security or anxiety of attachment that eventually develops (Ainsworth & Bell, 1969). Indeed, this analysis seemed to redefine the meaning of "demand" feeding—letting infant behavioral cues determine not only when feeding is begun but also when it is terminated, how the pacing of feeding proceeds, and how new foods are introduced.

Our findings do not permit us to attribute overriding importance to any one context of mother–infant interaction. Whether the context is feeding, close bodily contact, face-to-face interaction, or indeed the situation defined by the infant's crying, mother–infant interaction provides the baby with opportunity to build up expectations of the mother and, eventually, a working model of her as more or less accessible and responsive. Indeed, our findings suggest that a mother who is sensitively responsive to signals in one context tends also to be responsive to signals in other contexts.

Practical Implications for Intervention

What I have so far summarized about research findings pertaining both to contexts of interaction and to qualitative differences in infant-mother attachment has implications for parenting education, for intervention by professionals to help a mother to achieve better interaction with her baby, and for the practices of substitute caregivers. I cannot go into detail here—and indeed such detail would need to be based on much fuller reports of the relevant research than I am able to include here. Among the intervention programs with which I am familiar, some parent-child development centers have reported success in the application of our research findings in improving and sustaining the rate of development of very young children through improving the quality of mother–infant interaction (e.g., Andrews, Blumenthal, Bache, & Wiener, Note 2). Furthermore, the expert clinical interventions of Fraiberg and her associates with families at risk have focused on increasing maternal responsiveness to infant behavioral cues (e.g., Shapiro, Fraiberg, & Adelson, 1976). It may be that such intervention, although obviously expensive, provides the most effective mode of helping dyads in which the difficulty stems from deep-seated difficulties in the mother's personality, such as the aversion to bodily contact characteristic of our Group A mothers.

Using the Mother as a Secure Base from Which to Explore

Attachment theory conceives of the behavioral system serving attachment as only one of several important systems, each with its own activators, terminators, predictable outcomes, and functions. During the prolonged period of human infancy, when the protective function of attachment is especially important, its interplay with exploratory behavior is noteworthy. The function of exploration is learning about the environment—which is particularly important in a species possessing much potential for adaptation to a wide range of environments. Attachment and exploration support each other. When attachment behavior is intensely activated, a baby tends to seek proximity/contact rather than exploring; when attachment behavior is at low intensity a baby is free to respond to the pull of novelty. The presence of an attachment figure, particularly one who is believed to be accessible and responsive, leaves the baby open to stimulation that may activate exploration.

Nevertheless, it is often believed that somehow attachment may interfere with the development of independence. Our studies provide no support for such a belief. For example, Blehar et al. (Note 1) found that babies who respond positively to close bodily contact with their mothers also tend to respond positively to being put down again and to move off into independent exploratory play. Fostering the growth of secure attachment facilitates rather than hampers the growth of healthy self-reliance (Bowlby, 1973).

Response to Separation from Attachment Figures

Schaffer (1971) suggested that the crucial criterion for whether a baby has become attached to a specific figure is that he or she does not consider this figure interchangeable with any other figure. Thus, for an infant to protest the mother's departure or continued absence is a dependable criterion for attachment (Schaffer & Callender, 1959). This does not imply that protest is an invariable response to separation from an attachment figure under all circumstances; the context of the separation influences the likelihood and intensity of protest. Thus there is ample evidence, which cannot be cited here, that protest is unlikely to occur, at least initially, in the case of voluntary separations, when the infant willingly leaves the mother in order to explore elsewhere. Protest is less likely to occur if the baby is left with another attachment figure than if he or she is left with an unfamiliar person or alone. Being left in an unfamiliar environment is more distressing than comparable separations in the familiar environment of the home—in which many infants are able to build up expectations that reassure them of mother's accessibility and responsiveness even though she may be absent. Changes attributable to developmental processes affect separation protest in complex ways. Further research will undoubtedly be able to account for these shifts in terms of progressive cognitive achievements.

Major separations of days, months, or even years must be distinguished from the very brief separations, lasting only minutes, that have been studied most intensively both in the laboratory and at home. Securely attached infants may be able to tolerate very brief separations with equanimity, yet they are likely to be distressed in major separations, especially when cared for by unfamiliar persons in unfamiliar environments. Even so, Robertson and Robertson (1971) showed that sensitive substitute parenting can do much to mute separation distress and avert the more serious consequences of major separations.

Despite a steady increase in our understanding of the complexities of response to and effects of separation from attachment figures in infancy and early childhood, it is difficult to suggest clear-cut guidelines for parents and others responsible for infant and child care. So much depends on the circumstances under which separation takes place, on the degree to which the separation environment can substitute satisfactorily for home and parents, on the child's stage of development and previous experience, and on the nature of his or her relationship with attachment figures. No wonder that the issue of the separations implicit in day care is controversial. Further research is clearly needed. Meanwhile, it would seem wise for parents—if they have

a choice—to move cautiously rather than plunging into substitute-care arrangements with a blithe assumption that all is bound to go well.

Other Attachment Figures

Many have interpreted Bowlby's attachment theory as claiming that an infant can become attached to only one person—the mother. This is a mistaken interpretation. There are, however, three implications of attachment theory relevent to the issue of "multiple" attachments. First, as reported by Ainsworth (1967) and Schaffer and Emerson (1964), infants are highly selective in their choices of attachment figures from among the various persons familiar to them. No infant has been observed to have many attachment figures. Second, not all social relationships may be identified as attachments. Harlow (1971) distinguished between the infant–mother and peer–peer affectional systems, although under certain circumstances peers may become attachment figures in the absence of anyone more appropriate (see, e.g., Freud & Dann, 1951; Harlow, 1963). Third, the fact that a baby may have several attachment figures does not imply that they are all equally important. Bowlby (1969) suggested that they are not—that there is a principal attachment figure, usually the principal caregiver, and one or more secondary figures. Thus a hierarchy is implied. A baby may both enjoy and derive security from all of his or her attachment figures but, under certain circumstances (e.g., illness, fatigue, stress), is likely to show a clear preference among them.

In recent years there has been a surge of interest in the father as an attachment figure, as reported elsewhere in this issue. Relatively lacking is research into attachments to caregivers other than parents. Do babies become attached to their regular baby-sitters or to caregivers in day-care centers? Studies by Fleener (1973), Farran and Ramey (1977), and Ricciuti (1974) have suggested that they may but that the preference is nevertheless for the mother figure. Fox (1977) compared the mother and the *metapelet* as providers of security to kibbutz-reared infants in a strange situation, but surely much more research is needed into the behavior of infants and young children toward caregivers as attachment figures in the substitute-care environment.

Consequences of Attachment

A number of investigators, including Main (1973, Note 3), Matas, Arend, and Sroufe (1978), and Waters, Wittman, and Sroufe (in press), having assessed the quality of 1-year-olds' attachment, have followed children through to ascertain whether this assessment bears a significant relationship to later behavioral measures in the second, third, or even sixth year of life. We (Ainsworth et al., 1978) have reviewed these investigations in some detail; only a brief summary can be given here.

In comparison with anxiously attached infants, those who are securely attached as 1-year-olds are later more cooperative with and affectively more positive as well as less aggressive and/or avoidant toward their mothers and other less familiar adults. Later on, they emerge as more competent and more sympathetic in interaction with peers. In free-play situations they have longer bouts of exploration and display more intense exploratory interest, and in problem-solving situations they are more enthusiastic, more persistent, and better able to elicit and accept their mothers' help. They are more curious, more self-directed, more ego-resilient—and they usually tend to achieve better scores on both developmental tests and measures of language development. Some studies also reported differences between the two groups of anxiously attached infants, with the avoidant ones (Group A) continuing to be more aggressive, noncompliant, and avoidant, and the ambivalent ones (Group C) emerging as more easily frustrated, less persistent, and generally less competent.

Conclusion

It is clear that the nature of an infant's attachment to his or her mother as a 1-year-old is related both to earlier interaction with the mother and to various aspects of later development. The implication is that the way in which the infant organizes his or her behavior toward the mother affects the way in which he or she organizes behavior toward other aspects of the environment, both animate and inanimate. This organization provides a core of continuity in development despite changes that come with developmental acquisitions, both cognitive and socioemotional.

This is not to insist that the organization of attachment is fixed in the first year of life and is insensitive to marked changes in maternal behavior or to relevant life events occurring later on. Nor is it implied that attachments to figures other than the mother are unimportant as supplementing or compensating for anxieties in infant–mother attachment—although too little is yet known about how various attachments relate together to influence the way in which infants organize their perception of and approach to the world. Despite the need for further research, however, the yield of findings to date provides relevant leads for policies, education in parenting, and intervention procedures intended to further the welfare of infants and young children.

Notes

1. Blehar, M. C., Ainsworth, M. D. S., & Main, M. *Mother–infant interaction relevant to close bodily contact.* Monograph in preparation, 1979.
2. Andrews, S. R., Blumenthal, J. B., Bache, W. L., III, & Weiner, G. *Fourth year report: New Orleans Parent-Child Development Center.* Unpublished document, March 1975. (Available from Susan R. Andrews, 6917 Glenn Street, Metairie, Louisiana 70003.)
3. Main, M., & Londerville, S. B. *Compliance and aggression in toddlerhood: Precursors and correlates.* Paper in Preparation. 1979.

References

Ainsworth, M. D. S. *Infancy in Uganda: Infant care and the growth of love.* Baltimore, Md.: Johns Hopkins Press, 1967.

Ainsworth, M. D. S. Attachment as related to mother–infant interaction. In J. S. Rosenblatt, R. A. Hinde, C. Beer, & M. Busnel (Eds.), *Advances in the study of behavior* (Vol. 9). New York: Academic Press, 1979.

Ainsworth, M. D. S., & Bell, S. M. Some contemporary patterns of mother–infant interaction in the feeding situation. In A. Ambrose (Ed.), *Stimulation in early infancy.* London: Academic Press, 1969.

Ainsworth, M. D. S., Blehar, M. C., Waters, E., & Wall, S. *Patterns of attachment: A psychological study of the strange situation.* Hillsdale, N.J.: Erlbaum, 1978.

Bell, S. M., & Ainsworth, M. D. S. Infant crying and maternal responsiveness. *Child Development,* 1972, *43,* 1171–1190.

Blurton Jones, N. G. Comparative aspects of mother–child contact. In N. G. Blurton Jones (Ed.), *Ethological studies of child behavior.* London: Cambridge University Press, 1972.

Bowlby, J. *Attachment and loss: Vol. 1. Attachment.* New York: Basic Books, 1969.

Bowlby, J. *Attachment and loss: Vol. 2. Separation: Anxiety and anger.* New York: Basic Books, 1973.

Brazelton, T. B., Koslowski, B., & Main, M. The origins of reciprocity: The early mother–infant interaction. In M. Lewis & L. A. Rosenblum (Eds.), *The effect of the infant on its caregiver.* New York: Wiley, 1974.

Caldwell, B. M. The effects of infant care. In M. L. Hoffman & L. W. Hoffman (Eds.), *Review of child development research* (Vol. 1). New York: Russell Sage Foundation, 1964.

Connell, D. B. *Individual differences in attachment: An investigation into stability, implications, and relationships to the structure of early language development.* Unpublished doctoral dissertation, Syracuse University, 1976.

Farran, D. C., & Ramey, C. T. Infant day care and attachment behavior toward mother and teachers. *Child Development,* 1977, *48,* 1112–1116.

Fleener, D. E. Experimental production of infant-maternal attachment behaviors. *Proceedings of the 81st Annual Convention of the American Psychological Association,* 1973, *8,* 57–58. (Summary)

Fox, N. Attachment of kibbutz infants to mother. *Child Development,* 1977, *48,* 1228–1239.

Fraiberg, S. *Insights from the blind.* New York: Basic Books, 1977.

Freud, A., & Dann, S. An experiment in group upbringing. *Psychoanalytic Study of the Child,* 1951, *6,* 127–168.

Harlow, H. F. The maternal affectional system. In B. M. Foss (Ed.), *Determinants of infant behaviour* (Vol. 2) New York: Wiley, 1963.

Harlow, H. F. *Learning to love.* San Francisco: Albion, 1971.

Konner, M. J. Maternal care, infant behavior, and development among the !Kung. In R. B. Lee & I. DeVore (Eds.), *Kalahari hunter–gatherers.* Cambridge, Mass.: Harvard University Press, 1976.

Main, M. *Exploration, play, and level of cognitive functioning as related to child-mother attachment.* Unpublished doctoral dissertation, Johns Hopkins University, 1973.

Main, M. Avoidance in the service of proximity. In K. Immelmann, G. Barlow, M. Main, & L. Petrinovich (Eds.), *Behavioral development: The Bielefeld Interdisciplinary Project.* New York: Cambridge University Press, in press.

Matas, L., Arend, R. A., & Sroufe, L. A. Continuity of adaptation in the second year: The relationship between quality of attachment and later competence. *Child Development*, 1978, *49*, 547–556.

Ricciuti, H. N. Fear and the development of social attachments in the first year of life. In M. Lewis & L. A. Rosenblum (Eds.), *The origins of fear*. New York: Wiley, 1974.

Robertson, J. & Robertson, J. Young children in brief separation: A fresh look. *Psychoanalytic Study of the Child*, 1971, *26*, 264–315.

Schaffer, H. R. *The growth of sociability*. London: Penguin Books, 1971.

Schaffer, H. R., & Callender, W. M. Psychological effects of hospitalization in infancy. *Pediatrics*, 1959, *25*, 528–539.

Schaffer, H. R., & Emerson, P. E. The development of social attachments in infancy. *Monographs of the Society for Research in Child Development*, 1964, *3* (Serial No. 94).

Shapiro, V., Fraiberg, S., & Adelson, E. Infant-parent psychotherapy on behalf of a child in a critical nutritional state. *Psychoanalytic Study of the Child*, 1976, *31*, 461–491.

Stayton, D. J., & Ainsworth, M. D. S. Individual differences in infant responses to brief, everyday separations as related to other infant and maternal behaviors. *Developmental Psychology*, 1973, *9*, 226–235.

Stern, D. N. Mother and infant at play: The dyadic interaction involving facial, vocal, and gaze behaviors. In M. Lewis & L. A. Rosenblum (Eds.), *The effect of the infant on its caregiver*. New York: Wiley, 1974.

Walters, R. H., & Parke, R. D. The role of the distance receptors in the development of social responsiveness. In L. P. Lipsitt & C. C. Spiker (Eds.), *Advances in child development and behavior*. New York: Academic Press, 1965.

Waters, E., Vaughn, B. E., & Egeland, B. R. Individual differences in infant–mother attachment relationships at age one: Antecedents in neonatal behavior in an urban economically disadvantaged sample. *Child Development*, in press.

Waters, E., Wittman, J., & Sroufe, L. A. Attachment, positive affect, and competence in the peer group: Two studies in construct validation. *Child Development*, in press.

Development in Early Childhood

The Co-ordination of Perspectives

Jean Piaget, Bärbel Inhelder, and Edith Mayer

Developmental psychologist Jean Piaget (1896–1980) and his student Bärbel Inhelder (b. 1913) collaborated on child development research in Switzerland for over 40 years. In the 1940s Albert Einstein encouraged Piaget to study the child's emerging understanding of time, velocity, and movement. Piaget did so, and the texts *The Child's Conception of Time* (1946) and *The Child's Conception of Movement and Speed* (1946) were the result. Piaget then became further interested in children's understanding of "space" in general. Professor of human development Howard Gardner would call this "spatial intelligence," or the comprehension of the relations of objects in three-dimensional space.

Piaget and Inhelder's text *The Child's Conception of Space* was first published in France in 1948 and then in England in 1956. The following excerpt is taken from chapter 8 of that book, "The Co-ordination of Perspectives," which was written in collaboration with Edith Mayer, and it includes Piaget's famous "three-mountain" research methodology. The excerpt refers to one of his most famous developmental concepts, "egocentrism" (or "egocentric constructions"). In Piaget's work the term *egocentrism* does not refer to selfishness but rather to the cognitive limitation of children in Stage II (the preoperational stage) of not being able to take the perspective of others. This inability has important implications for parents, teachers of the young, and child-care workers: we would not want to think of children as being willfully selfish if they are simply cognitively immature.

Piaget never made strong claims concerning the age ranges of his stages. In fact, he emphasized that age is not a stage, that children differ significantly in their rate of cognitive development. Some children have the ability to take others' perspectives by age 4 or 5; others cannot until age 7 or 8.

Key Concept: egocentrism and perspective taking

*P*erspective appears at a relatively late stage in the child's psychological development. In this respect our experiments merely confirm what had already been demonstrated through direct observation of children's drawing. . . . '[I]ntellectual realism' is not superseded by 'visual realism' until about the age of 8 or 9. Not until then does the child draw things 'as he really sees them', according to his perspective as an actual observer. Well known though this may be, it is nevertheless surprising, and for two good reasons.

First, assuming that projective relations are geometrically more complex than topological relations, and assuming that their construction requires a set of axioms equivalent to those of euclidean geometry, then in terms of psychological development one might expect the operations leading to their elaboration to appear somewhat in advance, and to be promoted by experience of perspective in visual perception. But on the contrary, what we actually find is that the order of psychological development runs concurrent with that of axiomatic, theoretical construction, perspective appearing relatively late in the child's approach to geometrical problems. It does not appear, and this is the interesting point, until he reaches the stage where he begins to form co-ordinate systems or systems of reference. Hence perspective would appear to depend upon operational concepts rather than upon familiarity born of intuition and experience.

Second, and this is even more puzzling, since the relationships inherent to perspective are already operative in the realm of direct perception they might be taken to express the child's own viewpoint in the simplest and most immediate fashion. Yet we know very well that the child's outlook is at first completely egocentric and tends to change appearances which are in fact purely relative to his own perception and activity, into false or spurious absolutes.

The question therefore arises as to why the child is so slow to master simple perspective relations and only does so when he is able to co-ordinate a number of possible points of view. The answer is that a perspective system entails his relating the object to his own viewpoint, as one of which he is fully conscious. Here as elsewhere, to become conscious of one's own viewpoint involves distinguishing it from other viewpoints, and by the same token, co-ordinating it with them. Thus it is evident that the development of perspectives requires a comprehensive, global construct, one which enables objects to be linked together in a co-ordinate system, and viewpoints to be linked by projective relations corresponding to various potential observers.

The experiments performed thus far have dealt only with perspective or projection for successive positions of a single object, whether seen by the child or by an imaginary observer. We must now proceed to examine the perspective of a group of objects as envisaged by an observer from different positions, or alternatively by a number of observers. The experiments which follow have two aims. Firstly, to study the construction of a global system linking together a number of perspectives. Secondly, to examine the relationships which the child establishes between his own viewpoint and those of other observers. These experiments involve multiple perspectives of the sort which it is possible to imagine when standing before a mountain massif, or group of mountains which can be seen from various different positions.

The problem is therefore no longer one concerned simply with changes in apparent shape and size of objects, but mainly with the positions of objects relative to one another and to various observers (or the same observer in different positions). Hence we shall be concerned chiefly with the relations of before-behind, left-right, relations of within two of the three dimensions operative in imaginary perspectives.

Now although these are based on . . . topological relations, . . . it is obvious that the introduction of the observer's own viewpoint serves to differentiate them from the latter. In a system of topological relations, the expressions 'to the left' or 'to the right' can only refer to alternative directions of travel along a linear series. They remain purely arbitrary so far as the viewpoint of an observer is concerned (this is well illustrated by the way in which some of the younger children reverse a series as if it were seen in a mirror). In a projective system, however, 'left' and 'right' are relative to the viewpoint of the observer, and the type of problem posed by the perspectives of a group of mountains involves several objects and several observers at the same time. It will be seen to depend, therefore, on a global projective system directly comparable to the type of co-ordinate system required in constructing maps or plans in the realm of euclidean geometry. . . .

Technique and General Results

A pasteboard model, one metre square and from twelve to thirty centimetres high, was made to represent three mountains (see Fig. 18.1). From his initial position in front of the model (A) the child sees a green mountain occupying the foreground a little to his right. The summit of this mountain is topped by a little house. To his left he sees a brown mountain, higher than the green one and slightly to its rear. This mountain is distinguished not only by its colour but also by having a red cross at the summit. In the background stands the highest of the three mountains, a grey pyramid whose peak is covered in snow. From position C (opposite position A) a zigzag path can be seen running down the side of the green mountain, while from position B (to the right of the model, relative to position A) a little rivulet is seen to descend the brown mountain. Each mountain is painted in a single colour, except for the snow cap of the grey mountain, and the only reference points are those described.

The children are also shown a collection of ten pictures, measuring 20x28 cm. These represent the mountains seen from different viewpoints and are painted in the same colours as the model. They are clearly distinguishable and are large enough for particular features such as the cross, the house and the snow-capped peak to be easily visible. The children are also given three pieces of cardboard, shaped and coloured the same as each of the mountains, and these may be arranged to represent the mountains as seen in a given perspective.

Finally, the apparatus includes a wooden doll 2 or 3 cm. in height. The head of the doll is a plain wooden ball with no face painted on it so that the child can ignore the doll's line of sight and need only consider its position. This doll is put in a number of different places and the child's task is to discover what perspective the doll will 'see' in each of the different positions. It is not the child who moves around the group of mountains—except to check his answers—but the doll which is supposed to be doing the travelling. The child has the problem of trying to imagine, and to reconstruct by a process of inference, the changes in perspective that will accompany the doll's movements, or the different positions which the doll must occupy to suit the various perspectives.

For this purpose we employed three separate but complementary methods of questioning the child. Firstly, the child is given the three pieces of shaped cardboard and asked to reconstruct the kind of 'snapshot' which could be taken of the group of mountains from position A, laying the pieces in appropriate positions on the table. Next, the doll is put at position C and the child asked to make the kind of picture which the doll, or he himself, could take from that position. This procedure is repeated for positions B and D. After this the child is told to sit at B (or C or D) and asked to show with the pieces of cardboard, the picture he could take from there. He is also asked to reconstruct the picture he has already made from A or other positions he has occupied previously. With older children it is of course possible to arrange the doll in more complicated positions in order to differentiate the perspectives more clearly. Conversely, with the younger children, the emphasis is laid more on the child's own

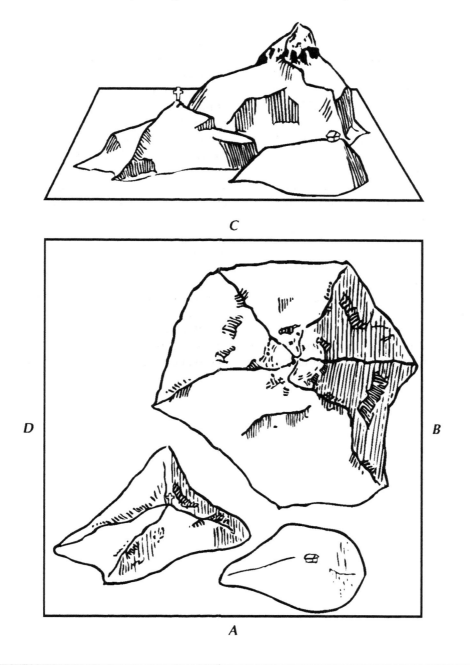

C

D

B

A

Figure 18.1   The Three Mountains

changes of position and on the co-ordination of his own changing perspectives.

In the second type of experiment we no longer ask the child to construct imaginary snapshots of the mountains, but show him the set of pictures, asking him to pick out the one which is most suited to the view seen by the doll. As a rule, all the ten pictures are shown at the same time, though naturally the questions only deal with four or five positions to avoid boredom and routine answers.

The third experiment is the converse of the second. Instead of trying to find the picture which corresponds to the position of the doll, the child selects one of the pictures

and then decides what position the doll would have to occupy to take a snapshot similar to it.

These experiments were carried out on a hundred children, 21 between 4 and 6;6 years, 30 between 6;7 and 8 years, 33 between 8 and 9;6 years, and 16 between 9;6 and 12 years. The results may be classified as follows.

[In the following paragraphs, the authors refer to stages of child development that were developed in greater detail in the original text. Stage II is the preoperational stage, so named because the child cannot yet perform logical operations upon objects and thus cannot coordinate two perspectives at once. In Substage IIA the child is not yet developed enough to

understand someone else's perspective. In Substage IIB the child begins to understand and realize that others do have a different viewpoint, but the child is unable to successfully take that viewpoint. Stage III is Piaget's concrete operations stage, during which the child is able to coordinate two perspectives at once and is able to take the perspective of others.—Eds.]

Throughout Stage II the child distinguishes hardly or not at all between his own viewpoint and that of other observers (represented by the doll in different positions). At Substage IIA Method (1) for instance, each time the doll is moved the child makes a new picture with his bits of cardboard as if to reproduce the observer's point of view. Nevertheless, when examined, each of these pictures turns out to be the same. They all show the mountains from a single point of view, that of the child himself. During Substage IIB the child shows some attempt at discrimination but usually relapses into the egocentric constructions of Substage IIA.

Throughout Substage IIA Method (2) also results in the choice of a picture corresponding to the child's own viewpoint, or else in a random choice indicating that, so far as the child is concerned, all the pictures are equally suitable for all points of view, so long as they show three mountains. Conversely, Method (3) shows a complete lack of discrimination between different positions of the doll in relation to the different pictures. The doll is placed anywhere at random or simply left in the same place all the time, because the child thinks the doll can see the three mountains from any position, regardless of perspective. During Substage IIB, Methods (2) and (3) reveal the child engaged in an attempt to separate the various points of view. But, as he fails to relate the relevant factors in the correct way his efforts are doomed to failure.

Stage III, on the other hand (7–8 to 11–12 years), shows a progressive discrimination and co-ordination of perspectives. At Substage IIIA (averaging 7–8 to 9 years) certain relationships are varied with changes in the position of the observer, but there is still no comprehensive co-ordination of viewpoints. This is not achieved until Substage IIIB (about 9–10 years), at which point the mastery of simple perspective is complete (as has already been seen) and perspective has begun to appear in drawing.

The Genetic Roots of Thought and Speech

L. S. Vygotsky

L. S. Vygotsky (1896–1934) is generally considered the greatest Russian developmental psychologist. He earned a degree in law from Moscow University, but he also studied such disparate topics as linguistics, psychology, general social science, literature, and philosophy. Following graduation he took employment teaching psychology at a teacher's college in western Russia. This work brought him in contact with children with developmental and perceptual disabilities. His compassion for these children led him to focus on cognitive developmental psychology in his search to help them fulfill their potential. Later, Vygotsky accepted a position at the Moscow Institute of Psychology. He was an authentic Marxist, aiming to help construct the new socialist state through a radical new psychology. Unfortunately, he died of tuberculosis at the young age of 38, only 10 years into his systematic research in developmental psychology.

Vygotsky's *Thought and Language*, published posthumously in Russia in 1934, was too radical for the guardians of Soviet doctrine and was suppressed from 1936 to 1956; it was first published in English in 1962. The following excerpt comes from chapter 4, "The Genetic Roots of Thought and Speech," of *Thought and Language*. In this selection, "genetic" means developmental, or emergent, not simply hereditary.

Of focal concern to many psychologists is the development of inner speech. Early in his career, Jean Piaget put forth that inner speech arose as egocentrism decreased. Behaviorists argued that "inner speech" was simply nonobservable slight movements of the muscles related to speaking. Vygotsky, however, taking the notion of "consciousness" seriously, viewed inner speech as the internalization of human dialogue, which differed significantly from the approaches of both Piaget and the behaviorists.

Key Concept: inner speech

No matter how we approach the controversial problem of the relationship between thought and speech, we shall have to deal extensively with *inner speech*. Its importance in all our thinking is so great that many psychologists, [John] Watson among others, even identify it with thought—which they regard as inhibited, soundless speech. But psychology still does not know how the change from overt to inner speech is accomplished, or at what age, by what process, and why it takes place.

Watson says that we do not know at what point of their speech organization children pass from overt to whispered and then to inner speech because that problem has been studied only incidentally. Our own researches lead us to believe that Watson poses the problem incorrectly. There are no valid reasons to assume that inner speech develops in some mechanical way through a gradual decrease in the audibility of speech (whispering).

It is true that Watson mentions another possibility: "Perhaps," he says, "all three forms develop simultaneously" [1, p. 322]. This hypothesis seems to us as unfounded

from the genetic [developmental, not hereditary] point of view as the sequence: loud speech, whisper, inner speech. No objective data reinforce that *perhaps*. Against it testify the profound dissimilarities between external and inner speech, acknowledged by all psychologists including Watson. There are no grounds for assuming that the two processes, so different *functionally* (social as opposed to personal adaptation) and *structurally* (the extreme, elliptical economy of inner speech, changing the speech pattern almost beyond recognition), may be *genetically* parallel and concurrent. Nor (to return to Watson's main thesis) does it seem plausible that they are linked together by whispered speech, which neither in function nor in structure can be considered a transitional stage between external and inner speech. It stands between the two only phenotypically, not genotypically.

Our studies of whispering in young children fully substantiate this. We have found that structurally there is almost no difference between whispering and speaking aloud; functionally, whispering differs profoundly from inner speech and does not even manifest a tendency toward the characteristics typical of the latter. Furthermore, it does not develop spontaneously until school age, though it may be induced very early: Under social pressure, a three-year-old may, for short periods and with great effort, lower his voice or whisper. This is the one point that may seem to support Watson's view.

While disagreeing with Watson's thesis, we believe that he has hit on the right methodological approach: To solve the problem, we must look for the intermediate link between overt and inner speech.

We are inclined to see that link in the child's egocentric speech, described by [Jean] Piaget, which, besides its role of accompaniment to activity and its expressive and release functions, readily assumes a planning function, i.e., turns into thought proper quite naturally and easily.

If our hypothesis proves to be correct, we shall have to conclude that speech is interiorized psychologically before it is interiorized physically. Egocentric speech is inner speech in its functions; it is speech on its way inward, intimately tied up with the ordering of the child's behavior, already partly incomprehensible to others, yet still overt in form and showing no tendency to change into whispering or any other sort of half-soundless speech.

We should then also have the answer to the question of *why* speech turns inward. It turns inward because its function changes. Its development would still have three stages—not the ones Watson found, but these: external speech, egocentric speech, inner speech. We should also have at our disposal an excellent method for studying inner speech "live," as it were, while its structural and functional peculiarities are being shaped; it would be an objective method since these peculiarities appear while speech is still audible, i.e., accessible to observation and measurement.

Our investigations show that speech development follows the same course and obeys the same laws as the development of all the other mental operations involving the use of signs, such as counting or mnemonic memorizing. We found that these operations generally develop in four stages. The first is the primitive or natural stage, corresponding to preintellectual speech and preverbal thought, when these operations appear in their original form, as they were evolved at the primitive level of behavior.

Next comes the stage which we might call "naïve psychology," by analogy with what is called "naïve physics"—the child's experience with the physical properties of his own body and of the objects around him, and the application of this experience to the use of tools: the first exercise of the child's budding practical intelligence.

This phase is very clearly defined in the speech development of the child. It is manifested by the correct use of grammatical forms and structures before the child has understood the logical operations for which they stand. The child may operate with subordinate clauses, with words like *because, if, when,* and *but,* long before he really grasps causal, conditional, or temporal relations. He masters syntax of speech before syntax of thought. Piaget's studies proved that grammar develops before logic and that the child learns relatively late the mental operations corresponding to the verbal forms he has been using for a long time.

With the gradual accumulation of naïve psychological experience, the child enters a third stage, distinguished by external signs, external operations that are used as aids in the solution of internal problems. That is the stage when the child counts on his fingers, resorts to mnemonic aids, and so on. In speech development it is characterized by egocentric speech.

The fourth stage we call the "in growth" stage. The external operation turns inward and undergoes a profound change in the process. The child begins to count in his head, to use "logical memory," that is, to operate with inherent relationships and inner signs. In speech development this is the final stage of inner, soundless speech. There remains a constant interaction between outer and inner operations, one form effortlessly and frequently changing into the other and back again. Inner speech may come very close in form to external speech or even become exactly like it when it serves as preparation for external speech—for instance, in thinking over a lecture to be given. There is no sharp division between inner and external behavior, and each influences the other.

In considering the function of inner speech in adults after the development is completed, we must ask whether in their case thought and linguistic processes are necessarily connected, whether the two can be equated. . . . [A]s in the case of animals and of children, we must answer "No."

Schematically, we may imagine thought and speech as two intersecting circles. In their overlapping parts, thought and speech coincide to produce what is called verbal thought. Verbal thought, however, does not by any means include all forms of thought or all forms of speech. There is a vast area of thought that has no direct relation to speech. The thinking manifested in the use of tools belongs in this area, as does practical intellect in general. Furthermore, investigations by psychologists of the Wuerzburg school have demonstrated that thought can function without any word images or speech movements detectable through self-observation. The latest experiments show also that there is no direct correspondence between inner speech and the subject's tongue or larynx movements.

Nor are there any psychological reasons to derive all forms of speech activity from thought. No thought process may be involved when a subject silently recites to himself a poem learned by heart or mentally repeats a sentence supplied to him for experimental purposes—Watson notwithstanding. Finally, there is "lyrical" speech prompted by emotion. Though it has all the earmarks of speech, it can scarcely be classified with intellectual activity in the proper sense of the term.

We are therefore forced to conclude that fusion of thought and speech, in adults as well as in children, is a phenomenon limited to a circumscribed area. Nonverbal thought and nonintellectual speech do not participate in this fusion and are affected only indirectly by the processes of verbal thought. . . .

We shall now summarize our investigation of inner speech. . . . [W]e considered several hypotheses, and we came to the conclusion that inner speech develops through a slow accumulation of functional and structural changes, that it branches off from the child's external speech simultaneously with the differentiation of the social and the egocentric functions of speech, and finally that the speech structures mastered by the child become the basic structures of his thinking.

This brings us to another indisputable fact of great importance: Thought development is determined by language, i.e., by the linguistic tools of thought and by the sociocultural experience of the child. Essentially, the development of inner speech depends on outside factors; the development of logic in the child, as Piaget's studies have shown, is a direct function of his socialized speech. The child's intellectual growth is contingent on his mastering the social means of thought, that is, language.

We can now formulate the main conclusions to be drawn from our analysis. If we compare the early development of speech and of intellect—which . . . develop along separate lines both in animals and in very young children—with the development of inner speech and of verbal thought, we must conclude that the later stage is not a simple continuation of the earlier. *The nature of the development itself changes,* from biological to sociohistorical. Verbal thought is not an innate, natural form of behavior but is determined by a historical-cultural process and has specific properties and laws that cannot be found in the natural forms of thought and speech. Once we acknowledge the historical character of verbal thought, we must consider it subject to all the premises of historical materialism, which are valid for any historical phenomenon in human society. It is only to be expected that on this level the development of behavior will be governed essentially by the general laws of the historical development of human society.

The problem of thought and language thus extends beyond the limits of natural science and becomes the focal problem of historical human psychology, i.e., of social psychology.

Reference

Watson, J., *Psychology from the Standpoint of a Behaviorist.* Philadelphia and London, G. B. Lippincott, 1919.

Social Participation Among Pre-School Children

Mildred B. Parten

Mildred B. Parten was a researcher affiliated with the Institute of Child Welfare at the University of Minnesota. She referred to her particular research interest as "genetic sociology," which is now more commonly termed "social development." Most of us have fond memories of "play" during our early childhood years. We can remember watching others play, being alone in play, playing alongside others, and actively playing games. As students of human development, however, we might ask ourselves, Is there an actual development sequence of social relationships during play?

Parten carefully studied this question during the 1920s by observing 42 children at play. The results of her study were published in 1932 in "Social Participation Among Pre-School Children," *The Journal of Abnormal and Social Psychology*, from which the following selection has been taken. Are the stages of play that she identified still valid today? Research following Parten's model was performed 40 years later, and it was found that the sequence of stages was still common but that American children were spending less time interacting socially during play. Do you have a hypothesis concerning why that is?

Key Concept: stages of play

$\mathcal{G}$enetic [developmental, not hereditary] Sociology is as yet a little developed field of science. Investigators of social behavior have overlooked the period when adjustment to the group is first acquired and practiced. In so doing, they have ignored a source that ought to contribute not only to the explanation of child behavior, but to the understanding of adult group habits which persist from childhood. By the time individuals have acquired their "human nature," their overt group responses are determined by such a multiplicity of factors such as customs, mores, traditions, social controls, past experience in groups, emotions and native equipment, that many scientists have despaired of ever finding any uniformities in their behavior. The genetic approach to the study of social motivation and adjustment promises to reveal group behavior which is only slightly affected 148 by these complex social factors. The reactions of children are more or less spontaneous and overt and therefore perceptible to investigators.

Most of the investigations on the genesis of social behavior that have been made up to the present time are to be found in the psychological and educational rather than in the sociological literature.

Description of Subjects and of Method of Observation

This investigation was carried on in the Nursery School of the Institute of Child Welfare at the University of Minnesota. The applicability of the findings of this study to children as a whole is a function of the similarity of the subjects studied to children in general. In so far as these individuals are representative children, and if the sample is sufficient, the generalizations should hold true. . . .

The 42 children observed were given intelligence tests which . . . seem to indicate that their average mental ability is above normal, although the I.Q.'s range from 81 to 145. The occupations of the fathers are representative of the economic groups of the city of Minneapolis, except for the fact that there is an over-weighting with children from the professional classes. The children were from mixed national stock and came from families where the number of children ranged from one to five.

Period of Observation

The observations extended from October 26, 1926, to June 10, 1927, with the majority of the observations during the months from January to April. The records from October to January were made when the technique of observing was being developed. During May and June the records were not kept daily because weather conditions permitted the children to play outside and it was thought that elements might enter into outside play which did not exist in indoor play. To complete records, however, some observations on outdoor play were made for subjects who entered the nursery school late in the year.

In order to provide a minimum of variation in the conditions of observation, the investigation was carried on at the same hour every day that the children were in the nursery school. The hour selected for observation was a morning period from 9:30 to 10:30 during the free-play period. At this hour every child is permitted to play with any toys he wishes and with any children, or with none at all, as he desires. The teachers make relatively few suggestions to the children, but are in sight of the children in order to help settle any problems that may arise. The sandboxes are opened at the beginning of the hour, the kiddie-kars are placed in the gymnasium upstairs, and practically all toys are accessible to the children without assistance from adults in the room. Since there are not enough toys of every type to supply each child, there is a ruling that the child who gets a toy first, may play with it until he leaves it, or in the case of the swings and large apparatus, the children must take turns. A few activities are directed by adults during this hour, such as painting water-color pictures, washing dolls' clothes, or making valentines; but in no case are the children solicited to join in these activities. If they do join, it is of their own volition.

There are about two assistants or teachers to every room. Occasionally there are four or five observers who sit quietly near the door, and who do not speak to anyone except to nod a reply to the questions from the children. As a rule, the players are quite oblivious to the presence of adults and pursue their activities as if no grown-ups were around.

Categories of Social Participation

Two aspects of social participation may be considered, *extensity,* or the number of social contacts made by an individual, and *intensity,* or the kind of groups participated in and the rôle of the individual in those groups. The number of social contacts may be measured by recording the number of different groups in which a child played. Such a record, however, fails to bring out the differences in social participation between the child who is actively playing in a group and one who is merely

an accidental member. Intensity of participation may be determined in two ways: first, by the extent of group integration, i.e., whether the group is organized in such a way that certain duties and responsibilities are demanded of its members, or whether it is only a congregation of independent individuals; and second, by the status of the individual in the group, i.e., whether or not he is helping to shape the plans and activities of the group, i.e., that is to say, his leadership.

After several weeks of preliminary observation of the children at play the extensity and group integration were combined in such a way that a scale of social participation with rigidly defined categories was worked out. One child, for example, did not seem to be playing at all. He usually stood in the middle of the room, pulling at a handkerchief which was tied to his blouse. His head dropped from one shoulder to the other. If asked what he wanted to do, he would merely shake his head; if a toy were placed in front of him, he would not look at it. This type of behavior was called *unoccupied,* although the child was really playing in the manner designated by Stern as the play limited to the child's own body. In order not to confuse this type of play with solitary play, unoccupied behavior was defined as follows:

> *Unoccupied behavior*—The child apparently is not playing, but occupies himself with watching anything that happens to be of momentary interest. When there is nothing exciting taking place, he plays with his own body, gets on and off chairs, just stands around, follows the teacher, or sits in one spot glancing around the room.

Closely related to the unoccupied behavior is the play in which the child observes a group of children playing, but he himself does not overtly enter into the play activity. He is an *onlooker.* Such behavior was described as follows:

> *Onlooker*—The child spends most of his time watching the other children play. He often talks to the children whom he is observing, asks questions, or gives suggestions, but does not overtly enter into the play himself. This type differs from the unoccupied in that the onlooker is definitely observing particular groups of children rather than anything that happens to be exciting. The child stands or sits within speaking distance of the group so that he can see and hear everything that takes place.

A third type of play behavior is that which is usually called playing alone or *solitary play.* Contrary to general opinion there is no clear-cut distinction between group and solitary play. This is particularly true when the play space available for thirty-six children is too meager to permit them to get out of speaking or hearing distance of one another. For this reason, in borderline cases, a purely arbitrary distinction was used to discriminate between group and non-group play. It was decided that a child who played with toys different from those of the children within speaking distance of himself, and one who centered his interest upon his own play, making no effort to get close to and speak to other children, was playing alone. This play was defined thus:

Solitary independent play—The child plays alone and independently with toys that are different from those used by the children within speaking distance and makes no effort to get close to other children. He pursues his own activity without reference to what others are doing.

Closely related to such individual play is a type of group play which was called:

Parallel activity—The child plays independently, but the activity he chooses naturally brings him among other children. He plays with toys that are like those which the children around him are using, but he plays with the toy as he sees fit, and does not try to influence or modify the activity of the children near him. He plays *beside* rather than *with* the other children. There is no attempt to control the coming or going of children in the group.

A common example of this type of play may be observed in the group who congregate around the sandbox. Several children stand close to one another around the sandbox, each child going after and using the toys with which he wishes to play in the sand (usually cups). Children come and go all the time, but those remaining at the sandbox pay no attention to the movements of others; they are absorbed in their own activities. This type of play is not solitary play, yet it is independent play in a group. To what extent children choose to play with toys because they bring them into physical proximity to other children one can not observe; only the overt facts, not the motives, are observable. Suffice it to say that parallel play better resembles group play, and is a more socialized form of play than solitary independent play.

Two other types of group play were *associative* play and *coöperative* or *organized supplementary play*. Associative play is group play in which there is an overt recognition by the group members of their common activity, interests, and personal associations. Organized supplementary play is the most highly organized group activity in which appears the elements of division of labor, group censorship, centralization of control in the hands of one or two members, and the subordination of individual desire to that of the group. Associative play is a less well organized form of the group activity in which the children play with one another, while organized supplementary play is the type in which the efforts of one child are supplemented by those of another for the attainment of a final goal. They were characterized as follows:

Associative play—The child plays with other children. The conversation concerns the common activity; there is a borrowing and loaning of play material; following one another with trains or wagons; mild attempts to control which children may or may not play in the group. All the members engage in similar if not identical activity; there is no division of labor, and no organization of the activity of several individuals around any material goal or product. The children do not subordinate their individual interests to that of the group; instead each child acts as he wishes. By his conversation with the other children one can tell that his interest is primarily in his associations, not in his activity. Occasionally, two or three children are engaged in no activity of any duration, but are merely doing whatever happens to draw the attention of any of them.

Coöperative or organized supplementary play—The child plays in a group that is organized for the purpose of making some material product, or of striving to attain some competitive goal, or of dramatizing situations of adult and group life, or of playing formal games. There is a marked sense of belonging or of not belonging to the group. The control of the group situation is in the hands of one or two of the members who direct the activity of the others. The goal as well as the method of attaining it necessitates a division of labor, taking of different rôles by the various group members and the organization of activity so that the efforts of one child are supplemented by those of another.

To illustrate the difference between parallel, associative and organized supplementary play, the sandbox situation may be cited.

Sandbox Situation

Parallel activity—Several children are engaged in filling cups in the sandbox. Each child has his own cup and fills it without reference to what the other children are doing with their cups. There is very little conversation about what they are making. No one attempts to tell who may or may not come to the sandbox, so children are coming and going all the time. Occasionally one finds a child who remains at the sandbox during the entire period. The children play *beside* rather than *with* one another.

Associative play—The children begin to borrow one another's cups, they explain why they need two cups; they advise and offer sand to one another. They call a child to the sandbox, and ask those present to make room for him. The others may or may not move over, depending upon their own wishes. No child or children dictate what the various children shall make, but each makes whatever he pleases. Someone may suggest that they all make a road but in that case each child makes his own road, or none at all, as he chooses, and the other children do not censor him. There is much conversation about their common activity.

Organized supplementary play—One child suggests that they are all making supper. Soon the various family rôles are assigned or adopted and the children speak about their shares in preparing the meal. Domination by one or more of the children occurs, one child being informed that he can't cook because he's the baby. The group becomes closed to some children and open to others, depending upon the wishes of the leaders. The children are criticized by one another when they do not play their rôles correctly. They are not permitted to leave the sandbox unless it is known what they are going to do next.

Imitation of Film-Mediated Aggressive Models

Albert Bandura, Dorothea Ross, and Sheila A. Ross

Albert Bandura was born in Canada in 1925. He earned his bachelor's degree at the University of British Columbia and his Ph.D. at the University of Iowa. He has taught psychology at Stanford University since 1953. Bandura initially worked within the behaviorist paradigm, and his work on "observational learning" through "vicarious reinforcement" substantially modified the traditional direct reinforcement theories of behaviorism. He is considered the premier researcher on modeling and observational learning, which he initially summarized in his classic text *Social Learning Theory* (Prentice Hall, 1977). Bandura's own search for truth in psychology led him even further afield from behaviorism. His focus on the internal cognitive events that mediate behavior led to his magnum opus, *Social Foundations of Thought and Action: A Social Cognitive Theory* (Prentice Hall, 1986). Additionally, his published research on human aggression and self-efficacy are some of the best known works in those areas of social psychology.

The following excerpt is taken from "Imitation of Film-Mediated Aggressive Models," *Journal of Abnormal and Social Psychology* (1963), which details research performed in collaboration with Dorothea Ross and Sheila A. Ross and which illustrates Bandura's concepts of modeling and observational learning. It also deals with a critically important societal question, one that many parents and teachers wonder about: Does watching violent television programs lead children to commit violence?

When interpreting the study's statistical results, keep in mind that a probability level less than .05 ($p < .05$) indicates a statistically significant difference among the scores for the experimental groups and the control group (or between the boys and the girls in this study). A probability level less than .01 ($p < .01$) gives one even more confidence in the results ($p < .05$ means that there are 5 chances in 100 that there is not a true difference between groups; $p < .01$ means that there is only 1 chance in 100 that there is not a true difference between groups; $p < .001$ means that there is only 1 chance in 1,000 that there is not a true difference between groups).

Key Concept: observational learning, modeling, and aggression

In a test of the hypothesis that exposure of children to film-mediated aggressive models would increase the probability of Ss' [Subjects—i.e., children] aggression to subsequent frustration, 1 group of experimental Ss observed real-life aggressive models, a 2nd observed these same models portraying aggression on film, while a 3rd group viewed a film depicting an aggressive cartoon character. Following the exposure treatment, Ss were mildly frustrated and tested for the amount of imitative and nonimitative aggression in a different experimental setting. The overall results provide evidence for both the facilitating and the modeling influence of film-mediated aggressive stimulation. In addition, the findings reveal that the effects of such exposure are to some extent a function of the sex of the model, sex of the child, and the reality cues of the model. . . .

A recent incident (San Francisco Chronicle, 1961) in which a boy was seriously knifed during a re-enactment of a switchblade knife fight the boys had seen the previous evening on a televised rerun of the James Dean movie, *Rebel Without a Cause*, is a dramatic illustration of the possible imitative influence of film stimulation. Indeed, anecdotal data suggest that portrayal of aggression through pictorial media may be more influential in shaping the form aggression will take when a person is instigated on later occasions, than in altering the level of instigation to aggression.

In an earlier experiment (Bandura & Huston, 1961), it was shown that children readily imitated aggressive behavior exhibited by a model in the presence of the model. A succeeding investigation (Bandura, Ross, & Ross, 1961), demonstrated that children exposed to aggressive models generalized aggressive responses to a new setting in which the model was absent. The present study sought to determine the extent to which film-mediated aggressive models may serve as an important source of imitative behavior.

Aggressive models can be ordered on a reality-fictional stimulus dimension with real-life models located at the reality end of the continuum, nonhuman cartoon characters at the fictional end, and films portraying human models occupying an intermediate position. It was predicted, on the basis of saliency and similarity of cues, that the more remote the model was from reality, the weaker would be the tendency for subjects to imitate the behavior of the model. . . .

To the extent that observation of adults displaying aggression conveys a certain degree of permissiveness for aggressive behavior, it may be assumed that such exposure not only facilitates the learning of new aggressive responses but also weakens competing inhibitory responses in subjects and thereby increases the probability of occurrence of previously learned patterns of aggression. It was predicted, therefore, that subjects who observed aggressive models would display significantly more aggression when subsequently frustrated than subjects who were equally frustrated but who had no prior exposure to models exhibiting aggression.

Method

The subjects were 48 boys and 48 girls enrolled in the Stanford University Nursery School. They ranged in age from 35 to 69 months, with a mean age of 52 months.

Two adults, a male and a female, served in the role of models both in the real-life and the human film-aggression condition, and one female experimenter conducted the study for all 96 children.

General Procedure

Subjects were divided into three experimental groups and one control group of 24 subjects each. One group of experimental subjects observed real-life aggressive models, a second group observed these same models portraying aggression on film, while a third group viewed a film depicting an aggressive cartoon character. The experimental groups were further subdivided into male and female subjects so that half the subjects in the two conditions involving human models were exposed to same-sex models, while the remaining subjects viewed models of the opposite sex.

Following the exposure experience, subjects were tested for the amount of imitative and nonimitative aggression in a different experimental setting in the absence of the models.

The control group subjects had no exposure to the aggressive models and were tested only in the generalization situation.

Subjects in the experimental and control groups were matched individually on the basis of ratings of their aggressive behavior in social interactions in the nursery school. The experimenter and a nursery school teacher rated the subjects on four five-point rating scales which measured the extent to which subjects displayed physical aggression, verbal aggression, aggression toward inanimate objects, and aggression inhibition. The latter scale, which dealt with the subjects' tendency to inhibit aggressive reactions in the face of high instigation, provided the measure of aggression anxiety. Seventy-one percent of the subjects were rated independently by both judges so as to permit an assessment of interrater agreement. The reliability of the composite aggression score, estimated by means of the Pearson product-moment correlation, was .80. . . .

Experimental Conditions

Subjects in the Real-Life Aggressive condition were brought individually by the experimenter to the experimental room and the model, who was in the hallway outside the room, was invited by the experimenter to come and join in the game. The subject was then escorted to one corner of the room and seated at a small table which contained potato prints, multicolor picture stickers, and colored paper. After demonstrating how the subject could design pictures with the materials provided, the experimenter escorted the model to the opposite corner of the room which contained a small table and chair, a tinker toy set, a mallet, and a 5-foot inflated Bobo doll. The experimenter explained that this was the model's play area and after the model was seated, the experimenter left the experimental room.

The model began the session by assembling the tinker toys but after approximately a minute had elapsed, the model turned to the Bobo doll and spent the remainder of the period aggressing toward it with highly novel responses which are unlikely to be performed by children independently of the observation of the model's behavior. Thus, in addition to punching the Bobo doll, the model exhibited the following distinctive aggressive acts which were to be scored as imitative responses:

The model sat on the Bobo doll and punched it repeatedly in the nose.

The model then raised the Bobo doll and pommeled it on the head with a mallet.

Following the mallet aggression, the model tossed the doll up in the air aggressively and kicked it about the room. This sequence of physically aggressive acts was repeated approximately three times, interspersed with verbally aggressive responses such as, "Sock him in the nose . . . ," "Hit him down . . . ," "Throw him in the air . . . ," "Kick him . . . ," and "Pow."

Subjects in the Human Film-Aggression condition were brought by the experimenter to the semi-darkened experimental room, introduced to the picture materials, and informed that while the subjects worked on potato prints, a movie would be shown on a screen, positioned approximately 6 feet from the subject's table. The movie projector was located in a distant corner of the room and was screened from the subject's view by large wooden panels.

The color movie and a tape recording of the sound track was begun by a male projectionist as soon as the experimenter left the experimental room and was shown for a duration of 10 minutes. The models in the film presentations were the same adult males and females who participated in the Real-Life condition of the experiment. Similarly, the aggressive behavior they portrayed in the film was identical with their real-life performances.

For subjects in the Cartoon Film-Aggression condition, after seating the subject at the table with the picture construction material, the experimenter walked over to a television console approximately 3 feet in front of the subject's table, remarked, "I guess I'll turn on the color TV," and ostensibly tuned in a cartoon program. The experimenter then left the experimental room. The cartoon was shown on a glass lens screen in the television set by means of a rear projection arrangement screened from the subject's view by large panels. . . .

In both film conditions, at the conclusion of the movie the experimenter entered the room and then escorted the subject to the test room.

Aggression Instigation

In order to differentiate clearly the exposure and test situations subjects were tested for the amount of imitative learning in a different experimental room which was set off from the main nursery school building.

The degree to which a child has learned aggressive patterns of behavior through imitation becomes most evident when the child is instigated to aggression on later occasions. Thus, for example, the effects of viewing the movie, *Rebel Without a Cause*, were not evident until the boys were instigated to aggression the following day, at which time they re-enacted the televised switchblade knife fight in considerable detail. For this reason, the children in the experiment, both those in the control group, and those who were exposed to the aggressive models, were mildly frustrated before they were brought to the test room.

Following the exposure experience, the experimenter brought the subject to an anteroom which contained a varied array of highly attractive toys. The experimenter explained that the toys were for the subject to play with, but, as soon as the subject became sufficiently involved with the play material, the experimenter remarked that these were her very best toys, that she did not let just anyone play with them, and that she had decided to reserve these toys for some other children. However, the subject could play with any of the toys in the next room. The experimenter and the subject then entered the adjoining experimental room. . . .

Test for Delayed Imitation

The experimental room contained a variety of toys, some of which could be used in imitative or nonimitative aggression, and others which tended to elicit predominantly nonaggressive forms of behavior. The aggressive toys included a 3-foot Bobo doll, a mallet and peg board, two dart guns, and a tether ball with a face painted on it which hung from the ceiling. The nonaggressive toys, on the other hand, included a tea set, crayons and coloring paper, a ball, two dolls, three bears, cars and trucks, and plastic farm animals. . . .

The subject spent 20 minutes in the experimental room during which time his behavior was rated in terms of predetermined response categories by judges who observed the session through a one-way mirror in an adjoining observation room. The 20-minute session was divided in 5-second intervals by means of an electric interval timer, thus yielding a total number of 240 response units for each subject. . . .

Results

The mean imitative and nonimitative aggression scores for subjects in the various experimental and control groups are presented in Table 21.1.

Since the distributions of scores departed from normality and the assumption of homogeneity of variance could not be made for most of the measures, the Freidman two-way analysis of variance by ranks was employed for testing the significance of the obtained differences.

Total Aggression

The mean total aggression scores for subjects in the real-life, human film, cartoon film, and the control groups are 83, 92, 99, and 54 respectively. The results of the analysis of variance performed on these scores reveal that the main effect of treatment conditions is significant ($Xr^2 = p < .05$), confirming the prediction that exposure of subjects to aggressive models increases the probability that subjects will respond aggressively when instigated on later occasions. Further analyses of pairs of scores by means of the Wilcoxon matched-pairs signed-ranks test show that subjects who viewed the real-life models and the film-mediated models do not differ from each other in total aggressiveness but all three experimental groups expressed significantly more aggressive behavior than the control subjects. . . .

Influence of Sex of Model and Sex of Child

In order to determine the influence of sex of model and sex of child on the expression of imitative and nonimitative aggression, the data from the experimental groups were combined and the significance of the differences between groups was assessed by *t* tests for uncorrelated means. In statistical comparisons involving relatively

Table 21.1 Mean Aggression Scores for Subgroups of Experimental and Control Subjects

| | Experimental Groups | | | | | |
| | Real-life Aggressive | | Human Film Aggressive | | Cartoon Film Aggressive | Control Group |
Response Category	F Model	M Model	F Model	M Model		
Total aggression						
Girls	65.8	57.3	87.0	79.5	80.9	36.4
Boys	76.8	131.8	114.5	85.0	117.2	72.2
Imitative aggression						
Girls	19.2	9.2	10.0	8.0	7.8	1.8
Boys	18.4	38.4	34.3	13.3	16.2	3.9
Mallet aggression						
Girls	17.2	18.7	49.2	19.5	36.8	13.1
Boys	15.5	28.8	20.5	16.3	12.5	13.5
Sits on Bobo doll*						
Girls	10.4	5.6	10.3	4.5	15.3	3.3
Boys	1.3	0.7	7.7	0.0	5.6	0.6
Nonimitative aggression						
Girls	27.6	24.9	24.0	34.3	27.5	17.8
Boys	35.5	48.6	6.8	31.8	71.8	40.4
Aggressive gun play						
Girls	1.8	4.5	3.8	17.6	8.8	3.7
Boys	7.3	15.9	12.8	23.7	16.6	14.3

*This response category was not included in the total aggression score.

skewed distributions of scores the Mann-Whitney U test was employed.

Sex of subjects had a highly significant effect on both the learning and the performance of aggression. Boys, in relation to girls, exhibited significantly more total aggression ($t = 2.69$, $p < .01$), more imitative aggression ($t = 2.82$, $p < .005$), more aggressive gun play ($z = 3.38$, $p < .001$), and more nonimitative aggressive behavior ($t = 2.98$, $p < .005$). Girls, on the other hand, were more inclined than boys to sit on the Bobo doll but refrained from punching it ($z = 3.47$, $p < .001$).

The analyses also disclosed some influences of the sex of the model. Subjects exposed to the male model, as compared to the female model, expressed significantly more aggressive gun play ($z = 2.83$, $p < .005$). The most marked differences in aggressive gun play ($U = 9.5$, $p < .001$), however, were found between girls exposed to the female model ($M = 2.9$) and males who observed the male model ($M = 19.8$). Although the overall model difference in partially imitative behavior, Sits on Bobo, was not significant, Sex x Model subgroup comparisons yielded some interesting results. Boys who observed the aggressive female model, for example, were more likely to sit on the Bobo doll without punching it than boys who viewed the male model ($U = 33$, $p < .05$). Girls reproduced the nonaggressive component of the male model's aggressive pattern of behavior (i.e., sat on the doll without punching it) with considerably higher frequency than did boys who observed the same model

($U = 21.5$, $p < .02$). The highest incidence of partially imitative responses was yielded by the group of girls who viewed the aggressive female model ($M = 10.4$), and the lowest values by the boys who were exposed to the male model ($M = 0.3$). This difference was significant beyond the .05 significance level. These findings, along with the sex of child and sex of model differences reported in the preceding sections, provide further support for the view that the influence of models in promoting social learning is determined, in part, by the sex appropriateness of the model's behavior (Bandura et al., 1961)....

Discussion

The results of the present study provide strong evidence that exposure to filmed aggression heightens aggressive reactions in children. Subjects who viewed the aggressive human and cartoon models on film exhibited nearly twice as much aggression than did subjects in the control group who were not exposed to the aggressive film content....

Filmed aggression, not only facilitated the expression of aggression, but also effectively shaped the form of the subjects' aggressive behavior. The finding that children modeled their behavior to some extent after the film characters suggests that pictorial mass media, particularly television, may serve as an important source of social behavior. In fact, a possible generalization of responses originally learned in the television situation to the experimental film may account for the significantly greater amount of aggressive gun play displayed by subjects in the film condition as compared to subjects in the real-life and control groups. It is unfortunate that the qualitative features of the gun behavior were not scored since subjects in the film condition, unlike those in the other two groups, developed interesting elaborations in gun play (for example, stalking the imaginary opponent, quick drawing, and rapid firing), characteristic of the Western gun fighter.

References

Bandura, A., & Huston, Aletha C. Identification as a process of incidental learning. *J. abnorm. soc. Psychol.*, 1961, **63**, 311–318.

Bandura, A., Ross, Dorothea, & Ross, Sheila A. Transmission of aggression through imitation of aggressive models. *J. abnorm. soc. Psychol.*, 1961, **63**, 575–582.

San Francisco Chronicle. "James Dean" knifing in South City. *San Francisco Chron.*, March 1, 1961, 6.

Child Care Practices Anteceding Three Patterns of Preschool Behavior

Diana Baumrind

Diana Baumrind (b. 1927) studied at Hunter College and at the University of California, Berkeley, where she earned her Ph.D. in 1951. Although certified and licensed to practice psychology, she has spent most of her career as a researcher of human development. She has held various project directorships at Berkeley, mostly concentrating on contextual issues in family socialization. She is best known for her work on describing parental styles of child care and discipline and how those styles differentially influence child behavior.

It is universally agreed that parents (primary caregivers) have the biggest influence on the development of their children. One of the most frequently asked questions in courses on developmental psychology and human development is, What is the best way to raise my (current or future) son or daughter? To answer this question as a social scientist, one must reliably identify several forms or styles of parenting, observe the behavior of children subjected to those parenting styles, and compare the results. This is just what Baumrind did. Her research is discussed in the following selection, taken from "Child Care Practices Anteceding Three Patterns of Preschool Behavior," *Genetic Psychology Monographs* (1967).

Key Concept: parenting styles

Introduction

The major objective of the present investigation is to study systematically childrearing practices associated with competence in the young child. In order to do this a group of preschool children were identified who were self-reliant, self-controlled, explorative, and content (Pattern I in this investigation). The childrearing practices of their parents were contrasted with those of parents whose children were discontent, withdrawn, and distrustful (Pattern II), and those of parents whose children had little self-control or self-reliance and tended to retreat from novel experiences (Pattern III). Multiple assessment procedures were used to measure parental control, maturity demands, clarity of communication, and warmth. Observations were made in natural and structured settings and data obtained on parents and children independently.

The conceptual approach to parent-child relations from which the study proceeds starts with the assumption that the physical, cognitive, and social development of middle-class preschool children in America is largely a function of parental childrearing practices. With varying degrees

of consciousness and conscientiousness, parents create their children psychologically as well as physically. The child's energy level, his willingness to explore and will to master his environment, and his self-control, sociability, and buoyancy are set not only by genetic structure but by the regimen, stimulation, and kind of contact provided by his parents. The child's inherent cognitive potential can be fully developed by a rich, complex environment or inhibited by inadequate and poorly timed stimulation. The young child learns from his parents how to think as well as how to talk, how to interpret and use his experience, how to control his reactions, and how to influence other people. Children learn from their parents how to relate to others, whom to like and emulate, whom to avoid and derogate, how to express affiliation and animosity, and when to withhold response. The parents' use of reinforcement, whether punishment or reward, alters the child's behavior and affects his future likes and dislikes. Parents differ in the degree to which they wish to influence their children, and they differ in their effectiveness as teachers and models. Some parents attempt to maximize and others to minimize the direct influence that they have upon their children. Some parents enjoy prolonged and intense contact and others are discomforted by such contact. Parents differ in their ability to communicate clearly with their children and in their desire to reason with and listen to the ideas and objections of their offspring. They vary in the frequency and kinds of demands that they make of their children. Some parents require of their preschool children that they participate in household chores, or that they care for themselves and their rooms, or that they control their feelings, while others seek to prolong the early period of dependency, immaturity, and spontaneous expression of feelings.

The parent variables assess the childrearing practices described above, and were selected for their theoretical importance as predictors of competence in preschool children. A great deal of attention has been given in the past to the negative effects on children of too much control. The disciplinary variables selected for study reflected this particular bias. An effort was made in this investigation to define the control variables separately from the restrictive variables and then to study the interaction of control with nurturance rather than restrictiveness with nurturance.

Subjects

Selection of Subjects

Subjects were 32 three- and four-year-olds chosen from among children enrolled at the Child Study Center, Institute of Human Development, University of California, Berkeley during the Fall semester of 1961.

The 110 children enrolled at the Child Study Center were assessed along five dimensions: namely, self-control, approach-avoidance tendency, self-reliance, subjective mood, and peer affiliation. In conferences attended by nursery school teachers and the observer staff, each dimension of child behavior was given concrete meaning by reference to relevant time sample categories and illustrated by instances of actual observed behavior. After 14 weeks of observation, the children in the four participating nursery school groups were ranked on each dimension by their nursery school teacher and the observing psychologist. Where the nursery school teacher and psychologist disagreed about the placement of a child, the disagreement was resolved by conference or the child was disqualified. A respectful relationship existed between nursery school staff and the team of psychologists, each group of whom had the opportunity to observe the children from a different perspective and thus contribute to the discussion in important ways and on an equal footing. Fifty-two children, who received among the five highest or among the five lowest rankings on two or more dimensions, after conference, composed the first pool of potential subjects. These children were further observed in a laboratory setting where they were exposed to standardized stimuli. For example, the children were presented by a psychologist with three puzzles graded in difficulty

so that each child experienced easy success, probable success, and certain failure. Their responses to success and failure were observed and rated by the testing psychologist and another psychologist who in each case had also observed and ranked the children in the nursery school setting. The psychologist responsible for initial selection of the child had the opportunity then to see the child function in a second and entirely different type of setting. In order for the child to remain in the study, the observing psychologist's ratings of the child in the two settings had to concur and to be confirmed by the psychologist who presented the children with the structured stimuli. By using multiple assessment procedures, groups of children with clear-cut, stable patterns of interpersonal attributes were obtained.

All children who were reliably rated over settings and had one of the patterns of high and low scores designated . . . were used as subjects. A total of 32 subjects met these criteria. The three patterns of children were selected in order that a set of hypotheses concerning the interacting effects of parental control, parental maturity demands, parent child communication, and parental nurturance could be tested. Children who were ranked high on mood, self-reliance, and approach or self-control were designated as Pattern I ($N = 13$). Children who were ranked low on the peer affiliation and mood dimensions and were not ranked 164 high on the approach dimension were designated as Pattern II ($N = 11$). Children who were ranked low on self-reliance and low on self-control or approach were designated as Pattern III ($N = 8$). . . .

Child Behavior Dimensions

The five dimensions of child behavior used in establishing pattern membership were chosen to assess aspects both of socialized behavior and independent behavior.

Self-Control

Self-control is defined as the tendency, in a consistent and reliable fashion, to suppress, redirect, inhibit, or in other ways control the impulse to act, in those situations where self-restraint is appropriate. In order for an instance of self-restraint to be treated as an index of self-control, the child must be motivated to engage in an act and there must be adaptive reasons for restraint in the form of an adult prohibition or a safety rule.

Aspects of self-control assessed were (*a*) obedience to school rules that conflict with an action that the child is motivated to perform, under circumstances where such prohibitions are known to the child; (*b*) ability to sustain a work effort; (*c*) capacity to wait his turn in play with other children or in use of washroom facilities; (*d*) ability to restrain those expressions of excitement or anger that would be disruptive or destructive to the peer group; and (*e*) low variability of self-control as shown by absence of explosive emotional expression or swings between high and low control.

Approach-Avoidance Tendency

Approach-Avoidance tendency measures the extent to which the child reacts to stimuli that are novel, stressful, exciting, or unexpected, by approaching these stimuli in an explorative and curious fashion (contrasted to avoiding these stimuli or becoming increasingly anxious when challenged to approach them).

Aspects of approach assessed were (a) vigor and involvement with which child reacts to his normal environment; (b) preference for stimulating activities, such as rough and tumble games or climbing and balancing; (c) interest in exploring the potentialities of a new environment (noted in particular when the child is invited to come to the laboratory to participate in the structured observation); (d) tendency to seek out experiences with challenge (e.g., tasks which are new for him, or cognitive problems at the upper limits of his ability); and (e) tendency to attack an obstacle to a goal rather than retreat from the goal.

Subjective Mood (Buoyant-Dysphoric)

This dimension refers to the predominant affect expressed by the child with regard to the degree of pleasure and zest shown. A buoyant mood is demonstrated behaviorally by happy involvement in nursery school activities. If the child is outgoing, he may appear lively and perhaps aggressively good-humored. If less outgoing, the child may appear contemplative and privately engrossed, in a contented, secure manner. A dysphoric mood is expressed by anxious, hostile, and unhappy peer relations and low involvement in nursery school activities. If the child is outgoing he may appear angry, punishing, and obstructive, when dysphoric. If less outgoing, the child may appear fearful, bored, or subdued.

Self-Reliance

Self-reliance refers to the ability of the child to handle his affairs in an independent fashion relative to other children his age. As this variable is defined, realistic help-seeking may be regarded as an aspect of self-reliance rather than dependency when the child actively searches for help in order to perform a task too difficult for him to accomplish alone. The child rated high in self-reliance, however, does not seek help as a way of relating to others or of avoiding effort, but as a means of achieving a goal or learning a new technique.

Aspects of self-reliance assessed were (a) ease of separation from parents; (b) matter-of-fact rather than dependent manner of relating to nursery school teachers, especially when seeking help; (c) willingness to be alone at times; (d) pleasure expressed in learning how to master new tasks; (e) resistance to encroachment of other children; (f) leadership interest and ability; and (g) interest expressed in making decisions and choices which affect him.

Peer Affiliation

This dimension refers to the child's ability and desire to express warmth toward others of his own age.

Aspects assessed were (a) expressions of trust in peers and expectation of being treated by them in an affiliative manner; (b) expressions of affection congruent with the particular peer relationship; (c) cooperative engagement in group activities; and (d) absence of sadistic, hostile, or unprovoked aggressive behavior toward playmates.

Parent Behavior Dimensions

. . . The dimensions studied are parental control, parental maturity demands, parent-child communication, and parental nurturance. The dimensions of parent-child interaction were assessed during home visits, structured observation, and interviews. The individual variables that defined the dimensions operationally are described. The operational definitions of each dimension appear beneath the conceptual definition and consist of the component variables listed under Home Visit Sequence Analysis (HVSA) and Summary Ratings for the Structured Observation (SRSO). . . .

Parental Control

The term parental control refers to the socializing functions of the parent: that is, to those parental acts that are intended to shape the child's goal-oriented activity, modify his expression of dependent, aggressive, and playful behavior, and promote internalization of parental standards. Parental control as defined here is not a measure of restrictiveness, punitive attitudes, or intrusiveness. Parental control included such variables as consistency in enforcing directives, ability to resist pressure from the child, and willingness to exert influence upon the child. . . .

Parental Maturity Demands

Maturity demands refer both to the pressures put upon the child to perform at least up to ability in intellectual, social, and emotional spheres (independence-training) and leeway given the child to make his own decisions (independence-granting). . . .

Parent-Child Communication

By clarity of parent-child communication is meant the extent to which the parent uses reason to obtain compliance, solicits the child's opinions and feelings, and uses open rather than manipulative techniques of control. . . .

Parental Nurturance

The term nurturance is used to refer to the caretaking functions of the parent: that is, to those parent acts and attitudes that express love and are directed at guaranteeing the child's physical and emotional well-being.

Nurturance is expressed by warmth and involvement. By warmth is meant the parent's personal love and compassion for the child expressed by means of sensory stimulation, verbal approval, and tenderness of expression and touch. By involvement is meant pride and pleasure in the child's accomplishments, manifested by words of praise and interest, and conscientious protection of the child's welfare. (We speak of the child's welfare from the parent's perspective.) . . .

Conceptual Approach

The propositions upon which the study hypotheses are based will be presented in this section. A general statement of the expected related effects of parental control, parental maturity demands, parent-child communication, and parental nurturance is as follows: parents who are both controlling and demanding (referred to as nonpermissive), but also nurturant and communicative, should generate in their children self-reliant, self-assertive, and self-controlled (Pattern I) behavior; parents who are nonpermissive and non-nurturant should generate moderately self-reliant and self-controlled, but also dysphoric and disaffiliative (Pattern II), behavior; and parents who are noncontrolling and nondemanding (permissive) should promote dependence, avoidance of stress, and low self-control (Pattern III) behavior. . . .

Proposition A: Nonpermissive, nurturant parents are more effective reinforcing agents for their children than are nonpermissive, nonnurturant or permissive, nurturant parents. . . .

Proposition B: Nonpermissive, nurturant parents will effectively model behavior that is self-assertive (approach-oriented and self-reliant) and affiliative. . . .

Proposition C: Low maturity demands will result in low self-reliance, especially if the parent is nurturant. . . .

Proposition D: High maturity demands will result in higher aspirations, greater self-reliance, and a more buoyant attitude when the parents are nurturant than when they are nonnurturant. . . .

Proposition E: Clarity of communication accompanying high parental control will promote the development of conformity without loss of self-assertiveness. . . .

Procedures

To permit internal validation of results, multiple measures were used. Each measure was devised to perform a slightly different function. The structured observation was devised to maximize the crucial group differences by presenting, to each mother-child pair, standard stimuli designed to elicit influence attempts by the parent and resistance from the child. A rating instrument, the Parent Behavior Rating Scales (PBRS), was devised to provide the latitude needed for clinical inference, and as a convenient way of summarizing information gathered during the home visit. The Home Visit Sequence Analysis

(HVSA) measured parent-child interactions directly and discretely. Data obtained from this source are minimally affected by halo, since each variable from the HVSA is associated with a theoretical dimension of parent-child interaction via an inferential chain unknowable to the coder. Additional information about childrearing practices and attributes was obtained by interviewing each parent separately.

Although the data obtained on child training practices from the several sources were not collected independently, the data obtained from these sources were defined so differently that they could reasonably be used as corroborative. . . . In no case did results obtained by the different methods contradict one another.

All parents and children selected for study agreed to participate. They were promised feedback about results which they received in the form of a report, describing the hypotheses and general results. In approaching the family to participate, we acknowledged gratefully the extent of our debt to the subjects and the initial discomfort that subjects and observers alike might be expected to experience during the home visit. . . .

Results and Discussion. . . .

Summary of Results

In order that the reader might have a visual picture of the total results the variables measuring each dimension were composited for the HVSA and SRSO and are presented in Figure 22.1. . . . The two measures, very different in unit and setting, give nearly identical pictures of between-group differences. Parents of Pattern I children are uniformly high on all dimensions by comparison with other parents. Pattern II and Pattern III show reverse relationships on the control and nurturance scores. Parents of the disaffiliated and dysphoric children were more controlling and less nurturant, while the opposite is true for parents of immature children. This relationship between the control and nurturance composites is more striking than the between-group difference on either dimension. Of particular interest is the similarity of parents of both contrast groups on communication scores, when compared to the parents of Pattern I children whose scores are very much higher. . . .

Discussion

Childrearing Practices Associated With Pattern I Child Behavior. Pattern I children were both socialized and independent. They were self-controlled and affiliative on the one hand and self-reliant, explorative, and self-assertive on the other hand. They were realistic, competent, and content by comparison with Pattern II and Pattern III children. Boys and girls were equally represented, as were children of different birth orders. The differences between Pattern I children and children in the other

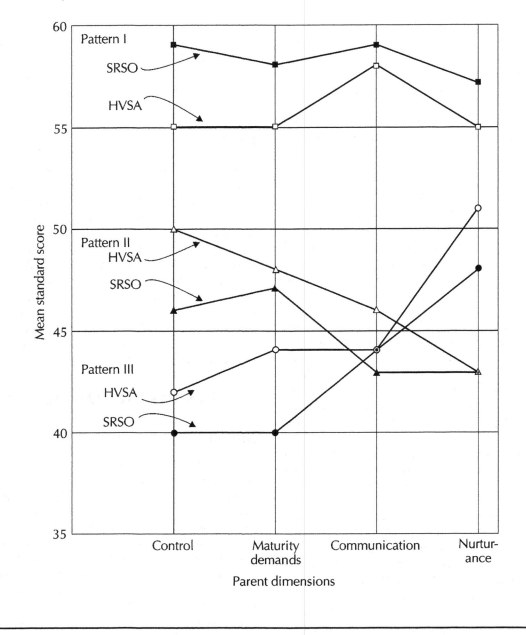

Figure 22.1 Profile of Composited Parent Dimension Scores from the Summary Ratings for the Structured Observation (SRSO) and the Home Visit Sequence Analysis (HVSA) for Each Pattern

patterns were far more pronounced than were the differences between children in Patterns II and III.

The magnitudes of group differences for their parents were similarly discrepant. In the home setting, parents of Pattern I children were markedly consistent, loving, conscientious, and secure in handling their children. They respected the child's independent decisions but demonstrated remarkable ability to hold to a position once they took a stand. They tended to accompany a directive with a reason. On the SRSO, mothers of Pattern I children demonstrated firm control and demanded a good deal of their children. They also were more supportive and communicated more clearly with their children than did parents of children in Patterns II and III. Despite vigorous and at times conflictful interactions, their homes were not marked

by discord or dissensions. The above findings were true when parents of Pattern I children were compared with parents of children in either Pattern II or Pattern III. Parents of Pattern I children balanced high nurturance with high control and high demands with clear communication about what was required of the child. Under the conditions pertaining in their homes, Pattern I children were not adversely affected by their parents' socialization and maturity demands and, indeed, seemed to thrive under the pressure imposed. We are inclined to think that by using reason to accompany a directive and by encouraging verbal give and take, these parents were able to maintain control without stimulating rebellion or passivity.

By comparison with parents of Pattern III children in the home setting, parents of Pattern I children had firmer control over the actions of their children, engaged in more independence training and did not baby their children. It is clear from the PBRS that the Pattern I household by comparison with the Pattern III household was better coordinated, that there were fewer instances of disciplinary friction, and the policy of regulations was clearer and more effectively enforced. Power was used in an open and nonmanipulative fashion by parents of Pattern I children, and yet the child was more satisfied by interactions with his parents than was the Pattern III child. According to interview data, by comparison with fathers of Pattern III children, fathers of Pattern I children accepted a more important role in the disciplining of their children. Both parents of Pattern I children expressed greater feeling of control over the behavior of their children and less internal conflict about disciplinary procedures than did parents of Pattern III children.

Childrearing Practices Associated With Pattern II Child Behavior.

Pattern II children were significantly less content, more insecure and apprehensive, less affiliative toward peers, and more likely to become hostile or regressive under stress than Pattern I children. They were more inclined to do careful work and functioned at a higher cognitive level than Pattern III children. The group was composed, by comparison with Pattern III, of (significantly) more first-born and only children of one- and two-child families, and (nonsignificantly) more girls.

Parents of Pattern II children were, by comparison with parents of the other two groups, less nurturant and involved with their children. They exerted firm control and used power freely, but offered little support of affection. They did not attempt to convince the child through use of reason to obey a directive, nor did they encourage the child to express himself when he disagreed. According to interview data, the mother was more inclined to give an absolute moral imperative as a reason for her demands than were Pattern I parents. Her expressed attitudes were less sympathetic and approving and she admitted more to frightening the child. Her expressed nonnurturant attitudes were reflected in her observed behavior on HVSA and SRSO measures.

Childrearing Practices Associated With Pattern III Child Behavior.

Pattern III children were lacking in self-control and self-reliance by comparison with children in the other groups.

By comparison with parents of Pattern I children, the parents of Pattern III children behaved in a markedly less controlling manner and were not as well organized or effective in running their households. They were self-effacing and insecure about their ability to influence their children, lacking the qualities of a strong model. Neither parent demanded much of the child and fathers were lax reinforcing agents. They engaged in less independence training and babied their children more. There are some indications that by comparison with parents of Pattern I children these parents were less intensely involved with

their children and used love manipulatively. Mothers used withdrawal of love and ridicule rather than power or reason as incentives.

The most significant difference between parents of Pattern II and Pattern III children was that the former were the more controlling. Since parents of Pattern III children were the warmer, the control-nurturance ratios are in opposite directions: parents of the dysphoric and disaffiliated children were controlling and not at all warm, while parents of the immature children were not at all controlling and comparatively warm.

The prototypic child-centered parent who is both permissive (noncontrolling and nondemanding) and warm did not appear. The most mature and competent children sampled certainly did not have child-centered parents. But neither did the least mature and self-reliant group of children.

The Interacting Effects of Control and Warmth.

The interacting effects of control and warmth clearly differ from the interacting effects of restrictiveness and warmth. Becker (1, p. 198) summarized the interactions of restrictiveness *vs.* permissiveness with warmth *vs.* hostility. He reported that warm-restrictive parents tend to have dependent, well socialized, submissive children. In this study warm-controlling parents were not paired with submissive, dependent children, but rather with assertive, self-reliant children. Parents of Pattern I children enforced directives and resisted the child's demands, but they did not overprotect or overrestrict the child. The children were well socialized but not passive-dependent. Apparently early control, unlike restrictiveness, does not lead to "fearful, dependent, and submissive behaviors, a dulling of intellectual striving and inhibited hostility" (1, p. 197). Becker reports that children of warm-nonrestrictive parents were socially outgoing, successfully aggressive, independent, and friendly. In this study, children of warm-noncontrolling parents were immature and avoidant. They were not self-assertive and self-reliant, as were children of warm-nonrestrictive parents.

Restrictiveness and control, then, relate to quite different behaviors and have contrasting effects on self-assertiveness and self-reliance in young children. In order to understand the effects of either control or restrictiveness in child behavior, a configurational analysis that takes into account interactions with nurturance variables is necessary.

Summary

Childrearing practices of parents with self-reliant, self-controlled, approach-oriented, buoyant children were contrasted with childrearing practices of other parents whose children were drawn from the same preschool population. There were two contrast groups of children. Members of one contrast group were dysphoric and disaffiliated, while members of the other group were immature. Parent dimensions measured were parental control, parental maturity demands, parent-child communication, and parental nurturance.

Parent-child interaction data were obtained by means of focussed interviews, home visits, and structured observations. The home visits offered the opportunity to observe the family in a natural setting, while the structured observation confronted the mother and child with a standard set of arousal stimuli designed to elicit responses of theoretical interest.

Certain hypotheses were tested about the effects of childrearing practices using data obtained from independent observations of parents and children in natural and contrived situations.

The following points should be kept in mind when generalizing from the findings. It does not follow from these results that either parental control or nurturance bears a positive linear relationship to competence in preschool children. The total range is not represented. Parents of subjects with scores in the middle range on the child attributes measured may have even more extreme scores on the parent dimensions measured. Also the directions of cause-effect relationships were inferred only from the successful predictions of these relationships.

The following are conclusions about the subgroups studied. Parents of the most competent and mature boys and girls (Pattern I children) were notably firm, loving, demanding, and understanding. Parents of dysphoric and disaffiliative children (Pattern II children) were firm, punitive, and unaffectionate. Mothers of dependent, immature children (Pattern III children) lacked control and were moderately loving. Fathers of these children were ambivalent and lax. The spontaneity, warmth, and zest of Pattern I children were not affected adversely by high parental control.

Reference

Becker, W. C. Consequences of different kinds of parental discipline. In M. L. Hoffman & L. W. Hoffman (Eds.), *Review of Child Development Research (Vol. 1)*. New York: Russell Sage Foundation, 1964. Pp. 169–208.

Cognitive Development in Middle Childhood

Verbal Behavior

B. F. Skinner

B. F. Skinner (1904–1990) was born in Pennsylvania and received his doctorate in psychology from Harvard University in 1931. He became a member of the Harvard faculty in 1948, where he stayed until his death. Skinner is the most influential member of the behaviorist movement, which dominated American psychology for most of the twentieth century. He published many texts and research papers, including *The Behavior of Organisms* (1938), *Science and Human Behavior* (1953), *Walden Two* (1961), *Beyond Freedom and Dignity* (1971), and *About Behaviorism* (1974).

Although Skinner is not considered a "developmental psychologist," his work has been very influential among psychologists studying human development. In particular, his explanation of "operant conditioning," based on reinforcement and punishment, is often invoked to explain the acquisition of new behavior in the developing human. One of the greatest concerns in the field of human development is language development. How is it that humans come to speak and understand speech? In Skinner's classic text *Verbal Behavior* (1957), he provided the behaviorist explanation. He later summarized his findings concerning the development of verbal behavior in chapter 6 of *About Behaviorism*, from which the following excerpt has been taken.

Key Concept: verbal behavior

Relatively late in its history, the human species underwent a remarkable change: its vocal musculature came under operant control. Like other species, it had up to that point displayed warning cries, threatening shouts, and other innate responses, but vocal operant behavior made a great difference because it extended the scope of the social environment. [Language was born, and with it many important characteristics of human behavior for which a host of mentalistic explanations have been invented.]

The very difference between "language" and "verbal behavior" is an example. Language has the character of a thing, something a person acquires and possesses. Psychologists speak of the "acquisition of language" in the child. The words and sentences of which a language is composed are said to be tools used to express meanings, thoughts, ideas, propositions, emotions, needs, desires, and many other things in or on the speaker's mind. A much more productive view is that verbal behavior is behavior. It has a special character only because it is reinforced by its effects on people—at first other people, but eventually the speaker himself. As a result, it is free of the spatial, temporal, and mechanical relations which prevail between operant behavior and nonsocial consequences. If the opening of a door will be reinforcing, a person may grasp the knob, turn it, and push or pull in a given way, but if, instead, he says, "Please open the door," and a listener responds appropriately, the same reinforcing consequence follows. The contingencies are different, and they generate many important differences in the behavior which have long been obscured by mentalistic explanations.

How a person speaks depends upon the practices of the verbal community of which he is a member. A verbal repertoire may be rudimentary or it may display an elaborate topography under many subtle kinds of stimulus control. The contingencies which shape it may be indulgent (as when parents respond to their children's crude approximations to standard forms) or demanding (as in the teaching of diction). Different verbal communities shape and maintain different languages in the same speaker, who then possesses different repertoires having similar effects upon different listeners. Verbal responses are classified as requests, commands, permissions, and so on, depending upon the reasons why the listener responds, the reasons often being attributed to the speaker's intentions or moods. The fact that the energy of a response is not proportional to the magnitude of the result has contributed to the belief in verbal magic (the magician's "Presto chango" converts a handkerchief into a rabbit). Strong responses appear in the absence of an appropriate audience, as Richard III demonstrated when he cried, "A horse! a horse! my kingdom for a horse!" although there was no one to hear him.

Apart from an occasional relevant audience, verbal behavior requires no environmental support. One needs a bicycle to ride a bicycle but not to say "bicycle." As a result, verbal behavior can occur on almost any occasion. An important consequence is that most people find it easier to say "bicycle" silently than to "ride a bicycle silently." Another important consequence is that the speaker also becomes a listener and may richly reinforce his own behavior.

Meaning and Reference

The term "meaning," though closely associated with verbal behavior, has been used to make some of the distinctions already discussed. Those who have confused behaviorism with structuralism, in its emphasis on form or topography, have complained that it ignores meaning. What is important, they contend, is not what a person is doing but what his behavior means to him; his behavior has a deeper property not unrelated to . . . purpose, intention, or expectation. . . . But the meaning of a response is not in its topography or form (that is the mistake of the structuralist, not the behaviorist); it is to be found in its antecedent history. The behaviorist is also accused of describing the environmental setting in physical terms and overlooking what it means to the responding person, but here again the meaning is not in the current setting but in a history of exposure to contingencies in which similar settings have played a part.

In other words, meaning is not properly regarded as a property either of a response or a situation but rather of the contingencies responsible for both the topography or behavior and the control exerted by stimuli. To take a primitive example, if one rat presses a lever to obtain food when hungry while another does so to obtain water when thirsty, the topographies of their behaviors may be indistinguishable, but they may be said to differ in meaning: to one rat pressing the lever "means" food; to the other it "means" water. But these are aspects of the contingencies which have brought behavior under the control of the current occasion. Similarly, if a rat is reinforced with food when it presses the lever in the presence of a flashing light but with water when the light is steady, then it could be said that the flashing light means food and the steady light means water, but again these are references not to some property of the light but to the contingencies of which the lights have been parts.

The same point may be made, but with many more implications, in speaking of the meaning of verbal behavior. The over-all function of the behavior is crucial. In an archetypal pattern a speaker is in contact with a situation to which a listener is disposed to respond but with which he is not in contact. A verbal response on the part of the speaker makes it possible for the listener to respond appropriately. For example, let us suppose that a person has an appointment, which he will keep by consulting a clock or a watch. If none is available, he may ask someone to tell him the time, and the response permits him to respond effectively. The speaker sees the clock and announces the time; the listener hears the announcement and keeps his appointment. The three terms which appear in the contingencies of reinforcement generating an operant are divided between two people: the speaker responds to the setting, and the listener engages in the behavior and is affected by the consequences. This will happen only if the behaviors of speaker and listener are supported by additional contingencies arranged by the verbal community.

The listener's belief in what the speaker says is like the belief which underlies the probability of any response ("I believe this will work") or the control exerted by any stimulus ("I believe this is the right place"). It depends on past contingencies, and nothing is gained by internalizing them. To define interpersonal trust as "an expectancy held by an individual or a group that the word, promise, verbal or written statement of another individual or group can be relied on" is to complicate matters unnecessarily.

The *meaning of a response for the speaker* includes the stimulus which controls it (in the example above, the setting on the face of a clock or watch) and possibly aversive aspects of the question, from which a response brings release. The *meaning for the listener* is close to the meaning the clock face would have if it were visible to him, but it also includes the contingencies involving the appointment, which make a response to the clock face or the verbal response probably at such a time. A person who will leave for an appointment upon seeing a certain position of the hands of a clock will also leave upon hearing a response made by a person whose responses in the past have been accurately controlled by the position of the hands and which for that reason control strong responses now.

One of the unfortunate implications of communication theory is that the meanings for speaker and listener are the same, that something is made common to both of them, that the speaker conveys an idea or meaning, transmits information, or imparts knowledge, as if his mental possessions then become the mental possessions of the listener. There are no meanings which are the same in the speaker and listener. Meanings are not independent entities. We may look for the meaning of a word in the dictionary, but dictionaries do not give meanings; at best they give other words having the same meanings. We must come to a dictionary already "provided with meanings."

A referent might be defined as that aspect of the environment which exerts control over the response of which it is said to be the referent. It does so because of the reinforcing practices of a verbal community. In traditional terms, meanings and referents are not to be found in words but in the circumstances under which words are used by speakers and understood by listeners, but "used" and "understanding" need further analysis.

Verbal responses are often said to be taken by the listener as signs, or symbols, of the situations they describe, and a great deal has been made of the symbolic process. . . . Certain atmospheric conditions may be a "sign of rain," and we respond to them to avoid getting wet. We usually respond in a slightly different way in escaping from the rain itself if we have had no sign of it in advance. We can say the same thing about the weatherman's verbal responses, which are no more a sign or symbol of rain than the atmospheric change.

Metaphor. We have seen that a stimulus present when a response is reinforced acquires some control over the probability that that response will occur, and that this effect generalizes: stimuli sharing some of its properties also acquire some control. In verbal behavior one kind of response evoked by a merely similar stimulus is called a metaphor. The response is not transferred from one situation to another, as the etymology might suggest; it simply occurs because of a similarity in stimuli. Having come to say "explode" in connection with firecrackers or bombs, a person may describe a friend who suddenly behaves in a violent manner as "exploding in anger." Other figures of speech illustrate other behavioral processes.

Abstraction. A characteristic feature of verbal behavior, directly attributable to special contingencies of reinforcement, is abstraction. It is the listener, not the speaker, who takes practical action with respect to the stimuli controlling a verbal response, and as a result the behavior of the speaker may come under the control of properties of a stimulus to which no practical response is appropriate. A person learns to react to red things under the nonsocial contingencies of his environment, but he does so only by emitting a practical response for each red thing. The contingencies cannot bring a single response under the control of the property of redness alone. But a single property may be important to the listener who takes many kinds of practical action on many different occasions because of it and who therefore reinforces appropriately when a given object is called red. The referent for red can never be identified in any one setting. If we show a person a red pencil and say, "What is that?" and he says, "Red," we cannot tell what property evoked his response, but if we show him many red objects and he always says, "Red," we can do so—and with increasing accuracy as we multiply cases. The speaker is always responding to a physical object, not to "redness" as an abstract entity, and he responds "red" not because he possesses a concept of redness but because special contingencies have brought that response under the control of that property of stimuli.

There is no point in asking how a person can "know the abstract entity called redness." The contingencies explain the behavior, and we need not be disturbed because it is impossible to discover the referent in any single instance. We need not . . . deny that abstract entities exist and insist that such responses are merely words. What exist are the contingencies which bring behavior under the control of properties or of classes of objects defined by properties. (We can determine that a single response is under the control of one property by naming it. For example, if we show a person a pencil and say, "What *color* is this?" he will then respond to the property specified as color—provided he has been subject to an appropriate history of reinforcement.)

Concepts. When a class is defined by more than one property, the referent is usually called a concept rather than an abstract entity. That concepts have real referents has been pointed out by saying that "they are discoveries rather than inventions—they represent reality." In other words, they exist in the world before anyone identifies them. But discovery (as well as invention) suggests mental action in the production of a concept. A concept is simply a feature of a set of contingencies which exist in the world, and it is discovered simply in the sense that the contingencies bring behavior under its control. The statement "Scientific concepts enable certain aspects of the enormous complexity of the world to be handled by men's minds" is vastly improved by substituting "human beings" for "men's minds."

Sentences and Propositions

The traditional notion of meaning and referent runs into trouble when we begin to analyze larger verbal responses under the control of more complex environmental circumstances. What are the referents of sentences—not to mention paragraphs, chapters, or books? A sentence surely means more than its separate words mean. Sentences do more than refer to things; they *say* things. But what are the things they say? A traditional answer is "Propositions." But propositions are as elusive as meanings. Bertrand Russell's view has been paraphrased as follows: "The significance of a sentence is that which is common to a sentence in one language and its translation into another language. For example, 'I am hungry' and 'J'ai faim' have in common elements which constitute the significance of a sentence. This common element is the proposition." But what *is* this common element? Where is it to be found? A dictionary that gave the meanings of sentences would simply contain other sentences having the same meanings.

A translation can best be defined as a verbal stimulus that has the same effect as the original (or as much of the same effect as possible) on a different verbal community. A French translation of an English book is not another statement of a set of propositions; it is another sample of verbal behavior having an effect upon a French reader similar to the effect of the English version on an English reader. The same interpretation may be made of a translation from one medium into another. It has been said that the Prelude to *Tristan and Isolde* is "an astonishingly intense and faithful translation into music of the emotions which accompany the union of a pair of lovers." Rather than try to identify the feeling, let alone the proposition, which is thus translated, we may say simply that the music has something of the same effect as physical union.

The concept of expression and communication may be treated in a similar way. A speaker or a listener responds to conditions of his body which he has learned to call feelings, but what he says or hears is behavior, due to contingencies of which the felt conditions may be by-products. To say that music expresses "what is inexpressible in cognitive, and especially in scientific, language" is to say that it has an effect that verbal behavior cannot have. Verbal behavior does not communicate feelings, though it may result in conditions similarly felt. It does not communicate propositions or instructions. To "instruct" a mother cat to desert her young by delivering an electric shock to a part of her brain does not communicate an instruction that was first held in the mind of the scientist; the shock simply has an effect (a dash of cold water would have produced the same result). [Austrian zoologist Karl von] Frisch's account of the language of bees (an account which is becoming increasingly suspect) did not make him a Champollion, reading a Rosetta stone.

The concept of stimulus control replaces the notion of referent with respect not only to responses which occur in isolation and are called words (such as nouns and adjectives) but also to those complex responses called sentences. Possibly could be said to describe "fact" a referent to the latter, although its suggestion of truth versus falsity raises difficulties. The child responds in sentences to events in his environment—events involving more than one property or thing, or relations among things, or relations of actor and acted upon, and so on, and his responses contain elements which he never has any occasion to emit alone. The linguist assigns these elements to syntax or grammar. He does so as part of an analysis of the practices of a given verbal community, from which he extracts rules which may be used in the construction of new sentences. . . .

The Manipulation of Words and Sentences

Structuralism has been strongly encouraged in linguistics because verbal behavior often seems to have an independent status. We are inclined to give special attention to its form because we can report it easily, and rather accurately, simply by modeling it, as in a direct quotation. The report "He said, 'hammer' " gives a much more complete description of the topography of his behavior than "He was hammering." In teaching a child to talk, or an adult to pronounce a difficult word, we produce a model—that is, we say the word and arrange contingencies under which a response having similar properties will be reinforced. There is nothing especially verbal about modeling (in teaching sports or the dance, the instructor "shows a person what to do" in the sense of doing it himself), but with the invention of the alphabet, it became possible to record verbal behavior, and the records, free of any supporting environment, seemed to have an independent existence. A speaker is said to "know" a poem or an oath or a prayer. Early education in China and Greece was largely a matter of memorizing literary works. The student seemed to know the wisdom expressed by the work, even though his behavior was not necessarily under the control of the conditions which induced the original speaker or writer, or an informed listener, to respond in a given way.

Verbal behavior has this kind of independent status when it is in transmission between speaker and listener— for example, when it is the "information" passing over a telephone wire or between writer and reader in the form of a text. Until fairly recently, linguistics and literary criticism confined themselves almost exclusively to the analyses of written records. If these had any meaning, it was the meaning for the reader, since the circumstances under which the behavior had been produced by the writer had been forgotten, if they were ever known.

The availability of verbal behavior in this apparently objective form has caused a great deal of trouble. By dividing such records into words and sentences without regard to the conditions under which the behavior was emitted, we neglect the meaning for the speaker or writer, and almost half the field of verbal behavior therefore escapes attention. Worse still, bits of recorded speech are moved about to compose new "sentences," which are then analyzed for their truth or falsity (in terms of their effect on a reader or listener), although they were never generated by a speaker. Both logician and linguist tend to create new sentences in this way, which they then treat as if they were the records of emitted verbal behavior. If we take the sentence "The sun is a star" and put the word "not" in the proper place, we transform it into "The sun is not a star" but no one has emitted this instance of a verbal response, and it does not describe a fact or express a proposition. It is simply the result of a mechanical process.

Perhaps there is no harm in playing with sentences in this way or in analyzing the kinds of transformations which do or do not make sentences acceptable to the ordinary reader, but it is still a waste of time, particularly when the sentences thus generated could not have been emitted as verbal behavior. A classical example is a paradox, such as "This sentence is false," which appears to be true if false and false if true. The important thing to consider is that no one could ever have emitted the sentence as verbal behavior. A sentence must be in existence before a speaker can say, "This sentence is false," and the response itself will not serve, since it did not exist until it was emitted. What the logician or linguist calls a sentence is not necessarily verbal behavior in any sense which calls for a behavioral analysis.

The transformational rules which generate sentences acceptable to a listener may be of interest, but even so it is a mistake to suppose that verbal behavior is generated by them. Thus, we may analyze the behavior of small children and discover that, for example, part of their speech consists of a small class of "modifiers" and a larger class of "nouns." (This fact about verbal behavior is due to the contingencies of reinforcement arranged by most verbal communities.) It does not follow that the child "forms a noun phrase of a given type" by "selecting first one word from the small class of modifiers and selecting second one word from the large class of nouns." This is a linguist's reconstruction after the fact.

The analysis of verbal behavior, particularly the so-called discovery of grammar, came very late. For thousands of years no one could have known he was speaking according to rule. . . .

Development. An undue concern for the structure of verbal behavior has encouraged the metaphor of development or growth. Length of utterance is plotted as a function of age, and semantic and grammatical features are observed as they "develop." The growth of language in a child is easily compared with the growth of an embryo, and grammar can then be attributed to rules possessed by the child at birth. A program in the form of a genetic code is said to "initiate and guide early learning . . . as a child acquires language." But the human species did not evolve because of an inbuilt design: it evolved through selection under contingencies of survival, as the child's verbal behavior evolves under the selective action of contingencies of reinforcement. As I have noted, the world of a child develops, too.

A child does seem to acquire a verbal repertoire at an amazing speed, but we should not overestimate the accomplishment or attribute it to invented linguistic capacities. A child may "learn to use a new word" as the effect of a single reinforcement, but it learns to do nonverbal things with comparable speed. The verbal behavior is impressive in part because the topography is conspicuous and easily identified and in part because it suggests hidden meanings.

If the structuralists and developmentalists had not confined themselves so narrowly to the topography of behavior at the expense of the other parts of the contingencies of reinforcement, we should know much more about how a child learns to speak. We know the words a child first uses and the characteristic orders in which they tend to be used. We know the length of utterances at given ages, and so on. If structure were enough, that would be the whole story. But a record of topography needs to be supplemented by an equally detailed record of the conditions under which it was acquired. What speech has the child heard? Under what circumstances has he heard it? What effects has he achieved when he has uttered similar responses? Until we have this kind of information, the success or failure of any analysis of verbal behavior cannot be judged.

Creative Verbal Behavior

In verbal behavior, as in all operant behavior, original forms of response are evoked by situations to which a person has not previously been exposed. The origin of behavior is not unlike the origin of species. New combinations of stimuli appear in new settings, and responses which describe them may never have been made by the speaker before, or heard or read by him in the speech of others. There are many behavioral processes generating "mutations," which are then subject to the selective action of contingencies of reinforcement. We all produce novel forms—for example, in neologisms, blends, portmanteau words, witty remarks involving distortion, and the mistakes of hasty speech.

A great deal has been made of the fact that a child will "invent" a weak past tense for a strong verb, as in saying "he goed" instead of "he went." If he has never heard the form "goed" (that is, if he as associated only with adults), he must have created a new form. But we do not speak of "creation" if, having acquired a list of color words and a list of object words, he for the first time says "purple automobile." The fact that the terminal "-ed" suggests "grammar" is unnecessarily exciting. It is quite possible that it is a separable operant, as a separate indicator of the past tense or of completed action in another language might be, and that "go" and a terminal "-ed" are put together, as "purple" and "automobile" are put together, on a novel occasion.

A Review of B. F. Skinner's Verbal Behavior

Noam Chomsky

Noam Chomsky (b. 1928) earned his Ph.D. at the University of Pennsylvania in 1955 and then joined the faculty at the Massachusetts Institute of Technology, where he has been headquartered ever since.

Chomsky's work in linguistics is considered some of the most brilliant and creative of the twentieth century, and he has had a tremendous impact in the disciplines of psychology, anthropology, linguistics, philosophy, and literature, as well as other fields. In human development he is most noted for his theory of the "language acquisition device" (LAD), an innate ability of humans to understand language. He explained how the grammar of all languages have a "deep structure" in common, which explains why any infant brought up in any culture will learn, without formal instruction, the language of that culture.

In the 1950s the vast majority of American psychologists had adopted the behaviorist approach to studying psychology. B. F. Skinner, being the main spokesperson for this school of thought, had published the text *Verbal Behavior* (1957), in which he theorized and summarized his research (mostly with rats and pigeons) on how humans develop their language behavior. His focus was entirely on the environmental stimuli that reinforce (strengthen) or punish (weaken) verbal utterances.

The following excerpt is from Chomsky's famous criticism of Skinner's approach, "A Review of B. F. Skinner's *Verbal Behavior*," which was published in the journal *Language* in 1959.

Key Concept: language development

The system that Skinner develops specifically for the description of verbal behavior . . . is based on the notions 'stimulus', 'response', and 'reinforcement'. . . . I think it is important to see in detail how far from the mark any analysis phrased solely in these terms must be and how completely this system fails to account for the facts of verbal behavior.

Consider first the term 'verbal behavior' itself. This is defined as 'behavior reinforced through the mediation of other persons' (2).* The definition is clearly much too broad. It would include as 'verbal behavior', for example, a rat pressing the bar in a Skinner-box, a child brushing his teeth, a boxer retreating before an opponent, and a mechanic repairing an automobile. Exactly how much of ordinary linguistic behavior is 'verbal' in this sense, however, is something of a question: perhaps, as I have pointed out above, a fairly small fraction of it, if any substantive

meaning is assigned to the term 'reinforced'. This definition is subsequently refined by the additional provision that the mediating response of the reinforcing person (the 'listener') must itself 'have been conditioned *precisely in order to reinforce* the behavior of the speaker' (225, italics his). This still covers the examples given above, if we can assume that the 'reinforcing' behavior of the psychologist, the parent, the opposing boxer, and the paying customer are the result of appropriate training, which is perhaps not unreasonable. A significant part of the fragment of linguistic behavior covered by the earlier definition will no doubt be excluded by the refinement, however. Suppose, for example, that while crossing the street I hear someone shout *Watch out for the car* and jump out of the way. It can hardly be proposed that my jumping (the mediating, reinforcing response in Skinner's usage) was conditioned (that is, I was trained to jump) precisely in

---

* [All page numbers in parentheses refer to Skinner's *Verbal Behavior.*—Eds.]

order to reinforce the behavior of the speaker. Similarly for a wide class of cases, Skinner's assertion that with this refined definition 'we narrow our subject to what is traditionally recognized as the verbal field' (225) appears to be grossly in error.

V erbal operants are classified by Skinner in terms of their 'functional' relation to discriminated stimulus, reinforcement, and other verbal responses. A *mand* is defined as a 'verbal operant in which the response is reinforced by a characteristic consequence and is therefore under the functional control of relevant conditions of deprivation or aversive stimulation' (35). This is meant to include questions, commands, etc. Each of the terms in this definition raises a host of problems. A mand such as *Pass the salt* is a class of responses. We cannot tell by observing the form of a response whether it belongs to this class (Skinner is very clear about this), but only by identifying the controlling variables. This is generally impossible. Deprivation is defined in the bar-pressing experiment in terms of length of time that the animal has not been fed or permitted to drink. In the present context, however, it is quite a mysterious notion. No attempt is made here to describe a method for determining 'relevant conditions of deprivation' independently of the 'controlled' response. It is of no help at all to be told (32) that it can be characterized in terms of the operations of the experimenter. If we define deprivation in terms of elapsed time, then at any moment a person is in countless states of deprivation. It appears that we must decide that the relevant condition of deprivation was (say) salt-deprivation, on the basis of the fact that the speaker asked for salt (the reinforcing community which 'sets up' the mand is in a similar predicament). In this case, the assertion that a mand is under the control of relevant deprivation is empty, and we are (contrary to Skinner's intention) identifying the response as a mand completely in terms of form. The word 'relevant' in the definition above conceals some rather serious complications.

In the case of the mand *Pass the salt*, the word 'deprivation' is not out of place, though it appears to be of little use for functional analysis. Suppose however that the speaker says *Give me the book*, *Take me for a ride*, or *Let me fix it*. What kinds of deprivation can be associated with these mands? How do we determine or measure the relevant deprivation? I think we must conclude in this case, as before, either that the notion 'deprivation' is relevant at most to a minute fragment of verbal behavior, or else that the statement 'X is under Y-deprivation' is just an odd paraphrase for 'X wants Y', bearing a misleading and unjustifiable connotation of objectivity.

The notion 'aversive control' is just as confused. This is intended to cover threats, beating, and the like (33). The manner in which aversive stimulation functions is simply described. If a speaker has had a history of appropriate reinforcement (e.g. if a certain response was followed by 'cessation of the threat of such injury—of events

which have previously been followed by such injury and which are therefore conditioned aversive stimuli') then he will tend to give the proper response when the threat which had previously been followed by the injury is presented. It would appear to follow from this description that a speaker will not respond properly to them and *Your money or your life* (38) unless he has a past history of being killed. But even if the difficulties in describing the mechanism of aversive control are somehow removed by a more careful analysis, it will be of little use for identifying operants for reasons similar to those mentioned in the case of deprivation.

It seems, then, that in Skinner's terms there is in most cases no way to decide whether a given response is an instance of a particular mand. Hence it is meaningless, within the terms of his system, to speak of the *characteristic* consequences of a mand, as in the definition above. Furthermore, even if we extend the system so that mands can somehow be identified, we will have to face the obvious fact that most of us are not fortunate enough to have our requests, commands, advice, and so on characteristically reinforced (they may nevertheless exist in considerable 'strength'). These responses could therefore not be considered mands by Skinner. In fact, Skinner sets up a category of 'magical mands' (48–9) to cover the case of 'mands which cannot be accounted for by showing that they have ever had the effect specified or any similar effect upon similar occasions' (the word 'ever' in this statement should be replaced by 'characteristically'). In these pseudo mands, 'the speaker simply describes the reinforcement appropriate to a given state of deprivation or aversive stimulation'. In other words, given the meaning that we have been led to assign to 'reinforcement' and 'deprivation', the speaker asks for what he wants. The remark that 'a speaker appears to create new mands on the analogy of old ones' is also not very helpful.

Skinner's claim that his new descriptive system is superior to the traditional one 'because its terms can be defined with respect to experimental operations' (45) is, we see once again, an illusion. The statement 'X wants Y' is not clarified by pointing out a relation between rate of bar-pressing and hours of food-deprivation; replacing 'X wants Y' by 'X is deprived of Y' adds no new objectivity to the description of behavior. His further claim for the superiority of the new analysis of mands is that it provides an objective basis for the traditional classification into requests, commands, etc. (38–41). The traditional classification is in terms of the intention of the speaker. But intention, Skinner holds, can be reduced to contingencies of reinforcement, and, correspondingly, we can explain the traditional classification in terms of the reinforcing behavior of the listener. Thus a question is a mand which 'specifies verbal action, and the behavior of the listener permits us to classify it as a request, a command, or a prayer' (39). It is a request if 'the listener is independently motivated to reinforce the speaker'; a command if 'the listener's behavior is . . . reinforced by reducing a threat'; a prayer if the mand 'promotes reinforcement by generating an emotional disposition'. The mand is advice if the listener is positively reinforced by the consequences of mediating the reinforcement of the speaker; it is a warning if 'by carrying out the behavior specified by the speaker the listener escapes from aversive stimulation'; and so on. All this is obviously wrong if Skinner is using the words 'request', 'command', etc., in anything like the sense of the corresponding English words. The word 'question' does not cover commands. *Please pass the salt* is a request (but not a question), whether or not the listener happens to be motivated to fulfill it; not everyone to whom a request is addressed is favorably disposed. A response does not cease to be a command if it is not followed; nor does a question become a command

if the speaker answers it because of an implied or imagined threat. Not all advice is good advice, and a response does not cease to be advice if it is not followed. Similarly, a warning may be misguided; heeding it may cause aversive stimulation, and ignoring it might be positively reinforcing. In short, the entire classification is beside the point. A moment's thought is sufficient to demonstrate the impossibility of distinguishing between requests, commands, advice, etc., on the basis of the behavior or disposition of the particular listener. Nor can we do this on the basis of the typical behavior of all listeners. Some advice is never taken, is always bad, etc., and similarly with other kinds of mands. Skinner's evident satisfaction with this analysis of the traditional classification is extremely puzzling.

Conservation of Continuous Quantities

Jean Piaget

One of the most renowned of developmental psychologist Jean Piaget's experiments is the conservation of volume experiment, which he performed with glass beakers. Conservation, the understanding that substances maintain the same quantity even after changing shape, has implications for the learning of arithmetic and geometry, as well as other aspects of spatial reasoning, such as shape, mass, area, and so on. The following excerpt, taken from *The Child's Conception of Number* (W. W. Norton, 1965), was first published in French in 1941 and in English in 1952. The chapter from which the selection was taken, "Conservation of Continuous Quantities," was originally published in 1939 in *Journal de Psychologie*.

In most secondary sources (like a standard college textbook on human development), the beaker experiment is described as being performed with two squat, identical beakers and one tall, narrow beaker. Note that in Piaget's original experiment, however, the setup is slightly different. Should this make any difference in the outcome of the study? Also note that children's names are followed by parentheses with semicolons, such as (5;3)—this means that the child was 5 years and 3 months old at the time of questioning. In this study, what Piaget refers to as Stage I corresponds to his preoperational stage; Stage II is a transitional stage between preoperations and the concrete operational stage; and Stage III is the concrete operational stage.

Key Concept: conservation of volume

Every notion, whether it be scientific or merely a matter of common sense, presupposes a set of principles of conservation, either explicit or implicit. It is a matter of common knowledge that in the field of the empirical sciences the introduction of the principle of inertia (conservation of rectilinear and uniform motion) made possible the development of modern physics, and that the principle of conservation of matter made modern chemistry possible. It is unnecessary to stress the importance in every-day life of the principle of identity; any attempt by thought to build up a system of notions requires a certain permanence in their definitions. In the field of perception, the schema of the permanent object presupposes the elaboration of what is no doubt the most primitive of all these principles of conservation. Obviously conservation, which is a necessary condition of all experience and all reasoning, by no means exhausts the representation of reality or the dynamism of the intellectual processes, but that is another matter. Our contention is merely that conservation is a necessary condition for all rational activity, and we are not concerned with whether it is sufficient to account for this activity or to explain the nature of reality.

This being so, arithmetical thought is no exception to the rule. A set or collection is only conceivable if it remains unchanged irrespective of the changes occurring in the relationship between the elements. For instance, the permutations of the elements in a given set do not change its value. A number is only intelligible if it remains identical with itself, whatever the distribution of the units of which it is composed. A continuous quantity such as a length or a volume can only be used in reasoning if it is a permanent whole, irrespective of the possible arrangements of its parts. In a word, whether it be a matter of continuous or discontinuous qualities, of quantitative relations perceived in the sensible universe, or of sets and numbers conceived by thought, whether it be a matter of the child's earliest contacts with number or of the most refined axiomatizations of any intuitive system, in each and every case the conservation of something is postulated as a necessary condition for any mathematical understanding.

From the psychological point of view, the need for conservation appears then to be a kind of functional *a priori* of thought. But does this mean that arithmetical notions acquire their structure because of this conservation, or are we to conclude that conservation precedes any numerical or quantifying activities, and is not only a function, but also an *a priori* structure, a kind of innate idea present from the first awareness of the intellect and the first contact with experience? It is experiment that will provide the answer, and we shall try to show that the first alternative is the only one that is in agreement with the facts.

Technique and General Results

This [essay] will be devoted to experiments made simultaneously with continuous and discontinuous quantities. It seemed to us essential to deal with the two questions at the same time, although the former are not arithmetical. . . .

The child is first given two cylindrical containers of equal dimensions (A1 and A2) containing the same quantity of liquid (as is shown by the levels). The contents of A2 are then poured into two smaller containers of equal dimensions (B1 and B2) and the child is asked whether the quantity of liquid poured from A2 into (B1 + B2) is still equal to that in AI. If necessary, the liquid in B1 can then be poured into two smaller, equal containers (C1 and C2), and in case of need, the liquid in B2 can be poured into two other containers C3 and C4 identical with C1 and C2. Questions as to the equality between (C1 + C2) and B2, or between (C1 + C2 + C3 + C4) and A1, etc., are then put. In this way, the liquids are subdivided in a variety of ways, and each time the problem of conservation is put in the form of a question as to equality or non-equality with one of the original containers. Conversely, as a check on his answers, the child can be asked to pour into a glass of a different shape a quantity of liquid approximately the same as that in a given glass, but the main problem is still that of conservation as such.

The results obtained seem to prove that continuous quantities are not at once considered to be constant, and that the notion of conservation is gradually constructed by means of an intellectual mechanism which it is our purpose to explain. By grouping the answers to the various questions, it is possible to distinguish three stages. In the first, the child considers it natural for the quantity of liquid to vary according to the form and dimensions of the containers into which it is poured. Perception of the apparent changes is therefore not corrected by a system of relations that ensures invariance of quantity. In the second stage, which is a period of transition, conservation gradually emerges, but although it is recognized in some cases, of which we shall attempt to discover the characteristics, it is not so in all. When he reaches the third stage, the child at once postulates conservation of the quantities in each of the transformations to which they are subjected. Naturally this does not mean that this generalization of constancy extends at this stage beyond the limits of the field studied here.

In our interpretation of these facts, we can start from the following hypotheses, some of which directed the research of this chapter while others arose in the course of our experiments. The question to be considered is whether the development of the notion of conservation of quantity is not one and the same as the development of the notion of quantity. The child does not first acquire the notion of quantity and then attribute constancy to it; he discovers true quantification only when he is capable of constructing wholes that are preserved. At the level of the first stage, quantity is therefore no more than the asymmetrical relations between qualities, i.e., comparisons of the type 'more' or 'less' contained in judgements such as 'it's higher', 'not so wide', etc. These relations depend on perception, and are not as yet relations in the true sense, since they cannot be co-ordinated one with another in additive or multiplicative operations. This co-ordination begins at the second stage and results in the notion of 'intensive' quantity, i.e., without units, but susceptible of logical coherence. As soon as this intensive quantification exists, the child can grasp, before any other measurement, the proportionality of differences, and therefore the notion of extensive quantity. This discovery, which alone makes possible the development of number, thus results from the child's progress in logic during these stages.

Stage I: Absence of Conservation

For children at the first stage, the quantity of liquid increases or diminishes according to the size or number of the containers. The reasons given for this non-conservation vary from child to child, and from one moment to the next, but in every case the child thinks that the change he sees involves a change in the total value of the liquid. Here we have some examples:

Blas (4;0). 'Have you got a friend?—*Yes, Odette.*—Well look, we're giving you, Clairette, a glass of orangeade (A1, ¾ full), and we're giving Odette a glass of lemonade (A2, also ¾ full). Has one of you more to drink than the other?—*The same.*—This is what Clairette does: she pours her drink into two other glasses (B1 and B2, which are thus half filled). Has Clairette the same amount as Odette?—*Odette has more.*—Why?—*Because we've put less in* (She pointed to the levels in B1 and B2, without taking into account the fact that there were two glasses).—(Odette's drink was then poured into B3 and B4.) *It's the same.*—And now (pouring Clairette's drink from B1 + B2 into L, a long thin tube, which is then almost full)?—*I've got more.*—Why?—*We've poured it into that glass* (pointing to the level in L), *and here* (B3 and B4) *we haven't.*—But were they the same before?—*Yes.*—And now?—*I've got more.'* Clairette's orangeade was then poured back from L into B1 and B2: 'Look, Clairette has poured hers like Odette. So, is all the lemonade (B3 + B4) and all the orangeade (B1 + B2) the same?—*It's the same* (with conviction).—Now Clairette does this (pouring B1 into C1 which is then full, while B2 remains half full). Have you both the same amount to drink?—*I've got more.*—But where does the extra come from?—*From in there* (B1).—What must we do so that Odette has the same?—*We must take that little glass* (pouring part of B3 into C2).—And is it the same now, or has one of you got more?—*Odette has more.*—Why?—*Because we've poured it into that little glass (C2).*—But is there the same amount to drink, or has one got more than the other?—*Odette has more to drink.*—Why?—*Because she has three glasses* (B3 almost empty, B4 and C2, while Clairette has C1 full and B2).'. . .

Stage II. Intermediary Reactions

Between the children who fail to grasp the notion of conservation of quantity and those who assume it as a physical and logical necessity, we find a group showing an intermediary behaviour (not necessarily found in all children) which will characterize our second stage. Two at least of these transitional reactions are worthy of note. The first of these shows that the child is capable of assuming that the quantity of liquid will not change when it is poured from glass A into two glasses B1 and B2, but when three or more glasses are used he falls back on to his earlier belief in nonconservation. The second reaction is that of the child who accepts the notion of conservation when the differences in level, cross section, etc., are slight, but is doubtful when they are greater. Here we have some examples of the first type:

Edi (6;4): 'Is there the same in these two glasses (A1 and A2)?—*Yes.*—Your mummy says to you: Instead of giving you your milk in this glass (A1), I give it to you in these two (B1 and B2), one in the morning and one at night. (It is poured out.) Where will you have most to drink, here (A2) or there (B1 + B2)?—*It's the same.*—That's right. Now, instead of giving it to you in these two (B1 and B2), she gives it to you in three (pouring A2 into C1, C2 and C3), one in the morning, one at lunchtime and one at night. Is it the same in the two as in the three, or not?—*It's the same in 3 as in 2. . . No, in 3 there's more.*—Why?—. . .— (B1 and B2 were poured back into A1.) And if you pour the three (C1 + C2 + C3) back into that one (A2) how far up will it come?—(He pointed to a level higher than that in A1.)—And if we pour these 3 into 4 glasses (doing so into C1 + C2 + C3 + C4, with a consequent lowering of the level) and then pour it all back into the big one (A2), how far up will it come?—(He pointed to a still higher level.)—And with 5?—(He showed a still higher level.)—And with 6?—*There wouldn't be enough room in the glass.*'

Pie (5;0): 'Is there the same amount here (A1) and there (A2)?—(He tested the levels.) *Yes.*—(A1 was poured into B1 + B2. Is there the same amount to drink in these two together as in the other?—(He examined the levels in B1 and B2, which were higher than in A1.) *There's more here.*—Why?—*Oh yes, it's the same.*—And if I pour the two glasses (B1 and B2) into these three (C1 + C2 + C3), is it the same?—*There's more in the 3.*—And if I pour it back into the 2?—*Then there'll be the same* (B1 + B2) *as there* (A2).'

Here is an example of the second type:

Fried (6;5) agreed that A1 = A2. A1 was poured into B1 + B2. 'Is there as much lemonade as orangeade?—

Yes.—Why?—*Because those* (B1 + B2) *are smaller than that* (A2).—And if we pour the orangeade (A2) as well into two glasses (doing so into B3 + B4, but putting more in B3 than in B4), is it the same?—*There's more orangeade than lemonade.*'—(B3 + B4 thus seemed to him more than B1 + B2).

A minute later he was given A1 half full, and A2 only a third full. 'Are they the same?—*No, there's more here* (A1).—(A1 was then poured into several glasses C.) *It's the same now as there* (A2).' He finally decided, however: '*No, it doesn't change, because it's the same drink* (i.e. A1 = C1 + C2 + C3 + C4 and A1 < A2).'. . .

Stage III: Necessary Conservation

In the replies characteristic of the third stage children state immediately, or almost immediately, that the quantities of liquid are conserved, and this irrespective of the number and nature of the changes made. When the child discovers this invariance, he states it as something so simple and natural that it seems to be independent of any multiplication of relations and partition. . . .

Here are some examples:

Aes (6;6). A1 and A2 were ¾ filled, and then A1 was poured into P1, which was wide and low. 'Is there still as much orangeade as there was in the other glass?—*There's less.*—(A2, which was supposed to be his glass, was poured into P2.) Will you still have the same amount to drink now?—*Oh yes! It's the same, It seems as if there's less, because it's bigger* (= wider), *but it's the same.*—(P1 and P2 were poured back into A1 and A2 and A1 was then poured into B1 + B2.) Has Roger got more than you now?—*He's got the same* (definitely).—And if I pour yours into 4 glasses (A2 into C1 + C2 + C3 + C4)?—*It'll still be the same.*'

Geo (6;6). Her glass was A1, ½ full, and A2, only ⅓ full was supposed to be Madeleine's. 'Who has more?—*I've got more.*—That's right. But Madeleine wants to have the same amount. She divides hers by pouring it into two glasses (C1 + C2) and says: "Now I've got more, or at any rate the same amount as you."—Who has more now?— (After some thought) *It's still me.*—She then pours it into 3 glasses (C1 + C2 + C3). Who has more now?—*Still me.*—Then she pours it into a lot of glasses (C1, C2 and C3 were poured back into A2, the contents of which were then divided between 6 little glasses C). Who has more now?—*Madeleine has more, because it's been poured into the other glasses.*—And if we put it all back into here (A2) where will it come up to?—(She reflected.) *No, Madeleine has less. I thought she had more, but she hasn't.*—Can't it be more?—*No.*—(Glasses C were poured back into A2, then A2 was poured into 8 little glasses.) And now?—*No, it's still the same. It's the same all the time.*' Finally she was given two new glasses A3 and A4, both half-full, and A3 was poured into B1 + B2 : '*She has the same.*—Are you sure it's the same?—*Yes, it's only been poured out.*'

Bert (7;2): 'The orangeade (A1, ⅔ full) is for Jacqueline, the lemonade (A2, ½ full) is for you. Who has more?—*Jacqueline.*—You pour yours (A2) into these two (B1 + B2, which were then full). Who has more?—*It's still Jacqueline.*—Why?—*Because she has more.*—And if you pour this (B1) into those (C1 + C2)?—*It's still Jacqueline, because she has a lot.*—Every change produced the same result: *'It's Jacqueline, because I saw before that she had more.'* Then A3, equal to A4, was poured into C1 + C2 : *'It's still the same, because I saw before in the other glass that it was the same. —But how can it still be the same?—You empty it and put it back in the others!'*

Social and Personality Development in Middle Childhood

Children's Ideas About Friendship: A New Theory

Robert L. Selman and Anne P. Selman

Robert L. Selman and Anne P. Selman are a husband-and-wife research team working out of Harvard University. They have studied children's social development over several decades. Robert Selman teaches developmental psychology at the Harvard Graduate School of Education and has directed the Harvard–Judge Baker Social Reasoning Project. Anne Selman, formerly a preschool teacher, is currently a freelance writer and editor.

Although much research has been performed in the twentieth century on the socialization and social psychology of children and adolescents, until the Selmans' studies were published, very little was available in the research literature on the development trends in childhood friendships.

In some ways this is surprising because there is little in life that is more important to us than good friendship. The article "Children's Ideas About Friendship: A New Theory," *Psychology Today* (October 1979), from which the following selection has been excerpted, is a summary of the Selmans' work concerning the stages that children and youth advance through in making and sustaining friendships. A greatly expanded version of this brief research report, entitled *The Growth of Interpersonal Understanding*, was published by Robert Selman in 1980 through Academic Press.

Key Concept: stages of friendship

Children's understanding of friendship—their reasoning about it, their conceptions and theories about what it is and how it works—is dramatically different from that of adults. Of course, many people are aware that children see the world differently. What is not so obvious is that the differences are not just based on misunderstandings or lack of information. Children have their own original theories for interpreting the events in their lives—theories that change as they grow up. They "know" a lot about friendship. It's simply not the same as what we adults know.

In describing children's changing theories of friendship, our work ultimately addresses how these theories relate to children's social interactions. Just as Lawrence Kohlberg, the Harvard psychologist, described in "The Child as a Moral Philosopher" (*Psychology Today*, September 1968) we believe the child may be properly called a friendship philosopher. Like Kohlberg, in our theory we draw on Piaget's notion that children's cognitive development passes through stages. We, too, have been influenced by George Herbert Mead's emphasis on the growth

of the human capacity to view one's own thoughts, feelings, and actions from another's perspective.

Together with a team of graduate students, we have studied the friendship thinking of over 250 subjects, age three to 45, to determine whether all youngsters pass through distinct stages in their understanding of friendship and, if they do, to identify the distinguishing characteristics of each stage. At the same time, we have attempted to discern whether their changing notions of friendship parallel, in overall form and content, changes in other areas of interpersonal understanding, such as parent-child and peer-group relations. We are also exploring the relation of these concepts, expressed in the calm of interviews, to how children reason in everyday situations. And we are gaining experience in ways to counsel disturbed youngsters who have difficulty getting along with peers—a form of therapy that might be called friendship counseling.

We have found that children's understanding of friendship, like their understanding of justice, does develop in a relatively universal and orderly sequence of stages, each characterized by a distinct, formal structure of thought, which does parallel stages in their thinking about relationships with others in general. More specifically, we have identified five separate stages in their thinking about friendship (the ages are rough guidelines):

Stage 0 (ages three to seven): This is the stage of Momentary Playmateship. The child has difficulty distinguishing between a physical action, such as grabbing a toy, and the psychological intention behind this action. He cannot distinguish between his viewpoint and those of others. Friends are valued for their material and physical attributes and defined by proximity. As one child told us, "He is my friend" Why? "He has a giant superman doll and a real swing set."

Stage 1 (ages four to nine): At this stage, the child can differentiate between his own perspective and those of others. However, he does not yet understand that dealing with others involves give-and-take between people. This is the stage of One-Way Assistance. In a "good" friendship, one party does what the other party wants one to. Assessments of friendship deal with the viewpoint, needs, or satisfaction of only one party. Said one child, "She is not my friend anymore." Why? "She wouldn't go with me when I wanted her to."

Stage 2 (ages six to 12): The child has the ability to see interpersonal perspectives as reciprocal, each person taking into account the other's perspective. This is the stage of Two-Way Fair-Weather Cooperation. Conceptions of friendship include a concern for what each person thinks about the other—it is much more a two-way street. Friendship is not seen as working unless both friends participate. However, the limitation of this stage is that the child still sees the basic purpose of friendship as serving many separate self-interests, rather than mutual interests. "We are friends," said one youngster. "She likes me and I like her. We do things for each other."

Stage 3 (ages nine to 15): Not only can the child take the other's point of view, but by now he or she can also step outside the friendship and take a generalized third-person perspective on it. This is the stage of Intimate, Mutually Shared Relationships. With the ability to take a third-person perspective, the child can view friendship as an ongoing, systematic relationship. There is a shift from seeing friendship as reciprocal cooperation for each person's self-interests to seeing it as collaboration with others for mutual and common interests. Friends share more than secrets, agreements, or plans. Friends share feelings, help each other to resolve personal and interpersonal conflicts, and help each other solve personal problems. The reasoning at this stage can also limit young people's thinking, because close friendship is viewed as an exclusive, intimate, and rather possessive connection. An example: "He is my best friend. We can tell each other things we can't tell anyone else; we understand each other's feelings. We can help each other when we are needed."

Stage 4 (age 12 and older): This is the stage of Autonomous Interdependent Friendships. The individual sees

relationships as complex and often overlapping systems. In a friendship, the adolescent or adult is aware that people have many needs and that in a good friendship each partner gives strong emotional and psychological support to the other, but also allows the friend to develop independent relationships. Respecting needs for both dependency and autonomy is seen as being essential to friendship. According to one child, "One thing about a good friendship is that it's a real commitment, a risk you have to take. You have to be able to support and trust and give, but you have to be able to let go, too."

To get at our subjects' reasoning and derive these five-stage descriptions, we used open-ended, semi-structured interviews, a common technique in developmental descriptive research. In each interview, we presented a dilemma, a story with no ending, to encourage our subjects to share their thoughts, and not just tell us what they thought we wanted to hear. We interviewed more than 50 pilot subjects of widely varying ages. Studying the literature of philosophy and social psychology, and what friendship means to different groups of children and clinicians who work with them, we identified six issues that are critical in children's friendships: 1) formation (making friends), 2) closeness and intimacy, 3) trust and reciprocity, 4) jealousy and exclusion, 5) conflicts and their resolution, and 6) termination (ending friendships).

We then used these issues as a basis for questions in more formal interviews, between 20 and 45 minutes long, with 93 subjects aged three through 34. The subjects either heard or saw a filmstrip of a commonplace interpersonal dilemma geared to their age level. In one of our stories, for example, Kathy has been asked by Jeannette, a new girl in town, to go to an ice-skating show with her the next afternoon. But Kathy has already made a date with her long-time best friend, Debby, to plan a puppet show. To complicate matters, it is clear that Debby does not like Jeannette.

Following the presentation of this dilemma, we asked the children a flexible series of questions related to each of the six friendship issues. For instance, when discussing Kathy's dilemma, they talked about how friendships begin, how a decision to go to the ice show might affect the old friendship, and so on. Each of these questions became a starting point from which to investigate a child's thinking about related personal experiences. We tried to find out not only what the children would do in the dilemma, but also the reasoning behind it. The structure of their thinking, we found, was more evident in the justifications, the arguments, and the explanations for choices than it was in the "answer" to the question of whether Kathy should go with Jeannette.

To see just how important probing the "why" of children's answers can be, consider the following:

Both a 15-year-old and a five-year-old were asked how Kathy might decide whether Jeannette was a good friend. Both responded that it would depend on whether the two were "close to each other." Do these children really have the same beliefs and attitudes about friendship? To find out, the interviewer probed a little deeper, asking, "What do you mean by 'close to each other'?" The 15-year-old responded, "Someone who shares lots of the same values as you." The five-year-old said, "If she moves down the street, real close, they can play a lot."

We analyzed the approximately 1,000 pages of transcribed data from our 93 interviews for regular patterns of thought about the nature of friendship. We described each issue in terms of the five stages previously outlined. Take, for example, the two issues of trust/reciprocity and jealousy/exclusion. At Stage 0, children equate trust with physical capabilities rather than psychological intentions. One four-year-old told us he trusted his friend because "if I give him my toy, he won't break it. He isn't strong enough." Considerations of jealousy and exclusion also emphasize the physical. Responding to the ice-show dilemma, one five-year-old assured us, "Jeannette cannot play because Debby and Kathy are already playing and there is no more room."

On issues of both trust and jealousy, children at Stage 1 realize that feelings and intentions, not just physical characteristics, keep friends together or divide them. But they are still concerned with the experience of only one party rather than both. As one seven-year-old said, "You trust a friend if he does what you want." Jealousy, here, is seen as more than simply a Stage 0 concept of not enough room to play; it is a feeling held by the excluded or rejected person. "Debby will feel bad if Kathy goes with Jeannette," one child told us. Why? "Because she wanted to go, too." But children still perceive that Debby will be unhappy because she is denied what she wants, not because she is upset at being rejected.

By Stage 2, conceptions of both jealousy and trust encompass the feelings or intentions of both parties. "Trust," one nine-year-old observed, "means if you want to do things for him he will want to do things for you." Similarly, youngsters who reason at Stage 2 understand jealousy to mean the excluded child has feelings of being left out. "Debby will feel left out," many children noted, "because Kathy chose someone else over her."

At Stage 3, mutual commitment within a relationship, rather than simple two-way reciprocity or détente between parties, is the major organizing principle around which children think about issues in friendship. Children feel that both trust and jealousy are related to the bond of commitment between two friends, an exclusive bond that does not easily allow for intrusions by others. The emergence of this level of understanding roughly corresponds to that period of preadolescence or early adolescence when children often form powerful attachments to one particular chum. A 12-year-old noted, "Trust is everything in a friendship. You tell each other things that you don't tell anyone else, how you really feel about personal things. It takes a long time to make a close friend, so you really feel bad if you find out that he is trying to make other close friends, too."

Only after the preadolescent or early adolescent child finishes with this period, when he conceives of friendship with such intensity, can he move to a Stage 4 understanding. The older adolescent now believes friends can be mutually close yet grant each other a certain degree of autonomy and independence. "If you are really close friends and trust each other, you can't hold on to everything. You gotta let go once in a while," said one youngster. "Give each other a chance to breathe," he advised. Social circumstances that may prompt jealousy are also more clearly understood at Stage 4. For example, one may understand that people can envy others because of their status in the community.

If valid, the five stages of development should appear at about the same time across issues, only in their prescribed order, under a variety of circumstances, and in the lives of all children interviewed. To determine the model's validity according to these criteria, we interviewed a new sample of 152 subjects, ages three through 40. Of these, 24 came from schools for disturbed children. Of the remaining normal subjects, 48 were interviewed three times over a five-year period. Although a detailed report of our findings is still in progress, we can say that evidence supports the validity of the stages of friendship understanding as we describe them.

Our tests for validity also suggest that the levels of development are hierarchically organized; that is, they form an increasingly comprehensive set of insights. This means that as individuals move to higher levels of interpersonal understanding, they do not discard lower or earlier stages but build upon them. A child capable of reasoning at Stage 2 (for example, of seeing that jealousy can occur because of feeling rejected by another person) does not forget all earlier understanding (for example, that one may be jealous of a friend's physical capabilities or material possessions). However, the child with a higher level of understanding may find the physical, material kind of jealousy not as critical to a friendship as does the child capable of only lower-level understanding.

This does not imply that a child with lower-level understanding will not actually feel jealous if a valued playmate rejects him for another. It suggests, however, that the younger child naturally transforms a psychological experience of personal rejection into physical or material terms and concepts that he can comprehend more readily. Thus, a five-year-old who fears the loss of his playmate to another child says, "There is no more room," even when there is a huge play area, not because he is lying but because this is the way he actually experiences and understands the nature of exclusion in a friendship.

*H*aving established some validity for our model, we have turned from description to application, determining how these stages can be applied to the world beyond the interview session. One widely used educational application is an outgrowth of our data-collection method. We have developed, for example, a curriculum model for elementary and junior high school students that uses the dilemma approach to stimulate discussion among children.

Educators (as well as therapists) may benefit from comparing the level of a child's understanding of friendship, as demonstrated in an interview, with his actual relationships with peers. This relation is probably not simple and straightforward. Still, we might, for example, expect children with higher levels of interpersonal understanding to have friendships that are more meaningful, close, stable, or mature. Our observations suggest that for the most part, this is the case. But recently, we have discovered that some children may be too advanced in their understanding to get along well with peers.

This conclusion emerges from such studies as the one we're doing with four groups of third- and fifth-grade girls in weekly after-school activities. The girls begin each group meeting by planning the day's activity; they then work together for up to an hour and end the meeting with a review discussion of how much was accomplished and how well they cooperated with one another. We are observing how they interact and are relating each girl's interaction to her stage of friendship and interpersonal understanding.

The data have yet to be fully analyzed, but we can informally report on Joannie, one child whose patterns of making friends and getting along in this particular group appear to be, in part, a function of a "too advanced" level of social understanding. Joannie (all the children's names have been changed) continually used Stage 3 strategies and interpretations to communicate with and influence the rest of her third-grade group. When conflicts arose, she exhorted the others to share their feelings, and complained bitterly at times about the "lack of team spirit."

Our data indicate that most children do not express this kind of Stage 3 understanding until seventh or eighth grade. Rather than having a salutary effect, Joannie's exhortations only confused, frustrated, and annoyed the other girls, most of whom were transitional between Stages 1 and 2. She was unable to persuade them to follow her lead. As the natural leader of the group said to us afterward, "Joannie was always doing things and giving the rest of us orders we can't understand."

Joannie did not make friends in this group. This does not mean that high levels of understanding limit a child's friendships, or that there is no relation between a child's level of friendship conception and her friendships. Joannie did, in fact, have a very close friend outside the group who, perhaps not coincidentally, also had a very advanced level of interpersonal understanding.

Much of the work in applying our model has been with children who have been put in clinic schools at least in part because of disturbances in their peer relationships. Our research has shown they have difficulties in achieving a level of interpersonal understanding that is appropriate to their age, or in consistently acting on such understanding. As a result, we include in the clinic school

program at Boston's Judge Baker Guidance Center a variety of situations that encourage children to provide support and feedback to one another, in order to help them think about friendship issues. In these contexts, we have observed a pattern of problems involving the child who is too far behind.

When Tommy was first admitted to a clinic school at age 14, he had a history of severe social deprivation and abuse; frequently, he hid under his desk for fear of teachers and peers. Gradually, he began to form a close tie to his teacher, but it was almost entirely a one-sided, you-give-I-take affair, characteristic of Stage 1 understanding. After a year, Tommy formed his first relationship with another child. Rather than being based on a Stage 3 bond of mutual trust, which is usual at his age, Tommy's relationship was based on playing with toy trucks with a younger child in the class, in a style typical of a Stage 1, one-way notion of friendship. In his occasional attempts to make new friends, Tommy would approach a child with a toy to share, or go up to other children and try to join in their play without any observable expression of reciprocity. If the others did not respond, he would become upset and leave, unaware of the inadequacy of his one-way social strategies.

Our model helps us place Tommy's behavior along a developmental continuum in which he can be compared with other children his age. Rather than focusing on his rebuff of the other child, our analysis looks at Tommy's strategies for interacting with others and sees him as not necessarily hostile or unfriendly, but as a child whose way of making friends is developmentally far behind that of others his age.

Another clinical anecdote illustrates how our model can clarify and help defuse interpersonal problems. During a clinic school session, two 13-year-olds, Ben and Steve, were playing catch on the sidelines while a softball game was taking place nearby. Waiting for his turn at bat, Hank left the game, came over to Ben and Steve, and said, "Throw it here, throw it, throw it." Steve hesitated, but Ben's response was, "Get the (expletive deleted) out of here. There's not enough room for another guy in our catch." Hank persisted and the confrontation escalated until the boys were fighting and their counselor had to separate them and bring them to a friendship-counseling session with the principal.

The first, and often the most difficult, phase of such a session is understanding exactly what happened. In this case, for five or 10 minutes Ben was in a rage, refusing to do anything but curse and threaten Hank, while Hank simply looked morose and sullen. Over the course of the next 15 minutes, however, both boys calmed down. Hank explained, "I asked him to throw me the ball, that's all." Ben's report was that "Hank barged in and screwed up what we were already doing. I told him there was no room for a third guy and he was already playing in the softball game anyway." According to Hank, Ben tried to order him away, and "Nobody does that to me."

Once feelings have subsided a bit and various versions of the facts are presented, the second phase of the crisis-counseling session can begin. Each child is asked to think about his or her own feelings during the fracas and what other events may have contributed to the problem. In this particular session, Ben acknowledged that he got angry and fought not only because there was no room in the catch for Hank but also because he felt that he and Steve were special friends and special friends need time without others bugging them; he felt jealous when Hank "butted in" to this time.

Ben's expression of this clearly Stage 3 conception of friendship, closeness, and jealousy was immediately useful to himself, his counselor, and the principal as a partial explanation for his strong feelings. His reasoning also gave them a sense of what Ben's developmental capacity was and what they could expect him to understand. Of course, other psychological knowledge was important to resolving the problem. For example, Hank was new in school and extremely sensitive to rejection.

In the final phase of the session, the counselors direct each child to look at the behavior and aims of every participant, and ask them (in more colloquial terms, of course) what strategies each might have used to achieve his respective aims more effectively. In this case, they asked Hank to consider different ways of asking to be included in the activity of the two boys—and advised him on what to do if rejected. They suggested to Ben that he consider how to communicate to a third party the importance of a special friendship in a way that would neither embarrass nor insult the other child.

We are not unrealistic. Counselors do not tell children that everyone can or should be friends; we adults wouldn't want to be preached to like that ourselves. Yet learning how to be able to form and maintain friendships, one of the most difficult processes for these children, must be given some systematic attention.

For some troubled children—those with long histories of maladaptive or immature strategies for making or maintaining friendships—discussions, crisis sessions, and the like are not enough. More long-term, intensive treatment is necessary. We have begun to develop new approaches to "friendship therapy" for such cases, working with pairs of children who have been either too withdrawn or too impulsive to form stable relationships with their peers. An adult works once or twice a week with a pair of youngsters to help each of them experience the process of making friends in practice as they play, and in theory as they reflect upon what has happened.

*T*here has been some evidence and much speculation that promoting the natural process of friendship in preadolescence is quite important for later, adult social development. Based on his clinical experience in the early 1950s, psychiatrist Harry Stack Sullivan labeled the normal shift during preadolescence from the concept of détentelike reciprocity typical of Stage 2 ("What should I do to get what I want?") to the concept of mutuality typical of Stage 3 ("How can I contribute to the feelings of worth of my friends?") as a Continental Divide in interpersonal relations. He predicted that those individuals who do not negotiate it successfully would continue as adults to view other people only as a source of self-gratification or as a cause of frustration.

Our own data also suggest that by late adolescence, most individuals intellectually understand the difference between trade-off reciprocity and psychological mutuality, although we still do not know all the factors that may encourage or inhibit the application of this higher-level understanding in people's lives.

Our interview data suggest, however, that where many late adolescents and adults (particularly the males in our sample) have the most difficulty is in making the transition not between Stages 2 and 3, but between 3 and 4. We found many young people reject the intense closeness of Stage 3, but are unable to move to Stage 4, which integrates independence and autonomy with the value of maintaining an intense, and hence vulnerable commitment to another person. This appears to leave these adolescents in a transitional state halfway between stages. We suspect that with time, such conceptual storms over intimacy resolve themselves, as do the emotional storms over intimacy that many young adults experience at this transitional time.

Although our stages describe the friendship conceptions of children growing up, it is intriguing to speculate that they may also explain the qualitative phases that any two adults go through in developing a friendship. As we noted, the individual, when moving to new stages of understanding, does not forget the reasoning of earlier stages. Thus adult friendships may in some way recall and recapitulate the development in childhood.

When meeting for the first time, for instance, two adults may appraise each other's physical appearance or assess the immediate benefits of forming an association with the other person, as in the child's Stage 0. This might be followed by a period in which they explore each other's superficial likes and dislikes, each finding satisfaction in the other's company, as in the childhood Stages 1 and 2. Then may come a tentative long-term sharing of deeper feelings and concerns.

In the end, our two adult friends may develop that combination of personal autonomy and interdependence characteristic of Stage 4. The level that any friendship attains would be based, in part, upon the level of understanding each party could provide.

Such speculation, no matter how plausible, awaits further study. But these questions and the many others raised in the study of friendship can be more thoroughly examined when the investigator is armed with knowledge of normally emerging stages in the understanding of friendship and the role they play in social relations.

The Moral Judgment of the Child

Jean Piaget

Although Swiss psychologist Jean Piaget (1896–1980) is most famous for his stages of cognitive development concerning scientific reasoning, he is also greatly acclaimed for his observational studies of children's moral development (see headnotes concerning Piaget elsewhere in this text). In particular, Piaget's work concerning development of the moral reasons for following rules is considered one of the greatest data-based studies of children's moral development. In his study, Piaget focused on the development of stages of justice reasoning by observing and interviewing Swiss boys playing marbles. First published in French in 1932, this study was not translated and published in English until 1965. The following selection is from that text, entitled *The Moral Judgment of the Child* (Free Press).

This seminal study by Piaget was unmatched in explicating the developmental nature of morality until the pioneering studies of Lawrence Kohlberg nearly 30 years later. Kohlberg's research was based upon Piaget's stages, and Kohlberg followed Piaget in focusing upon justice as the central issue in moral reasoning.

Key Concept: stages of following rules

From the point of view of the practice or application of rules four successive stages can be distinguished.

A first stage of a purely *motor* and *individual* character, during which the child handles the marbles at the dictation of his desires and motor habits. This leads to the formation of more or less ritualized schemas, but since play is still purely individual, one can only talk of motor rules and not of truly collective rules.

The second may be called *egocentric* for the following reasons. This stage begins at the moment when the child receives from outside the example of codified rules, that is to say, some time between the ages of two and five. But though the child imitates this example, he continues to play either by himself without bothering to find play-fellows, or with others, but without trying to win, and therefore without attempting to unify the different ways of playing. In other words, children of this stage, even when they are playing together, play each one "on his own" (everyone can win at once) and without regard for any codification of rules. This dual character, combining imitation of others with a purely individual use of the examples received, we have designated by the term Egocentrism.

A third stage appears between 7 and 8, which we shall call the stage of incipient *cooperation*. Each player now tries to win, and all, therefore, begin to concern themselves with the question of mutual control and of unification of the rules. But while a certain agreement may be reached in the course of one game, ideas about the rules in general are still rather vague. In other words, children of 7–8, who belong to the same class at school and are therefore constantly playing with each other, give, when they are questioned separately, disparate and often entirely contradictory accounts of the rules observed in playing marbles.

Finally, between the years of 11 and 12, appears a fourth stage, which is that of the *codification of rules*. Not only is every detail of procedure in the game fixed, but the actual code of rules to be observed is known to the whole society. There is remarkable concordance in the formation given by children of 10–12 belonging to the same class at school, when they are questioned on the rules of the game and their possible variations.

These stages must of course be taken only for what they are worth. It is convenient for the purposes of exposition to divide the children up in age classes or stages, but the facts present themselves as a continuum which cannot be cut up into sections. This continuum, moreover, is not linear in character, and its general direction can only be observed by schematizing the material and ignoring the minor oscillations which render it infinitely complicated in detail. So that ten children chosen at random will perhaps not give the impression of a steady advance which gradually emerges from the interrogatory put to the hundred odd subjects examined by us at Geneva and Neuchâtel.

If, now, we turn to the consciousness of rules we shall find a progression that is even more elusive in detail, but no less clearly marked if taken on a big scale. We may express this by saying that the progression runs through three stages, of which the second begins during the ego-centric stage and ends towards the middle of the stage of cooperation (9–10), and of which the third covers the remainder of this co-operating stage and the whole of the stage marked by the codification of rules.

During the first stage rules are not yet coercive in character, either because they are purely motor, or else (at the beginning of the egocentric stage) because they are received, as it were, unconsciously, and as interesting examples rather than as obligatory realities.

During the second stage (apogee of egocentric and first half of cooperating stage) rules are regarded as sacred and untouchable, emanating from adults and lasting forever. Every suggested alteration strikes the child as a transgression.

Finally, during the third stage, a rule is looked upon as a law due to mutual consent, which you must respect if you want to be loyal but which it is permissible to alter on the condition of enlisting general opinion on your side.

The correlation between the three stages in the development of the consciousness of rules and the four stages relating to their practical observance is of course only a statistical correlation and therefore very crude. But broadly speaking the relation seems to us indisputable. The collective rule is at first something external to the individual and consequently sacred to him; then, as he gradually makes it his own, it comes to that extent to be felt as the free product of mutual agreement and an autonomous conscience. And with regard to practical use, it is only natural that a mystical respect for laws should be accompanied by a rudimentary knowledge and application of their contents, while a rational and well-founded respect is accompanied by an effective application of each rule in detail.

There would therefore seem to be two types of respect for rules corresponding to two types of social behavior. This conclusion deserves to be closely examined, for if it holds good, it should be of the greatest value to the analysis of child morality. One can see at once all that it suggests in regard to the relation between child and adult. Take the insubordination of the child towards its parents and teachers, joined to its sincere respect for the commands it receives and its extraordinary mental docility. Could not this be due to that complex of attitudes which we can observe during the egocentric stage and which combines so paradoxically an unstable practice of the law with a mystical attitude towards it? And will not cooperation between adult and child, in so far as it can be realized and in so far as it is facilitated by co-operation between children themselves, supply the key to the interiorization of commands and to the autonomy of the moral consciousness? . . .

Third and Fourth Stages

Towards the age of 7–8 appears the desire for mutual understanding in the sphere of play (as also, indeed, in the conversations between children). This felt need for understanding is what defines the third stage. As a criterion of the appearance of this stage we shall take the moment when by "winning" the child refers to the fact of getting the better of others, therefore of gaining more marbles than the others, and when he no longer says he has won when he has done no more than to knock a marble out of the square, regardless of what his partners have done. As a matter of fact, no child, even from among the older ones, ever attributes very great importance to the fact of knocking out a few more marbles than his opponents. Mere competition is therefore not what constitutes the affective motive-power of the game. In seeking to win the child is trying above all to contend with his partners *while observing common rules*. The specific pleasure of the game thus ceases to be muscular and egocentric, and becomes social. Henceforth, a game of marbles constitutes the equivalent in action of what takes place in discussion in words: a mutual evaluation of the competing powers which leads, thanks to the observation of common rules, to a conclusion that is accepted by all.

As to the difference between the third and fourth stages, it is only one of degree. The children of about 7 to 10 (third stage) do not yet know the rules in detail. They try to learn them owing to their increasing interest in the game played in common, but when different children of the same class at school are questioned on the subject the discrepancies are still considerable in the information obtained. It is only when they are at play that these same children succeed in understanding each other, either by copying the boy who seems to know most about it, or, more frequently, by omitting any usage that might be disputed. In this way they play a sort of simplified game. Children of the fourth stage, on the contrary, have thoroughly mastered their code and even take pleasure in juridical discussions, whether of principle or merely of procedure, which may at times arise out of the points in dispute.

Let us examine some examples of the third stage, and, in order to point more clearly to the differentiating characters of this stage, let us begin by setting side by side the answers of two little boys attending the same class at school and accustomed to playing together. (The children were naturally questioned separately in order to avoid any suggestion between them, but we afterwards compared their answers with one another.)

Ben (10) and Nus (11, backward, one year below the school standard) are both in the fourth year of the lower school and both play marbles a great deal. They agree in regarding the square as necessary. Nus declares that you always place 4 marbles in the square, either at the corners or else 3 in the center with one on top (in a pyramid). Ben, however, tells us that you place 2 to 10 marbles in the enclosure (not less than 2, not more than 10).

To know who is to begin you draw, according to Nus, a line called the "coche" and everyone tries to get near it: whoever gets nearest plays first, and whoever goes beyond it plays last. Ben, however, knows nothing about the coche: you begin *"as you like.—*Isn't there a dodge for knowing who is to play first?—No.—Don't you try with the coche?—*Yes, sometimes.—*What is the coche?— . . . (he cannot explain)." On the other hand, Ben affirms that you "fire" the first shot at a distance of 2 to 3 steps from the square. A single step is not enough, and *"four isn't any good either."* Nus is ignorant of this law and considers the distance to be a matter of convention.

With regard to the manner of "firing," Nus is equally tolerant. According to him you can play "piquette" or "roulette," but *"when you play piquette everyone must play the same. When one boy says that you must play roulette, everyone plays that way."* Nus prefers roulette because *"that is the best way":* piquette is more difficult. Ben, however, regards piquette as obligatory in all cases. He is ignorant, moreover, of the term roulette and when we show him what it is he says: *"That is bowled piquette! That's cheating!"*

According to Nus everyone must play from the coche, and all through the game. When, after having shot at the square you land anywhere, you must therefore come back to the coche to "fire" the next shot. Ben, on the contrary, who on this point represents the more general usage, is of opinion that only the first shot should be fired from the coche: after that *"you must play from where you are."*

Nus and Ben thus agree in stating that the marbles that have gone out of the square remain in the possession of the boy who dislodged them. This is the only point, this and the actual drawing of the square, on which the children give us results that are in agreement.

When we begin to play, I arrange to stay in the square (to leave my shooter inside the enclosure). *"You are dished,* cries Ben, delighted, *you can't play again until I get you out!"* Nus knows nothing of this rule. Again, when I play carelessly and let the shooter drop out of my hand, Ben exclaims *"Fan-coup"* to prevent me from saying "coup-passé" and having another shot. Nus is ignorant of this rule.

At one point Ben succeeds in hitting my shooter. He concludes from this that he can have another shot, just as though he had hit one of the marbles placed in the square. Nus, in the same circumstances does not draw the same conclusions (each must play in turn according to him) but deduces that he will be able to play the first shot in the next game.

In the same way, Ben thinks that everyone plays from the place the last shot has led him to and knows the rule that authorizes the player to change places, saying *"du mien"* or *"un empan,"* whereas Nus, who has certainly heard those words, does not know what they mean.

These two cases, chosen at random out of a class of 10-year-old pupils, show straight away what are the two differential features of the second stage. 1) There is a general will to discover the rules that are fixed and common to all players (cf. the way Nus explains to us that if one of the partners plays piquette *"everyone must play the same"*). 2) In spite of this there is considerable discrepancy in the children's information.

A Cross-Cultural Analysis of Sex Differences in the Behavior of Children Aged Three Through Eleven

Beatrice Blyth Whiting and Carolyn Pope Edwards

Beatrice Blyth Whiting was a psychological-anthropologist research associate of the Laboratory of Human Development at Harvard University. She earned her doctorate in anthropology from Yale University in 1942 and has published a number of influential texts, including *Children of Different Worlds: The Formation of Social Behavior*, coauthored by Carolyn Edwards (Harvard University Press, 1988). Following the anthropological tradition, Whiting's research methods are ethnographic, which tend to be a form of qualitative, not quantitative, research. The goal of ethnographies is to systematically and meaningfully observe, record, and interpret culturally related behavior.

In the early 1950s there was a consensus among social scientists that no systematic and adequate study comparing child development in a variety of different cultures existed. To solve this problem the Committee on Social Behavior of the Social Science Research Council held a series of meetings that eventually resulted in a plan. When executed, this plan became known as the "Six Culture Study." Whiting, along with her husband, John Whiting, and their long-time colleague Richard Longabaugh, supervised this grand work, which resulted in the classic text *Children of Six Cultures* (Harvard University Press, 1975). It represents the knowledge gained from nearly two decades of planning, traveling to remote parts of the world, recording data, and analyzing those data.

Carolyn Pope Edwards is a professor of psychology and family and consumer sciences at the University of Nebraska, Lincoln. She earned her B.A. in anthropology (1969) and her Ed.D. in human development (1974) from Harvard, where she was a student of Professor Whiting's. She has conducted research on moral development and child social behavior in Kenya, she has studied the city-run systems of early childhood education and care in Italy, and since 1996 she has researched infant emotional development in Norway. Among her recent publications are *The Hundred Languages of Children: The Reggio Emilia Approach—Advanced Reflections*, 2d ed., coedited by Lella Gandini and George E. Forman (Ablex, 1998) and *Bambini: Italian Experiences of Infant and Toddler Care*, coedited by Lella Gandini (Teachers College Press, 2000).

The following selection is from "A Cross-Cultural Analysis of Sex Differences in the Behavior of Children Aged Three Through Eleven," *The Journal of Social Psychology* (1973). It is based on the fieldwork of Whiting et al.'s Six Culture Study, and it includes comparisons of child development in Kenya, Okinawa, India, the Philippines, Mexico, and New England.

Key Concept: cross-cultural development

Summary

Our study suggests that (*a*) there are universal sex differences in the behavior of children 3–11 years of age, but the differences are not consistent nor as great as the studies of American and Western European children would suggest; (*b*) socialization pressure in the form of task assignment and the associated frequency of interaction with different categories of individuals—i.e., infants, adults, and peers—may well explain many of these differences; (*c*) aggression, perhaps especially rough and tumble play, and touching behavior seem the best candidates for biophysical genesis; (*d*) all of the behaviors that are characteristic of males and females seem remarkably malleable under the impact of socialization pressures, which seem to be remarkably consistent from one society to another; and (*e*) the difference in many of the types of behavior seems to be one of style rather than intent: i.e., seeking help ("feminine") rather than attention ("masculine"), and justifying dominance by appealing to the rules ("feminine") rather than straight egoistic dominance ("masculine").

Although our findings do not speak for adolescent and adult male and female behavior, they should caution the social scientists and animal ethologists who are interested in possible evolutionary and survival theories not to underestimate the effect of learning environments. These learning environments may well be responsible for the behavior frequently attributed to the innate characteristics of male and female primates as inherited by their human descendants.

A. Introduction

This paper investigates the validity of the stereotypes of sex differences as evidenced by behavior of children between the ages of three and 11, observed in natural settings in seven different parts of the world.[1]

Females are frequently characterized as more dependent, passive, compliant, nurturant, responsible, and sociable than males, who in turn are characterized as more dominant, aggressive, and active. Assuming that these statements imply observable behaviors, the authors have attempted to define the stereotypes in such a way as to relate them to the categories of interactions which have been used in a series of observational studies of children in natural settings.

There are two major research issues: are these observable differences biological and genetically determined or the result of learning a society's definition of appropriate sex role behavior? To begin to answer these questions one can proceed by asking, first, whether or not the behaviors said to characterize the male and the female are present in all societies and, second, on the assumption that they are found in societies with a variety of cultures, are there associated universal sex role requirements and associated sex typed socialization pressures?

It is our assumption that sex differences reported for the United States or another Western-type culture may reflect only an idiosyncratic type of socialization. If, however, the same differences appear in societies with divergent cultures and life styles, the assumption of universality gains credence. To determine whether sex differences in behavior are biologically determined or the result of universal sex role requirements is far more difficult. Since our study does not include observations of neonates and young infants, it cannot speak to the possible influence and interaction of biological and social variables. It is possible, however, to note age changes during the 3- to 11-year age span and the presence of associated socialization pressures, and to consider the consistency of sex differences across samples of children.

B. Method

Six of the samples are the children of the Six Culture Study (8, 12), observed in 1954–56 by field teams who lived in communities located in Nyansongo in Kenya, Taira in Okinawa, Khalapur in India, Tarong in the Philippines, Juxtlahuaca in Mexico, and Orchard Town in New England.[2] The societies were selected by the field teams on the basis of interest. They vary in complexity as reflected in occupational specialization, political structure, and settlement pattern, and in social structure. Three societies favor patrilineal extended families, the other three nuclear families. In three societies children sleep and eat with their mother, father, and siblings; in three they share intimate space with other kin. [For detailed analysis of the cultures see Whiting and Whiting (13).]

The children were all three to 11 years of age, with 12 girls and 12 boys in four of the societies, 11 girls and 11 boys in Juxtlahuaca, and eight girls and eight boys in Nyansongo. The children were observed in natural settings, most frequently in their house or yard, on an average of 17 different times for five-minute periods over a period of six to 14 months. The observations were focused on one child at a time by one of the members of the field team plus a bilingual assistant. The social interaction recorded in these paragraphs was subsequently coded at the Laboratory of Human Development at Harvard University. The code was designed to identify the instigator and instigation, if any, to the child's act and the action immediately following his act. The analysis of the 8500 interactions was done on a computer. Of the more than 70 original types of interactions coded, 12 summary types were selected for analysis. [For detailed description of methodology, see Imamura (6, pp. 3–18), Whiting (12), and Whiting and Whiting (14, chap. 3)]. The 12 behaviors are (*a*) *Offering help*—offering food, toys, tools, or general help; (*b*) *Offering support*—offering emotional support and comfort; (*c*) *Seeking help and comfort*—seeking instrumental help or emotional support; (*d*) *Seeking attention and approval*—seeking approval or either positive or negative attention; (*e*) *Acting sociably*—greeting, initiating friendly interaction, or engaging in friendly interaction; (*f*) *Dominating*—attempting to change the ongoing behavior of another to meet one's own egoistic desires; (*g*) *Suggesting responsibly or prosocial dominance*—suggesting that another change his behavior in such a way as to meet the rules of the family or other group, or serve the welfare of the group; (*h*) *Reprimanding*—criticizing another's behavior after the fact; (*i*) *Seeking or offering physical contact*—nonaggressive touching or holding; (*j*) *Engaging in rough and tumble play*—playing which includes physical contact, wrestling, and playful aggression; (*k*) *Insulting*—verbally derogating another; (*l*) *Assaulting*—attempting to injure another.

In 1968–70 a sample of 70 children between the ages of two and 10 were observed in Ngecha, a village situated 20 miles north of Nairobi in Kenya. The children were observed by students for periods of 30 minutes over the course of two years, and their behavior was recorded in running paragraphs and then coded by the observers. The code used was a revised version of the six culture code. The children between three and 10 years of age have been selected for the analysis in this paper; there were 21 girls and 18 boys aged 3–6 years, and nine girls and nine boys aged 7–10.

In order to relate the stereotypes of female and male behavior to the behavior we have observed and coded in our studies, we have attempted to define the stereotypes operationally and then selected from our codes those categories that seem best to represent the definitions. To measure the sex differences in these behaviors, we have used the proportion scores of each child for each of the relevant types of observed behavior, and computed a set of group means from those individual proportion scores. The children have been divided into groups on the basis of sex, age (3–6 years old *versus* 7–11 years old), and cultural sample.

Comparisons between girls and boys in each culture are based on the differences between the mean proportion scores for the behavior types. Significance levels are based on *t* tests between the means of the sex age groups. The comparisons for the pooled samples are based on scores standardized by culture. Nyansongo and Juxtlahuaca, because of the smaller number of children (16 and 22, respectively), are slightly underrepresented when the standardized scores are pooled.

C. Results

1. "Dependency" (Stereotype: girls are more dependent than boys). There are three types of behavior which have been traditionally classified under this heading: (*a*) seeking help, (*b*) seeking attention, (*c*) seeking physical contact. In the six culture study, seeking for help included both asking for instrumental help—that is, requesting help in reaching a goal, asking for an object needed to reach a goal, or requesting food—and asking for comfort or reassurance. Seeking attention included bids for approval and attempts to call attention to oneself by boasting or by performing either praiseworthy or blameworthy acts with the intent of becoming the focus of another person's attention. The category of seeking or offering physical contact included behavior in which the child sought proximity to another, or touched, held, or clung to another.

Table 28.1 presents the comparisons. It can be seen that in five of the six societies girls aged 3–6 were observed to seek help more frequently than did the boys aged 3–6, and the difference between the pooled groups of younger girls and boys is significant at the .05 level. In the 7- to 11-year-old comparison, however, there is an equal split; in three societies girls were observed to seek help more than boys and in three the reverse was true.

Seeking attention is more characteristic of boys than girls. In four of the samples, boys 3–6 seek attention more

frequently than do girls, but for the pooled sample of six societies there is no significant difference. Among 7- to 11-year-olds in the four societies where there are differences, boys seek attention more frequently and the difference is significant at the .05 level.

Girls were observed to seek or offer physical contact more frequently than boys. For the young group as a whole there is a marked sex difference, girls seeking or offering physical contact more frequently than boys ($p < .01$).

In sum, the stereotype of female "dependency" holds for two of the types of behavior—seeking help and seeking or offering physical contact—but is especially true of the younger age groups, there being no significant difference in these behaviors in the 7- to 11-year-olds. Seeking attention, on the other hand, is a male form of "dependency," is clearly present in the 7- to 11-year-old group, and is the only type of "dependent" behavior in which there are significant differences in the older age group.

2. "Sociability" (Stereotype: girls are more sociable than boys). "Sociability," which includes greeting behavior and all acts judged to have the primary intent of seeking or offering friendly interaction, is correlated with "dependent" behavior. As can be seen in Table 28.1, there is a slight tendency for girls to be more sociable than boys but the differences are not significant.

3. "Passivity" (Stereotype: girls are passive). "Passivity" is frequently associated with dependency in the stereotypes of female behavior. This concept is more difficult to operationalize, and we have accepted the definitions of Kagan and Moss (7). They list among other behavioral indices of passivity in the preschool child: (*a*) retreat when dominated by a sibling; (*b*) no reaction when goal object is lost; (*c*) withdrawal when blocked from goal by environmental obstacle; and (*d*) withdrawal from mildly noxious or potentially dangerous situations. During the school years, their passivity measures included (*a*) withdrawal from attack or social rejection, and (*b*) withdrawal from difficult and frustrating situations.

The six culture code included instigational situations described as encountering difficulty, being blocked, having property taken away, being challenged to competition, being insulted or physically attacked, and being dominated. In these situations, if we accept the above definition of "passivity," girls should, according to the stereotype, respond by withdrawal. Two types of instigations occur with sufficient frequency to make analysis possible: (*a*) aggressive instigations, including being insulted, roughed up in a playful fashion, and being physically attacked by peers; and (*b*) dominant instigations. We have analyzed the proportion of responses that are compliant and the proportion of those that are counteraggressive. Table 28.1 presents the findings. "Withdrawal" includes behavior coded as complies, hides, avoids, breaks interaction, deprecates self, and acts shy. "Counteraggression" includes playful aggression or rough and tumble play,

Table 28.1 Difference Between the Mean Proportion Scores of Boys and Girls in the Six Culture Study

Behavior Category		Nyansongo	Juxtlahuaca	Tarong	Taira	Khalapur	Orchard Town	All
Dependency								
1. Seeks help	3–6	+	+	+	+	+*	–	+*
	7–11	–	–	+	+	–**	+	–
2. Seeks attention	3–6	+	–	–	–	–	+	–
	7–11	–	–**	–	–	–	–	–*
3. Physical contact	3–6	+	+	–	+	+	+	+**
	7–11	+	+	+	–	+	+	+
Sociability								
	3–6	+	–	–	+	+	+	+
	7–11	+	–	+	+	+*	–	+
Passivity								
1. Withdrawal from aggressive instigations	3–6	+	–	+	+	–	+	+
	7–11	–	+	+	–	+	–	+
2. Counteraggression in response to an aggressive instigation	3–6	–	–	+	+	+	–	–
	7–11	–	+	–	–*	–	–*	–**
3. Compliance to dominant instigations (prosocial and egoistic)	3–6	–	–	+	+	+	–	+
	7–11	+	+	+	–	–	–	+
4. Initiative (% of acts which are self-instigated)	3–6	–	–	+	–	+	–	–
	7–11	+	–	–	–*	+	+	–
Nurturance								
1. Offers help	3–6	–	+	+	+	+	–	+
	7–11	+	+	+**	–	+	+	+**
2. Gives support	3–6	–	+	+	+*	–	+	+
	7–11	+	+*	+	+	+	+	+***
Responsibility								
	3–6	+	+	+	+	+	+	+*
	7–11	–	+	–	+	–*	+	–
Dominance								
	3–6	–	–	+	–	–	–	–*
	7–11	–	+	–	–	–	–	–
Aggression								
1. Rough and tumble play	3–6	+	–	–	–	–	+	–*
	7–11	+	–	–	–	–	–	–*
2. Insults	3–6	–	–	–	–**	–	–	–**
	7–11	–	–	–	–**	–	+	–*
3. Assaults	3–6	–	–	–	–	–	+	–
	7–11	+	–	–	–	+	–	–

Note: A (+) indicates that the girls' score was higher than the boys'. A (–) indicates that the boys' score was higher than the girls'.
* $p < .05$.
** $p < .01$.
*** $p < .001$.

insulting behavior, and assaulting with the judged intent of injuring another.

It can be seen (Table 28.1) that there is no consistent trend in the six samples in relation to withdrawal from aggressive instigations of peers, although there is an over-all tendency for girls to withdraw more frequently than boys. If one contrasts the proportion of counteraggressive responses when attacked by peers, the findings are more consistent. There is no significant difference between girls and boys in the 3–6 age group but by 7–11 the boys react proportionately and significantly more frequently with counteraggression than do the girls (Table 28.1).

Sex differences in compliance to prosocial and egoistically dominant instigations (Table 28.1) are only slightly in the direction the stereotype would predict. There is one type of compliance which is significantly different for girls and boys: namely, obedience to the mother. In the 7–11 age group girls are significantly more compliant to their mothers' commands and suggestions ($p < .05$). However, this kind of compliance seems a much better operational measure of a variable that might be called "cooperativeness" than it does of passivity. One might interpret that the 7- to 11-year-old girls have identified with their mothers and their mothers' goals and are therefore willing to cooperate when their mothers assign tasks.

In sum, older boys respond more aggressively than girls to aggressive instigations, and there is a trend for boys to be less compliant than girls to the wishes of others. However, these differences are not as great as the literature would imply (1).

There is another dimension of behavior which might be considered the obverse of "passivity": namely, "initiative." As operationalized here, initiative is measured by a proportion score, the proportion of the child's acts that were judged to be self-instigated, rather than responses to the instigations of others. Table 28.1 presents the comparison. It can be seen that in the younger group the proportion of self-instigated acts is similar for boys and girls. In the older age group boys were judged to initiate interaction proportionately more frequently than were girls, but the difference between the two groups does not reach an acceptable level of significance. What accounts for this slight difference? It could either be that girls initiate fewer acts than boys or that they receive proportionately more instigations than do boys. Girls initiate social interaction somewhat more frequently than do boys as judged by rate scores. However, girls receive proportionately more *mands* from others than do boys. That is, other individuals interrupt and try to change the ongoing behavior of girls more than that of boys. It is this higher rate of interruptions or instigations received that makes the older girls have a slightly lower proportion of self-instigated acts than have the boys. Perhaps this higher rate of attempts to change girls' behavior sets is related to the Western stereotype of feminine "sensitivity" or "responsiveness" and to the reports that girls have greater awareness of their immediate environment than do boys (15).

4. "Nurturance" (Stereotype: girls are more nurturant than boys). Table 28.1 presents the difference between boys and girls on two components of this behavior system. It can be seen that in the 3- to 6-year-old period there are no consistent trends across the six societies and no significant differences. By 7–11, however, girls are observed to offer help and support significantly more than boys ($p < .01$ and $< .001$, respectively). That there are no sex differences in the early age group, but rather marked increases with age, does not fit the innate differences hypothesis.

5. "Responsibility" (Stereotype: girls are more responsible than boys). In the six culture study any attempt to change the behavior of others with the judged intent of seeing to the welfare of the group and the maintenance of socially approved behavior has been coded as "suggests responsibly" (prosocial dominance) and distinguished from

"dominance," which was defined as attempts to change the behavior of another to meet the egoistic desires of the actor. As can be seen in Table 28.1, in the 3- to 6-year-old group girls offered responsible suggestions more frequently than boys in all six samples, the difference significant at the .05 level of confidence. By 7–11, however, there is no difference, the boys having increased markedly.

6. "Dominance" (Stereotype: boys are more dominant than girls). Egoistic dominance (Table 28.1), on the other hand, as the stereotype would have it, was observed more frequently in boys. The level of significance is .05 for the young group and not significant in the 7–11 sample.

7. "Aggression" (Stereotype: boys are more physically aggressive than girls; girls are more verbally aggressive). We have coded three types of aggression: (*a*) rough and tumble play, aggression which has a strong sociable component; (*b*) verbal aggression, primarily verbal communications judged to be motivated by the desire to derogate and insult; and (*c*) assaulting, physical aggression judged to be motivated by the desire to cause pain and injury. As can be seen (Table 28.1), boys were observed in rough and tumble play significantly more frequently than girls in both age groups. They were also, contrary to the stereotype, significantly more insulting than girls—the level of significance reaching .01 for the young and .05 for the older group (Table 28.1). Assaulting wit the intent to injure (Table 28.1) was not observed with great enough frequency to make any definitive statement. In five of the samples, the 3- to 6-year-old boys assaulted more; by 7–11 the frequency of the behavior is roughly similar in four samples. The reader is referred back to the findings concerning responses to aggressive instigations. In sum, on all measures of aggression, boys score higher than girls but the differences are significant only in rough and tumble play and verbal aggression, and in the older group in counteraggression when attacked by peers.

D. Discussion

Insulting, rough and tumble play, and dominating egoistically are the most clearly "masculine" types of behavior in the 3- to 6-year-old age group, and seeking or offering physical contact, seeking help, and suggesting responsibly (or prosocial dominance) the most clearly "feminine." The fact that body contact is involved in both rough and tumble play and touching behavior suggests that they are alternative modes of establishing cutaneous contact. One may also dichotomize two types of dominance— straight commanding (dominates), the male mode, and dominance justified by rules of appropriate behavior (suggesting responsibly), the female mode. In the older age group nurturance becomes a clearly "feminine" characteristic, and the measures of aggression distinguish the boys. Seeking attention appears to be both a "masculine" form of dependency and, in its self-arrogating aspects, a measure of competitiveness.

Although it is obviously impossible to do more than speculate about biophysical determinants of these behaviors, the sex differences that are greatest in the younger group might be considered the best candidates for sex-linked characteristics. The age trends in the behavioral systems are presented in Table 28.2.

Seeking and offering of physical contact, a behavior that differentiates the sexes clearly in the 3- to 6-year-old group, decreases significantly with age. One might interpret this as a decrease in the desire for physical contact, contact which may have served as a pain and anxiety reducer at the younger age and now is less frequently needed. The significant increase of nurturance and responsibility with age suggests that these are behaviors which increase with socialization pressure. Nurturance increases significantly in girls, and responsibility or prosocial dominance increases in both girls and boys, at the .06 level of significance for girls and the .001 level for boys. Since by 7–11 years of age there is no significant sex difference in the proportion of responsible suggestions, the significant increase for the boys may indicate that pressure for responsibility begins at an earlier age for girls.[3] The proportionate increase of self-instigated acts of boys may reflect the fact that girls are assigned tasks that keep them closer to the house and adults, tasks and setting that are associated with more requests and demands from others.

There is evidence in our data of differential pressure on girls and boys to be nurturant. Older girls in our sample took care of children under 18 months of age more frequently than did boys ($p < .05$), and infant care is undoubtedly one of the variables contributing to the significant increase in the proportion of offering help and support. There is also evidence that more girls than boys in the younger age group are assigned responsible tasks. By the older age group, however, boys are engaged in animal husbandry, and both girls and boys are beginning to help in agricultural work. Boys feed and pasture animals significantly more frequently than girls ($p < .001$); girls do significantly more domestic chores (cleaning $p < .001$, food preparation, cooking, and grinding $p < .001$) and care for siblings. The number of tasks assigned to both boys and girls increases significantly with age (8).

These sex differences in assigned work are associated with the different frequency with which boys and girls interact with various categories of people: i.e., adults, infants, and peers. Caring for infants and performing domestic chores require that girls stay in the vicinity of the house and yard and hence remain more frequently in the company of adult females. Both young and older girls interact with female adults more frequently than do boys ($p < .05$ and $< .01$, respectively), and older girls interact with infants significantly more than do boys ($p < .01$). Herding and other animal husbandry chores take the boy away from the house. Boys interact less frequently with adults and infants and proportionately and significantly more with peers (3–4 years $p < .05$; 7–10 $p < .01$), especially male peers.

What can be said about the consequences of this difference in type of dyadic interaction? To answer this question we analyzed the types of behavior that children direct most frequently to adults, to infants, and to child peers. These three age grades of people seem to draw different types of behavior from children, and the behavior which children direct to a given category is remarkably similar across cultures (14). The acts most frequently directed toward adults are (a) seeking help, (b) seeking or offering physical contact, (c) seeking attention, and (d) seeking friendly interaction, or "sociability"—the first two of these being "feminine" type behavior (see Table 28.1). When interacting with infants, children most frequently offer help, support, and sociability—the first two again "feminine" type behaviors. In contrast, when interacting with peers, sociability, rough and tumble play, and derogatory and insulting interchanges are most frequent, the last two of these "masculine" type behaviors.

Two studies in Kenya and research in progress in Guatemala confirm our deduction that girls are at home more frequently than are boys (9, 10, 11). In Kenya, Sara Nerlove working in Nyansongo and Robert and Ruth Munroe working in Vihiga made observational studies of same-aged pairs of girls and boys. At the same times each day they sought out the children's whereabouts and measured their distance from home. The girls were found to be nearer to home significantly more often than the boys.

Table 28.2   Showing Significant Changes in the Mean of the Proportion Scores of the Behavior of Girls and Boys from Ages 3–6 to 7–11

Behavior	Girls	Boys
Offers help	+**	
Offers support	+*	
Responsibility		+***
Seeks or offers physical contact	−**	−***
Proportion of self-instigated acts		+*

Note: A (+) indicates an increase with age, a (−) indicates a decrease.
* $p < .05$.
** $p < .01$.
*** $p < .001$.

Although these findings may be interpreted to indicate that girls are innately more timid than boys, it seems more parsimonious to assume that they reflect socialization pressure and differential task assignment, girls being kept home to perform infant tending and domestic chores.

The question then becomes why girls are assigned domestic chores and the care of infants significantly more frequently than are boys. It is because girls are innately better suited to such tasks or does it simply reflect a universal sex typing and a preparation of young girls for their adult roles? In all the societies we have studied, women have the major responsibility for the care of infants and for domestic chores. This is in accord with the findings of cross-cultural studies on the division of labor (3). Assigning these chores to girls rather than boys may simply reflect the early training of girls for the expected female role.

This differential socialization pressure on girls is in accord with the findings of Barry, Bacon, and Child (2) in their cross-cultural study of sex differences in socialization, based on ratings made from published ethnographic reports of societies distributed around the world. They found that girls received more pressure to be nurturant, obedient, and responsible, boys more pressure to achieve and be self-reliant. In our sample the greater frequency in the proportion of nurturant behavior, its increase with age, and the greater compliance to mothers of girls are as one would predict from the Barry, Bacon, and Child findings. As noted above the greater amount of time spent caring for infants can be interpreted as greater pressure toward nurturance. Pressure toward obedience as reported by the mothers of the six cultures is greatest in those societies that assign infant care and similarly is exerted more on girls than on boys (13, 14). It is also greater in those societies in which children are engaged in animal husbandry. Responsible behavior, as we have measured it, does not show significant sex differences in the six culture samples, but does in recent observational studies in Kenya (see footnote 3). However, since there is a high correlation between the Barry, Bacon, and Child ratings on pressure toward responsibility and the number of chores assigned to girls and boys as reported in the ethnographic monographs, the significant difference in the number of chores assigned to girls and boys in the 3- to 6-year-old age group is in accord with their findings. In the older group there is great variation from one society to another. The crucial variable seems to be economic; in societies with animal husbandry or agricultural work that can be assigned to boys, there are no sex differences in amount of work required of girls and boys after 7–8 years of age.

Our measures of achievement-oriented and self-reliant behavior are less direct, but are also in accord with the sex differences in socialization reported by Barry, Bacon, and Child. Seeking attention as we have coded it includes self-arrogation and boasting. In the older age group, as reported above, boys are proportionately significantly higher than girls in this type of behavior. If we assume that these behaviors are motivated by achievement

needs, the findings are as predicted. The proportion of self-instigated acts might be considered a measure of self-reliance. There is a trend, as reported above, for boys 7–11 to be proportionately higher in acts that were not judged to be clearly instigated by the actions of others. It should be noted again here, however, that this measure may simply reflect the fact that boys are interrupted less frequently by the *mands* of others than are girls. The ethnographic sources make it difficult to distinguish between being allowed to do what one wishes unsupervised by others and self-reliance.[4]

In sum, our evidence suggests that the nature of the tasks assigned to girls is the best predictor of four of the five primary types of "feminine" behavior (see Table 28.1), since (*a*) the tasks require more frequent interaction with infants and adults and (*b*) the nature of the tasks themselves involves care of others—offering help and comfort to infants, preparing and offering food to the entire family—all work focused on the needs of others and the welfare of the family. These tasks clearly require a child to be compliant—to be willing to service the requests of others and to obey task-related instructions. Furthermore, all of these tasks require the girl to be tolerant of interruptions and demands for succorance, and require her to be constantly alert to the motivational states of others—behaviors possibly related to field dependence, a quality commonly attributed to women (15).

It is interesting to note here societal differences in "femininity" scores. Orchard Town girls, for example, score low in offering help and support and do significantly less infant care than girls in other societies.

Further insight into the possible consequences of task assignment can be gained by looking at the "masculine" and "feminine" profiles of boys who are assigned domestic chores and the care of infants. There are many societies in which young boys are required to do such work. Among these are East African societies in which women are the agriculturalists, men traditionally the pastoralists and warriors. In these societies young boys are classified with women and girls until they approach pubescence, at which time they are frequently initiated into manhood in formal *rites de passage*. Nyansongo, one of the six cultures, is an example of such a society. The women, who work four or five hours a day in the gardens, assign the care of infants to a designated older sibling and the tending of the cooking fire and the washing of utensils to the same or some other child of the family. Although mothers prefer girl nurses, it is not considered inappropriate to delegate the responsibility to a boy if there is no female of the proper age—in this case under 10 years of age—since older girls are either in school or helping in agricultural work.

Our evidence suggests that requiring boys to tend babies and perform domestic chores reduces sex differences in the mean proportion scores of "masculine" and "feminine" behavior in two of these East African societies. In Nyansongo half of the boys aged five and over took care of infants and half helped with domestic chores. When one contrasts the mean proportion scores of the boys and girls, the magnitude of the sex differences is smaller than in any of the six societies with the exception of Orchard Town, which will be discussed later. Nyansongo boys score higher than would be predicted on offering help and offering support, young boys scoring higher than young girls on both types of behavior. Nyansongo girls are aberrantly high in rough and tumble play, younger girls in assaulting, and boys retreat from aggressive attacks from peers as frequently as do girls. The comparisons are similar in Ngecha, our other East African sample. In the Ngecha sample, the older boys offer help and support somewhat more frequently than do the girls ($p < .22$), the younger boys seek sociability significantly more than do the girls ($p < .05$), the older girls seek attention slightly more frequently than do the boys ($p < .23$), and the girls of both ages were observed in rough and tumble play as frequently as the boys.

A more detailed analysis of the effect of assigning "feminine" tasks to boys has been presented by Carol Baldwin Ember (5). In 1968 when she was working in Oyugis in Western Kenya, by a fluke of sex ratio there were an unusually large number of households in which there was no girl of the appropriate age to care for an infant sibling, and hence there was quite a large sample of boys who were acting as nurses and doing domestic chores. Using this unusual opportunity Carol Ember undertook an observational study of these boys. She compared them to a matched sample of boys who were not responsible for "feminine" chores, as well as to a sample of girls. She used a code similar to that used in the six culture study. Her observations were made when the children were not working.

Her findings based on a linear regression of the means for the three groups—boys who did little child tending or domestic chores which kept them inside the homestead, boys who did many such tasks, and girls—show significant differences between the three samples. Boys high on feminine work had behavior profiles that were more "feminine" than boys who did not perform such work. They were more responsible (prosocially dominant), less aggressive (including assaulting and insulting), less dependent (including seeking help, support, attention, information, and material goods),[5] and less egoistically dominant (including dominating, reprimanding, and prohibiting action egoistically) (all differences significant at the .01 level). The differences were not great, however, when Ember compared boys who were and who were not assigned "feminine" chores which took them *outside* the homestead: i.e., carrying water, fetching wood, digging root crops, picking vegetables, and going to the market to mill flour. Her data do not show the predicted differences in nurturant behavior.

In sum, in societies where boys take care of infants, cook, and perform other domestic chores, there are fewer sex differences between boys and girls, and this decrease is due primarily to the decrease in "masculine" behavior

in boys; boys are less egoistically dominant, score proportionately lower in some forms of aggression, seek attention proportionately less frequently, and score higher on suggesting responsibly. On the other hand, the 3- to 6-year-old girls in these societies are high on assaulting and miscellaneous aggression, and both younger and older girls score low on sociability (14).

Although there are no samples of girls in any of the six cultures who do "masculine" type tasks, the girls of Orchard Town, New England, as mentioned above, do very little infant care. Since most New England families consist of two children averaging around two years apart in age, and since there are no courtyard cousins, young nieces, nephews, or half-siblings as in extended and polygynous families, there is little opportunity for Orchard Town girls to care for infants except as paid baby sitters. In general, however, Orchard Town mothers do not hire baby sitters under 11 years of age, Orchard Town girls are also more strongly committed to education and may aspire to jobs that are considered appropriate to both sexes. Their work in school is practically identical with that of boys. It is interesting, therefore, to see how this sample of U.S. girls who have been observed in natural settings fits the predicted patterns on the behaviors which we have found to be significantly different between boys and girls in the pooled samples. As in Nyansongo, the magnitude of the differences is small. The direction of the insignificant differences is as expected with one exception, the young girls scoring higher than the boys in the proportion of attention seeking, "masculine" type behavior. They also score higher than any other sample of girls on this type of behavior— behavior which in general is higher among the children of the more complex societies (Orchard Town, Khalapur, and Taira) where schooling and achievement are more highly valued (14). It is a type of behavior which, when directed toward adults, is frequently motivated by a desire for approval and, as discussed above, when directed toward peers may have affiliation or self-arrogation as its goal. It is a frequent behavior in New England classrooms.

As noted above, the Orchard Town girls score the lowest of the samples of girls on offering help and support, "feminine" traits, and have one of the lowest percentages of interaction with infants.

In sum, in both the East African societies where "feminine" work is assigned to boys and in Orchard Town, New England, where less "feminine" work is assigned to girls and where there is less difference in the daily routine of boys and girls, the behavior of girls and boys does not show as great differences as in other societies.

Notes

1. This study is based on the field work of the six culture study, financed by the Behavioral Science Division of the Ford Foundation, and on field work in Kenya by the Child Development Research Unit, financed by the Carnegie Corporation. The analysis of the data has been made possible by a United States Public Health Grant, MH-0196.

2. Observations were gathered by Robert L. LeVine and Barbara LeVine, Thomas and Hatsumi Maretzki, Leigh Minturn, William and Corrine Nydegger, A. Kimball and Romaine Romney, and John and Ann Fischer.
3. In Ember's study in Western Kenya and in the ongoing research in Kenya there are significant sex differences in prosocial dominance, girls scoring significantly higher than boys in the 7- to 11-year age groups.
4. For discussion of the problem, and data on achievement and self-reliance among the !Kung Bushmen of the Khalahari, see Patricia L. Draper (4).
5. It is unfortunate that dependency as operationally defined by Ember included both the masculine and feminine modes.

References

1. Bardwick, J. M. Psychology of Women: A Study of Biocultural Conflicts. New York: Harper & Row, 1971.
2. Barry, H., III, Bacon, M. K., & Child, I. L. A cross-cultural survey of some sex differences in socialization. *J. Abn. & Soc. Psychol.*, 1957, **55**, 327–332.
3. D'Andrade, R. G. Sex differences and cultural institutions. In E. E. Maccoby (Ed.), *The Development of Sex Differences*. Stanford, Calif.: Stanford Univ. Press, 1966.
4. Draper, P. L. !Kung Bushman childhood: A review of the Barry, Child, and Bacon hypothesis regarding the relation of child training practices to subsistence economy. Paper presented at the annual meetings of the American Anthropological Association, New York. November, 1971.
5. Ember, C. R. The effect of feminine task assignment on the social behavior of boys. *Ethos*, 1973, in press.
6. Imamura, S. Mother and Blind Child: The Influence of Child Rearing Practices on the Behavior of Preschool Blind Children. New York: Amer. Found. for Blind, 1965.
7. Kagan, J., & Moss, H. A. Birth to Maturity. New York: Wiley, 1962.
8. Minturn, L., & Lambert, W. W. Mothers of Six Cultures: Antecedents of Child Rearing. New York: Wiley, 1964.
9. Munroe, R. L., & Munroe, R. H. Effect of environmental experience on spacial ability in an East African society. *J. Soc. Psychol.*, 1971, **83**, 15–22.
10. Nerlove, S. B. Private communication, 1971.
11. Nerlove, S. B., Munroe, R. H., & Munroe, R. L. Effect of environmental experience on spatial ability: A replication. *J. Soc. Psychol.*, 1971, **84**, 3–10.
12. Whiting, B. B., *Ed.* Six Cultures: Studies of Child Rearing. New York: Wiley, 1963.
13. Whiting, B. B., & Whiting, J. W. M. Task assignment and personality: a consideration of the effect of herding on boys. In W. W. Lambert & R. Weisbrod (Eds.), *Comparative Perspectives on Social Psychology*. Boston: Little, Brown, 1971.
14. Whiting, J. W. M., Whiting, B. B., & Longabaugh, B. Children of six cultures. In press.
15. Witkin, H. A., Dyk, R. B., Faterson, H. R., Goodenough, D. R., & Karp, S. A. Psychological Differentiation. New York: Wiley, 1962.

Physical and Cognitive Development in Adolescence

Psychological Correlates of Somatic Development

Mary Cover Jones

Mary Cover Jones (1896–1987) studied at Vassar College and earned her Ph.D. from Columbia University. Most of her career as a research psychologist was spent at the University of California, Berkeley.

Although the following selection concerns her work correlating physical development with psychological development, Jones had an earlier claim to fame: She was the first to scientifically document the behavioral extinction of fear in a child (the case of "Peter"). She was inspired in this work by her close association with James Watson, the founder of behaviorism, and her observation of Watson's famous movie documenting the fear conditioning of "Little Albert."

The most valuable research design in the field of human development, and also the most difficult to accomplish, is the "longitudinal design." Jones is to be applauded for accomplishing a well-respected longitudinal study spanning research of the same group of males from the 1930s into the 1960s. The following selection, which details this research, is taken from "Psychological Correlates of Somatic Development," *Child Development* (1965). In it, Jones summarizes her work comparing the rate of physical maturation in adolescent boys with the later psychological attributes of these boys, now grown into men.

Key Concept: somatic development

his longitudinal study relates rate of physical maturing to psychological variables using a number of somatic criteria and personality measures. The boy who is accelerated in physical development is socially advantaged in the peer culture. In adulthood the same success pattern continues. He is poised, responsible, achieving in conformity with society's expectations. He may be conventional in cognitive patterns and in attitudes. The boy whose pubescence came late is active and exploring with evidence of compensatory adaptations. In adulthood, he is insightful, independent, and impulsive. Individual differences indicate the complexity of personal and social interactions with influence development.

This study continues a series that has dealt with the relationship between some aspects of rate of physical maturing in adolescent boys and certain behavioral and personality characteristics. Since the 1950 report on physical maturing among boys as related to behavior (M. C. Jones & Bayley, 1950), there have been more than a dozen publications that use the Oakland Growth Study sample and deal with some psychological concomitants of

rate of maturing as defined by skeletal age. The published studies were reviewed in 1963 (Eichorn).

The Sample

Members of this longitudinal study (H. E. Jones, 1938) are now in their early 40's. They were observed, measured, and tested as school children and studied again at intervals in adulthood (H. E. Jones, Macfarlane, & Eichorn, 1960). Evaluation of the adult sample as compared to the original has shown that although death, distance, and disinclination have attenuated the sample of 150 who were with the study at high-school graduation to 99 in the 1958–60 follow-up, there has been no consistent bias that would seem to account for dropouts (M. C. Jones, 1957).

The adult study members did not differ from the original sample in (*a*) general intelligence as measured by the Terman Group Test of Mental Ability, (*b*) socioeconomic status (Edwards, 1933), (*c*) childhood family size, and (*d*) some selected adolescent personality variables (Haan, 1962; Stewart, 1962).

The Procedure

The purpose of this report is threefold: first, to consider the value of using age measures of maturing other than consistent skeletal age for comparisons on personality measures; second, to specify the contributions of certain physical characteristics associated with pubescence, such as stature, strength, and sexual development to behavior; third, to report on recent available psychological measures from an intensive follow-up when the groups were in their late 30's.

Psychological Comparisons Based on Age Measures

To examine age measures of maturity other than consistent skeletal age, the following were used:

1. The Stolzes' (1951) Analysis of the Physical Characteristics of This Same Sample. The assessments used by the Stolzes began at around the eleventh year. (Skeletal-age measures were not available until age 14.) A comparison of extreme groups using the Stolzes' indexes of chronological age at the onset, at the apex, and at the end of puberal growth in height enabled a comparison at stages within the puberal-growth cycle to determine whether some periods were more predictive than others of certain psychological behaviors. There are, of course, overlapping cases in all of these extreme group samples. (Comparisons were also made between early or late-maturing boys and those who matured at an average rate. The relationships were not as pronounced nor as consistent as those that emerged from comparing extreme groups.)

Chronological Age at Reaching 90 Per Cent Mature Height. Nicolson and Hanley's (1953) factor-analytic study of 11 indicators of adolescent-maturation rate found this to be the best single measure of the general factor, which was sufficient to account for all reliable covariations. Correlational procedures were used with this measure and included the entire sample of 88 boys.

For all of these comparisons using age indexes, only two psychological measures will be reported. These are observational ratings of individuals in small, like-sexed groups in a free-play setting in adolescence (Newman & H. E. Jones, 1946) and the California Personality Inventory (CPI) scale (Gough, 1960) scores at age 33.

Free-Play Ratings in Adolescence. Free-play ratings were compared at yearly intervals (ages 13 through 16) for three groups of individuals who are contrasted in rate of maturing at the onset (average age for the total group 12½ years), at the apex (average age 14), and at the end (average age 15½) of the growth period for height.

One-tenth of the cases considered here in the early maturing category appear in all three distributions; 16 per cent appear at two levels each. Among the late developers the overlap is greater, the corresponding percentages being 24 in all three categories, 61 per cent in the onset and end group, 52 per cent common to the apex and end categories. The number of cases in each group varied from 12 to 22.

Those who represent opposite extremes of the maturity distribution at the onset of puberty show the most strikingly differentiated patterns, and these are most marked near the end of their high-school years. These individuals were conspicuously disparate at the beginning of the race toward maturity, and some continued in this relative position throughout adolescence. The reinforcing effect of this continued variation in development might be expected to reveal pronounced behavioral concomitants. In this respect they resemble those who were consistently deviate in skeletal maturity. Table 29.1 presents the significance of the difference in standard scores on the free-play ratings for the index of puberal height, for the consistently early or late in skeletal maturity, and for correlations with the total sample of 88 boys at the age of reaching 90 per cent mature height.

The over-all pattern that emerges is consistent with that described in the first published report in 1950. The early maturing are rated as having superior physique and physical abilities. "Good physique" is representative of 14 items in these categories. Differences first appear in contrasting groups at age 14 and are significant at later ages for all three groups (those whose growth in height was early at the onset, the apex, or the end of their puberal period). By the end of high school, these boys are also rated as more "poised," "relaxed," "good natured," and "unaffected." The late-maturing boys are expressive, dynamic, and bouyant. However, they are also rated as more "tense" and "affected" in their high-school years.

Peskin (1963), with rather similar findings based on interview data for boys in the Guidance Study (Macfarlane, 1938), considers the activity and zestfulness of the late maturer to be evidence of his freedom to experiment and resist confining social rules which would circumscribe his behavior.

The description of the late maturer in the Oakland Growth Study sample likewise could be interpreted to indicate that he is more explanatory and tolerant of impulse, especially in the light of the CPI scale scores in adulthood (Table 29.2).

CPI Measures in Adulthood

The *California Personality Inventory Manual* (Gough, 1960) groups the first six scales under the heading "Measures of Poise, Ascendancy, and Self-Assurance." All of these scales show higher scores for those who matured early by one or another of the three criteria. The second series of six scales are labeled "Measures of Socialization, Maturity, and Responsibility." Again the early maturers earn higher scores. The third CPI scale score group— "Measures of Achievement Potential and Intellectual

Table 29.1 Free-Play Ratings—Comparison of Three Maturity Measures

High Ratings	Puberal-Height Index				Skeletal		r
	Age				Age		(90% Mature
	13	14	15	16	14	16	Height)
Early maturers rate high:							
Good physique		*	***	***	***	**	_*
Masculine physique		*	***	***	*	***	_*
Physical efficiency		*	**	**	**	***	_*
Sex appeal			*	**	**	***	...
Matter of fact				**	...	**	...
Relaxed				***	...	***	...
Late maturers rate high:							
Talkative	...	...	...	**	...	...	...
Active	...	...	...	**	**	*	...
Peppy	...	...	...	**	...	...	*
Busy	...	...	...	*	...	...	**
Eager	*	**	...	***	**	**	**
Social	...	...	...	**	...	...	...
Submissive	...	...	**	...	...	...	...
Carefree	...	**	...	...	...	...	...
Good natured	...	**a	...	...	...	***b	...
Unaffected	...	*a	...	...	...	**a	...

aLate.
bEarly.
*Significant at the .10 level.
**Significant at the .05 level.
***Significant at the .01 level.

Efficiency"—is meaningful chiefly in indicating that early maturers achieve via conformity.

Scores are slightly higher for the later maturers on the scale "Achievement via Independence." (We have found no significant differences in tested mental ability for the late as contrasted with the early maturers.) The implication is that difference in rate of maturing may be related to different modes of expressing intellectual competencies. This is further suggested in the late maturers' higher scores on psychological mindedness and flexibility.

The most clear-cut differentiation occurs on the psychoneurotic scale developed by Jack Block (1961a). Since the late developers score near the average, this means that the accelerated mark fewer diagnostic items on this scale. The early maturers' denial of negative feelings is in keeping with their tendency to mark items positively, which give them high scores on the good-impression scale.

The CPI scale scores at age 33 for the various maturity groups reflect the greatest differentiation for those who were consistently early or late to mature by the skeletal age criterion, the measure used in the earliest publications. There are more significant differences here than reported earlier, due to the fact that three additional cases in each extreme group came in late for study and were added to the sample for this report. Also, some changes and additions have been made in the CPI scales.

Psychological Comparisons Based on Physical Indexes Related to Maturity Status

What were some of the external signs of maturity that served to alert these growing individuals to their developmental progress? A question in the follow up interview when the subjects were in their late 30's was: "Do you think you developed earlier, at about the same time as, or later than the boys of your age?"

Most individuals answered correctly in terms of our corroborating data. This is evident from their retrospective memories concerning size, strength, weight, growth of pubic hair and of sex organs.

Some of the somatic characteristics associated with maturing as suggested by these psychological picture that emerges in the contrasting groups. The extreme groups compared here were:

1. The Stolz sample of those who were tallest as contrasted with those who were shortest at the onset and at the end of the puberal period.
2. Boys with a fat period as contrasted with those who had no fat period—a group selected by the Stolzes for this report.
3. Those with a puberal period of short duration as contrasted with those with a long puberal period.

Table 29.2 CPI Scale Scores Comparison of Three Maturity Measures

| High Ratings | Puberal-Height Index | | | Consistent Skeletel Age | | | r |
	Early	Late	Signifance	Early	Late	Signifance	90% Mature Height)
No. of cases	13	12		12	15		58
Early are high:							
Dominance	33	27	*	33	26	*	***
Capacity for status	22	21	...	23	21	**	...
Sociability	27	23	**	28	25	*	**
Well being	41	38	*	41	39	...	**
Responsibility	34	30	**	33	30	*	*
Socialization	41	34	***	40	34	**	***
Self-control	33	28	...	34	29	**	...
Good impression	23	16	***	24	17	***	***
Achievement via conformity	31	27	...	32	28	**	**
Late are high:							
Psychologically minded	12	15	**	13	14	...	...
Flexible	10	14	*	10	15	**	...
Psychoneurotic	4	8	**	5	8	**	***

*Significant at the .10 level.
**Significant at the .05 level.
***Significant at the .01 level.

4. Those who were contrasted in pubic-hair rating near the onset of puberty and also half way through the puberal cycle at age 15 when ratings were most disparate.

5. Those whose onset and cessation of growth of the glans penis was early or late.

6. The H. E. Jones (1949) sample of those consistently strong or weak during adolescence.

Again free-play ratings and CPI scores were used for the comparisons.

Free-Play Ratings. The behavioral characteristics associated with strength are very similar to those for early maturity. Shortness yields ratings comparable to those for late maturity. Boys with a fat period are seen as more phlegmatic and feminine than those with whom they are compared. Pubic-hair ratings for this sample are less differentiating than would have been predicted, since they are frequently used as a measure of maturity status. Most productive was the correlation of free-play ratings with the assessment of the pubic-hair index near the onset of puberty. Early growth of the glans penis is associated with many favorable ratings of behavior and personality. (Table 29.3).

CPI Measures. The data on groups contrasted in physical characteristics for the CPI scores conform to that for the maturity groups, though the differences are fewer. The tall and strong resemble the early maturing in their scores, the weak tend to earn scores similar to those of the late maturing. The other categories yield only tentative findings in line with expectations.

Measures of Adult Interviews

Of all the criteria examined in this effort to relate somatic variation to psychological characteristics, both in adolescence and in adulthood, our first selection, that of being a consistently early or late developer by skeletal-age criteria, still seemed as satisfactory as any other. Therefore, it was the classification used to examine measures available from the follow-up study when the members were approximately 38 years old.

Impressions in the form of ratings have been recorded for these individuals as they related their life histories in interviews and as they retrospectively described themselves as adolescents. Four separate rating schemes have been used by the institute staff.

First to be examined were ratings of retropective memories (in 17 categories) made by the interviewer and another psychologist, neither of whom had had previous contact with the subject. The material was provided by the study members as they answered questions pertaining to their adolescent social behavior, relation to parents, school experiences, and self concepts.

Differences between the two maturity groups (those consistently accelerated or retarded in skeletal age) appear, with the early developers remembering enjoyment of social activities, of being early to develop, and of having a pleasant affect in regard to being physically mature at an early age (Table 29.4).

The late maturing are rated as having reported a significantly greater number of memories concerning their heterosexual or social-sex development. But examination of protocols indicates that, without exception, this

Table 29.3 Comparison of Free-Play Ratings for Extreme Groups on Five Physical Variables

	Tall	Short	Strong	Weak	Not Fat	Fat	Pubic-Hair Ratings (r)	Early Onset Growth Glans Penis
No. of cases	18	13	10	10	28	22	88	12
Eager	...	**	...	...	**	...	_**	*
Good natured	...	*	*	...	**	...	...	**
Social	...	**	...	...	***	...	_*	*
Popular	...	**	**	...	*	...	...	**
Enjoys games	...	*	...	...	**	...	_*	...
Leader	...	...	...	...	...	...	...	***
Effect on group	...	...	*	...	...	...	_*	**
Confident	...	...		...	...	...	...	***
Uninhibited	...	...		...	...	...	_**	*
Assured	...	...	...	...	...	...	...	***
Matter of fact	...	...	...	...	...	...	**	...
Relaxed	...	...	***	...	...	...	...	**
Cheerful	...	...	...	...	...	...	...	**
Carefree	...	**	**	...	...	...	...	**
Laughing	...	...	...	...			**	...
Good physique	...	...	**		**	...	*	***
Good grooming	...	...	*	...	...	**	*	**
Masculine physique	...	...	***	...	...	...	...	***
Sex appeal	...	...	***	...	...	...	*	***
Physical efficiency	...	...	**	...	...	...	...	***

*Significant at the .10 level.
**Significant at the .05 level.
***Significant at the .01 level.

Table 29.4 Ratings of Interview Protocols at Age 38: Consistently Early or Late Skeletal-Age: Ratings of Retrospective Adolescent Memories

	Scores		
	Early	Late	Significance
No. of cases	9	8	...
Developed early	4.5	2.9	*
Positive effect for developmental status	4.3	2.6	*
Enjoyed social life	5.0	3.6	*
Social-sex development	3.0	4.8	*

*Significant at the .05 level.

greater verbalization was laden with concern about peer rejection, shyness, and ineptness.

A second source of data from the interviews is the Kroeber-Haan ratings of ego mechanisms (Haan, 1963). Few significant differences can be reported, but the analysis suggests that with the 20 alternative coping and defense mechanisms rated, the late maturing are seen as more often using the coping devices: "tolerance of ambiguity," "selective awareness," "playfulness in the service of the ego," and "egalitarian attitudes." This supports the evidence from the CPI scores showing greater perceptiveness and insight for the late maturing.

Justification for continuing the examination for the remaining two rating schedules cannot be made on statistical grounds because of the paucity of the relationships. But the few findings to be reported are clearly in line with what would have been predicted.

From Block's Q sorts (1961b), composed of 100 items, those contrasts that do emerge are consistent with the descriptions from other measures. The early maturing boy is more often represented in adulthood (a) as priding himself on being objective and rational and (b) as judging himself to be conventional. These two items can be related to the CPI scale for achievement via conformity, on which the early developers scored higher. The early maturer is rated as "power oriented," as "condescending," and as "satisfied with his appearance." The CPI scales indicating dominance and ascendance and the ability to make a good impression are suggested by these variables.

Those who developed late are rated as "initiating humor,"—clearly allied to early adolescent ratings of emotional buoyancy, to the Playfulness (Haan, 1961) and Flexibility scales on the CPI, and to the ego-mechanism rating of playfulness in the service of the ego. His "vulnerability to threat" recalls the frequent appearance of differences between extreme groups in various somatic categories on the psychoneurotic scale.

Reichard's (1961) extensive system of ratings of dynamic- and cognitive-personality variables yielded several plausible relationships. The early maturers are rated as more "moralistic," reflecting the responsible, socialized, conventional syndrome reported for CPI responses.

The "conscious negative identification with mother" of the late developers recalls their adolescent TAT stories of rejection by parents (Mussen & M. C. Jones, 1957). It reflects, also the lower scores on the CPI Socialization and Social-Control scales on which the late maturing less often checked items pertaining to a happy family life. Finally, the following two differences on the Reichard scale regarded this search through some 70 items: the early developers are rated as having "premature identity formation," late developers as having "delayed identity formation." This suggests support for the theoretical formulation that accelerated developers escape prematurely into adulthood while the retarded take more time in which to integrate their impulses and capacities.

Discussion of Interview Ratings

The extreme maturity groups are less differentiated by the rating of intensive interview material from the late 30's than by the observational ratings in adolescence or the self-report inventory scores when the subjects were 33.

These are possible explanations: First, the sample is further attenuated by the lapse of an additional 5 years. Although the shrinking sample seems not to have been qualitatively altered, there are fewer cases for comparison at each extreme. A second possibility is that the additional 5 years of time have erased some of the differences that had persisted from adolescence to the thirty-third year of life when the CPI was administered. One would not expect this to be a major factor in view of the greater stability of life patterns over the 5-year space in the 30's as contrasted with the numerous changes involving war service, occupational choices, and the beginning of family life between the end of high school and the early 30's. A third possibility is that the rating of interviews represents a different methodology than that employed in observational ratings or self-report techniques (Radke-Yarrow, 1963). The explicit purpose of the follow-up interviews was to plumb areas of deeper and more dynamic import than had been possible in the earlier explorations of personality in adolescence. Perhaps in these more theoretically oriented classifications of personality, physical maturity variations have less import, or their influence is less readily discernable through indirect assessment of interview material.

Discussion of Group Findings

What has this study contributed to information or understanding concerning the psychological correlates of maturity status? For the early maturing boys, conclusions do not require an alteration of earlier findings. As a group, early maturing boys have assets that are valued by the peer culture.

The picture continues in adulthood (Jones, 1958; Ames, 1957). Men who matured early describe themselves on the CPI as able to make a good impression, as poised, responsible, achieving in conformity with society's expectations, and as relatively free from neurotic symptoms. They may be somewhat rigid in cognitive processes and in attitudes as contrasted with the average and with the late maturing in this sample.

The boys whose pubescence came late cling to a little-boy type of activity which may be salutary in respect to impulse expression. It is accompanied by more tense and attention-getting behavior in the high-school years.

The CPI measures support the earlier findings (M. C. Jones, 1957) for the late maturers by adding significant differences for some somatic categories on related scales. In addition, the interview ratings suggest that the later maturer has the ability to cope—with humor, with tolerance of ambiguity and of individual idiosyncrasies, with perceptiveness, and with playfulness in the service of the ego. However this adaptability is accompanied by a certain fearfulness and vulnerability to threat.

When growth timing within the adolescent period is considered, differences in maturity at the onset phase are most productive of psychological relationships. However, these behavior differences may not be evident concomitantly with the growth phase but may become increasingly significant and tend to be most pronounced in the later high-school years. A consistently extreme maturity status in adolescence is most promising of predictive value for adult measures.

This is a predominantly urban, middle-class, Western sample. It is not possible to generalize to other classes, times, or climes. The number of cases compared in our extreme groups is small, and there is some overlapping in the various categories. Correlational procedures with the total sample have confirmed the results for extreme groups. But the tentative findings await verification from other populations.

Individual Differences

We have been discussing group trends to which not all cases conform. This is obvious when we look at the distribution of scores that contribute to the statistical average.

Figure 29.1 shows the scores for individuals in the two extreme maturity groups on the CPI Psychoneurotic Scale. Late developers score higher on this scale, but the group average for later maturers is very near the average for the total sample. It is the early maturers who show exceptionally low scores. The highest psychoneurotic score is earned by a professor, as is the lowest score among the late developers. These two men are at occupational

Figure 29.1 Psychoneurotic Scale

Figure 29.2 Good Impression Scale

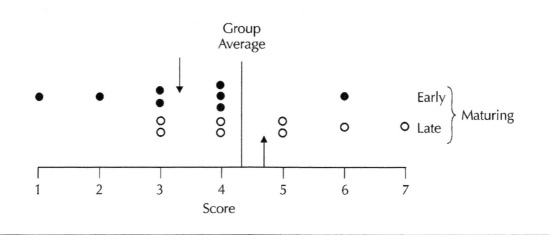

Figure 29.3 Tolerance of Ambiguity

levels far above their fathers'. The second highest and the second lowest scores of the late maturers belong to men with drinking problems who are among the most downward mobile of our group. How do we generalize from these facts?

More in line with expectations are the scores on the Good Impression Scale (Figure 29.2). The two highest scores on the Psychoneurotic Scale were made by the same late developers who have the lowest score on the Good Impression Scale, and vice versa; the lowest psychoneurotic score belongs to the business executive with the highest score on the Good Impression Scale.

Figure 29.3 shows the ego-mechanism ratings at age 38 for tolerance of ambiguity. The highest score was earned by a late maturer, but the next highest belong one each to an early and a late maturer. A professor is one of these. And the business executive with the lowest score, who presumably can make the best impression and has the lowest psychoneurotic score, is rates as the least able to tolerate ambiguity.

To explain scores as different as these we need to consider the complexity of human growth and the multiplicity of factors, cultural and psychological as well as physical, that produce the individual adjustment patterns of late- and early-maturing boys.

References

Ames, R. Physical maturing among boys as related to adult social behavior. *Calif. J. educ. Res.*, 1957, **8**, 67–75.

Block, J. A. psychoneurotic scale. California personality inventory. Berkeley: Univer. of Calif. Institute of Human Development, 1961. (a)

Block, J. *The Q sort method in personality assessment and psychiatric research.* Springfield, Ill.: Charles C Thomas, 1961. (b)

Edwards, A. A social and economic grouping of the gainful workers of the United States. *J. Amer. statis. Ass.*, 1933, **28**, 377–387.

Eichorn, Dorothy. Biological correlates of behavior. In H. Stevenson (Ed.), *Yearb. nat. Soc. Stud. Educ.*, 1963, Part I, 4–61.

Gough, H. G. *California personality inventory manual.* Palo Alto, Calif.: Consulting Psychologist Pr., 1960.

Hann, Norma. A playfulness scale. California personality inventory. Unpublished manuscript. Berkeley: Institute of Human Development, Univers. of Calif., 1961.

Haan, Norma. Some comparisons of various Oakland growth study sub-samples on selected variables. Unpublished manuscript. Berkeley: Institute of Human Development, Univ. of Calif., 1962.

Hann, Norma. Proposed model of ego functioning: coping and defense mechanisms in relationships to IQ change. *Psychol. Monogr.*, 1963, **77**; No. 8 (Whole No. 571).

Jones, H. E. The California adolescent growth study. *J. educ. Res.*, 1938, **31**, 561–567.

Jones, H. E. *Motor performance and growth.* Berkeley: Univ. of Calif. Pr., 1949.

Jones, H. E., Macfarlane, Jean W., & Eichorn, Dorothy H. A progress report on growth studies at the University of California. *Vita Humana*, 1960, **3**, 17–31.

Jones, Mary C. The later careers of boys who were early- or late-maturing. *Child Develpm.*, 1957, **28**, 113–128.

Jones, Mary C. A study of socialization patterns at the high school level. *J. genet. Psychol.*, 1958, **93**, 87–111.

Jones, Mary C., & Bayley, Nancy. Physical maturing among boys as related to behavior. *J. educ. Psychol.*, 1950, **41**, 129–148.

Macfarlane, Jean W. Studies in child guidance. I. Methodology of data collection and organization. *Monogr. Soc. Res. Child Develpm.*, 1938, **3**, 254.

Mussen, P. H., & Jones, Mary C. Self-conceptions, motivations, and interpersonal attitudes of late- and early-maturing boys. *Child Develpm.*, 1957, **28**, 243–265.

Newman, Frances B., & Jones, H. E. The adolescent in social groups. *Appl. Psychol. Monogr.*, 1946, **9**, 94.

Nicholson, Arline B., & Hanley, C. Indices of physiological maturity: derivation and interrelationships. *Child Develpm.*, 1953, **24**, 3–28.

Peskin, H. Possible relations of growth and maturity to early psychic experiences. In *Biological Time*, Sympos., Soc. Res. Child Develpm. mtgs., Berkeley, Calif., 1963.

Radke-Yarrow, Marian. The elusive evidence. Presidential address given at Amer. Psychol. Ass., Philadelphia, Pa., September, 1963.

Reichard, Suzanne. Dynamic and cognitive personality variables. Oakland growth study. Unpublished manuscript. Berkeley: Institute of Human Development, Univer. of Calif., 1961.

Stewart, L. Social and emotional adjustment during adolescence as related to the development of psychosomatic illness in adulthood. *Genet. Psychol. Monogr.*, 1962, **65**, Part I, 175–215.

Stolz, H. R., & Stolz, Lois M. *Somatic development of adolescent boys.* New York: Macmillan Co., 1951.

The Mental Development of the Child

Jean Piaget

Jean Piaget (1896–1980), perhaps the greatest of all developmental psychologists, was the first stage-theorist to clearly demarcate, through observational studies and the semiclinical interviewing method, the cognitive differences between adolescence and middle childhood.

Piaget called the stage of adolescent cognitive development the "formal" stage because in the teen years most people begin to be able to think abstractly. These young adults are able to perform mental operations on the "form" of an idea and do not need to rely on concrete observations and representations. Piaget called this type of thinking "hypothetico-deductive," which indicates that it is the beginning of scientific thought. An adolescent can draw conclusions (deductions) from hypotheses (premises) without ever seeing concrete data. On the practical side, this is why algebra is not taught until the teenage years.

Piaget wrote about the formal operational stage in many of his texts and research reports over a span of many decades. The following extract is taken from a text that was first published in French in 1964, when Piaget was nearly 70 years old. It was later published in 1968 as *Six Psychological Studies* by Vintage Books.

Several other selections in this volume are from the works of Piaget. You may wish to refer to the headnotes of these selections for more background on Piaget.

Key Concept: formal operations and hypothetico-deductive thinking

Adolescence

[One might] think that mental development is completed at eleven to twelve years of age and that adolescence is simply a temporary crisis, resulting from puberty, that separates the child from the adult. It is true that the maturation of the sexual instinct is marked by a momentary disequilibrium that lends a characteristic affective coloration to this last period of psychological evolution. But these well-known facts . . . far from exhaust the analysis of adolescence. Indeed, pubertal changes would play only a very secondary role if the thinking and emotions characteristic of adolescents were accorded their true significance. We shall describe the structures of these final forms of thought and of the affective life, rather than the problems of adolescence. In addition, while there is provisional disequilibrium, one must not forget that every transition from one stage to another is likely to provoke temporary oscillations. In reality, appearance notwithstanding, adolescence assures thought and affectivity of an equilibrium superior to that which existed during middle and late childhood. Abilities multiply, and at first these additional capacities are troubling to both thought and affectivity, but subsequently they strengthen them. . . .

Thought and Its Operations

By comparison with a child, an adolescent is an individual who constructs systems and "theories." The child does not build systems. Those which he possesses are unconscious or preconscious in the sense that they are unformulable or unformulated so that only an external observer can understand them, while he himself never "reflects" on them. In other words, he thinks concretely, he deals with each problem in isolation and does not integrate his solutions by means of any general theories from which he could abstract a common principle. By contrast, what is striking in the adolescent is his interest in theoretical problems not related to everyday realities. He is frequently occupied with disarmingly naïve and chimeric ideas concerning the future of the world. What is particularly surprising is his facility for elaborating abstract theories. Some write; they may create a philosophy, a political tract, a theory of aesthetics, or whatever. Others do not write; they talk. The majority talk only about a small part of their personal creations and confine themselves to ruminating about them intimately and in secret. But all of them have systems and theories that transform the world in one way or another.

The eruption of this new kind of thinking, in the form of general ideas and abstract constructions, is actually much less sudden than it would seem. It develops in relatively continuous fashion from the concrete thinking of middle childhood. The turning point occurs at about the age of twelve, after which there is rapid progress in the direction of free reflection no longer directly attached to external reality. At eleven or twelve years of age there is a fundamental transformation in the child's thinking which marks the completion of the operations constructed during middle childhood. This is the transition from concrete to "formal" thinking, or, in a barbarous but clear term, "hypothetico-deductive" thinking.

Up to this age (eleven–twelve), the operations of intelligence are solely "concrete," i.e., they are concerned only with reality itself and, in particular, with tangible objects that can be manipulated and subjected to real action. When at the concrete level, thinking moves away from tangible reality, absent objects are replaced by more or less vivid representations, which are tantamount to reality. If a child at this level is asked to reason about simple hypotheses, presented verbally, he immediately loses ground and falls back on the prelogical intuition of the preschool child. For example, all children of nine or ten can arrange colors into series even better than they can arrange sizes, yet they are completely unable to answer the following question, even when it is put in writing: "Edith has darker hair than Lily. Edith's hair is lighter than Susan's. Which of the three has the darkest hair?" In general, they reply that since Edith and Lily are dark-haired and Edith and Susan are light-haired, Lily is the darkest, Susan the lightest, and Edith in between. On the verbal plane, they succeed in producing only a series of uncoordinated pairs, as children of five or six do when they attempt to seriate a set of size-graded objects. That is why in school they have such difficulty in resolving arithmetic problems, even though such problems involve operations well known to them. If the children were able to manipulate objects, they would be able to reason without difficulty, whereas apparently the same reasoning on the plane of language and verbal statements actually constitutes other reasoning that is much more difficult because it is linked to pure hypotheses without effective reality.

As of eleven to twelve years, formal thinking becomes possible, i.e., the logical operations begin to be transposed from the plane of concrete manipulation to the ideational plane, where they are expressed in some kind of language (words, mathematical symbols, etc.), without the support of perception, experience, or even faith. In the previous example—"Edith has darker hair than Lily, etc."—three fictive personages are presented in the abstract as pure hypotheses, and thinking involves reasoning about these hypotheses. Formal thought is "hypothetico-deductive," in the sense that it permits one to draw conclusions from pure hypotheses and not merely from actual observations. These conclusions even have a validity independent of their factual truth. This explains why formal thinking represents so much more difficulty and so much more mental work than concrete thought.

What, in effect, are the conditions for the construction of formal thought? The child must not only apply operations to objects—in other words, mentally execute possible actions on them—he must also "reflect" these operations in the absence of the objects which are replaced by pure propositions. This "reflection" is thought raised to the second power. Concrete thinking is the representation of a possible action, and formal thinking is the representation of a representation of possible action. It is not surprising, therefore, that the system of concrete operations must be completed during the last years of childhood before it can be "reflected" by formal operations. In terms of their function, formal operations do not differ from concrete operations except that they are applied to hypotheses or propositions. Formal operations engender a "logic of propositions" in contrast to the logic of relations, classes, and numbers engendered by concrete operations. The system of "implications" that governs these propositions is merely an abstract translation of the system of "inference" that governs concrete operations.

Only after the inception of formal thought, at around the age of eleven or twelve, can the mental systems that characterize adolescence be constructed. Formal operations provide thinking with an entirely new ability that detaches and liberates thinking from concrete reality and permits it to build its own reflections and theories. With the advent of formal intelligence, thinking takes wings, and it is not surprising that at first this unexpected power is both used and abused. The free activity of spontaneous reflection is one of the two essential innovations that distinguish adolescence from childhood.

. . . [E]ach new mental ability starts off by incorporating the world in a process of egocentric assimilation. Only later does it attain equilibrium through a compensating accommodation to reality. The intellectual egocentricity of adolescence is comparable to the egocentricity of the infant who assimilates the universe into his own corporal activity and to that of the young child who assimilates things into his own nascent thought (symbolic play, etc.). Adolescent egocentricity is manifested by belief in the omnipotence of reflection, as though the world should submit itself to idealistic schemes rather than to systems of reality. It is the metaphysical age *par excellence*; the self is strong enough to reconstruct the universe and big enough to incorporate it.

Then, just as the sensorimotor egocentricity of early childhood is progressively reduced by the organization of schemata of action and as the young child's egocentric thinking is replaced with the equilibrium of concrete operations, so the metaphysical egocentricity of the adolescent is gradually lessened as a reconciliation between formal thought and reality is effected. Equilibrium is attained when the adolescent understands that the proper function of reflection is not to contradict but to predict and interpret experience. This formal equilibrium surpasses by far the equilibrium of concrete thought because it not only encompasses the real world but also the undefined constructions of rational deduction and inner life.

Forms of Intellectual and Ethical Development in the College Years

William G. Perry, Jr.

William G. Perry's research on the development of undergraduate college students is the foundational work that has informed nearly all studies on the development of the intellect and of ethics among college students for the last 35–40 years. It is the seminal study; the research most likely to be cited regarding the development of college-age adults in nearly any culture that publishes such investigations.

Bill Perry was a Harvard man for most of his life. He earned both bachelor's (Greek and English, 1935) and master's degrees (English, 1940) from Harvard University. He then taught history and English at the Rivers School in Brookline, MA and then Williams College, but he returned to Harvard in 1946 to set up the Bureau of Study Counsel and was the director of that Bureau for thirty-three years. During those years he was also professor of education at the Harvard Graduate School of Education and a member of the Faculty of Arts and Sciences. He counseled Harvard College students, supervised the counseling of graduate students, and established himself as a premier researcher and theoretician of the development of college students.

Perry's classic text, *Forms of Intellectual and Ethical Development in the College Years: A Scheme*, was first published in 1970. Its influence was so strong that twenty-eight years later (1998) a new edition was published, with an introduction by Lee Knefelkamp, a close colleague of Perry's and a professor at Teachers College, Columbia University. This book charts the cognitive and moral growth of college students through nine developmental positions (note that Perry preferred to call his levels of growth "positions" and not stages). Perry's developmental scheme begins with "Position 1: Basic Duality," in which students see the world in concrete black and white, move through several positions of "Multiplicity," then two forms of Relativism at Position 5, and then four positions related to Commitment. Descriptions of these nine positions are excerpted below.

Key Concept: intellectual and ethical development in the college years

Position 1:

Basic Duality

The structure we designate as Position 1 delineates the simplest set of assumptions about the nature of knowledge and values of which we found evidence in our records. The outlook is one in which the world of knowledge, conduct and values is divided as the small child divides his world between the family and the vague inchoate outside. From this position, a person construes all issues of truth and morality in the terms of a sweeping and unconsidered differentiation between in-group vs. outgroup. This division is between the familiar world

of Authority-right-we, as against the alien world of illegitimate-wrong-others. In the familiar world, morality and personal responsibility consist of simple obedience. Even "learning to be independent," as Authority asks one to, consists of learning self-controlled obedience. In the educational aspect of this world, morality consists of committing to memory, through hard work, an array of discrete items—correct responses, answers, and procedures, as assigned by Authority. In this structure's most primitive form, Authority's omniscience is so taken-for-granted that no distinction is made between Authority and the Absolute. "Truth" and "what They say" function as tautological alternatives of expression, as do "right" and "what They want."

Position 2:

Multiplicity Pre-Legitimate

The structure of Position 2 delineates in closer detail the first steps in that journey from innocence forecast in broad terms in the latter part of the descriptions of Position 1. This detail reveals a point of paradoxical incongruity between a process in personal development and the nature of modern liberal education.

In the past, a young person freed himself from his embeddedness in the homogeneity of family and community through "adolescent revolt." In this traditional revolt a person laid hold of the diversity of opinion in the larger world and used it as a weapon against the orthodoxy from which he struggled to emerge. The individuation which he achieved in this revolt then faced him with the complexities and responsibilities of his freedom. Well into the present century, this often productive revolt could be carried on through the college years, since each professor claimed to be teaching *the* truth, *the* facts of his subject.

The decline of orthodoxies and the intrusion of a loose pluralism into community and home has caused at least one writer to regret with well founded nostalgia the loss of this strengthening experience of revolt (Friedenberg, *The Vanishing Adolescent,* 1959). In a modern liberal arts college, however, the change has involved more than a mere decline of orthodoxies. The majority of the faculty has gone beyond differences of absolutistic opinion into teachings which are deliberately founded in a relativistic epistemology (see discussion of examination questions in Chapter 1).

In this current situation, if a student revolts against "the Establishment" before he has familiarized himself with the analytical and integrative skills of relativistic thinking, the only place he can take his stand is in a simplistic absolutism. He revolts, then, not against homogeneous lower-level orthodoxy but against heterogeneity. In doing so he not only narrows the range of his materials, he rejects the second-level tools of critical analysis, reflection and comparative thinking—the tools through which the successful rebel of a previous generation moved forward to productive dissent.

The irony is clear in our records. The student who, at these early levels of development, takes his stand in Opposition to what he perceives globally as the "hemming and hawing" and "vague theorizing" of academic Authorities takes a bold forward step in personal individuation, but he then quickly finds that he has painted himself into a corner. In contrast, the student who more blandly presumes that Authority knows its business and is presenting all these complexities as mere exercises for the students' own good—this student takes a far less radical step in personal development but finds himself later in a much more flexible position for further growth. As a final twist, in perceiving all of Authority's "on-the-one-hands" and "on-the-other-hands" as a mere obstacle course set

out to help students learn how to reach *the* Truth on their own, this trusting soul is misperceiving the issue just as thoroughly as the most stubborn rebel.

The structures of Position 2 illustrate the origins of this paradox in the two minimal adaptations through which those of our students who were moving forward from Position 1 first accorded meaning to diversity. In the first of these, diversity and complexity are still perceived as *alien* but as elements introduced *within* the community by willful Authorities who are failing of their mediational role. Where no contrasting "good" Authorities can be found, and where the student is either isolated among his peers or finds support only in a like-minded minority, he perceives diversity and complexity not so much as alien to the community but alien to *him*. It is this perception that seems to lead most forcibly to the student's relocating his own stance within the structure by taking a stand in Opposition. . . .

Position 3:

Multiplicity Subordinate

A sophomore-to-be is speaking of his preference for physics:

> S. I'd feel (*laughs*) rather insecure thinking about these philosophical things all the time and not coming up with any definite answers. And definite answers are, well, they, they're sort of my foundation point. In physics you get definite answers to a point. Beyond that point you know there *are* definite answers, but you can't reach them.

In the concession "but you can't reach them," this student makes room in his epistemology for a legitimate human uncertainty. It is a grudging concession and does not affect the nature of truth itself (only man's relation to it!), but the accommodation has loosened the tie between Authority and the Absolute. Uncertainty is now unavoidable, even in physics. As a consequence, a severe procedural problem becomes unavoidable too. How, in an educational institution where the student's every answer is evaluated, are answers judged? Where even Authority doesn't know the answer yet, is not any answer as good as another?

This is the problem which preoccupies students looking at the world from the structure of Position 3, a structure in which uncertainty and complexity are no longer considered mere exercises or impediments devised by Authority but seen as realities in their own right, plumb in the middle of Authority's world. The new perception seems in some cases to derive from direct observation of instructors involved in that very act of puzzling previously thought fit only for students—"Here was this great professor, and he was groping *too!*" Often it is mediated by such vehicles as the history of science or current discoveries which imply (so obviously in retrospect) that many "answers" are yet to be revealed. In any case, it is understandable that the first issue raised should be of evaluation. It affects the student right in the midst of the guidelines of his daily work.

The blow is considerable. So far Authority has been perceived as grading on amount of rightness, achieved by honest hard work, and as adding an occasional bonus for neatness and "good expression." But in the uncertainty of authorized Multiplicity, coupled with a freedom that leaves "amount" of work "up to you" and Authority ignorant of how much you do, rightness and hard work vanish as standards. Nothing seems to be left but "good expression":

S. If I present it in the right manner it is well received. Or it is received . . . I don't know, I still haven't exactly caught onto what, what they want.

And:

S. I've been handing in papers that if I were grading I would have given an extremely low mark. Some of them perhaps I wouldn't even have passed. But they've been coming back in many cases with extremely good marks. So since I can't explain that, I certainly can't explain how any marks, ah, would be worked out. . . .

Here in considering Position 4, we take up the outlook characteristic of the modal developmental position of the students in our study at the time when they first talked with us at the end of the freshman year. The mean point of development of freshmen of the Class of '58 (computed from the judged interviews) fell between Positions 3 and 4; for the Classes of '62 and '63, it fell between Positions 4 and 5. Position 4 represents therefore the modal "starting point" in our students' accounts, the view of the world from which they most typically reported in the Spring of their freshman year. Of the two structures of this Position, I shall consider the more Oppositional alternative first.

Multiplicity Correlate

In Position 3, the student perceived Multiplicity as a temporary fuzziness in Authority's domain—a limited area of ambiguity in which They will someday soon uncover the underlying Laplacean order. However, a student with a bit of Oppositional gumption in him will recognize a playground when he sees one. As long as the area of ambiguity remains, he will have a right to his own opinion in it, and They will have *no right* to call him wrong. Moreover, as he finds the area to be ever larger than he expected, and the day of revelation of The Truth ever more remote, he may claim for Multiplicity a domain of its own, over against Authority's domain, and of equal epistemological legitimacy. Then, in Authority's domain, where Absolute answers are known, epistemological and moral law may still read, absolutely, "You're either right or you're wrong"; but in the domain of Multiplicity, where answers are (as yet) unknown, the epistemological and moral law will read, with equal absolutism, "Everyone has a right to his own opinion."

This restructuring provides for a recapitulation and broadening, at an abstract philosophical level, of an earlier adolescent revolt which had been limited to a reactive espousal of the *opposite* to whatever Authority said. The raising of Multiplicity from a subordinate status to that of a legitimate domain of its own seems to promise freedom from the bondage of simple reaction, and the energy of revolt can now be invested in an imperialistic extension of the domain of total freedom at the expense of Authority's claims.

Authority, in which the self takes a stand in chaos, will provide (once contextual thought is discovered to provide some order) a platform from which certain Authorities may be viewed with entirely new eyes.

By whatever means it is discovered, the bridge to the new world of comparative thought lies in the distinction between an opinion (however well "expressed") and a *supported* opinion. One item on CLEV read, "Where authorities differ, a student's opinion should be graded only on how well it is expressed." A freshman who had agreed in the fall and disagreed in the spring remarks:

S. Well—it's an opinion, but it's got to be an educated opinion. Have something behind it, not just a hearsay opinion. I mean, you can't form an opinion unless you have some knowledge behind it, I suppose.

In this transitional statement it is not yet clear that a better opinion would not still be one which simply has "more" knowledge behind it in the purely quantitative sense; and yet an "educated" opinion is surely something else than a right answer or a wrong answer or *any* opinion. The step to truly qualitative comparison is now a short one.

Relativism Subordinate

There is, however, another pathway from Position 3 to the vision of Relativism. This path, which the majority of our students followed, does not involve setting Multiplicity, as a world of its own, over against the world of Authority. Rather, it allows the discovery of Relativism in Multiplicity to occur in the context of Authority's world where Multiplicity is still something "They want us to work on":

S. Another thing I've noticed about this more concrete and complex approach—you can get away without . . . trying to think about what they want—ah, think about things the *way* they want you to think about them. But if you try to use the approach the course outlines, then you find yourself thinking in *complex terms*: weighing more than one factor in trying to develop your own opinion. Somehow, for me, just doing that has become extended beyond the courses. . . . Somehow what I think about things now seems to be more—ah, it's hard to say right or wrong— but it seems (*pause*) more *sensible*.

Here the correction from "what They want" to "the *way* They want you to think" signals the discovery of the articulation of the "concrete" with the "complex" in "weighing" in Multiplicity—a mode of thought which is the structural foundation of Relativism. The weighing of "more than one factor," or, as this student later explained, "more than one approach to a problem," forces a comparison of patterns of thought, that is, a thinking about thinking. For most students, as for this student, the event seems to be conscious and explicit; that is, the initial discovery of meta-thought occurs vividly in foreground, as figure, against the background of previous ways of thinking, and usually as an item in the context of "what They want."

Now the capacity to compare different approaches to a problem in "developing one's own opinion" is presumably the ordinary meaning of "independent thought." The paradox for liberal education lies in the fact that so many of our students learned to think this way because it was "the way They want you to think," that is, out of a desire to conform. Can one learn to think independently out of obedience to Authority's demand? . . .

Position 5:

Relativism Correlate, Competing, or Diffuse

Our scheme must now account for a drastic revolution. Up to this point the students have been able to assimilate the new, in one way or another, to the fundamental dualistic structure with which they began. The new, to the extent that it has been anomalous or contradictory, has naturally forced them to make certain accommodations in the structure, but these have been achieved either by the elaboration of dualism into a dual dualism or by the addition of a new subcategory of "critical thinking" to the general category of "what Authority wants."

These developments, however, have been enough to make the system unwieldy. Like the Ptolemaic cosmology, it has become overelaborate, and it has taken into itself incongruities which are the seeds of its own destruction. The time is ripe for a more economical address. The students will find this address in the radical reperception of all knowledge as contextual and relativistic.

The students appear to achieve this revolution in their view of the world by making a transposition in the hierarchy or forms of Position 4. They promote Relativism from its status as a special case (or subordinate part within a broad dualistic context) to the status of context, and within this new context they consign dualism to the subordinate status of a special case.

This form of revolutionary restructuring has been revealed as a characteristic of the evolution of scientific theory (Kuhn, 1962). Strangely enough, we have found no explicit description of this kind of transformation as a phenomenon in human personal development. As a strategy of growth it would seem to deserve a prominent place, not only in theory of cognitive development but also in consideration of emotional maturation and the formation of identity.

In our scheme of development this striking event takes place between Position 4 and Position 6. In Position 4, the student had assimilated Multiplicity and Relativism into the framework of a world he still assumed to be dualistic. In Position 6 he will apprehend the implications of personal choice in a world he assumes to be relativistic. This revolution is precipitated by the failure of a dualistic framework to assimilate the expanding generalization of Relativism. . . .

A student who saw Relativism as "subordinate" in Position 4 saw it as a special way of thinking about certain special problems. He had discovered that a comparison among several interpretations of data (e.g., the wording and metrics of a poem, the offices and powers of a governmental system, the complexities within an economic or historical event) is the *way* They want you to think about such things." He had discovered not only a Multiplicity of points of view *about* such matters as literature, history or politics, but a patterning *within* each point of view, an interdependency of parts within the whole, which gave each "point of view" its special character, its coherence, its integrity.

The discovery brought him a new sense of power. Not only had he "caught on" in his studies, he could now think about thought: he could spot a false dichotomy, talk about assumptions and frames of reference, and argue about the degree of coherence of interpretations or their congruence with data.

But in making this new discovery, the student had, by necessity, to assimilate it in some way to the extant major structure of his previous world view. To perceive it at all, he had to construe it from where he stood, in short, to see it as a particular, a figure seen against the old background.

He saw Relativism, therefore, as a special case: a way of thinking about a certain class of problems, a way of "making sense" in otherwise chaotic Multiplicity, and most of all, a special procedure (among other procedures) that "They want here."

The old dualism was still intact. It was of course a complex, or dual, dualism. On the one hand there were still those things that are either right or wrong, and to which "They know the answers"; on the other hand were those indeterminate matters about which "They want you to think" in the new relativistic ways. The latter "ways" had not yet challenged the former. Authority still reigned, asking for performance in both.

In sum, the student perceived Relativism as an item *in the old dualistically structured context.*

In the next step, Relativism is perceived as the common characteristic of *all* thought, all knowing, all of man's relation to his world. Against this ground, dualistic right-or-wrong thinking, and even "ideas of absolutes" become special cases *in the new relativistically structured context.*

This event, presented us with a paradox: the revolution is both the most violent accommodation of structure in the entire development, and at the same time the most quiet. It involves a complete transposition between part and whole, figure and ground, and yet almost no student in our sample referred to it as a conscious event, a discrete experience, a "realization."

The inferences suggested by the reports of students in Position 5, however gain in credibility by offering as their corollary an explanation of the paradox itself. What seems to happen is this. Relativistic thinking, self-conscious in its newness in Position 4, gradually becomes habitual. This seems to occur first in those specific courses or situations in which the student has perceived such thinking as appropriate. At the same time, however, the student discovers new areas in which it is appropriate, perhaps in bull sessions in his dormitory on subjects like religion, politics or morals.

Position 6:

Commitment Foreseen

A sense of identity seems to require some feeling of continuity in what "I" know and what "I" value (Erikson, 1959). If one comes to look upon all knowing and all valuing as contingent on context, and if one is then confronted with an infinite universe of potential contexts for truth and care, one is threatened with loss of identity. From one context to another what one will see as true and what one will care about will be discontinuous; one will not know who "I" am. Reciprocally, for lack of a stable locus, or "point of view" for the observer, whatever is seen "out there" will swim also.

If one construes knowledge and values as relativistic, one is therefore threatened with the possibility of humanly unbearable disorientation. Other than denying relativism itself, the ways of preventing this disaster would seem limited to three. Two of these are defensive, involving denials of responsibility. As forms of alienation, they will be considered in detail in the section on Escape. Briefly they are: (1) To "go limp," denying any need for meaning beyond one's immediate, passive responses; to leave responsibility for context, and thus meaning, to the vagaries of environment; to drift from context to context without acknowledging one's wish to reconcile incongruities. In this mode, orientation can be adequate within each moment; the cost is to know one's self as a self through time. Furthermore, this cost must carry with it a cost to knowing, in any deeper sense, other peoples' selves. (2) To exploit the situation deliberately by becoming an active, self-avowed opportunist. Here a limited selfhood is achieved ("I am an opportunist"); the loss is to depth of feeling and to the social responsibility that springs from compassion.

The third solution is transcendent, taking the form of Commitments. In this study the term "Commitment" refers to an act, or ongoing activity relating a person as agent and chooser to aspects of his life in which he invests his energies, his care and his identity. In common usage the word often refers more narrowly to the object of Commitment alone rather than to the whole act or relation. Thus, "a man's commitments" may suggest his wife, children, job, and whatever obligations or causes or expectancies he has undertaken. If, however, one includes not only these external objects but also a man's acts of choice, and the personal investment he makes in them, the word refers to an affirmatory experience through which the man continuously defines his identity and his involvements in the world (cf. Polanyi, 1958).

The word "Commitments," then, refers to affirmations: in all the plurality of the relativistic world—truths, relationships, purposes, activities, and cares, in all their contexts—one affirms what is one's own. As ongoing creative activities, Commitments require the courage of responsibility, and presuppose an acceptance of human limits, including the limits of reason.

Commitments are creative in that through choice and affirmation the individual generates meanings and relationships neither presupposed nor entailed by the structure of the relativistic world itself. The structures of Relativism (as distinct from the chaos of Multiplicity) do provide, by definition, wide opportunity for the exercise of reason. Reason reveals relations within any given context; it can also compare one context with another on the basis of meta-contexts established for the purpose. But there is a limit. In the end, reason itself remains reflexively a property that turns reason back upon reason's own its farthest reaches, then, reason alone will leave the thinker with legitimate contexts and no way of choosing among them—no way, at least, that he can justify through reason alone. If he then throws reason entirely, he retreats to the irresponsible in Multiplicity ("Anyone has a right to his opinion"). If he is still to honor reason he must now also transcend it; he must affirm his own position from within himself in full awareness that reason can never completely justify him or assure him. In affirming his values, reason may help, but it will not in itself convince him that these values are better than any others; he must commit himself through his own faith. In choosing his career, he must risk his life to his own best guess; reason can never tell him fully about the roads not taken. Yet in the nature of the world as he has come to see it, he must commit himself or abrogate responsibility.

Position 6 in our scheme describes the moment of this realization. In Position 5, Relativism had become the diffuse property permeating man's ways of knowing and caring in his universe. Against this background now appears, as figure, the responsibility of the individual in relating himself to such a world. The word "Commitment" as we use it refers to the structural properties of this figure-ground relation. . . .

Positions 7, 8, and 9:

(7) Initial Commitment; (8) Orientation in Implications of Commitment; (9) Developing Commitment(s)

In the drama of maturation we have been observing, the setting has now become stabilized. From this point onwards, our records reveal no major restructuring of the background of life. The assumption is established that man's knowing and valuing are relative in time and circumstance, and that in such a world the individual is faced with the responsibility for choice and affirmation in his life.

The drama of development now centers on this theme of responsibility. The hero makes his first definition of himself by some engagement undertaken at his own risk. Next he realizes in actual experience the implications of his initial Commitments. Then, as he expands the arc of his engagements and pushes forward in the impingements and unfoldings of experience, he discovers that he has undertaken not a finite set of decisions but a way of life.

The development is therefore more qualitative than structural, and its steps are not readily demarked by major changes in forms. Accordingly, Positions 7, 8, and 9 express degrees of ripening in an art. They describe degrees of seasoning which we felt to be broadly distinguishable in our students' reports.

Position 7 describes that state in a student's life in which he has undertaken to decide on his own responsibility who he is, or who he will be, in some major area of his life (for example, "I have decided on medicine"). He is at the moment rather taken up with the impact of the content of the Commitment. Internally he typically experiences a relief in settled purpose, and at the same time he feels strongly *defined by* the external forms typifying the role he has chosen (for example, medical student, doctor).

Position 8 describes a level of experience in which the stylistic issues of Commitment have emerged in greater prominence over external forms (for example, "So I've decided to be a doctor but how many ways are there of doing *that?*—and the rest of life!"). Position 9 describes a maturity in which a person has developed an experience of "who he is" in his Commitments both in their content and in his style of living them. At the same time that this experience has "settled" him, it has left him aware that, to a degree that is partly his own to determine and partly in the hands of fate, he is to be forever on the move. His past decisions may have settled to some degree what he is doing, what he may do, and what he can never do; but how he does it emerges from himself in the particulars of each moment. He will be far too busy, of course, to contemplate each moment in these terms, but the fact that he takes many of his responsibilities for granted does not reduce them for him. Indeed the very degree to which he will balance his emersion in action with times of contemplation will express in itself one of his Commitments to "the kind of person I am."

We hardly felt that the circumstance of being a college student would provide a basis in experience for the seasoning described by Position 9. Rather, it seemed to round out the scheme by extrapolation much as did Position 1 in the other direction, and its inclusion seemed also to enlighten the character of Position 8. As it turned out, the judges did use Position 9 on occasion—thirteen times out of a total of 120 ratings of the twenty senior interviews in the sample of four-year reports. In discussion, the Judges revealed that they looked on such a rating as a kind of tribute—a statement that a given student expressed a degree of maturity beyond the judge's own: "I just wanted to say, 'You're a better man than I am'!"

Social and Personality Development in Adolescence

Development and Validation
of Ego-Identity Status

James E. Marcia

James E. Marcia completed his Ph.D. in psychology at Ohio State University and went on to teach at Simon Fraser University in British Columbia. He became keenly interested in Erik Erikson's psychosocial stage theory, especially the adolescent stage, known as the identity versus role confusion stage. For his doctoral dissertation, Marcia decided to perform an empirical study in which he examined a method of assessing levels of achievement of ego identity, as described by Erikson.

By basing his work on Erikson's psychosocial stage theory, Marcia was placing himself in the Freudian, psychoanalytic tradition. Erikson borrowed Sigmund Freud's psychosexual concept of "ego" and transformed it into a social construct based on the ego's development of an "identity." Erikson framed identity as primarily coming from one's chosen career or profession but also as being greatly influenced by such factors as one's religious or sexual identification as well. Marcia then built upon Erikson's work by empirically delineating four different conditions, or statuses, of ego identity establishment.

Marcia condensed the results of his dissertation into journal article format, and it was published in the *Journal of Personality and Social Psychology* in 1966. This article, "Development and Validation of Ego-Identity Status," has since become a modern classic, and the following is a reprinting of it. At its core, this is scientific research into the age-old teenagers' question, "Who am I?"

Key Concept: identity statuses

Four modes of reacting to the late adolescent identity crisis were described, measured, and validated. Criteria for inclusion in 1 of 4 identity statuses were the presence of crisis and commitment in the areas of occupation and ideology. Statuses were determined for 86 college male Ss by means of individual interviews. Performance on a stressful concept-attainment task, patterns of goal setting, authoritarianism, and vulnerability to self-esteem change were dependent variables. Ss higher in ego identity performed best on the concept-attainment task; those in the status characterized by adherence to parental wishes set goals unrealistically high and subscribed significantly more to authoritarian values. Failure of the self-esteem condition to discriminate among the statuses was attributed to unreliability in self-esteem measurement.

Ego identity and identity diffusion (Erikson, 1956, 1963) refer to polar outcomes of the hypothesized psychosocial crisis occurring in late adolescence. Erikson views this phase of the life cycle as a time of growing occupational and ideological commitment. Facing such imminent adult tasks as getting a job and becoming a citizen, the individual is required to synthesize childhood identifications in such a way that he can both establish a reciprocal relationship with his society and maintain a feeling of continuity within himself.

Previous studies have attempted to determine the extent of ego-identity achievement by means of an adjustment measure and the semantic differential technique (Bronson, 1959) a Q-sort measure of real-ideal-self discrepancy (Gruen, 1960), a measure of role variability based on adjective ranking (Block, 1961), and a questionnaire (Rasmussen, 1964). While these studies have investigated self-ratings on characteristics that should follow if ego identity has been achieved, they have not dealt explicitly with the psychosocial criteria for determining degree of ego identity, nor with testing hypotheses regarding direct behavioral consequences of ego identity.

To assess ego identity, the present study used measures and criteria congruent with Erikson's formulation of the identity crisis as a *psychosocial* task. Measures were a semi-structured interview and an incomplete-sentences blank. The interview (see Method section) was used to determine an individual's specific identity status: that is which of four concentration points along a continuum of ego-identity achievement best characterized him. The incomplete-sentences blank served as an overall measure of identity achievement. The criteria used to establish identity status consisted of two variables, crisis and commitment, applied to occupational choice, religion, and political ideology. Crisis refers to the adolescent's period of engagement in choosing among meaningful alternatives; commitment refers to the degree of personal investment the individual exhibits.

"Identity achievement" and "identity diffusion" are polar alternatives of status inherent in Erickson's theory. According to the criteria employed in this study, an identity-achievement subject has experienced a crisis period and is committed to an occupation and ideology. He has seriously considered several occupational choices and has made a decision on this own terms, even though his ultimate choice may be a variation of parental wishes. With respect to ideology, he seems to have reevaluated past beliefs and achieved a resolution that leaves him free to act. In general, he does not appear as if he would be overwhelmed by sudden shifts in his environment or by unexpected responsibilities.

The identity-diffusion subject may or may not have experienced a crisis period; his hallmark is a lack of commitment. He has neither decided upon an occupation nor is much concerned about it. Although he may mention a preferred occupation, he seems to have little conception of its daily routine and gives the impression that the choice could be easily abandoned should opportunities arise elsewhere. He is either uninterested in ideological matters or takes a smorgasbord approach in which one outlook seems as good to him as another and he is not averse to sampling from all.

Two additional concentration points roughly intermediate in this distribution are the moratorium and foreclosure statuses. The moratorium subject is *in* the crisis period with commitments rather vague; he is distinguished from the identity-diffusion subject by the appearance of an active struggle to make commitments. Issues often described as adolescent preoccupy him. Although his parents' wishes are still important to him, he is attempting a compromise among them, society's demands, and his own capabilities. His sometimes bewildered appearance stems from his vital concern and internal preoccupation with what occasionally appear to him to be unresolvable questions.

A foreclosure subject is distinguished by not having experienced a crisis, yet expressing commitment. It is difficult to tell where his parents' goals for him leave off and where his begin. He is becoming what others have prepared or intended him to become as a child. His beliefs (or lack of them) are virtually "the faith of his fathers living still." College experiences serve only as a confirmation of childhood beliefs. A certain rigidity characterizes his personality; one feels that if he were faced with a situation in which parental values were nonfunctional, he would feel extremely threatened.

Previous studies have found ego identity to be related to "certainty of self-conception" and "temporal stability of self-rating" (Bronson, 1959), extent of a subject's acceptance of a false personality sketch of himself (Gruen, 1960), anxiety (Block, 1961), and sociometric ratings of adjustment (Rasmussen, 1964). Two themes predominate in these studies: a variability-stability dimension of self-concept, and overall adjustment. In general, subjects who have achieved ego identity seem less confused in self-definition and are freer from anxiety.

Four task variables were used to validate the newly constructed identity statuses: a concept-attainment task administered under stressful conditions, a level of aspiration measure yielding goal-setting patterns, a measure of authoritarianism, and a measure of stability of self-esteem in the face of invalidating information.

The hypotheses investigated were these:

1. Subjects high in ego identity (i.e., identity-achievement status) will receive significantly lower (better) scores on the stressful concept-attainment task than subjects lower in ego identity. Subjects who have achieved an ego identity, with the internal locus of self-definition which that implies, will be less vulnerable to the stress conditions of evaluation apprehension and over-solicitousness (see Method section).
2. Subjects high in ego identity will set goals more realistically than subjects low in ego identity on a level of aspiration measure. The increment to overall ego strength following identity achievement should be reflected in the ego function of reality testing.
3. Subjects in the foreclosure status will endorse "authoritarian submission and conventionality" items to a greater extend than subjects in the other statuses.
4. There will be a significant positive relationship between ego identity measures and a measure of self-esteem.
5. Subjects high in ego identity will change less in self-esteem when given false information about their personalities than subjects low in ego identity.
6. There will be a significant relationship between the two measures of ego identity: the identity-status interview and the incomplete-sentences blank.

Method

Subjects

Subjects were 86 males enrolled in psychology, religion, and history courses at Hiram College.

Confederate Experimenters

Due to the possibility of contamination by subject inter-communication on a small campus, the study employed 10 confederate (task) experimenters who administered the concept-attainment task in one 12-hour period to all subjects. These task experimenters, 7 males and 3 females, were members of the author's class in psychological testing and had taken three or more courses in psychology. They had previously assisted in a pilot study, and had been checked twice by the author on their experimental procedure. The use of a sample of experimenters, none of whom were aware of the subjects' standings on crucial independent variables, also has advantages in terms of minimizing the effects of experimenter bias (Rosenthal, 1964).

Identity Status. Identity status was established by means of a 15–30 minute semistructured interview. All interviews followed the same outline, although deviations from the standard form were permitted in order to explore some areas more thoroughly. In most cases, the criteria for terminating an interview involved the completion of the prescribed questions as well as some feeling of certainty on the interviewer's part that the individual had provided enough information to be categorized. Interviews were tape-recorded and then replayed for judging. Hence, each interview was heard at least twice, usually three or four times.

A scoring manual (Marcia, 1964) was constructed using both theoretical criteria from Erikson and empirical criteria from a pilot study. Each subject was evaluated in terms of presence or absence of crisis as well as degree of commitment for three areas: occupation, religion, and politics—the latter two combined in a general measure of ideology. The interview judge familiarized himself with the descriptions of the statuses provided in the manual and sorted each interview into that pattern which it most closely resembled. Analysis of interjudge reliability for the identity statuses of 20 randomly selected subjects among three judges yielded an average percentage of agreement of 75. One of the judges was essentially untrained, having been given only the scoring manual and the 20 taped interviews.

A multiple question in the occupational area was:

How willing do you think you'd be to give up going into ——if something better came along?

Examples of typical answers for the four statuses were:

[Identity achievement] Well, I might, but I doubt it. I can't see what "something better" would be for me.

[Moratorium] I guess if I knew for sure I could answer that better. It would have to be something in the general area—something related.

[Foreclosure] Not very willing. It's what I've always wanted to do. The folks are happy with it and so am I.

[Identity diffusion] Oh sure. If something better came along, I'd change just like that.

A sample question in the religious area was:

Have you ever had any doubts about your religious beliefs?

[Identity achievement] Yeah, I even started wondering whether or not there was a god. I've pretty much resolved that now, though. The way it seems to me is. . . .

[Moratorium] Yes, I guess I'm going through that now. I just don't see how there can be a god and yet so much evil in the world or. . . .

[Foreclosure] No, not really, our family is pretty much in agreement on those things.

[Identity diffusion] Oh, I don't know. I guess so. Everyone goes through some sort of stage like that. But it really doesn't bother me much. I figure one's about as good as the other!

Overall Ego Identity. The Ego Identity Incomplete Sentences Blank (EIISB) is a 23-item semistructured projective test requiring the subject to complete a sentence "expressing his real feelings" having been given a leading phrase. Stems were selected and a scoring manual designed (Marcia, 1964) according to behaviors which Erikson (1956) relates to the achievement of ego identity. Empirical criteria were gathered during a pilot study. Each item was scored 3, 2, 4 or 1 and item scores summed to yield an overall ego-identity score. Two typical stems were: If one commits oneself—and, When I let myself go I—Scoring criteria for the latter stem are:

3—Nondisastrous self-abandonment. Luxurlating in physical release. For example, have a good time and do not worry about others' thoughts and standards, enjoy almost anything that has laughter and some physical activity involved, enjoy myself more.

2—Cautiousness, don't know quite what will happen, have to be careful. Defensive or trivial. For example, never know exactly what I will say or do, sleep, might be surprised since I don't remember letting myself go.

1—Goes all to pieces, dangerous, self-destructive, better not to. For example, think I talk too much about myself and my personal interests, tend to become too loud when sober and too melodramatic when drunk, sometimes say things I later regret.

Analysis of interscorer reliability for 20 protocols among three judges yielded an average item-by-item correlation of $r = .76$, an average total score correlation of $r = .73$, and an average percentage of agreement of 74.

Measures of Task Variables

Concept Attainment Task Performance. The Concept Attainment Task (CAT) developed by Bruner, Goodnow, and Austin (1956) and modified by Weick (1964), requires the subject to arrive at a certain combination of attributes of cards. The subject may eliminate certain attributes by asking whether a card is positive or negative for the concept and he may guess the concept at any time. He is penalized 5 points for every request, 10 points for every guess, and 5 points for every 30 seconds that passes before he attains the concept. Level of aspiration was obtained by informing the subject of his previous time and asking him to estimate his time on the next problem.

Quality of performance on the CAT was assessed by the following measures: overall CAT scores (points for time plus points for requests and guesses), points for time alone, points for requests and guesses alone, number of "give-ups" (problems which the subject refused to complete). The main level of aspiration measure was attainment discrepancy or *D* score, the algebraic average of the differences between a subject's stated expectancy for a problem and his immediately preceding performance on a similar problem.

A combination of two stress conditions (stress defined here as externally imposed conditions which tend to impair performance) were used: evaluation apprehension and oversolicitousness. Evaluation apprehension refers to a subject's feeling that his standing on highly valued personal characteristics is to be exposed. The characteristic chosen for this study was intellectual competence, unquestionably salient for college students. Oversolicitousness was chosen as a logical complement to evaluation apprehension. It was assumed that unnecessary reassurance would validate and, hence, augment whatever anxiety the subject was experiencing.

Pilot study data indicated that the stress conditions were effective. Using the same task experimenters as in the final study, 56 subjects (27 males and 29 females) took the CAT under stress and nonstress (i.e., stress omitted) conditions. Each experimenter ran about 3 stress and 3 nonstress subjects. Stressed subjects performed significantly more poorly than nonstressed ones ($t = 2.61$, $df = 54$, $p < .02$).

Self-Esteem Change and Authoritarianism. The Self-Esteem Questionnaire (SEQ-F) is a 20-item test developed by deCharms and Rosenbaum (1960) on which the subject indicates his degree of endorsement of statements concerning general feelings of self-confidence and worthiness.

In addition, statements reflecting authoritarian submission and conventionality, taken from the California F Scale (Adorno, Frenkel-Brunswik; Levinson, & Sanford, 1950), which were originally filler items, are used here as a dependent variable. The SEQ-F was administered twice, the first time in a classroom setting the second, during the experimental situation following an invalidated self-definition.

The treatment condition of "invalidated self-definition" (ISD) followed the CAT and directly preceded the second administration of SEQ-F. It consisted of giving the subject false information concerning the relationship between his alleged self-evaluation and his actual personality.

Procedure

Following is the experimental procedure: Subjects completed the EI-ISB and SEQ-F in class. Each subject was interviewed to determine his identity status. (This interviewing period lasted about 2 months.) On the day of the experiment, each subject went through the following conditions: *(a)* Administration of the CAT under stress by the task experimenter. *Evaluation apprehension* was created by the task experimenter's saying:

> By the way, I thought you might be interested to know that this test is related to tests of intelligence[1] and that it's been found to be one of the best single predictors of success in college. So of course, you'll want to do your very best.

Oversolicitousness was created during CAT performance by the task experimenter's hovering over the subject, asking him if he were comfortable, advising him not to "tense up," not to "make it harder on yourself." *(b)* Following the CAT, the subject was seated in the author's office where he was given either a positive or negative (randomly assigned) invalidated self-definition. The subject found the experimenter intently scanning a data sheet and was told:

> I've been looking over some of the data and it seems that while you consider yourself less [more] mature than other subjects, you actually come out as being more [less] mature. Is there any way you can account for this discrepancy? [Pause for the subject's response.] This seems to hold up also for self-confidence. It seems that you consider yourself as having less [more] self-confidence than other subjects, yet you actually come out having more [less].

(c) The subject was then sent to another room where he took the SEQ-F for the second time. The following day each subject received a postcard from the experimenter explaining the false information.

Results

Performance on CAT

The relationship between the identity statuses and CAT performance was investigated by means of individual *t* tests. These are found in Table 32.1 and support the hypothesis of significant differences in CAT performance between subjects high and low in ego identity.

For all three indices of CAT performance identity-achievement subjects perform significantly[2] better than identity-diffusion subjects (p's ranging from .01 to .05)* and identity achievement subjects perform significantly better than the other three statuses combined (p's ranging from .02 to .05).

Data involving the number of problems on which the subjects in the different identity statuses gave up are presented in Table 32.2.

---

* [When interpreting the statistical results, keep in mind that a probability level less than .05 ($p < .05$) indicates a statistically significant difference between or among the groups being tested. A probability level less than .01 ($p < .01$) gives one even more confidence in the results. A $p < .05$ means only 5 chances in 100 that there is not a true difference between groups; $p < .001$, only one chance in 1,000 that there is not a true difference between groups.—Eds.]

Table 32.1   Differences Between Identity Statuses in CAT Performance

	N	M Time	SD	M requests + Guesses	SD	M overall Score	SD	t
Identity status								
Identity achievement (A)	18	18.17	7.94	599.17	186.63	791.94	244.15	
Moratorium (B)	22	24.50	15.77	807.14	495.58	1024.82	612.04	
Foreclosure (C)	23	34.20	13.84	875.82	285.44	1147.83	407.98	
Identity diffusion (D)	21	29.73	18.52	767.38	266.43	1078.57	352.38	
Groups compared								
Time								
A versus D								2.39*
A versus B + C + D								2.41**
A versus C								2.90***
A + B + D versus C								2.24*
Requests + guesses								
A versus D								2.19*
A versus B + C + D								2.28*
A versus C								3.47***
A + B + C versus C								1.69
Overall score								
A versus D								3.47***
A versus B + C + D								2.45**
A versus C								3.19***
A + B + D versus C								1.63

* $p \leq .05$.
** $p \leq .02$.
*** $p \leq .01$.

Table 32.2   Number of CAT Problems on Which Subjects in Each Identity Status Gave Up

	Identity Status				
	Identity Achievement	Moratorium	Foreclosure	Identity Diffusion	All Other
Give-ups	1	7	13	11	31
Completions	107	125	131	109	365
	$\chi^2 = 8.93$				$\chi^2 = 5.69*$

* $p < .02$.

Comparing identity-achievement subjects with other subjects, significantly fewer instances of giving up on CAT problems are found for the identity-achievement subjects. This, together with the previous findings concerning the relationship between identity status and CAT performance under stress, provides substantial confirmation of Hypothesis 1.

An interesting supplementary finding is that moratorium subjects were significantly more variable in overall CAT scores than subjects in the other three statuses combined ($F_{max} = 2.62$, $df = 21/61$, $p < .05$; See McNemar, 1955, pp. 244–247).

Correlations between all three CAT performance measures and the EIISB, while in the expected direction, failed to reach significance. The Pearson r between overall CAT performance and EI-ISB scores was $-.14$ ($df = 82$).

Level of Aspiration

The D, or attainment discrepancy score, reflects the difference between a subject's aspirations and his actual performance. An overall positive D score means that the subject tends to set his goals higher than his attainment; a negative D score means the opposite.

Inspection of original data revealed that no status obtained a negative average D score, the range being from 3.60 for identity achievement to 5.06 for foreclosure. Analysis of variance indicates a significant difference among statuses in D score ($F = 5.10$, $df = 3/80$, $p < .01$). The t tests presented in Table 32.3 show the foreclosure subjects exhibiting higher D scores than identity-achievement subjects ($t = 3.35$, $df = 38$, $p < .01$) and higher D scores than the other statuses combined ($t = 3.70$, $df = 82$, $p < .001$).

Table 32.3 Differences in D Score Between Identity Statuses

	N	M	SD	t
Identity status				
Identity achievement (A)	18	3.60	.80	
Moratorium (B)	22	4.11	.72	
Foreclosure (C)	23	5.06	1.65	
Identity diffusion (D)	21	3.91	1.49	
Groups compared				
C versus A				3.35*
C versus A + B + D				3.70**
B versus A				1.90
C + B + D versus A				.57

* $p \leq .01$.
** $p \leq .001$.

It appears that foreclosure subjects tend to maintain high goals in spite of failure.

Authoritarian Submission and Conventionality (F)

The t tests presented in Table 32.4 show that foreclosure subjects received significantly higher F scores than identity-achievement subjects ($t = 3.88, df = 38, p < .001$) and also significantly higher F scores than the other statuses combined ($t = 3.75, df = 82, p < .001$).

Self-Esteem

The significant relationship found here was between EI-ISB scores and the initial SEQ ($r = .26, df = 84, p < .01$). No significant differences among identity statuses for SEQ were found ($F = .66, df = 3/82$, ns [not significant]). In addition, self-esteem appeared to be unrelated to authoritarian submission and conventionality ($r = -.03, df = 84$, ns) and to CAT performance ($r = -.03, df = 82$, ns).

Change in SEQ Following ISD

Although differences in the expected direction were found (i.e., identity achievement changed less than identity diffusion), these were not significant ($t = 1.39, df = 37, p < .20$). Observer ratings of subjects' reactions to the invalidated self-definition indicated that this treatment condition was effective. The failure to obtain significant results may have been due to unreliability in the self-esteem measure engendered by the 2-month span between the first and second administration. There was a tendency for foreclosure subjects given negative information to show a greater decrease in self-esteem than identity-achievement subjects under similar conditions ($t = 2.60, df = 19, p < .02$).

No relationship was found between EI-ISB scores and self-esteem change ($r = .001, df = 84$, ns).

Table 32.4 Differences in F Scores Between Identity Statuses

	N	M	SD	t
Identity status				
Identity achievement (A)	18	34.28	8.99	
Moratorium (B)	23	37.57	8.05	
Foreclosure (C)	24	45.17	9.01	
Identity diffusion (D)	21	38.67	10.19	
Groups compared				
C versus A				3.88*
C versus A + B + D				3.75*
D versus A				.44
B versus A				1.20

* $p \leq .001$.

Table 32.5 Differences Between Identity Statuses in EI-ISB Scores

	N	M	SD	t
Identity status				
Identity achievement (A)	18	48.28	5.10	
Moratorium (B)	23	48.09	4.23	
Foreclosure (C)	24	46.17	4.62	
Identity diffusion (D)	21	43.33	3.52	
Groups compared				
A versus C				1.37
B versus C				1.41
B versus D				3.94*
A versus D				3.89*
A + C + B versus D				3.61*

* $p \leq .001$.

EI-ISB Scores and Identity Status

Two techniques were employed to assess the relationship between overall ego identity as measured by EI-ISB and identity status. These were an analysis of variance among the four statuses ($F = 5.42, df = 3/82, p < .01$), and t tests among the individual statuses. The latter are found in Table 32.5.

Identity-achievement subjects received significantly higher EI-ISB scores than did identity-diffusion subjects ($t = 3.89, df = 37, p < .001$), and the first three identity statuses taken together received significantly higher EI-ISB scores than did identity diffusion ($t = 3.62, df = 84, p < .001$). Thus, the distinctive group with respect to EI-ISB scores appears to be identity diffusion. These findings lend some support to the hypothesized relationship between overall ego identity and identity status.

Discussion

Of the two approaches to the measurement of ego identity, the interview, based on individual styles, was more successful than the incomplete-sentences test, which treated ego identity as a simple linear quality.

Particularly interesting was the relationship between such apparently diverse areas as performance in a cognitive task and commitment to an occupation and ideology. The interview and the CAT tapped two prime spheres of ego function: the infrapsychic, seen on the CAT which required the individual to moderate between pressing internal stimuli (stress-produced anxiety) and external demands (completion of the task), and the psychosocial, seen in the interview which evaluated the meshing of the individual's needs and capabilities with society's rewards and demands. The relationship between these two spheres contributes validity to both the identity statuses and to the generality of the construct, ego.

No confirmation of the hypothesis relating ego identity to resistance to change in self-esteem was obtained, possibly because the length of time between the first and second SEQ administration was 2 months. The variability in subjects' self-esteem over this period of time may have obscured differences due to treatment alone.

Following are experimentally derived profiles of each status:

1. Identity achievement. This group scored highest on an independent measure of ego identity and performed better than other statuses on a stressful concept attainment task—persevering longer on problems and maintaining a realistic level of aspiration. They subscribed somewhat less than other statuses to authoritarian values and their self-esteem was a little less vulnerable to negative information.

2. Moratorium. The distinguishing features of this group were its variability in CAT performance and its resemblance on other measures to identity achievement.

3. Foreclosure. This status' most outstanding characteristic was its endorsement of authoritarian values such as obedience, strong leadership, and respect for authority. Self-esteem was vulnerable to negative information and foreclosure subjects performed more poorly on a stressful concept-attainment task than did identity-achievement subjects. In addition, their response to failure on this task was unrealistic, maintaining, rather than moderating, unattained high goals. This behavior pattern is referred to by Rotter (1954) as "low freedom of movement [and is associated with] the achievement of superiority through identification [pp. 196–197]"—an apt description for one who is becoming his parents' alter ego.

4. Identity diffusion. While this status was originally considered the anchor point for high-low comparisons with identity achievement it occupied this position only in terms of EI-ISB scores. CAT performance was uniformly poorer than that of identity achievement, although not the lowest among the statuses. The identity-diffuse

individuals to which Erikson refers and identity-diffusion subjects in this study may be rather different with respect to extent of psychopathology. A "playboy" type of identity diffusion may exist at one end of a continuum and a schizoid personality type at the other end. The former would more often be found functioning reasonably well on a college campus. While having tapped a rather complete range of adjustment in the other statuses, the extent of disturbance of an extreme identity diffusion would have precluded his inclusion in our sample. Hence, it is the foreclosure, and not the identity-diffusion, subject who occupies the lowest position on most task variables.

In conclusion, the main contribution of this study lies in the development, measurement, and partial validation of the identity statuses as individual styles of coping with the psychosocial task of forming an ego identity.

Notes

1. In fact, intelligence test scores gleaned from the subjects' college files did correlate significantly with CAT performance ($r = 55$, $df = 82$, $p < .0005$). However, no significant relationship was found between intelligence and identity status.
2. All significance levels for t tests are based on two-tailed tests.

References

Adorno, T.W., Frenkel-Brunswik, E., Levinson, D. J., & Sanford, R. N. *The authoritarian personality.* New York: Harper, 1950.

Block, J. Ego identity, role variability, and adjustment. *Journal of Consulting Psychology.* 1961, **25**, 392–397.

Bronson, G. W. Identity diffusion in late adolescents. *Journal of Abnormal and Social Psychology,* 1959, **59**, 414–417.

Bruner, J. S., Goodnow, I. J., & Austin, G. A. *A study of thinking.* New York: Wiley, 1956.

deCharms, R., & Rosenbaum, M. E. Status variables and matching behavior. *Journal of Personality,* 1960, **28**, 492–502.

Erikson, E. H. The problem of ego identity. *Journal of the American Psychoanalytic Association,* 1956, **4**, 56–121.

Erikson, E. H. *Childhood and society.* (2nd ed.) New York: Norton, 1963.

Gruen, W. Rejection of false information about oneself as an indication of ego identity. *Journal of Consulting Psychology,* 1960, **24**, 231–233.

Marcia, J. E. Determination and construct validity of ego identity status. Unpublished doctoral dissertation, Ohio State University, 1964.

McNemar, Q. *Psychological statistics.* (2nd ed.) New York: Wiley, 1955.

Rasmussen, J. E. The relationship of ego identity to psychosocial effectiveness. *Psychological Reports,* 1964, **15**, 815–825.

Rosenthal, R. Experimenter outcome-orientation and the results of the psychological experiment. *Psychological Bulletin,* 1964, **61**, 405–412.

Rotter, J. B. *Social learning and clinical psychology.* Englewood Cliffs, N. J.: Prentice-Hall, 1954.

Weick, K. E. Reduction of cognitive dissonance through task enhancement and effort expenditure. *Journal of Abnormal and Social Psychology,* 1964, **68**, 533–539.

Pathognomic Versus Developmentally Appropriate Self-Focus During Adolescence

Michael L. Penn and Debra J. Witkin

Michael L. Penn, the great-grandson of an American slave, was born in Winston Salem, North Carolina, but spent most of his childhood in New York City. He first studied philosophy at Brandeis University, then earned his B.A. in psychology, history, and religion from the University of Pennsylvania in 1986. He earned his M.A. and Ph.D. in clinical psychology from Temple University in Philadelphia, Pennsylvania, in 1988 and 1991, respectively. He is currently an associate professor of psychology at Franklin and Marshall College in Lancaster, Pennsylvania.

Penn has published articles in a wide range of psychology-related fields, including adolescent psychopathology, public health, cultural psychology, women's studies, peace psychology, substance abuse treatment, and the psychology of homelessness. He is the author of *Desecration of the Temple: The Global Problem of Violence Against Women and Girls* (Rowman & Littlefield, 1997).

Debra J. Witkin was an undergraduate at Franklin and Marshall College when she received a Hackman Scholar Research Fellow Award to assist Dr. Penn in his research. Their collaboration produced the following selection.

As established by Erik H. Erikson, identity is the critical psychosocial issue of adolescence. To be aware of one's identity, one must focus one's cognition upon one's self to some degree. Penn and Witkin contend, however, that self-focused attention has also been associated with psychopathology, such as depression, alcohol abuse, suicide, eating disorders, and anxiety. The following selection, which is from "Pathognomic Versus Developmentally Appropriate Self-Focus During Adolescence: Theoretical Concerns and Clinical Implications," *Psychotherapy* (Summer 1994), helps the reader to differentiate between healthy self-focus and pathological self-focus during the developmental period of adolescence.

Key Concept: adolescent identity issues and psychopathology

*S*elf-focused attention has been associated with a number of psychopathological and distress related conditions—including depression, alcohol abuse, suicide, eating disorders, anxiety, and loneliness. Ironically, however, increased self-focus is also regarded as a normative aspect of adolescent functioning. Elkind for example, has described adolescent egocentrism as developmentally appropriate and a number of empirical investigations have found that among normal adolescent samples, self-focus increases dramatically between pre- and post-stages of adolescent development. Given the widely recognized link between self-focus and psychopathology, as well as the heightened degree of self-focus that characterizes normative adolescent functioning, it is important to distinguish between normative, adaptive self-focus during adolescence and abnormal or pathological self-focus.

In this article distinctions are made between the adaptive and developmentally appropriate aspects of

adolescent self-focus and the maladaptive pattern of self-focus manifested by clinical samples. It is argued that self-focus, whether adaptive or pathological, may vary along six dimensions: 1) content; 2) valence; 3) intensity; 4) duration; 5) consistency; and 6) purpose. It is in modifying these dimensions of self-focus among adolescents seeking therapy that positive psychological outcomes can be effected. Before these themes are elaborated upon further, a description of the nature of self-focus in general, and of adolescent self-focus in particular, is in order.

On the Nature of Self-Focus

Carver (1979) defined self-focused attention in the following way:

When attention is self-directed, it sometimes takes the form of focus on internal perceptual events, that is, information from those sensory receptors that react to changes in bodily activity. Self-focus may also take the form of an enhanced awareness of one's present or past physical behavior, that is, a heightened cognizance of what one is doing or what one is like. Alternatively, self-attention can be an awareness of the more or less permanently encoded bits of information that comprise, for example, one's attitudes. (p. 1255)

Self-focused attention is thus characterized by an awareness of internally generated, self-relevant information and may include physical, cognitive, affective or behavioral aspects of the self.

Self-Focus During Adolescence

For a variety of reasons, self-focus during adolescence may be especially high. For example, adolescence is a stage marked by rapid physical and psychosocial development. Indeed, at no time in the life cycle, other than perhaps infancy, is transformation of every aspect of the self as profound as it is during adolescence. The physical changes taking place during adolescence are collectively labeled *puberty* and are manifested in five highly salient phenomena: a rapid acceleration in growth; the further development of the gonads; the appearance of secondary sex characteristics including development of the genitals and breasts, and the growth of pubic, facial and body hair; changes in the distribution of fat and muscle; and changes in both the circulatory and respiratory systems, which facilitate increased strength and tolerance for exercise (Marshall, 1978). Puberty, then, initiates a dramatic transformation in appearance in a relatively short period of time. Given the variety and intensity of these morphological changes, individuals may spend more time focused on physical aspects of the self during adolescence than during other periods of development.

In addition to morphological changes, both the cognitive and social changes that take place during adolescence may lead to increased attention to self-relevant information. The cognitive maturation that takes place during adolescence, for example, results in a greater capacity for, and therefore a greater propensity toward, self-scrutiny and introspection. Elkind (1976) has pointed out that adolescents' newly emerging cognitive capacities often give rise to certain cognitive limitations that may be summarized in the term "adolescent egocentrism." There are two components to adolescent egocentrism that bear particular relevance to this discussion—*imaginary audience,* a type of heightened self-consciousness, and the *personal fable.*

Imaginary audience is characterized by a heightened concern for how the adolescent appears in the eyes of others. Thus, an adolescent who is concerned that "everyone will notice" some superficial physical flaw is exhibiting imaginary audience behavior in its classic form. The tendency to engage in imaginary audience behavior increases the salience of the self by making the self the center of everyone else's attention. As Elkind (1976) explains, the emergence of formal operational thought make it possible for young people to think about other people's thinking. This newly emerging ability, however, is said to be constrained by an inability to distinguish between what is of interest to others and what is of interest to the self. Since the young adolescent is preoccupied with his or her own self, he or she assumes that everyone else has the same concern. As a consequence, adolescents are vulnerable to high levels of self-scrutiny and self-inspection.

A second aspect of adolescent egocentrism, the *personal fable,* revolves around the adolescent's erroneous belief that his or her experiences are unique. In its more positive form, the personal fable may lead to feelings of invulnerability, optimism, and confidence. For example, adolescents tend to overestimate their capacities while underestimating their vulnerability to certain kinds of risks. In its negative form, the personal fable may result in self-absorption, self-pity and/or an exaggerated sense of self-importance that serves to disconnect the adolescent from others. Often times, in the adolescent's mind, others do not and cannot understand his or her perspective and experiences. The self is perceived as disconnected and alone.

Beyond these aforementioned physical and cognitive impeti, the developmental tasks of adolescence—including identity development and the assumption of personal responsibility—may require elevated levels of self-consciousness. Because the acquisition of self-knowledge (or a sense of identity) is such a salient aspect of adolescent development, adolescence is that time of life when self-awareness can precipitate great opportunities for growth, as well as numerous opportunities for the development of psychological problems.

Self-focus during adolescence is thus fueled by physical development, emerging cognitive capacities, and the assumption of new responsibilities. When increased self-focus serves the larger goal of self-development, self-awareness can facilitate enhancement of self-control, the clarification of values and possible career paths, and the development of a sense of identity and purpose. When self-focus is unhealthy, however, it tends to thwart, rather than facilitate, such processes.

Pathological/Pathognomic Self-Focus

Ingram (1990) has reviewed a number of studies that suggest that self-focused attention may contribute to the intensification and/or initiation of psychopathology. He wrote: "Self-focused attention . . . may contribute to both the intensification and initiation of psychopathology. Thus, with regard to initiation, self-focused attention would serve to contribute to the constellation of variables that bring about disorder. In particular, chronically high levels of self-focused attention across a variety of situational contexts may constitute a cognitive diathesis in a diathesis–stress relation with psychopathology" (p. 162). Since increased self-focus may be both normative and adaptive during adolescence, it is largely the nature and purpose of self-focus which will govern whether it is adaptive or harmful. Self-focus, whether adaptive or pathological, may vary along six dimensions: *content, valence, intensity, duration, consistency,* and *purpose.*

Content

The *content* of self-focus may consist of an awareness of behavioral, psychological, or physical aspects of the self. Adaptive self-regulation and self-development depend upon an individual's ability to monitor each of these domains while also attending to non-self–related processes. When self-focus becomes constricted to one aspect of the self, personality and/or behavioral pathologies may begin to emerge.

Excessive somatic self-focus, for example, can lead to, or be symptomatic of, anxiety and/or eating and self-perception disorders such as anorexia and/or bulimia nervosa and body dysmorphic disorder. These disorders may be prevalent among adolescent populations because pubertal processes render somatic self-focus more likely. Whether such focus is negative in valence and exclusive in content depends upon the psychosocial context in which adolescents come of age.

An example of how pubertal processes can render individuals vulnerable to pathological somatic self-focus is provided by Peterson (1985) and her colleagues. Peterson et al. evaluated interactions between pubertal development and local social norms by randomly sampling pubertal boys and girls from two suburban school districts that were similar in social class. They found that while boys from both communities and girls from one community all reported similar satisfaction with their weight and feelings of attraction, the girls of one community were very dissatisfied with their weight and felt unattractive. These differences persisted even when actual weight was controlled for. In discussing these findings, Peterson et al. noted that local social norms governing attractiveness rendered pubertal girls in one community negatively focused on one aspect of the self—physical appearance. In addition, as compared with both boys and girls from the former community, girls from the latter community proved to be less active in various school activities. Thus, these girls had fewer opportunities to develop the full range of their identities and sense of self; instead, they tended to focus excessively on appearance.

In another study that sought to explain why sex differences in depression may begin to emerge during adolescence, Girgus, Nolen-Hoeksema & Seligman (1989) found that while males tend to like the changes in their bodies that come with puberty, girls tend to dislike the changes that they undergo. According to the researchers, girls' body dissatisfaction was related to the loss of "the long, lithe, pre-pubescent look that is idealized in modern fashion" (p. 3) and tended to render them more somatically focused. Increased somatic focus, in turn, tended to render dissatisfied girls more vulnerable to external stress; as a consequence, they were more vulnerable to depression.

Valence

Five factors contribute to the *valence* of self-focus: physical and psychological health; judgments about one's competence; the degree to which one feels physically attractive; the degree to which one feels that he or she belongs; and the extent to which one perceives one's self to be evolving and developing. When the valence of self-focus is positive, individuals experience a sense of well-being and contentment. By contrast, negative self-focus is precipitated by the onset of physical or psychological illness, concerns about one's psychological and/or physical qualities, profound loneliness and disconnection, or concerns that one is no longer growing and developing in important ways.

When adolescents seek therapy, it is usually because some aspect of the self is seen in a negative light. Some aspect of the self is perceived as injured, or inadequate, or stuck. One of the primary goals of the therapist is to facilitate the restoration of a positive view of the self so that the adolescent will have the courage to continue the difficult work that is involved in self development. During adolescence, in particular, the individual will encounter a great deal of information about the self that can be disconcerting. In adolescence one begins to get a sense for how complex life is and how small we are as compared with our responsibilities. One gets a sense of the future and thus can feel like shrinking from the many demands that the future will make. One makes many mistakes of judgment; one says and does things that are later regretted. All of these kinds of experiences do battle against a positive view of the self.

Intensity

The energy, power, or force released by self-awareness is captured by the idea of *intensity*. When the intensity of self-awareness is high and the valence is positive, one experiences what Maslow (1962) has referred to as a "peak experience." The self is perceived as powerful, focused, alive, and in harmony with itself and the world. When, however, intensity is high and valence is negative one experiences the self in its most radical negativity. If one has ever been publicly embarrassed, or done something that was in sharp contrast to one's values, one has had an acute experience of self-awareness that is high in intensity and negative in valence. Regret, shame, and guilt all arise out of high-intensity, negative valence self-awareness. It is the intensity of negative self-awareness that motivates the desire to escape from the self.

That individuals are motivated to escape aversive self-awareness is supported by a number of findings.

For example, working under the assumption that a mirror or camera makes a person aware of him or herself, Duval & Wicklund (1972) found that subjects receiving negative evaluations chose to spend less time in front of a camera or mirror than subjects who received positive evaluations. Gibbons & Wicklund (1976) found that a putdown or rejection from a female confederate caused male subjects to avoid tape recordings of their own voices; and Steenbarger & Aderman (1979) have shown that people escaped from a mirrored room more quickly after receiving discouraging feedback. Beyond the laboratory, Hull and his colleagues (Hull, 1981; Hull, et al., 1983; Hull & Young, 1983) have shown that alcohol reduces self-awareness and is often used to achieve that effect. In addition, Baumeister has persuasively argued that sexual masochism (Baumeister, 1981; Baumeister & Sher, 1988) and suicidal processes (Baumeister, 1990; Baumeister, 1991) may be precipitated by a desire to escape aversive self-awareness.

Comparatively high rates of suicide among adolescents may result, in part, from high-intensity, negative valence self-focus. Indeed, over the last several decades epidemiologists have documented significant temporal or secular trends in the prevalence of completed and attempted suicides by adolescents. Such increases parallel sociological trends that reflect an increase in the salience of the self for all Western people, and particularly for adolescents (Baumeister & Sher, 1988; Levin, 1987).

For example, whereas in generations prior to the Renaissance people acquired their identities largely from their social and professional roles, following the Renaissance, and particularly after industrialization, the search for identity became increasingly important as part of the psychosocial agenda of adolescence (Guidano, 1987). In addition, uniqueness and individuality were increasingly emphasized. As a result, the salience of the self, and the burdens that attend self-awareness, have dramatically increased. As evidence of this, one need only peruse the growing number of professional and lay articles, magazines, and books written in the last three decades that discuss self-related pathologies and concerns.

Duration

The duration of self-focus captures the amount of time individuals spend focused on self-related tasks and concerns. As has been noted, the general valence of self-focus will reflect an individual's sense of self-worth or self-esteem. Adolescents with a positive self-image tend to spend less time focused on the self than do poor self-image adolescents. That this is so is substantiated by Salmela-Aro (1992), who found that as compared with normals, adolescents with psychological problems tended to describe self-related projects when they listed goals. Normals, by contrast, tended to list task-related goals. In addition, Rosenthal & Simeonsson (1989) have found that, while nondisturbed adolescents show a general decline in self-consciousness throughout adolescence, the self-consciousness of disturbed adolescents tends to remain high. Last, and perhaps most relevant to this discussion, Natale, Dahlberg & Jaffe (1978) have found an inverse relation between use of self-references and improvement in psychotherapy.

Consistency

The *consistency* of self-focus involves the extent to which self-focus occurs across a range of situations. Ingram (1990) discussed the adaptive function of being able to shift focus in order to accommodate various situational demands. When one lacks the ability to shift focus between internal and external states according to a given situation, the result can be maladaptive. With certain pathologies, this apparent "inflexibility" of self-focus may exist either in specific situations, or generally, across all situations. For example, an adolescent with test anxiety may only have high-intensity, negative valence self-awareness when in testing situations. On the other hand, the depressed adolescent is self-concerned in almost all situations. The more situations self-focus encompasses, the more detrimental it may be to an adolescent's functioning and psychosocial well-being.

Purpose

Purpose of self-focus refers to the explicit or implicit motive for self-directed attention. Inasmuch as increased self-focus during adolescence can facilitate the processes of identity development, self-regulation and self-directed growth, it may serve important adaptive functions. Self-focus that is not guided and motivated by these purposes, however, is likely to be destructive. Since the therapeutic process has the potential of enhancing self-focus, it is important for the therapist to be sure that he or she is not simply prescribing more of the pathogen. One safeguard against this is to take a developmental approach to the adolescent's self-exploration. A developmental approach presents an opportunity to convert the crisis of high-intensity, negative valence self-awareness into an opportunity for self-discovery and growth. Following is an example of the use of a developmental approach to psychotherapy that takes into account the various dimensions of self-focus.

Case Illustration

A 20-year-old Caucasian male whom I will call Daniel was brought to our outpatient clinic by his parents. Daniel's parents were concerned that he would carry out an oft-stated promise that he would kill himself on his 21st birthday. At the time of initial assessment, Daniel evidenced depression and corroborated his parents' fears stating his intention to kill himself on his birthday in two months.

In addition to depressive symptoms, Daniel evidenced poor impulse control. Although he had never hurt another person, Daniel often did things to inflict pain upon himself. One thing that he did often was to light a cigarette in the bridge connecting two people's forearms. The first person to move his/her arm was the loser. When Daniel arrived for his first session, he proudly displayed a third-degree burn from this exercise.

Daniel is the eldest of two children born in a middle-class suburb of Philadelphia. He reported having a "decent" relationship with his seventeen-year-old sister, but a stormy and intense relationship with his parents. According to his parents, Daniel suffered no unusual physical, social, or psychological trauma during his early childhood, and enjoyed normal peer relations. Although Daniel did graduate from high school with his cohort, he did not do well academically. Much of Daniel's failure was attributed to his decade-long history of drug use which began at age nine. Approximately a year-and-a-half before our initial interview, Daniel was successful at treatment for drug use. Daniel also underwent cosmetic surgery to have some of the fat removed from his pectoralis muscles before the initial session. Daniel was employed in a small plastics and fiberglass company (owned by a close friend), working sporadically whenever he needed money. Since Daniel still lived with his parents, his economic responsibilities were limited to maintaining his own supply of pocket-money. Although Daniel's cognitive and physical development was that of a man, his emotional and social development was clearly delayed. These developmental delays may have been the result of excessive drug use and/or permissive parenting.

The initial and most pressing goal of treatment was to reduce suicide risk. Several factors in the patient's history suggested that he did not desire to kill himself. Daniel had successfully completed a drug treatment program and had maintained sobriety for more than a year. In addition, he attended nearly every session with me—even though our meetings were scheduled for 7:00 A.M. Last, as was noted earlier, Daniel had just undergone cosmetic surgery.

Working with the theory of suicide developed by Roy Baumeister we proceeded on the assumption that Daniel did not have a desire to die, but to escape noxious self-awareness. Thus, the risk was high-intensity, negative valence self-awareness. Within this theoretical framework, I regarded Daniel's drug use as earlier attempts to decrease noxious self-awareness. When the escape provided by drug use proved to be insufficiently gratifying, Daniel abandoned it and began to see suicide as another viable option.

The first step in treatment was for Daniel to sign a contract ensuring me that he would not kill himself. Then I began the more difficult process of helping Daniel recognize that he did not like the person he had become. I set out to convince him that he could change his own life in meaningful ways and could become the kind of person that he could honor and respect. The first step in changing ourselves, I said, is in acknowledging the areas in which we need to change. I spoke with him about his parents' permissiveness and its effect on his maturation.

His childish behavior, I noted, precluded the development of a positive sense of self.

In order to reinforce the idea that he could change, I designed a self-report instrument that enabled Daniel to reflect upon himself. We resolved that every day he would work to improve in each of these areas. We also noted that each day life would give him opportunities to further develop himself.

In order further to reinforce Daniel's belief in his ability to change, I used hypnotic suggestions and positive visualizations. Deep relaxation and hypnosis were also used to expand awareness of the complexity of the self and to metabolize some of the anger (negative valence) he seemed to have toward himself, his parents, and perhaps the world. Each day (we met for one hour, five days a week for six weeks), we spent at least twenty minutes in meditation, deep relaxation, or hypnosis.

Finally, on the weekend before his birthday, I recounted to Daniel the progress that had been made. I told him how proud I was of him, but how I feared that he might make a suicide attempt just to save face. I told him that avoiding this attempt was perhaps the ultimate test of his newly gained maturity and self-control.

The next Monday, on his birthday, Daniel called me to tell me that he had driven to Florida to spend some time with his favorite aunt. Two days later, he returned from Florida and resumed his daily sessions with me. From that point onward, his psychosocial, behavioral, and emotional progress was exceptional. Before he ended the program, he had rented his own apartment and was going to work regularly. In addition, his depressive symptoms and suicidal ideation had completely subsided.

Discussion and Conclusion

Daniel's bout with drug addiction, his cosmetic surgery, self-inflicted burns, and repeated fantasies of suicide all represent somatically focused attempts to deal with noxious self-awareness. In the absence of any understanding of how to effect meaningful self-improvement, Daniel's only recognized option was to destroy himself, as well as those whom he held responsible for his condition. The functions of the self-report measure were to diversify the content of Daniel's self-focus and to enable him to become conscious of aspects of the self that had theretofore been largely neglected. By helping to shift the content of Daniel's focus to nonsomatic aspects of the self, avenues for growth that had not been previously considered were opened up. In addition, although initially ego-dystonic, the intensity of Daniel's negative self-awareness was used to fuel the processes necessary for critical self-analysis and growth. Because Daniel's efforts at self-control and self-development were recognized and praised, the valence of self-awareness became increasingly positive. Ultimately, as Daniel's ability to monitor, understand, and control himself increased there was much more energy available for non-self–related tasks. Thus, the duration of self-focus began to decrease and Daniel was able to spend more time at work and in service to others.

As can be gleaned from this case illustration, attention to the six dimensions of self-focus may serve as a heuristic for guiding the clinical interview and for monitoring and catalyzing improvements in an adolescent's view of the self. Many adolescents who either volunteer for psychotherapy, or are brought to treatment by their parents or the judicial system, are, like Daniel, angry, confused, and desperately longing to make something of themselves. An increasing number of them, however, haven't the slightest idea about how to go about doing this. By helping adolescents to understand, appreciate, and enhance self-related qualities, psychotherapists can contribute significantly to the ability of adolescents to complete the difficult, but important psychosocial agenda of the adolescent stage of development.

References

Baumeister, R. F. (1990). Suicide as escape from self. *Psychological Review, 97,* 90–113.

Baumeister, R. F. (1986). *Identity: Cultural change and the struggle for self.* New York: Oxford University Press.

Baumeister, R. F. (1991). *Escaping the self.* New York: Basic.

Baumeister, R. F. & Sher, S. J. (1988). Self-defeating behavior patterns among normal individuals: Review and analysis of common self-destructive tendencies. *Psychological Bulletin, 104,* 3–22.

Brennan, T. (1982). Loneliness in adolescence. *In* L. A. Peplau and D. Perlman (Eds.), *Loneliness, a sourcebook of current theory, research and therapy* (pp. 269–290). New York: John Wiley.

Buss, A. (1980). *Self-consciousness and social anxiety.* San Francisco: Freeman.

Carver, C. (1979). A cybernetic model of self-attention processes. *Journal of Personality and Social Psychology, 37,* 1251–1281.

Carver, C. S. & Scheier, M. F. (1986). Functional and dysfunctional responses to anxiety: The interaction between expectancies and self-focused attention. *In* R. Schwarzer (Ed.), *Self-related cognitions in anxiety and motivation* (pp. 111–141). Hillsdale, NJ: Erlbaum.

Duval, S. & Wicklund, R. A. (1972). *A theory of objective self-awareness.* New York: Academic.

Eccles, J. S. (1987). Adolescence: Gateway to gender role transcendence. *In* D. B. Carter (Ed.), *Current conceptions of sex roles and sex typing* (pp. 225–241).

Eccles, J. S. & Midgley, C. (1988). Stage/environment fit: Developmentally appropriate classrooms for early adolescents. *In* R. E. Ames and C. Ames (Eds.), *Research on motivation in education* (Vol. 3, pp. 139–186). San Diego: Academic.

Elkind, D. (1976). Understanding the young adolescent. *Adolescence, 13,* 127–134.

Elkind, D. (1979). Imaginary audience behavior in children and adolescents. *Developmental Psychology, 15,* 38–44.

Gibbons, F. X. & Wicklund, R. A. (1976). Selective exposure to self. *Journal of Research in Personality, 10,* 98–106.

Girgus, J. S., Nolen-Hoeksema, S. & Seligman, M. E. P. (1989). *Why do sex differences in depression emerge during adolescence?* Paper presented at the American Psychological Association National Conference, New Orleans, August.

Guidano, V. E. (1987). *Complexity of the self: A developmental approach to psychopathology and therapy.* New York: Guilford.

Higgins, E. T. & Eccles-Parsons, J. (1983). Social cognition and the social life of the child: Stages as subcultures. *In* E. T. Higgins, D. N. Ruble and W. W. Hartup (Eds.), *Social cognition and social development* (pp. 15–62). Cambridge, England: Cambridge University Press.

Hull, J. G. (1981). A self-awareness model of the causes and effects of alcohol consumption. *Journal of Abnormal Psychology, 90,* 586–600.

Hull, J. G., Levinson, R. W., Young, R. D. & Sher, K. J. (1983). Self-awareness-reducing effects of alcohol consumption. *Journal of Personality and Social Psychology, 44,* 461–473.

Hull, J. G. & Young, R. D. (1983). The self-awareness-reducing effects of alcohol: Evidence and implications. *In* J. Suls and A. G. Greenwald (Eds.), Psychological perspectives on the self. (Vol 2., pp. 159–190). Hillsdale, NJ: Erlbaum.

Ingram, R. E. (1990). Self-focused attention in clinical disorders: Review and a conceptual model. *Psychological Bulletin, 107,* 156–176.

Lerner, R. M., Lerner, J. V. & Tubman, J. (1989). Organismic and contextual bases of development. *In* G. R. Adams, R. Montemayor and T. P. Galotta (Eds.), *Biology of adolescent behavior and development* (pp. 11–37).

Levin, M. D. (1987). *Pathologies of the modern self.* New York: New York University Press.

Lewinsohn, P. M., Hoberman, H., Teri, L. & Hautzinger, M. (1985). An integrative theory of depression. *In* S. Reiss and R. Bootzin (Eds.), *Theoretical issues in behavior therapy* (pp. 331–359). New York: Academic.

Marshall, W. (1978). Puberty. *In* F. Falkner and J. Tanner (Eds.), *Human growth* (Vol. 2). New York: Plenum.

Maslow, A. (1962). *Toward a new psychology of being.* New York: Van Nostrand.

Musson, R. F. & Alloy, L. B. (1988). Depression and self-directed attention. *In* L. B. Alloy (Ed.), *Cognitive processes in depression* (pp. 193–220). New York: Guilford.

Muuskovic, B. (1988). Loneliness and adolescent alcoholism. *Adolescence, 23,* 503–515.

Natale, M., Dahlberg, C. C. & Jaffe, J. (1978). The relationship of defensive language behavior in patient monologues in the course of psychoanalysis. *Journal of Clinical Psychology, 34,* 466–470.

Peterson, A. (1985). Pubertal development as a cause of disturbance: Myths, realities, and unanswered questions. *Genetic, Social and General Psychology Monographs, 111,* 205–232.

Peterson, A. C., Schulenberg, J. E., Abramowitz, R., Offer, D. & Jarcho, H. (1984). A self-image questionnaire for young adolescents (SIQYA): Reliability and validity studies. *Journal of Youth and Adolescence, 13,* 93–111.

Pyszcynski, T. & Greenberg, J. (1985). Depression and preference for self-focusing stimuli after success and failure. *Journal of Personality and Social Psychology, 50,* 95–106.

Rosenthal, S. L. & Simeonsson, R. J. (1989). Emotional disturbance and the development of self-consciousness in adolescence. *Adolescence, 24,* 689–698.

Salmela-Aro, K. (1992). Struggling with self: The personal projects of students seeking psychological counseling. *Scandanavian Journal of Psychology, 33,* 330–338.

Sarason, I. G. (1975). Anxiety and self-preoccupation. *In* I. G. Sarason and C. D. Spielberger (Eds.), *Stress and anxiety* (Vol. 2, pp. 129–151). New York: Hemisphere.

Sarason, I. G. (1986). Test anxiety, worry, and cognitive interference. *In* R. Schwarzer (Ed.), *Self-related cognitions in anxiety and motivation* (pp. 19–33). Hillsdale, NJ: Erlbaum.

Steenbarger, B. N. & Aderman, D. (1979). Objective self-awareness as a nonaversive state: Effect of anticipating discrepancy reduction. *Journal of Personality, 47,* 330–339.

Wine, J. (1971). Test anxiety and direction of attention. *Psychological Bulletin, 76,* 92–104.

Wine, J. (1982). Evaluation anxiety: A cognitive-attentional construct. *In* H. W. Krohne and L. Laux (Eds.), *Achievement, stress, and anxiety* (pp. 207–219). Washington, DC: Hemisphere.

Cognitive Development in Early and Middle Adulthood

Subjective Knowledge: The Quest for Self

Mary Field Belenky et al.

At the time of the publication of *Women's Ways of Knowing: The Development of Self, Voice, and Mind* (Basic Books, 1986), lead author Mary Field Belenky was one of the principal investigators of "Listening Partners," an application and research project at the University of Vermont that encouraged the intellectual development of rural women. The book was coauthored by Blythe McVicker Clinchy, who was a professor of psychology at Wellesley College, a liberal arts college for women near Boston, Massachusetts; Nancy Rule Goldberger, who was a member of the faculty at the Fielding Institute in Santa Barbara, California; and Jill Mattuck Tarule, who was a professor of clinical psychology at Lesley College Graduate School in Cambridge, Massachusetts.

In the late 1970s Belenky et al. became concerned with, among other things, the need to better represent the cognitive development of women in the academic literature on human development. They launched a research project that included 135 women participants, 90 of whom were currently attending one of six different colleges, and 45 of whom were seeking information from family agencies about, or assistance with, parenting. This research led Belenky et al. to define seven "ways of knowing" that are characteristic of women: (1) "Silence," in which women feel mindless, voiceless, and controlled by others; (2) "Received Knowledge: Listening to the Voices of Others," in which women feel capable of copying knowledge from the "all-knowing authorities" but not of creating it on their own; (3) "Subjective Knowledge: The Inner Voice" and (4) "Subjective Knowledge: The Quest for Self," in which truth and knowledge are seen as personal, private, and intuited; (5) "Procedural Knowledge: The Voice of Reason" and (6) "Procedural Knowledge: Separate and Connected Knowing," in which women focus on acquiring and communicating objective knowledge; and (7) "Constructed Knowledge: Integrating the Voices," in which women realize that knowledge is dependent on context and that they can create knowledge, and wherein they value both subjectivist and objectivist approaches to knowing.

As you turn your attention to the following selection, which is from *Women's Ways of Knowing*, note that it focuses primarily on the fourth way of knowing, "Subjective Knowledge: The Quest for Self." This cognitive approach is typical of women in young, as well as middle, adulthood.

Key Concept: women's ways of knowing

Right now I'm busy being born.
—Teresa
Twenty-four years old

$\mathcal{W}$hat follows a woman's discovery of personal authority and truth is, of course, a blend of her own unique life circumstances and attributes. But as we listened to many stories, we began to hear how a newly acquired subjectivism led the woman into a new world, which she insisted on shaping and directing on her own. As a result, her relationships and self-concept began to change.

Severance of Connections: "Walking Away from the Past"

Over half of the large group of subjectivists had recently taken steps to end relationships with lovers or husbands, to reject further obligations to family members, and to move out and away on their own. They seemed to be saying to us that if firsthand experience was the route to knowing, then they were going to amass experiences. Although subject to an extraordinary range of emotional pushes and pulls—anxiety, anger, insecurity, guilt, depression, exhilaration—most of the women were making these changes with a stubborn determination. Some realized they faced loneliness ahead, but they did not seem to care. It was easy to be impressed by the courage of some, by the recklessness of others. Certainly it was clear that as they began to think and to know, they began to act. Some were even driven to action by their inner voice.

There were almost no women in this group who were not actively and obsessively preoccupied with a choice between self and other, acting on behalf of self as opposed to denying the self and living for and through others. In younger, single, advantaged women, this took the familiar turn of an adolescent push for freedom from "oppressive" or "stagnant" parental and community influences, bolstered by going away to school. For some of the women from close-knit ethnic communities, it meant moving out of the old neighborhood to avoid the pressure to conform. Although a few of the older women with established families felt unable to leave the economic and emotional security of home, most were planning to retreat or actually had retreated from old responsibilities and connections to others. They had thrown out husbands or left home themselves, usually but not always taking the children with them.

In many ways, these women are like the youths in fairy tales (as we recall, usually male) who set out from the family homestead to make their way in the world, discovering themselves in the process. Our women set out on this developmental journey with a sense of power in their intuitive processes and a newfound energy and openness to novelty.

We see in the women's stories the dilemma that [professor of human development] Carol Gilligan [asserts is] central in women's morality. Women are drawn to the role of caretaker and nurturer, often putting their own needs at the bottom of the list, preceded by other people, husband, and children. At the position of received knowledge, using the either/or thinking so characteristic of the position, women believe that "to get something for oneself" is abhorrent and selfish because others are bound to be deprived as a result. Gilligan believes that for people operating within a responsibility orientation, the initiation of actions on behalf of the self signifies the transition into mature moral thought, a late-occurring developmental shift in which the self is included as an equal claimant in any moral decision. We, however, disagree with Gilligan on this point, having examined the stories of subjectivist women who were beginning to get something for themselves but who did not yet appear to be developing a coherent, reflective moral maturity in Gilligan's terms.

With subjectivist women, there is minimal forethought and reason in their decision to "walk away from their pasts." The claims of others, for years so salient for them, are often suddenly disregarded when the women begin to assert their own authority and autonomy. They leap at the first chance to escape and go it alone without thinking

much at all about the consequences; perhaps, for some, the escape is an overly eager promotion of the self at the expense of others.

It is important to keep in mind the broader cultural context in assessing the meaning of such changes in women's priorities. During the 1970s there was a widespread cultural sanction of self-indulgence, self-actualization, and opportunism. Promotion of self was in vogue and assumed the status of a new social phenomenon, being tagged a symptom of the "me-decade" by Tom Wolfe (1976) and the "cult of narcissism" by Christopher Lasch (1979). The time was ripe for the development of subjectivist thought and the severance of ties and responsibilities to others.

Some of the women we interviewed had both the financial resources and the personal willfulness to launch themselves into the world at large. They were the will-o'-the-wisps, the wanderers, the world travelers. Assertive and self-absorbed, they had thrown themselves into life, taken risks others would not, tried out new selves as their contexts changed. By the time of the interview, many of them had already changed their contexts several times in their quest for self—they had shifted schools, lived in communes, traveled to foreign countries, taken wilderness trips, worked a variety of jobs.

One young woman we call Abby related the change in her assessment of her responsibilities in her marriage after the birth of her child.

> Being married to him was like having another kid. I was his emotional support system. After I had my son, my maternal instincts were coming out of my ears. They were filled up to here! I remember the first thing I did was to let all my plants die. I couldn't take care of another damn thing. I didn't want to water them, I didn't want to feed anybody. Then I got rid of my dog.

Two events—the birth of her child and a solitary month-long wilderness trip—had put Abby in touch with "the divine forces" within her and changed her "whole way of looking at the world." Abby divorced her husband, moved to a new community with their son, and had just entered into a lesbian relationship at the time of the interview.

Looking more closely at some of the life stories, we saw that often the subjectivist's escape from parents or inhibiting marriages and relationships had all the aspects of what Erik Erikson (1968) calls a "negative identity," that is, a definition of yourself primarily in terms of opposition to others or what you are not. One woman from a small midwestern community and religious family quietly and with considerable trepidation began to redefine herself in opposition to her family's values. She first chose a liberal eastern arts-oriented college over her state university and, at the time of her interview, was contemplating leaving college with her black boyfriend to live in the rural southern town from which he came. Another college student, who described her uneducated parents as stagnant and banal, was about to set out to find herself by moving to

Europe and establishing a career in the theater, entertaining a vision of herself that her parents would find unfathomable and shocking. Yet another woman related with bitter humor how she considered herself to be a careless, impetuous slob who was the exact opposite of what her perfectionistic and methodical father expected her to be.

The eventual path a woman takes is, in large measure, a function of the familial and educational environments in which she is struggling with these problems. Families and schools differ tremendously in the degree to which they reinforce risk taking or conformity behavior in women. Erica's options might have been broadened significantly by her hard-working, self-denying mother who communicated to her daughter her own unrealized wish to go to Spain. Certainly the college Erica chose for herself was an optimal environment for intellectual and psychological awakening in its explicit support for questioning and adventurous thinking and exploring. Abby was brought up in a very traditional, male-oriented family in which she sought paternal approval and was "geared to pleasing men." She was given money to explore the world but not the paternal sanction to step out of the stereotyped female role as nurturer.

All too often neither the family, whether the family of origin or of reproduction, nor the educational institution she attends, recognizes or nurtures the budding subjectivist's impetus toward change, redefinition, and application of her new ways of knowing and learning. The family's reaction to a woman's return to school can be painful for her. One woman described her tearful daughter berating her: "You used to stay home to do needlepoint." Another told us how her angry husband had first hidden then burned her schoolbooks.

As women begin to act on their new conceptions of truth and to forge new rules and boundaries in their relationships, some become distinctly antimale. Negative attitudes toward specific men in their pasts—lovers, fathers, husbands, teachers—become generalized to all men, whom they perceive as controlling, demanding, negating, and life suppressing. Their attitude is not so much that of retreating from others—the attitude "I will go it alone"—as it is the attitude "I will go it without men."

Other subjectivist women we interviewed assumed a much more antagonistic stance toward men.

> There are men who can't stand the fact that I am female, as young as I am, doing the things that I do. I sometimes feel that they are trying to pull me down but I am not going to let that happen. . . . I'm going to be my own person. I don't have to live with and depend on men.
>
> I deal with men when I have to, when I can't avoid it. I'm not friendly nor am I unfriendly. I'm just eager to get it over with. I have no desire to waste any time or energy on men at all.
>
> I find I can do better without men. Definitely better without men! I have to let them know that I'm not the sweet little girl from the all-girls' college that you think I am. If you walk on me, then I'll get up and walk back on

you. I won't be rude but I'll give you a taste of your own medicine.

We heard a number of stories from women who spoke in these terms and who turned all men out of their lives, and many other stories from women for whom heterosexual relationships and intimacy were on hold. For most, there was the early adherence to traditional sex roles; the stress of never getting anything for themselves; the angry, even dismissive feelings toward others whom they experienced as clinging tyrants; the impulsive yet determined throwing out and breaking ties; and the launching of new intentions and new directions. Yet throughout this turmoil and tumultuous effort to claim the self, we saw many signs that women were still invested in connections to others: their children, their reliable and supportive friends (usually female), new groups and organizations that "understood" their motives and objectives, and, for some, a new man "who is on my side."

Nevertheless, there is something tentative and unsettled in the view of the self that is characteristic of women at the subjectivist position. They sense the enormity of the steps they have taken. Relationships feel unstable and the future is dim. As Abby put it, "It's hard to foresee anything, because the whole structure of our lives can change overnight. I can say, 'Now I see myself changing in this way or that way,' but I really don't know what's going to happen to me." These women sojourners have been propelled into action and are committed to continuing their developmental journey; the way ahead appears foggy.

Concepts of the Self

The instability and flux that subjectivist women experience when they contemplate their future is due, in part, to the lack of grounding in a secure, integrated, and enduring self-concept. Whereas in the position of received knowledge, women derive a sense of "who I am" from the definitions others supply and the roles they fill, subjectivist women shift away from this perspective and experience a wrenching away of the familiar contexts and relationships within which the old identity has been embedded. Their place in life is no longer a matter of adopting the values of the community and fulfilling the expectations of those they care about. The women in subjectivism often seemed bewildered over the sense of loss of themselves once they distanced themselves from the feedback and reinforcement that family and community provided. If, as Gilligan and [J. B.] Miller claim, women tend to define themselves in the context of relationships, then it is not surprising that women making a break with their pasts and former relationships may enter a period in which there is considerable flux in self-concept. If new relationships and new self-definitions have not yet emerged or been articulated, past images or labels that others supplied may have a peremptory hold on the woman's experience of herself. Sadly, some women looking back on their lives recalled themselves in painfully negative terms, revealing as they talked how little the people with whom they lived valued them. They felt trapped by the negative images from the past or splintered into vaguely sensed parts and subject to kaleidoscopic shifts in self-picture that kept them off balance.

A young, unmarried woman with two sons, having just begun the transition into subjective knowing, revealed such a negative self-image. "Unfortunately, I've never felt much about myself. I guess I was brought up to think everybody else was better than I was, and unfortunately I kind of still feel that way, you know. If I'm walking down the aisle and meet someone, I'll get out of the way." Another early subjectivist had an equally hard time believing that she had a self other than vaguely sensed negative traits: "How would I describe myself to myself? I—I—that's really just a blank. I wouldn't know what to say. I can pretend something or try to portray something, but I never really think of myself. I never talk to myself. If I did, it would be a negative type of thing."

No matter what their pasts were, most subjectivist women found it difficult to reflect upon or even describe themselves clearly. Like so many other aspects of their lives that were changing, so, too, was the image they held of themselves. Having entered the era of subjective truth, in which knowing is a matter of internal groping and intuition, these women had few words available to them to communicate something about an inner self that still was so novel, so hidden from public view. At best they resorted to a string of images or metaphors when asked to describe themselves, leaving the job of integration to the listener. A young college student revealed the private and connotative language often used during the period of subjectivism.

> The easiest way for me to see myself is in images. Images of flowers, in Winnie the Pooh, sea gulls. I don't know if I could ever do it using words. A lot of times you see something in your own mind. Other times you see it and there's no word connection. It's just . . . bonk . . . and it's there and it's really a true form of understanding. It's hard to use words.

She did, in fact, use words as she talked to us, but like many women in this group she reported that she found talking about herself an almost impossible task.

The majority of women we interviewed and classified as subjective knowers, even though they experienced fluctuations in their sense of who they were, which contributed to their uneasiness, also valued this instability as a sign that they were now open to novelty. We heard again and again how openness to change and novelty had become the fulcrum around which their new identities revolved. Some women used the imagery of birth, rebirth, and childhood to describe their experience of a nascent self.

> The person I see myself as now is just like an infant. I see myself as beginning. Whoever I can become, that's a wide-open possibility.

> I actually think that the person I am now is only about three or four years old with all these new experiences. I always was kind of led, told what to do. Never really thought much about myself. Now I feel like I'm learning all over again.

> I've never had a personality. I've always been someone's daughter, someone's wife, someone's mother. Right now I'm so busy being born, discovering who I am, that I don't know who I am. And I don't know where I'm going. And everything is going to be fine.

These were women for whom the birth of the self was occurring as late as thirty or forty, even fifty. Along with their reported sense of being newly born were significant indicators of an impetus toward action, change, and risk taking. They seemed propelled by an inner fire, communicating to us a feeling of exhilaration and optimism as they plunged ahead toward some dim future.

> It's hard to say who I am because I don't really think about more than tomorrow. In the future I'll probably have a better understanding, because now I simply don't know. I think it will really be a fun thing to find out. Just do everything until I find out.

> I'm a different person each day. It's the day, I guess, depending on how it is outside or how my body feels.

> I'm only the person that I am at this moment. Tomorrow I'm somebody different, and the day after that I'm somebody different. . . . I'm always changing. Everything is always changing.

New Connections: The Role of Inward Watching and Listening

For all women the shift into subjectivism is an adaptive move in that it is accompanied by an increased experience of strength, optimism, and self-value. Nevertheless, we were concerned, as we heard their stories, about maladaptive consequences. Paradoxically, in spite of their basic commitment and responsiveness to others, their fervent insistence on "going it alone" contributed to their isolation from others. We wondered how trapped women might become in their subjectivist philosophy, how lonely they would become if they excluded others from their lives in an attempt at self-protection. We also wondered what or who might engage them in further questioning their assumptions about truth and knowing, propel them into further growth, and lead them to move beyond their distrust of external influence.

Certainly a few of the women impressed us as entrenched in their subjective world. They were stubbornly committed to their view of things and unwilling to expose themselves to alternative conceptions. Although they might have described themselves as generous and caring, they could be, in fact, impatient and dismissive of other people's interpretations. They easily resorted to expletives when faced with others' viewpoints—"That's bullshit!" "That teacher was an asshole. He didn't know what he was talking about!" These were women at their most belligerent, oppositional, and argumentative. They were similar to the males whom Perry called "oppositional multiplists," who were adept at turning the tables on authorities by bludgeoning them with wordy, offensive arguments. In the classroom as in life, they warded off others' words and influence via ploys to isolate, shout down, denigrate, and undo the other.

It was difficult to imagine how such entrenched subjectivists might advance to a more adaptive and differentiated way of knowing. Perry speculated that perhaps oppositional multiplists become "entrapped by their own argumentativeness" (1970, p. 99), implying that the route to further development was the pressure others exerted to provide reasons and evidence for opinions recklessly thrown about.

In our study, few women were as outspoken and confrontative as Perry's male multiplists. Even when the women held strongly to their own way of doing things, they remained concerned about not hurting the feelings of their opponents by openly expressing dissent. They reported that they were apt to hide their opinions and then suffer quietly the frustration of not standing up to others. Some women described feeling either a petulant, private resentment of others or self-admonishment for being so unassertive. Once again we saw that sustaining connections with others prevail in the stories of women.

An additional consequence of the entrenched subjectivist position appeared in only a few of our cases. A kind of existential loneliness and despair pervaded the interviews of these few women who had not found bridges back to other people. One depressed college sophomore told us about her discovery that there were multiple truths and multiple realities. She had concluded that, since no one could know anything for sure and each person was locked in her own world, there was no way and no reason for people to try to reach each other or communicate. She believed that "it's a case of knowing too much. . . . My question to you, Why do people live?"

Most of the subjective knowers we interviewed were neither entrenched and oppositional nor depressed and despairing. They were, as we described earlier, forward-looking, positive, and open to new experiences. They were curious people and, from the moment they turned inward to listen to the "still small voice," found a new and fascinating object for study: the self. When we asked subjectivists how they learned best, they frequently mentioned knowledge obtained by observing the self as well as observing others. Women at the position of received knowledge, in contrast, were limited to listening to others and imitating because there was little inner experience of self. During the period of subjectivism, the predominant learning mode is one of *inward* listening and watching. The women associated this mode with a sense of change.

> I'm turning in. I try and watch myself more. Like if I had watched myself years ago, it would have been pretty boring because I really wasn't doing anything. I wasn't changing.

> I keep discovering things inside myself. I am seeing myself all the time in a different light.

Given the unsettled sense of an ever-changing self, it is not surprising that observation and listening serve an important function for these women. They are the primary means they have available for articulation and differentiation of the self. They watch and listen to themselves and begin to notice inner contradictions; they watch and listen to others and begin to draw comparisons between their own and other people's experience. They become aware of other as "other" in contrast to the more conformist women who diffuse distinctions between self and other and perceive people primarily in stereotypic terms.

To some extent listening to others is self-serving. It is a way of learning about the self without revealing the self; however, good listeners draw others to them. Watching, listening subjectivists attract other persons' trust, in part because they listen and in part because they seem nonjudgmental. Many of our women told us about this important skill and how it kept them connected to others. Yet some also clearly indicated that it was the knowledge they gained about themselves that they valued rather than the mutual exchange of experience.

Women's emphasis on beginning to hear themselves think, while gathering observations through watching and listening, is the precursor to reflective and critical thought characteristic of the other positions we will discuss. During the period of subjective knowing, women lay down procedures for systematically learning and analyzing experience. But what seems distinctive in these women is that their strategies for knowing grow out of their very embeddedness in human relationships and their alertness to the details of everyday life. Subjectivist women value what they see and hear around them and begin to feel a need to understand the people with whom they live and who impinge on their lives. Though they may be emotionally or intellectually isolated from others at this point in their history, they begin to actively analyze their past and current interactions with others. Although they may not have taken the next step of speaking out to others about their perceptions of the world, of acquiring a public voice, they engage in self-expression by talking to themselves, talking to their diaries, and even, with one woman, talking to her cats about her inner secrets. These women are "gaining a voice" and a knowledge base from which they can investigate the world. We will see as we consider the rest of our story how significant "really listening" and "really talking" can be for women.

References

Erikson, E. H. (1968). *Identity: Youth and crisis.* New York: Norton.

Lasch, C. (1979). *The culture of narcissism: American life in an age of diminishing expectations.* New York: Warner Books.

Perry, W. G. (1970). *Forms of intellectual and ethical development in the college years.* New York: Holt, Rinehart & Winston.

Wolfe, T. (1976). The me-decade and the third great awakening. *New York Magazine, 9,* 34, 26–33.

Age Differences in Primary Mental Ability Factors

John L. Horn and Raymond B. Cattell

Raymond B. Cattell was an exceptionally prolific researcher in the fields of factor analysis (a statistical method) and trait psychology. He earned his Ph.D. in psychology in 1929 from Kings College in London, where he studied under the founder of factor analysis, Charles Spearman. Cattell came to America and taught at Clark and Harvard Universities before settling down for several decades of research and teaching at the University of Illinois. John L. Horn, who coauthored the following selection with Cattell, was a graduate student of Cattell's at the University of Illinois. He later became a professor at the University of Denver.

One of the hottest debates and areas of research in the field of human development concerns efforts to describe the nature of human intelligence and to characterize its development. Horn's and Cattell's research in this area was fairly innovative. They posited two main factors, or two main types, of intelligence: fluid and crystallized intelligence. The following selection is from "Age Differences in Primary Mental Ability Factors," which was published in 1967 in the *Journal of Gerontology*. In it, Horn and Cattell use a cross-sectional research method to demonstrate the different rates of the growth, stabilization, and decline of these two forms of intelligence across the life span.

Key Concept: fluid and crystallized intelligence

The study reported here ... aimed at providing a sound theoretical basis for integrating evidence on relationships between aging and intellectual performances. The principles guiding this effort are those contained in the theory of fluid and crystallized intelligence. (Cattell, 1941; 1950; 1957a; 1963; Horn, 1965; Horn & Cattell, 1965). . . .

A full development of this theory runs to book length (Horn, 1965) and thus is well beyond the scope of this paper, but in very general terms the central hypothesis of the theory states that, because of influences operating throughout development, intellectual processes come to be organized at a general level along two principal dimensions. These dimensions indicate two kinds of ability, each so broad and pervasive relative to other abilities and each so much involving performances commonly said to indicate intelligence that each is worthy of the name "intelligence"—hence the terms "fluid intelligence" (Gf) and "crystallized intelligence" (Gc). The former is an operationally based concept . . . [and] is most closely related to biological influences operating in development, whereas Gc more directly reflects cohesiveness and individual differences in a broad set of experiential learning influences. . . .

In verbal terms the two general factors may be described more fully as follows:

(a) Fluid intelligence involves the processes of perceiving relations, educing correlates, and maintaining span of immediate awareness in concept formation and attainment, reasoning, and abstracting. Here these processes are assessed in tasks in which the problem fundaments tend to be either novel for all persons being measured or else extremely common, over-learned elements of the culture of these persons. In a task such as the Letter Series, which defines Inductive Reasoning (I), for example, the alphabet fundaments are over-learned by most adults, whereas the figural fundaments of a task, such as the Figure Series, defining CFR [Figural Relations] are novel to most adults. It will be noted, too, that the tasks defining Gf involve several kinds of content, including figural, symbolic, and semantic, as defined by Guilford (1959). Likewise, the function is not peculiar to speeded tests: in the tasks of Intellectual Level (IL), the S is not at all penalized for working slowly, and several of the other tasks which define Gf are administered under powerlike conditions. In fact, speeded measures are apt to assess, besides Gf, a general speediness function, Gs. . . .

The concept of fluid intelligence is quite similar to Spearman's concept of "G" (Spearman, 1927; Spearman & Jones, 1950), although many of the tests which Spearman regarded as among the best operational measures of "G" are not among the purest markers for Gf but are instead markers for Gc.

(b) Crystallized intelligence is like Gf in that it is also a broad dimension of intellect involving the processes of education and perception of relations, reasoning and abstracting, etc. But unlike Gf it is assessed in tasks which require considerable pre-training in skills which constitute the more esoteric aspects of the collective intelligence of a culture. In a task such as Abstruse Word Analogies of the primary factor CMR, Semantic Relations, for example, the S must perceive relationships between concepts like denizen and indigenous, but success with the problem is dependent to a large extent, also, upon having an education which allows one to become aware of the existence of concepts like denizen and indigenous. Crystallized intelligence can be measured in speeded tasks involving fluency and originality in the use of concepts or generalized solution instruments or aids (Cattell, 1963; Horn, 1965), but again, as in the case of Gf, speediness is not an essential aspect of the function. If measured in speeded tasks alone, Gc scores will contain variance on the general speediness and fluency functions described in subsequent paragraphs. . . .

According to theory, both Gf and Gc develop rapidly in childhood, the former because neural structures are maturing at a rapid rate, the latter for this reason, partly, since the development of Gc is dependent upon the development of Gf, but mainly because the factors producing acculturation are intense during this period. The rate of development of Gf slows to a stop at the point where neural maturation ceases, whereas in Gc this slowing occurs as the intensity of educational effort drops off. The two factors are virtually indistinguishable in the very early periods of development. They come to be distinguished as a function of different kinds of influence operating in development.

On the one hand there are influences which directly affect the neurological-physiological functioning and structure upon which intelligence must be seen to be constructed, viz., influences operating through the agencies of inheritance and injury. On the other hand, there are influences which affect neurological-physiological functioning and structure only indirectly through learning. The development of Gf is crudely the sum of the first set of influences; Gc is a sum of these plus the second set.

At the outset of development there is the basic structure given by heredity. There follows an unfolding of this maturation. The development of Gf is largely determined by these factors. But superimposed upon these influences are those resulting from injuries, particularly to the central nervous system (CNS), but also to other physiological structures. Such injuries occur throughout life and, since they are often irreversible, they may be seen to accumulate, both within a given individual and within groups of individuals over which means for intellectual performances can be computed.

There are innumerable ways in which small CNS injuries can occur, for example, carbon monoxide poisoning, lead poisoning, high fever, blows to the head, anoxia resulting from a wide variety of causes, etc. These may be seen to accumulate within individuals. The large, easily detected injuries, which, however, leave a person viable, are not so clearly seen to accumulate within individuals, but they become statistically more frequent as the average age of Ss [subjects] increases and thus may be seen to accumulate in groups of individuals. In either case it is implied that, insofar as measurements of intelligence are dependent upon and reflect the integrity of the CNS, the averages for the measurements will decline as age progresses.

In the means computed in the early years of development the influence of injuries on intellectual performance is largely masked by the influence due to the rapid growth occurring in these years. However, as growth stops the injury effects are manifested in the averages. Thus in adulthood there occurs, according to this theory, a drop in the average level of performance on the tasks which define fluid intelligence.

Likewise, superimposed upon the basic inherited structures are a number of influences which determine the extent of acculturation of individuals. These influences are, at least in part, independent of both the inherited potential and that determined by CNS and other injuries. As a paradigm for the process postulated here, one may consider the acquisition of learning sets in an experiment such as that described by Harlow (1949). In this experiment the Ss were given an exceptional educational experience. It is probable that in their natural environment the monkeys used in Harlow's studies would never have acquired the particular skills he taught them. These animals were given an opportunity to acquire an aspect of intelligence which had been previously developed within a culture, viz., human culture. According to Ferguson's (1956) transfer theory, the effects of this acculturation would spread throughout development to the learning of concepts and aids which otherwise would not have been acquired. As compared with monkeys who were not given these educational opportunities, Harlow's monkeys would thus acquire a new component of intelligence. Tests of intelligence which contained a large proportion of problems that could be solved by application of the abilities of this component would tend to form a functional unity.

In human development the accumulation of aspects of the intelligence developed within a culture tends to occur throughout life. The rate of accumulation may decrease, as noted above, but there is no necessary reason why some accretion should not occur over the entire span of development. Thus on this basis the theory predicts that the average level of crystallized intelligence recorded for adults at different age levels will tend to rise with age.

But the theory must take some account of the possibility of memory loss or other change which might produce reduction in ability to utilize that which would otherwise be Gc. For example, decline of Gf will eventually, if rather indirectly, show in a slowing of the rate of development of Gc. Thus if the rate of accumulation of the effects of acculturation drops much below the rate of decline in Gf, there may result a decline also in Gc. It would seem that if this occurs, however, it shows in the averages for ability performances only at a rather late stage of development, i.e., beyond age 60 (Horn, 1965).

. . . The general purpose of the study was to examine the implications of this theory by comparisons of performances of adults of different ages. More specifically, it was predicted that

(1) The means at different age levels for primary abilities defining Gf almost exclusively, i.e., the relatively pure markers for Gf, would not increase in adulthood, but instead would usually decrease from the late teens onward.

(2) The means at different age levels for primary abilities defining Gc most purely would not decrease, but instead would usually increase from the late teens into the sixties.

(3) Primary abilities which have variance split nearly evenly between Gf and Gc, as determined by prior factor analyses, would show a variable relationship to aging. . . .

Subjects.   The tests listed in Table 35.1 were administered to a sample of 297 persons from Stateville, Pontiac, and Dwight State Prisons in Illinois, the Illinois Soldiers' and Sailors' Children's School, Canon City State Penitentiary in Colorado, and the Colorado State Employment Office in Denver. All Ss were volunteers. They were offered information about their performances as an inducement for giving their time and doing their best.

The age range for the sample was 14 to 61 years. But there was only one 14-year-old, two persons aged 61, and

one each aged 56, 55, and 52; the bulk of the sample thus was between 15 and 51 years of age. The mean age was 27.6, and the standard deviation for this variable was 10.6.

For purposes of analysis the Ss were divided into five age groupings. This breakdown into categories was intended primarily to provide groups wherein the N was large enough to yield reasonably stable statistics. But the groupings were also intended to represent theoretically interesting phases of intellectual development from late childhood into adulthood. Thus, for example, because it is rather widely held that intellectual development reaches a peak sometime between age 14 and 21, the rather limited sample of Ss in this age range was divided into two groups: the mid-teeners, including persons aged 14 through 17 (N = 46), the late-teeners, including those aged 18 through 20 (N= 51). Using this terminology, the other groupings are: the twenties (ages 21 through 28, N = 81), the thirties (ages 29 through 39 with N = 73) and the over-forties (ages 40 through 61 and N = 46).

Results

. . . [T]he results indicate that:

1. The abilities classified (by prior factor analyses) as "fluid" have a different pattern of association with age than have the abilities classified as "crystallized." It would seem that the fluid abilities do not reach full development until the late teens, but decline steadily beginning in the twenties, whereas crystallized abilities improve throughout the span of adulthood here considered. . . .

2. Visualization abilities seem to reach a peak in development somewhat later than fluid abilities and somewhat earlier than crystallized abilities.

3. Speed of intellectual and clerical performance has a rather complex relationship to aging. IL [Intellectual Level], a pure power measure in the Gf pattern, shows the same pattern of decline with aging as do other fluid abilities; Fi [Ideational Fluency] and Fa [Associational Fluency], on the other hand, both speeded functions in the Gc factor, show much the same pattern of improvement with age as do other crystallized abilities. Speed

Table 35.1   The Tests

	Tests Combined to Measure Primary
I. Fluid intelligence (Gf) primaries & tests	
1. Induction (I)	Letter grouping and number series
2. Figural relations (CFR)	Figure series, figure classification, matrices, and topology
3. Associative memory (Ma)	Paired related words and nonsense equations
4. Intellectual speed (ISp)	Furneaux speed operations
5. Intellectual level (IL)	Furneaux level operations
II. Crystallized intelligence (Ge) primaries and tests	
6. Verbal comprehension (V)	Vocabulary and general information
7. Mechanical knowledge (Mk)	Mechanical information and tool identification
8. Ideational fluency (Fi)	Things round and ideas
9. Experiential evaluation (EMS)	Social situations
10. Associational fluency (Fa)	Controlled associations

of arithmetical operations tends to be greater for older persons, but the simple clerical speed tasks show some decline after the twenties. If the sum over the six simple speeded functions is taken, there is suggestion of very slight decline in speed of performance beginning in the thirties.

4. The relation of carefulness to age is highly variable, depending on the task on which the carefulness score is based. When recorded in fluid ability tasks, such as Figure Classification and Matrices, there would appear to be some decline after the twenties, whereas if the score is based on crystallized skills, such as Practical Estimates and Arithmetic, it seems that the pattern is like that for Gc.

Discussion

The results from this investigation thus support hypotheses which originate from the general theory of fluid and crystallized intelligence. They indicate, also, why results from many previous studies of aging and intelligence have often been regarded as contradictory and difficult to interpret. The distinction between Gf and Gc has not been clearly recognized in previous studies. . . .

Summary

The theory of fluid and crystallized intelligence was outlined and discussed in terms of some recent findings from higher order factor analytic investigations and with regard to its relevance from understanding relationships between aging and changes in intellectual performances. Estimates of a broad sample of primary mental abilities were obtained for a sample in which the age groupings extended from the teens (ages 14–17) to "over-40" (ages 40–61). The abilities were grouped according to whether they were primarily fluid, primarily crystallized, a mixture of these two, or markers for general visualization, speediness, carefulness or fluency dimensions. The primary abilities classified as "primarily fluid" showed decline with age beginning in the early twenties; primaries classified as "primarily crystallized" showed improvement with age throughout the period here considered.

References

Cattell, R. B.: Some theoretical issues in adult intelligence testing. (Abstract). *Psychol. Bull., 38:* 592, 1941.

Cattell, R. B.: *Personality.* McGraw-Hill, New York, 1950, 689 pp.

Cattell, R. B.: *Personality and motivation structure and measurement.* World Book, New York, 1957, pp. 492–499. (a)

Cattell, R. B.: Theory of fluid and crystallized intelligence: a critical experiment. *J. educ. Psychol., 54:* 1–22, 1963.

Ferguson, G. A.: On transfer and the abilities of man. *J. Canad. Psychol., 10:* 121–131, 1956.

Guilford, J. P.: Three faces of intellect. *Amer. Psychol., 14:* 469–479, 1959.

Harlow, H. F.: The formation of learning sets. *Psychol. Rev., 56:* 51–65, 1949.

Horn, J. L.: *Fluid and crystallized intelligence: a factor analytic study of the structure among primary mental abilities.* Ph.D. thesis, Univ. Illinois, Urbana, 1965, 357 pp.

Horn, J. L., and R. B. Cattell: *Refinement and test of the theory of fluid and crystallized intelligence.* Reps. Psychol. Dept., Univ. Denver, Denver, 1965.

Spearman, C.: *The abilities of man.* Macmillan & Co., New York, 1927, 408 pp.

Spearman, C., and L. W. Jones: *Human ability.* Macmillan, London, 1950, 198 pp.

Critical Consciousness: An Alternative Pathway for Positive Personal and Social Development

Elena Mustakova-Possardt

Elena Mustakova-Possardt earned her B.A. (1982) and M. A. (1983) in English at Sofia University in Bulgaria, and her doctorate in human development from the University of Massachusetts, Amherst (1996). She received the Henry A. Murray Dissertation Award, Radcliffe College, Harvard University in 1995 to support her cross-cultural research project on "Social Responsibility and Critical Consciousness in Bulgarian Midlifers," which explored adult social consciousness and citizenship in the context of economic, political, and social transformation. Her doctoral dissertation, "The Ontogeny of Critical Consciousness," which was based on that research, earned the Outstanding Dissertation Award from the International Association for Moral Education in 1998. While teaching at the Department of Psychology of the State University of West Georgia, she was awarded the Carter Partnership Award 2003 (a $10,000 award from President Jimmy Carter's Center in Atlanta, Georgia) for her work founding the Latino Initiative of State University of West Georgia, aimed at applying the insights of critical and community psychology theory and praxis to assisting the new Latino immigrant population of rural Carroll County, GA, in its empowerment, in improving its quality of life, and integrating into the life of the larger community.

Her award-winning dissertation work was summarized in a journal article, "Critical Consciousness: An Alternative Pathway for Positive Personal and Social Development," published in the *Journal of Adult Development* (1998), and has been included in this volume below. The expanded version of this work came out as a book in 2003; *Critical Consciousness: A Study of Morality in Global Historical Context* (Greenwood Publishers).

Mustakova defines *critical consciousness* as a moral awareness that empowers us to be able to dissemble ourselves from our cultural, social, and political environment, and engage in a responsible critical moral dialogue with that environment in our own minds and hearts, and with others. Critical consciousness is created through the synergistic interaction between the structural development of the mind (similar to Piaget's stages) and moral motivation. Mustakova's mapping of the development of critical consciousness is grounded in her empirical work through interviews with both Bulgarian and American adult research participants.

Key Concept: critical consciousness

Introduction

The ability of individuals to take perspective on their immediate cultural, social, and political environment, to engage in critical dialogue with it, bringing to bear fundamental moral commitments including concerns for justice and equity, and to define their own place with respect to surrounding reality, constitutes an important human faculty. Freire (1973) referred to this ability as critical consciousness (CC), and built a social movement for literacy and empowerment around it. There have been philosophical attempts to describe the phenomenon of CC (Marcuse, 1989a, 1989b, 1989c, 1989d; Fromm, 1959, 1989; Jung, 1933; Jung, as discussed in Progoff, 1973; Kierkegaard, as discussed in Webb, 1988), as well as phenomenological studies (Bembow, 1994) and applied psychological studies of some of its aspects (Walker, 1995). A diverse body of literatures also bear on the phenomenon of CC. Of these literatures, the neo-Piagetian and Vygotskian developmental approaches (Kohlberg, 1984; Wertsch, 1985) are particularly relevant to the approach adopted in this paper.

I define CC as an integrative psychological construct which unites private aspects of adult meaning-making with more public aspects of adults' actions in the larger social world. The study to be reported here looked at CC as a unifying structure, which can be analyzed in terms of component elements of structural development and moral motivation but cannot be reduced to the sum total of those two components. Structural development is understood in terms of four dimensions: (1) at least formal operational understanding of causality (see Commons & Richards, 1984); (2) ability to identify social patterns within concrete social situations (see Weinstein & Alschuler, 1985); (3) a differentiated sense of self (Kegan, 1982; Lahley, Souvaine, Kegan, Goodman, & Felix, 1988); (4) at least conventional social system and conscience orientation (Kohlberg, 1984). Moral motivation is defined as the overall predominance of moral over expediency concerns.

Sources of My Construct of CC and Research Design

My thinking about the construct of critical consciousness began inductively, as I tried to organize my observations on social responsibility and citizenship in the several different societies and cultures in which I lived and worked: Bulgaria, Libya, The United Arab Emirates, Zimbabwe, and the U.S. The question was what accounted for the fact that some people, both educated and not so well educated, brought moral understanding to the social, cultural, and political realities and allegiances of their lives, and sought to establish morally responsible relationships with those realities, while others were willing to adapt to an unjust social reality and make the best of it.

My main conceptual source has been Freire's (1973) work. Freire believed that "one can only know to the extent that one "problematizes" the natural, cultural and historical reality in which s/he is immersed" (p. ix). He called this capacity "critical consciousness," differentiating it from the technocrat's "problem-solving stance" (p. ix). He described it in the following way:

The critically transitive consciousness is characterized by depth in the interpretation of problems; by the substitution of causal principles for magical explanations; by the testing of one's "findings" and by openness to revision; by the attempt to avoid distortion when perceiving problems and to avoid preconceived notions when analyzing them; by refusing to transfer responsibility; by rejecting passive positions; by soundness of argumentation; by the practice of dialogue rather than polemics; by receptivity to the new for reasons beyond mere novelty and by the good sense not to reject the old just because it is old—by accepting what is valid in both old and new. (Freire, 1973, p. 18)

Freire (1973) described the development of this type of consciousness through three stages: "semi-intransitive magical," "naive transitive," and critical consciousness. He also described a possible deflection from this development in the movement from naive transitive consciousness to "fanaticized consciousness" instead of CC. Here is how Freire (1973) described each of these early types of social consciousness:

Men of semi-intransitive consciousness cannot apprehend problems situated outside their sphere of biological necessity. Their interests center almost totally around survival, and they lack a sense of life on a more historical plane. His sphere of perception is limited . . . he is impermeable to challenges situated outside the sphere of biological necessity. In this sense only, semi-intransitivity represents a new disengagement between men and their existence. (p. 17)

Magical consciousness . . . simply apprehends facts and attributes to them a superior power by which it is controlled and to which it must therefore submit. (p. 44)

Naive transitivity . . . is characterized by an oversimplification of problems; by a nostalgia for the past; by underestimation of the common man; by a strong tendency to gregariousness; by fragility of argument; by the practice of polemics rather than dialogue. (p. 18)

There is a close potential relationship between naive transitivity and massification. If a person does not move from naive transitivity to a critical consciousness but instead falls into a fanaticized consciousness, he will become even more disengaged from reality. . . . In fanaticized consciousness the distortion of reason makes men irrational. The possibility of dialogue diminishes markedly. Men are defeated and dominated, though they do not know it; they fear freedom though they believe themselves to be free. They follow general formulas and prescriptions as if by their own choice. They are directed, they do not direct themselves. Their creative power is impaired. They are objects, not subjects. (pp. 19–20)

Freire's (1973) work suggested a developmental model of CC prior to the last 20 years of advances in structural-developmental theory. My analysis of Freire's understanding of CC suggested a neo-Piagetian social-cognitive developmental evolution of how people make sense of their social world and their own relatedness to it, and of the increasing responsibility they take for this process with advancing development.

Among the many characteristics of CC that Freire (1973) described, and which appear to refer to structural developmental properties, I identified as central three recurring components, which became fundamental to my definition of CC. First, CC is *a way of knowing* which he considered the only true way of knowing. It *involves critical analysis of reality*: "The more accurately men grasp true causality, the more critical their understanding of reality will be" (Freire, 1973, p. 44). Second, it involves retaining and *experiencing the sense of connectedness with reality*, i.e., analyzing as a participant not as an observer.

To be human is to engage in relationships with others and with the world. . . . As men emerge from time, discover temporality and free themselves from "today," their relationships with the world become impregnated with consequence. . . . As men relate to the world by responding to the challenges of the environment, they begin to dynamize, to master, and to humanize reality. (Freire, 1973, pp. 3–)

Third, it is *a process of collective dialogue,* of *co-construction in the course of dynamic social interaction.*

> As men amplify their power to perceive and respond to suggestions and questions arising in their context, and increase their capacity to enter into dialogue not only with other men but with their world, they become "transitive." . . . Transitivity of consciousness makes man "permeable." It leads him to replace his disengagement from existence with almost total engagement. (Freire, 1973, p. 17)
>
>   Dialogue is an I-Thou relationship, and thus necessarily a relationship between two Subjects. (Freire, 1973, p. 52)

There have been many efforts to translate Freire's general philosophical understanding of the movement from early forms of social consciousness to critical consciousness into specific approaches to education and consciousness-raising in the Western world (Bailey, 1976; Elias, 1976; Schipani, 19840. Critical pedagogy (Shor & Freire, 1987) has explored the potential of education and praxis to bring about large-scale transformations in the direction of CC. Smith (1975, 1976) operationalized the definition of *conscientizacao,* and developed a coding system which breaks down the developmental process of conscientization into a system of verbal responses characteristic of each stage. He organized his coding system around three main existential tasks in the oppressor/oppressed relationship: naming the problem, reflecting, acting on it. This coding system describes in significant detail the internal behaviors exhibited by people of various educational and class backgrounds in Ecuador at each stage, and highlights convergencies with biographical data on the life of Malcolm X.

Against the background of these diverse philosophical and behavioral approaches to the phenomenon of CC, I began to study its psychological and social nature, the specific psychological processes underlying the stage movement in conscientization, and the contextual conditions that may foster the evolving of a more differentiated and integrated social consciousness.

Various bodies of literature informed by research: (a) developmental theory (neo-Piagetian and Vygotskian), (b) the critical theorists (Bronner & Kellner, 1989), (c) postmodern thought (Foucault, 1984), (d) moral psychology (Hoffman, 1989, 1991; Kohlberg, 1984; Maslow, 1959), (e) research on social activism (Bellah, 1985; Bembow, 1994; Colby & Damon, 1992; Wuthnow, 1991). In an effort to build grounded theory (Glaser & Strauss, 1967; Strauss & Corbin, 1990), relying on existing qualitative data, I also performed a preliminary thematic and an informal structural analysis of life histories from three sources: Gandhi's (1927) Autobiography, Colby and Damon's (1992) case studies of moral exemplars, and Bembow's (1994) phenomenological case studies of social activists. These studies suggested to me that CC may not be

the automatic outcome of the development of systemic thought and its application to understanding social reality (see Commons & Richards, 1984). Rather, CC appeared to be a moral pathway in the evolution of social consciousness. Hence, I conceptualized the formation of social consciousness as the outcome of the interplay between motivation and structural development.

In the subsequent cross-cultural interview research described below, I set out to elaborate and explore the value of this conceptual model. I studied the possibility for ordinary people in Western contexts to follow a CC pathway, and I tried to identify the ways in which the CC pathway may be distinct form other pathways of development of social consciousness. The study explored the patterns of interactions between social conditions and ordinary midlife individuals' experiences in the domains of work, family, social and political life, and moral and religious thinking, which may have led the individuals to:

1. Question the set of social relations and the larger social environment in which they find themselves
2. Feel compelled to make active efforts to transform their relationship with those social conditions in congruence with their understanding
3. Seek an alternative vision of how things should be on grounds of explicit concerns with issues of justice and equity

Method

Subjects

The study relied on two samples, one from the U.S. and one from Bulgaria. The U.S. sample was part of Colby and Damon's (1994) on-going study of Midlife Social Responsibility, supported by the MacArthur Foundation Research Program on Successful Midlife Development (MIDMAC). Colby and Damon's study relied on a national sample of 100 people, roughly half men and half women, residing in or around five urban areas throughout the country, namely, Atlanta, Chicago, Boston, San Francisco, and Phoenix. My interviews represented the Boston subsample of the Social Responsibility study. That sample consisted of 20 midlifers, 7 women and 13 men, aged 35 to 60.

The Bulgarian sample of eight subjects was selected separately, through a study on Social Responsibility and Critical Consciousness in Bulgarian Midlifers supported by the 1995 Henry A. Murray Dissertation Award (Mustakova-Possardt, 1995). I selected the participants in an effort to have them represent a range of diverse sectors of Bulgarian social life. Four people were from the capital of Sofia, and four from a small country town. There were four men and four women. In spite of my efforts, the Bulgarian sample ended up being biased along the education criterion, with a higher average length of education than the U.S. population.

Interview Format

The cross-cultural data were collected using Colby and Damon's (1994) Social Responsibility in-depth semiclinical interview format. The interview falls into six parts. In the first part, the participants are invited to construct the story of their lives as they see it, dividing it into several main chapters. They focus on the main themes, events, and relationships that in their own understanding contributed to who they believe they are, as well as on the links that connect the various chapters. Then they focus on critical events and significant people. This overview sheds some light on the family and other circumstances which contributed to the way these individuals prioritize their experience in their social world.

The second part revisits in greater detail each of the main areas of social responsibility, namely: work, family, volunteering and donations, and political involvement. It focuses on the ways in which individuals prioritize their commitments and sense of responsibility, their motivations, and the personal meaning they make of their choices. It also sheds light on how they think of themselves in relation to others, and how their sense of responsibility to others influences their self-definitions.

The third part focuses explicitly on the participants' moral reasoning and moral sense of self. The fourth focuses on their sense of community involvement, and the place of communities in relation to their sense of self. The fourth focuses on the participants' religion and/or personal philosophies. The last part inquires into the participants' motivations for agreeing to participate in the interview. For the purpose of the Bulgarian interviews, I translated the Colby and Damon interview tool into Bulgarian.

Data Analysis

My approach to the data analysis was a "grounded theory" (Strauss & Corbin, 1990) approach. Building grounded theory is a hermeneutic enterprise (Van Manen, 1990), which united my conceptions of the political, social, and personal nature of CC with my best understanding of neo-Piagetian and Vygotskian developmental theory (see Mustakova-Possardt, 1996).

I applied three types of analytic procedures: (a) qualitative coding techniques for conceptualizing the data (Strauss & Corbin, 1990), (b) a more quantifiable informal developmental data analysis, (c) biographical analysis. Space limitations do not allow me to elaborate each analytic procedure beyond the brief summaries offered below.

Thematic Analysis

The interview data on how people made meaning of their lives and commitments was analyzed using Strauss and Corbin's (1990) four levels of thematic coding of qualitative data. With the help of this method, I identified an initial broad range of categories of analysis, which were then elaborated into subcategories of properties and dimensions. The next step was to group these categories and dimensions into core categories and themes. Finally, I was able to map the relationship between themes, categories, and dimensions within a template of what I identified as the core category of motivation.

Structural Developmental Analysis

This part of the data analysis relied on four neo-Piagetian theoretical frameworks, which I found most pertinent to the salient structural developmental aspects of Freire's (1973) definition of CC. Those aspects were (a) reasoning about causality, (b) understanding of one's social experience, (c) ways in which the self relates to social experience, and (d) moral reasoning. To address them, I relied on my understanding of adult development theory, and informally applied (a) Commons and Rodriguez's (1990) general stage theory, (b) Weinstein and Alschuler's (1985) model of the development of self-knowledge, (c) Kegan's (1982) subject/object model of the evolving self (Lahey et al, 1988), and (d) Kohlberg's (1984) theory of the evolution of moral reasoning.

On the basis of Freire's (1973) definition of CC and adult development theory, I hypothesized a structural developmental threshold for CC as an adult phenomenon: formal operational grasp of causality, the ability to identify abstract patterns in one's social environment, a differentiated sense of self as an internal institution relatively independent of interpersonal pressures, conventional moral reasoning with a social system and conscience orientation. I drew on the above four theoretical frameworks to describe the developmental evolution in levels of CC.

Biographical Analysis

I sought thematic overlaps in the cross-cultural biographical accounts, which could shed some light on the origins of the individuals' motivation in childhood experience, family background, and significant models; I relied on my general clinical understanding to generate plausible interpretations.

My understanding is informed by Vygotskian theory of socialization, discourse mediation, and internalization in the formation of individual social consciousness (Wertsch, 1985). I sought instances of moral induction, moral internalization, and self-attribution (Hoffman, 1989), as well as the developmental transformation of goals (Colby & Damon, 1992).

Results and Discussion

Distinction Between Predominantly Moral and Expediency Motivation

In my thematic analysis, I focused on the category of motivation in order to explore the value of conceptualizing the formation of social consciousness as the outcome of the interplay between motivation and structural development. I conceptualized motives as reflecting a continuum between predominantly moral and predominantly expediency motivation. I understand moral motivation in terms of a centrality of moral and critical normative ends and ontological concerns, as opposed to expediency motivation, in which pragmatic ends are central and moral and critical normative ends are peripheral (Marcuse, 1989a). Within this motivational continuum, I found four central motives: (1) the motive to establish a sense of identity; (2) motives to negotiate external and internal authority, personal responsibility, and agency; (3) motives shaping relationships with others and one's environment; (4) motives related to the understanding of the meaning and purpose of life. I conceptualized these motives as the four moral motivational dimensions around which individual social consciousness is formed. In some cases, these dimensions were elaborated with a centrality of moral concerns, while in others they were colored mostly by expediency concerns and narrowly conceived self-interest.

Each motivational dimension itself represents a moral-expediency continuum, along which the individual can be approximately placed. These four continuums allowed me to understand the interview data not just in terms of the current way of being of the individual, but in terms of the potential for dynamic change. Each interview revealed a unique configuration of these four motivational dimensions, with different dimensions prevalent in the lives of different individuals. However, some level of CC (as defined in this study) appeared to be present only to the degree that all four motivational dimensions were predominantly morally colored, even if some were more so than others. On this basis, I developed a motivational template of the four dimensions of continuum between moral and expediency motivation, presented in Table 36.1.

The four motivational dimensions are best understood in terms of the clusters of themes obtained from thematic analysis, and shown in the expanded motivational template in Table 36.2.

In order to illustrate my approach to the understanding of motivation, and the role of motivational dimensions in the overall motivational configuration of an individual, I will examine briefly the first dimension. The space limitations of this paper do not allow similar discussions of each dimension; those can be found in Mustakova-Possardt, 1996.

Identity

I started the data analysis relying on Kohlberg's (1984) account of the development of morality as progressive personal reconstructions and internalization of collective moral norms, leading to the formation of social identity. Hence, I expected to see elements of social and moral responsibility as increasingly central to the individual's self-identifications with the establishing of conventional moral reasoning.

I found that in some cases the formation of social identity is mediated by moral concerns which have a central role and can precede the conscious formation of social identity. In contrast, other cases suggested direct socialization (Marcuse, 1989a) into pervasive social configurations, unmediated by moral tensions.

The cases of Danton and Ada from my Bulgarian sample offer an example of a sense of identity rooted respectively primarily in moral concepts and realities, or in social configurations. Both Danton and Ada described a rootedness in a solid patriarchal culture and tradition. However, what they saw as defining their own identities in that tradition was substantially different in each case.

Danton was a Bulgarian Jew and a well-respected psychotherapist, who traversed a long and painstaking journey from a secure career in what he saw as the inhumane practices of psychiatry under the communist establishment, to a financially and professionally risky orientation toward what he saw as the respect for people and personal freedom as characterizing the philosophical foundation of psychotherapy. The first self-identification that Danton spoke of was his clan or extended family, which in his memories was held together by a morally defined

Table 36.1   Motivational Template of the Dimensions of the Moral/Expediency

Dimensions	Expediency Motivation	Moral Motivation
1. Identity	Identity predominantly rooted in social conventions (*social identity*) *and lack of moral imperative*	Identity predominantly rooted in *moral values* (*moral identity*) *and moral imperative*
2. Authority, responsibility, and agency	*Limited personal authority and responsibility; lack of agency* (fear, helplessness, skepticism in the face of external authority)	*Personal moral authority and critical discernment of external authority; expanding sense of moral responsibility; moral agency*
3. Relationships	Lack of empathy, *alienation, impermeability,* lack of concern for justice and not hurting	*Empathy relatedness, permeability, concerns for justice and not hurting*
4. Meaning of life	*Self-referential frames of reference and limited goals*	*Larger frames of reference* as vantage point for critical discernment and self-reflection; *life purpose greater than self*

Table 36.2 Expanded Motivational Template

Dimension	Expediency Motivation	Moral Motivation

1. Identity	*Social identity*
	  a. Rooted in social conventions, unmedated by values, precarious
	  b. Lack of moral character grounded in virtues
	  c. Centrality of self-image and appearance concerns
	  d. Self-absorbed, instrumental consumer concerns
	  e. Absence of habitual morality
	  f. No moral imperative
		Moral identity
		  a. Rooted in universal moral values, solid, mediated socialization.
		  b. Strong character grounded in vitues
		
		  c. Periphaeal self-image concerns
		
		  d. Normative ends
		
		  e. Habitual morality
		  f. Moral imperative

2. Agency and responsibility	*Lack of agency and limited responsibility*
	  a. Absence (or scarcity) of figures of authentic moral authority; no models
	  b. Lack of interest to compare and discern authentic authority; lack of respect for it
	  c. Either no moral self-attribution and sense of personal moral authority of its opposity; self-righteousness
	  d. Limited sense of moral responsibility, mostly derived form social and cultural stereotypes
	  e. No internal conversation around issues of moral authority and responsibility
	  f. No examples of true agency translate into skepticism, helplessness, fear in the face of external authority
		Moral agency and expanding moral responsibility
		  a. Figures authentic moral authority; models internalized
		  b. Intuitive moral sense grows into critical discernment of and respect for authentic authority
		  c. Moral self-attrition and sense of internal moral authority
		
		  d. Expanding personal moral responsibility continuously reconstructed
		
		  e. Centrality of internal conversation around moral authority and responsibility
		  f. Examples of moral agency translate into personal moral agency

3. Relationships	*Lack of empathy, alienation, impermeability, no concerns with justice and not hurting*
	  a. Hostile environment stifles empathy and relatedness
	  b. Lack of/limited empathy
	  c. Isolated, individualistic way of being, in competition with others
	  d. Lack of mostly casual relationships; just contacts; deficiency of attachments
	  e. Centrality of receiving
	  f. Inner place not inclusive of others
	
	  g. No common purpose with others; no sense of community
	  h. Cognitive and affective provincialism; limited membership in immediate interest groups; no sense of belonging to a larger humanity
	  i. Limited communication and sharing
	
	  j. Impermeabillity to meaningful social relationships
		Empathy, relatedness, permeability, concerns with justice and not hurting
		  a. Benevolent, empathic environment fosters empathy and relatedness
		  b. Levels of empathy
		  c. Rootedness in relatedness
		
		  d. Engaged in relationships on every level
		
		  e. Centrality of giving
		  f. Inner place inclusive of others and larger world
		  g. Fulfillment derived from common purpose with others and sense of community
		  h. Cognitive and affective decentering sense of belonging to a larger humanity
		
		  i. Value placed on open communication and permeability to others
		  j. Permeability to meaningful social relationships

Table 36.2   (continued)

Dimension	Expediency Motivation	Moral Motivation
	k. Compartmentalization and prejudice	k. Lack of compartmentalization and prejudice
	l. Split between public and private life and alienation form public life	l. Integration of private and public life
	m. No concerns with justice and equity and not hurting	m. Concerns with justice and equity and not hurting
	n. No social consciousness	n. Social consciousness
	o. No basics for enduring commitments beyond self, or work for the betterment of society	o. Enduring commitments beyond self work for the betterment of society
4. Meaning of life	*Self-referential frames of reference and limited goals*	*Larger frames of reference and life purpose as vantage point for critical discernment and self-reflection*
	a. Sense of meaninglessness of life; no search or questions about meaning	a. Faith in meaning and wisdom of life; search for it and on-going questions
	b. No larger purpose that individual self	b. Life purpose seen in aligning oneself with life's meaning and wisdom as best understood
	c. Peripheral concerns with right/wrong, good/bad, true/false; no vantage point outside self-interest	c. Continuous elaboration of connections between right and wrong, good and bad, true and false as vantage point
	d. Negative criticism	d. Critical discernment
	e. Reliance on habit and ritual	e. Self-reflection
	f. No interest in establishment consistency in one's understanding of life; no grappling with contradictions	f. Efforts to integrate understanding of reality and grappling with contradictions
	g. Embeddedness in sociocultural reality; status quo taken for absolute; tendency to be satisfied with opinions, stereotypes, polemics and fragile arguments	g. Problematizing of sociocultural reality from point of view of larger moral framework
	h. Impermeability to suggestions and questions arising from context	h. Permeability to suggestions and questions arising from context
	i. Surface functioning	i. Depth dimension of existence activated
	j. Disengaged and alienated from one's world	j. Engaged in wholesome and immediate relationships with reality

Jewish identity, centered around uprightness, honesty, hard work, loyalty, and excellence, as well as around the prominent moral authority figures of the grandfathers. In adolescence, the ethnic Jewish factor was enriched by peer group and class—Danton identified with a group of friends, all intellectually minded young men consumed with ideas and experiencing themselves as outsiders to mainstream communist society. He described his identity as powerfully influenced by Jewish existentialist philosopher Martin Wuder, who rejected "Israeli chauvinism," and "sought dialogue between people in the direction of an evolving global human culture." Again, the class factor appeared primarily morally defined. In adulthood, Danton identified with his profession, but as he spoke of who he was, he described

himself as "someone who always tends to seek out opportunities to sit and talk with people" because he is "so moved by people."

In contrast, Ada, a prominent and committed pediatrician, related as her first identification being "the daughter of the village doctor whom everybody respected and was in awe of." Social status appeared prominent. Ada grew up trying to live up to that self-image, and to be smarter than the village kids, and later smarter than her college peers, more achieving, more serious, more morally upright, etc. In other words, the values of honesty, uprightness, hard work, and accomplishment in her case seemed to serve as status identifiers. Concern with status, and accompanying self-righteousness, ran through all her later identification.

For example, Ada defined as the guiding preoccupation in most of her professional choices normative rather than instrumental, careeristic concerns, identifying herself as a morally minded professional. She said she distrusted the pompous sloganeering and ulterior career motives of open communist party meetings in the workplace, and remained ideologically aloof. However, the conversation revealed consistent status identifiers throughout her life story. She identified with her professional achievements and ensuing status within the communist medical establishment to the point where the fall of the communist regime, and her subsequent loss of status as a result of the disintegration of all government establishments (including the medical one), brought about a sudden strong identification with the communist establishment and a bitter, dismissive, and intolerant attitude to the social unrest accompanying the changes in Bulgarian society.

Overall, Danton's motivation revealed a relative consistency of moral concerns related to his primarily moral sense of identity. Ada's motivation around most of her life choices exhibited strong inconsistencies, and an overall tendency toward self-interest, related to the prominence of status in her self-identification.

In the overall sample of 28 participants, I identified nine cases of clear moral motivation, 15 cases of expediency motivation, and four cases which seemed too close to call.

Structural-Developmental Analysis

The informal structural-developmental assessment of the interviews indicated the following distribution of structural-developmental levels: preconventional—seven cases; conventional—13 cases; postconventional—eight cases. The thematic analysis revealed two different types of social consciousness for each developmental level, corresponding to the two types of motivation discussed above. These types of social consciousness were expressed in qualitatively different understandings of social responsibility and citizenship. In clarifying the nature of these differences, I expanded by conception of the evolution of social consciousness as a continuum between CC and non-CC along the dimensions of composite structural development and motivation.

The CC developmental pathway reveals the evolving of morally responsible citizenship through a *dynamic synergy* between moral motivation and structural development, its two main components. The interaction between them produces three levels of social consciousness in the life-span, *pre-CC, transitional CC,* and *CC.* Each level is a unique combination of motivation and structures of thought, and *cannot be reduced to either.* At each level, the person negotiates a substantially different range of tasks, concerns, and limitations. At each level, moral motivation seems to spur structural development, while structural development provides the social skills and understanding required to put one's intuitive moral interest into practice, and to become a moral agent for positive social change.

My impression from the 28 cases is that the ego-transcending nature of moral motivation brings to structural development a distinctive energy, which foreshadows the complete evolving of ego-transcending motivation with Authentic consciousness (Wade, 1996). In this way, moral motivation serves to spur structural development, while without the dominant presence of moral motivation, lifelong structural development depends for its motivational source on the evolving negotiation of immediate self-interest, and appears to be more vulnerable to social circumstances and more uneven. Such an understanding helps explain the particular agency and resilience of CC individuals across the developmental spectrum; in them, moral motivation is developmentally elaborated into an unusually expansive range of moral and social concerns and engagements. I did not observe a comparably committed citizenship among the non-CC interviewees.

Summary Descriptions of Each Level of CC

Pre-CC

The period of pre-CC is the time of the formation of the four dimensions of moral motivation, and the reaching of the structural-developmental threshold for CC. Ideally, this begins to happen in early childhood and continues into young adulthood. However, if the structural-developmental threshold is not fully reached but moral motivation has formed the individual is likely to continue to operate with Pre-CC into biological adulthood. I encountered two such cases.

If the formation of moral motivation does not occur, the individual embarks on a non-CC pathway of development. In this case, there appears to be the possibility for circumstances to occur later in life which can stimulate the moral elaboration of one or another of the motivational dimensions. Such a development may have a snowball effect and bring about the progressive moral elaboration of the other motivational dimensions, allowing the person to move to the CC pathway. However, my data did not include full-blown cases of such transformations, but just glimpses into the possible beginnings of such a process (see Mustakova-Possardt, 1996).

Transitional CC

People who exhibit transitional CC continue to negotiate moral identity, authority, and responsibility, but, with the advent of formal operational thinking, these questions are taken beyond concrete situations. The individual is now able to identify increasingly generalized patterns in his/her immediate social reality; s/he feels implied in these social patterns, and is therefore asking pressing questions about personal role and responsibility. In the context of this growing critical discernment, we also see people with transitional CC deal with a lot of internal contradictions. The incomplete decentering of a person with conventional morality (Kohlberg, 1984) accounts for frequent conflicts between prejudice and stereotypical thinking in some areas of social life, and the general striving toward establishing meaningful and wholesome relationships within an ever-expanding social radius.

The person exhibiting transitional CC has a structure of the self characterized by a predominantly interpersonal (Kegan, 1982) subject/object epistemology. The lack of a fully differentiated Institutional (Kegan, 1982) self accounts for limited self-reflection, a typically limited sense of agency, and a certain ambivalence in defining a stance amid conflicting interpersonal loyalties and pressures. Nevertheless, the striving toward consistency, integrity, service, and compassion is strong enough to foster the gradual evolving of a social consciousness oriented toward positive social change in the direction of all-inclusive justice and equity.

Hence, the main achievement of transitional CC is the birth of problematizing and increasingly dialogical relationships with social reality, as Freire (1973) defined them. The successful progressive shedding of contradictions, stereotypes, and prejudices, and the expansion of permeability, seem to depend on the strength of moral motivation, and on the degree to which "the depth dimension of existence" (Marcuse, 1989a) has been activated. Overall, transitional CC is characterized by embeddedness in conventional realities and efforts to operate morally and responsibly within them, finding legal and caring ways within the existing social paradigm. The main limitation of transitional CC is its lack of systemic understanding, the result of which is that multiple social patterns and pathways of activism may be experienced as overwhelming when one is committed to bringing about positive change. In this sense, what is generally considered the mark of CC, i.e., dereification (Bembow, 1994), has not yet occurred. This is a phenomenon that characterizes the liberating movement toward CC.

In my sample of 28, I found four cases of transitional CC, three from the U.S. and one from Bulgaria, and nine cases of conventional non-CC, eight from the U.S. and one from Bulgaria. These distinctions between transitional CC and conventional non-CC will be illustrated below, by the cases of William and Agnes.

CC

The level of CC represents the full formation of CC proper, i.e., a social consciousness disembedded from, and able to deconstruct, its immediate social milieu, engaged in a progressively expanding critical moral dialogue with its socio-historical world. The central moral motivational dimension elaborated throughout this period is the progressively expansive reconstruction of the meaning and purpose of life, and the evolving of a principled philosophical, historical, and global vision.

Individuals at this level exhibit an identity characterized by relative unity of self and morality. They speak of moral responsibility and agency in the socio-political

domain. They appear relatively disembedded from and engaged in relationships with their social environment; and they relate to socio-political allegiances, growing permeability to meaningful social relationships, social consciousness, and possibly socio-political activism. These people problematize their social environment, bringing moral frames of reference to it. They often attempt to apply spiritual understanding to socio-political reality, and rely heavily on self-reflection in their efforts to bring inner and outer life into harmony.

This is a period of gradual integration of the above moral motivational dimensions into a paradigmatic understanding of an increasingly activated depth dimension of existence (Marcuse, 1989a). With it, we see the advent of integrated and interconnected personhood, which shows increasingly less compartmentalization of public and private concerns, and a consistent moral agency across domains. The CC pathway culminates in what Freire (1973) described as emancipated subjects, rather than objects, of history, able to "perceive epochal themes" and "act upon the reality within which these themes are generated" (p. 5).

To illustrate the above, I offer a few quotes form one of the CC individuals interviewed (for more detailed case studies, see Mustakova-Possardt, 1996):

> When others turn to me in need, I do what I believe is right. I don't know if I want to call that help. It's more of a mutual thing, they learn from me and I learn from them. These relationships are gifts. . . . I share what I know about waters and feeding and mental health. . . . I try to help others not feel like victims of their lives. . . . But I cannot talk about volunteering help. For me, *to do something good, and then to remember it and talk about it, is already about something else;* it's about your ego, not about others. I simple *engage with the other person's world,* and it is something beautiful and enriching for both of us.
>
> In order to judge a particular political line or group, I have to understand and feel the thinking of the whole nation. The current state of things is the outcome of the whole complex of people, with all its groups. Nothing happens accidentally. What we have is what we need at the moment. That's how it is with everything in life. It's another question how I see the future, a future without fear. Fear is at the core of all human misery. In order *to do away with fear, we have to all understand who we are, where we are going, what life is about, and that life does not end here.* Then we will have global change. *Global change will mean that things are done without self-interest,* that international help is given for the right reasons and in the right way. . . . Every nation has its values and the help given has to respect those values.

In my sample of 28, I found six cases of CC, four from Bulgaria and two from the U.S. and two cases of postconventional non-CC.

The limitations of this paper do not allow me to offer vignettes of the two alternative types of consciousness at each developmental level. I have chosen to do that only for the level of conventional thought, because we know that this is the most common level among adult populations (Cook-Greuter, 1990), and it seems important to understand the distinctions between CC and non-CC in the majority of conventional adults.

William and Agnes

Agnes and William were both recently retired competent professionals. Agnes was an elementary school teacher in the same public school system for over 20 years; William did not complete his engineering degree, but was a qualified computer service representative with IBM for 31 years. Both showed consistency and pride in their careers; both were valued by, and loyal to, their respective employers. Both divorced partners to whom they had long-standing commitments, and went through self-doubts and inner struggle around their decisions; in neither case was divorce something lightly undertaken. Both individuals proved to be responsible and successful parents of children who turned into "good people" in their parents' descriptions.

According to my informal structural assessment, and as illustrated below, both Agnes and William were conventional thinkers (Kohlberg, 1984), who seemed to operate out of predominantly institutional self-systems [Kegan 4/3 or 4(3); Kegan, 1982] and construct their own understanding of their social roles and the norms by which they lived. At the same time, their sense of identity appeared to be somewhat interpersonally derived from belonging to a particular group, class, occupation. They both exhibited achievement consciousness (Wade, 1996).

In the case of Agnes, her pride in and control over her own self as "institution" came through in her descriptions of how she kept her unfaithful former husband at arm's length and did not agree to get back together with him in spite of his repeated invitations to do so over the years. She remained on friendly terms with him, and let him visit and see the children, but cautiously avoided any complications. She maintained here independence and protected her property, with a firm belief that "slow and steady, wins the race." Asked about the happiest time in her life, she pointed to the years when she was an elementary teacher, and raised her kids alone: "They [the kids] were manageable, and I loved my job. I felt important and needed." Her occupation gave her a sense of identity: "[Y]ou know, when you were teaching, you were employed, you were somebody. Those kids depended on you."

William's institutional self-definitions got expressed in many ways: from the personal moral norms which he established and lived by, frequently notably against the tide, to the pride he took in organizing this present life as a retired person around the setting and achieving of goals with his second wife. His goals centered around the successful investment and managing of financial resources. He was a member of a lodge, and was elected a trustee. Like Agnes, William's occupation gave him a sense of identity. He took pride in his competency, in being "the best technician, the best person I could," satisfying his customers, and "being appreciated." He liked "working with people, and doing the job."

Both Agnes and William operated successfully within the social system, with a sense of self relatively separate form social reality, and saw themselves as honest, hard-working, law-abiding citizens. Throughout the conversation, however, their critical discernment was mostly directed outward, and they exhibited limited self-knowledge.

In spite of their developmental similarities and common conservative tastes and tendencies, Agnes and William represented two significantly different categories of people in terms of CC. I see William as exhibiting transitional CC, and Agnes as operating from its convention non-CC counterpart, with a more uneven developmental profile.

Agnes came closest from the U.S. sample to exhibiting a consistent lack of development along the four moral motivational dimensions, without being a dysfunctional antisocial personality. She struck me as a very lonely and isolated human being, deprived of genuinely moral frames of reference, and struggling to confront the egocentric trap which personal history and cultural heritage seemed to have combined to create in her life. In contrast, William appeared happy, self-fulfilled, inspired, and hopeful. One of his main goals was to learn more about life. He came across as a generative human being, whose CC had equipped him to deal with the challenges in life.

Agnes had *compartmentalized her own consciousness and her life* to the point that her children did not know anything about her "family history," or that her "mother was a whore." She didn't keep in touch with her extended family, or even with her brothers. Agnes used a striking metaphor to describe her life:

> I started to run my life like a post-office. Incidents and events that I couldn't do anything about that there were bothering me, I just had to put them in the slot, and put them away, forget about them, and not dwell on them, because it was hurting me too much.

Agnes seemed to have *no internal frames of reference larger than the self*. All *her frames of reference were external*, notably materialistic and lifestyle-oriented. Her children's success was measured by the fact they were "gainfully employed." She manifested *class and role stereotypes*, and disdain for working-class people ("If I hadn't, where would I be today? Probably at work in some factory, marrying some hometown boy"). She expressed no interest or concern about others in the larger social world, but felt fine when she was *socialized into a carefully chosen, protected environment*. Faced with cancer and a sense of losing control for the first time in her adult life, she frantically sought external solutions to the acute anxiety attacks she experienced every morning. Yet, she remained *isolated in her individualism*, taking care of "numero uno first," and responding to others only upon request and in guarded ways.

In Agnes, the combination of expediency motivation and conventional thought translated into extremely limited expressions of social responsibility and citizenship, and no real dialogue with social reality. She did the minimum, within the accepted institutional cultural norm, to give back to society (she contributed to a few charities), making sure not to engage emotionally or to commit to any demands on her time and comfort. She had no interest in politics or social issues, and revealed *bigotry* and *self-righteousness* as she talked about morality. (For example, she considered herself "a great one to dictate morals and morality; that's how my kids were brought up.")

Overall, Agnes did not engage in creative and responsible relationships with the wider world, which would have allowed her to come to know it. She was impermeable and alienated, and did not enter into real dialogue with others, or problematize her social experience.

William's strong moral motivation was primarily expressed in his *sense of personal and social moral responsibility,* which permeated all his decisions, from parenting and resisting the cultural tide in raising his six children, to keeping himself informed on current issues, understanding their moral implications, and voting his conscience. His *moral imperative and critical discernment extended* to every issue, within the limits of what I believe was his early formal operational reasoning. He differentiated between *respecting authority* and being able to *question authority,* he *questioned the dominant cultural tendency* to couple critical questioning of authority with an unwillingness to respect any authority. Below is an example of his thinking about international issues such as the war in Bosnia:

Let's stop the fighting. Let's get together. What are the issues here? There's no sense in what they are doing. . . . The nonsense that's going on in the world. . . . Killing of innocent people. What? Just a political cause? You don't believe in the other person, what they're doing is right? They're just as right as you are. Or your faith is a little different than somebody else's faith? People have been killed in the name of God, it's ridiculous. It's terrible. I'm sure God didn't want that.

Another example of how William's *moral motivation prompted him to problematize social reality* within his structural limitations is the interesting distinction he drew between the ideological significance that's placed on practically every issue, and its common sense value. His lack of systemic thinking rendered him unable to appreciate the political, economic, and international complexities of the issue at hand. Yet, he cut right through it:

We have to get back to basics and common sense again. I think we've lost that. Everything has become too politicized. You *have to do what's good for the country and what's good for the world, what's good for us.* . . . The budget issue is common sense, and yet we're trying to make big politics out of it. . . . One party won't give in to the other because it's not their issue. They've taken over an issue. We've got to get together; we *have one issue:* the budget.

William's position on welfare was another example of how he examined issues in a thoughtful way, which defied simplifications:

I think we've gone overboard in welfare. People lost sense of their work ethic because of welfare. . . . We have to have common sense in that, because I think welfare is just a gift from people to another group. It's a way of redistribution of the wealth, but it's actually a gift. . . . Roosevelt instituted some type of welfare, social security, but as I remember, it was a civilian conservation corps, the public works projects, where he gave people jobs, and that wasn't welfare because they worked, they were given job so they could exist and pull themselves up. Now you don't have to work. We've lost that work ethic. . . . It's great to give, but you got to be careful.

A theme that ran throughout William's life was: *I am what I can give, what I can share with others!* Narrow self-interest was notably lacking in his priorities; his *sense of self appeared united with his sense of morality.* Asked how his family life contributed to his sense of who he was, he turned the question around: "How did my family life contribute? I think, how did I contribute to my family life, *how did I contribute?"*

William's moral motivation interacted with his structures of thought producing what I see as typical expressions of transitional CC in terms of citizenship. He sought opportunities to do positive social work within the existing system: He visited veterans, distributes Christmas baskets to the poor, volunteered time to his lodge to manage its facilities and resources, and helped raise funds for charities, contributing regularly to United Way, the Red Cross, and a children's hospital. He summarized his own sense of social responsibility and citizenship in the following way:

I know we can't all run for President. We all can't be CEOs. But in our own way, we hope we contribute to society, whether that be with our own families, with our work and our organizations, with whatever people we come in contact with. And we hope we impart certain positive things. I don't think we have to be big politicians or corporate managers to do that

William's structural limitations (discussed above) confined him to person-to-person work for social change. His self-knowledge was limited, although he searched himself with integrity and grappled with his contradictions. William took nothing for granted, and engaged in an on-going moral dialogue with his world, although from a limited socio-historical perspective. He was a good example of why CC cannot be reduced to moral motivation only, nor to structures of thought, but is a synergistic outcome of the on-going interaction between the two.

Themes and Patterns from Personal History and Biography

I saw some overlapping themes and patterns which appear related to possible sources of motivational dimensions, which will not be discussed in this paper beyond a very brief overview. (For elaboration, see Mustakova-Possardt, 1996.)

Identity

Predominantly moral or expediency thinking and doing seems to be related to who one thinks one is. The formation of a sense of identity appears to be a process of developing rootedness in implicitly modeled realities, internalized to some degree as character, and explicitly taught concepts, which serve as organizers of experience and develop into sources of conscious identification. Modeling and teaching, character and identity formation, appear in constant interplay. Ideally, the two would be in harmony, but every person's history reveals a different configuration of the two.

The concepts central to the daily discourse in the immediate family and, later, in the larger social environment can be predominantly universal moral and/or spiritual values, such as honesty, justice, righteousness, service, generosity, humility, compassion, etc., which mediate and color the way social experience is understood. Conversely, they can be predominantly oriented toward current social conventions, such as class, race, national or other group interests, social or gender roles, etc. The people who exhibited rootedness predominantly in universal moral values seemed less vulnerable to changes in social circumstances, whereas people socialized directly into the prevalent social configurations exhibited a sense of identity less secure and more prone to overwhelming self-image concerns.

Where people described an environment which relied on moral induction (Hoffman, 1983, 1989, 1991), moral self-attribution seems to have developed, along with stronger empathic feelings, habitual morality (Colby & Damon, 1992), and moral imperative. The resulting predominant preoccupation with normative rather than instrumental concerns (Marcuse, 1989a) in time began to operate as a vantage point for critical discernment. Where a genuine concern with the spiritual dimensions of life was part of the early environment, it appears to have activated a depth dimension of experience, fostering what Marcuse (1989b) described as "a consciousness capable of breaking through the material veil of the affluent society in which liberation seems to be predicated upon the opening and activation of the depth dimension of human existence" (p. 281).

These people's self-identifications exhibited a quiet and enduring sense of inherent nobility, a heart-felt respect for the nobility of other human beings regardless of social distinctions.

Authority, Responsibility, Agency

This motivational dimension reflects the tendency for authentic external moral authority in a child's life to be internalized, and gradually reconstructed as personal moral authority, responsibility, and agency. The populatedness with, versus scarcity of, figures of authentic moral authority in a child's life appears to be a significant motivational factor. In fact, it seems that the degree and nature of agency in adulthood is proportional to the agency modeled by the significant sources of authentic moral authority in childhood. Individuals who seemed deprived of such figures in childhood consistently exhibited struggles with personal agency and a very limited sense of personal moral responsibility.

The models provided by figures of authentic moral authority inevitably come into contrast with other authority figures. Thus, the intuitive moral sense of the young person has the opportunity to develop into critical discernment of and respect for authentic moral authority. The on-going negotiation of such contrasts seems to generate an internal conversation around issues of moral authority and responsibility, which becomes central to the person and strengthens his/her preoccupation with normative concerns and moral imperative.

Relationships

This motivational dimension reflects the importance of experiencing oneself in relationships in terms of the overall formation of moral motivation. The nature of the relationships a person learns to establish with his/her environment appears to be a powerful motivating factor in terms of becoming a caring, engaged moral agent for positive social change. People who described compartmentalized, self-interest-oriented, or casual relationships, with limited or no empathy, seemed to become estranged from themselves first, and, as a natural outcome, tended to engage less and less fully with their world. Altogether, the ability and inclination to engage in meaningful, wholesome relationships with one's environment, and to be moved by expanding levels of empathy, permeability, and concerns with justice and equity, appears to be a reflection of environments, and the degree to which they foster empathy, relatedness, and a common purpose with others. It also appears important who and what the person's circle of relatedness includes—whether it includes a sense of belonging to a larger humanity and an awareness of one's connectedness with nature, or it is provincial and includes only limited interest groups. Agnes was a compelling example of a person struggling with her own limited ability to relate, which reflected the limitations of her specific early relationships (Mustak-ova-Possardt, 1996).

Meaning of Life

Whether a person asks and values questions regarding the meaning of life, i.e., whether ontological, rather than solely instrumental, concerns are central to his/her experience of life, is another significant motivational dimension. The search for authentic meaning in life through the continuous elaboration of the connections between right and wrong, good and bad, true and false, provides a larger frame of reference that serves as a vantage point from which to reflect on self and experience. Engaging in a genuine dialogue with reality draws on the mind, expands its capacities, and eventually develops into principled, philosophical, historical, and global vision.

This search for meaning larger than the self seems to be fostered by a moral and/or spiritual environment which operates with faith in the meaning and wisdom of life, and recognizes one's responsibility to align oneself with it. The search for self-transcending meaning has proven to be a powerful integrating factor in personality development, as supported by the findings of Colby and Damon (1992). I also found that the sense of transcendence appears proportional to the sense of agency of the individual. Where the belief system is strictly ethical, with no "intimation of transcendence" (Colby & Damon, 1992, p. 311), there seems to be a less complete unity between self and morality, and moral agency exhibits a stronger reasoning factor.

In summary, most individuals who exhibited some level of CC gave evidence of a configuration of intellectual, moral, and spiritual education, which interacted with their intuitive moral sense and capacity for development and produced a potentially liberating CC way of being. In contrast, the individuals who did not exhibit CC related circumstances of intellectual, moral, or spiritual deprivation and spent their lives developing compensatory mechanisms and trying to combat a sense of inner void. Those individuals related experiences in which their intuitive moral sense, instead of being developed and fostered into fully formed moral motivation, was squelched by hostile, unempathic, or amoral environments, and, over time, was poised in opposition to the growing sense of immediate self-interest.

Conclusions

An important outcome of this study is its clarification of CC not just as a particular way of being, but as a life-long pathway. When we think of CC, it seems easiest to imagine it in its advanced, fully developed form, combining enlightened critical discernment and the ability to deconstruct socio-cultural realities along with insightful introspection and creative moral agency. However, tracking motivational dimensions, as was done in this study, enables us to see how CC begins to evolve early in life. At every level, the synergistic interplay between moral motivation and the structural development produces a type of consciousness which appears to be an alternative to non-CC.

This paper suggests the importance of moral motivation in overall positive adult development. Instead of looking at morality as purely a matter of structural development, contrasts between moral and expediency motivation at all levels suggest the centrality of authentic moral

concerns in the formation of consciousness. Although the four moral motivational dimensions are continuously elaborated throughout development, the predominance of moral over expediency concerns seems not to be necessarily an outcome of development.

On the other hand, CC is not the equivalent of moral motivation, by virtue of the fact that consciousness cannot be described by motivation only; it is the product of the interaction between motivation and evolving structures of thought, where each component continuously shapes the other. Such an understanding of CC, as both a moral and an intellectual phenomenon, is consistent with Freire's (1973) understanding of CC as a way of being which establishes relationships with the world impregnated with consequence.

This study has contributed to a conceptualization of a "CC pathway." I believe that further study of how people enter and leave this pathway, as well as progress through it, is needed. Such study may have important implications for life-long education, counseling, and the transformation of socio-political reality.

References

Bailey, J. P. (1976). Consciousness raising groups for women: Implications of Paolo Freire's theory of critical consciousness for psychotherapy and education (Doctoral dissertation, University of Massachusetts, Amherst, 1976). *Dissertation Abstracts International, 38,* 01A:0164.

Bellah, R. et al. (1985). *Habits of the heart: Individualism and commitment in American life.* CA: University of California Press

Bembow, J. (1994). Coming to know: A phenomenological study of individuals actively committed to radical social change (Doctoral dissertation, University of Massachusetts, Amherst, 1994). *Dissertation Abstracts International, 55,* 03A:0528.

Bronner, S., & Kellner, D. (Eds.). (1989). *Critical theory and society: A reader.* New York: Routledge, Chapman and Hall.

Colby, A., & Damon, W. (1992). *Some do care.* New York: Macmillan.

Colby, A., & Damon, W. (1994). *Social responsibility at midlife: research plane for 1994–95.* Unpublished manuscript.

Commons, M. L., & Richards, F. A. (1984). A general model of stage theory. In M. L. Commons, F. A. Richards, & C. Armon (Eds.), *Beyond formal operations: Vol. 1. Late adolescent and adult cognitive development.* New York: Praeger.

Commons, M. L. & Rodrigues, J. A. (1990). Equal access without "establishing" religion: The necessity for aggressing social perspective-taking skills and institutional atmosphere. *Developmental Review, 10,* 323–340.

Cook-Greiter, S. (1990). Maps for living: Ego development stages from symbiois to conscious universal embeddedness. In Commons et al. *Adult Development: Models and methods in the study of adolescent and adult thought.* 2. New York: Cambridge University Press.

Elias, J. L. (1976). *Conscientization and deschooling: Freire's and Illich's proposals for the reshaping of society.* Philadelphia: Westminster Press.

Foucault, M. (1984). What is Enlightenment? In Paul Rabinow (Ed.) *The Foucault Reader.* New York: Plenum.

Freire, P (1973). *Education for critical consciousness.* New York: Continuum.

Fromm, E. (1959). Value, psychology, and human existence. In A. A. Maslow (Ed.), *New knowledge in human values* (pp. 151–165). New York: Harper & Brothers.

Fromm, E. (1989). Politics and psychoanalysis. In S. Broner & D. Kellner (Eds.), *Critical theory and society: A reader* (pp. 213–219). New York: Routledge, Chapman and Hall.

Gandhi, M. K. (1927). *An autobiography or the story of my experiments with truth.* Ahmedabad-14; India Navajivan.

Glaser, B. C., & Strauss, A. L. (1967). *The discovery of grounded theory: Strategies for qualitative research.* Chicago: Aldine.

Hoffman, M. L. (1983). Affective and cognitive processes in moral internalization. In E. T Higgins, D. N. Ruble, & W. W. Hartup (eds.), *Social cognition and social development: A sociocultural perspective.* Cambridge: Cambridge University Press.

Hoffman, M. L. (1989). Empathy and prosocial activism. In N. Eisenberg, J. Reykowski, & E. Staub (Eds.), *Social and moral values* (pp. 65–87). Hillsdale, NJ: Erlbaum.

Hoffman, M. L. (1991). Commentary. *Journal of Human Development, 34,* 105–110.

Jung, C. G. (1933). *Modem man in search of a soul.* New York: Harcourt, Brace and World.

Kegan, R. (1982). *The evolving self: Problem and process in human development.* Cambridge, MA: Harvard University Press.

Kohlberg, L. (1984). *The psychology of moral development: Essays on moral development* (Vol. 2). San Francisco: Harper & Row.

Lahey, L., Souvaine, E., Kegan, R., Goodman, R., & Felix, S. (1988). *A guide to the subject-object interview: Its administration and interpretation.* Cambridge, MA: The Subject-Object Workshop.

Marcuse, H. (1989a). From ontology to technology: Fundamental tendencies of industrial society. In S. Bronner & D. Kellner (Eds.), *Critical theory and society: A reader* (pp. 119–128). New York: Routledge, Chapman and Hall.

Marcuse, H. (1989b). Liberation from the affluent society. In S. Bronner & D. Kellner (Eds.), *Critical theory and society: A reader* (pp. 276–288). New York: Routledge, Chapman and Hall.

Marcuse, H. (1989c). The obsolescence of the Freudian concept of man. In S. Bronner & D. Kellner (Eds.), *Critical theory and society: A reader* (pp. 233–247). New York: Routledge, Chapman and Hall.

Marcuse, H. (1989d). Philosophy and critical theory. In S. Bronner & Kellner, D. (Eds.), *Critical theory and society: A reader* (pp. 58–77). New York: Routledge, Chapman and Hall.

Maslow, A. (Ed.). (1959). *New knowledge in human values.* New York: Harper & Brothers.

Mustakova-Possardt, E. (1995). *Critical consciousness and social responsibility among Bulgarian midlifers: Research proposal for the Henry A. Murray Dissertation Award.* Unpublished manuscript.

Mustakova-Possardt, E. (1996). Ontogeny of critical consciousness (Doctoral dissertation, University of Massachusetts, Amherst, 1996). *Dissertation Abstracts International, 57,* 10B:6616.

Progoff, I. (1973). *Jung, synchronicity, & human destiny: Noncausal dimensions of human experience.* New York: Julian Press.

Schipani, D. S. (1984). *Conscientization and creativity: Paolo Freire and Christian education.* Lanham, MD: University Press of America.

Shor, I. & Freire, P. (1987). *A pedagogy for liberation: dialogues on transforming education.* South Hadley, MA: Bergin & Garvey.

Smith, W. A. (1975). Conscientizacao: an operational definition (Doctoral dissertation, University of Massachusetts, Amherst, 1975). *Dissertation Abstracts International, 37,* 01A:0205.

Smith, W. A. (1976). *The meaning of conscientizacao: The goal of Paolo Freire's pedagogy.* Amherst: Center for International Education, University of Massachusetts.

Strauss, A., & Corbin, J. (1990). *Basics of qualitative research.* Newbury Park, CA: Sage.

Van Manen, M. (1990). *Researching lived experience: Human science for an action sensitive pedagogy.* Albany: State University of New York Press.

Wade, J. (1996). *Changes of mind: A holonomic theory of the evolution of consciousness.* Albany: State University of New York Press.

Walker, S. J. (1995). College students, alcohol and drugs, and culture: An application of the theories and practices of Robert Kegan and Paolo Freire (Doctoral dissertation, Harvard University, 1995). *Dissertation Abstracts International, 56,* 06A:2140.

Webb, E. (1988). *Philosophers of consciousness.* Seattle: University of Washington Press.

Weinstein, G., & Alschuler, A. (1985). Educating and counseling for self-knowledge development. *Journal of Counseling and Development, 64,* 19–25.

Wertsch, J. V. (1985). *Vygotsky and the social formation of the mind.* Cambridge, MA: Harvard University Press.

Wuthnow, R. (1991). *Acts of compassion.* New Jersey: Princeton University Press.

Social and Personality Development in Early and Middle Adulthood

A Conception of Adult Development

Daniel J. Levinson

Daniel J. Levinson worked most of his life as a professor of psychology in the Department of Psychiatry at Yale University. He also served as director of psychology of the Connecticut Mental Health Center and director of the Research Unit for Social Psychology and Psychiatry. Prior to working at Yale, he taught at Case Western Reserve University and Harvard University.

In 1978 Levinson published a best-selling nonfiction text on human development entitled *The Seasons of a Man's Life*. In that text he introduced to the American public the concept of the human "life cycle," using the metaphor of the seasons to illustrate the spring, summer, autumn, and winter of a man's life. Following that text Levinson published *The Seasons of a Woman's Life*, in which he expanded and refined his notions of the human life cycle. In the second book Levinson used examples from the lives of adult women, whereas he only used examples from men in his earlier text. Based on his decades of research into the adult life cycle, and after the completion of those two texts, Levinson summarized his views in "A Conception of Adult Development," *American Psychologist* (January 1986), which is excerpted in the following selection.

Key Concept: the life cycle

The Life Course

Life course is one of the most important yet least examined terms in the human sciences. It is a descriptive term, not a high-level abstraction, and it refers to the concrete character of a life in its evolution from beginning to end. Both words in this term require careful attention.

The word *course* indicates sequence, temporal flow, the need to study a life as it unfolds over the years. To study the course of a life, one must take account of stability and change, continuity and discontinuity, orderly progression as well as stasis and chaotic fluctuation. It is not enough to focus solely on a single moment; nor is it enough to study a series of three or four moments widely separated in time, as is ordinarily done in longitudinal research. It is necessary, in Robert White's (1952) felicitous phrase, to examine "lives in progress" and to follow the temporal sequence in detail over a span of years.

The word *life* is also of crucial importance. Research on the life course must include all aspects of living: inner wishes and fantasies; love relationships; participation in family, work, and other social systems; bodily changes; good times and bad—everything that has significance in a life. To study the life course, it is necessary first to look at a life in all its complexity at a given time, to include all its components and their interweaving into a partially integrated pattern. Second, one must delineate the evolution of this pattern over time.

The study of the life course has presented almost insuperable problems to the human sciences as they are now constituted. Each discipline has claimed as its special domain one aspect of life, such as personality, social role, or biological functioning, and has neglected the others. Every discipline has split the life course into disparate segments, such as childhood or old age. Research has been done from such diverse theoretical perspectives as biological aging, moral development, career development, adult socialization, enculturation, and adaptation to loss or stress, with minimal recognition of their interconnections. The resulting fragmentation is so great that no discipline or viewpoint conveys the sense of an individual life and its temporal course.

The recognition is slowly dawning that the many specialties and theoretical approaches are not isolated entities but aspects of a single field: the study of the individual life course. During the next decade, this study will emerge as a new multidisciplinary field in the human sciences, linking the various disciplines. With the formation of a more comprehensive, systematic conception of the life course, the parts will become less isolated and each part will enrich the others.

The Life Cycle

The idea of the life cycle goes beyond that of the life course. In its origin this idea is metaphorical, not descriptive or conceptual. It is useful to keep the primary imagery while moving toward more precise conceptualization and study. The imagery of "cycle" suggests that there is an underlying order in the human life course; although each individual life is unique, everyone goes through the same basic sequence. The course of a life is not a simple, continuous process. There are qualitatively different phases or seasons. The metaphor of seasons appears in many contexts. There are seasons in the year. Spring is a time of blossoming, and poets allude to youth as the springtime of the life cycle. Summer is the season of greatest passion and ripeness. An elderly ruler is "the lion in winter." There are seasons within a single day—dawn, noon, twilight, the full dark of night—each having its counterpart in the life cycle. There are seasons in love, war, politics, artistic creation, and illness.

The imagery of the life cycle thus suggests that the life course evolves through a sequence of definable forms. A season is a major segment of the total cycle. Change goes on within each season, and a transition is required for the shift from one to the next. Every season has its own time, although it is part of and colored by the whole. No season is better or more important than any other. Each has its necessary place and contributes its special character to the whole.

What are the major seasons in the life cycle? Neither popular culture nor the human sciences provide a clear answer to this question. The modern world has no established conception—scientific, philosophical, religious, or literary—of the life cycle as a whole and of its component phases. There is no standard language that demarcates and identifies several gross segments of the life cycle. The predominant view, rarely stated explicitly, divides it into three parts: (a) an initial segment of about 20 years, including childhood and adolescence (preadulthood); (b) a final segment starting at around 65 (old age); and (c) between these segments, an amorphous time vaguely known as adulthood.

A good deal is known about the preadult years, which for a century have been the main province of the field of human development. The developmental perspective has been of crucial importance here. The idea is now accepted that in the first 20 years or so all human beings go through an underlying sequence of periods—prenatal, infancy, early childhood, middle childhood, pubescence, and adolescence. Although all children go through common developmental periods, they grow in infinitely varied ways as a result of differences in biological, psychological, and social conditions. In its concrete form, each individual life course is unique. The study of preadult development seeks to determine the universal order and the general developmental principles that govern the process by which human lives become increasingly individualized.

Historically, the great figures in the study of child development, such as Freud and Piaget, have assumed that development is largely completed at the end of adolescence. Given these assumptions, they had no basis for concerning themselves with the possibilities of adult development or with the nature of the life cycle as a whole. An impetus to change came in the 1950s when geriatrics and gerontology were established as fields of human service and research. Unfortunately, gerontology has not gone far in developing a conception of the life cycle. One reason, perhaps, is that it skipped from childhood to old age without examining the intervening adult years. Present understanding of old age will be enhanced when more is known about adulthood; thus, old age can be connected more organically to the earlier seasons.

There is now very little theory, research, or cultural wisdom about adulthood as a season (or seasons) of the life cycle. We have no popular language to describe a series of age levels after adolescence. Words such as *youth, maturity,* and *middle age* are ambiguous in their age linkages and meanings. The ambiguity of language stems from the lack of any cultural definition of adulthood and how people's lives evolve within it. In the human sciences, too, we have no adequate conception of the nature of adulthood. We have a detailed picture of many trees but no view of the forest and no map to guide our journey through it.

I turn now to my own view of the life cycle. It derives from my research and draws upon the work of earlier investigators such as Erikson (1950, 1969), Jung, von Franz, Henderson, Jacobi, and Jaffe (1964), Neugarten (1968), Ortega y Gasset (1958), and van Gennep (1960). (For a fuller review, see Levinson & Gooden, 1985.)

Eras: The Macrostructure of the Life Cycle

I conceive of the life cycle as a sequence of *eras*. Each era has its own biopsychosocial character, and each makes its distinctive contribution to the whole. There are major changes in the nature of our lives from one era to the next, and lesser, though still crucially important, changes within eras. They are partially overlapping: A new era begins as the previous one is approaching its end. A *cross-era transition*, which generally lasts about five years, terminates the outgoing era and initiates the next. The eras and the cross-era transitional periods form the macrostructure of the life cycle, providing an underlying order in the flow of all human lives yet permitting exquisite variations in the individual life course.

Each era and developmental period begins and ends at a well-defined modal age, with a range of about two years above and below this average. The idea of age-linked phases in adult life goes against conventional wisdom. Nevertheless, these age findings have been consistently obtained in the initial research and in subsequent studies. The idea of age-linked eras and periods now has the status of an empirically grounded hypothesis that needs further testing in various cultures.

The first era, *Preadulthood*, extends from conception to roughly age 22. During these "formative years" the individual grows from highly dependent, undifferentiated infancy through childhood and adolescence to the beginnings of a more independent, responsible adult life. It is the era of most rapid biopsychosocial growth. The first few years of life provide a transition into childhood. During this time, the neonate becomes biologically and psychologically separate from the mother and establishes the initial distinction between the "me" and the "not me"—the first step in a continuing process of individuation.

The years from about 17 to 22 constitute the *Early Adult Transition*, a developmental period in which preadulthood draws to a close and the era of early adulthood gets underway. It is thus part of both eras, and not fully a part of either. A new step in individuation is taken as the budding adult modifies her or his relationships with family and other components of the preadult world and begins to form a place as an adult in the adult world. From a childhood-centered perspective, one can say that development is now largely completed and the child has gained maturity as an adult. The field of developmental (i.e., child) psychology has traditionally taken this view. Taking the perspective of the life cycle as a whole, however, we recognize that the developmental attainments of the first era provide only a base, a starting point from which to begin the next. The Early Adult Transition represents, so to speak, both the full maturity of preadulthood and the infancy of a new era. One is at best off to a shaky start, and new kinds of development are required in the next era.

The second era, *early adulthood*, lasts from about age 17 to 45 and begins with the Early Adult Transition. It is the adult era of greatest energy and abundance and of greatest contradiction and stress. Biologically, the 20s and 30s are the peak years of the life cycle. In social and psychological terms, early adulthood is the season for forming and pursuing youthful aspirations, establishing a niche in society, raising a family, and as the era ends, reaching a more "senior" position in the adult world. This can be a time of rich satisfaction in terms of love, sexuality, family life, occupational advancement, creativity, and realization of major life goals. But there can also be crushing stresses. Most of us simultaneously undertake the burdens of parenthood and of forming an occupation. We incur heavy financial obligations when our earning power is still relatively low. We must make crucially important choices regarding marriage, family, work, and life-style before we have the maturity or life experience to choose wisely. Early adulthood is the era in which we are most buffeted by our own passions and ambitions from within and by the demands of family, community, and society from without. Under reasonably favorable conditions, the rewards of living in this era are enormous, but the costs often equal or even exceed the benefits.

The *Midlife Transition*, from roughly age 40 to 45, brings about the termination of early adulthood and the start of middle adulthood. The distinction between these two eras, and the concept of Midlife Transition as a developmental period that separates and connects them, are among the most controversial aspects of this schema. The research indicates, however, that the character of living always changes appreciably between early and middle adulthood (Holt, 1980; Gooden, 1980; Levinson, 1977, 1984, in press). Similar observations, based on different methods and evidence, are given in the work of Jung, Ortega, Erikson and others, noted earlier. The process of change begins in the Midlife Transition (though the forms and degree of change vary enormously) and continues throughout the era. One developmental task of this transition is to begin a new step in individuation. To the extent that this occurs, we can become more compassionate, more reflective and judicious, less tyrannized by inner conflicts and external demands, and more genuinely loving of ourselves and others. Without it, our lives become increasingly trivial or stagnant.

The third era, *middle adulthood*, lasts from about age 40 to 65. During this era our biological capacities are below those of early adulthood but are normally still sufficient for an energetic, personally satisfying and socially valuable life. Unless our lives are hampered in some special way, most of us during our 40s and 50s become "senior members" in our own particular worlds, however grand or modest they may be. We are responsible not only for our own work and perhaps the work of others, but also for the development of the current generation of young adults who will soon enter the dominant generation.

The next era, *late adulthood*, starts at about age 60. The *Late Adult Transition*, from 60 to 65, links middle and late adulthood and is part of both. I will not discuss late adulthood here. My speculations regarding this era (and a subsequent one, late late adulthood) are given in Levinson (1977).

The Life Structure and Its Development in Adulthood

My approach to adult development grows out of, and is shaped by, the foregoing views regarding the life course and the life cycle. I am primarily interested in apprehending the nature of a person's life at a particular time and the course of that life over the years. Personality attributes, social roles, and biological characteristics are aspects of a life; they should be regarded as aspects and placed within the context of the life.

The key concept to emerge from my research is the *life structure*: the underlying pattern or design of a person's life at a given time. It is the pillar of my conception of adult development. When I speak of periods in adult development, I am referring to periods in the evolution of the life structure. I will first introduce the concept of life structure and then describe my theory and findings about its evolution in adulthood.

The meaning of this term can be clarified by a comparison of life structure and personality structure. A theory of personality structure is a way of conceptualizing answers to a concrete question: "What kind of person am I?" Different theories offer numerous ways of thinking about this question and of characterizing oneself or others; for example, in terms of traits, skills, wishes, conflicts, defenses, or values.

A theory of life structure is a way of conceptualizing answers to a different question: "What is my life like now?" As we begin reflecting on this question, many others come to mind. What are the most important parts of my life, and how are they interrelated? Where do I invest most of my time and energy? Are there some relationships—to spouse, lover, family, occupation, religion, leisure, or whatever—that I would like to make more satisfying or meaningful? Are there some things not in my life that I would like to include? Are there interests and relationships, which now occupy a minor place, that I would like to make more central?

In pondering these questions, we begin to identify those aspects of the external world that have the greatest significance to us. We characterize our relationship with each of them and examine the interweaving of the various relationships. We find that our relationships are imperfectly integrated within a single pattern or structure.

The primary components of a life structure are the person's *relationships* with various others in the external world. The other may be a person, a group, institution or culture, or a particular object or place. A significant relationship involves an investment of self (desires, values, commitment, energy, skill), a reciprocal investment by the other person or entity, and one or more social contexts that contain the relationship, shaping it and becoming part of it. Every relationship shows both stability and change as it evolves over time, and it has different functions in the person's life as the life structure itself changes.

An individual may have significant relationships with many kinds of others. A significant other might be an actual person in the individual's current life. We need to study interpersonal relationships between friends, lovers, and spouses; between parents and their adult offspring at different ages; between bosses and subordinates, teachers and students, and mentors and protégés. A significant other might be a person from the past (e.g., Ezra Pound's vital relationship with the figure of Dante) or a symbolic or imagined figure from religion, myth, fiction, or private fantasy. The other might not be an individual but might be a collective entity such as a group, institution, or social movement; nature as a whole, or a part of nature such as the ocean, mountains, wildlife, whales in general, or Moby Dick in particular; or an object or place such as a farm, a city or country, "a room of one's own," or a book or painting.

The concept of life structure requires us to examine the nature and patterning of an adult's relationships with all significant others and the evolution of these relationships over the years. These relationships are the stuff our lives are made of. They give shape and substance to the life course. They are the vehicle by which we live out—or bury—various aspects of our selves and by which we participate, for better or worse, in the world around us. Students of the life course seek to determine the character of each relationship, its place within the person's evolving life, and the meaning of this life for the person and his or her world.

At any given time, a life structure may have many and diverse components. We found, however, that only one or two components—rarely as many as three—occupy a central place in the structure. Most often, marriage—family and occupation are the central components of a person's life, although wide variations occur in their relative weight and in the importance of other components. The central components are those that have the greatest significance for the self and the evolving life course. They receive the largest share of the individual's time and energy, and they strongly influence the character of the other components. The peripheral components are easier to change or detach; they involve less investment of self and can be modified with less effect on the fabric of the person's life.

In terms of open systems theory, life structure forms a boundary between personality structure and social structure and governs the transactions between them. A boundary structure is part of the two adjacent systems it connects, yet is partially separate or autonomous. It can be understood only if we see it as a link between them. The life structure mediates the relationship between the individual and the environment. It is in part the cause, the vehicle, and the effect of that relationship. The life structure grows out of the engagement of the self and the world. Its intrinsic ingredients are aspects of the self and aspects of the world, and its evolution is shaped by factors in the self and in the world. It requires us to think conjointly about the self and the world rather than making one primary and the other secondary or derivative. A theory of life structure must draw equally upon psychology and the social sciences.

Developmental Periods in Early and Middle Adulthood

In tracing the evolution of the life structure in the lives of men and women, I have found an invariant basic pattern (with infinite manifest variations): The life structure develops through a relatively orderly sequence of age-linked periods during the adult years. I want to emphasize that this is a finding, not an a priori hypothesis. It was as surprising to me as to others that the life structure should show such regularity in its adult development, given the absence of similar regularity in ego development, moral development, career development, and other specific aspects of the life.

The sequence consists of an alternating series of *structure-building* and *structure-changing* (transitional) periods. Our primary task in a structure-building period is to form a life structure and enhance our life within it: We must make certain key choices, form a structure around them, and pursue our values and goals within this structure. Even when we succeed in creating a structure, life is not necessarily tranquil. The task of building a structure is often stressful indeed, and we may discover that it is not as satisfactory as we had hoped. A structure-building period ordinarily lasts 5 to 7 years, 10 at the most. Then the life structure that has formed the basis for stability comes into question and must be modified.

A *transitional* period terminates the existing life structure and creates the possibility for a new one. The primary tasks of every transitional period are to reappraise the existing structure, to explore possibilities for change in the self and the world, and to move toward commitment to the crucial choices that form the basis for a new life structure in the ensuring period. Transitional periods ordinarily last about five years. Almost half our adult lives is spent in developmental transitions. No life structure is permanent—periodic change is given in the nature of our existence.

As a transition comes to an end, one starts making crucial choices, giving them meaning and commitment, and building a life structure around them. The choices are, in a sense, the major product of the transition. When all the efforts of the transition are done—the struggles to improve work or marriage, to explore alternative possibilities of living, to come more to terms with the self—choices must be made and bets must be placed. One must decide "This I will settle for," and start creating a life structure that will serve as a vehicle for the next step in the journey.

Within early and middle adulthood, the developmental periods unfold as follows (see Figure 37.1). We have found that each period begins and ends at a well-defined average age; there is a variation of plus or minus two years around the mean.

1. The *Early Adult Transition*, from age 17 to 22, is a developmental bridge between preadulthood and early adulthood.
2. The *Entry Life Structure for Early Adulthood* (22 to 28) is the time for building and maintaining an initial mode of adult living.
3. The *Age 30 Transition* (28 to 33) is an opportunity to reappraise and modify the entry structure and to create the basis for the next life structure.
4. The *Culminating Life Structure for Early Adulthood* (33 to 40) is the vehicle for completing this era and realizing our youthful aspirations.
5. The *Midlife Transition* (40 to 45) is another of the great cross-era shifts, serving both to terminate early adulthood and to initiate middle adulthood.

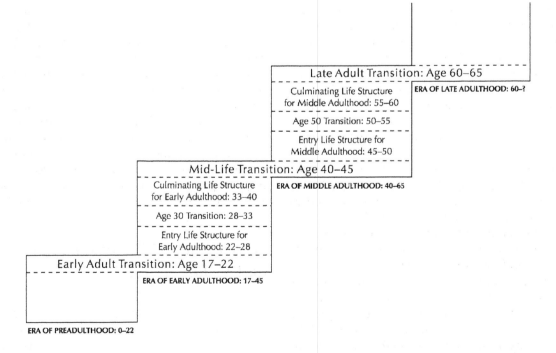

Note: From *The Seasons of a Man's Life* by D. J. Levinson with C. N. Darrow, E. B. Klein, M. H. Levinson, and B. McKee, 1978. New York: Alfred A. Knopf, Inc. Copyright 1978 by Daniel J. Levinson. Reprinted by permission of Alfred A. Knopf, Inc.

Figure 37.1   Developmental Periods in the Eras of Early and Middle Adulthood.

6. The *Entry Life Structure for Middle Adulthood* (45 to 50), like its counterpart above, provides an initial basis for life in a new era.
7. The *Age 50 Transition* (50 to 55) offers a mid-era opportunity for modifying and perhaps improving the entry life structure.
8. The *Culminating Life Structure for Middle Adulthood* (55 to 60) is the framework in which we conclude this era.
9. The *Late Adult Transition* (60 to 65) is a boundary period between middle and late adulthood, separating and linking the two eras.

The first three periods of early adulthood, from roughly 17 to 33, constitute its "novice phase." They provide an opportunity to move beyond adolescence, to build a provisional but necessarily flawed entry life structure, and to learn the limitations of that structure. The two final periods, from 33 to 45, form the "culminating phase," which brings to fruition the efforts of this era.

A similar sequence exists in middle adulthood. It, too, begins with a novice phase of three periods, from 40 to 55. The Midlife Transition is both an ending and a beginning. In our early 40s we are in the full maturity of early adulthood and are completing its final chapter; we are also in the infancy of middle adulthood, just beginning to learn about its promise and its dangers. We remain novices in every era until we have had a chance to try out an entry life structure and then to question and modify it in the mid-era transition. Only in the period of the Culminating Life Structure, and the cross-era transition that follows, do we reach the conclusion of that season and begin the shift to the next. During the novice phase we are, to varying degrees, both excited and terrified by the prospects for living in that era. To varying degrees, likewise, we experience the culminating phase as a time of rich satisfactions and of bitter disappointments, discovering as we so often do that the era ultimately gives us much more and much less than we have envisioned.

This sequence of eras and periods holds for men and women of different cultures, classes, and historical epochs. There are, of course, wide variations in the kinds of life structures people build, the developmental work they do in transitional periods, and the concrete sequence of social roles, events, and personality change. The theory thus provides a general framework of human development within which we can study the profound differences that often exist between classes, genders, and cultures.

References

Erikson, E. H. (1950). *Childhood and society*. New York: Norton.

Erikson, E. H. (1969). *Ghandi's truth*. New York: Norton.

Gooden, W. E. (1980). *The adult development of Black men*. Unpublished doctoral dissertation, Yale University, New Haven, CT.

Holt, J. (1980). *An adult development psychobiography of C. G. Jung*. Unpublished senior thesis, Yale University School of Medicine, New Haven, CT.

Jung, C. G., von Franz, M.-L., Henderson, J. L., Jacobi, J., & Jaffe, A. (1964). *Man and his symbols*. New York: Doubleday.

Levinson, D. J. (1977). The mid-life transition. *Psychiatry, 40*, 99–112.

Levinson, D. J. (1984). The career is in the life structure, the life structure is in the career: An adult development perspective. In M. B. Arthur, L. Bailyn, D. J. Levinson, & H. Shepard, *Working with careers* (pp. 49–74). Columbia University, School of Business.

Levinson, D. J. (in press). *The seasons of a woman's life*. New York: Knopf.

Levinson, D. J., & Gooden, W. E. (1985). The life cycle. In H. I. Kaplan & B. J. Sadock (Eds.), *Comprehensive textbook of psychiatry* (4th ed., pp. 1–13). Baltimore, MD: Williams and Williams.

Neugarten, B. L. (1968). Adult personality: Toward a psychology of the life cycle. In B. L. Neugarten (Ed.), *Middle age and aging: Reader in social psychology* (pp. 137–147). Chicago: University of Chicago Press.

Ortega y Gasset, J. (1958). *Man and crisis*. New York: Norton. (Original work published 1933).

van Gennep, A. (1960). *The rites of passage*. Chicago: University of Chicago Press. (Original work published 1908).

White, R. W. (1952). *Lives in progress*. New York: Holt, Rinehart & Winston.

Self-Actualizing People:
A Study of Psychological Health

Abraham H. Maslow

Abraham H. Maslow (1908–1970) was born in Brooklyn, New York, and studied at the City College of New York and the University of Wisconsin. Maslow spent the majority of his research and teaching career at Brandeis University in Waltham, Massachusetts. He was a leading exponent of the "humanistic" school of psychology, sometimes referred to as the "third forces" (Sigmund Freud's psychoanalysis and B. F. Skinner's behaviorism being the first and second "forces"). Maslow's writings include *Toward a Psychology of Being* (1962) and *Farther Reaches of Human Nature* (1971).

Humanistic psychology judges orthodox behaviorism and psychoanalysis to be too rigidly theoretical and overly concerned with mental illness instead of psychological health. From the humanistic perspective, Maslow developed a theory of motivation that describes the process by which an individual progresses from basic needs such as food and shelter, to social needs such as belongingness (love) and esteem, to the highest needs of what he called self-actualization, or the self-directed fulfillment of one's inner potential. Humanistic psychotherapy, usually in the form of group therapy, seeks to help the individual progress through these stages.

Of particular concern to the field of human development is Maslow's concept of self-actualization, what other humanistic psychologists, such as Carl Rogers, call "self-realization."

The following selection focuses upon Maslow's research and his description of self-actualized people. It is taken from chapter 11, "Self-Actualizing People: A Study of Psychological Health," of the third edition of his most frequently cited book, *Motivation and Personality* (Harper & Row, 1954).

Key Concept: self-actualization

The study to be reported in this [essay] is unusual in various ways. It was not planned as an ordinary research; it was not a social venture but a private one, motivated by my own curiosity and pointed toward the solution of various personal moral, ethical, and scientific problems. I sought only to convince and to teach myself rather than to prove or to demonstrate to others. . . .

Quite unexpectedly, however, these studies have proved to be so enlightening to me, and so laden with exciting implications, that it seems fair that some sort of report should be made to others in spite of its methodological shortcomings.

In addition, I consider the problem of psychological health to be so pressing that *any* suggestions, *any* bits of data, however moot, are endowed with great heuristic value. This kind of research is in principle so difficult—involving as it does a kind of lifting oneself by one's own

norms—that if we were to wait for conventionally reliable data, we should have to wait forever. It seems that the necessary thing to do is not to fear mistakes, to plunge in, to do the best that one can, hoping to learn enough from blunders to correct them eventually. At present the only alternative is simply to refuse to work with the problem. Accordingly, for whatever use can be make of it, the following report is presented with due apologies to those who insist on conventional reliability, validity, sampling, and the like.

The Study

Subjects and Methods

The subjects were selected from among personal acquaintances and friends, and from among public and historical figures. In addition, in a first research with young people, three thousand college students were screened, but yielded only one immediately usable subject and a dozen or two possible future subjects ("growing well").

I had to conclude that self-actualization of the sort I had found in my older subjects perhaps was not possible in our society for young, developing people.

Accordingly, in collaboration with E. Raskin and D. Freedman, a search was begun for a panel of *relatively* healthy college students. We arbitrarily decided to choose the healthiest 1 percent of the college population. This research, pursued over a two-year period as time permitted, had to be interrupted before completion, but it was, even so, very instructive at the clinical level.

It was also hoped that figures created by novelists or dramatists could be used for demonstration purposes, but none were found that were usable in our culture and our time (in itself a thought-provoking finding).

The first clinical definition, on the basis of which subjects were finally chosen or rejected, had a positive as well as a merely negative side. The negative criterion was an absence of neurosis, psychopathic personality, psychosis, or strong tendencies in these directions. Possibly psychosomatic illness called forth closer scrutiny and screening. Wherever possible, Rorschach tests were given, but turned out to be far more useful in revealing concealed psychopathology than in selecting healthy people. The positive criterion for selection was positive evidence of self-actualization (SA), as yet a difficult syndrome to describe accurately. For the purposes of this discussion, it may be loosely described as the full use and exploitation of talents, capacities, potentialities, and the like. Such people seem to be fulfilling themselves and to be doing the best that they are capable of doing, reminding us of Nietzsche's exhortation, "Become what thou art!" They are people who have developed or are developing to the full stature of which they are capable. These potentialities may be either idiosyncratic or species-wide.

This criterion implies also gratification, past or present, of the basic needs for safety, belongingness, love, respect, and self-respect, and of the cognitive needs for knowledge and for understanding, or in a few cases, conquest of these needs. This is to say that all subjects felt safe and unanxious, accepted, loved and loving, respect-worthy and respected, and that they had worked out their philosophical, religious, or axiological bearings. It is still an open question as to whether this basic gratification is a sufficient or only a prerequisite condition of self-actualization. . . .

The subjects have been divided into the following categories:

CASES: Seven fairly sure and two highly probably contemporaries (interviewed)

   Two fairly sure historical figures (Lincoln in his last years and Thomas Jefferson)

   Seven highly probably public and historical figures (Albert Einstein, Eleanor Roosevelt, Jane Addams, William James, Albert Schweitzer, Aldous Huxley, and Benedict de Spinoza)

PARTIAL CASES: Five contemporaries who fairly certainly fall short somewhat but who can yet be used for study

Collection and Presentation of Data

Data here consist not so much in the usual gathering of specific and discrete facts as in the slow development of a global or holistic impression of the sort that we form of our friends and acquaintances. It was rarely possible to set up a situation, to ask pointed questions, or to do any testing with my older subjects (although this *was* possible and was done with younger subjects). Contacts were fortuitous and of the ordinary social sort. Friends and relatives were questioned where this was possible.

Because of this and also because of the small number of subjects as well as the incompleteness of the data for many subjects, any quantitative presentation is impossible: only composite impressions can be offered for whatever they may be worth.

The Observations

Holistic analysis of the total impressions yields the following characteristics of self-actualizing people for further clinical and experimental study: perception of reality, acceptance, spontaneity, problem centering, solitude, autonomy, fresh appreciation, peak experiences, human kinship, humility and respect, interpersonal relationships, ethics, means and ends, humor, creativity, resistance to enculturation, imperfections, values, and resolution of dichotomies.

Perception of Reality

The first form in which this capacity was noticed was an unusual ability to detect the spurious, the fake, and the dishonest in personality, and in general to judge people correctly and efficiently. In an informal experiment with a group of college students, a clear tendency was discerned for the more secure (the more healthy) to judge their professors more accurately than did the less secure students, that is, high scorers in the S-I test (Maslow, 1952). . . .

Acceptance

A good many personal qualities that can be perceived on the surface and that seem at first to be various and unconnected may be understood as manifestations or derivatives of a more fundamental single attitude, namely, of a relative lack of overriding guilt, of crippling shame, and of extreme or severe anxiety. This is in direct contrast with the neurotic person who in every instance may be described as crippled by guilt and/or shame and/or anxiety. Even the normal member of our culture feels unnecessarily guilty or ashamed about too many things and has anxiety in too many unnecessary situations. Our healthy individuals find it possible to accept themselves and their own nature without chagrin or complaint or, for that matter, even without thinking about the matter very much. . . .

Spontaneity

Self-actualizing people can be described as relatively spontaneous in behavior and far more spontaneous than that in their inner life, thoughts, impulses, and so on. Their behavior is marked by simplicity and naturalness, and by lack of artificiality or straining for effect. This does not necessarily mean consistently unconventional behavior. If we were to take an actual count of the number of times that self-actualizing people behaved in an unconventional manner the tally would not be high. Their unconventionality is not superficial but essential or internal. It is their impulses, thought, and consciousness that are so unusually unconventional, spontaneous, and natural. Apparently recognizing that the world of people in which they live could not understand or accept this, and since they have no wish to hurt them or to fight with them over every triviality, they will go through the ceremonies and rituals of convention with a good-humored shrug and with the best possible grace. Thus I have seen a man accept an honor he laughed at and even despised in private, rather than make an issue of it and hurt the people who thought they were pleasing him. . . .

Problem Centering

Our subjects are in general strongly focused on problems outside themselves. In current terminology they are problem centered rather than ego centered. They generally are not problems for themselves and are not generally much concerned about themselves (e.g., as contrasted with the ordinary introspectiveness that one finds in insecure people). These individuals customarily have some mission in life, some task to fulfill, some problem outside themselves which enlists much of their energies (Bühler & Massarik, 1968; Frankl, 1969). . . .

Solitude

For all my subjects it is true that they can be solitary without harm to themselves and without discomfort. Furthermore, it is true for almost all that they positively *like* solitude and privacy to a definitely greater degree than the average person. . . .

Autonomy

One of the characteristics of self-actualizing people, which to a certain extent crosscuts much of what we have already described, is their relative independence of the physical and social environment. Since they are propelled by growth motivation rather than by deficiency motivation, self-actualizing people are not dependent for their main satisfactions on the real world, or other people or culture or means to ends or, in general, on extrinsic satisfactions. Rather they are dependent for their own development and continued growth on their own potentialities and latent resources. Just as the tree needs sunshine and water and food, so do most people need love, safety, and the other basic need gratifications that can come only from without. But once these external satisfiers are obtained, once these inner deficiencies are satiated by outside satisfiers, the true problem of individual human development begins, namely self-actualization. . . .

Fresh Appreciation

Self-actualizing people have the wonderful capacity to appreciate again and again, freshly and naively, the basic goods of life, with awe, pleasure, wonder, and even ecstasy, however stale these experiences may have become to others—what C. Wilson has called "newness" (1969). Thus, for such a person, any sunset may be as beautiful as the first one, any flower may be of breathtaking loveliness, even after a million flowers have been seen. The thousandth baby seen is just as miraculous a product as the first. A man remains as convinced of his luck in marriage 30 years after his marriage and is as surprised by his wife's beauty when she is 60 as he was 40 years before. For such people, even the casual workaday, moment-to-moment business of living can be thrilling, exciting, and ecstatic. These intense feelings do not come all the time; they come occasionally rather than usually, but at the most unexpected moments. The person may cross the river on the ferry ten times and at the eleventh crossing have a strong recurrence of the same feelings, reaction of beauty, and excitement as when riding the ferry for the first time (Eastman, 1928). . . .

Peak Experiences

Those subjective expressions that have been called the mystic experience and described so well by William James (1958) are a fairly common experience for our subjects, though not for all. The strong emotions described in the previous section sometimes get strong, chaotic, and widespread enough to be called mystic experiences. My interest and attention in this subject was first enlisted by several of my subjects who described their sexual orgasms in vaguely familiar terms, which later I remembered had been used by various writers to describe what *they* called the mystic experience. There were the same feelings of limitless horizons opening up to the vision, the feeling of being simultaneously more powerful and also more helpless than one ever was before, the feeling of great ecstasy and wonder and awe, the loss of placing in time and space with, finally, the conviction that something extremely important and valuable had happened, so that the subject is to some extent transformed and strengthened even in daily life by such experiences.

It is quite important to dissociate this experience from any theological or supernatural reference, even though for thousands of years they have been linked. Because this experience is a natural experience, well within the jurisdiction of science, I call it the peak experience. . . .

Human Kinship

Self-actualizing people have a deep feeling of identification, sympathy, and affection for human beings in general. They feel kinship and connection, as if all people were members of a single family. One's feelings toward siblings would be on the whole affectionate, even if they were foolish, weak, or even if they were sometimes nasty. They would still be more easily forgiven than strangers. Because of this, self-actualizing people have a genuine desire to help the human race. . . .

Humility and Respect

All my subjects without exception may be said to be democratic people in the deepest possible sense. I say this on the basis of a previous analysis of authoritarian (Maslow, 1943) and democratic character structures that is too elaborate to present here; it is possible only to describe some aspects of this behavior in short space. These people have all the obvious or superficial democratic characteristics. They can be and are friendly with anyone of suitable character regardless of class, education, political belief, race, or color. As a matter of fact it often seems as if they are not even aware of these differences, which are for the average person so obvious and so important. . . .

Interpersonal Relationships

Self-actualizing people have deeper and more profound interpersonal relations than any other adults (although not necessarily deeper than those of children). They are capable of more fusion, greater love, more perfect identification, more obliteration of the ego boundaries than other people would consider possible. There are, however, certain special characteristics of these relationships. In the first place, it is my observation that the other members of these relationships are likely to be healthier and closer to self-actualization than the average, often *much* closer. There is high selectiveness here, considering the small proportion of such people in the general population. . . .

Ethics

I have found none of my subjects to be chronically unsure about the difference between right and wrong in their actual living. Whether or not they could verbalize the matter, they rarely showed in their day-to-day living the chaos, the confusion, the inconsistency, or the conflict that are so common in the average person's ethical dealings. This may be phrased also in the following terms: these individuals are strongly ethical, they have definite moral standards, they do right and do not do wrong. Needless to say, their notions of right and wrong and of good and evil are often not the conventional ones. . . .

Humor

One very early finding that was quite easy to make, because it was common to all my subjects, was that their sense of humor is not of the ordinary type. They do not consider funny what the average person considers to be funny. Thus they do not laugh at hostile humor (making people laugh by hurting someone) or superiority humor (laughing at someone else's inferiority) or authority-rebellion humor (the unfunny, Oedipal, or smutty joke). Characteristically what they consider humor is more closely allied to philosophy than to anything else. It may also be called the humor of the real because it consists in large part in poking fun at human beings in general when they are foolish, or forget their place in the universe, or try to be big when they are actually small. This can take the form of poking fun at themselves, but this is not done in any masochistic or clownlike way. Lincoln's humor can serve as a suitable example. Probably Lincoln never made a joke that hurt anybody else; it is also likely that many or even most of his jokes had something to say, had a function beyond just producing a laugh. They often seemed to be education in a more palatable form, akin to parables or fables. . . .

Creativity

This is a universal characteristic of all the people studied or observed. . . . There is no exception. Each one shows in one way or another a special kind of creativeness or originality or inventiveness that has certain peculiar characteristics. . . . For one thing, it is different from the special-talent creativeness of the Mozart type. We may as well face the fact that the so-called geniuses display ability that we do not understand. All we can say of them is that they seem to be specially endowed with a drive and a capacity that may have rather little relationship to the rest of the personality and with which, from all evidence, the individuals seem to be born. Such talent we have no concern with here since it does not rest upon psychic health or basic satisfaction. The creativeness of the self-actualized person seems rather to be kin to the naive and universal creativeness of unspoiled children. It seems to be more a fundamental characteristic of common human nature—a potentiality given to all human beings at birth. Most human beings lose this as they become enculturated, but some few individuals seem either to retain this fresh and naive, direct way of looking at life, or if they have lost it, as most people do, they later in life recover it. Santayana called this the "second naiveté," a very good name for it. . . .

Imperfections

The ordinary mistake that is made by novelists, poets, and essayists about good human beings is to make them so good that they are caricatures, so that nobody would like to be like them. The individual's own wishes for perfection and guilt and shame about shortcomings are projected upon various kinds of people from whom average people demand much more than they themselves give. Thus teachers and ministers are sometimes conceived to be rather joyless people who have no mundane desires and who have no weaknesses. It is my belief that most of the novelists who have attempted to portray good (healthy) people did this sort of thing, making them into stuffed shirts or marionettes or unreal projections of unreal ideals, rather than into the robust, hearty, lusty individuals they really are. Our subjects show many of the lesser human ailings. They too are equipped with silly, wasteful, or thoughtless habits. They can be boring, stubborn, irritating. They are by no means free from a rather superficial vanity, pride, partiality to their own productions, family, friends, and children. Temper outbursts are not rare.

Our subjects are occasionally capable of an extraordinary and unexpected ruthlessness. It must be remembered that they are very strong people. This makes it possible for them to display a surgical coldness when this is called for, beyond the power of average people.

The man who found that a long-trusted acquaintance was dishonest cut himself off from this friendship sharply and abruptly and without any observable pangs whatsoever. A woman who was married to someone she did not love, when she decided on divorce, did it with such decisiveness that looked almost like ruthlessness. Some of them recover so quickly from the death of people close to them as to seem heartless. . . .

Values

A firm foundation for a value system is automatically furnished to self-actualizers by their philosophic acceptance of the nature of self, of human nature, of much of social life, and of nature and physical reality. These acceptance values account for a high percentage of the total of their individual value judgments from day to day. What they approve of, disapprove of, are loyal to, oppose or propose, what pleases them or displeases them can often be understood as surface derivations of this source trait of acceptance.

Adult Life Stages: Growth Toward Self-Tolerance

Roger Gould

Roger Gould earned his undergraduate degree at the University of Wisconsin and his M.D. at Northwestern University. He later joined the University of California, Los Angeles, as assistant director of the UCLA Psychiatric Outpatient Department. His clients ranged in age from the late teens to late adulthood. Gould's first study in human development was based on his insight that his patients' major concerns all seemed age related: teens were concerned with parents; patients in their 20s were concerned with vocational choice or their new roles as spouses or parents, or their lack of these roles; those in their 30s complained of feeling stuck and stagnant, and the questions of their 20s seemed vague and unclear; most of those in their late 30s and mid-40s felt intensely discontented and had a sense of urgency to figure out what their lives had meant so far and what they could still be.

Following his insight, Gould designed a research study to systematically examine the life concerns and challenges of his patients. He recruited several coresearchers who helped him interview the outpatient clients by age group for six months. This research revealed distinct patterns of human development. Gould then wondered if he would discover similar findings in "nonpatients." He therefore launched a major study, conducted over several years that included 524 white, middle-class people, ranging in age from 16 to 50. The results of this study are included in the following selection, which was taken from "Adult Life Stages: Growth Toward Self-Tolerance," *Psychology Today* (February 1975). A more expansive explanation of this study was published by Gould and his associates in a 1977 book entitled *Transformations*.

Key Concept: adult life stages

The evolution of a personality continues through the fifth decade of life. A person does not possess the full range of his uniqueness after merely passing through adolescence, which is the last stage of mental development that many psychologists officially recognize. The process of formation continues through stages of life that we are just beginning to recognize. I began the research reported here to take a new look at the complex process of change in adulthood.

Although a 20-year-old may feel fully formed and mentally well-equipped to cope with life, that same person at 40 will ask how he managed to get through the last 20 years.

Many a man in his 40s wishes he had not been so blinded by his ambition in his 20s. His need to prove himself deprived him of irreplaceable experiences with his wife and children. "If I had only known then what I know now about what is important in living. It takes such a long time to find out what it is all about."

Many a woman in her 40s wonders why she was so foolish in her 20s. She lived up to the rules of householding and child rearing that were in vogue then, but sees them as unimportant now. "I was young then. I did what the doctor told me. I didn't pick the baby up when he was crying even though I knew I should. If only I had followed my own judgment."

Throughout the years of adulthood, there is an ever-increasing need to win permission from oneself to continue developing, through a process I will touch on later in this article. The direction of change is toward becoming more tolerant of oneself, and more appreciative of the complexity of both the surrounding world and of the mental milieu but there are many things that can block, slow down, or divert that process.

Each role in life can lead to two opposite results in the change process. A role can be an opportunity to come to a more comprehensive understanding of oneself in action or a role can become a simplified definition of the self that does not do justice to the whole complex human being. In that sense, a role that may be vitalizing at one period of life can become justifying at another.

We are many years away from having the experience and the studies necessary for an in-depth understanding of the adult period comparable to our current understanding of childhood and adolescence, and my formulations at this point are at best tentative. A number of other researchers are looking at various aspects of adult growth, and all of these studies are adding to our previously impoverished fund of knowledge about the subject.

Escape from Dominance

My colleagues and I began our search for adult life phases by observing and recording patients in group therapy at the UCLA psychiatric outpatient clinic. There were seven age-graded groups, with ranges of 16 to 18, 18 to 22, 22 to 28, 29 to 34, 35 to 43 and 50 and over. Our descriptions were not psychologically elegant. We sought a level of psychological description that would be intelligible to a layman. Most of the observations were both consistent among observers and congruent with common sense, which encouraged us.

We found, for example, that the youngest age group was at a period when escape from parental dominance was the predominant theme of their discussions. This concealed the feelings of dependence and anxiety that resulted from preparing to leave the sanctuary of the family. The future was both distant and unknown to these people. The next age group, those between 18 and 22 years, substituted friends for family, and thus continued to grow independent of their family.

The 22- to 28-year-olds definitely felt that they were the now generation. Now was the time to live, and now was the time to build for the future, both professionally and personally. These people concentrate their energies and will power on becoming competent in the real world, and as they develop self-reliance they make less use of their friends as a substitute for the family.

This assurance about what to do wavered somewhat among the 29- to 34-year-olds, who often were questioning what they were doing and why they were doing it. As they became more self-reflective, this group found deeper strivings that had been put aside during their 20s when building a workable life structure had been the most important task.

The continuing expansion of the personality and life structure continued in a leisurely fashion in the early 30s, but changed to quiet urgency in the 35-to-43 set. Time, once shrugged off as infinite, was now visibly finite and the view was often worrisome.

People between the ages of 43 and 50 had come to terms with time, and with themselves as stable personalities. What is done is done; the die is cast. Children previously cherished as extensions of oneself are now to be respected as individuals as they become young adults.

The circle closes, as the adult raises a child who again becomes an adult.

Death: A New Presence

By 50, there is a mellowing of feelings and relationships. Children are a satisfaction, and parents are no longer the cause of one's personality problems. People of this age seemed to focus on what they have accomplished in half a century, and they were unrushed by the sense of urgency that accompanied the achieving 30s. At the same time, they were more eager to have "human" experiences, such as sharing the joys, sorrows, confusions and triumphs of everyday life rather than searching for the glamor, the glitter, the power or the abstract. Precious moments of contact and deep feeling define the value of being in touch. Death becomes a new presence for this age group.

With these general descriptions in mind, I devised a questionnaire to find the more exact periods during which people underwent a transition, and the nature of the things that concerned them the most. The original age categories were somewhat arbitrary, and the original subjects were those receiving psychiatric care. I wanted to see what age groupings would be distinguishable in the responses to the questionnaire, and whether the generalized sentiments found among the patients would be sustained by specific findings on a small sample of the nonpatient population.

I asked eight medical students to listen to tape recordings of the original patient discussions, and to list the statements about personal feelings that they felt stood out. I then grouped these statements into eight sections, covering relationships to parents, friends, children and spouses, and feelings about their own personality, job, time, and sexual behavior.

Each section had 16 questions. People ranked the questions from most to least applicable to their lives. There were no right or wrong answers, only changes in the importance of particular statements to people of various ages. Questions rose and fell in rank like the tide on a beach, providing a sensitive measure of the times of transition—and the tribulations.

The 524 white, middle-class people who filled out questionnaires had seven distinguishable phases: 16 to 17, 18 to 21, 22 to 28, 29 to 36, 37 to 43, 44 to 50 and 51 to 60. There were approximately 20 people (divided equally by sex) for each year between 16 and 33, and 20 for each three years between 33 and 60, with women disproportionately represented over age 45.

For most questions, the rankings stabilized between the ages of 22 and 29, and remained steady throughout life. Certain questions, however, brought distinctly different responses from adjacent age groups, and it was these questions that defined the phases of adult life.

The responses of the 16- and 17-year-olds were almost identical to the stable patterns of those 22 to 29. The young people are still a part of their families, and they think of themselves more as family members than as individuals. In contrast, the 18- to 22-year-olds responded in a pattern quite distinguishable from that of the age set on either side of them.

As other studies previously showed, people in this age group have a unique psychology and subculture. They are more open to new ideas about the world, and are less repressive. When they get back to the mainstream of adult life in the 20s, they give the same pattern of popular responses that characterize the remainder of the population.

The Spring to the 40s

The late 20s are an interesting and active time. Marriage absorbs and reflects many of the stresses and strains, and the statement, "I wish my mate would accept me for what I am as a person" takes a sharp upward excursion between the ages of 28 and 32, while there is decreasing agreement that "For me, marriage has been a good thing." Children, on the other hand, become increasingly important during this time, displacing parents in priority as the person's focus shifts from the generation behind to the one ahead.

There is a clear focus on the family in the 30s. An active social life seems less important, while feelings about one's mate and offspring increase in significance. The 30s are a period of very active psychological change, a gathering of mental muscles with which to spring into the 40s. After age 29, there is a decline in the feeling that "I would be quite content to remain as old as I am now," a harbinger of the feeling in the early 30s that life looks a bit more complex and difficult than it did back in the roaring 20s.

In the early 30s, there is suddenly a feeling that "I don't make enough money to do what I want." Although this statement is undoubtedly true for almost everyone, the significance here is signaled by a sharp increase in the relative importance of this feeling to those in their early 30s. There is also an increasing tendency to feel that parents are the cause of many unsolved, stubborn personality problems that are being faced at this age.

The 40s seem to begin in the late 30s, and I distinguish a series of shared sentiments spanning the ages 37 to 43. In this age period, personal comfort decreases, and marital comfort remains at a low level. Between 40 and 43, there are several temporary departures from previous levels on statements dealing with personal comfort, suggesting that the 40s are an unstable and uncomfortable time. Later in the 40s both friends and loved ones become increasingly important. Children continue to be very important, and there is a sharp rise in regrets for "my mistakes in raising my children."

Money, so bothersome because of its insufficiency in the early 30s, becomes less important, and there is an accompanying feeling that it is "Too late to make any major change in my career." Coupled to the first downward shift in the feeling that "There's still plenty of time to do most of the things I want to do," these responses show a 40s phase of reconciliation of what is with what might have been.

The sharp sense that "My personality is pretty well set" in the 41- to 43-year-old group establishes a dramatic beginning to the 44 to 50 period. In the span from 44 to 50, life settles down. With a slight sigh, there is an acceptance of the new ordering of things. Life is even. Not even better, not even worse, but simply even up.

Stability fraught with concern marks the 50s, and the concern is largely about time. With one's allotment of life more than half used up, people respond with increasing pessimism to the statement that "There's sill plenty of time to do most of the things I want to do," and with increasing agreement that "I try to be satisfied with what I have and not to think so much about the things I probably won't be able to get." Concerns about health rise, and there is increasing agreement that "I can't do things as well as I used to do."

The Adult Butterfly

It is important to realize that the above descriptions are generalizations, reflecting the average of considerable personal variation. While I believe the sequence to be true for the majority of people, the precise ages at which changes occur are a product of an individual's total personality, lifestyle and subculture. How these changes are expressed and dealt with varies considerably from person to person; it's what you face, not how you face it, that is the common denominator.

The prevailing concepts of adulthood have obscured not only what is being faced, but also the fact that an adult needs to engage in any kind of continuing growth process at all. Like a butterfly, an adult is supposed to emerge fully formed and on cue, after a succession of developmental stages in childhood. Equipped with all the accouterments, such as wisdom and rationality, the adult supposedly remains quiescent for another half century or so. While children change, adults only age. My research demonstrates a need to overhaul our current view of adulthood, and to recognize that there is a developmental sequence in the early and middle-adult years.

Many researchers have previously pointed out isolated times of change in adult life, such as parenthood or the mid-life crisis. While helpful, none of these studies identifies the progression of phases that might link such changes together.

Yet I feel that there is such a progression. Childhood delivers most people into adulthood with a view of adults that few could ever live up to. A child's idealized image of an adult can become the adult's painful measure of himself. Without an active, thoughtful confrontation of this image, the impressions of childhood will prevail. An adult who doesn't undertake this thinking and confrontation lives out his or her life controlled by the impossible attempt to satisfy the magical expectations of a child's world.

Thoughtful Confrontation

The process of change means coming to new beliefs about oneself and the world. Habitually unorganized beliefs are more felt than thought, yet these beliefs must be thought about before they can be modified by experiences.

Many people hold themselves accountable for being perfect even when they have decided that the limiting conditions of a particular situation made the "perfect" act inappropriate, unwise, unnecessary or impossible. On one hand they believe that the decision that shaped their action was correct, but on the other hand they continue to feel (and on some level believe) that something is wrong with them for not having acted at some arbitrary level of perfection.

The belief that is felt—I should have done the impossible—is often not raised to a high enough level of consciousness to be thought about. The incomplete and inexact form of the thought is usually substituted, "Somehow I should have been able to do it better" and is left dangling, unexamined, and therefore unmodified.

The proper next step in a thoughtful confrontation would be, "I have always felt I should do things perfectly regardless of the circumstances; but this time I *decided* to do things differently for this and this reason." In that statement the conflict between the past and present beliefs are joined and resolution becomes possible between two *operative* and contending beliefs of the self. Neither of these operative beliefs represents mere intellectualized conclusions that are also called beliefs. They are valid and valuable parts of the self that have to be reconciled before a new value can be created that is reflective of the adult experience.

The process of confrontation involves thinking honestly about what one really feels. Modern psychologies have not been of much help in delineating the persistently obscure relationship between feelings and thinking. There has been a tendency to see feeling and thinking as two unconnected realms, yet my observations as a psychoanalyst are that thinking can and does modify feelings. I believe that it is through the constant examination and reformulation of beliefs embedded in feelings that people substitute their own conception of adulthood for their childhood legacy.

This process of thinking through is a cumulative one, and it should really come as no surprise that there are certain similarities in what people experience and when they experience it. The passing of time sets the stage for several interacting processes that combine to produce the adult life phases I suggest. In addition to substituting an alternate reality for the childhood view, increasing age also brings changes in biological functioning, changes in the ages of one's parents and children, and changes in the cultural expectations about what a person should be doing.

My colleagues and I found that, in addition to the individualized process of changing childhood feelings about adulthood, there were enough experiences common to all adults to make it possible to find similarities in the way these people felt at different ages.

While children mark the passing years by their changing bodies, adults change their minds. Passing years and passing events slowly accumulate, like a viscous wave, eventually releasing their energy and assuming new forms in altered relationships with both time and people. By recognizing the patterns, we may gain some control over the forces by smoothing the transitions and muting the peaks and valleys of adult life phases.

Christian Maturity Through Ignatian Spirituality

William A. Barry, S. J.

The article that is included below is based on the classic developmental work of Ignatius of Loyola, who was born in 1491, the youngest son in a noble Basque family. Destined for the clergy, he nonetheless became a courtier at one of the princely houses in Spain and a soldier. Severely wounded in battle, he had a conversion experience while recuperating at the Loyola castle. As a result he decided to pursue a life in imitation of Christ and the saints. A nine month stay in the small town of Manresa, Spain, led him through a series of religious experiences that culminated in his writing *The Spiritual Exercises*. This book is one of the most influential texts on human development of the past 450 years and has guided the religious, spiritual, and psychological development of many millions of people. Ignatius of Loyola eventually became the founder of the Society of Jesus, the Jesuits, a religious congregation in the Roman Catholic Church. He died in 1556 and was canonized as a saint in 1622.

The author or coauthor of 18 books, William A. Barry, S. J. has been a Jesuit for 56 years and a priest for 44. He earned a doctorate in clinical psychology from the University of Michigan in 1968. He has taught at Weston Jesuit School of Theology, the University of Michigan and Boston College. From 1988–1991 he was rector of the Jesuit Community at Boston College and on the Board of Trustees. At present he is codirector of a nine-month program for Jesuit priests and brothers prior to their final vows and gives retreats and spiritual direction at Campion Renewal Center, Weston, MA. He is also Editor-in-Chief of the quarterly *Human Development*, and we include below his article, "Christian Maturity Through Ignatian Spirituality," taken from that journal. This article gives some context to the developmental journey explicated by Ignatius of Loyola, and connects it to the psychosocial stages described by Erik Erikson.

Keyword: Christian spiritual development

Some of the articles in this issue of HUMAN DEVELOPMENT concern formation. Perhaps because of my training as a clinical psychologist I think in terms of personal and interpersonal development as part of the formation of a person toward Christian maturity. As a result, I have come to believe that the process of making the full Ignatian *Spiritual Exercises* can be likened to the development of a friendship, in this case, a friendship with God, and in particular with the Son of God.

It is intriguing to explore the idea that God creates us human beings for friendship. Liz Carmichael, an Anglican priest and a medical doctor, has written a scholarly study of the notion of friendship with God through the history of Christianity. The book, *Friendship: Interpreting Christian Love,* shows how the idea of friendship with God has had periods of brilliant illumination in this history followed by long periods of a seeming loss of memory of the idea. It seems that the idea of friendship with God both

intrigues us and worries us. But some very solid theologians have held the thesis that we are created for friendship with God, including Aelred of Rivaulx and Thomas Aquinas. I have found the idea stimulating and challenging both in my own prayer life and in my thinking. I have used it in my work as a director of the *Spiritual Exercises* and in helping others to become directors. So far, God has not indicated that I am mistaken on this one.

We begin with a description of the development of any friendship. There are some clear steps and stages in the developing of a deep friendship. First, there needs to be an initial attraction. Without some initial attraction we will not take the time and expend the energy to become a friend of another. When something about the other attracts or intrigues us, we do something to initiate contact. You walk over to the person and introduce yourself, for example, or you ask to be introduced. At first, the conversation will be somewhat superficial. You exchange names and some data about yourselves. If the relationship is to develop into a friendship, the two of you will begin to talk about more important things in your lives. For example, you want to know not only how many brothers and sisters the other has, but also which ones she liked and which ones she found more difficult to like, not only what type of work she does, but also how she likes it and what she gets from it.

A Matter of the Heart

Friendship is a matter of the heart, of revealing what is in one's heart to the other in mutuality. It is a gradual process as each of you feels your way in this new relationship. Of course, eventually you both want to know how the other feels about you, another risk in transparency. If all goes well, there follows something like a honeymoon period when both of you delight in one another's company and want to spend as much time together as possible.

This idyllic period is disrupted when negative feelings arise. One of you becomes angry at the other; or one of you wonders if the other would still want to be a friend if she knew some secret that is shameful. The temptation is to keep this disturbing aspect secret. The trouble with such disturbing thoughts and emotions, however, is that one cannot leave them behind and get on with the relationship as though they never occurred. They are like magnets that attract other emotions and thoughts to them so that eventually you talk only about superficial things because the unspoken emotion or thought cannot be mentioned. The only way forward in the friendship is to take the risk of speaking about these disturbances with one another. The risk is that the budding friendship will be destroyed; the gain, however, is that a friendship can actually bloom. This stage can be likened to psychologist Erik Erikson's stage of intimacy where people grow in their ability to love and be loved as adults.

Eventually the two friends may have so solidified their friendship that they begin to think of doing something together. One outcome for a man and a woman would be to decide to get married and have a family. But friends can also engage in other projects together. At this stage their friendship focuses less on themselves and more on the larger world; they are at what Erikson calls the generative stage of development. Their conversations and self-revelations often are about the project or the family rather than about their relationship itself, though that is never forgotten.

Sharing Painful Times

Any friendship that lasts a long time faces the pain of sickness and the death of one of the friends. When serious illness strikes, the friendship faces a new crisis; will the two be able to continue to share deeply during this painful and anxiety-provoking time? Even the closest of friends find it difficult to confront pain and debilitating illness; in addition, each may want to spare the other from knowing how difficult it is either to have the illness or to watch it in the other. If they do not share their pain and suffering, they may find themselves growing distant from one another, leading to even more pain and loneliness. Again, growth in the friendship can only come through mutual self-revelation, and at this time the mutual self-revelation can be painful indeed. But it can also be a time of recalling the good times and of thanking one another and God for the blessings of the friendship. In spite of the present pain it is much better "to have loved and lost than never to have loved at all." This final growth in the relationship can lead to something like the wisdom Erikson posits as the final stage, a wisdom whose opposite is despair.

Now let's see if this analogy works as a descriptor for the progression one can experience in friendship with God through the experience of making the full *Spiritual Exercises.* Ignatius begins the process with a reflection on "The Principle and Foundation," a rather dry and almost catechism-like paragraph.

> Human beings are created to praise, reverence, and serve God our Lord, and by means of doing this to save their souls.
>
> The other things on the face of the earth are created for the human beings, to help them in the pursuit of the end for which they are created.
>
> From this it follows that we ought to use these things to the extent that they help us toward our end, and free ourselves from them to the extent that they hinder us from it.
>
> To attain this it is necessary to make ourselves indifferent to all created things, in regard to everything which is left to our free will and is not forbidden. Consequently, on our own part we ought not to seek health rather than sickness, wealth rather than poverty, honor rather than dishonor, a long life rather than a short one, and so on in all other matters.
>
> Rather, we ought to desire and choose only that which is more conducive to the end for which we are created (*Spiritual Exercises,* n. 23).

One can reflect on these words and come to the realization that they are true, but I do not think that they have their desired effect without an experience of God, an experience that makes God supremely attractive. I believe that this abstract statement is based on Ignatius' experience of God as the mysterious Other who creates us out of overwhelming and generous love and continues to sustain us at every moment of our lives. Ignatius believed that all human beings have experiences of God's creative and sustaining love and that if we pay attention to these experiences we will find that during them we desire God with all our heart and, at the same time, feel an enormous sense of well-being. Caught up in this experience we do feel that everything and everyone beside the object of this desire pales in comparison; we want this Mystery more than we want anything or anyone else. We become, for the moment at least, "indifferent" in the sense Ignatius means the word; we would not want to choose anything that would take us away from the object of this desire for "we know not what" the Mystery we call God. A long life or a short life, sickness or health, riches or poverty, these are all relative in comparison to the Mystery we desire.

Closer Relationship with God

I believe that this experience of being created out of love and for love underlies the abstract words of the Principle and Foundation. If we pay attention to experiences such as these, we recognize that we are being drawn into a closer relationship with God, to friendship. When we relish such experiences, we desire to be with God, and we engage in something like a "honeymoon" period in our relationship with God. These experiences reflected on and savored provide the firm foundation upon which we and God can build a deepening friendship.

However, there are many people who find it difficult to believe in such experiences of God as caring and loving. Poor and abusive parenting leaves some people with an image of father or mother as someone to be feared; this image is easily transferred to God. For others, teaching about God in childhood leaves them with an image of God who is terrifying and threatening. For some reason, one of the men who became one of the first Jesuits, Pierre Favre (Peter Faber), had a terrible image of God when he met Ignatius when both were students in Paris. Ignatius worked with him for four years before he would allow him to make the *Exercises*. I presume that Ignatius was helping him to trust in experiences of God as caring and loving, whose plans are for our good, not to try us and find us wanting. Eventually, through what we might call pastoral counseling or spiritual direction, Pierre was ready to enter the *Exercises*. He had the foundation of an experienced-based trust in God's desire for his good and his friendship that enabled him to engage with God in the *Spiritual Exercises*. I have worked with such scrupulous people to help them to such an experienced-based trust in God. It is difficult work, but rewarding when through experience a new image of God begins to take hold. The process that a person engages when making the *Spiritual Exercises* requires a deep trust in God's love and care. One needs to have an experience of God creating us because of a desire for closeness and friendship with us.

(An aside: in the *Spiritual Exercises* Ignatius gives a number of suggestions for prayer. One of them advises the retreatant, just before beginning a prayer period, to "raise my mind and think how God our Lord is looking at me, and other such thoughts" (*Spiritual Exercises* n. 75). Ignatius presumes that God is always interested in us, always aware of us. Recently, when I used this long-forgotten advice, I found myself awed by the thought that God was waiting for me to be aware of God. In other words, God always wants us and our friendship.)

Realizing We Have Fallen Short

After some time of enjoyment of this "honeymoon" period we become aware that something is amiss. We know that we are all created for friendship with God and that God wants a world in which human beings share in this friendship and live harmoniously with God, one another and with the environment. But the world is not like this, and we realize that the world and we have fallen short of what God wants. A disturbance is introduced into the relationship with God. In the story of the Garden of Eden in the Book of Genesis the garden itself and the fact that the humans are naked and unashamed before God and one another depicts the way things were created to be. The disturbance I am speaking about is depicted after the first human beings have eaten the forbidden fruit in an effort to become like God. They become afraid, clothe themselves and go into hiding from God. They feel ashamed and unworthy of God's friendship and expect punishment. In the *Spiritual Exercises* the retreatant who begins to feel this way is embarking on what Ignatius calls the "First Week," a period of facing up to one's sins and failures and the sins and failures of our human world. The question faced is a stark one: "Does God still want my friendship after all that I have done? Does God still love our human world given the mess we humans have made of it?"

Moreover, because I cannot see my own sinfulness, I have to ask God to reveal my sins to me, to reveal how God sees me and the world. To ask God for such revelation is impossible unless one has had an experience of God as caring and loving; hence, the need of the "principle and foundation" experience. Even with that experience in hand, people find it difficult to ask God for such a revelation. But when they do ask, they find that the revelation is for their good, that God wants to forgive them and still wants their friendship. In the *Exercises* Ignatius advises the retreatant who has a felt knowledge of sin to have a conversation with Jesus on the cross, and adds: "A colloquy (conversation) is made, properly speaking, in the way one friend speaks to another, or a servant to one in authority—now begging a favor, now accusing oneself of some misdeed, now telling one's concerns and asking counsel about them:" Notice the first analogy, "friend to friend" Those who can look Jesus in the eyes and find in them love and forgiveness feel a great sense of relief. People who ask God to show them their sins and the sinfulness of the world discover, to their delight, that, along with the shame and tears they experience for the way they have lived, they are freed of a tremendous burden. With a great sigh of relief they realize that God still loves them and the world, still wants their friendship. They have traversed the stage of intimacy and the difficulties of realizing how far they and the world have fallen short of what God wants and still feel loved and welcomed by God.

Desiring to Know Jesus More Intimately

For those who are making the full *Spiritual Exercises* the next step comes with the welling up of the desire to know Jesus more intimately in order to love him more and to follow him more closely. They want Jesus to reveal himself, what makes him tick, what he loves and hates, what he dreams, and thus to fall in love with him and work with him. They enter the stage of generativity, if you will. They now want to walk the road of life with Jesus as their friend and companion. This stage, too, has its ups and downs as it becomes clearer what being a companion of Jesus will entail. After all, if we become his companions, we are liable to meet the same obstacles and enmity he met and suffer the same fate.

Persevering in Friendship with Jesus

The director of the *Exercises* helps the retreatant deal with the attraction and the repulsion of being a companion of Jesus. Those who persevere in this growing friendship with Jesus find themselves becoming freer of the attachments that hinder them from following the way of Jesus, of joining him in pursuing God's project in this world. They deepen their friendship with Jesus and want to be with him, no matter the consequences. Those who come this far in friendship with Jesus have that emotional maturity Freud spoke of; they have the ability to love and to work.

Retreatants who walk with Jesus to Jerusalem find themselves wanting, and perhaps dreading, to share with him his passion and death. They are ready to enter what Ignatius calls the "Third Week" of the *Spiritual Exercises*. Again they are asking Jesus to reveal himself to them, but this time it is the hard revelation of what it was like for him to go through this terrible week trusting in his Father when he had no one else in whom to trust.

Retreatants will find this period of the *Exercises* difficult. It is painful to see Jesus, who has now become a close friend, go through this agony, abandoned by his friends, betrayed by one of them, accused of leading the people astray by the leaders of his own religion, flogged, beaten and hung naked on a Roman cross to die a horrible death. Those who contemplate these scenes often find themselves resisting the revelation they desire. They may focus on all the other characters in the scenes rather than on Jesus; they may find themselves angry with God for allowing this horror. If they continue to ask Jesus to reveal himself, they will find themselves drawn into a deeper love for him and a deeper sympathy. One woman whom I directed wept with relief when Jesus finally died. In this week it becomes most clear that consolation does not necessarily mean feeling joyful and happy because here the consolation we ask for brings a heavy load. But as with two friends who share the pain of illness and dying, it is consoling to share Jesus' pain and suffering and loneliness.

The Joy of the Resurrection

Moreover, it is the only real way to experience the joy of the resurrection. The risen Jesus tells the two disciples on the road to Emmaus: "Was it not necessary that the Messiah should suffer these things and then enter into his glory?" (Lk 24: 26). I take this necessity not as an eternal decree of God making it necessary, but as a statement that to be the Messiah he now is, he had to go through this suffering. He still has the wounds even in glory; the horror is not undone by the resurrection. Rather, with the resurrection we find that the crucifixion and death are not the last word. God, in Jesus, received the worst we humans could devise. This worst is the victory of God. And God has not retaliated against us by annihilating us. God is forgiving love, and even the worst we can do will not deter God from the desire to embrace us in friendship. The joy of the resurrection is the joy that Jesus is alive and well, that God has raised him bodily from the dead, and that his resurrection will be ours. Those who are given the grace to share in Jesus' joy through contemplation of the scenes of his resurrection can never despair, no matter what happens in their lives because they know in their bones that Jesus is risen and that they too are one with him. They have reached a high degree of spiritual and emotional maturity indeed.

The *Spiritual Exercises* end with the "Contemplation to Attain Love," a fitting climax to this progressive growth into a deep friendship with God. In this contemplation Ignatius makes two preliminary observations that underline the point I have been making throughout this article.

> First. Love ought to manifest itself more by deeds than by words.
>
> Second. Love consists in a mutual communication between the two persons. That is, the one who loves gives and communicates to the beloved what he or she has, or part of what one has or can have; and the beloved in return does the same to the lover. Thus, if the one has knowledge, one gives it to the other who does not; and similarly in regard to honors or riches. Each shares with the other (*S.E., n. 230–231*).

As will become clear, Ignatius is using the analogy of friends to speak of the relationship with God. It is extraordinary, when you think about it, to think that God wants our gifts just as much as we want God's gifts. God has created us for such mutuality. "Each shares with the other." In this contemplation, then, Ignatius proposes some points so that we can experience God's prolific generosity and realize that God wants our generosity, not as a demand, but as a token of friendship. In the points Ignatius asks us to ponder them, but, in reality, he hopes that we will "contemplate," that is, see, touch and sense what God is doing in the creation that is ongoing. The purpose of such contemplation is to draw out of us a corresponding love for God, a desire to give God all that we are, just as God has given us all that God is.

In the first of the four points retreatants are encouraged to remember all the gifts they have received. "I will ponder with deep affection how much God our Lord has done for me, and how much he has given me of what he possesses, how consequently how he, the same Lord, desires to give me even his very self, in accordance with his divine design" (*S.E.*, n. 234). Other translations of this last phrase make the statement almost poignant: "it is the Lord's wish, as far as he is able, to give me himself." God cannot give me all that God wants to give me because I am not God and also because I resist the self-gift. But God wants to give me as much of Godself as is possible. That is an amazing statement. In response the retreatant is encouraged to offer God all of oneself, liberty, memory, intelligence, understanding, one's entire will, "all that I have and possess." The mutuality is moving toward fullness.

In the other points I ask to experience how God dwells in everything, how God labors and works for me in all of creation, and how all good things and gifts come from God. If one comes to experience the world in this way, then one is a contemplative in action, that is, one finds God in all things. A person who comes close to this ideal has reached a high level of maturity indeed. The way to such maturity, as with all progress toward maturity, is through developing relationships, in this case the relationship with God. Engaging closely with God over time will transform us into people who are more like Christ, more like the images of God we are created to be.

Development During the Elder Years

Aging and IQ:
The Myth of the Twilight Years

Paul B. Baltes and K. Warner Schaie

Paul B. Baltes (b. 1939) is a developmental psychologist and gerontologist. He received his doctorate in psychology in 1967 from the University of Saarbrucken, Germany, and spent his next 12 years in America at West Virginia University, Pennsylvania State University, and Stanford University. In 1980 he became codirector of the Max Planck Institute for Human Development and Education in Berlin, Germany. Baltes is particularly well known for advancing the validity of research design in the study of human development and for his emphasis on the individual's capacity for significant change across the entire lifespan.

K. Warner Schaie, born in a Germanic part of Poland, emigrated to America in 1947. He studied at the University of California, Berkeley, and earned his doctorate at the University of Washington in Seattle. He has taught human development courses at a variety of universities and has published many books and papers in the field of developmental psychology. He is particularly well known for having initiated the Seattle Longitudinal Study, perhaps the best-designed long-term study of the development of human intelligence.

A long-standing question in human development concerns whether or not intelligence declines in old age. Does our intelligence increase, decrease, or stay the same as we advance from middle to late adulthood? The following selection, taken from Baltes and Schaie's article "Aging and IQ: The Myth of the Twilight Years," *Psychology Today* (March 1974), addresses this question and reviews a variety of studies performed by Baltes and Schaie, as well as other researchers, concerning the development of intelligence in late adulthood.

Key Concept: aging and IQ

News reporters never tire of pointing out that Golda Meir works 20-hour days, yet is in her mid-70s, and a grandmother. *Time*, in a recent story on William O. Douglas, noted that the blue eyes of the 75-year-old Justice "are as keen and alert as ever. So, too, is [his] intellect." This sort of well-intended but patronizing compliment betrays a widespread assumption that intelligence normally declines in advanced adulthood and old age, and that people like Meir and Douglas stand out as exceptions.

In our opinion, general intellectual decline in old age is largely a myth. During the past 10 years, we and our colleagues (particularly G.V. Labouvie and J.R. Nesselroade) have worked to gain a better understanding of intelligence in the aged. Our findings challenge the stereotyped view, and promote a more optimistic one. We have discovered that the old man's boast, "I'm just as good as I ever was," may be true, after all.

The Data on Decline

For a long time, the textbook view coincided with the everyday notion that as far as intelligence is concerned, what goes up must come down. The research that supported this view was cross-sectional in nature. The investigator administered intelligence tests to people of various ages at a given point in time, and compared the performance levels of the different age groups. Numerous studies of this type conducted during the '30s, '40s and '50s led researchers to believe that intelligence increases up to early adulthood, reaches a plateau that lasts for about 10 years, and begins to decline in a regular fashion around the fourth decade of life.

The first doubts arose when the results of longitudinal studies began to be available. In this type of study, the researcher observes a single group of subjects for a period of time, often extending over many years, and examines their performance at different ages. Early longitudinal studies suggested that intelligence during maturity and old age did not decline as soon as people had originally assumed.

As better intelligence tests became available, researchers began to realize that different intellectual measures might show different rates of decline. On measures of vocabulary and other skills reflecting educational experience, individuals seemed to maintain their adult level of functioning into the sixth, and even the seventh decade.

Resolving the Discrepancy

In 1956, one of us (Schaie) launched a major project aimed at resolving this disturbing discrepancy between the two kinds of study. Five hundred subjects, ranging in age from 21 to 70, received two intelligence tests, Thurstone and Thurstone's Primary Mental Abilities, and Schaie's Test of Behavioral Rigidity. Seven years later, we retested 301 of the subjects with the same tests.

The tests we used yielded 13 separate measures of cognitive functioning. Using factor-analysis methods, we found that the scores reflected four general, fairly independent dimensions of intelligence. 1) *Crystallized intelligence* encompasses the sorts of skills one acquires through education and acculturation, such as verbal comprehension, numerical skills, and inductive reasoning. To a large degree, it reflects the extent to which one has accumulated the collective intelligence of one's own culture. It is the dimension tapped by most traditional IQ tests. 2) *Cognitive flexibility* measures the ability to shift from one way of thinking to another, within the context of familiar intellectual operations, as when one must provide either an antonym or synonym to a word, depending on whether the word appears in capital or lower-case letters. 3) *Visuo-motor flexibility* measures a similar, but independent skill, the one involved in shifting from familiar to unfamiliar patterns in tasks requiring coordination between visual and motor abilities, e.g., when one must copy words but interchange capitals with lower-case letters. 4) Finally, *visualization* measures the ability to organize and process visual materials, and involves tasks such as finding a simple figure contained in a complex one or identifying a picture that is incomplete. The Schaie study did not contain sufficient measures of fluid intelligence, which encompasses abilities thought to be relatively culture free. Other researchers, e.g., Cattell and Horn, have reported a dramatic decline with age on fluid intelligence, though on the basis of cross-sectional data only.

If we analyze the data cross-sectionally (comparing the different age groups at a given point in time), we see the conventional pattern of early, systematic decline. But when we look at the results longitudinally (comparing a given age group's performance in 1956 with its performance in 1963), we find a definite decline on only one of the four measures, visuo-motor flexibility.

There is no strong age-related change in cognitive flexibility. For the most important dimension, crystallized intelligence, and for visualization as well, we see a systematic *increase* in scores for the various age groups, right into old age. Even people over 70 improved from the first testing to the second.

Intellectual Generation Gap

In cross-sectional studies, people who differ in age also differ in generation, since they were born in different years. This means that any measured differences in intelligence could reflect either age or generation differences, or both. Our study, however, allowed us to compare people from different generations at the same ages, because we tested people at two different points in time. For instance, we could compare subjects who were 50 in 1956 with subjects who were 50 in 1963. Our statistical analysis revealed that the differences between scores were due mainly to generational differences, not to chronological age. In other words, the important factor was the year a subject was born, rather than his age at the time of testing. Apparently, the measured intelligence of the population is increasing. The earlier findings of general intellectual decline over the individual life span were largely an artifact of methodology. On at least some dimensions of intelligence, particularly the crystallized type, people of average health can expect to maintain or even increase their level of performance into old age.

At present, we can only speculate about the reasons for generational differences in intelligence. We believe the answer lies in the substance, method and length of education received by different generations. When we consider the history of our educational institutions, and census data on the educational levels attained by members of specific generations, it seems fair to assume that the older people in our study were exposed to shorter periods of formal education. Furthermore, their education probably relied more heavily on principles of memorization, and less heavily on those of problem-solving.

However, there are other possibilities that must be reckoned with before we can offer a more definite interpretation. Members of different generations may differ in their sophistication in test-taking or their willingness to volunteer responses. They may differ in the extent to which they have been encouraged to achieve intellectually. And tests developed to measure the abilities of one generation may be invalid for another. In any case, the existence of differences between generations makes the search for "normal" aging phenomena a Sisyphean task.

Drop Before Death

Klaus and Ruth Riegel, psychologists at the University of Michigan, have recently suggested that when intellectual decline does occur, it comes shortly before death. In 1956, the Riegels gave intelligence tests to 380 German men and women between the ages of 55 and 75. Five years later they retested 202 of them. Some of the remainder had died, and others refused to be retested. When the Riegels looked back at the 1956 test scores of the subjects who had died, they discovered that on the average, the deceased subjects had scored lower than those who survived. Put another way, the low scores in 1956 predicted impending death.

The Riegels followed up their study in 1966 by inquiring into the fate of the people retested in 1961. Again, some people had died in the interim, and those who had died had lower scores than those who lived. Furthermore, people who had died since 1961 had declined in score from the first test session in 1956 to the second in 1961. These results pointed to a sudden deterioration during the five or fewer years immediately prior to natural death, or what the Riegels called a "terminal drop." Interestingly, the people who had refused to be retested in 1961 were more likely than the others to die before 1966. Perhaps their refusal reflected some kind of awareness of their own decline.

The Riegels' results may offer an alternative explanation for the general decline found by cross-sectional studies: the older groups may contain a higher percentage of people in the terminal drop stage, and their lower scores would not be typical of other older people. If the researcher could foresee the future and remove from his study those subjects nearing death, he might observe little or no change in the intelligence of the remaining group. In fact, the Riegels found that elderly subjects still alive in 1966 did as well, on the average, as persons at the presumed period of peak performance, 30 to 34 years, which of course, is consistent with our own data.

While it is tempting to speculate on the reasons for terminal drop, we feel that the present state of the art is such that interpretation must be tentative at best. Most researchers would probably tend to relate the drop in intellectual functioning to neurophysiological deterioration. However, this position overlooks the possibility that psychological variables contribute both to the drop and to biological death.

Aged-Biased IQ Tests

The nature of the tests used to assess intelligence may also contribute to the apparent decline that is sometimes observed. Sidney L. Pressey (who now lives as an octogenarian in a home for the elderly and continues to make occasional but insightful contributions to psychology) first pointed out that the concept of intelligence, as well as the instruments to measure it, are defined in terms of abilities most important during youth and early adulthood. This is not really surprising, since IQ tests came into existence for the purpose of predicting school performance. The format and content of these tests may simply be inappropriate for tapping the potential wisdom of the aged. For example, older people tend to do relatively

poorly on tests employing technical language such as the terminology of physics or computer programming. Their performance is better if items are worded in terms of everyday experiences.

Another problem is the distinction between a person's competence and his actual performance. Handicaps that have nothing to do with intrinsic ability may affect the way a person does on a test. For instance, Baltes and Carol A. Furry recently demonstrated that the aged are especially susceptible to the effects of fatigue; pretest fatigue considerably lowered the scores of older subjects, but did not affect the performance of younger ones.

Dwindling reinforcements may also affect the performance of the aged. Elderly individuals, because of their uncertain and shortened life expectancy, may cease to be sensitive to the sorts of long-range rewards that seem to control intellectual behavior in young people (e.g. education, career goals, and development of a reputation). Ogden Lindsley has proposed that the aged may become more dependent on immediate and idiosyncratic rewards.

Even when rewards are potentially effective, they may be unavailable to old people. Most researchers agree that the environment of the elderly is intellectually and socially impoverished. Family settings and institutions for the aged fail to provide conditions conducive to intellectual growth. The educational system discourages participation by the elderly, focusing instead on the young.

Recent work on age stereotypes indicates that some young people hold a negative view of old age. These views may influence them to withdraw reinforcements for competence in the elderly, or even to punish such competence. Aging persons may in time come to accept the stereotypes, view themselves as deficient, and put aside intellectual performance as a personal goal. In the process, the intellectual deficit becomes a self-fulfilling prophecy.

Compensatory Education for the Aged

Although educators have made massive attempts to overcome discrimination in early childhood, working through Government-funded compensatory programs, analogous efforts for the aged have barely begun. But, increasing numbers of gerontologists have felt encouraged enough by the reanalysis of intellectual decline to examine, probably for the first time in any vigorous manner, the degree to which intellectual performance can be bolstered. The results are still very sketchy, but they are promising.

Some researchers, working from a bio-behavioral perspective, have looked at the effects of physical treatments. For instance, hyperbaric oxygen treatment—the breathing of concentrated oxygen for extended periods to increase oxygen supply to the brain—seems to improve memory for recent events, although the outcome of such research is not at all free of controversy. Treatment of hypertension and conditioning of alpha waves also seem to be promising, and deserve careful study. Other researchers concentrate on studying the psychological aspects of the learning process; they experiment with the pacing of items, the mode of presentation (for instance, auditory versus visual), the amount of practice, the delivery of rewards, training in mnemonics, and so on.

The speed with which a person responds, which is important on many intellectual tests, is usually assumed to be a function of biological well-being. But in a series of pilot studies, Baltes, William Hoyer and Gisela V. Labouvie were able to improve the response speed of elderly subjects rather dramatically, using Green Stamps as a reward for faster performance in canceling letters, marking answer sheets and copying words. After as little as two hours of training, women 65 to 80 years of age increased their speed as much as 20 to 35 percent. The researchers compared the performance of these "trained" subjects with that of untrained controls on 11 different intelligence tests. Although the transfer of the speed training to test performance was not earthshaking, the overall pattern was encouraging.

In the interest of rectifying some of the social injustices that have resulted from the branding of the aged as deficient, social scientists must continue to explore, with vigor and optimism, the research avenues opened during the past few years. This research should be guided by a belief in the potential of gerontological intelligence, and a rejection of the rigid, biological view that assumes an inevitable decline. We should not be surprised to find that the socialization goals and mechanisms of a society are the most powerful influence on what happens to people, not only during childhood and adolescence but also during adulthood and old age.

Social roles and resources can be assigned without regard to age only when the deleterious aspects of aging are eliminated. Toward this end, in 1971 an American Psychological Association task force on aging made some specific recommendations for eliminating the unnecessary causes of decline in intellectual functioning. They included more forceful implementation of adult-education programs; funding of research and innovative programs in voluntary (rather than mandatory) retirement, second-career training, and leisure-time activity; and better utilization of skills that are unaffected by age.

When we consider the vast spectrum of negative conditions, attributes and expectations that most Western societies impose on older people, we must acclaim the impressive robustness of our older population in the face of adversity. At the same time, we hope that society, aided by geropsychology, soon finds ways to make life for the elderly more enjoyable and effective. Acknowledging that intellectual decline is largely a myth is, we hope, a step in the right direction.

Stages of Faith: The Psychology of Human Development and the Quest for Meaning

James W. Fowler

James W. Fowler earned his doctorate at Harvard Divinity School and is currently at Emory University in Georgia. Between 1972 and 1981 Fowler and his research associates conducted 359 structured "faith development interviews." The respondents ranged in age from 3 to 84, there were an equal number of males and females, and 98 percent of the sample was white. Regarding the religious background of the participants, 45 percent were Protestant, 37 percent were Catholic, and 11 percent were Jewish. Fowler's definition of "faith" goes beyond a religious orientation, claimed beliefs, creeds, or doctrines. Rooted in Paul Tillich's and Richard Niebuhr's theology, Fowler claims that whatever is "our ultimate concern" reveals our true faith. Fowler states that regardless of whether we believe in God, are agnostic, or are atheistic, we are concerned with what the purpose of our lives are, what is of true value, and what makes life worth living. He states that within the responses to those questions, we can discover the stage level of someone's faith.

The following selection is from Fowler's book *Stages of Faith: The Psychology of Human Development and the Quest for Meaning* (HarperSan-Francisco, 1981). As you turn your attention to this selection, it is important to know that Fowler has identified six stages of faith: (1) "Intuitive-Projective" faith, typical of young children, is based on fantasy and a blind belief in what adults tell us. (2) "Mythical-Literal" faith, typical of middle childhood, is based on concreteness and literalness and a concern for "facts." (3) "Poetic-Conventional" faith, typical of teens and many adults, is based on the beliefs of those we trust. (4) "Individuating-Reflective" faith is typical of middle and late adulthood but is sometimes found in young adults. At this stage, individuals assume responsibility for their beliefs and commitments and have "objective" understanding of creeds, doctrines, and so on. (5) "Paradoxical-Consolidation" faith is a level that most adults never reach, but if they do, it begins in midlife. At this stage, there is a recognition of one's own fallibility, an acceptance of those who have beliefs different from one's own, and a real understanding that humans all belong to one world community. (6) The final level, "Universalizing" faith, which few, even by late adulthood, ever reach, will be described in some detail in the following selection.

Key Concept: stages of faith

The movement from Stage 3 [Poetic-Conventional faith] to Stage 4 Individuative-Reflective faith is particularly critical for it is in this transition that the late adolescent or adult must begin to take seriously the burden of responsibility for his or her own commitments, lifestyle, beliefs and attitudes. Where genuine movement toward stage 4 is underway the person must face certain unavoidable tensions: individuality versus being defined by a group or group membership; subjectivity and the power of one's strongly felt but unexamined feelings versus objectivity and the requirement of critical reflection; self-fulfillment or self-actualization as a primary concern versus service to and being for others;

the question of being committed to the relative versus struggle with the possibility of an absolute.

Stage 4 most appropriately takes form in young adulthood (but let us remember that many adults do not construct it and that for a significant group it emerges only in the mid-thirties or forties). This stage is marked by a double development. The self, previously sustained in its identity and faith compositions by an interpersonal circle of significant others, now claims an identity no longer defined by the composite of one's roles or meanings to others. To sustain that new identity it composes a meaning frame conscious of its own boundaries and inner connections and aware of itself as a "world view." Self (identity) and outlook (world view) are differentiated from those of others and become acknowledged factors in the reactions, interpretations and judgments one makes on the actions of the self and others. It expresses its intuitions of coherence in an ultimate environment in terms of an explicit system of meanings. Stage 4 typically translates symbols into conceptual meanings. This is a "demythologizing" stage. It is likely to attend minimally to unconscious factors influencing its judgments and behavior.

Stage 4's ascendant strength has to do with its capacity for critical reflection on identity (self) and outlook (ideology). Its dangers inhere in its strengths: an excessive confidence in the conscious mind and in critical thought and a kind of second narcissism in which the now clearly bounded, reflective self overassimilates "reality" and the perspectives of others into its own world view.

Restless with the self-images and outlook maintained by Stage 4, the person ready for transition finds him- or herself attending to what may feel like anarchic and disturbing inner voices. Elements from a childish past, images and energies from a deeper self, a gnawing sense of the sterility and flatness of the meanings one serves— any or all of these may signal readiness for something new. Stories, symbols, myths and paradoxes from one's own or other traditions may insist on breaking in upon the neatness of the previous faith. Disillusionment with one's compromises and recognition that life is more complex than Stage 4's logic of clear distinctions and abstract concepts can comprehend, press one toward a more dialectical and multileveled approach to life truth.

Stage 5. Conjunctive Faith

I have not found or fabricated a simple way to describe Conjunctive faith. This frustrates me. I somehow feel that if I cannot communicate the features of this stage clearly, it means that I don't understand them. Or worse, I fear that what I call "Stage 5" really does not exist. I cannot accept either of these explanations. The truth, I believe, is that Stage 5, as a style of faith-knowing, *does* exist and it *is* complex. Moreover, while it has been—and is—exemplified in the lives of persons, in their writings and in writings about them, its structural features have not been adequately described, either in my own previous writings or in the writings of others.

As a way of opening our consideration of Conjunctive faith let me offer a few analogies, which may tease out an image of the character of the transition from Stage 4 to Stage 5. The emergence of Stage 5 is something like:

- Realizing that the behavior of light requires that it be understood both as a wave phenomenon *and* as particles of energy.
- Discovering that the rational solution or "explanation" of a problem that seemed so elegant is but a painted canvas covering an intricate, endlessly intriguing cavern of surprising depth.

- Looking at a field of flowers simultaneously through a microscope and a wide-angle lens.
- Discovering that a guest, if invited to do so, will generously reveal the treasured wisdom of a lifetime of experience.
- Discovering that someone who shares your identity also writes checks, makes deposits and stops payments on your checking account.
- Discovering that one's parents are remarkable people not just because they are one's parents.

Stage 5, as a way of seeing, of knowing, of committing, moves beyond the dichotomizing logic of Stage 4's "either/or." It sees both (or the many) sides of an issue simultaneously. Conjunctive faith suspects that things are organically related to each other; it attends to the pattern of interrelatedness in things, trying to avoid force-fitting to its own prior mind set. . . .

Let's sum up some of the central structural features of Conjunctive faith.

Stage 5 Conjunctive faith involves the integration into self and outlook of much that was suppressed or unrecognized in the interest of Stage 4's self-certainty and conscious cognitive and affective adaptation to reality. This stage develops "second naïveté" (Ricoeur) in which symbolic power is reunited with conceptual meanings. Here there must also be a new reclaiming and reworking of one's past. There must be an opening to the voices of one's "deeper self." Importantly, this involves a critical recognition of one's social unconscious—the myths, ideal images and prejudices built deeply into the self-system by virtue of one's nurture within a particular social class, religious tradition, ethnic group or the like.

Unusual before mid-life, Stage 5 knows the sacrament of defeat and the reality of irrevocable commitments and acts. What the previous stage struggled to clarify, in terms of the boundaries of self and outlook, this stage now makes porous and permeable. Alive to paradox and the truth in apparent contradictions, this stage strives to unify opposites in mind and experience. It generates and maintains vulnerability to the strange truths of those who are "other." Ready for closeness to that which is different and threatening to self and outlook (including new depths of experience in spirituality and religious revelation), this stage's commitment to justice is freed from the confines of tribe, class, religious community or nation. And with the seriousness that can arise when life is more than half over, this stage is ready to spend and be spent for the cause of conserving and cultivating the possibility of others' generating identity and meaning.

The new strength of this stage comes in the rise of the ironic imagination—a capacity to see and be in one's or one's group's most powerful meanings, while simultaneously recognizing that they are relative, partial and inevitably distorting apprehensions of transcendent reality. Its danger lies in the direction of a paralyzing passivity or inaction, giving rise to complacency or cynical withdrawal, due to its paradoxical understanding of truth.

Stage 5 can appreciate symbols, myths and rituals (its own and others') because it has been grasped, in some measure, by the depth of reality to which they refer. It also sees the divisions of the human family vividly because it has been apprehended by the possibility (and imperative) of an inclusive community of being. But this stage remains divided. It lives and acts between an untransformed world and a transforming vision and loyalties. In some few cases this division yields to the call of the radical actualization that we call Stage 6.

Stage 6. Universalizing Faith

As our structural-developmental theory of faith stages has emerged and undergone refinements, it has become clear that we are trying to do both descriptive and normative work. Our empirical studies have aimed at testing whether there is a predictable sequence of formally describable stages in the life of faith. The hypothesized stages with which we began, however, and the versions of them that have withstood empirical scrutiny exhibit an indisputably normative tendency. From the beginning of our work there has been a complex image of mature faith in relation to which we have sought for developmentally related prior or preparatory stages. It is this normative endpoint, the culminating image of mature faith in this theory, with which I want to work now. What *is* the normative shape of Stage 6 Universalizing faith?

In the little book *Life-Maps* I described Stage 6 in the following way:

In order to characterize Stage 6 we need to focus more sharply on the dialectical or paradoxical features of Stage 5 faith. Stage 5 can see injustice in sharply etched terms because it has been apprehended by an enlarged awareness of the demands of justice and their implications. It can recognize partial truths and their limitations because it has been apprehended by a more comprehensive vision of truth. It can appreciate and cherish symbols, myths and rituals in new depth because it has been apprehended in some measure by the depth of reality to which the symbols refer and which they mediate. It sees the fractures and divisions of the human family with vivid pain because it has been apprehended by the possibility of an inclusive commonwealth of being. Stage 5 remains paradoxical or divided, however, because the self is caught between these universalizing apprehensions and the need to preserve its own being and well-being. Or because it is deeply invested in maintaining the ambiguous order of a socioeconomic system, the alternatives to which seem more unjust or destructive than it is. In this situation of paradox Stage 5 must act and not be paralyzed. But Stage 5 acts out of conflicting loyalties. Its readiness to spend and be spent finds limits in its loyalty to the present order, to its institutions, groups and compromise procedures. Stage 5's perceptions of justice outreach its readiness to sacrifice the self and to risk the partial justice of the present order for the sake of a more inclusive justice and the realization of love.

The transition to Stage 6 involves an overcoming of this paradox through a moral and ascetic actualization of the universalizing apprehensions. Heedless of the threats to self, to primary groups, and to the institutional arrangements of the present order that are involved, Stage 6 becomes a disciplined, activist *incarnation*—a making real and tangible—of the imperatives of absolute love and justice of which Stage 5 has partial apprehensions. The self at Stage 6 engages in spending and being spent for the transformation of present reality in the direction of a transcendent actuality.

Persons best described by Stage 6 typically exhibit qualities that shake our usual criteria of normalcy. Their heedlessness to self-preservation and the vividness of their taste and feel for transcendentmoral and religious actuality give their actions and words an extraordinary and often unpredictable quality. In their devotion to universalizing compassion they may offend our parochial perceptions of justice. In their penetration through the obsession with survival, security, and significance they threaten our measured standards of righteousness and goodness and prudence. Their enlarged visions of universal community disclose the partialness of our tribes and pseudo-species. And their leadership initiatives, often involving strategies of nonviolent suffering and ultimate respect for being, constitute affronts to our usual notions of relevance. It is little wonder that persons best described by Stage 6 so frequently become martyrs for the visions they incarnate.

Before commenting on the passages I have just offered from *Life-Maps* let me share another effort to describe the shape of Stage 6, this time from a more recent writing. This will serve as our summary in advance:

Stage 6 is exceedingly rare. The persons best described by it have generated faith compositions in which their felt sense of an ultimate environment is inclusive of all being. They have become incarnators and actualizers of the spirit of an inclusive and fulfilled human community.

They are "contagious" in the sense that they create zones of liberation from the social, political, economic and ideological shackles we place and endure on human futurity. Living with felt participation in a power that unifies and transforms the world, Universalizers are often experienced as subversive of the structures (including religious structures) by which we sustain our individual and corporate survival, security and significance. Many persons in this stage die at the hands of those whom they hope to change. Universalizers are often more honored and revered after death than during their lives. The rare persons who may be described by this stage have a special grace that makes them seem more lucid, more simple, and yet somehow more fully human than the rest of us. Their community is universal in extent. Particularities are cherished because they are vessels of the universal, and thereby valuable apart from any utilitarian considerations. Life is both loved and held to loosely. Such persons are ready for fellowship with persons at any of the other stages and from any other faith tradition.

Even as I read these descriptions I am haunted—as I am sure you are—by memories of Jonestown, Guyana and the Reverend Jim Jones. Also in my mind, images of the deeply angry, mystical eyes of the aged Ayatollah Khomeini look out across the frenzied, impassioned mobs he inspires with his mixture of chauvinistic nationalism and religious absolutism. The followers of both these men—and those of many other persons like them—would likely hear my descriptions of Stage 6 as depictions of their revered, and feared, leaders. To hear the qualities of State 6 in these ways, however, is to miss some extremely important qualifications and dimensions of Stage 6 faith. Fascinated with the charisma, the authority and frequently the ruthlessness of such leaders, we must not fail to attend in the descriptions of Stage 6 to the criteria of inclusiveness of community, of radical commitment to justice and love and of selfless passion for a transformed world, a world made over not in *their* images, but in accordance with an intentionality both divine and transcendent.

When asked whom I consider to be representatives of this Stage 6 outlook I refer to Gandhi, to Martin Luther King, Jr., in the last years of his life and to Mother Teresa of Calcutta. I am also inclined to point to Dag Hammarskjöld, Dietrich Bonhoeffer, Abraham Heschel and Thomas Merton. There must be many others, not so well known to us, whose lives exhibit these qualities of Stage 6. To say that a person embodies the qualities of Stage 6 is not to say that he or she is perfect. Nor is it to imply that he or she is a "self-actualized person" or a "fully functioning human being"—though it seems that most of them are or were, if in somewhat different senses than Abraham Maslow or Carl Rogers intended their terms. Greatness of commitment and vision often coexists with great blind spots and limitations. Erik Erikson, writing his book on Gandhi, set out to illumine the religious and ethical power of Gandhi's doctrine of *satyagraha*, the reliance on nonviolent strategies in the aggressive pursuit of the social truth that is justice. In the middle of the book Erikson had to stop. He found it necessary to write a stern and sad letter of reprimand to the Mahatma—dead those twenty-five years—pointing out the unfairness and the muted violence of Gandhi's treatment of his wife, Kasturba, and of his sons. (Gandhi, in forming his ashram, had insisted on bringing Untouchables into the household. Kasturba had accepted this without complaint. She found it too much, however, when Gandhi insisted that she take on the job of removing their toilet wastes from the house—something he himself was patently unwilling to do.) To be Stage 6 does not mean to be perfect, whether perfection be understood in a moral, psychological or a leadership sense.

I do not believe that people set out to be Stage 6. That is not to say that some, who later come to fit that description, did not set out to be "saints." Thomas Merton while still a student at Columbia University came to be clear in his own mind that he wanted to become a saint. Students of his career, however, recognize that his growth toward what we are calling Stage 6, took paths and required difficulties that were unforeseen in Merton's early visions of sainthood. It is my conviction that persons who come to embody Universalizing faith are drawn into those patterns of commitment and leadership by the providence of God and the exigencies of history. It is as though they are selected by the great Blacksmith of history, heated in the fires of turmoil and trouble and then hammered into usable shape on the hard anvil of conflict and struggle.

The descriptions I have read to you of Stage 6 suggest another note of realism in our efforts to understand the normative endpoint of faith development in the Universalizing stage. Here I refer to what has been called the "subversive" impact of their visions and leadership. Even as they oppose the more blatantly unjust or unredeemed structures of the social, political or religious world, these figures also call into question the compromise arrangements in our common life that have acquired the sanction of conventionalized understandings of justice. King's "Letter from Birmingham Jail" was written not to "Bull" Connor or the Ku Klux Klan, but to a group of moderate and liberal religious leaders who had pled with King to meliorate the pressure his followers were exerting through nonviolent demonstrations on the city. King's assault on the more blatant features of a segregated city proved subversive to the genteel compromises by which persons of good will of both races had accommodated themselves in a racist society.

This subversive character of the impact of Stage 6 leadership often strikes us as arising from a kind of relevant irrelevance. Mother Teresa of Calcutta's ministry illustrates this powerfully. Mother Teresa, a foreign-born nun in her late thirties, head of a girls' boarding school, was going on retreat. As she traveled through the city she became overwhelmed by the sight of abandoned persons, lying in the streets, left to die. Some of these forgotten people were already having their not yet lifeless limbs gnawed by rodents. Under the impact of those grim sights she felt a call to a new form of vocation—a ministry of presence, service and care to the abandoned, the forgotten, the hopeless. In a nation and a world where scarcity is a fact of life, where writers and policy makers urge strategies of "triage" to ensure that resources are not "wasted" on those who have no chance of recovery and useful contribution, what could be less relevant than carrying these dying persons into places of care, washing them, caring for their needs, feeding them when they are able to take nourishment and affirming by word and deed that they are loved and valued people of God? But in a world that says people only have worth if they pull their own weight and contribute something of value, what could be *more* relevant?

In these persons of Universalizing faith these qualities of redemptive subversiveness and relevant irrelevance derive from visions they see and to which they have committed their total beings. These are not abstract visions, generated like utopias out of some capacity for transcendent imagination. Rather, they are visions born out of radical acts of identification with persons and circumstances where the futurity of being is being crushed, blocked or exploited. A Martin Luther King, Jr., prepared by familial and church nurture, by college, seminary and doctoral studies, influenced theologically and philosophically by Gandhi's teachings on nonviolent resistance, gets drawn into acts of radical identification with the oppressed when Rosa Parks refuses any longer to let her personhood be ground underfoot. Gandhi, steeped by a Jain mother with the doctrine of *ahimsa* (the doctrine of noninjury to being), influenced by a tradition of public service in his father's family, prepared by legal study in Britain, is physically abused and removed from the first-class section of a South African train. Through this shock of recognition of his identification with the oppressed and despised minority of a colonized people he is drawn eventually into the leadership of a nonviolent struggle for Indian independence.

We have already spoken of the identification with the hopeless and abandoned dying street people that launched Mother Teresa's vision of a ministry where one meets Christ in the person of the forgotten ones.

In such situations of concrete oppression, difficulty or evil, persons see clearly the forces that destroy life as it should be. In the direct experience of the negation of one's personhood or in one's identification with the negations experienced by others, visions are born of what life is *meant* to be. In such circumstances the promise of fulfillment, which is the birthright of each mother's child and the hope of each human community, cries out in affront at the persons and conditions that negate it. The visions that form and inform Universalizing faith arise out of and speak to such situations as these.

Reflections on the Last Stage—And the First

Erik Erikson

Erik Erikson (1902–1994) was born in Germany, studied psychoanalysis under Sigmund Freud and his daughter Anna Freud in Vienna, and moved to America in 1933, taking a position at Harvard Medical School. Based on his observations of human development in Europe and America, including his studies among the Sioux in South Dakota and the Yurok in northern California, he posited that social relationships are more influential on human development than the inner sexual tensions posited by Freud. He was also the first influential researcher in human development to emphasize stages of adult development beyond adolescence. Both Freud's psychosexual stages and Jean Piaget's cognitive-developmental stages end at puberty. Erikson, however, asserted that there are distinct stages of human functioning and interaction in young, middle, and late adulthood.

Erikson's theory of the eight stages of human development, spanning infancy to old age, was first published in his classic text *Childhood and Society* in 1950. The stage explored in the following selection, the last stage, is Integrity vs. Despair. In the two psychobiographies written by Erikson, *Young Man Luther: A Study in Psychoanalysis and History* (W. W. Norton, 1958) and *Gandhi's Truth on the Origins of Militant Nonviolence* (W. W. Norton, 1969), he addresses the psychology of aging. The following selection is from "Reflections on the Last Stage—And the First," which was published in *Psychoanalytic Study of the Child* in 1984 and is dedicated to the memory of Anna Freud. In it, Erikson examines the relationship between the "hope" generated in the first stage of life (Trust vs. Mistrust) and the wisdom generated in the last stage of life (Integrity vs. Despair).

Key Concept: Integrity vs. Despair: the final psychosocial stage crisis

*I*n wishing to make a contribution to this [work] in honor of Anna Freud, I find my thoughts somewhat dislocated by the fact that Joan Erikson's and my present studies do not concern childhood, but the very last stage of life: old age. To make the most of this I will attempt to restate and to reflect on an overall perspective of human development which promises to reveal some affinities between the end and the beginning of human life. Such a perspective becomes possible in our day when scientific, clinical, and public interest has, over several decades, shown special interest in a series of life stages. There was the Mid-Century White House Conference which was—no doubt in partial response to discoveries of psychoanalysis—dedicated to "a healthy personality for every child." There were the '60s when problems of identity so widely suggested themselves in the dramatic public behavior as well as in the psychopathology of youth and thus called for our psychosocial and historical considerations. And then, indeed, middle and early adulthood were discovered. Thus, the stages of life were highlighted by a historical relativity both in the ways in which they were experienced and in the methods used to

conceptualize them at different times by observers of varying ages and interests. Indeed, historical changes have recently mobilized a general, and somewhat alarmed, awareness of the rapidly changing conditions of old age and an intense interest in the special nature of this last stage. Together, these factors will never again permit us to treat masses of survivors as an accidental embarrassment: old age must eventually find a meaningful place in the economic and cultural order—meaningful to the old and to the occupants of all other age groups, beginning with childhood. But this permits us to look at the facts observed and the theories developed and discussed with the new hope that we may all learn to view infancy and childhood as the "natural" foundation of a truly desirable long life. This also means—and has meant for quite a while now—that we can no longer base our developmental perspectives preponderantly on clinical reconstructions of the past, on a search for regressions to and fixations on ever earlier stages and their conflicts and disbalances. Even our clinical orientation can only gain systematically from the additional study at each stage of life of the potentials for developmental recovery and genuine growth—and this up to the very last stage. There, even "elderlies" (and not only "elders"), rather than sporting a new childishness, may fulfill some of the promises of childhood like those which seem to be contained in such sayings as the biblical "Unless you turn and become like children. . . ." And some of these oldest all-human sayings may gain new meaning in our time when history reveals so shockingly what some (and primarily masculine) values of adulthood have contributed to the chances of a self-destruction of our species.

The timeless sayings of the past also serve to remind us that it is difficult to make any meaningful observations of the developmental details of human life without implying more or less conscious, large-scale configurations which back in Freud's time were still recognized and appreciated without much apology as part of a worker's *Weltanschauung*—that is, his or her way of viewing the design of the world and of human life within it. To begin with a prominent example: if the basic scheme is that of "developmental lines" (A. Freud, 1965), the outline of their details will clarify a firm direction in the linear growth of capacities from "lower" to "higher" stages of development. This naturally reflects the ethos of maturation implicit in the theories of psychosexuality and of the ego: and so the list ranges "from dependency to emotional self-reliance," "from egocentricity to peer relationships," or simply "from dependence to independence" and from "irrational to rational." This scheme has, of course, led to a wealth of observations.

Joan Erikson and I, in turn, have been trying to make explicit an "epigenetic" scheme of psychosocial development—epigenesis being a term first used in embryology. In our vocabulary (E. H. and J. M. Erikson, 1950), the overall term "life *cycle*" forces on our configurations a rounding out of the whole course of life which relates the last stage to the first both in the course of individual lives and in that of generations. We have, somewhat simplistically, designed a chart of stages which (some readers surely saw it coming) I must "once more" briefly present in order to clarify the epigenetic connection between old age and infancy. However, I employ such repetitiousness with ever fewer apologies, because we have learned over the years how difficult it is even for highly trained individuals to keep in mind the logic of a contextual conceptualization of developmental matters. And it is such contextuality which keeps a theory together and helps to make the observations based on it "comprehensible" in Einstein's sense, although they remain forever relative to the position of a single view within the viewpoints of its time and place.

So here is the chart of psychosocial stages. In its horizontals, we designate the stages of life, and this from the bottom up, in consonance with the image of growth and development: Infancy and Early Childhood, the Play Age and the School Age, Adolescence and Young Adulthood, Adulthood and Old Age. Along the diagonal we designate the basic *psychosocial crises*, each of which dominates

one stage, beginning in the lower left corner with Basic Trust vs. Basic Mistrust and ending with Integrity vs. Despair in the upper right corner. As can never be said too often, each stage is dominated both by a syntonic and a dystonic quality—that is: Mistrust as well as Trust and Despair as well as Integrity are essential developments, constituting together a "crisis" only in the sense that the syntonic should systematically outweigh or at least balance (but never dismiss) the dystonic. So the diagonal is not an "achievement" scale meant to show what we totally "overcome"—such a simplification comes all too easily in our optimistic culture—the dystonic part of each conflict. But, of course, the final balance of all stages of development must leave the syntonic elements dominant in order to secure a *basic strength* emerging from each overall crisis: at the beginning, it is Hope, and, at the end, what we are calling Wisdom.

Following the diagonal one step upward from the lower left corner we find the second psychosocial crisis to be that of Autonomy vs. Shame and Doubt, from which the strength Will emerges. Every diagonal step, however, leaves some as yet empty squares beneath, beside, and above it. Beneath Will and beside Hope we must assume some early development in which the crisis of Will is anticipated, while to the left of the Will crisis and thus contemporaneously with it, there must be a Hope already experienced enough to take conflicts of Will into account. Thus begins a vertical development along which Hope can be renewed and mature at every further stage—all the way up to the last stage where we will call it Faith. Indeed, by that time, the individual will have joined the generational cycle and will (with the crisis of Generativity vs. Stagnation) have begun to transmit some forms of faith to coming generations. All these stage-wise connections, on study, prove to be overriding necessities, as they provide the developmental impetus stage for stage in the dominant conflicts of life. In sum, this means that while each basic conflict dominates a particular stage along the diagonal, each has been there in some rudimentary form below the diagonal; and each, once having fully developed during its own dominant stage, will continue (above the diagonal) to mature further during all the subsequent stages and under the dominance of each stage-appropriate crisis.

These, then, are some of the epigenetic principles as applied to psychosocial development. But such development is, of course, systematically intertwined throughout not only with physical growth but also with the *psychosexual stages* which obey corresponding laws. This we will not pursue in this presentation. But it is obvious that in the beginning Hope must be truly "fed" with the libido verified in oral-sensory enjoyment, while in the second stage, the training of Will is invigorated by the experience of anal-muscular mastery. Correspondingly, it must be clear that the psychosexual stages, in turn, could not be fully actual without the contemporaneous maturation of the psychosocial strengths.

Table 43.1

	1	2	3	4	5	6	7	8
Old Age								Integrity vs. Despair. WISDOM
Adulthood							Generativity vs. Stagnation. CARE	
Young Adulthood						Intimacy vs. Isolation. LOVE		
Adolescence					Identity vs. Confusion. FIDELITY			
School Age				Industry vs. Inferiority COMPETENCE				
Play Age			Initiative vs. Guilt. PURPOSE					
Early Childhood		Autonomy vs. Shame, Doubt. WILL						
Infancy	Basic Trust vs. Basic Mistrust. HOPE							

In our review, this leads us to the question of the psychosexual status of the last two stages of life—adulthood and old age. For both, I have found it necessary as well as plausible to suggest a maturation beyond a mere fulfillment of *genitality*. For adulthood to which we ascribe the psychosocial crisis of Generativity vs. Stagnation (which vitalizes procreativity and productivity as well as creativity) I have claimed (exploring once more the full meaning of the Oedipus saga) a *procreative libido* without the satisfaction or sublimation of which, in fact, genitality could not really mature (Erikson, 1980). For presenile old age, in turn, I have claimed a psychosexual stage which keeps a *generalized sensuality* alive even as strictly genital expression weakens.

And so, in returning to the psychosocial stages, we must now account for two of our somewhat grandiose designations of old-age strengths, namely, Integrity (if "vs. Despair") and Wisdom. In comparison with these terms, the designation of Hope in the first stage makes sense enough: for how can one start living without a lot of ready trust, and how stay alive without some healthy mistrust? On the other hand (and in the other corner), despair certainly seems to be an almost too fitting dystonic "sense" for one who faces a general reduction of capacities as well as the very end of life. But the demand to develop Integrity and Wisdom in old age seems to be somewhat unfair, especially when made by middle-aged theorists—as, indeed, we then were. And we must ask: do the demands that "Integrity" suggests still hold when old age is represented by a fast-increasing, and only reasonably well-preserved group of mere long-lived "elderlies"?

So back to the chart and to the length and width of its four corners: how do they connect with each other? For the upper left corner, we have found a convincing syntonic term and concept: Faith. And here we can at last illustrate an experiential similarity in the chart's uppermost right and lowest left corners. Faith has been given cosmic worldwide contexts by religions and ideologies which offered to true believers some sense of immortality in the form of some unification with a unique historical or cosmic power which in its personalized form we may call an *Ultimate Other*. We can certainly find an experiential basis for such hope in the infant's meeting with the *maternal personage* faced "eye to eye" as what we may call the *Primal Other*. This basic visual mutuality as experienced at life's beginning and matured up through the stages may well continue to enliven in mature age the vision offered by more or less metaphysical vistas and vedas and of the countenances of prophets and great leaders in faiths and in ideologies, which (alas) confirm hopefulness as the most basic of all human strengths. The relation of (lower left corner) Hope and (upper left) Faith, then, contains a first example of an experiential similarity, namely, that of a mutual "meeting" with an all-important Other—which appears in some form on each stage of life, beginning with the maternal, but soon also the paternal

Other confirmed by visual and, indeed, various sensual experiences of rich mutuality.

It is, in this context, an ironical fact, that psychoanalysis has come to attach to this very Other the cold term "Object," which originally meant, of course, the aim of libidinal energy. By the end of life (this Primal Other having become an Ultimate Other), such deeply experienced faith is richly realized not only in religion, but also in mythology and in the arts; and it is confirmed by the detailed rituals and ritualizations which mark the beginning and the end of life in varying cultures—ritualizations that, in our time, must find new ways of expressing an all-human sense of existence and an anticipation of dying. For all this, I assume, the overall term Wisdom may still serve.

The experience of the Other, of course, appears in various forms and with varying certainty throughout life: and here we can refer to the literary evidence of Freud's friendship to [Wilhelm] Fliess. Freud called him, indeed, "der Andere," meaning the Other; and it is very clear that, for a time, they used each other in exchanges of wisdom well beyond professional conversation (Erikson, 1955). Thus, throughout development, a series of "others" will be encountered beginning with the fraternal and sororal others who are first and most ambivalently shared in childhood. Later, when identity is better defined, friends and comrades emerge. And then there is that territorial Other, the "Neighbor," who occupies his own (but often, alas, too close) territory. When he becomes the inimical Other, he can turn into a totally estranged Other, almost a member of another species: and, indeed, I have come to call this process pseudospeciation, a development of truly mandatory importance as human survival comes to depend on the inventive cultivation of shared neighborhoods.

This finally brings us to another basic experience for which we, I think, lack the right word. To truly meet others with whom to share a "We," one must have a sense of "I." In fact, one must have it before one can have the now much advertised "self." Freud obviously was concerned with this, for he at times wrote of an *"Ich,"* the English counterpart of which quite transparently is "I," although translation habitually turns it into "ego." This must be emphasized in these reflections because a sense of "I" becomes a most sensitive matter again in old age, as an individual's uniqueness gradually and often suddenly seems to have lost any leeway for further variations such as those which seemed to open themselves with each previous stage. Now non-Being must be faced "as is." But radically limited choices can make time appear forfeited and space depleted quite generally; while (to again follow the psychosocial strengths from left to right) the power of Will is weakened; Initiative and Purpose become uncertain; meaningful work is rare; and Identity restricted to what one has been. And if we follow the line to the adult stages and their bequest of Love (the fulfillment of a sense of "You") and of Care (which holds the generations together), we face that great inequality of fate which can limit the chances in old age of continued intimacy and of generative (and even "grand-generative") relationships. The resulting compulsive preoccupation with the repetition of meaningful memories, however, rather than being only symptomatic of mere helpless regression, may well represent a "regression in the service of development" in Peter Blos's (1980) term: for, in fact, there are now new age-specific conflicts for the sake of which the old person's sense of "I" must become free.

For these conflicts I can for the moment find only existential terms in contrast to strictly psychoanalytic ones. There is, on the border of Being and Not-Being, a sense of Dread in Kierkegaard's meaning, which is not explained by our present theories concerning anxiety; there is a sense of Evil which no classical sense of guilt necessarily covers; and there is, as we have just pointed out, a sense, or a lack of sense, of "I" or Existential Identity which our identity theories cannot fathom: these are all problems of Being, the open or disguised presence of which we must learn to discern in the everyday involvements of old people.

If we now have begun to connect (in an admittedly sweeping way) the first stage with the last, and both with a major collective institution—here belief systems—we could now assign major institutional trends to all the succeeding stages. To give just one more example—for I really promised only to clarify what I can in the relation of the last stage and the first—the basic need for Autonomy remains related throughout life to the universal human institution of the Law, which defines the leeway and the limits of individual Will, and with its punishments assigns Self-Doubt and Shame to transgressors—all of which, of course, influence the way in which right and wrong are taught to children in a given culture.

Epigenetically speaking, then, we can say that all the later age-specific developments are grounded or rooted in (and in fact dependent on) the strengths developed in infancy, childhood, and adolescence. And if the sense of autonomy "naturally" suffers grievously in old age, as the leeway of independence is constricted, there can also mature an active acceptance of appropriate limitations and a "wise" choice of involvements in vital engagements of a kind not possible earlier in life—and possibly (this we must find out) of potential value to a society of the future. Finally, just because I have been so active in outlining the development of Identity in adolescence, I may repeat that (a few squares to the right) the new and final sense of existential identity can convey a certain freedom from the despair associated with unlived or mislived—or, indeed, overdone—identity potentials.

So we return to what we claimed to be the dominant syntonic trait in the last stage, namely, Integrity. This in its simplest meaning is, of course, a sense of coherence and wholeness which is no doubt at risk under such terminal conditions of a loss of linkages in somatic, psychic, and social organization. What is demanded here could be simply called "Integrality," a readiness to "Keep things together," the best wording of which I owe to a little boy who had asked his mother what was going to happen when he died. "Your soul will go to heaven," she said, "and your body into the ground." "Mommy," he said, "if you don't mind, I'd like to keep my stuff together." Throughout life, then, we must allow for a human being's potential capacity under favorable conditions to let the integrative experience of earlier stages come to fruition; and so our chart allows along the right-most vertical, from infancy up, the gradual maturation of a quality of being, for which integrity does seem to be the right word.

Our anchor point in earliest childhood, however, remains the newborn's and the infant's developmental readiness for *mutuality*, which today is being demonstrated in all detail by the best workers in the area of child development and pediatrics: by which we mean the surprising power of potential unfolding born with this vulnerable creature, if only it is met in its readiness for energizing as well as instructive interplay, as it and its caretakers (literally) face each other. Only when such potentialities are studied exhaustively can clinical observers know what potentials are endangered in early situations at risk or where mutuality was, in fact, broken in misdevelopment.

We have circumscribed a lifetime, then. But the mere mention of mutuality will remind us of what is missing in this presentation, namely, a detailed discussion of Young Adulthood and its crisis of Intimacy and Isolation which is decisive in mobilizing the lifelong power of Love; and of Adulthood itself with its crisis of Generativity vs. Stagnation, which brings to maturation the adult strength of Care—and its demands for generational mutuality. This second-to-the-last stage on our diagonal bequeaths to the last what we called a grand-generative aspect of old age: a general grandparenthood, then, which must demand a useful and mutual place in the life of children, offering to the growing as well as to the old individuals an energizing as well as disciplined interaction according to the mores of technology and culture. As we reveal the potentials of early interplay, perhaps we will at last recognize what, in spite of such historical and cultural relativities, is invariantly human—that is, true for the whole human species and thus part of an indivisible specieshood which mankind can no longer afford to ignore.

References

Blos, P. (1980). The life cycle as indicated by the nature of the transference in the psychoanalysis of children. *Int. J. Psychoanal.*, 61: 146–151.

Erikson, E. H. (1955). Freud's 'The Origins of Psycho-Analysis.' *Int. J. Psychoanal.*, 36: 1–15.

——— (1980). On the generational cycle. *Int. J. Psychoanal.*, 61: 213–223.

——— (1982). *The Life Cycle Completed.* New York: Norton.

——— & Erikson, J. M. (1950). Growth and crisis of the "healthy personality." In *Symposium on the Healthy Personality*, ed. M. J. E. Senn. New York: Josiah Macy, Jr. Foundation, pp. 91–146.

Freud, A. (1965). Normality and pathology in childhood. *W.*, 6.

Freud, S. (1954). *The Origins of Psychoanalysis.* New York: Basic Books.

On Death and Dying

Elisabeth Kübler-Ross

Elisabeth Kübler-Ross, a psychiatrist, was born in 1926 in Zurich, Switzerland. She earned her M.D. at the University of Zurich in 1956. Shortly after that she moved to the United States, where she taught psychiatry at the University of Colorado and later at the University of Chicago.

The following selection consists of excerpts taken from five chapters of Kübler-Ross's most influential text, *On Death and Dying* (Macmillan, 1969): chapter 3, "First Stage: Denial and Isolation"; chapter 4, "Second Stage: Anger"; chapter 5, "Third Stage: Bargaining"; chapter 6, "Fourth Stage: Depression"; and chapter 7, "Fifth Stage: Acceptance." Kübler-Ross began the research on which this text is based in 1965, and she has continued to study the dying. She has reported her work in several texts, including *Death: The Final Stage of Growth* (1975), *Living With Death and Dying* (1982), *On Children and Death* (1983), and *AIDS: The Ultimate Challenge* (1987).

Researchers of human development are concerned with development throughout the lifespan. Scientifically, however, the last biological stage of life must be considered death. Most people are fascinated by, if not fearful and in awe of, this aspect of human development. Kübler-Ross has boldly entered this final territory of growth and decline and charted the stages of human psychological response to the realization of imminent death.

Key Concept: stages of dying

First Stage: Denial and Isolation

Among the over two hundred dying patients we have interviewed, most reacted to the awareness of a terminal illness at first with the statement, "No, not me, it cannot be true." This *initial* denial was as true for those patients who were told outright at the beginning of their illness as it was true for those who were not told explicitly and who came to this conclusion on their own a bit later on. One of our patients described a long and expensive ritual, as she called it, to support her denial. She was convinced that the X-rays were "mixed up"; she asked for reassurance that her pathology report could not possibly be back so soon and that another patient's report must have been marked with her name. When none of this could be confirmed, she quickly asked to leave the hospital, looking for another physician in the vain hope "to get a better explanation for my troubles." This patient went "shopping around" for many doctors, some of whom gave her reassuring answers, others of whom confirmed the previous suspicion. Whether confirmed or not, she reacted in the same manner; she asked for examination and reexamination, partially knowing that the original diagnosis was correct, but also seeking further evaluations in the hope that the first conclusion was indeed an error, at the same time keeping in contact with a physician in order to have help available "at all times" as she said.

This anxious denial following the presentation of a diagnosis is more typical of the patient who is informed prematurely or abruptly by someone who does not know the patient well or does it quickly "to get it over with" without taking the patient's readiness into consideration. Denial, at least partial denial, is used by almost all patients, not only during the first stages of illness or following confrontation, but also later on from time to time. Who was it who said, "We cannot look at the sun all the time, we cannot face death all the time"? These patients can consider the possibility of their own death for a while but then have to put this consideration away in order to pursue life.

I emphasize this strongly since I regard it a healthy way of dealing with the uncomfortable and painful situation with which some of these patients have to live for a long time. Denial functions as a buffer after unexpected shocking news, allows the patient to collect himself and, with time, mobilize other, less radical defenses. This does not mean, however, that the same patient later on will not be willing or even happy and relieved if he can sit and talk with someone about his impending death. Such a dialogue will and must take place at the convenience of the patient, when he (not the listener!) is ready to face it. The dialogue also has to be terminated when the patient can no longer face the facts and resumes his previous denial. It is irrelevant when this dialogue takes place. We are often accused of talking with very sick patients about death when the doctor feels—very rightly so—that they are not dying. I favor talking about death and dying with patients long before it actually happens if the patient indicates that he wants to. A healthier, stronger individual can deal with it better and is less frightened by oncoming death when it is still "miles away" than when it "is right in front of the door," as one of our patients put is so appropriately. It is also easier for the family to discuss such matters in times of relative health and well-being and arrange for financial security for the children and others while the head of the household is still functioning. To postpone such talks is often not in the service of the patient but serves our own defensiveness.

 enial is usually a temporary defense and will soon be replaced by partial acceptance. Maintained denial does not always bring increased distress if it holds out until the end, which I still consider a rarity. Among our two hundred terminally ill patients, I have encountered only three who attempted to deny its approach to the very last. Two of these women talked about dying briefly but only referred to it as "an inevitable nuisance which hopefully comes during sleep" and said "I hope it comes without pain." After these statements they resumed their previous denial of their illness. . . .

In summary, then, the patient's first reaction may be a temporary state of shock from which he recuperates gradually. When his initial feeling of numbness begins to disappear and he can collect himself again, man's usual response is "No, it cannot be me." Since in our unconscious mind we are all immortal, it is almost inconceivable for us to acknowledge that we too have to face death. Depending very much on how a patient is told, how much time he has to gradually acknowledge the inevitable happening, and how he has been prepared throughout life to cope with successful situations, he will gradually drop his denial and use less radical defense mechanisms.

We have also found that many of our patients have used denial when faced with hospital staff members who had to use this form of coping for their own reasons. Such patients can be quite selective in choosing different people among family members or staff with whom they discuss matters of their illness or impending death while pretending to get well with those who cannot tolerate the thought of their demise. It is possible that this is the

reason for the discrepancy of opinions in regard of the patient's needs to know about a fatal illness. . . .

Second Stage: Anger

If our first reaction to catastrophic news is, "No it's not true, no, it cannot involve me," this has to give way to a new reaction, when it finally dawns on us: "Oh, yes, it is me, it was not a mistake." Fortunately or unfortunately very few patients are able to maintain a make-believe world in which they are healthy and well until they die.

When the first stage of denial cannot be maintained any longer, it is replaced by feelings of anger, rage, envy, and resentment. The logical next question becomes: "Why me?" As one of our patients, Dr. G., puts it, "I suppose most anybody in my position would look at somebody else and say, 'Well, why couldn't it have been him?' and this has crossed my mind several times. . . . An old man whom I have known ever since I was a little kid came down the street. He was eighty-two years old, and he is of no earthly use as far as we mortals can tell. He's rheumatic, he's a cripple, he's dirty, just not the type of person you would like to be. And the thought hit me strongly, now why couldn't it have been old George instead of me?" (extract from interview of Dr. G.).

In contrast to the stage of denial, this stage of anger is very difficult to cope with from the point of view of family and staff. The reason for this is the fact that this anger is displaced in all directions and projected onto the environment at times almost at random. The doctors are just no good, they don't know what tests to require and what diet to prescribe. They keep the patients too long in the hospital or don't respect their wishes in regards to special privileges. They allow a miserably sick roommate to be brought into their room when they pay so much money for some privacy and rest, etc. The nurses are even more often a target of their anger. Whatever they touch is not right. The moment they have left the room, the bell rings. The light is on the very minute they start their report for the next shift of nurses. When they do shake the pillows and straighten out the bed, they are blamed for never leaving the patients alone. When they do leave the patients alone, the light goes on with the request to have the bed arranged more comfortably. The visiting family is received with little cheerfulness and anticipation, which makes the encounter a painful event. They then either respond with grief and tears, guilt or shame, or avoid future visits, which only increases the patient's discomfort and anger.

The problem here is that few people place themselves in the patient's position and wonder where this anger might come from. Maybe we too would be angry if all our life activities were interrupted so prematurely; if all the buildings we started were to go unfinished, to be completed by someone else; if we had put some hard-earned money aside to enjoy a few years of rest and enjoyment, for travel and pursuing hobbies, only to be confronted with the fact that "this is not for me." What else would we do with our anger, but let it out on the people who are most likely to enjoy all these things? People who rush busily around only to remind us that we cannot even stand on our two feet anymore. People who order unpleasant tests and prolonged hospitalization with all its limitations, restrictions, and costs, while at the end of the day they can go home and enjoy life. People who tell us to lie still so that the infusion or transfusion does not have to be restarted, when we feel like jumping out of our skin to be doing something in order to know that we are still functioning on some level! . . .

Third Stage: Bargaining

The third stage, the stage of bargaining, is less well known but equally helpful to the patient, though only for brief periods of time. If we have been unable to face the sad facts in the first period and have been angry at people and God in the second phase, maybe we can succeed in entering into some sort of an agreement which may postpone the inevitable happening: "If God has decided to take us from this earth and he did not respond to my angry pleas, he may be more favorable if I ask nicely." We are all familiar with this reaction when we observe our children first demanding, then asking for a favor. They may not accept our "No" when they want to spend a night in a friend's house. They may be angry and stamp their foot. They may lock themselves in their bedroom and temporarily express their anger by rejecting us. But they will also have second thoughts. They may consider another approach. They will come out eventually, volunteer to do some tasks around the house, which under normal circumstances we never succeeded in getting them to do, and then tell us, "If I am very good all week and wash the dishes every evening, then will you let me go?" There is a slight chance naturally that we will accept the bargain and the child will get what was previously denied.

The terminally ill patient uses the same maneuvers. He knows, from past experiences, that there is a slim chance that he may be rewarded for good behavior and be granted a wish for special services. His wish is most always an extension of life, followed by the wish for a few days without pain or physical discomfort. A patient who was an opera singer, with a distorting malignancy of her jaw and face who could no longer perform on the stage, asked "to perform just one more time." When she became aware that this was impossible, she gave the most touching performance perhaps of her lifetime. She asked to come to the seminar and to speak in front of the audience, not behind a one-way mirror. She unfolded her life story, her success, and her tragedy in front of the class until a telephone call summoned her to return to her room. Doctor and dentist were ready to pull all her teeth in order to proceed with the radiation treatment. She had asked to sing once more—to us—before she had to hide her face forever.

Another patient was in utmost pain and discomfort, unable to go home because of her dependence on injections for pain relief. She had a son who proceeded with his plans to get married, as the patient had wished. She was very sad to think that she would be unable to attend this big day, for he was her oldest and favorite child. With combined efforts, we were able to teach her self-hypnosis which enabled her to be quite comfortable for several hours. She had made all sorts of promises if she could only live long enough to attend this marriage. The day preceding the wedding she left the hospital as an elegant lady. Nobody would have believed her real condition. She was "the happiest person in the whole world" and looked radiant. I wondered what her reaction would be when the time was up for which she had bargained.

I will never forget the moment when she returned to the hospital. She looked tired and somewhat exhausted and—before I could say hello—said, "Now don't forget I have another son!"

The bargaining is really an attempt to postpone; it has to include a prize offered "for good behavior," it also sets a self-imposed "deadline" (e.g., one more performance, the son's wedding), and it includes an implicit promise that the patient will not ask for more if this one postponement is granted. None of our patients have "kept their promise"; in other words, they are like children who say, "I will never fight my sister again if you let me go." Needless to add, the little boy will fight his sister again, just as the opera singer will try to perform once more. She could not live without further performances and left the hospital before her teeth were extracted. The patient just described was unwilling to face us again unless we acknowledged the fact that she had another son whose wedding she also wanted to witness. . . .

Fourth Stage: Depression

When the terminally ill patient can no longer deny his illness, when he is forced to undergo more surgery or hospitalization, when he begins to have more symptoms or becomes weaker and thinner, he cannot smile it off anymore. His numbness or stoicism, his anger and rage will soon be replaced with a sense of great loss. This loss may have many facets: a woman with a breast cancer may react to the loss of her figure; a woman with a cancer of the uterus may feel that she is no longer a woman. Our opera singer responded to the required surgery of her face and the removal of her teeth with shock, dismay, and the deepest depression. But this is only one of the many losses that such a patient has to endure.

With the extensive treatment and hospitalization, financial burdens are added; little luxuries at first and necessities later on may not be afforded anymore. The immense sums that such treatments and hospitalizations cost in recent years have forced many patients to sell the only possessions they had; they were unable to keep a house which they built for their old age, unable to send a child through college, and unable perhaps to make many dreams come true.

There may be the added loss of a job due to many absences or the inability to function, and mothers and wives may have to become the breadwinners, thus depriving the children of the attention they previously had. When mothers are sick, the little ones may have to be boarded out, adding to the sadness and guilt of the patient.

All these reasons for depressions are well known to everybody who deals with patients. What we often tend to forget, however, is the preparatory grief that the terminally ill patient has to undergo in order to prepare himself for his final separation from this world. If I were to attempt to differentiate these two kinds of depressions, I would regard the first one a reactive depression, the second one a preparatory depression. The first one is different in nature and should be dealt with quite differently from the latter.

An understanding person will have no difficulty in eliciting the cause of the depression and in alleviating some of the unrealistic guilt or shame which often accompanies the depression. A woman who is worried about no longer being a woman can be complimented for some especially feminine feature; she can be reassured that she is still as much a woman as she was before surgery. Breast prosthesis has added much to the breast cancer patient's self-esteem. Social worker, physician, or chaplain may discuss the patient's concerns with the husband in order to obtain his help in supporting the patient's self-esteem. Social workers and chaplains can be of great help during this time in assisting in the reorganization of a household, especially when children or lonely old people are involved for whom eventual placement has to be considered. We are always impressed by how quickly a patient's depression is lifted when these vital issues are taken care of. . . .

The second type of depression is one which does not occur as a result of a past loss but is taking into account impending losses. Our initial reaction to sad people is usually to try to cheer them up, to tell them not to look at things so grimly or so hopelessly. We encourage them to look at the bright side of life, at all the colorful, positive things around them. This is often an expression of our own needs, our own inability to tolerate a long face over any extended period of time. This can be a useful approach when dealing with the first type of depression in terminally ill patients. It will help such a mother to know that the children play quite happily in the neighbor's garden since they stay there while their father is at work. It may help a mother to know that they continue to laugh and joke, go to parties, and bring good report cards home from school—all expressions that they function in spite of mother's absence.

When the depression is a tool to prepare for the impending loss of all the love objects, in order to facilitate the state of acceptance, then encouragements and reassurances are not as meaningful. The patient should not be encouraged to look at the sunny side of things, as this would mean he should not contemplate his impending death. It would be contraindicated to tell him not to be sad, since all of us are tremendously sad when we lose one beloved person. The patient is in the process of losing everything and everybody he loves. If he is allowed to express his sorrow he will find a final acceptance much easier, and he will be grateful to those who can sit with him during this state of depression without constantly telling him not to be sad. . . .

Fifth Stage: Acceptance

If a patient has had enough time (i.e., not a sudden, unexpected death) and has been given some help in working through the previously described stages, he will reach a stage during which he is neither depressed nor angry about his "fate." He will have been able to express his previous feelings, his envy for the living and the healthy, his anger at those who do not have to face their end so soon. He will have mourned the impending loss of so many meaningful people and places and he will contemplate his coming end with a certain degree of quiet expectation. He will be tired and, in most cases, quite weak. He will also have a need to doze off to sleep often and in brief intervals, which is different from the need to sleep during the times of depression. This is not a sleep of avoidance or a period of rest to get relief from pain, discomfort, or itching. It is a gradually increasing need to extend the hours of sleep very similar to that of the newborn child but in reverse order. It is not a resigned and hopeless "giving up," a sense of "what's the use" or "I just cannot fight it any longer," though we hear such statements too. (They also indicate the beginning of the end of the struggle, but the latter are not indications of acceptance.)

Acceptance should not be mistaken for a happy stage. It is almost void of feelings. It is as if the pain had gone, the struggle is over, and there comes a time for "the final rest before the long journey" as one patient phrased it. This is also the time during which the family needs usually more help, understanding, and support than the patient himself. While the dying patient has found some peace and acceptance, his circle of interest diminishes. He wishes to be left alone or at least not stirred up by news and problems of the outside world. Visitors are often not desired and if they come, the patient is no longer in a talkative mood. He often requests limitation on the number of people and prefers short visits. This is the time when the television is off. Our communications then become more nonverbal than verbal. The patient may just make a gesture of the hand to invite us to sit down for a while. He may just hold our hand and ask us to sit in silence. Such moments of silence may be the most meaningful communications for people who are not uncomfortable in the presence of a dying person. We may together listen to the song of a bird from the outside. Our presence may just confirm that we are going to be around until the end. We may just let him know that it is all right to say nothing when the important things are taken care of and it is only a question of time until he can close his eyes forever. It may reassure him that he is not left alone when he is no longer talking and a pressure of the hand, a look, a leaning back in the pillows may say more than many "noisy" words.

A visit in the evening may lend itself best to such an encounter as it is the end of the day both for the visitor and the patient. It is the time when the hospital's page system does not interrupt such a moment, when the nurse does not come in to take the temperature, and the cleaning woman is not mopping the floor—it is this little private moment that can complete the day at the end of the rounds for the physician, when he is not interrupted by anyone. It takes just a little time but it is comforting for the patient to know that he is not forgotten when nothing else can be done for him. It is gratifying for the visitor as well, as it will show him that dying is not such a frightening, horrible thing that so many want to avoid.

Acknowledgments

1.1 From *An Outline of Psychoanalysis* (pp. 25–32) by S. Freud, 1940 (J. Strachey, Trans.). New York: W. W. Norton. Translation copyright © 1949 by W. W. Norton & Company, Inc. Copyright © 1969 by The Institute of Psycho-Analysis and Alix Strachey. Reprinted by permission of W. W. Norton & Company, Inc.

1.2 From "The Genetic Approach to the Psychology of Thought" by J. Piaget, 1961, *Journal of Educational Psychology, 52*, pp. 275–281.

1.3 From *Childhood and Society*, 2d ed. (pp. 247, 249–256, 258–264, 266–269) by E. H. Erikson, 1963. New York: W. W. Norton. Copyright © 1950, 1963 by W. W. Norton & Company, Inc.; copyright renewed 1978, 1991 by Erik H. Erikson. Reprinted by permission of W. W. Norton & Company, Inc.

1.4 From "The Child as a Moral Philosopher" by L. Kohlberg, 1968, *Psychology Today, 214*, pp. 25–30. Copyright © 1968 by Sussex Publishers, Inc. Reprinted by permission of *Psychology Today*.

1.5 From *In a Different Voice: Psychological Theory and Women's Development* (pp. 5–23) by C. Gilligan, 1982. Cambridge, MA: Harvard University Press. Copyright © 1982, 1993 by Carol Gilligan. Reprinted by permission of Harvard University Press.

1.6 From "A Rounded Version" by H. Gardner and J. Walters, in *Multiple Intelligences: The Theory in Practice* (pp. 13–27) by H. Gardner, 1993. New York: Basic Books. Copyright © 1993 by Howard Gardner. Reprinted by permission of Basic Books, a member of Perseus Books, L.L.C. References omitted.

1.7 From *The Works of William Wordsworth* (pp. 587–590) by W. Wordsworth, 1994. Hertfordshire, England: Wordsworth Editions Ltd. Copyright © 1994 by Wordsworth Editions Ltd. Reprinted by permission.

2.1 From "The Spectrum of Development" by K. Wilber, in *Transformations of Consciousness: Conventional and Contemplative Pespectives on Development* (pp. 67–69, 71–74) ed. by K. Wilber, J. Engler, and D. P. Brown, 1986. Boston: New Science Library. Copyright © 1986 by Ken Wilber, Jack Engler, and Daniel P. Brown. Reprinted by permission of Shambhala Publications, Inc., Boston, MA. http://www.shambhala.com. References omitted.

2.2 From *The Seven Valleys and the Four Valleys* (pp. 4–9, 11–13, 17–18, 29–32, 36–39) by Bahá'u'lláh, 1976 (M. Gail, Trans.). Wilmette, IL: Bahá'í Publishing Trust. Copyright © 1945, 1952, 1973, 1975, 1978 by The National Spiritual Assembly of the Bahá'ís of the United States. Reprinted by permission.

2.3 From *A Source Book in Chinese Philosophy* (pp. 86–94) by K'ung Fu-Tzu, 1963 (Wing-Tsit Chan, Trans.). Princeton, NJ: Princeton University Press. Copyright © 1963 by Princeton University Press. Reprinted by permission. Notes omitted.

3.1 From "Heredity, Environment, and the Question 'How?'" by A. Anastasi, 1958, *Psychological Review, 65*, pp. 197–208.

3.2 From "The Origin of Personality" by A. Thomas, S. Chess, and H. G. Birch, 1970, *Scientific American, 223*, pp. 102–109. Copyright © 1970 by Scientific American, Inc. All rights reserved. Reprinted by permission.

4.1 From *The Origins of Intelligence in Children* (pp. 21, 23–27, 29–32, 47, 49–50, 147–152) by J. Piaget, 1952 (M. Cook, Trans.). New York: W. W. Norton. Copyright © 1952 by International Universities Press, Inc. Reprinted by permission. Notes omitted.

4.2 From "Infant–Mother Attachment" by M. D. S. Ainsworth, 1979, *American Psychologist, 34*, pp. 932–937. Copyright © 1979 by The American Psychological Association. Reprinted by permission.

5.1 From "The Co-ordination of Perspectives" by J. Piaget, B. Inhelder, and E. Mayer, in *The Child's Conception of Space* (pp. 209–213) by J. Piaget and B. Inhelder, 1956 (F. J. Langdon and J. L. Lunzer, Trans.). London: Routledge Kegan Paul. Copyright © 1956 by Routledge Kegan Paul. Reprinted by permission of Taylor & Francis Books Ltd.

5.2 From *Thought and Language* (pp. 44–48, 50–51) by L. S. Vygotsky, 1962 (E. Hanfmann and G. Vakar, Trans.). Cambridge, MA: MIT Press. Copyright © 1962 by MIT Press. Reprinted by permission.

5.3 From "Social Participation Among Pre-School Children" by M. B. Parten, 1932, *Journal of Abnormal and Social Psychology, 27*, pp. 243, 246–252.

Acknowledgments

Chapter 1

SELECTION 1   From AN OUTLINE OF PSYCHO-ANALYSIS, by Sigmund Freud, translated by James Strachey. Copyright © 1949 by W.W. Norton & Company, Inc. Copyright © 1969 by The Institute of Psycho-Analysis and Alix Strachey. Used by permission of W.W. Norton & Company, Inc.

SELECTION 2   From *The Journal of Educational Psychology*, 1961 (American Psychological Association).

SELECTION 3   From CHILDHOOD AND SOCIETY by Erik H. Erikson. Copyright © 1950, 1963 by W.W. Norton & Company, Inc., renewed © 1978, 1991 by Erik H. Erikson. Used by permission of W.W. Norton & Company, Inc.

SELECTION 4   From MEASURING EGO DEVELOPMENT, 1996, pp. 3–8. Copyright © 1996 by Lawrence Erlbaum Associates. Reprinted by permission.

SELECTION 5   Reprinted with permission from *Psychology Today* Magazine, Vol. 214, 1968, pp. 25–30. Copyright © 1968 by Sussex Publishers, Inc.

SELECTION 6   Reprinted by permission of the publisher from IN A DIFFERENT VOICE: Psychological Theory and women's Development by Carol Gilligan, pp. 5–23, Cambridge, Mass.: Harvard University Press, Copyright © 1982 by Carol Gilligan.

SELECTION 7   From MULTIPLE INTELLIGENCES: The Theory in Practice, 1993, pp. 13–27. Copyright © 1993 by Howard Gardner. Reprinted by permission of Basic Books, a member of Perseus Books Group, L.L.C.

SELECTION 8   From *American Psychologist*, Vol. 55, No. 1, January 2000, pp. 5–14. Copyright © 2000 by American Psychological Association. Reprinted by permission.

SELECTION 9   From THE WORKS OF WILLIAM WORDSWORTH (1807), pp. 587–590.

Chapter 2

SELECTION 10   From TRANSFORMATIONS OF CONSCIOUSNESS by Ken Wilber (Shambhala Publications, 1986, pp. 67–69, 71–74). Copyright © 1986 by Shambhala Publications, Inc. Reprinted by permission.

SELECTION 11   The "The Seven Valleys and the Four Valleys" by Bahaullah, 1862.

SELECTION 12   From A SOURCE BOOK IN CHINESE PHILOSOPHY, 1963, pp. 86–94. Copyright © 1963 by Princeton University Press. Reprinted by permission.

SELECTION 13   From BLACK PSYCHOLOGY, edited by Reginald L. Jones, Cobb & Henry Publishers, 2004. Copyright © 2004 by Cobb & Henry Publishers. Reprinted by permission.

Chapter 3

SELECTION 14   From *Psychological Review*, 1958 (American Psychological Association).

SELECTION 15   From *Scientific American*, August 1970, pp. 102–109. Copyright © 1970 by Scientific American, Inc. Reproduced with permission. All rights reserved. www.sciam.com

Index

A

abstraction, verbal behavior and, 136
acceptance: as stage of dying, 260–261; self-actualizing people and, 229–230
accommodation, cognitive development and, 6–7, 100–101, 102
adaptation, cognitive development and, 100–101, 102
adolescence: cognitive development in, 173–175; identity issues during, and psychopathology, 190–196
adult life stages, 233–236
African psychology, 70–82
age bias, in IQ tests, 245
agency, critical consciousness and, 211, 212, 218
aggression: cross-cultural analysis of sex differences in, 157–159, 162; modeling and observational learning and, 121–125
aging, intelligence and, 243–246
Ainsworth, Mary D. Salter, on infant-mother attachment, 104–109
Akbar, Na'im, on Black psychology, 70–82
amaurotic idiocy, 85
Anastasi, Anne, on environmental versus hereditary influences, 84–91
anger, as stage of dying, 258–259
assimilation, cognitive development and, 6–7, 100–101, 102
associative play, 120
attachment, infant-mother, 104–109
attention seeking, cross-cultural analysis of sex differences in, 157, 158, 160, 161
Aurobindo, Sri, 60–61
authenticity, positive psychology and, 52
authority, critical consciousness and, 211, 212, 218
autonomy: positive psychology and, 49; the psychosocial stages and, 10–11, 253; self-actualizing people and, 230; the stages of friendship and, 148, 149

B

Bahá u'lláh, on the stages of mystical development, 62–64
Baltes, Paul B., 50; on aging and intelligence, 243–246

Bandura, Albert, on modeling in aggression, 121–125
bargaining, as stage of dying, 259
Barry, William A., on spiritual development, 237–241
Baumrind, Diana, on parenting styles, 126–132
Belenky, Mary Field, on women's ways of knowing, 198–202
Benbow, Camilla, 50
bilingualism, environmental versus hereditary influences and, 87
Birch, Herbert G., on temperament, 92–96
Black psychology, 70–82
bodily-kinesthetic intelligence, 39–40
Buss, David, 48

C

Carruthers, Jacob, 73–74
Cattell, Raymond B., on fluid and crystallized intelligence, 203–206
causality, cognitive development and the concept of, 5
character strengths, positive psychology and, 44–54
Chess, Stella, on temperament, 92–96
child care practices: environmental versus hereditary influences and, 89; patenting styles and, 126–132
Chodorow, Nancy, 29, 30, 33
Chomsky, Noam, on language development, 139–141
Christian spiritual development, 237–241
coaching, environmental versus hereditary influences and, 87
codification of rules, 152, 153–154
cognitive development: development of inner speech and, 115–117; formal stage of, in adolescents, 173–175; genetic approach to, 4–8; sensorimotor stage of, 98–103
cognitive flexibility, intelligence and, 244
collectivism, Black psychology and, 73, 75, 78
competitive achievement, women's identity development and, 32–33
concepts, verbal behavior and, 136
confrontation, thoughtful, in adult life stages, 236

Confucius. *See* K'ung Fu-tzu
consciousness, the structure of, 59–61
conservation of volume, development of the concept of, 142–145
contemplation, stages of, 59–61
cooperation, rule following and, 152, 153–154
cooperative play, 120
creativity: positive psychology and, 50; self-actualizing people and, 231
critical consciousness (CC), personal and social development and, 207–220
crystallized intelligence, 244; fluid and, 203–206
Csikszentmihalyi, Mihaly, on positive psychology, 44–54
culture: moral reasoning and, 25–26; sex differences in children's behavior and, 155–163
cultural evolution, positive psychology and, 48

D

death, adult life stages and, 234
Deci, Edward, 49
Delle Fave, Antonella, 48
Demeter, 35
denial, as stage of dying, 257–258
dependency, cross-cultural analysis of sex differences in, 157, 158, 160, 161
depression, as stage of dying, 259–260
despair, the psychosocial stages and, 12–14, 252–256
Diener, Edward, 48
dominance, escape from, and adult life stages, 234
doubt, the psychosocial stages and, 10–11, 253
dying, the stages of, 257–263

E

eating disorders, adolescent self-focus and, 192
Edwards, Carolyn Pope, on cross-cultural analysis of sex differences in children's behavior, 155–163
ego development, 15–20; of women, 35